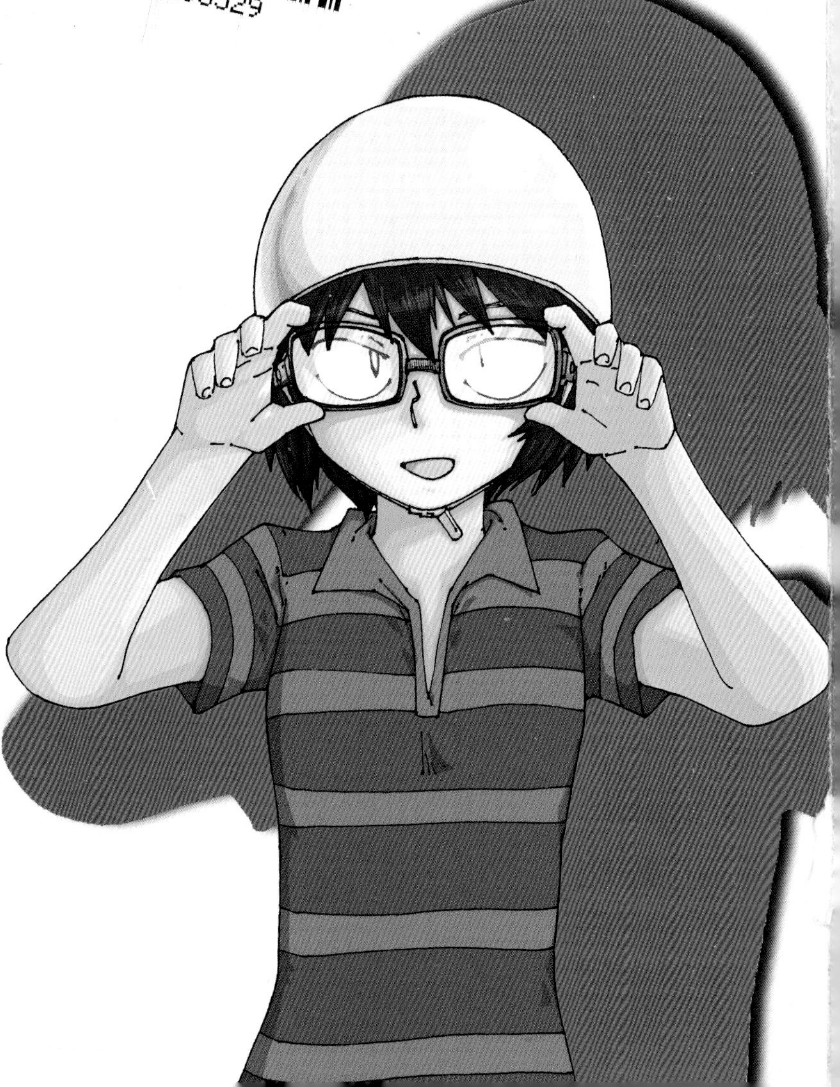

CONTENTS

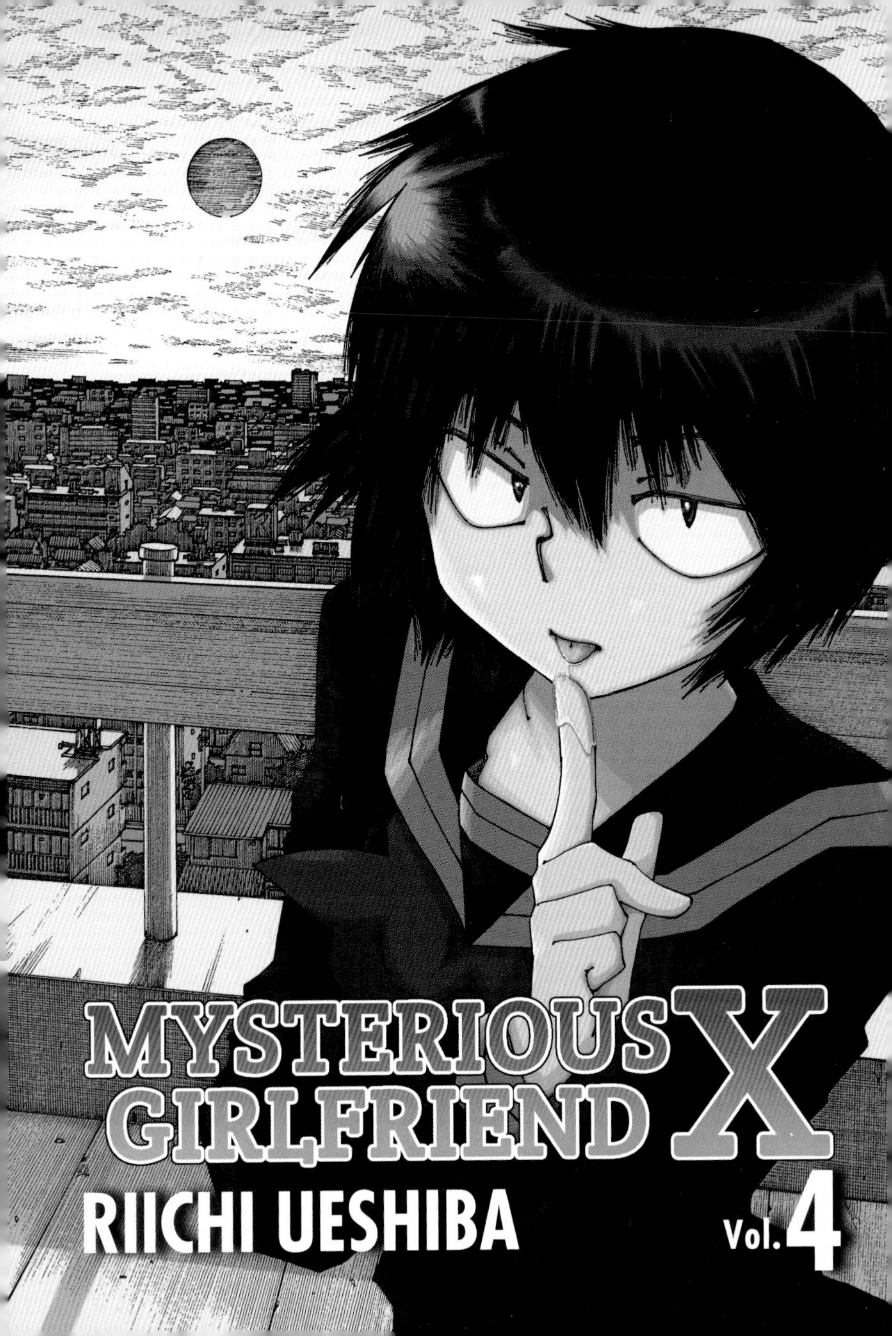
MYSTERIOUS GIRLFRIEND X
RIICHI UESHIBA
Vol. 4

MYSTERIOUS GIRLFRIEND X

Characters

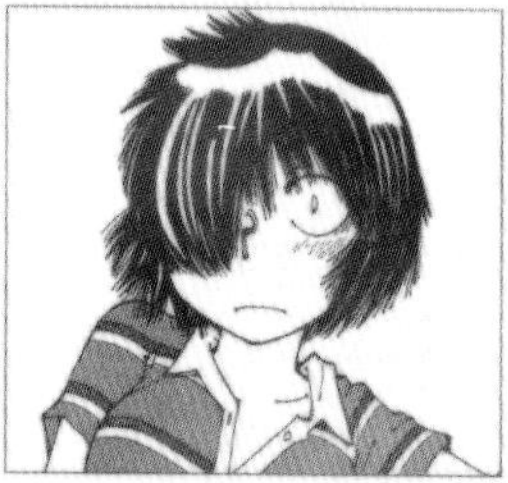

Mikoto Urabe (17)

A transfer student who joined Tsubaki's class. She can convey her own feelings through her drool, as well as pick up on Tsubaki's feelings through his. She's antisocial and everything she says and does is mysterious, but her ideas about love are very pure. Her hobby is using scissors, which she can use to cut up anything.

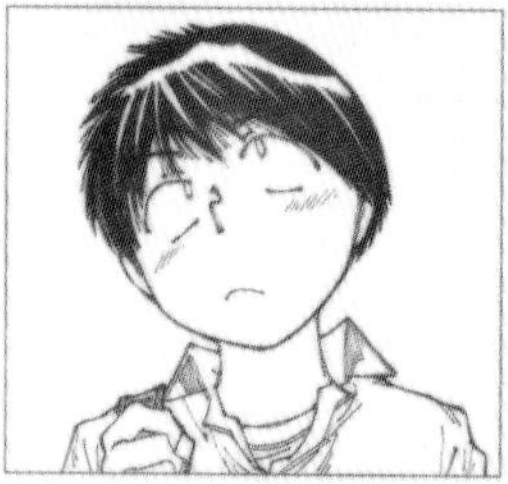

Akira Tsubaki (17)

The protagonist of the story. His bizarre relationship with Urabe began after he licked her drool one day. He is as interested in girls as any boy his age, but Urabe takes the lead in their relationship and Tsubaki can't seem to initiate any progress between them.

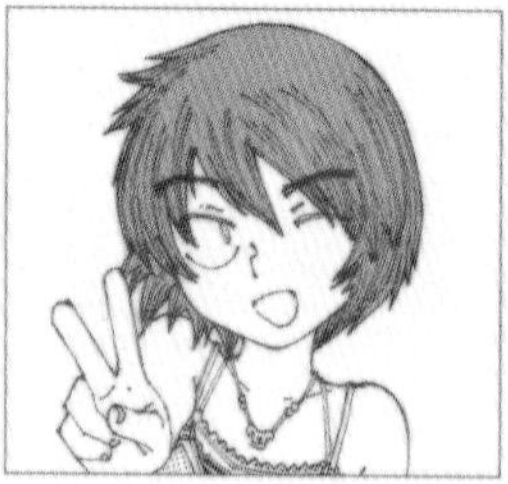

Momoka Imai (17)

An idol who looks just like Urabe. Longing to live the life of a "normal girl," she approached Urabe with a proposition that they switch places. She tends to overreact to things, and her best skill is her high kick. Her boobs are smaller than Urabe's.

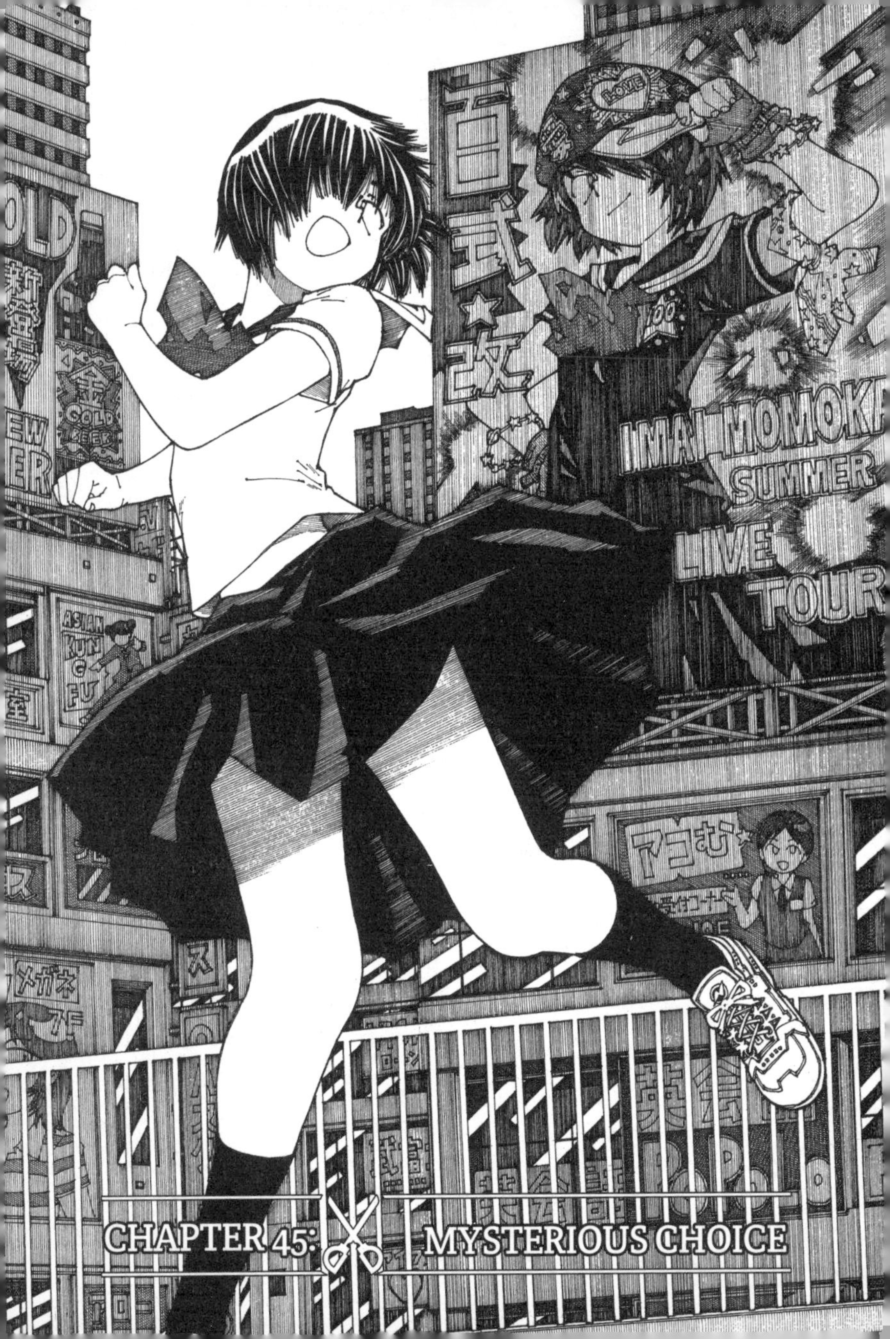
GOLD
GOLD BEER
ASIAN KUNG FU
LOVE
IMAI MOMOK
SUMMER
LIVE
TOUR
メガネ

CHAPTER 45: MYSTERIOUS CHOICE

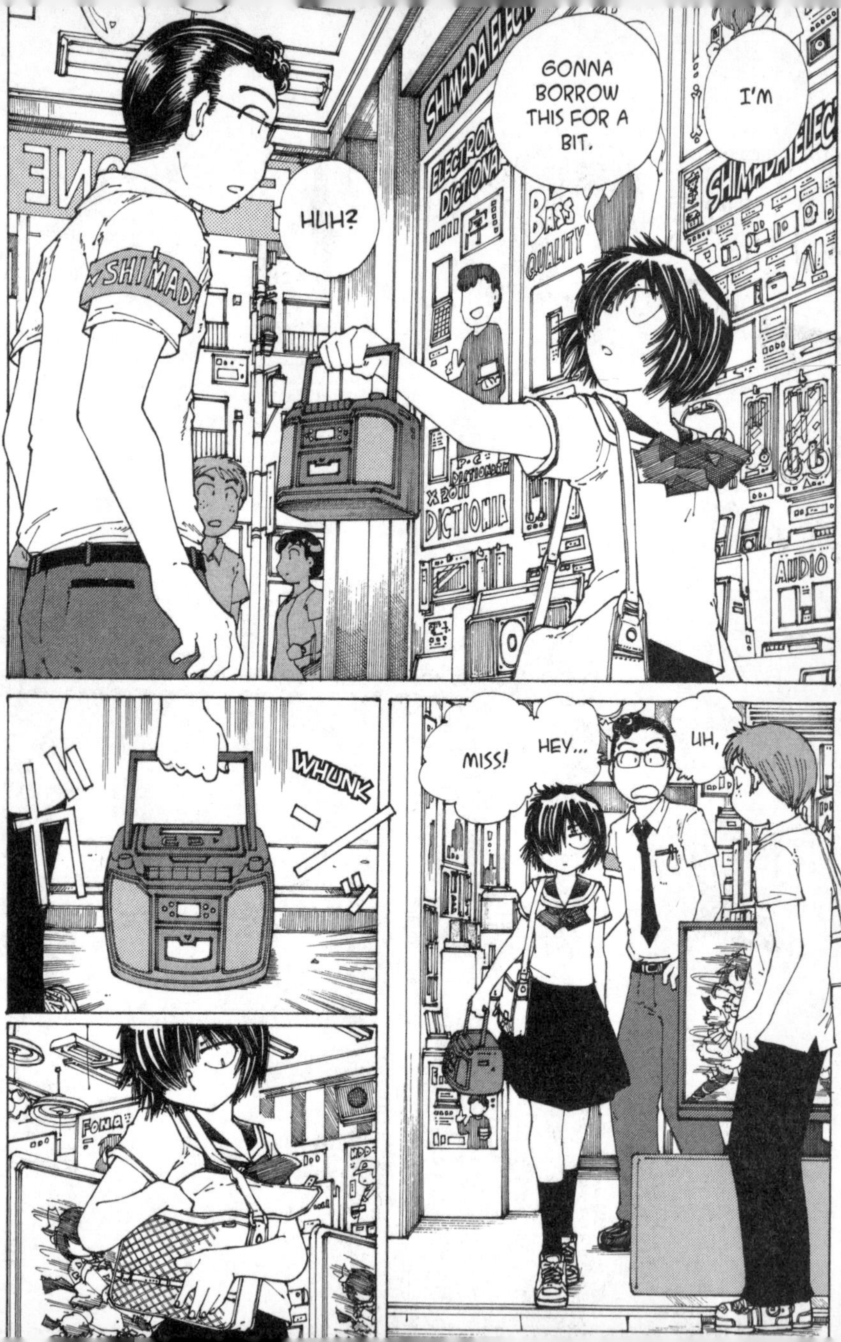
I'M
GONNA BORROW THIS FOR A BIT.
HUH?
UH,
HEY...
MISS!
WHUNK

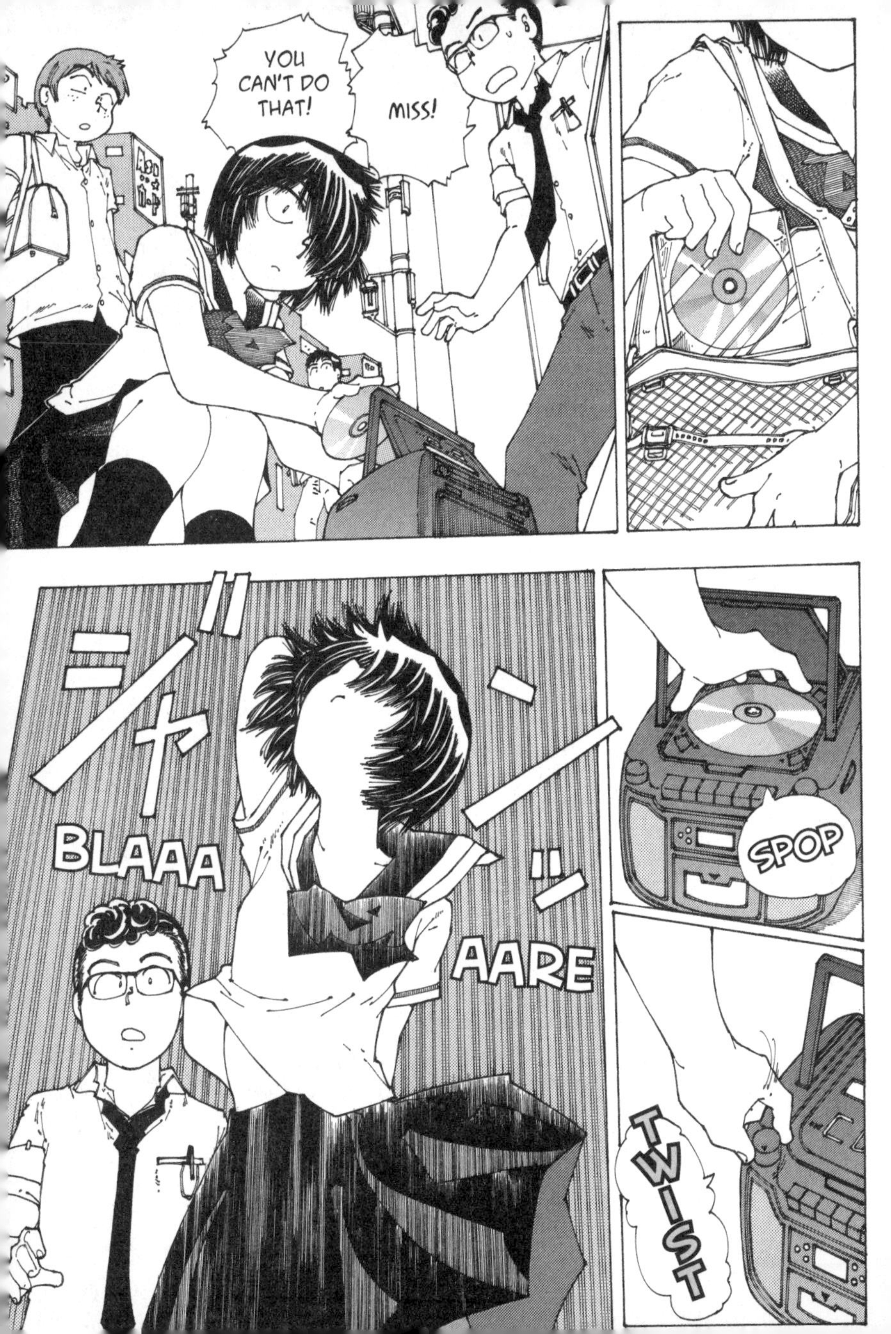
MISS!
YOU CAN'T DO THAT!
SPOP
TWIST
BLAAA
AARE

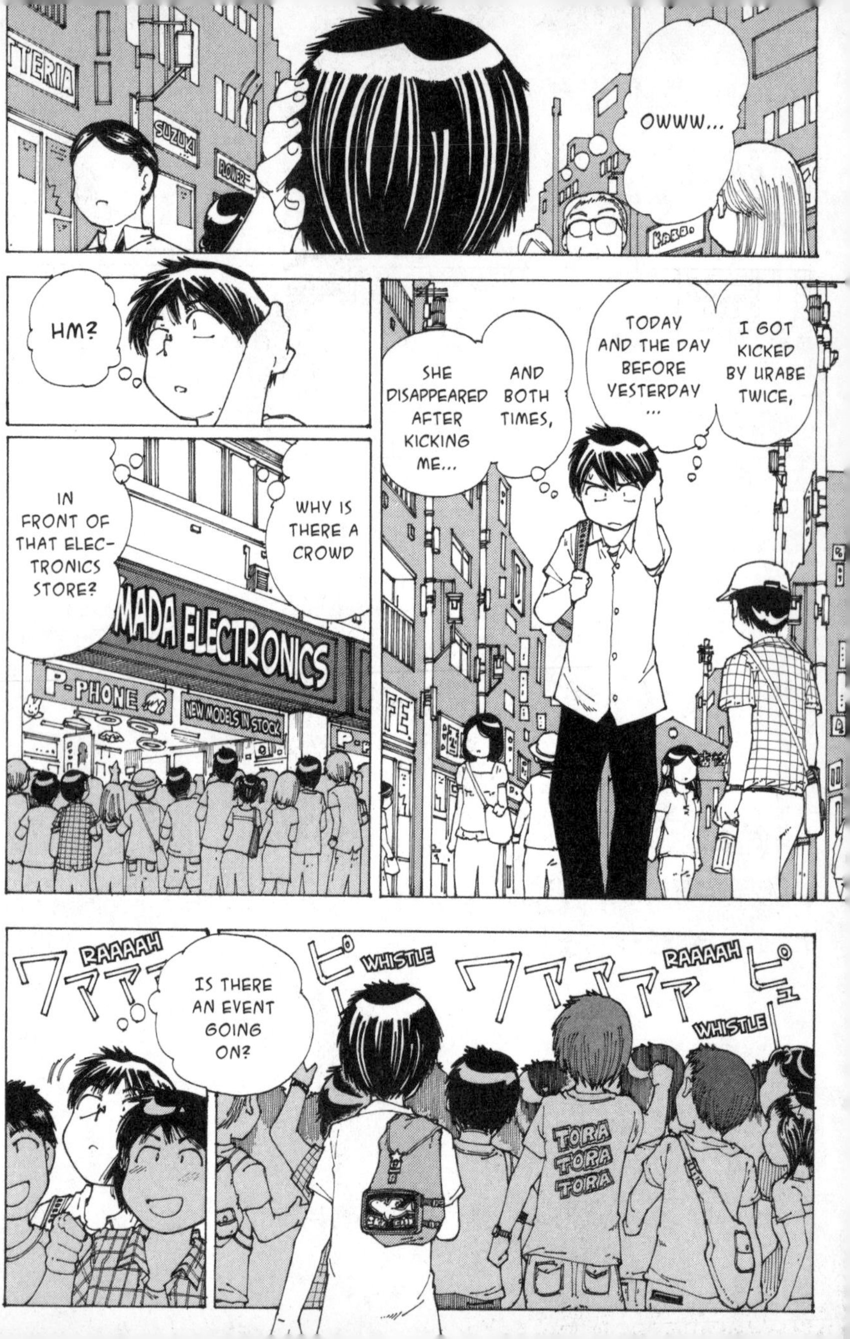
OWWW...
TTERIA
SUZUKI
I GOT KICKED BY URABE TWICE,
TODAY AND THE DAY BEFORE YESTERDAY ...
AND BOTH TIMES,
SHE DISAPPEARED AFTER KICKING ME...
HM?
WHY IS THERE A CROWD
IN FRONT OF THAT ELECTRONICS STORE?
MADA ELECTRONICS
P-PHONE
NEW MODELS IN STOCK
RAAAAH
WHISTLE
WHISTLE
TORA TORA TORA
RAAAAH
IS THERE AN EVENT GOING ON?

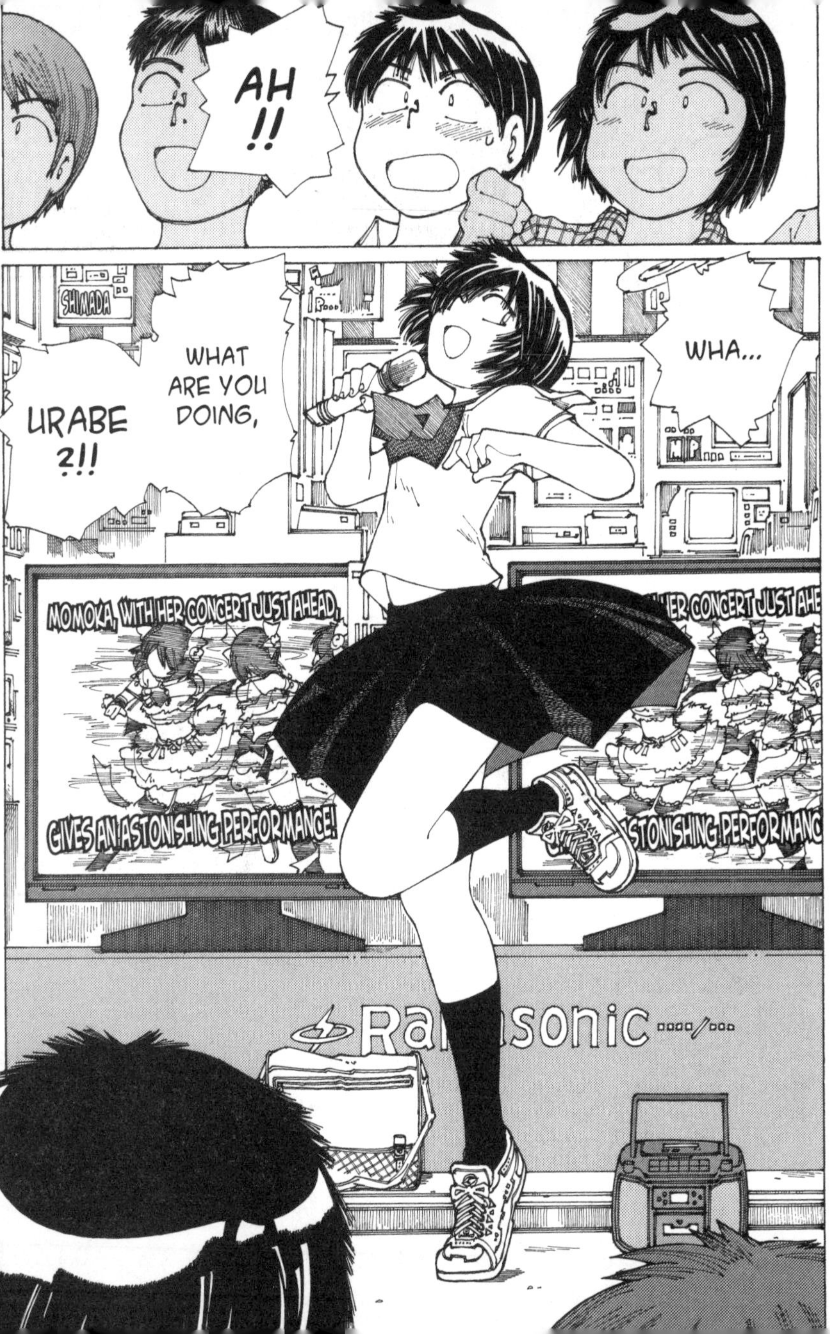
AH !!
WHA...
WHAT ARE YOU DOING,
URABE ?!!
SHIMADA
MOMOKA, WITH HER CONCERT JUST AHEAD,
GIVES AN ASTONISHING PERFORMANCE!

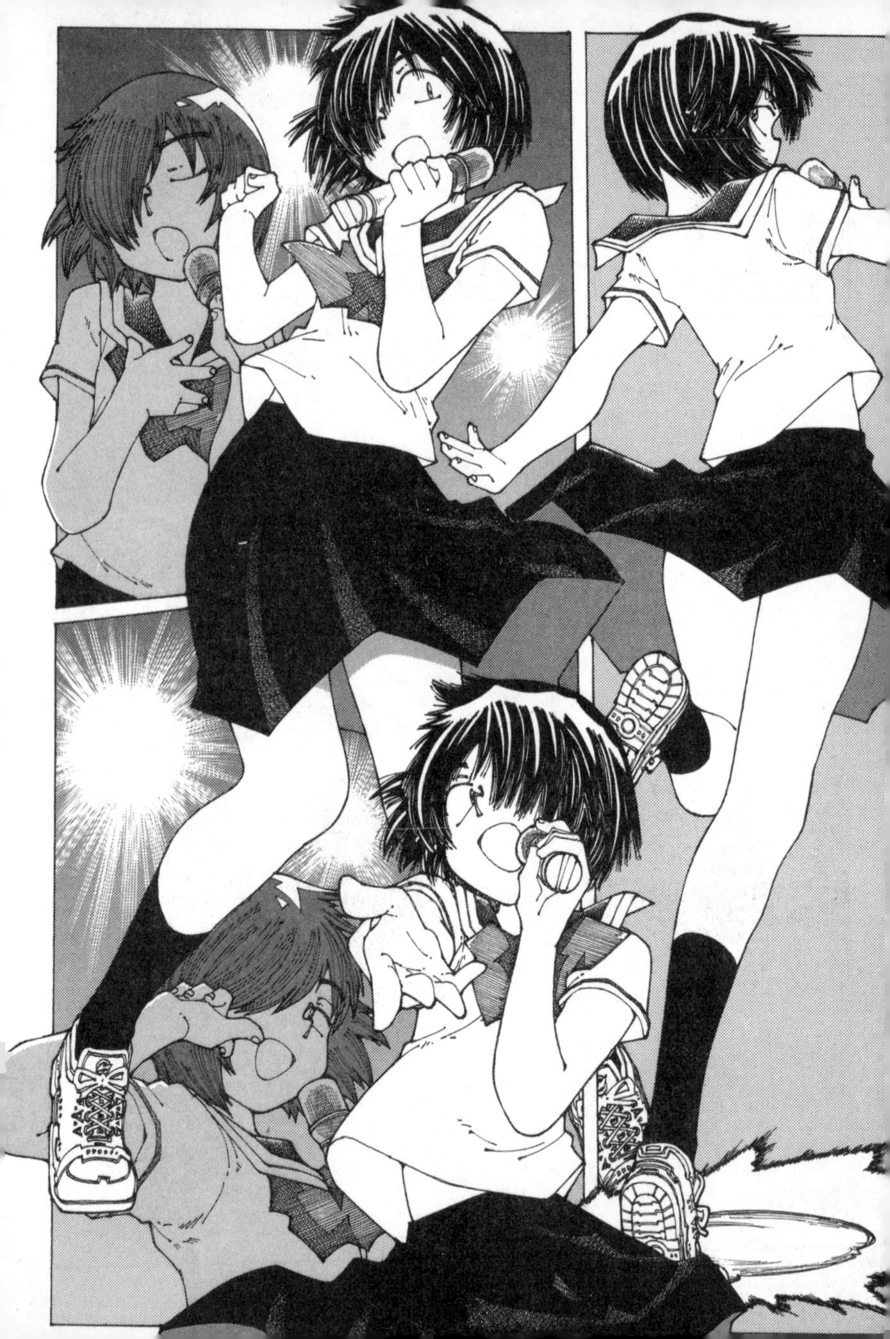

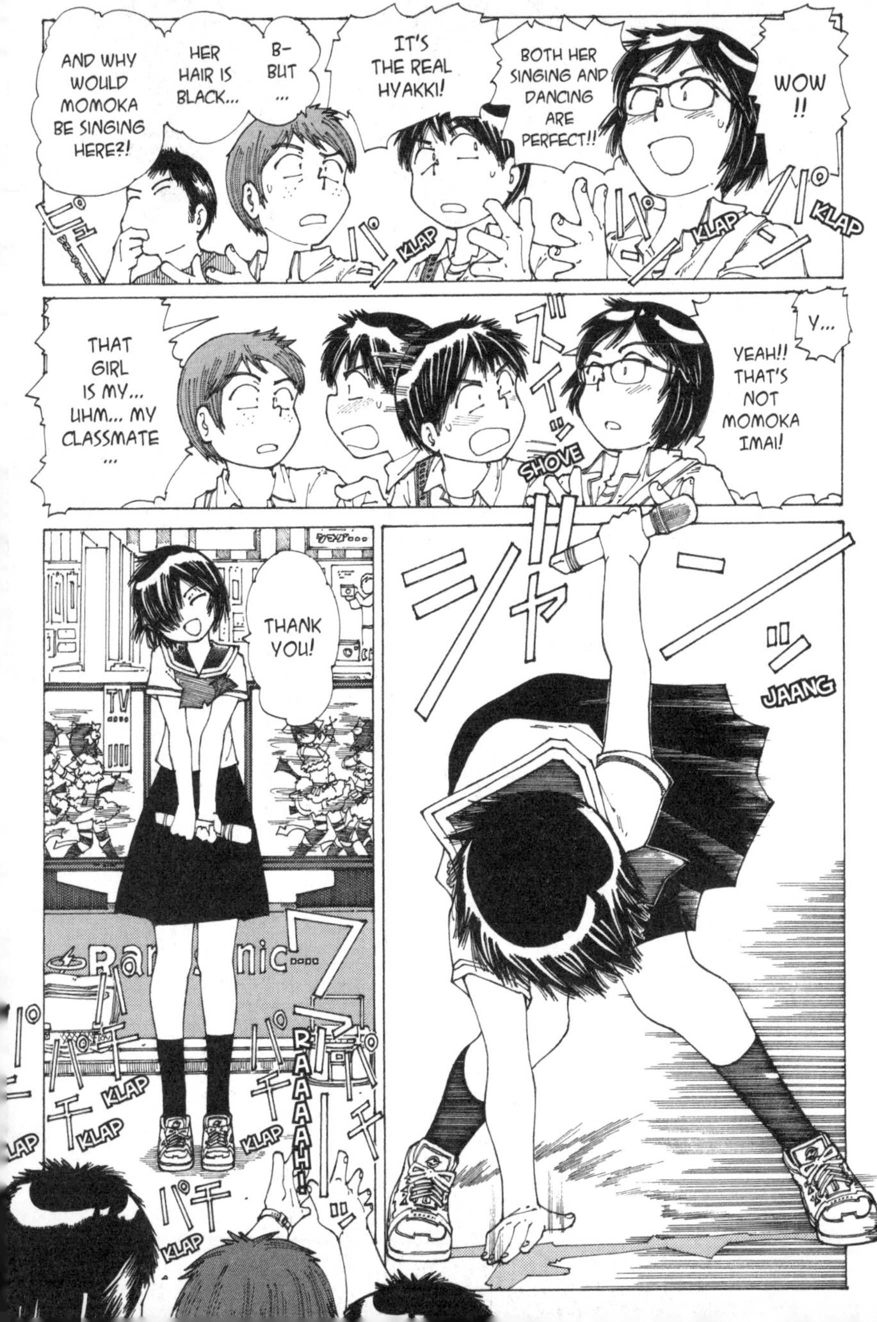
WOW!!
KLAP
KLAP
BOTH HER SINGING AND DANCING ARE PERFECT!!
IT'S THE REAL HYAKKI!
KLAP
B-BUT...
HER HAIR IS BLACK...
AND WHY WOULD MOMOKA BE SINGING HERE?!
Y...
YEAH!! THAT'S NOT MOMOKA IMAI!
SHOVE
THAT GIRL IS MY... UHM... MY CLASSMATE...
JAANG
THANK YOU!
RAAAAAH!
KLAP
KLAP
KLAP
KLAP
KLAP

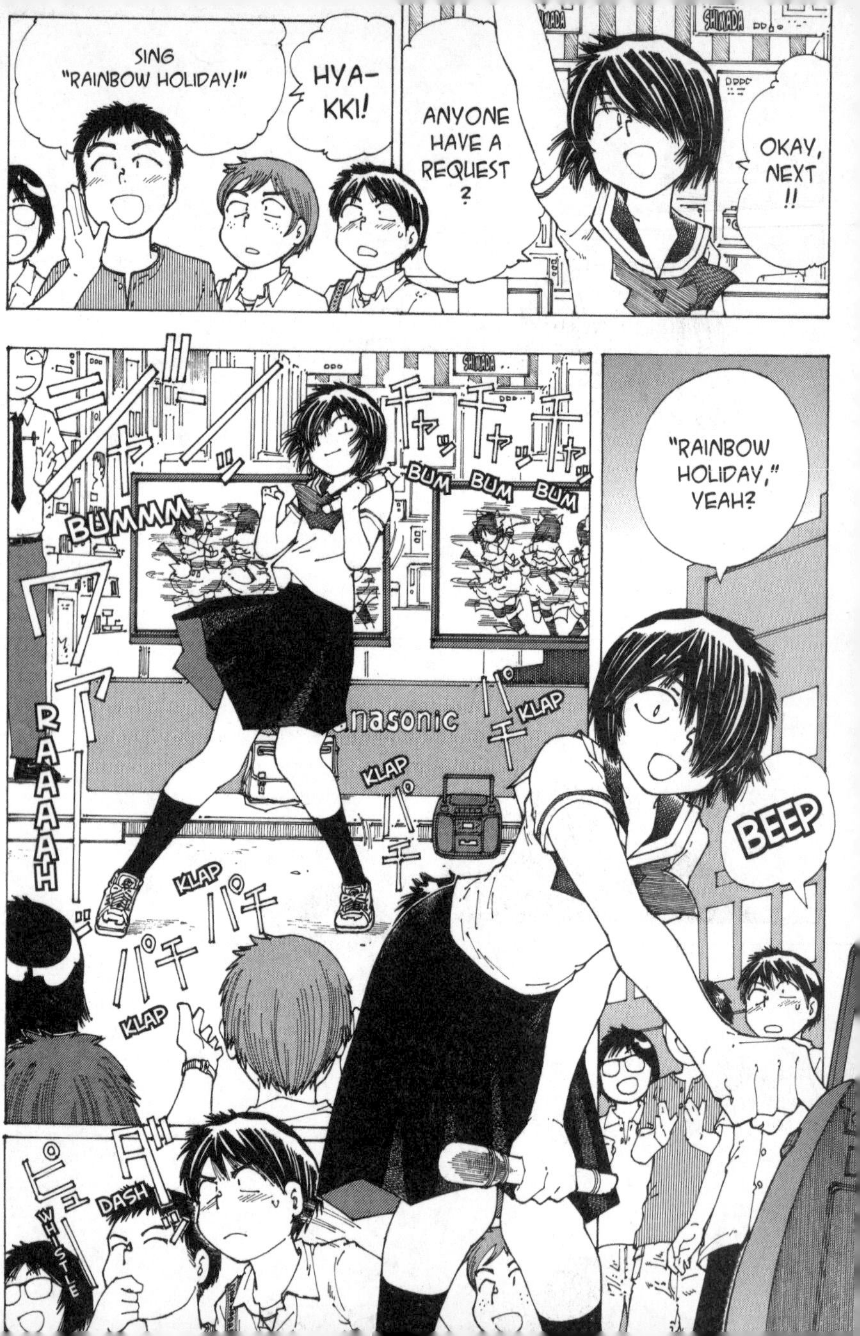
SHIMADA
OKAY, NEXT!!
ANYONE HAVE A REQUEST?
HYA-KKI!
SING "RAINBOW HOLIDAY!"
"RAINBOW HOLIDAY," YEAH?
BEEP
SHIMADA
チャッチャッチャッ
BUM BUM BUM
ジャーン
BUMMM
Panasonic
パチ
KLAP
KLAP
パチ
ワァアー
RAAAAAH
KLAP
パチ
パチ
KLAP
ダッ
DASH
ピュー
WHISTLE

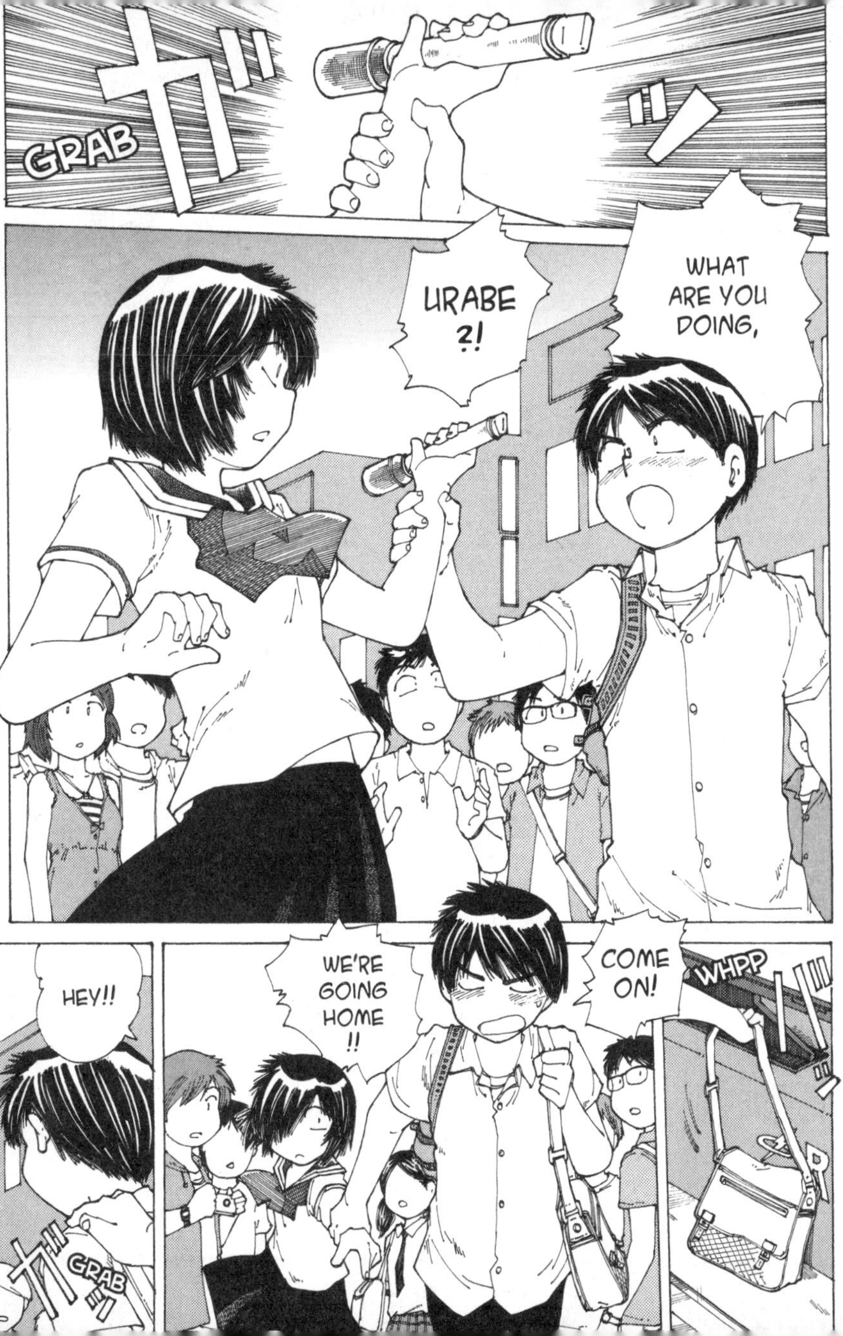
GRAB
WHAT ARE YOU DOING,
URABE ?!
WHPP
COME ON!
WE'RE GOING HOME !!
HEY!!
GRAB

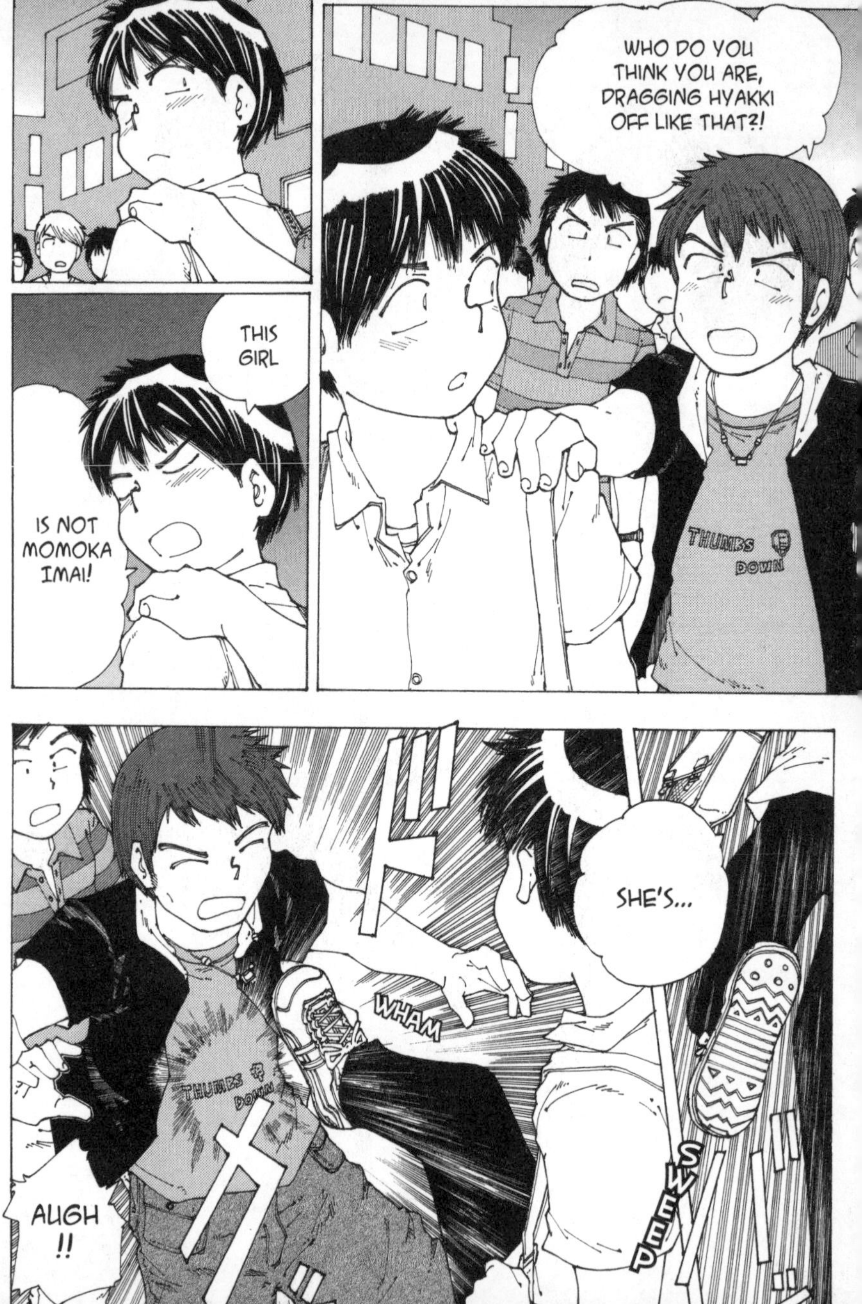
WHO DO YOU THINK YOU ARE, DRAGGING HYAKKI OFF LIKE THAT?!
THIS GIRL
IS NOT MOMOKA IMAI!
SHE'S...
WHAM
SWEEP
AUGH !!

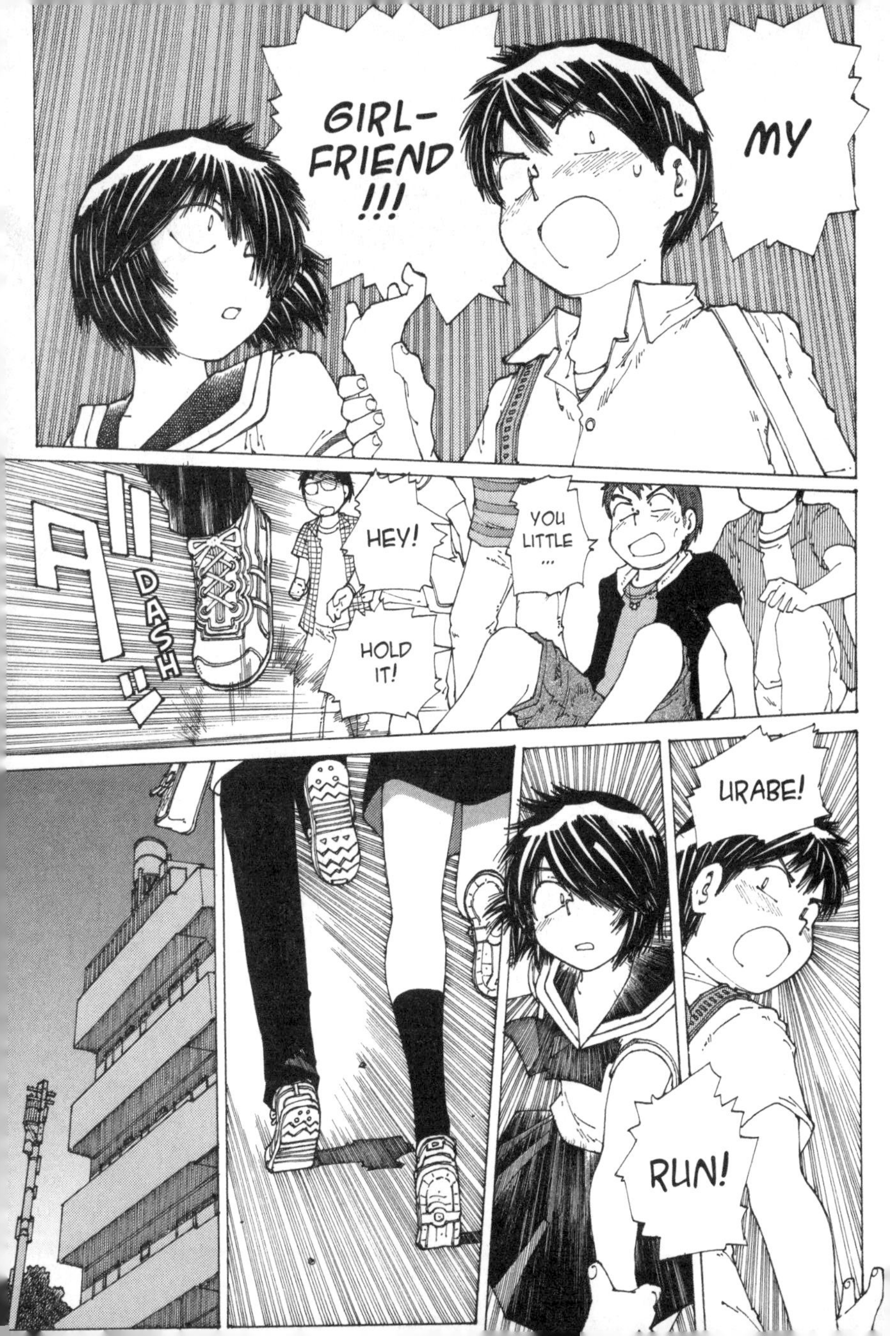
MY
GIRL-FRIEND!!!
YOU LITTLE ...
HEY!
HOLD IT!
DASH!!
URABE!
RUN!

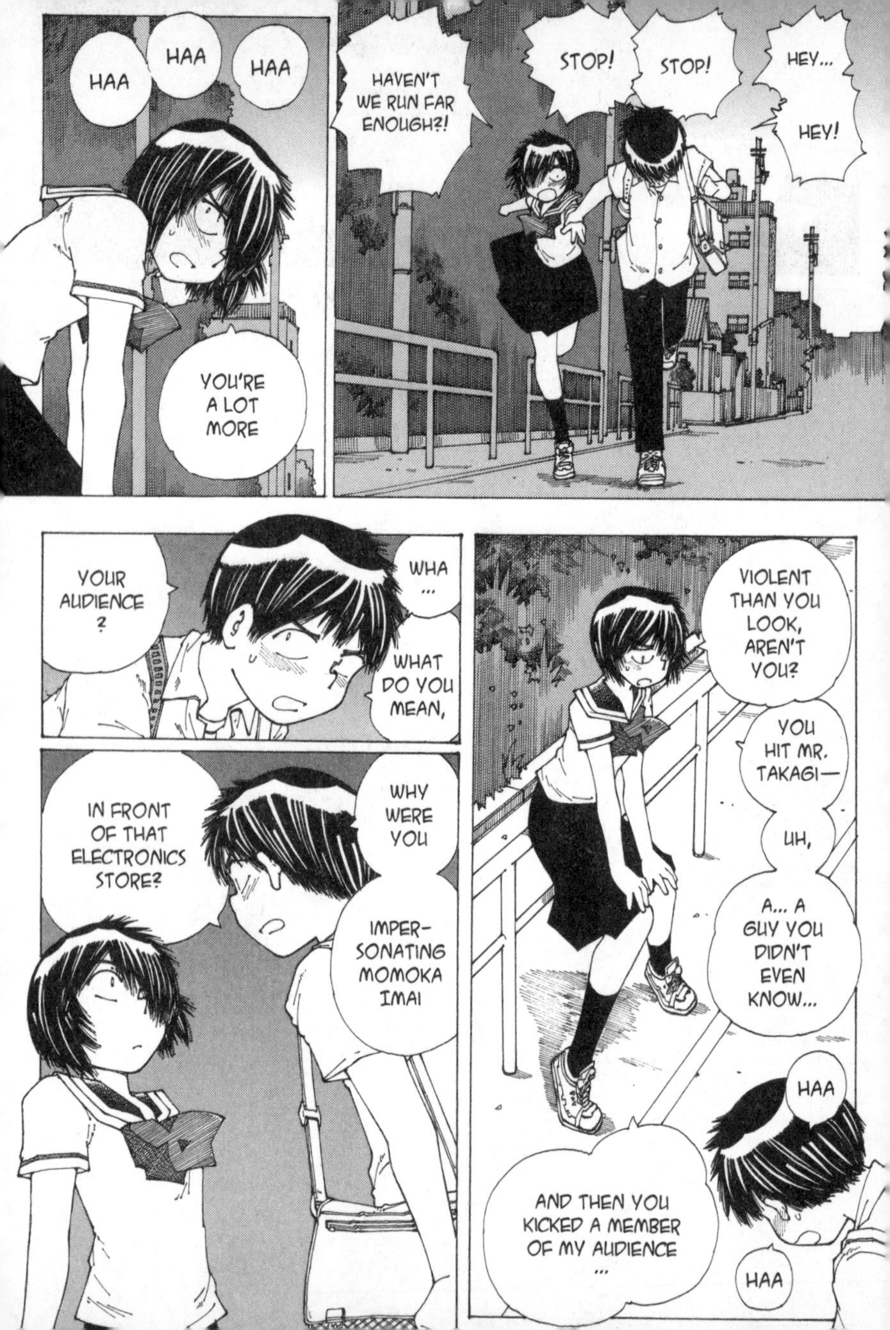
HEY...
HEY!
STOP!
STOP!
HAVEN'T WE RUN FAR ENOUGH?!
HAA
HAA
HAA
YOU'RE A LOT MORE
VIOLENT THAN YOU LOOK, AREN'T YOU?
YOU HIT MR. TAKAGI—
UH,
A... A GUY YOU DIDN'T EVEN KNOW...
HAA
AND THEN YOU KICKED A MEMBER OF MY AUDIENCE ...
HAA
WHA ...
WHAT DO YOU MEAN,
YOUR AUDIENCE ?
WHY WERE YOU
IMPERSONATING MOMOKA IMAI
IN FRONT OF THAT ELECTRONICS STORE?

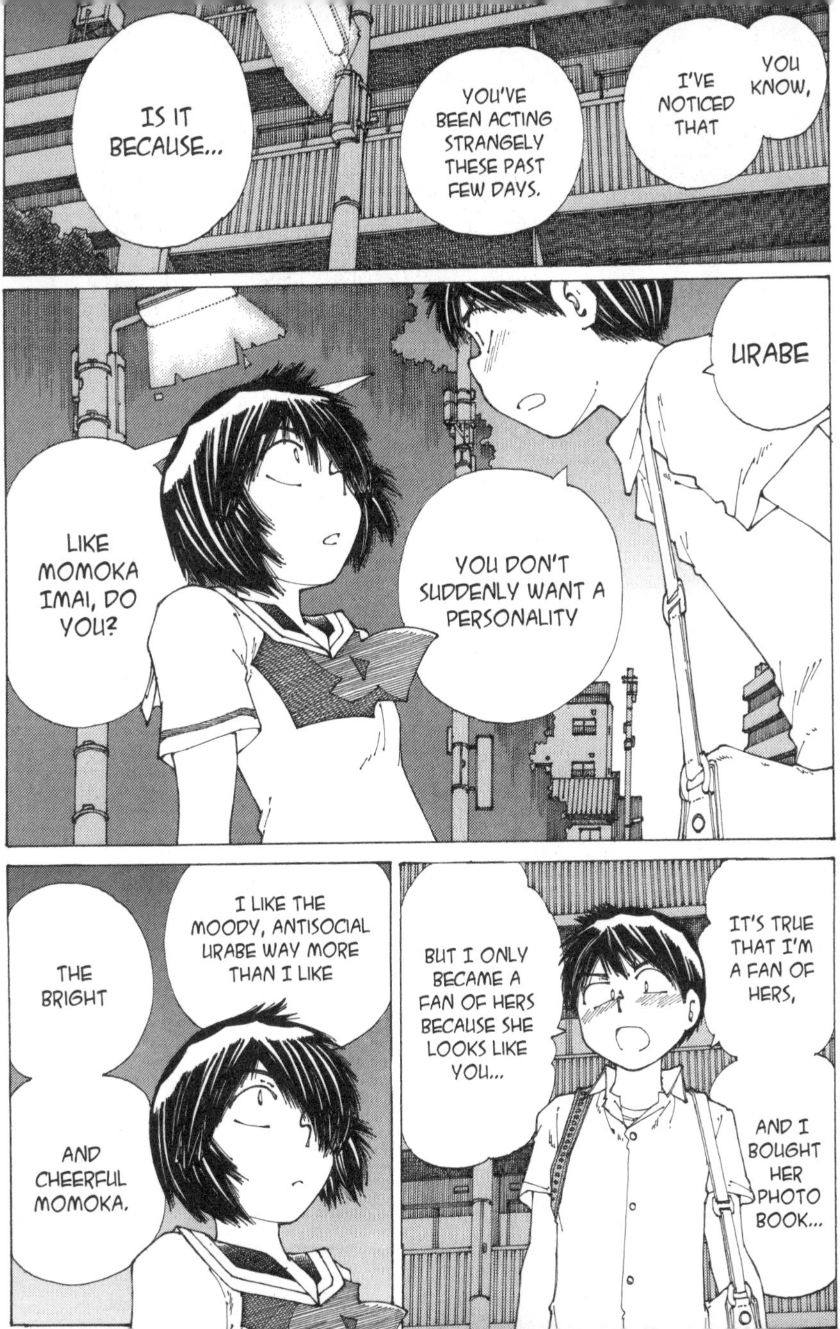
YOU KNOW,
I'VE NOTICED THAT
YOU'VE BEEN ACTING STRANGELY THESE PAST FEW DAYS.
IS IT BECAUSE...
URABE
YOU DON'T SUDDENLY WANT A PERSONALITY
LIKE MOMOKA IMAI, DO YOU?
IT'S TRUE THAT I'M A FAN OF HERS,
AND I BOUGHT HER PHOTO BOOK...
BUT I ONLY BECAME A FAN OF HERS BECAUSE SHE LOOKS LIKE YOU...
I LIKE THE MOODY, ANTISOCIAL URABE WAY MORE THAN I LIKE
THE BRIGHT
AND CHEERFUL MOMOKA.

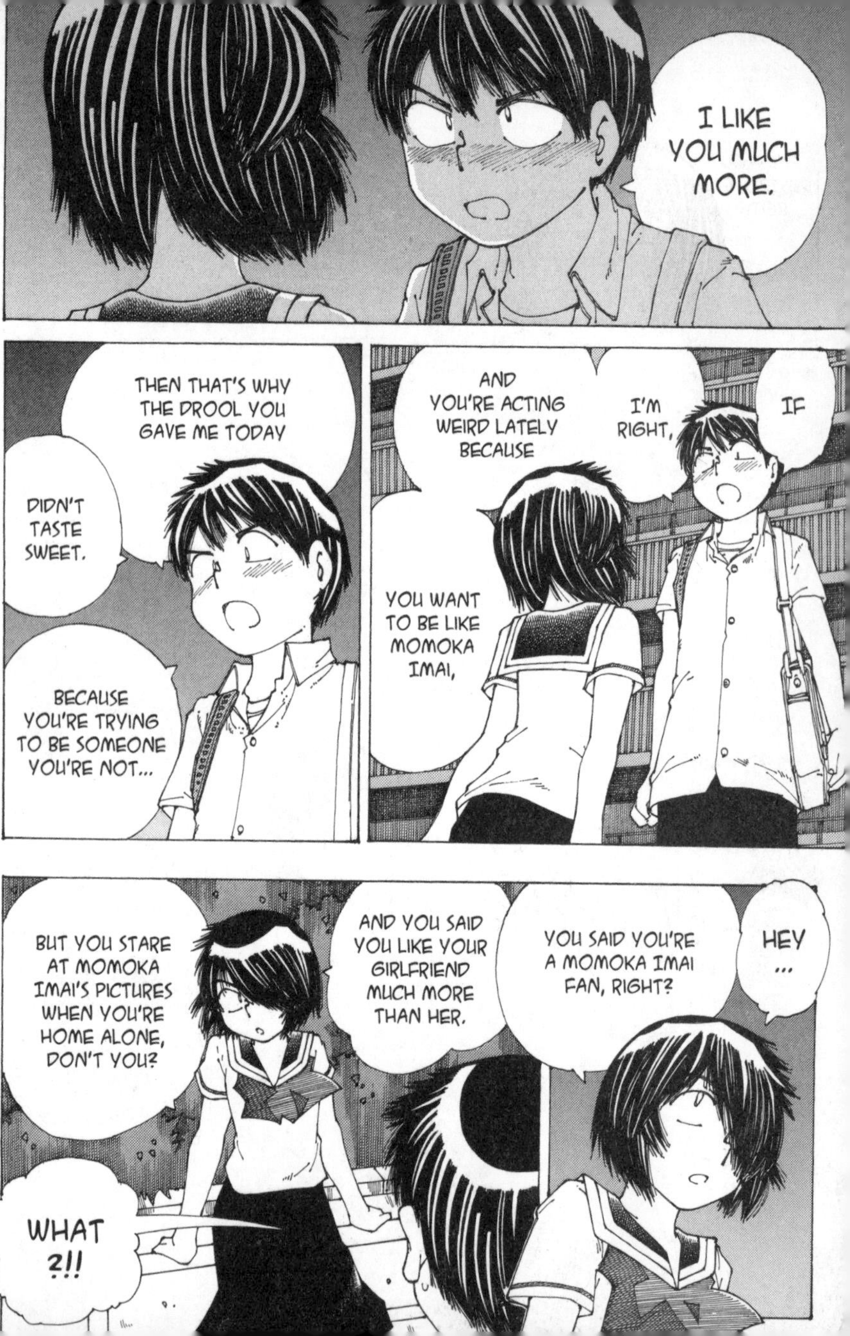
I LIKE YOU MUCH MORE.
IF
I'M RIGHT,
AND YOU'RE ACTING WEIRD LATELY BECAUSE
YOU WANT TO BE LIKE MOMOKA IMAI,
THEN THAT'S WHY THE DROOL YOU GAVE ME TODAY
DIDN'T TASTE SWEET.
BECAUSE YOU'RE TRYING TO BE SOMEONE YOU'RE NOT...
HEY ...
YOU SAID YOU'RE A MOMOKA IMAI FAN, RIGHT?
AND YOU SAID YOU LIKE YOUR GIRLFRIEND MUCH MORE THAN HER.
BUT YOU STARE AT MOMOKA IMAI'S PICTURES WHEN YOU'RE HOME ALONE, DON'T YOU?
WHAT ?!!

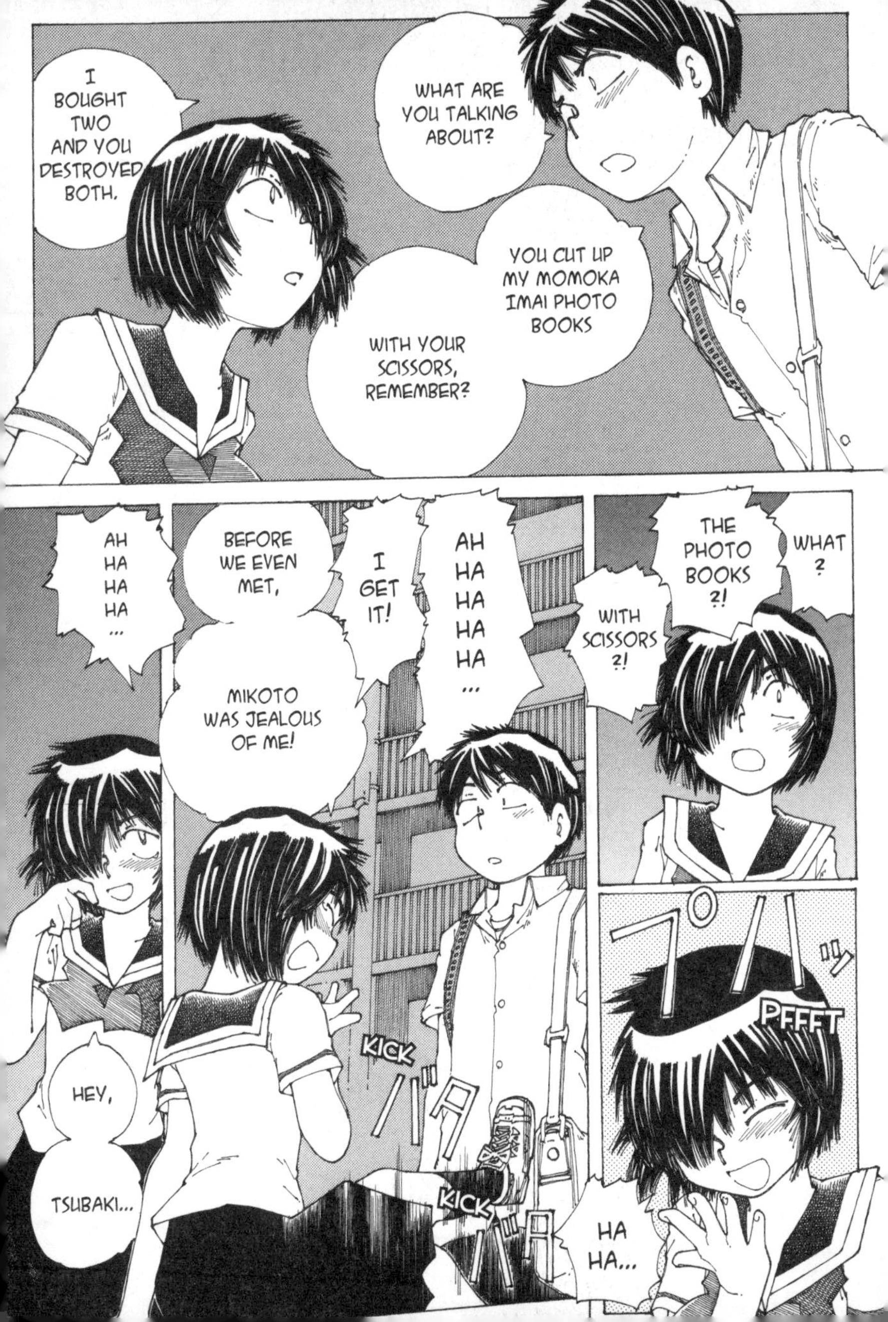
WHAT ARE YOU TALKING ABOUT?
YOU CUT UP MY MOMOKA IMAI PHOTO BOOKS
WITH YOUR SCISSORS, REMEMBER?
I BOUGHT TWO AND YOU DESTROYED BOTH.
WHAT?
THE PHOTO BOOKS?!
WITH SCISSORS?!
PFFFT
HA HA...
AH HA HA HA HA HA...
I GET IT!
BEFORE WE EVEN MET,
MIKOTO WAS JEALOUS OF ME!
KICK
KICK
AH HA HA HA...
HEY,
TSUBAKI...

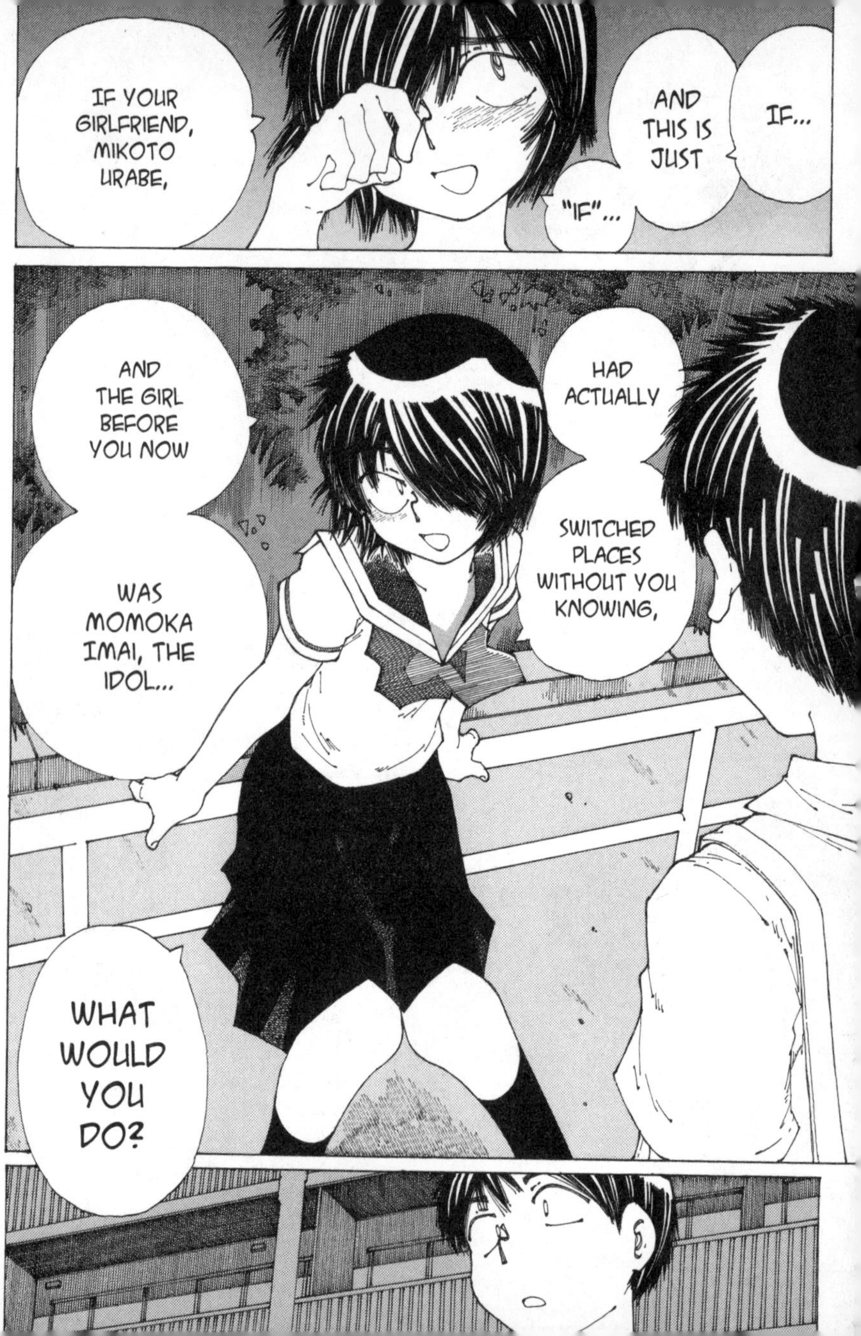
IF...
AND THIS IS JUST "IF"...
IF YOUR GIRLFRIEND, MIKOTO URABE,
HAD ACTUALLY SWITCHED PLACES WITHOUT YOU KNOWING,
AND THE GIRL BEFORE YOU NOW WAS MOMOKA IMAI, THE IDOL...
WHAT WOULD YOU DO?

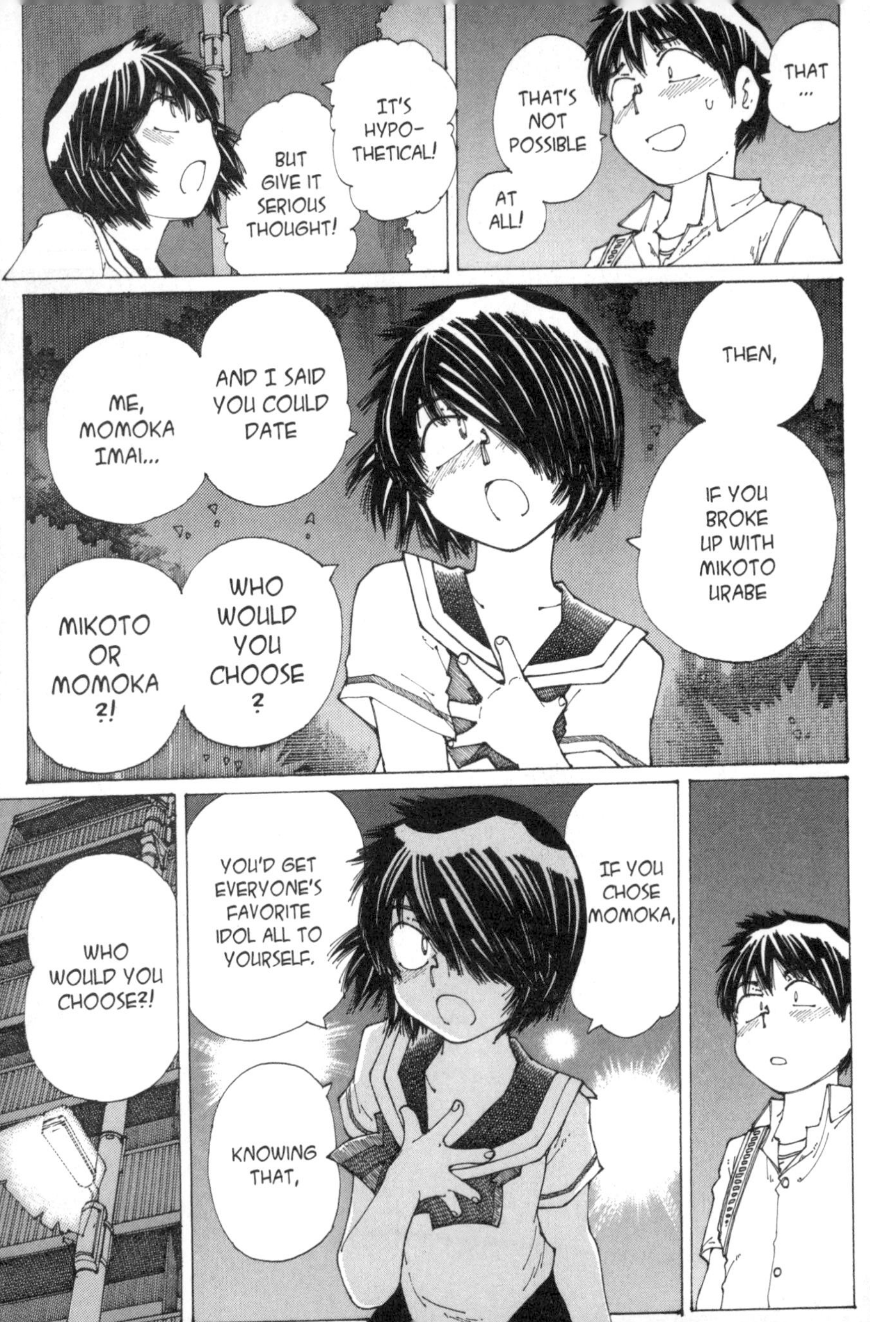
THAT ...
THAT'S NOT POSSIBLE
AT ALL!
IT'S HYPO-THETICAL!
BUT GIVE IT SERIOUS THOUGHT!
THEN,
IF YOU BROKE UP WITH MIKOTO URABE
AND I SAID YOU COULD DATE
ME, MOMOKA IMAI...
WHO WOULD YOU CHOOSE?
MIKOTO OR MOMOKA?!
IF YOU CHOSE MOMOKA,
YOU'D GET EVERYONE'S FAVORITE IDOL ALL TO YOURSELF.
KNOWING THAT,
WHO WOULD YOU CHOOSE?!

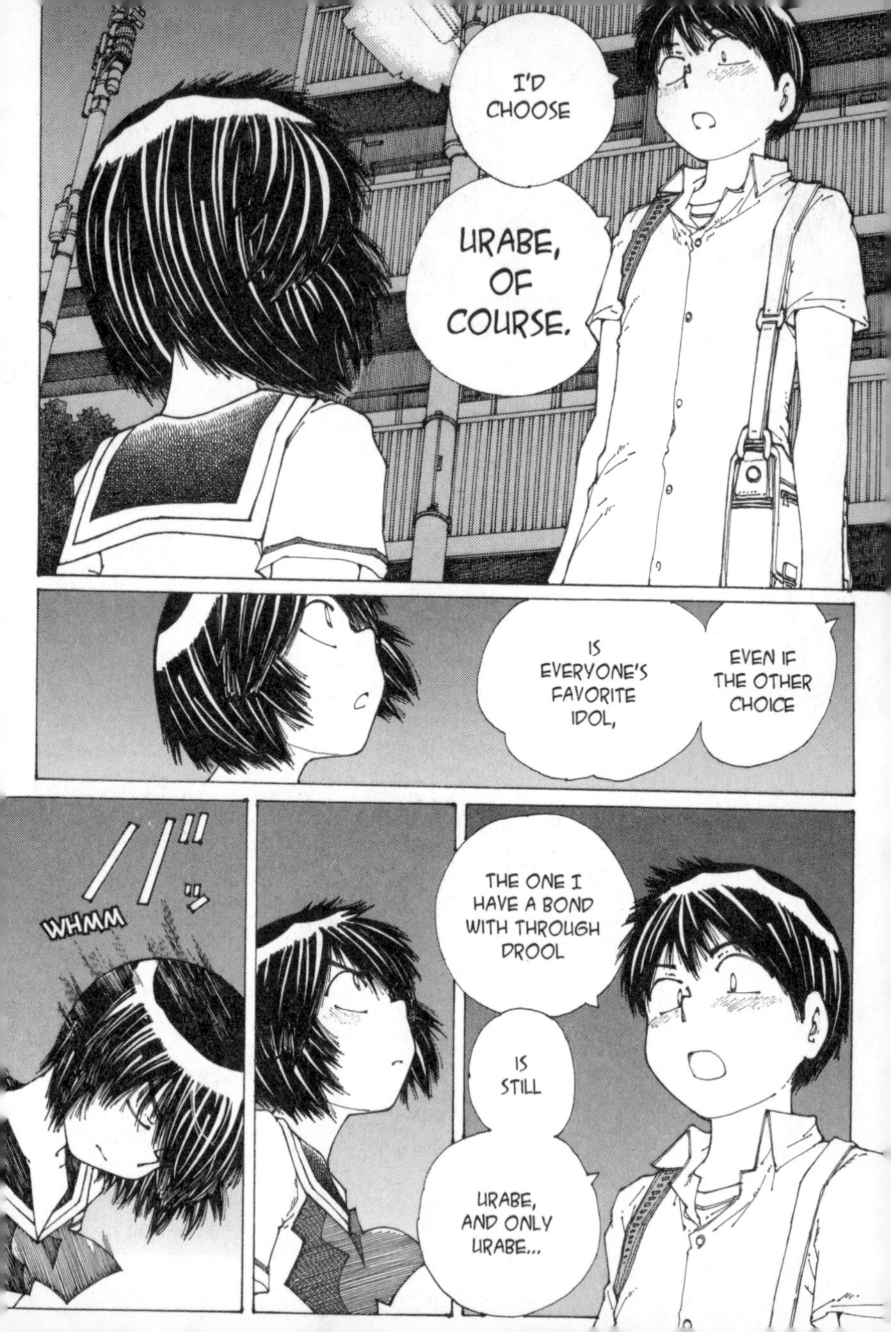
I'D CHOOSE
URABE, OF COURSE.
EVEN IF THE OTHER CHOICE
IS EVERYONE'S FAVORITE IDOL,
THE ONE I HAVE A BOND WITH THROUGH DROOL
IS STILL
URABE, AND ONLY URABE...
WHMM

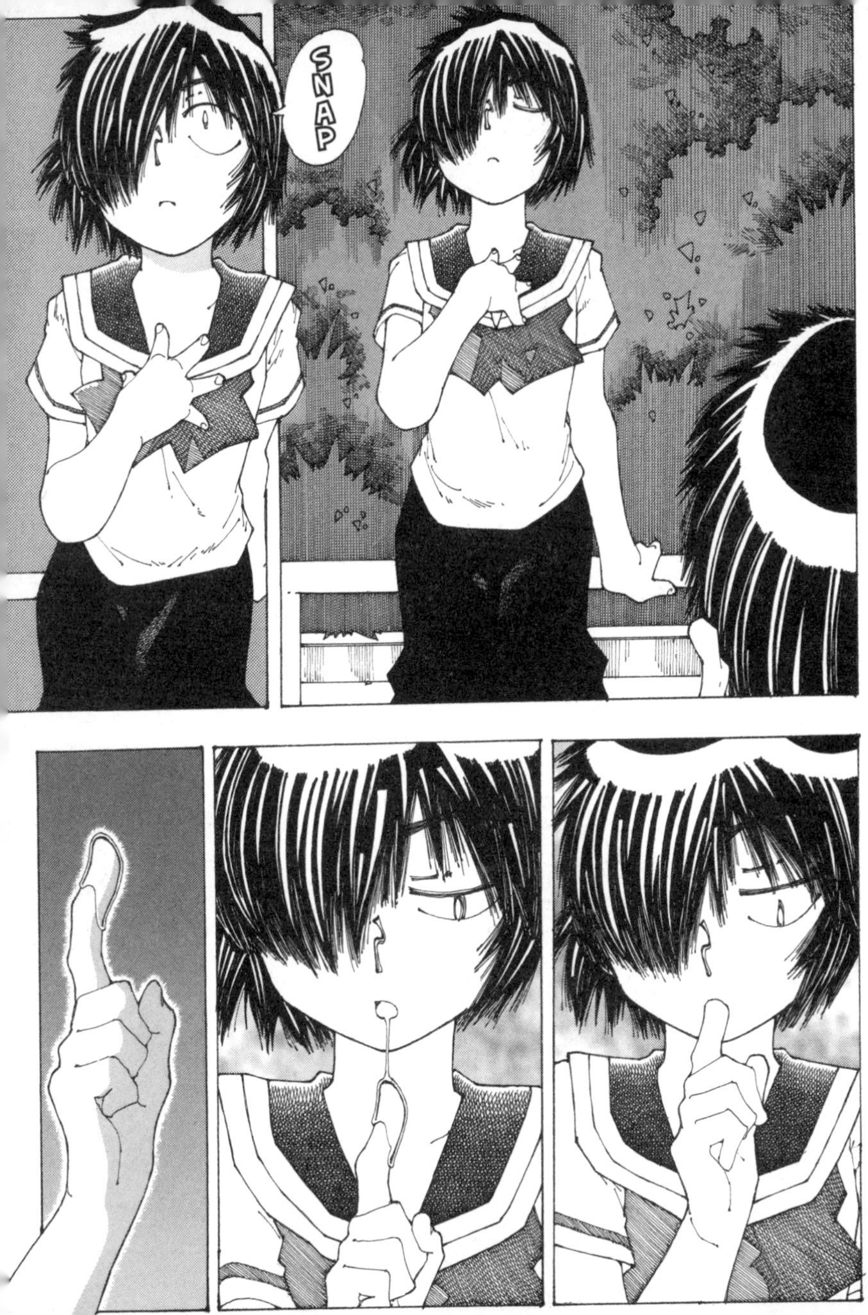
SNAP

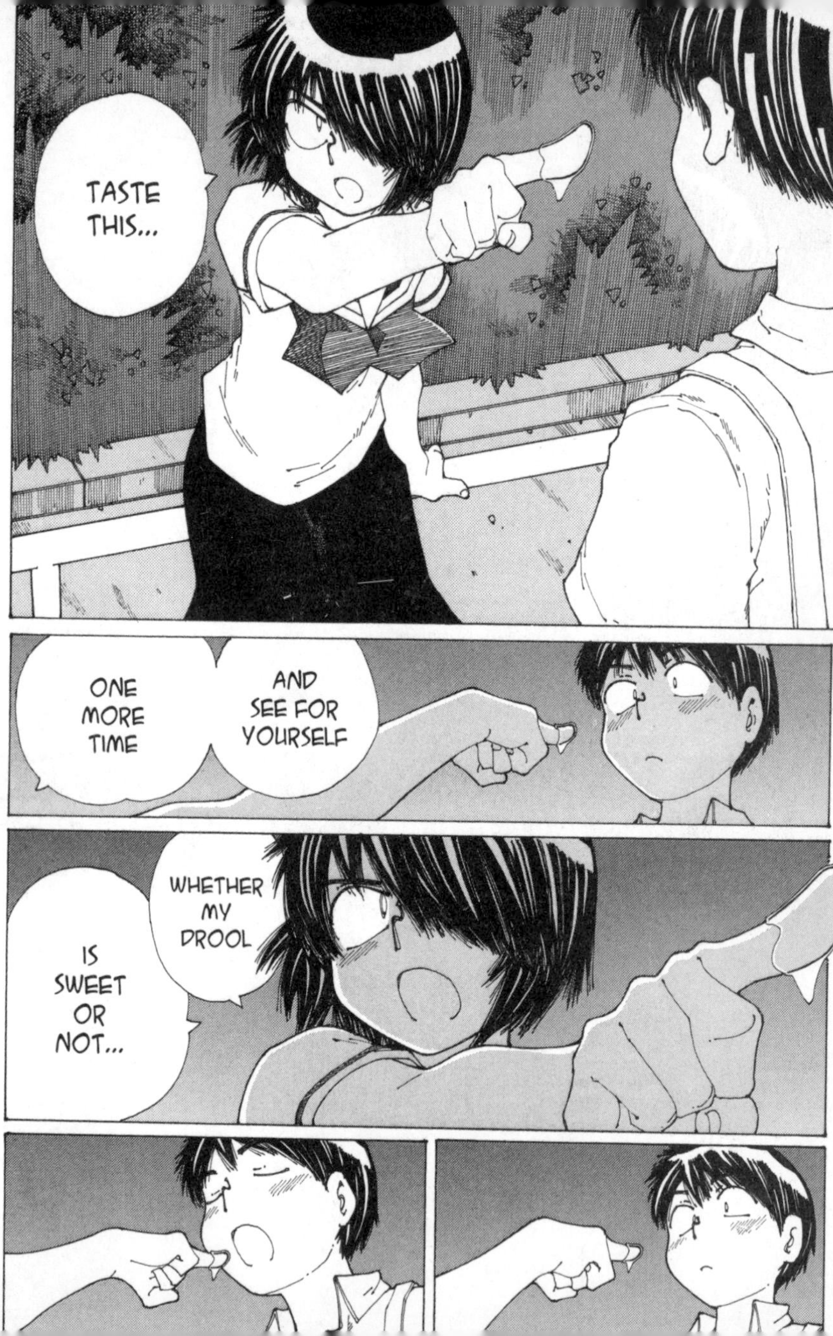
TASTE THIS...
AND SEE FOR YOURSELF
ONE MORE TIME
WHETHER MY DROOL
IS SWEET OR NOT...

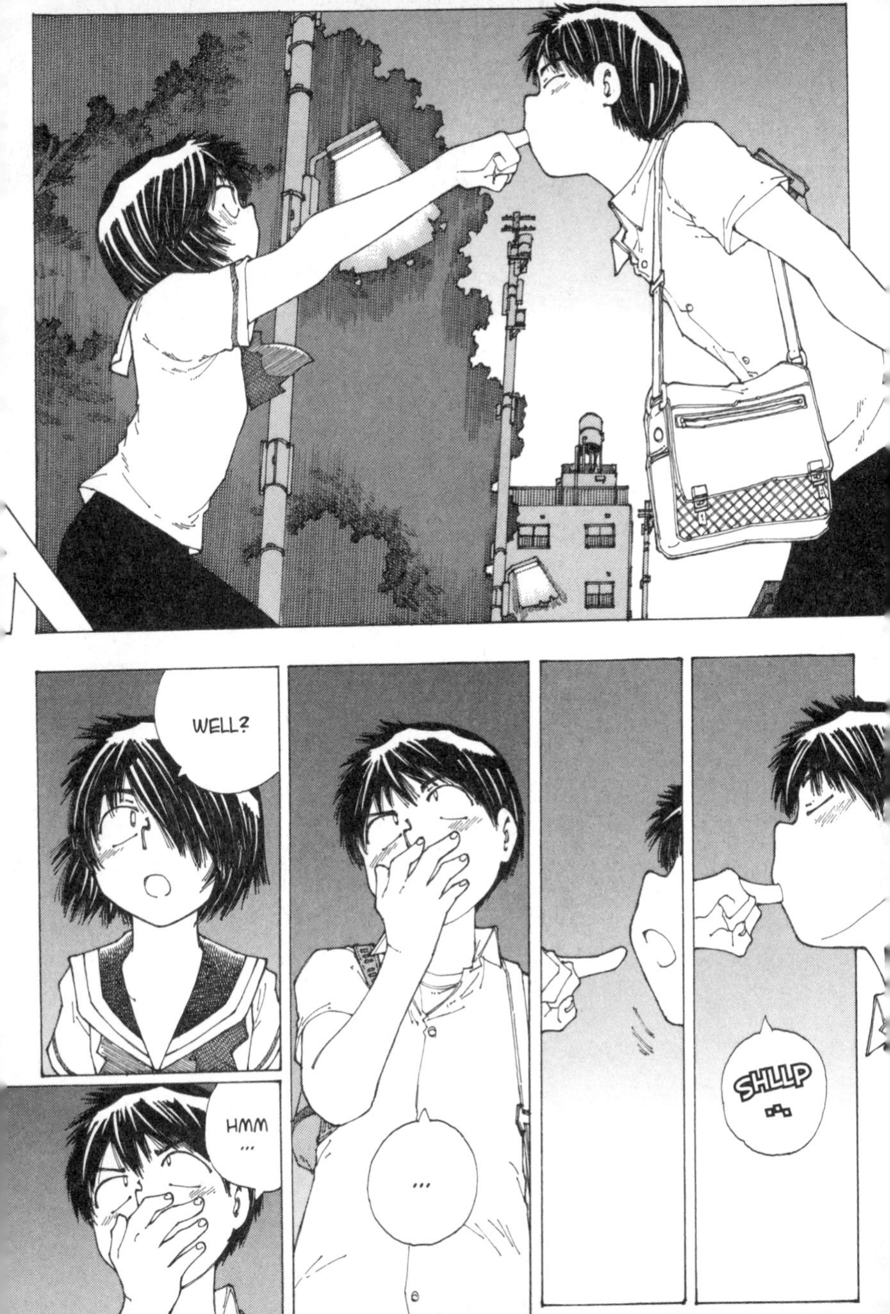
SHLLP
...
WELL?
HMM ...

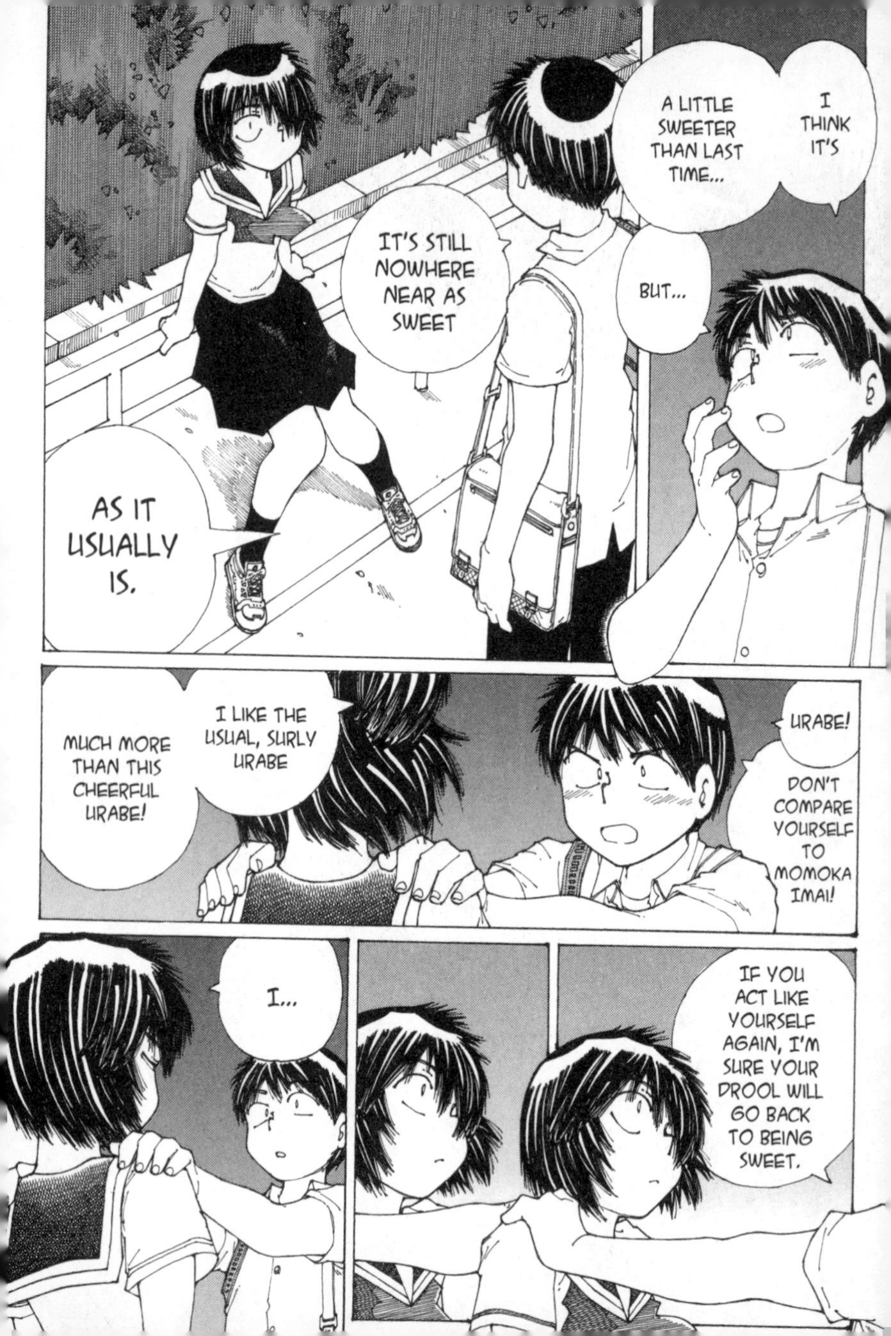
I THINK IT'S
A LITTLE SWEETER THAN LAST TIME...
BUT...
IT'S STILL NOWHERE NEAR AS SWEET
AS IT USUALLY IS.
URABE!
DON'T COMPARE YOURSELF TO MOMOKA IMAI!
I LIKE THE USUAL, SURLY URABE
MUCH MORE THAN THIS CHEERFUL URABE!
IF YOU ACT LIKE YOURSELF AGAIN, I'M SURE YOUR DROOL WILL GO BACK TO BEING SWEET.
I...

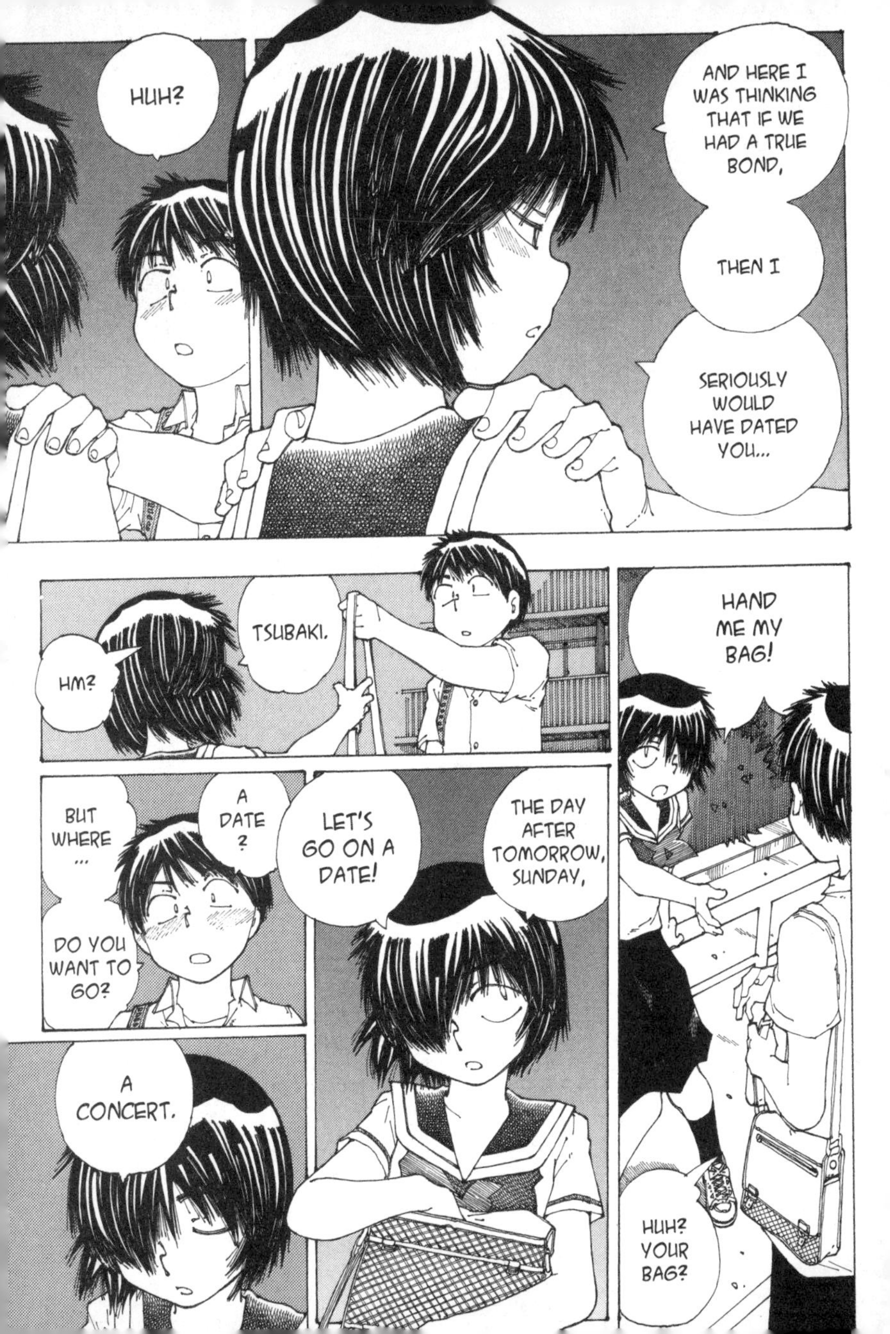
AND HERE I WAS THINKING THAT IF WE HAD A TRUE BOND,
THEN I
SERIOUSLY WOULD HAVE DATED YOU...
HUH?
HAND ME MY BAG!
HUH? YOUR BAG?
TSUBAKI.
HM?
THE DAY AFTER TOMORROW, SUNDAY,
LET'S GO ON A DATE!
A DATE?
BUT WHERE ...
DO YOU WANT TO GO?
A CONCERT.

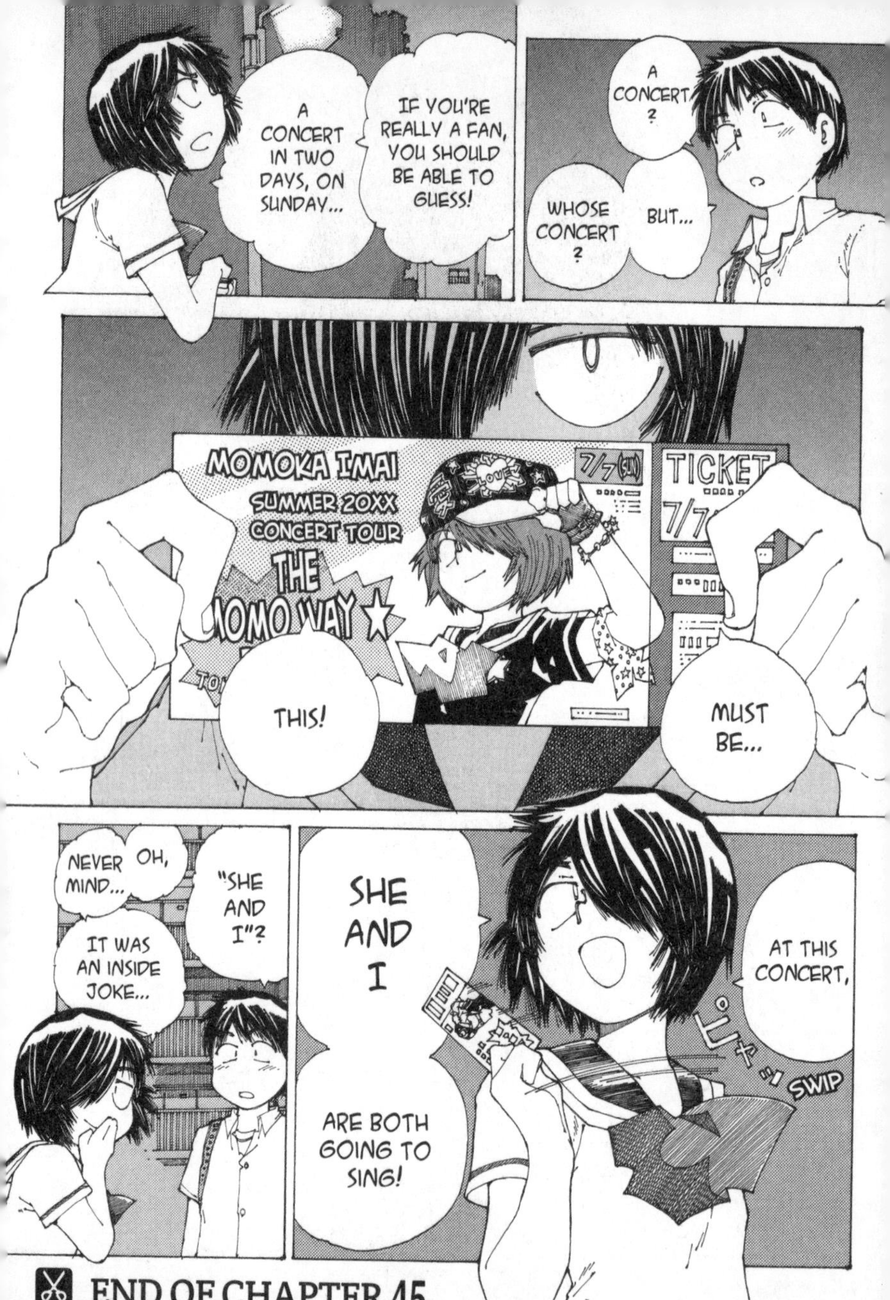
A CONCERT?
BUT...
WHOSE CONCERT?
IF YOU'RE REALLY A FAN, YOU SHOULD BE ABLE TO GUESS!
A CONCERT IN TWO DAYS, ON SUNDAY...
TICKET
MOMOKA IMAI
SUMMER 20XX CONCERT TOUR
THE MOMO WAY★
MUST BE...
THIS!
AT THIS CONCERT,
SWIP
SHE AND I
ARE BOTH GOING TO SING!
"SHE AND I"?
OH, NEVER MIND...
IT WAS AN INSIDE JOKE...

END OF CHAPTER 45

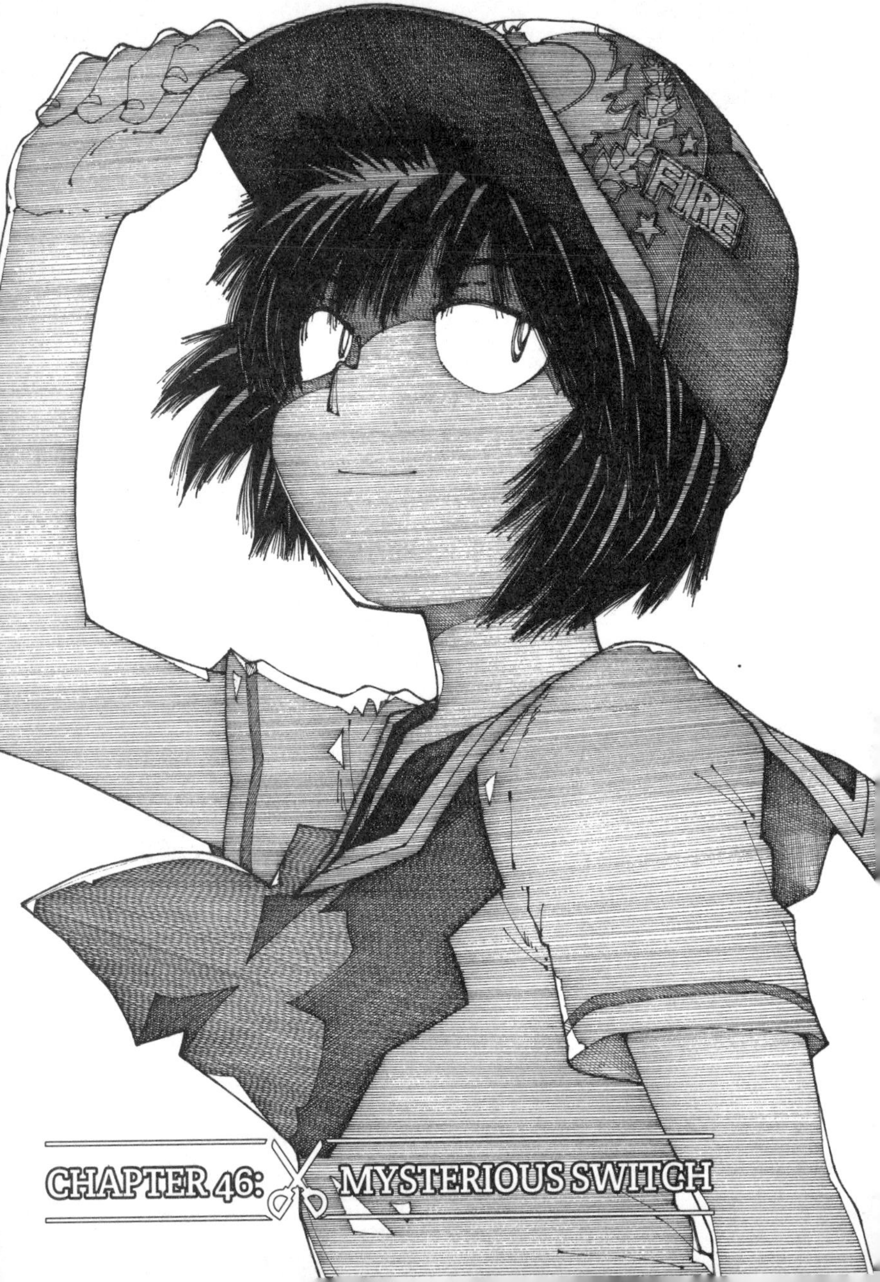
FIRE

CHAPTER 46: MYSTERIOUS SWITCH

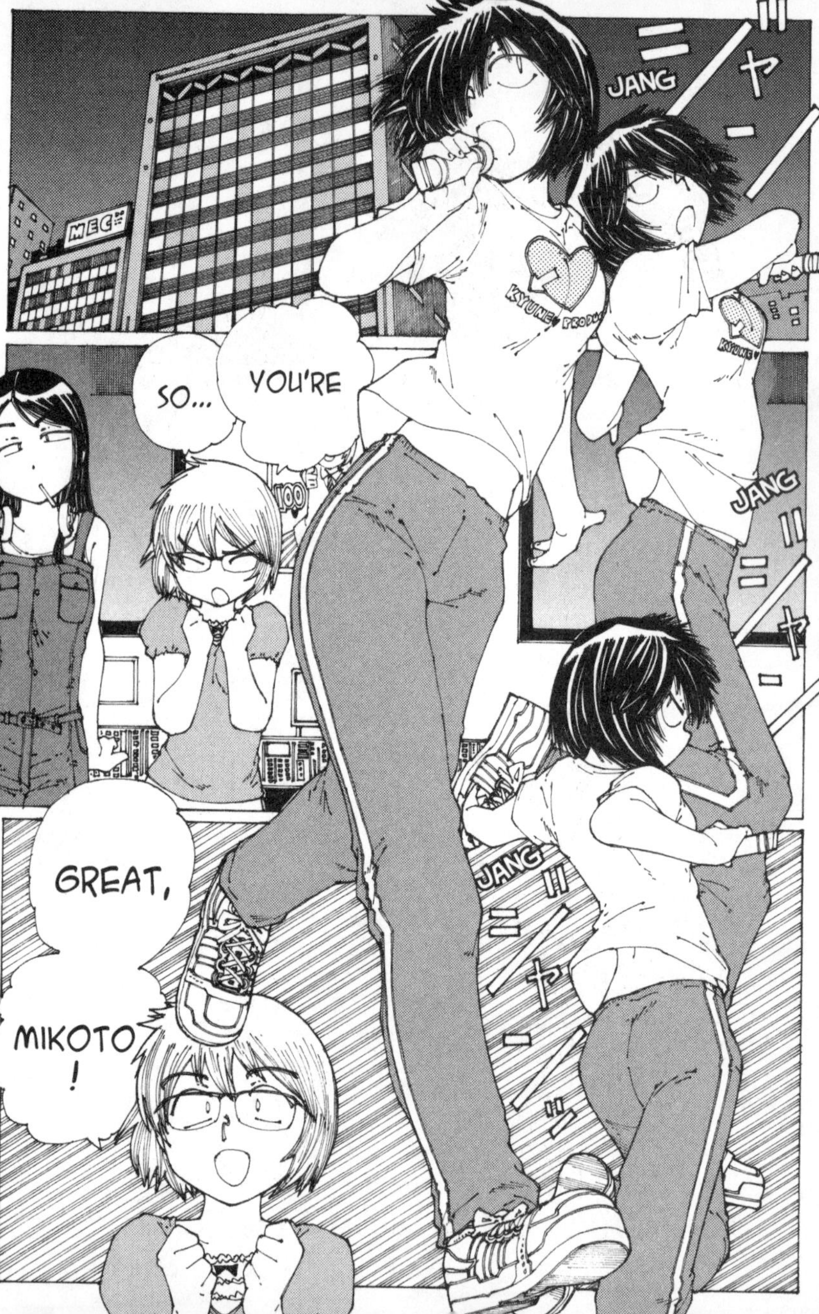
JANG
MEG
JANG
SO...
YOU'RE
JANG
GREAT,
MIKOTO!

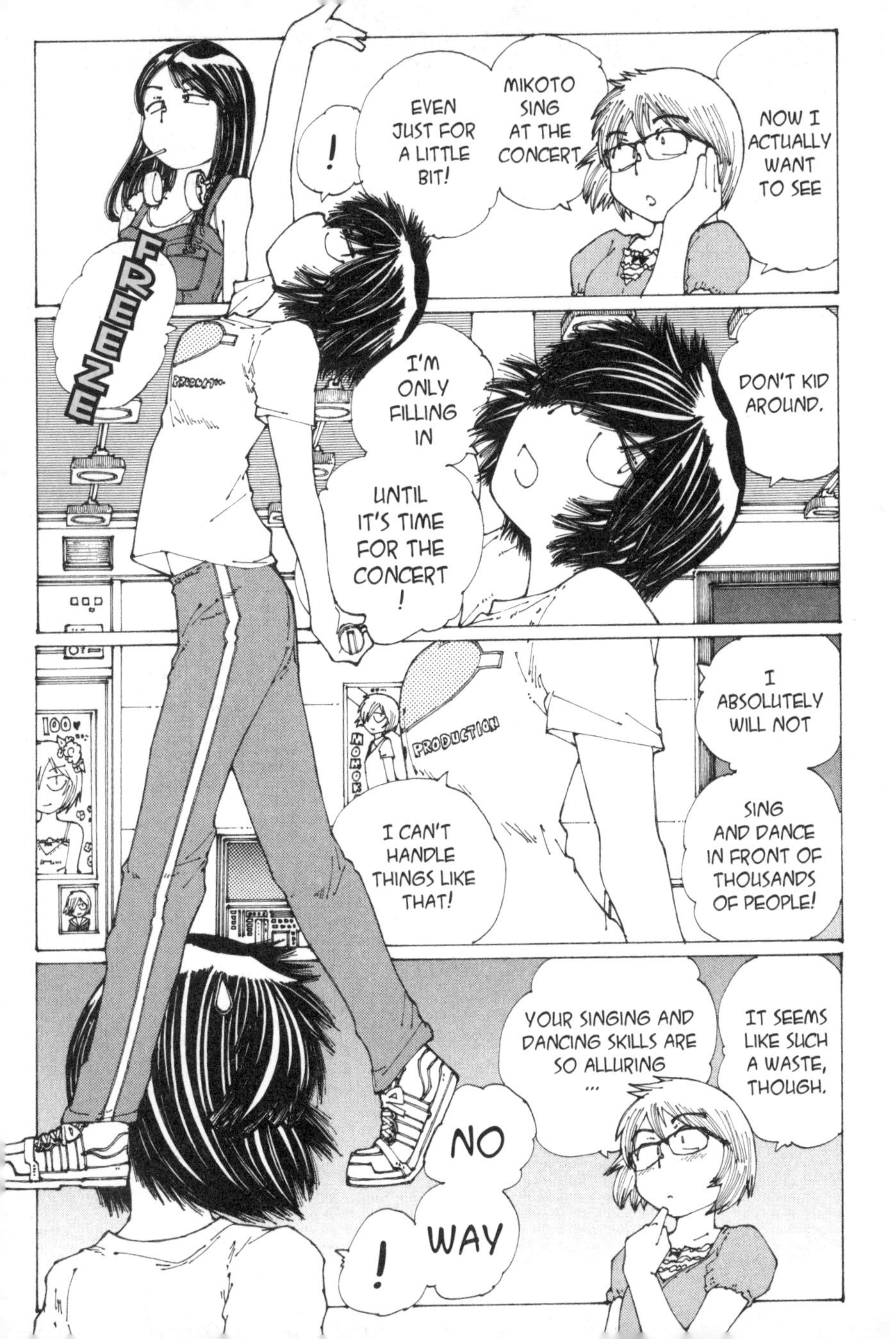
NOW I ACTUALLY WANT TO SEE
MIKOTO SING AT THE CONCERT
EVEN JUST FOR A LITTLE BIT!
!
FREEZE
DON'T KID AROUND.
I'M ONLY FILLING IN
UNTIL IT'S TIME FOR THE CONCERT !
I ABSOLUTELY WILL NOT
SING AND DANCE IN FRONT OF THOUSANDS OF PEOPLE!
PRODUCTION
I CAN'T HANDLE THINGS LIKE THAT!
IT SEEMS LIKE SUCH A WASTE, THOUGH.
YOUR SINGING AND DANCING SKILLS ARE SO ALLURING ...
NO WAY !

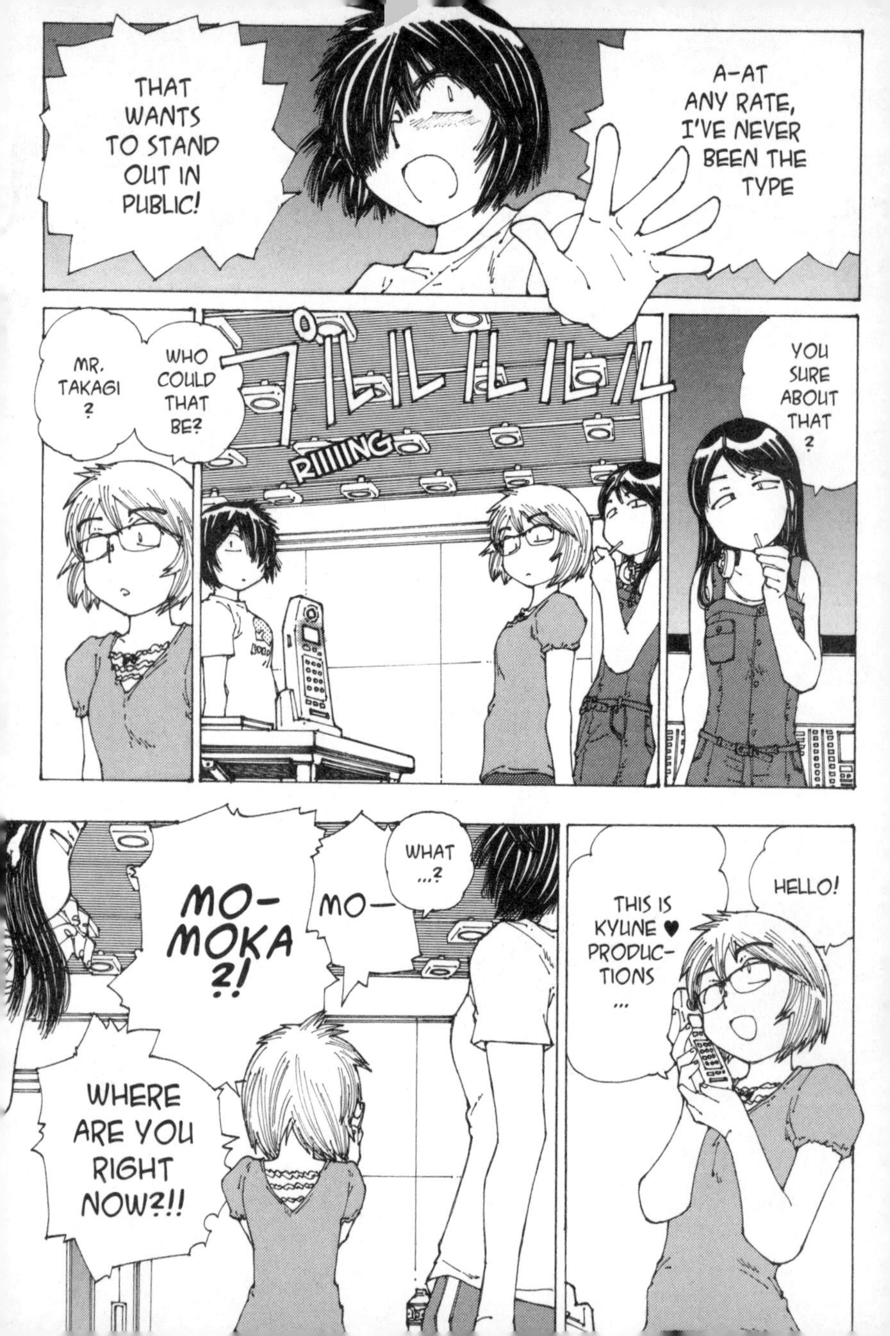
A-AT ANY RATE, I'VE NEVER BEEN THE TYPE
THAT WANTS TO STAND OUT IN PUBLIC!
YOU SURE ABOUT THAT?
プルルルル
RIIIING
WHO COULD THAT BE?
MR. TAKAGI?
HELLO!
THIS IS KYUNE ♥ PRODUCTIONS...
WHAT...?
MO—
MO-MOKA?!
WHERE ARE YOU RIGHT NOW?!!

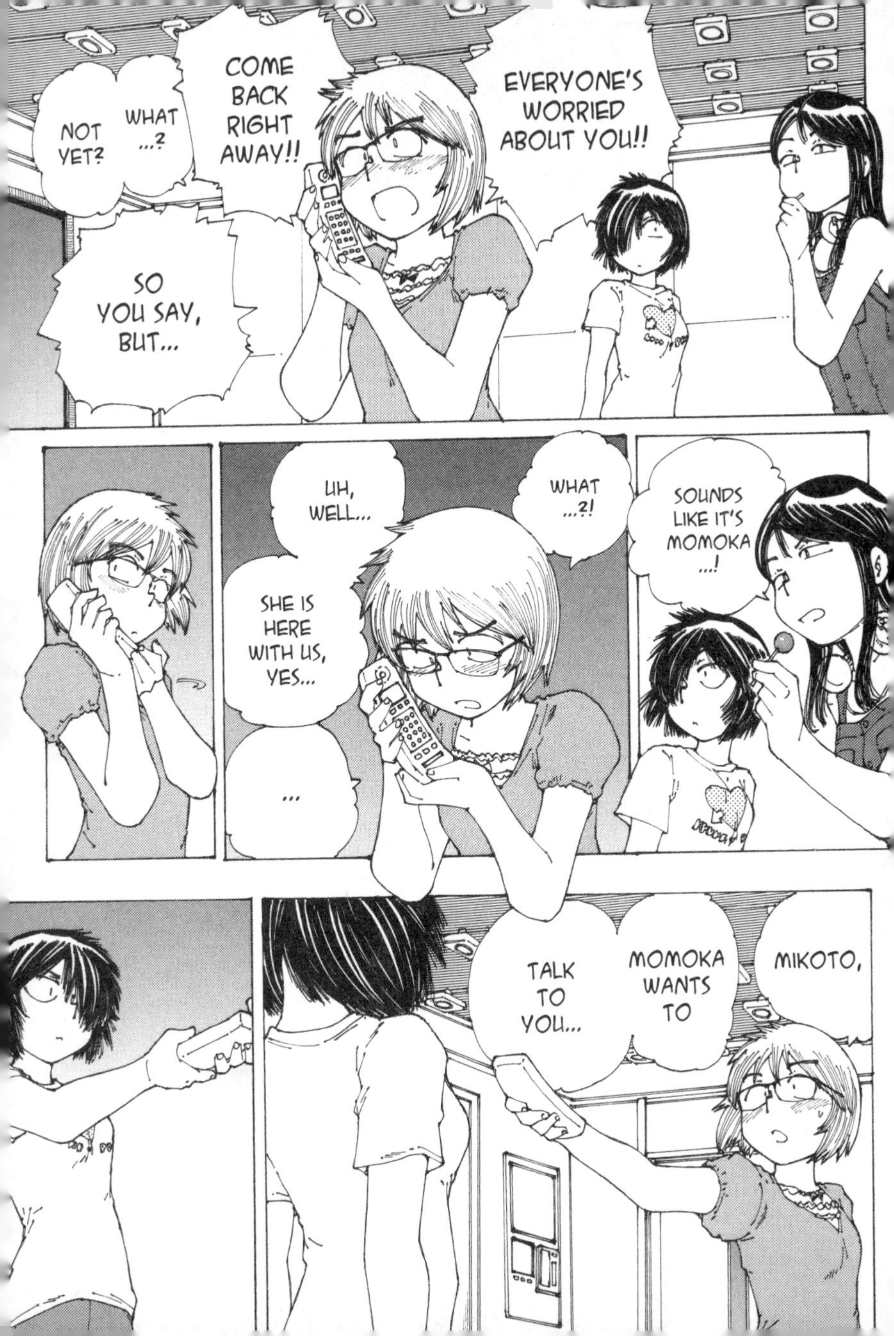
EVERYONE'S WORRIED ABOUT YOU!!
COME BACK RIGHT AWAY!!
WHAT ...?
NOT YET?
SO YOU SAY, BUT...
SOUNDS LIKE IT'S MOMOKA ...!
WHAT ...?!
UH, WELL...
SHE IS HERE WITH US, YES...
...
MIKOTO,
MOMOKA WANTS TO
TALK TO YOU...

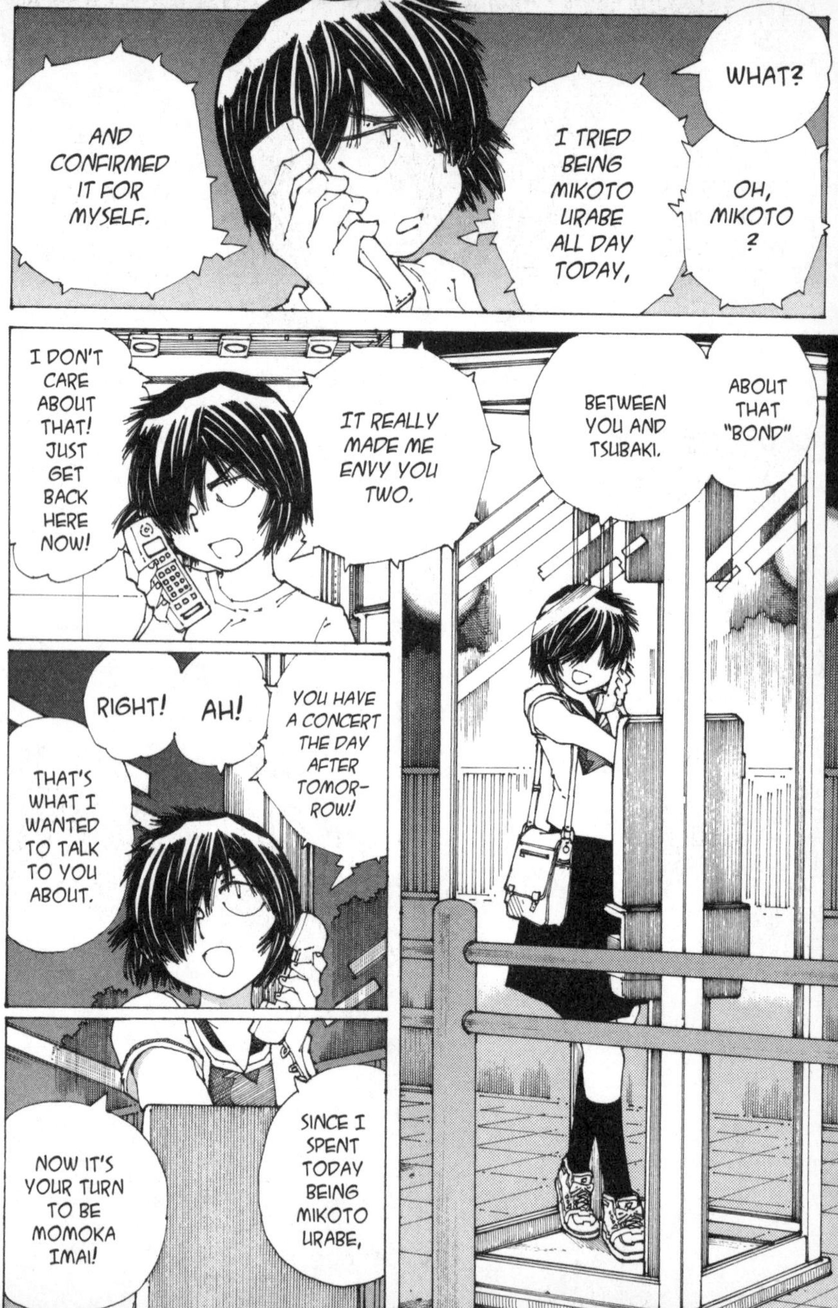
WHAT?
OH, MIKOTO?
I TRIED BEING MIKOTO URABE ALL DAY TODAY,
AND CONFIRMED IT FOR MYSELF.
ABOUT THAT "BOND"
BETWEEN YOU AND TSUBAKI.
IT REALLY MADE ME ENVY YOU TWO.
I DON'T CARE ABOUT THAT! JUST GET BACK HERE NOW!
YOU HAVE A CONCERT THE DAY AFTER TOMOR-ROW!
AH!
RIGHT!
THAT'S WHAT I WANTED TO TALK TO YOU ABOUT.
SINCE I SPENT TODAY BEING MIKOTO URABE,
NOW IT'S YOUR TURN TO BE MOMOKA IMAI!

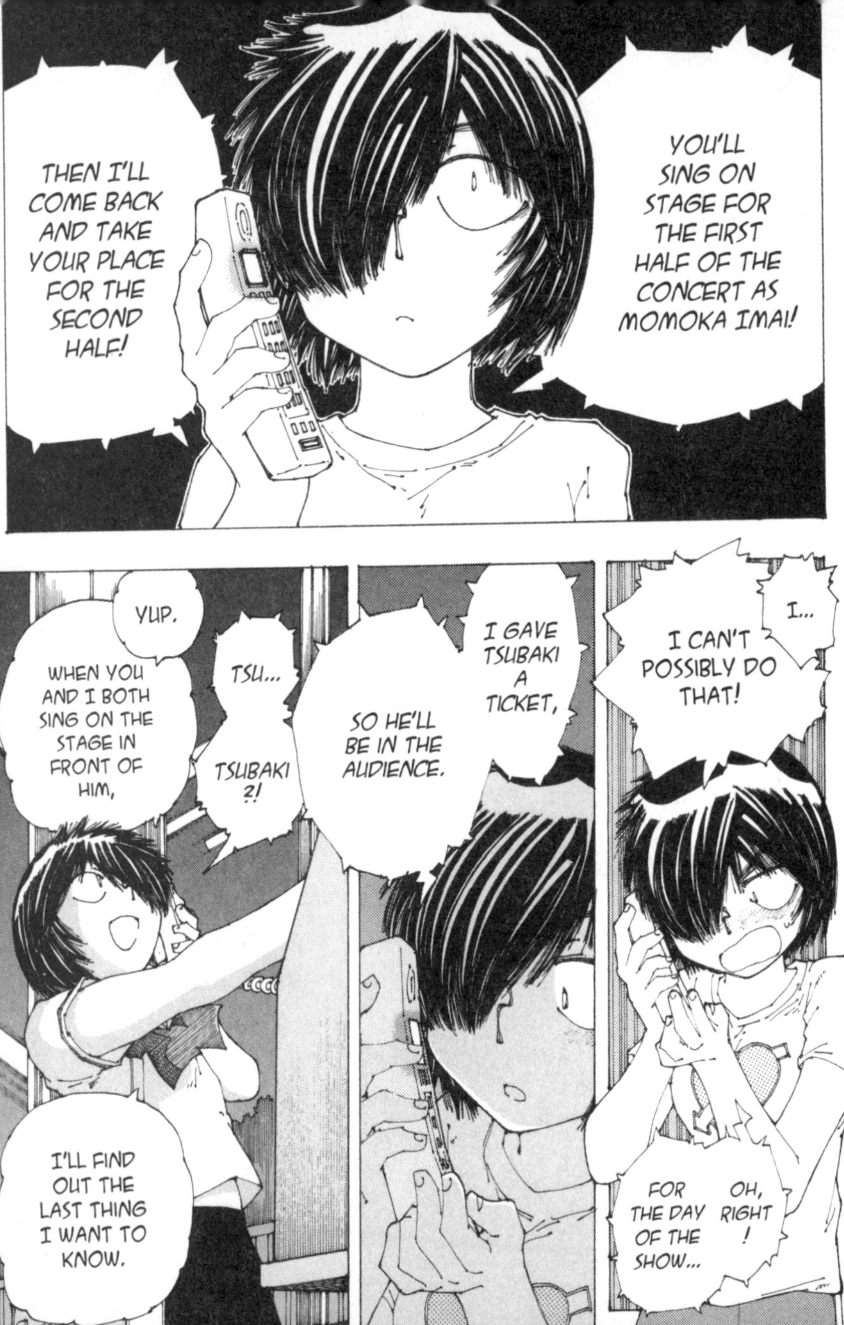
YOU'LL SING ON STAGE FOR THE FIRST HALF OF THE CONCERT AS MOMOKA IMAI!
THEN I'LL COME BACK AND TAKE YOUR PLACE FOR THE SECOND HALF!
I...
I CAN'T POSSIBLY DO THAT!
OH, RIGHT!
FOR THE DAY OF THE SHOW...
I GAVE TSUBAKI A TICKET,
SO HE'LL BE IN THE AUDIENCE.
TSU...
TSUBAKI ?!
YUP.
WHEN YOU AND I BOTH SING ON THE STAGE IN FRONT OF HIM,
I'LL FIND OUT THE LAST THING I WANT TO KNOW.

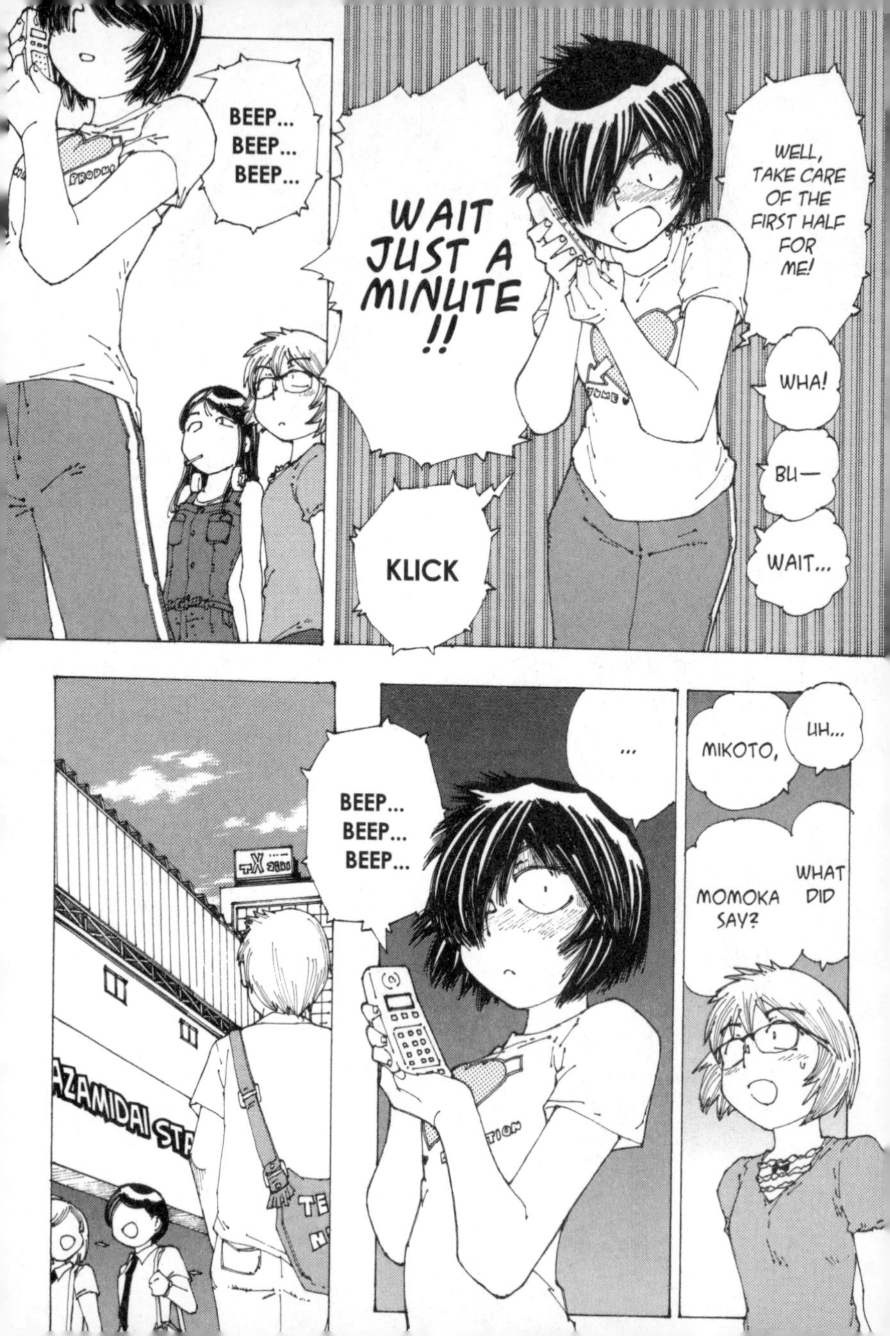
WELL, TAKE CARE OF THE FIRST HALF FOR ME!
WAIT JUST A MINUTE!!
WHA!
BU—
WAIT...
KLICK
BEEP... BEEP... BEEP...
UH... MIKOTO,
WHAT DID MOMOKA SAY?
...
BEEP... BEEP... BEEP...

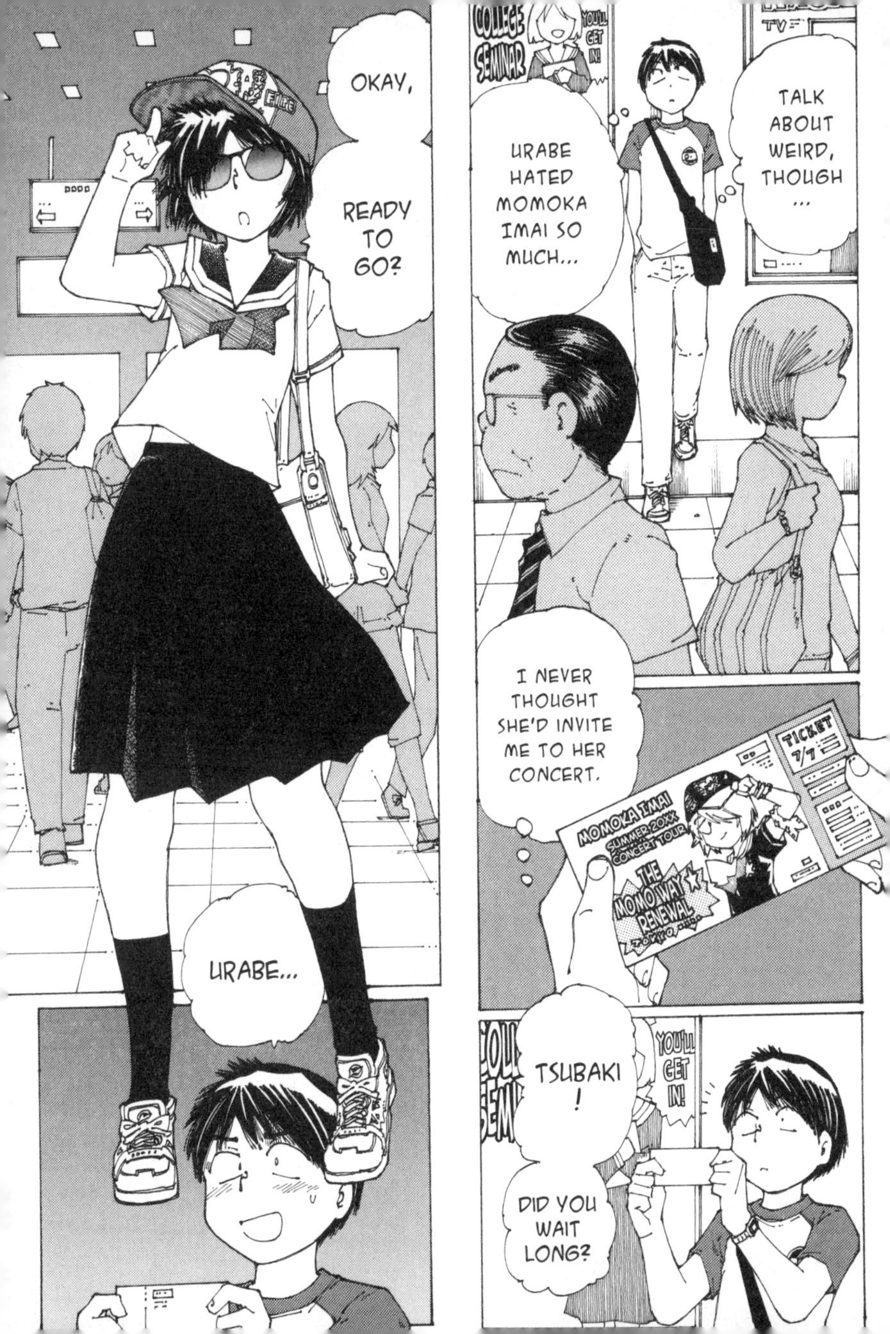
COLLEGE SEMINAR
YOU'LL GET IN!
TALK ABOUT WEIRD, THOUGH...
URABE HATED MOMOKA IMAI SO MUCH...
I NEVER THOUGHT SHE'D INVITE ME TO HER CONCERT.
TICKET 7/7
MOMOKA IMAI SUMMER 20XX CONCERT TOUR
THE MOMO WAY ★ RENEWAL
YOU'LL GET IN!
TSUBAKI!
DID YOU WAIT LONG?
OKAY,
READY TO GO?
URABE...

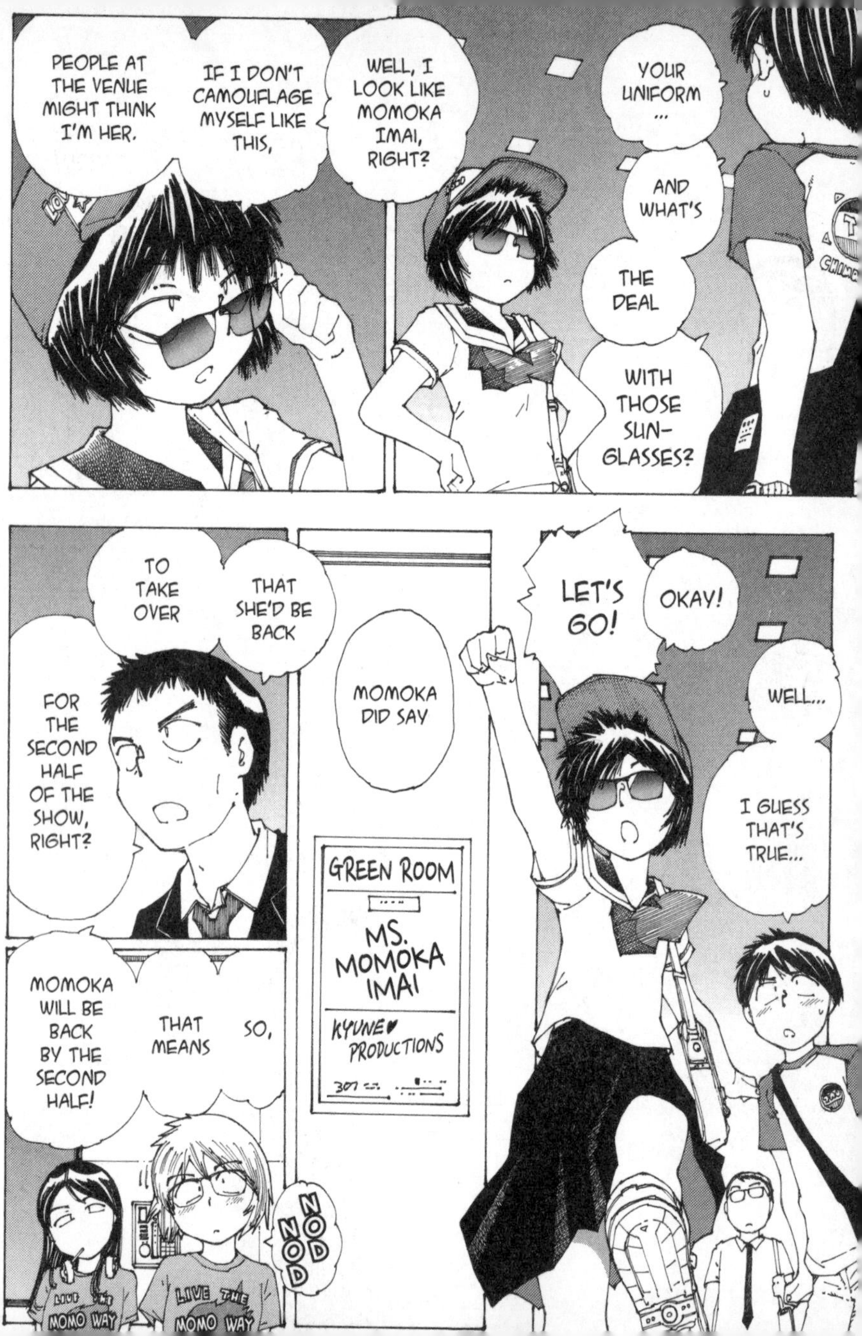
YOUR UNIFORM ...
AND WHAT'S
THE DEAL
WITH THOSE SUN-GLASSES?
WELL, I LOOK LIKE MOMOKA IMAI, RIGHT?
IF I DON'T CAMOUFLAGE MYSELF LIKE THIS,
PEOPLE AT THE VENUE MIGHT THINK I'M HER.
OKAY!
LET'S GO!
WELL...
I GUESS THAT'S TRUE...
GREEN ROOM
MS. MOMOKA IMAI
KYUNE♥ PRODUCTIONS
MOMOKA DID SAY
THAT SHE'D BE BACK
TO TAKE OVER
FOR THE SECOND HALF OF THE SHOW, RIGHT?
SO,
THAT MEANS
MOMOKA WILL BE BACK BY THE SECOND HALF!
NOD NOD
LIVE THE MOMO WAY
LIVE THE MOMO WAY

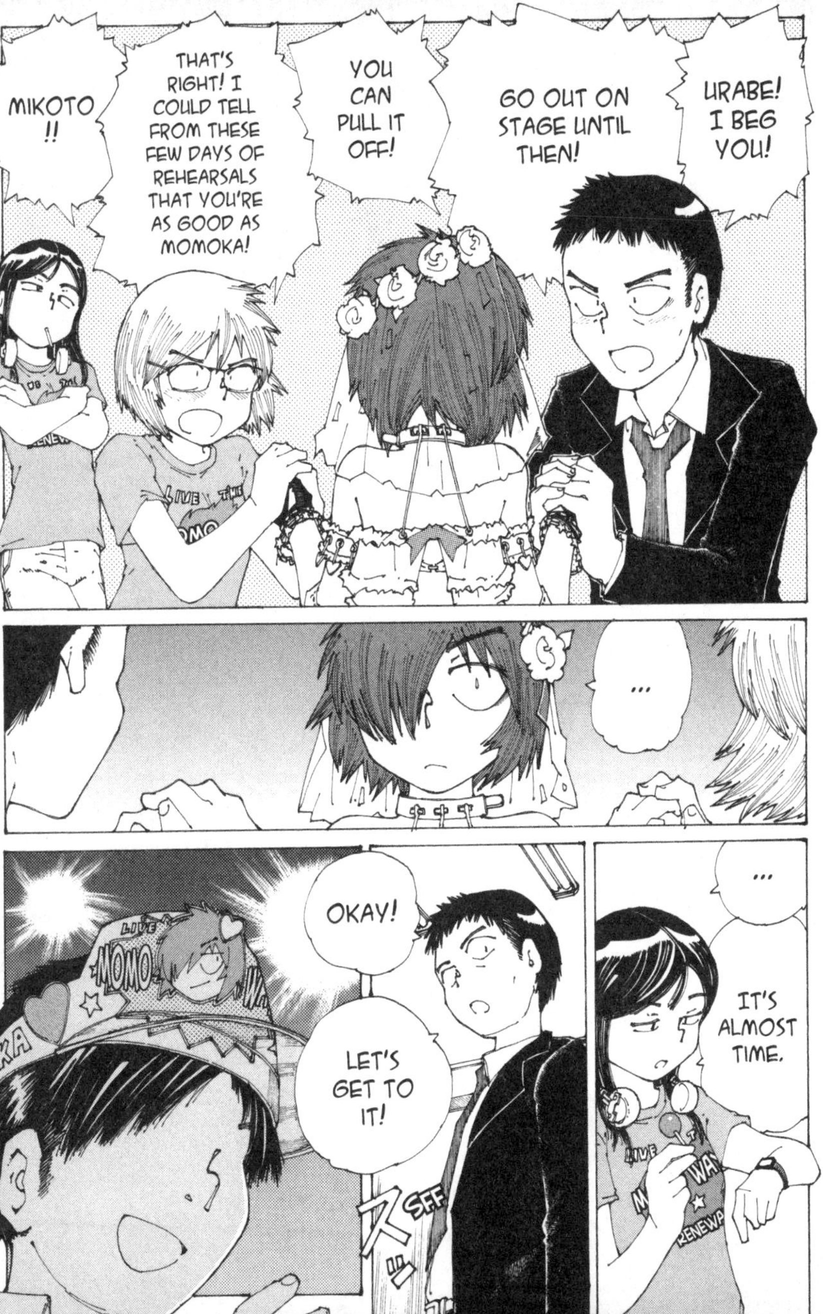
URABE! I BEG YOU!
GO OUT ON STAGE UNTIL THEN!
YOU CAN PULL IT OFF!
THAT'S RIGHT! I COULD TELL FROM THESE FEW DAYS OF REHEARSALS THAT YOU'RE AS GOOD AS MOMOKA!
MIKOTO !!
...
...
IT'S ALMOST TIME.
OKAY!
LET'S GET TO IT!
SFF

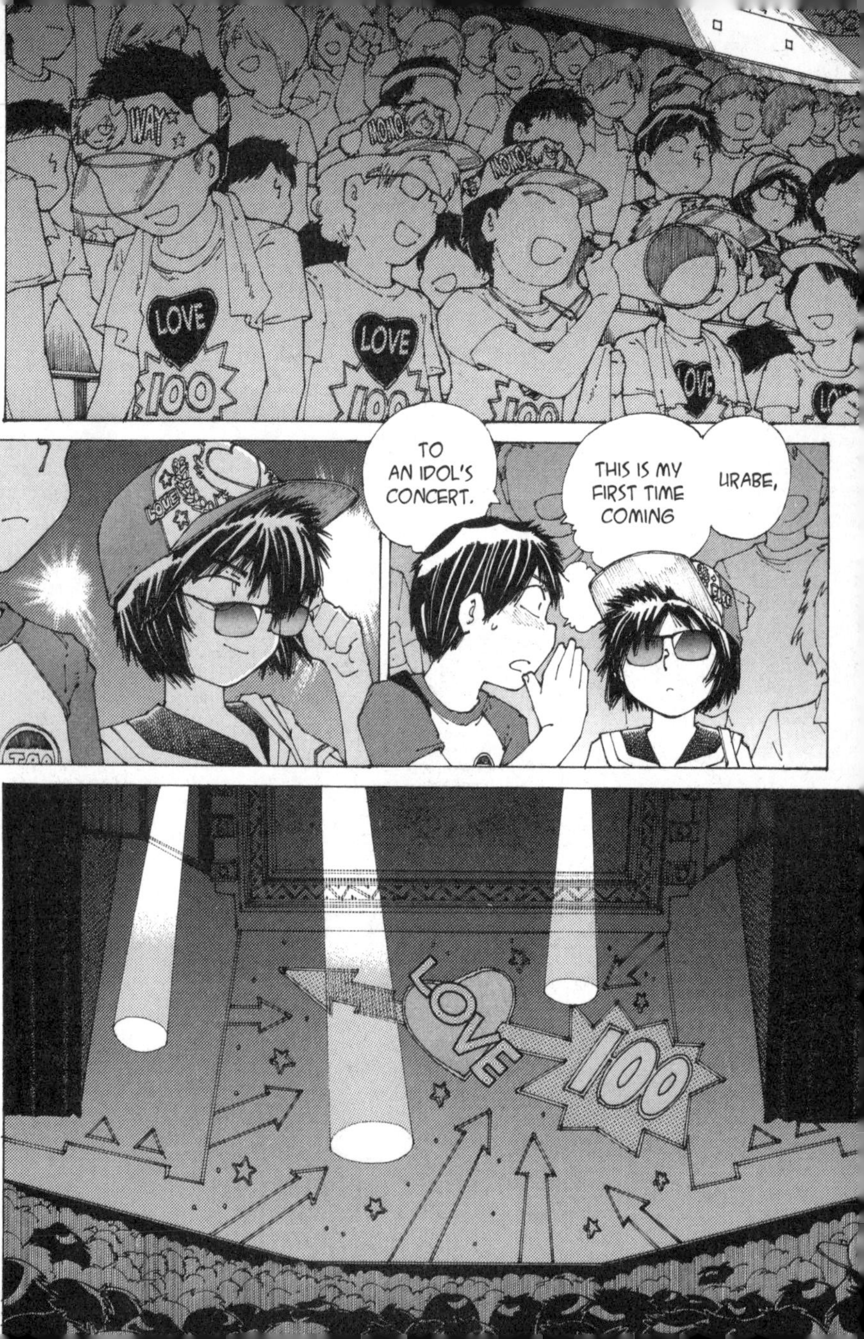
URABE,
THIS IS MY FIRST TIME COMING
TO AN IDOL'S CONCERT.

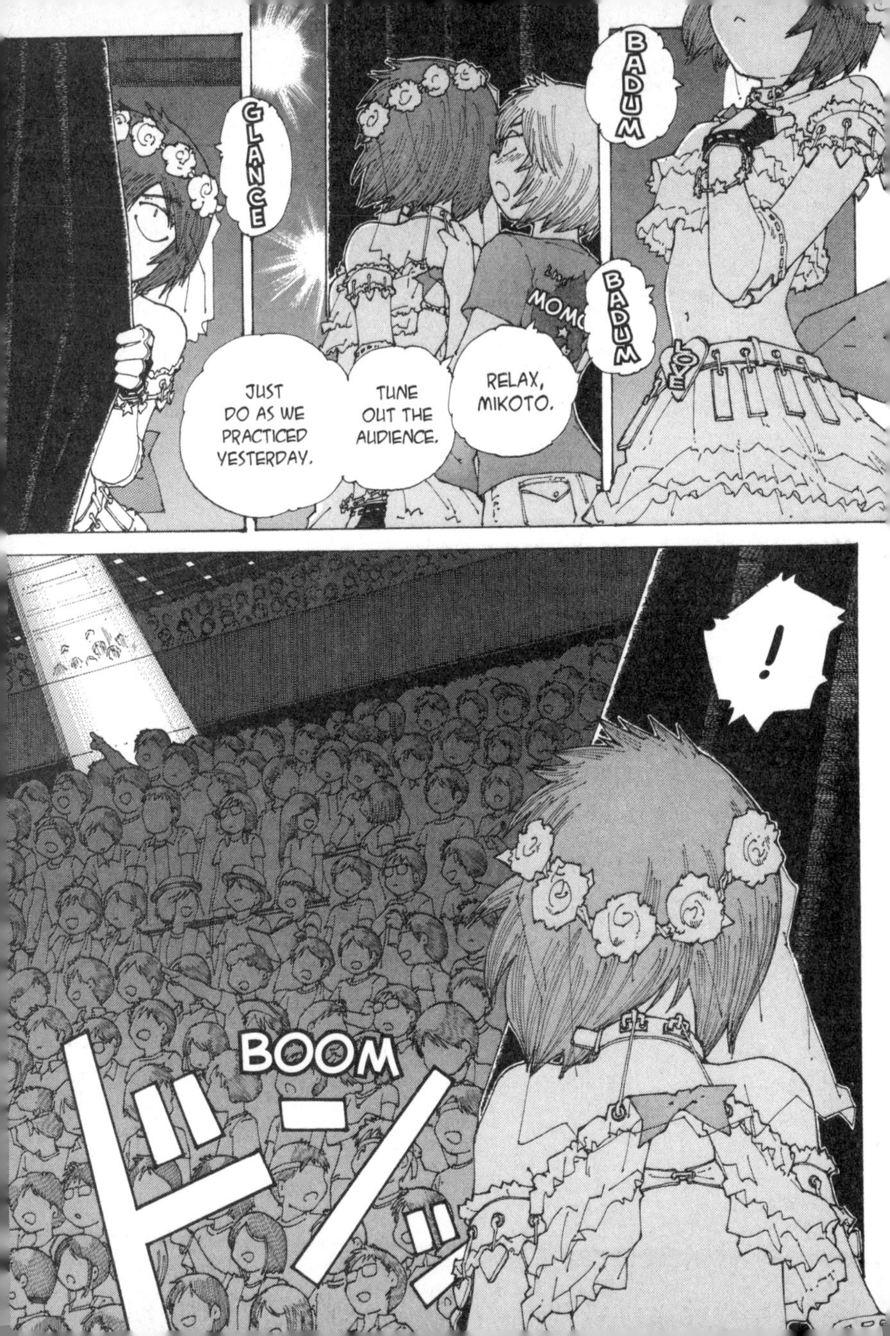
BADUM
BADUM
RELAX, MIKOTO.
TUNE OUT THE AUDIENCE.
JUST DO AS WE PRACTICED YESTERDAY.
GLANCE
MOMO
LOVE
!
BOOM

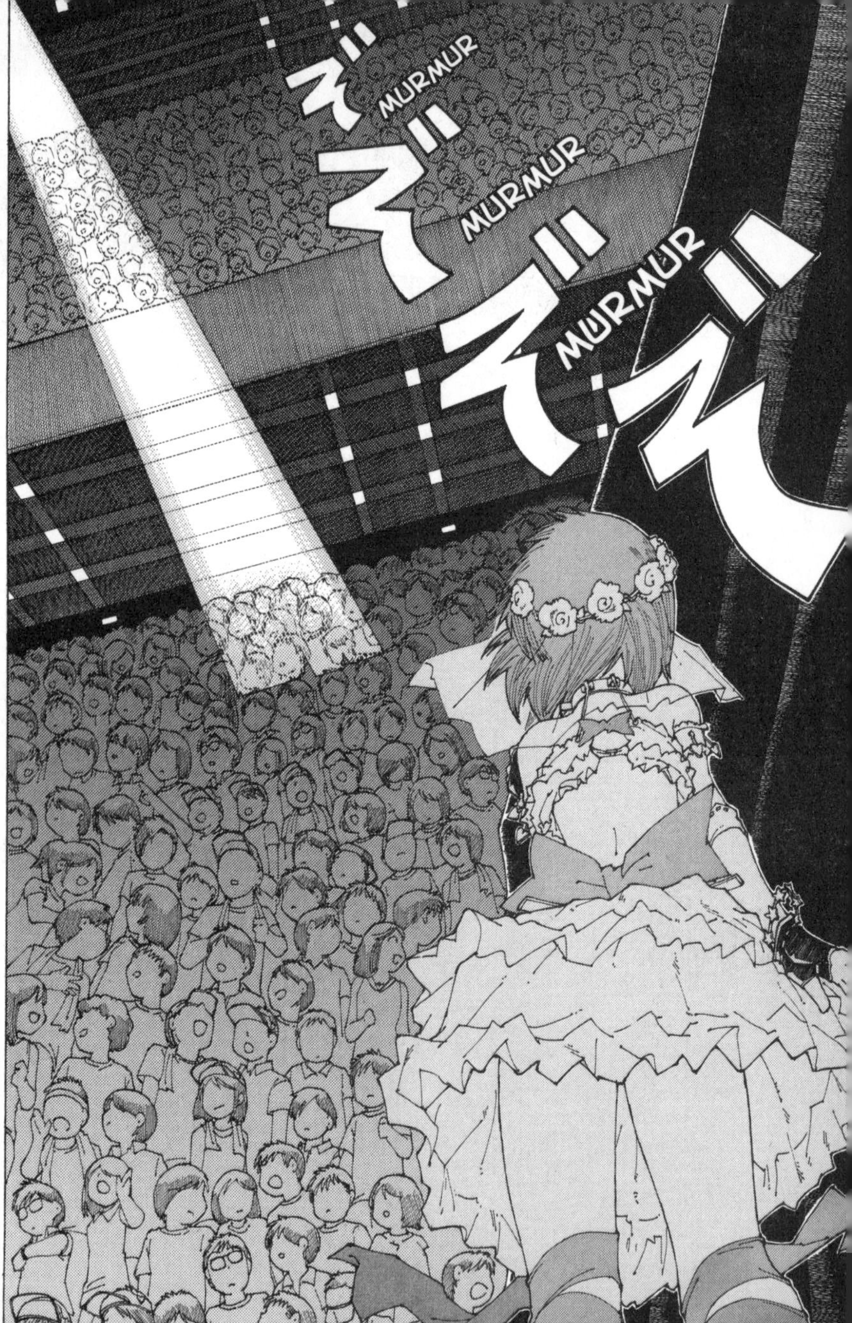
MURMUR
MURMUR
MURMUR
MURMUR

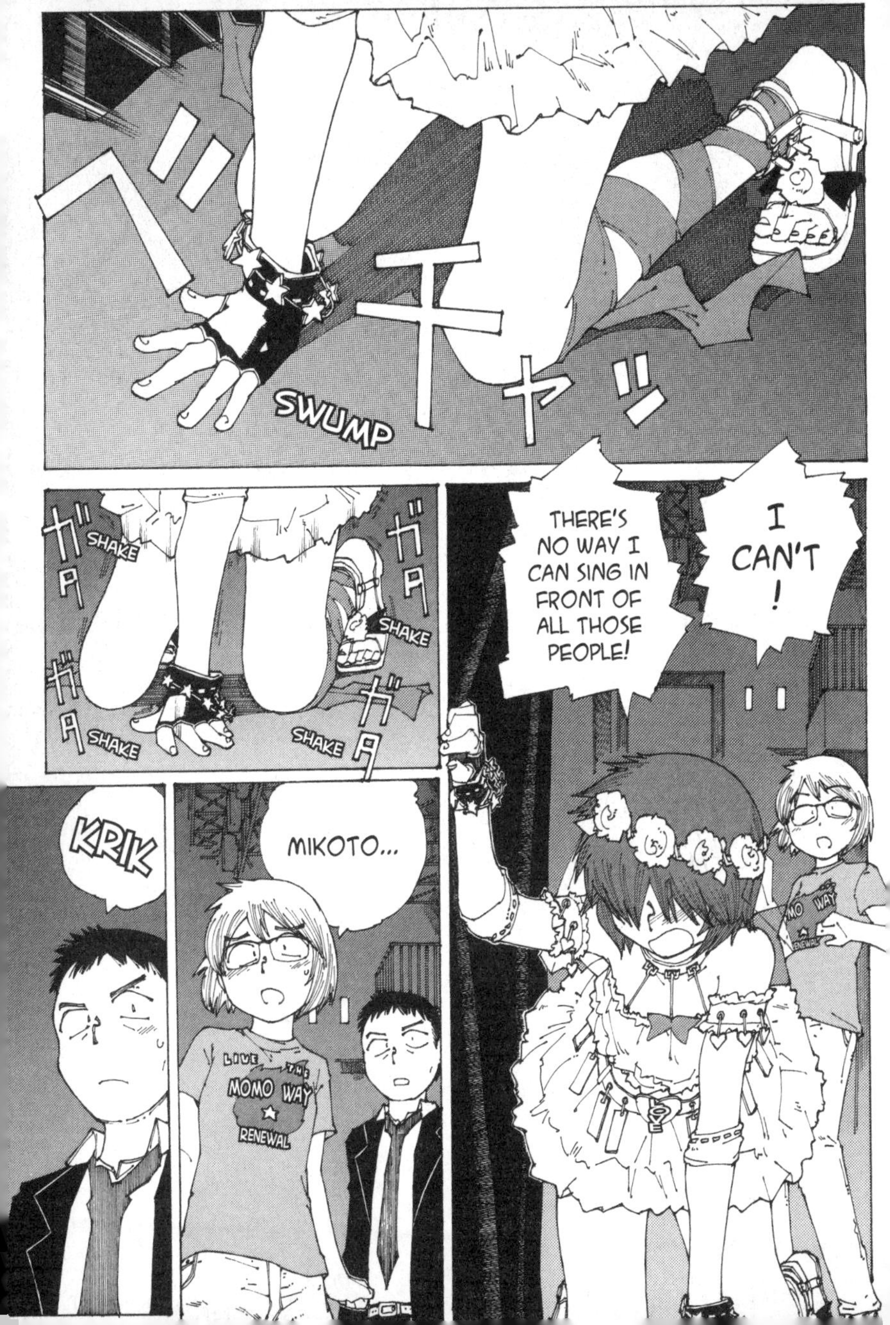
SWUMP
I CAN'T!
THERE'S NO WAY I CAN SING IN FRONT OF ALL THOSE PEOPLE!
SHAKE
SHAKE
SHAKE
SHAKE
MIKOTO...
LIVE THE MOMO WAY ☆ RENEWAL
KRIK

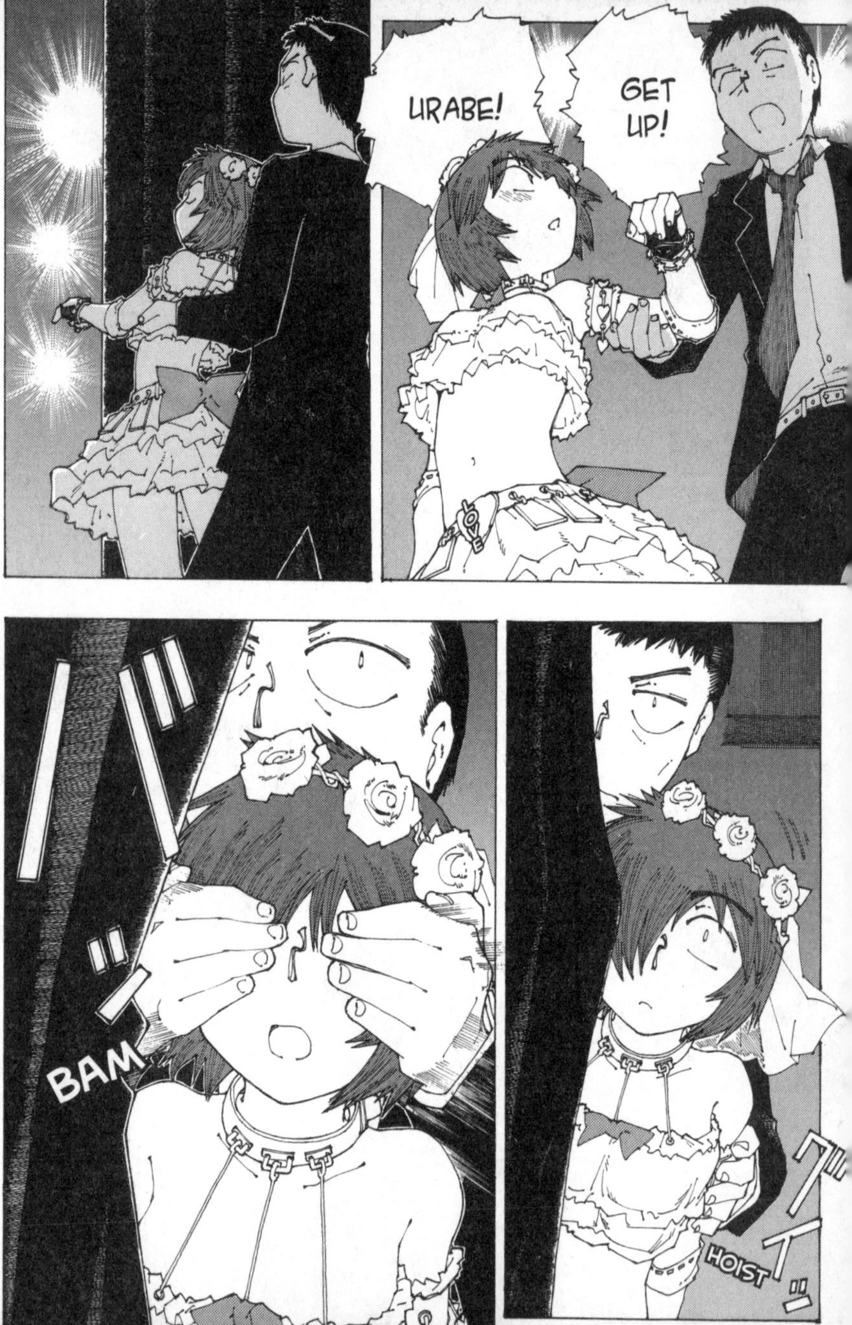
GET UP!
URABE!
HOIST
BAM

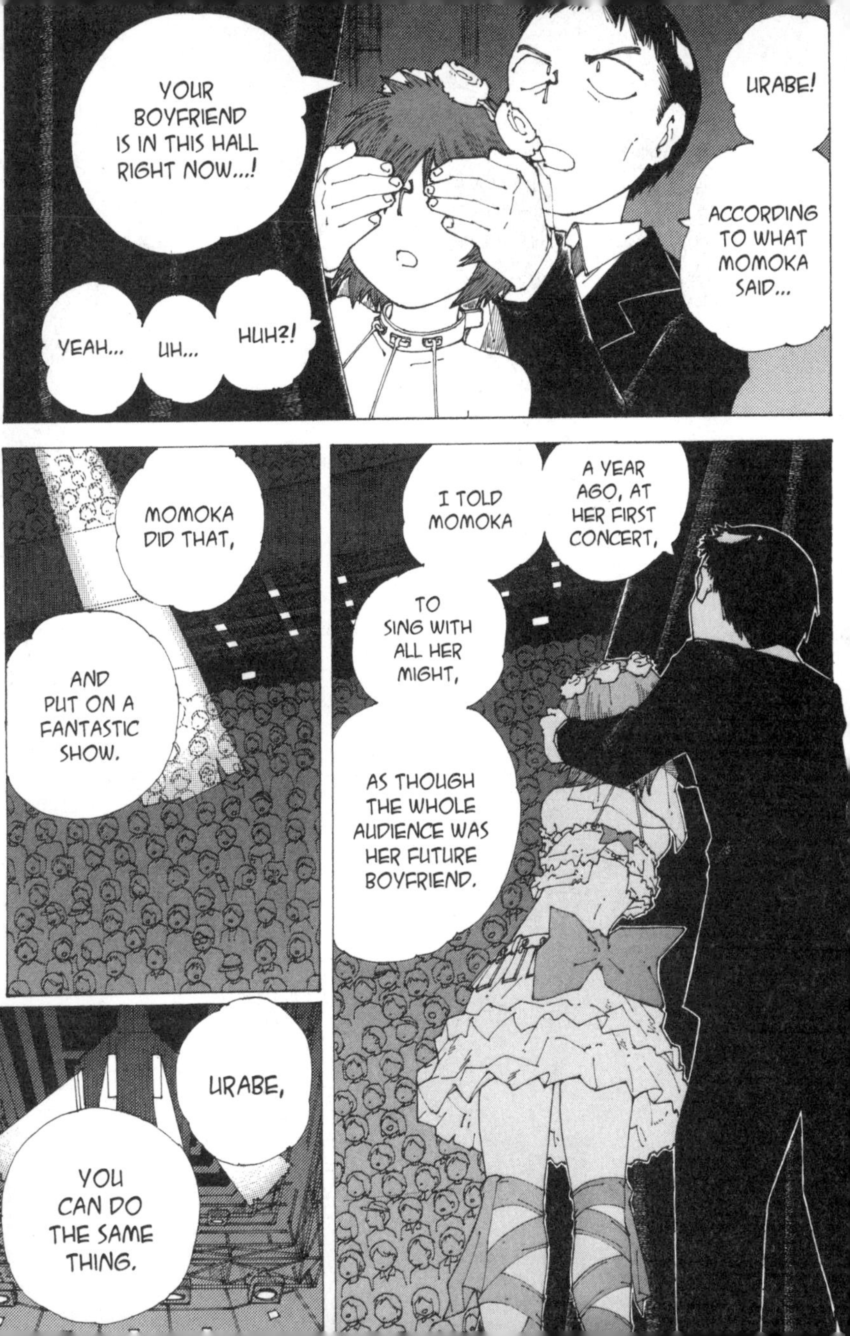
URABE!
ACCORDING TO WHAT MOMOKA SAID...
YOUR BOYFRIEND IS IN THIS HALL RIGHT NOW...!
HUH?!
UH...
YEAH...
A YEAR AGO, AT HER FIRST CONCERT,
I TOLD MOMOKA
TO SING WITH ALL HER MIGHT,
AS THOUGH THE WHOLE AUDIENCE WAS HER FUTURE BOYFRIEND.
MOMOKA DID THAT,
AND PUT ON A FANTASTIC SHOW.
URABE,
YOU CAN DO THE SAME THING.

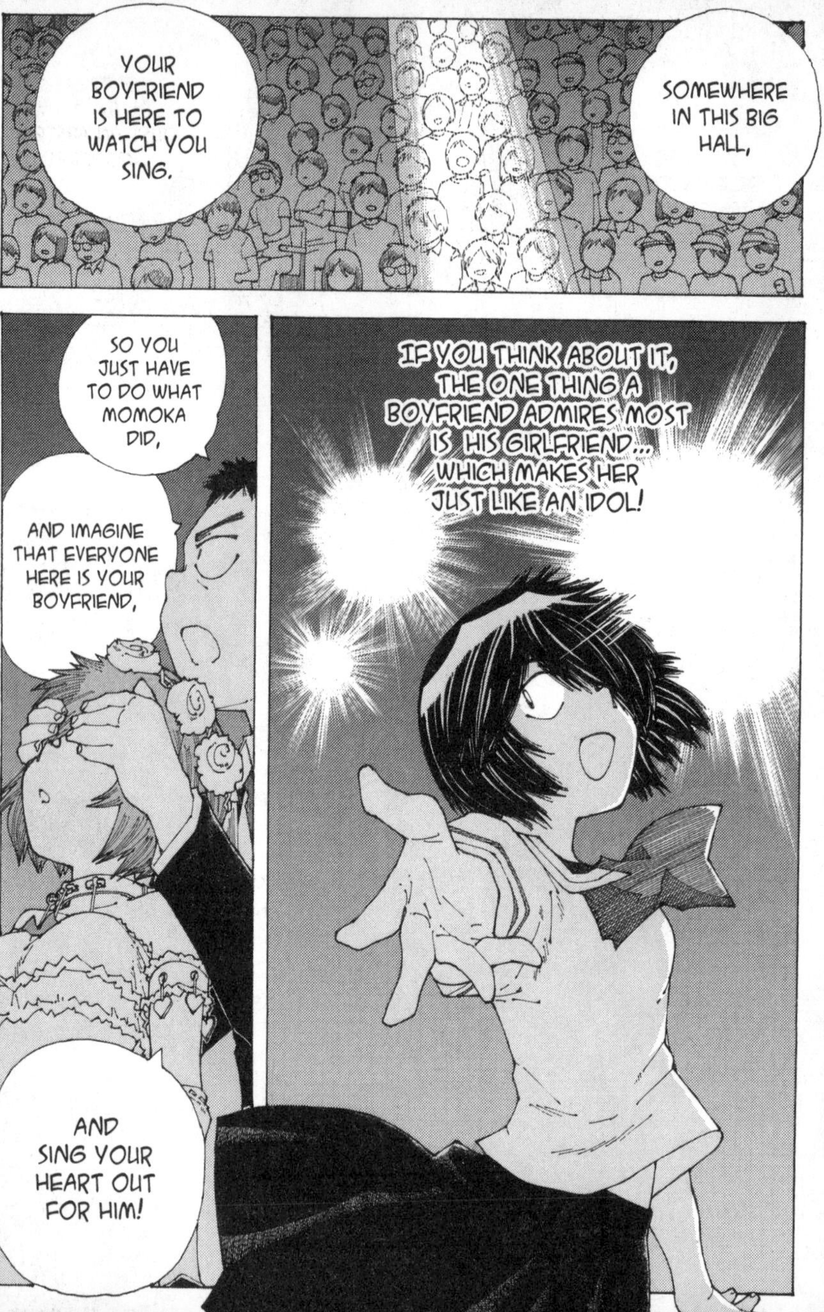
SOMEWHERE IN THIS BIG HALL,
YOUR BOYFRIEND IS HERE TO WATCH YOU SING.
IF YOU THINK ABOUT IT, THE ONE THING A BOYFRIEND ADMIRES MOST IS HIS GIRLFRIEND... WHICH MAKES HER JUST LIKE AN IDOL!
SO YOU JUST HAVE TO DO WHAT MOMOKA DID,
AND IMAGINE THAT EVERYONE HERE IS YOUR BOYFRIEND,
AND SING YOUR HEART OUT FOR HIM!

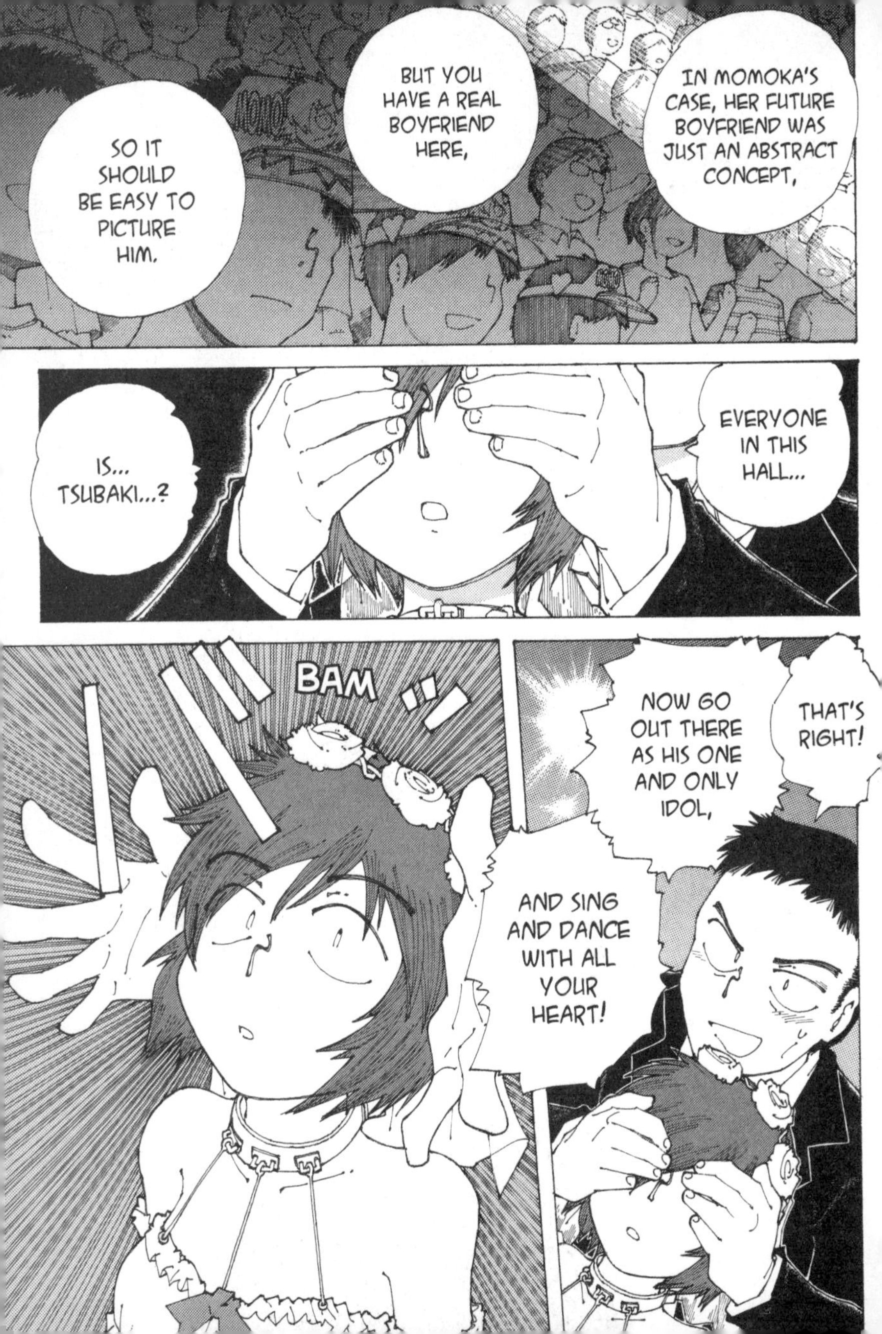
IN MOMOKA'S CASE, HER FUTURE BOYFRIEND WAS JUST AN ABSTRACT CONCEPT,
BUT YOU HAVE A REAL BOYFRIEND HERE,
SO IT SHOULD BE EASY TO PICTURE HIM.
EVERYONE IN THIS HALL...
IS... TSUBAKI...?
THAT'S RIGHT!
NOW GO OUT THERE AS HIS ONE AND ONLY IDOL,
AND SING AND DANCE WITH ALL YOUR HEART!
BAM

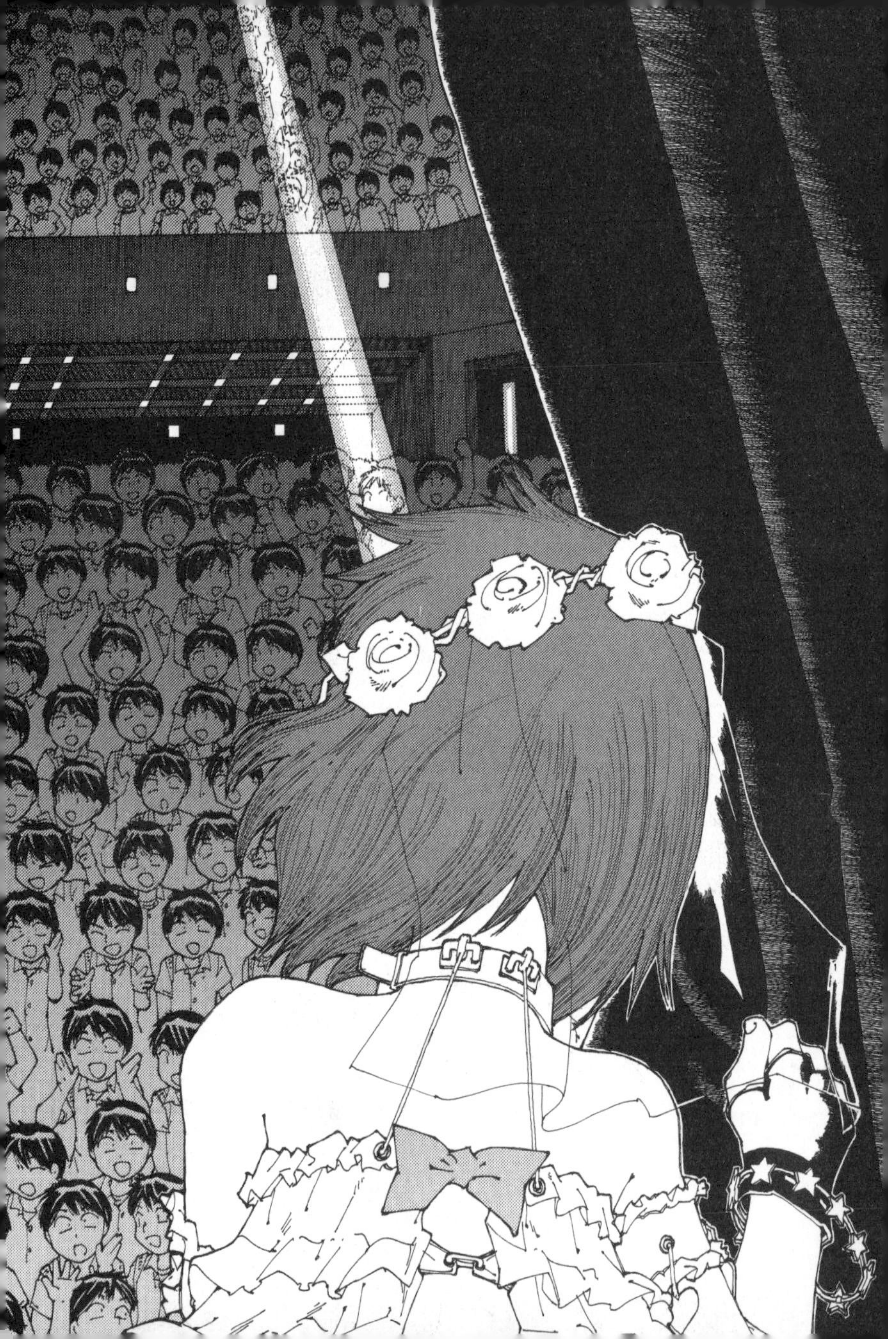

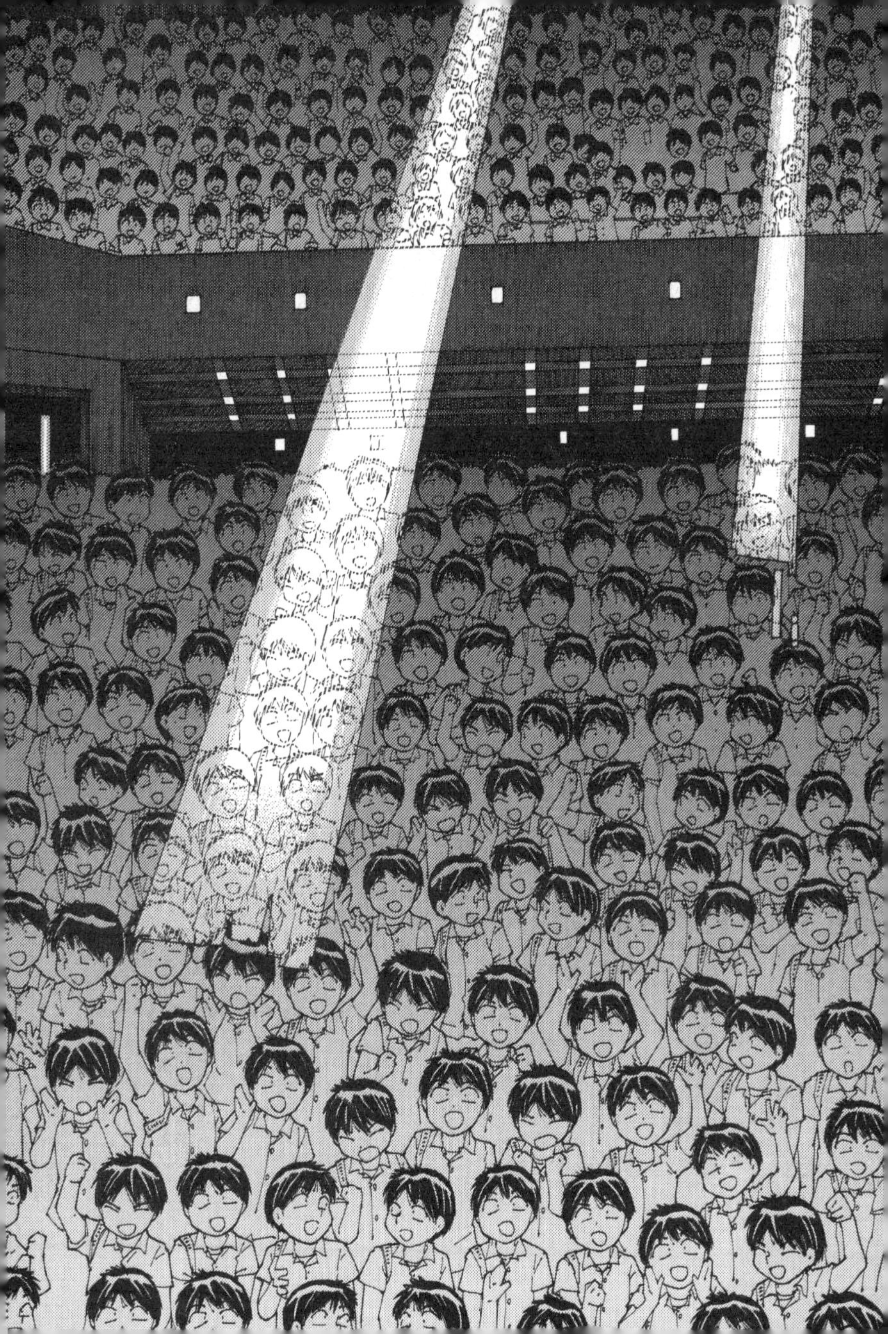

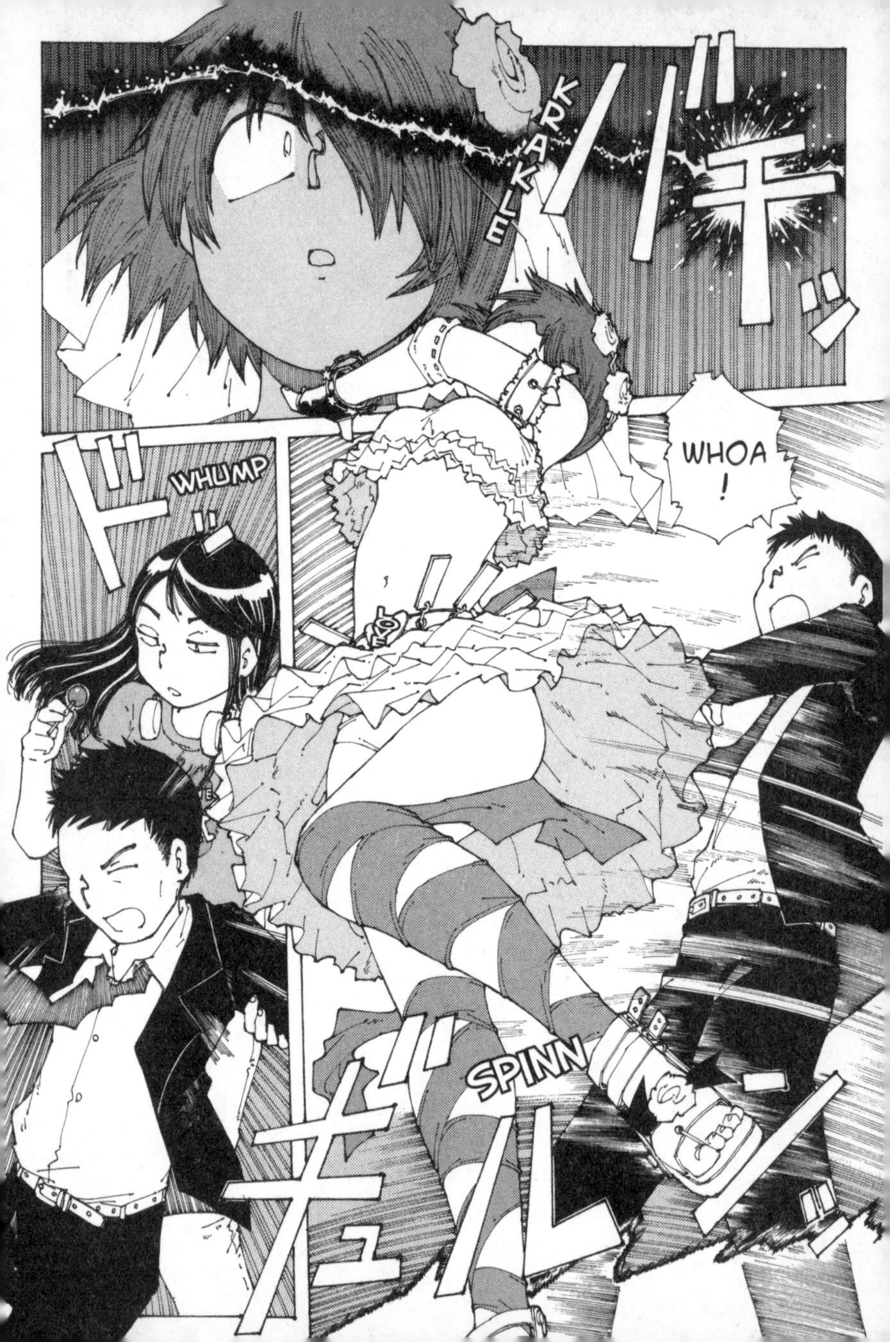

KRAKLE
バチッ
WHOA !
SPINN
ギュルンッ
WHUMP
ドッ

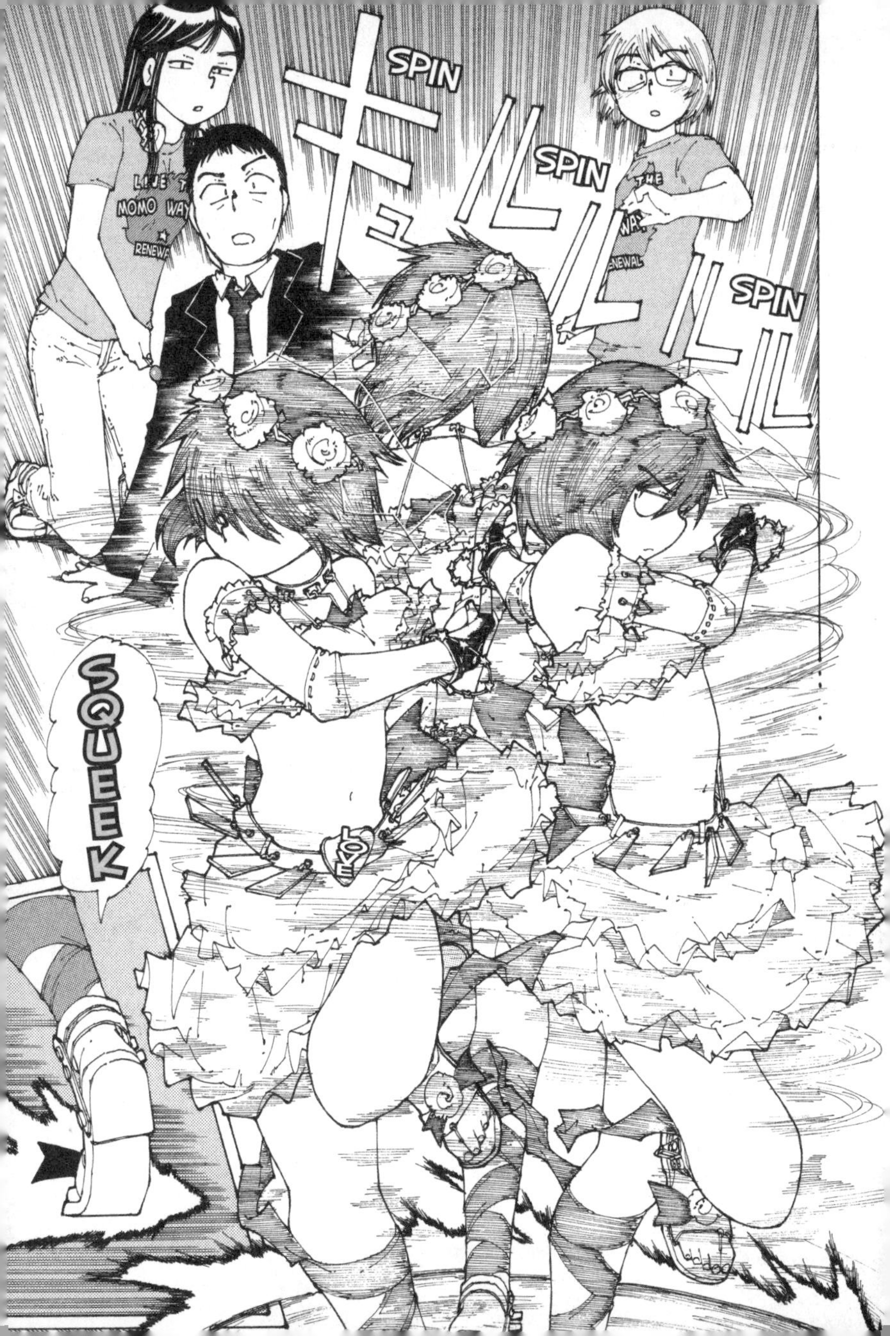
SPIN
SPIN
SPIN
キュルルル
LOVE
SQUEEK

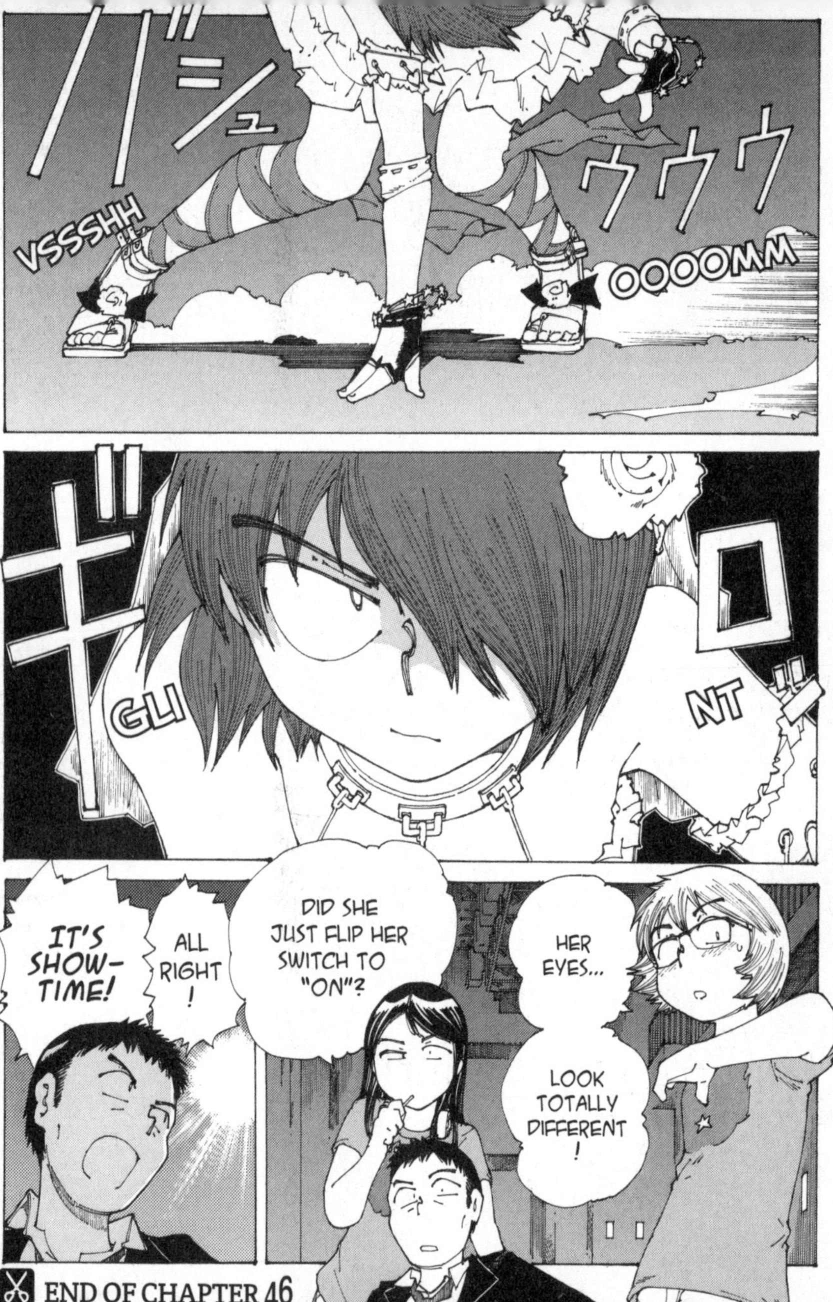
バジュウウウウ
VSSSHH
OOOOMM
ギロッ
GLI
NT
HER EYES...
LOOK TOTALLY DIFFERENT!
DID SHE JUST FLIP HER SWITCH TO "ON"?
ALL RIGHT!
IT'S SHOW-TIME!

END OF CHAPTER 46

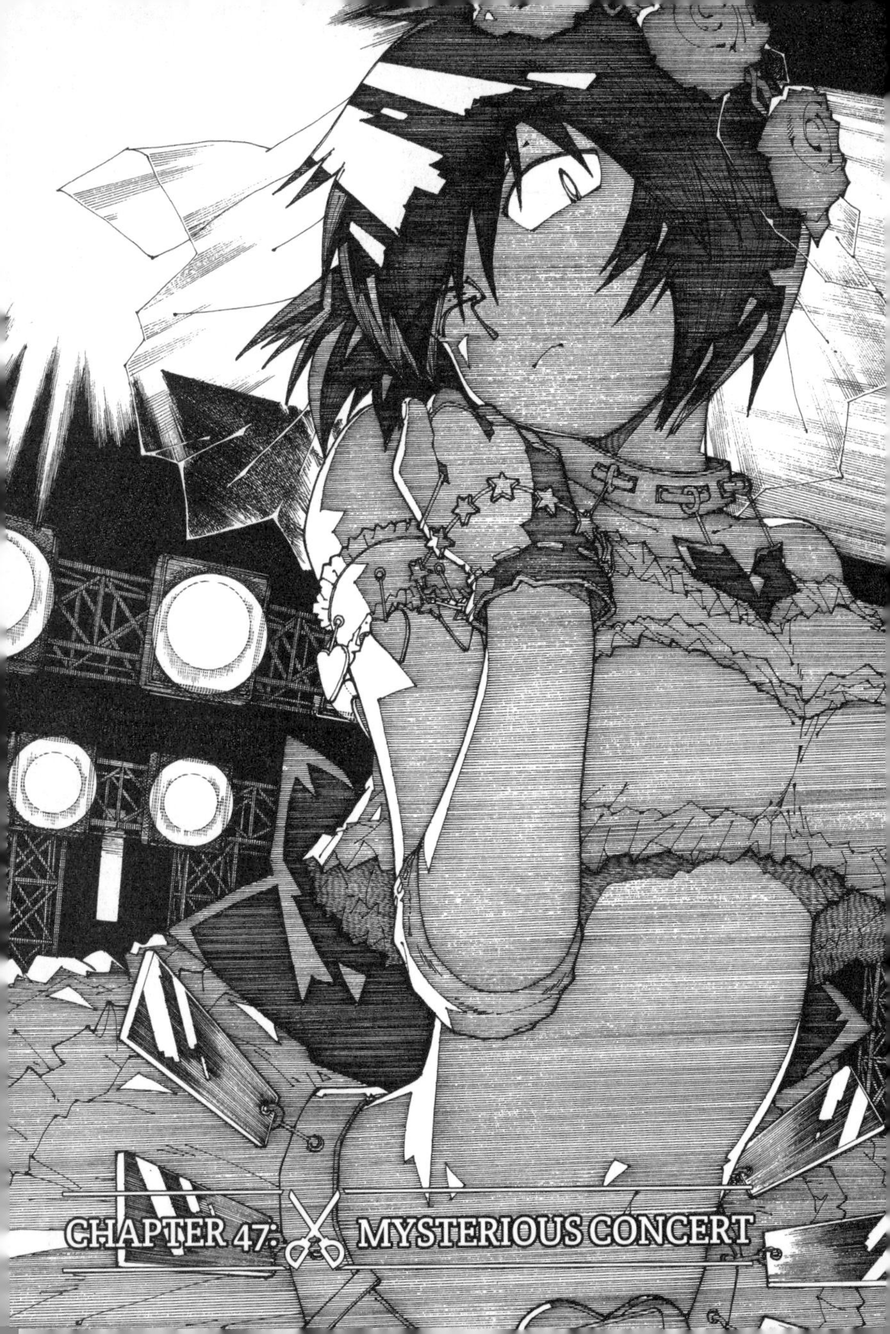
CHAPTER 47: MYSTERIOUS CONCERT

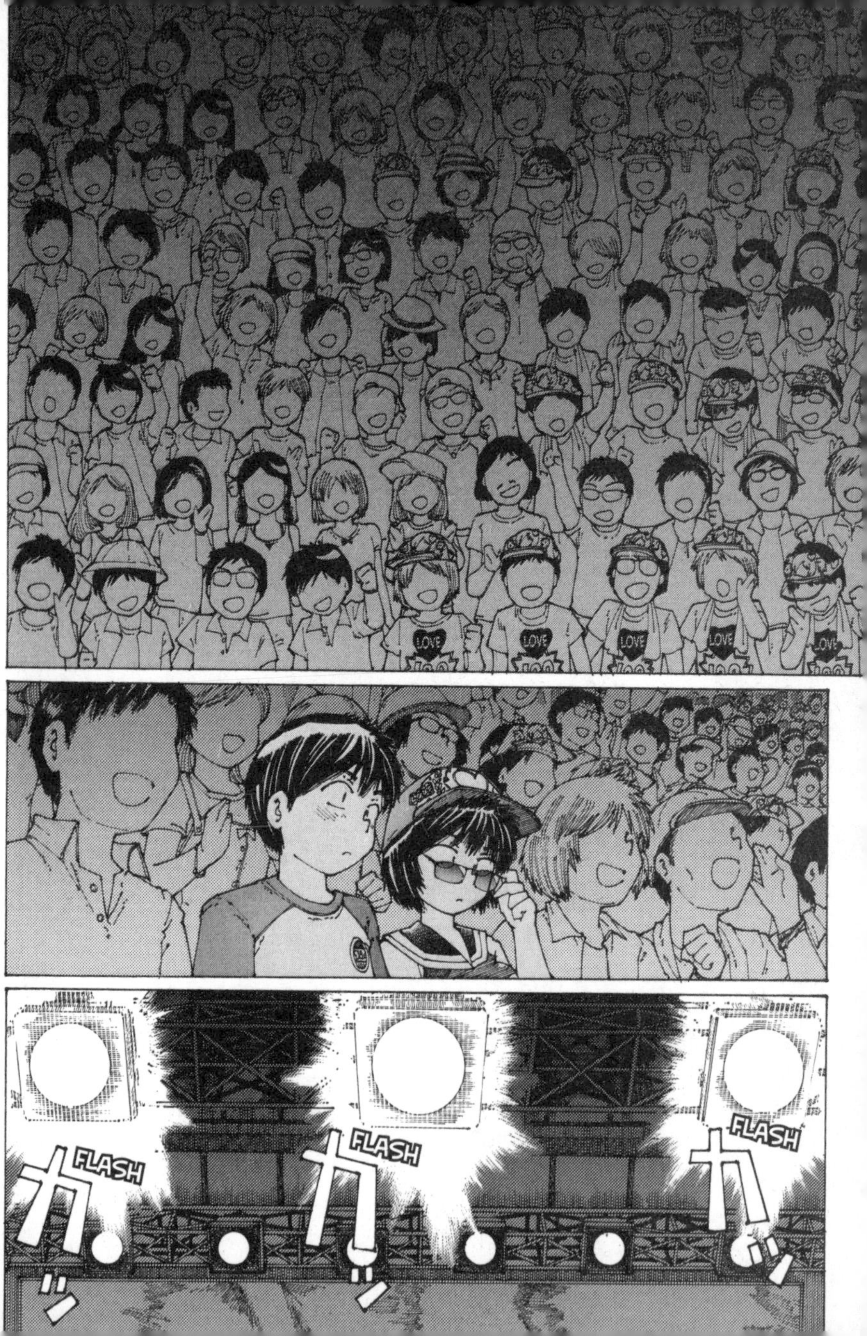
LOVE
LOVE
LOVE
LOVE
LOVE
カッ
FLASH
カッ
FLASH
カッ
FLASH

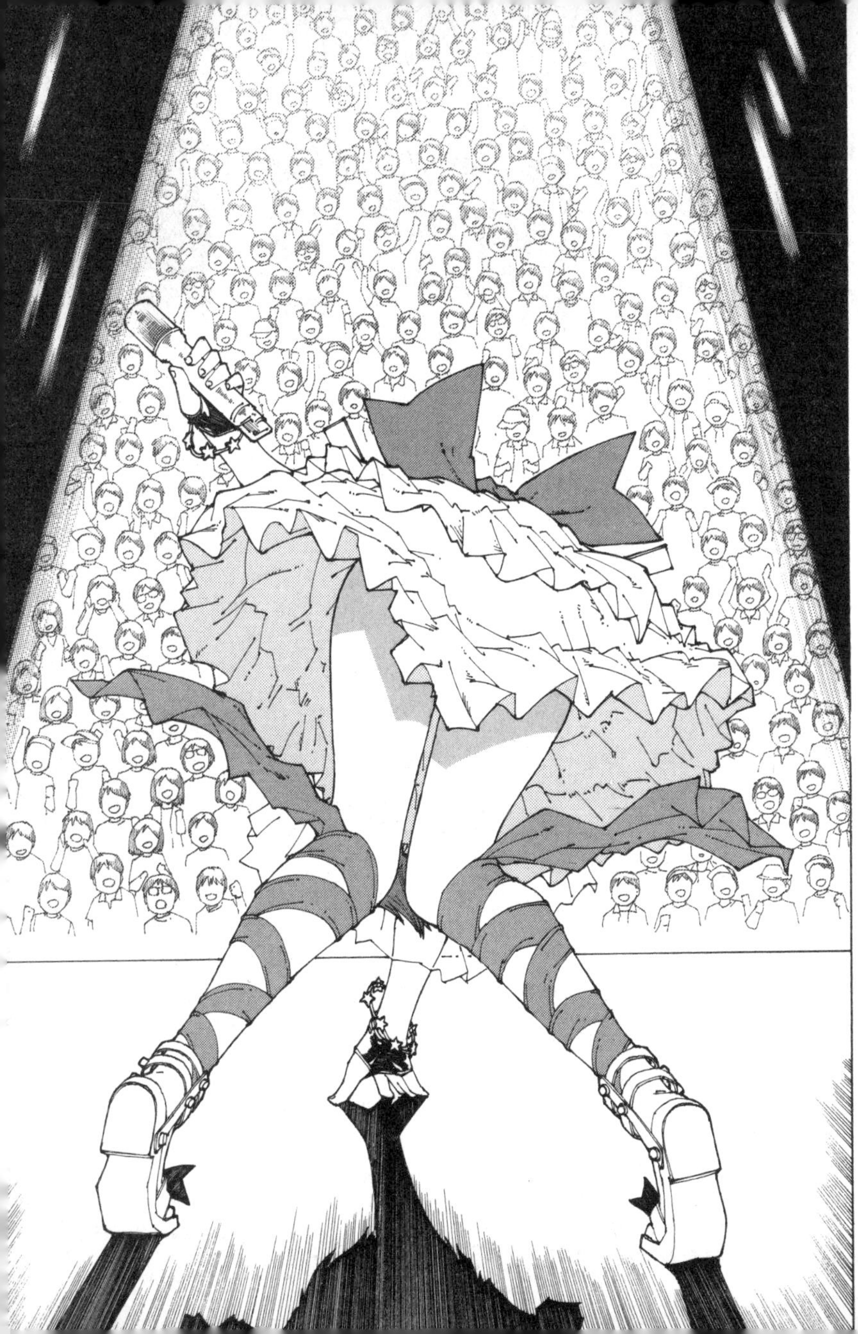

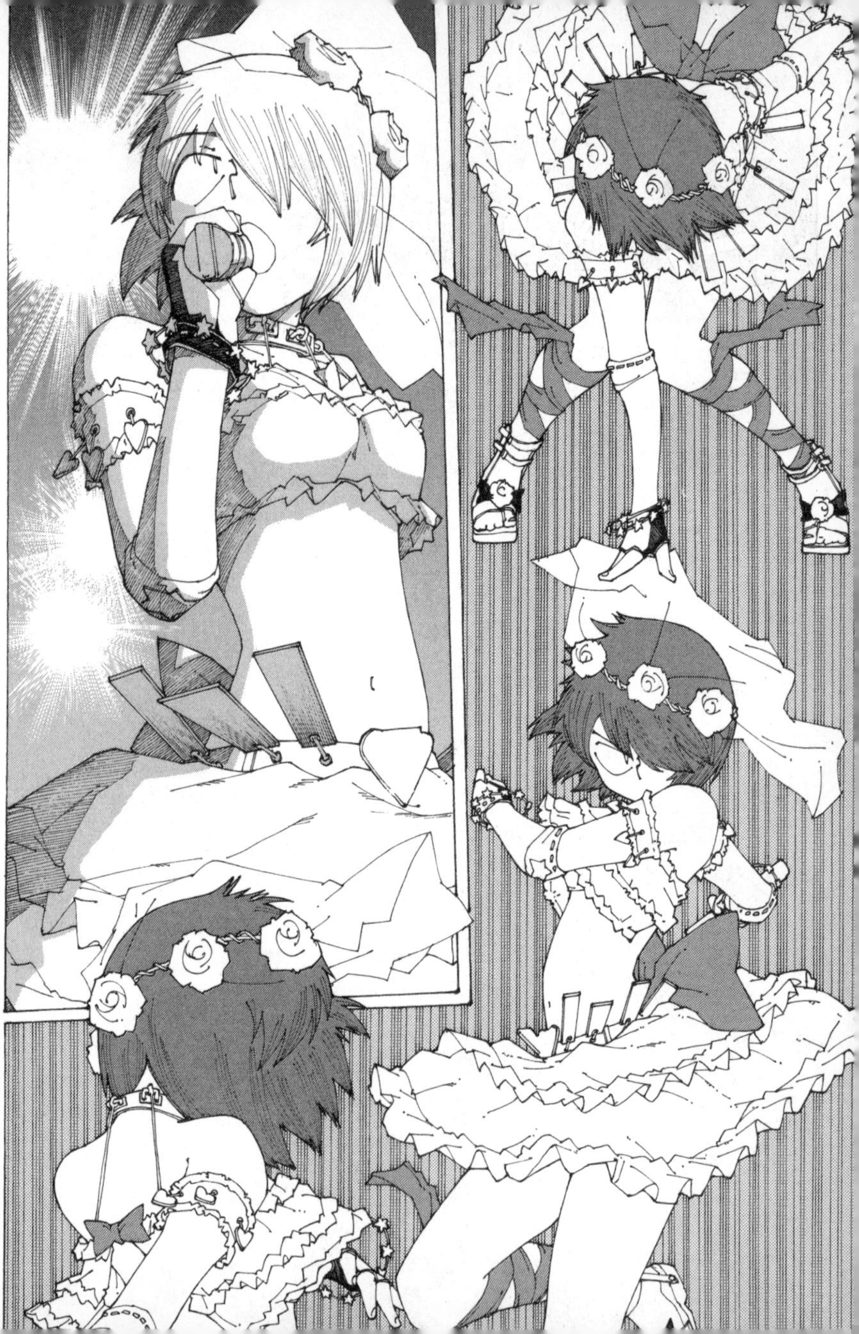

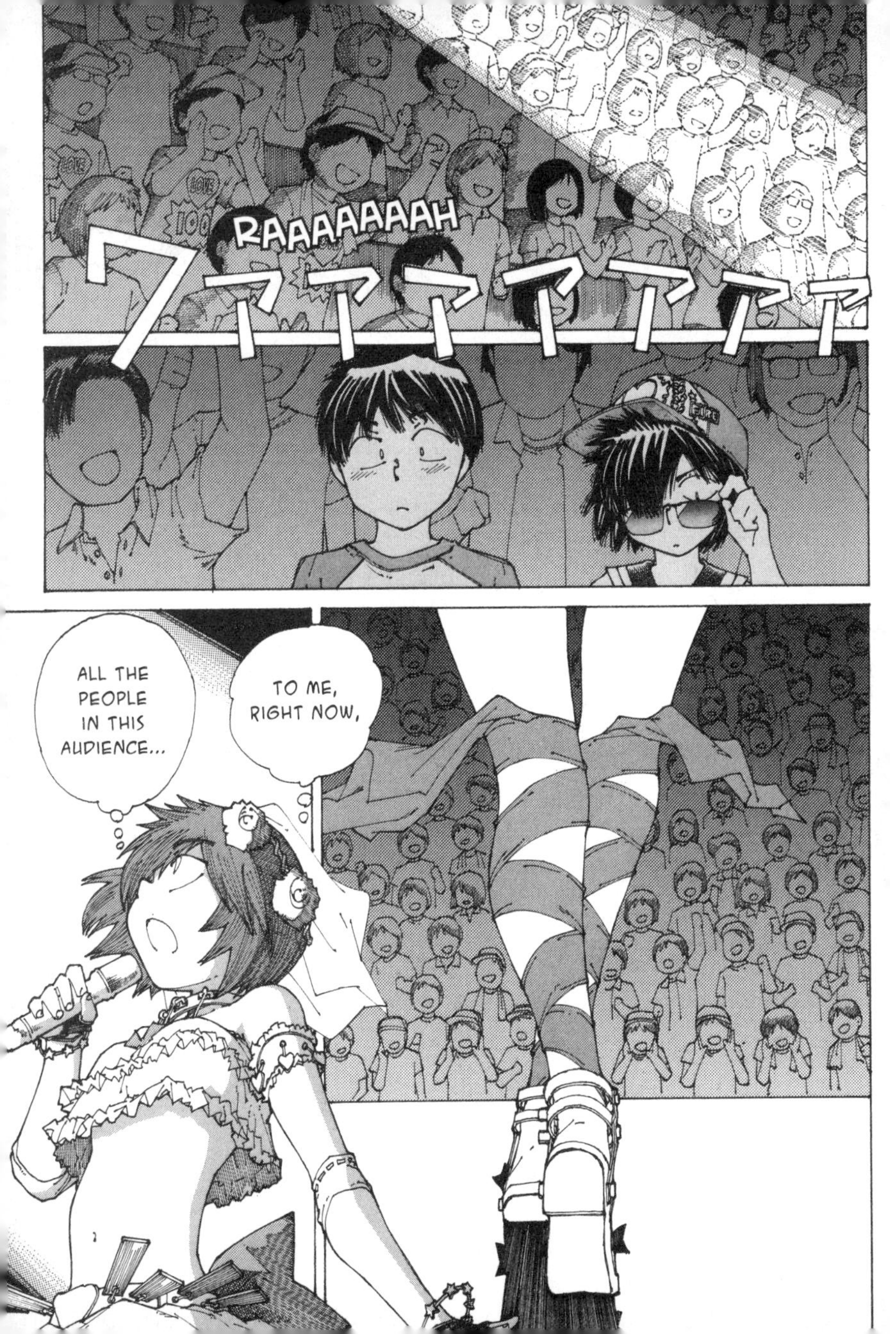
RAAAAAAAH
ワアアアアアア
TO ME, RIGHT NOW,
ALL THE PEOPLE IN THIS AUDIENCE...

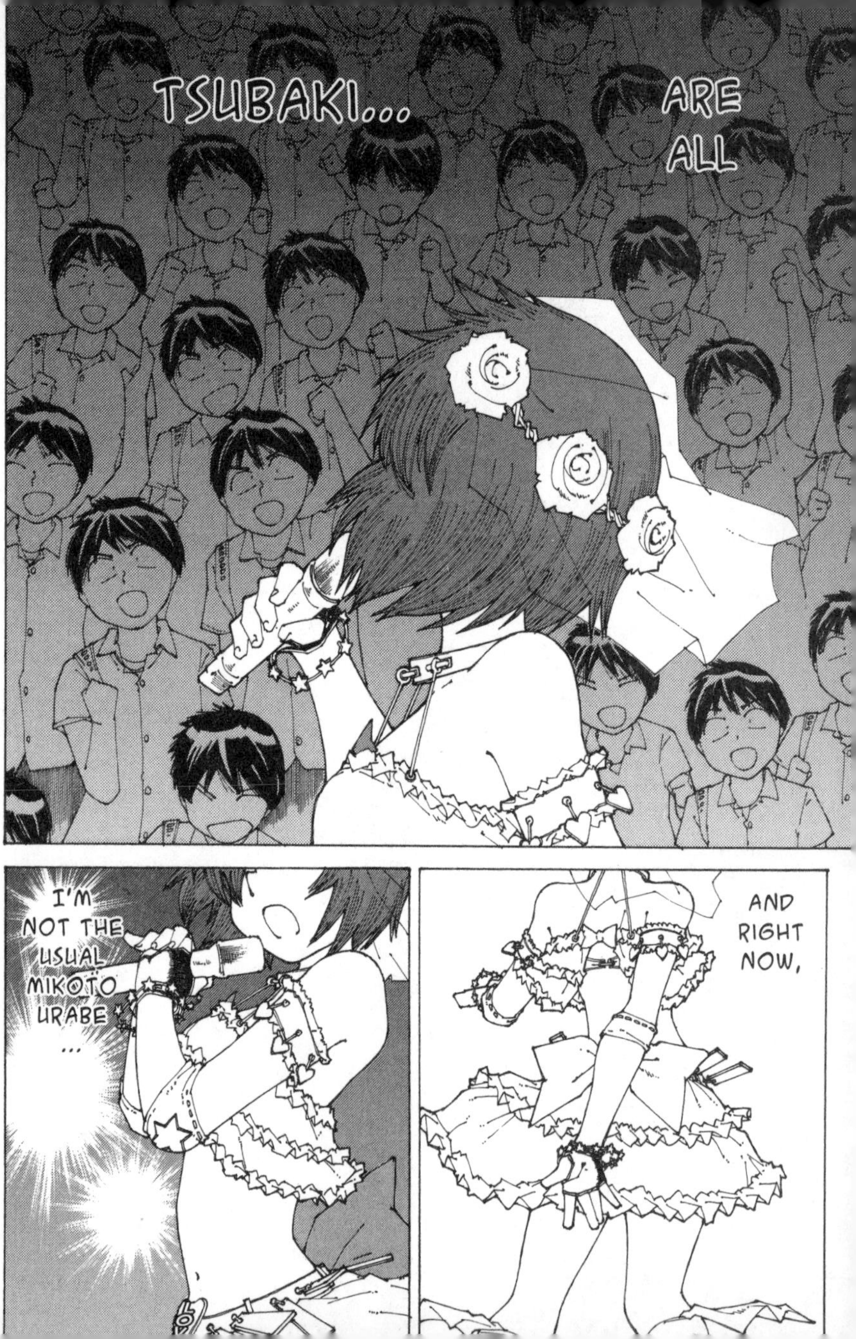
ARE ALL
TSUBAKI...
AND RIGHT NOW,
I'M NOT THE USUAL MIKOTO URABE ...

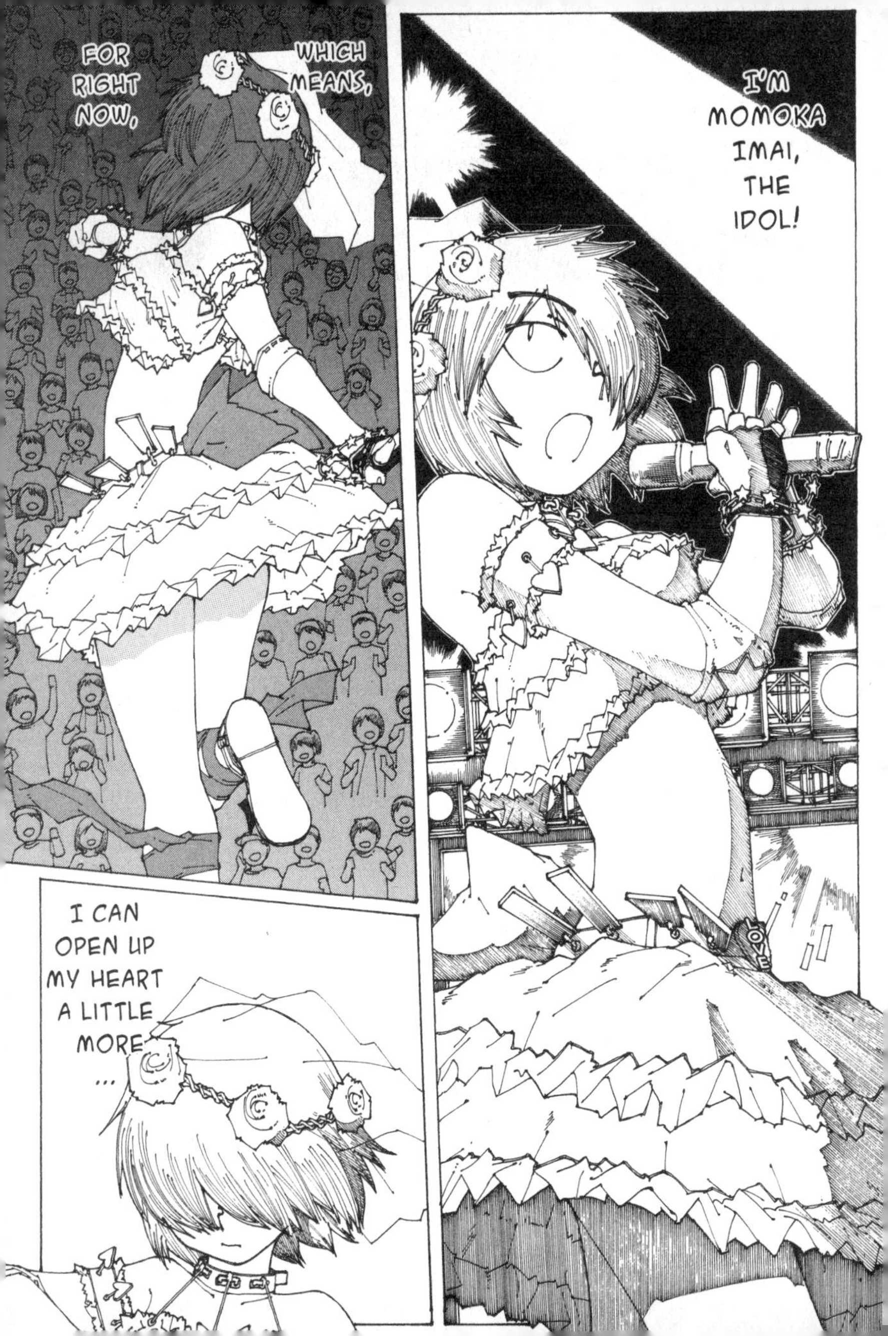
I'M MOMOKA IMAI, THE IDOL!
WHICH MEANS,
FOR RIGHT NOW,
I CAN OPEN UP MY HEART A LITTLE MORE ...

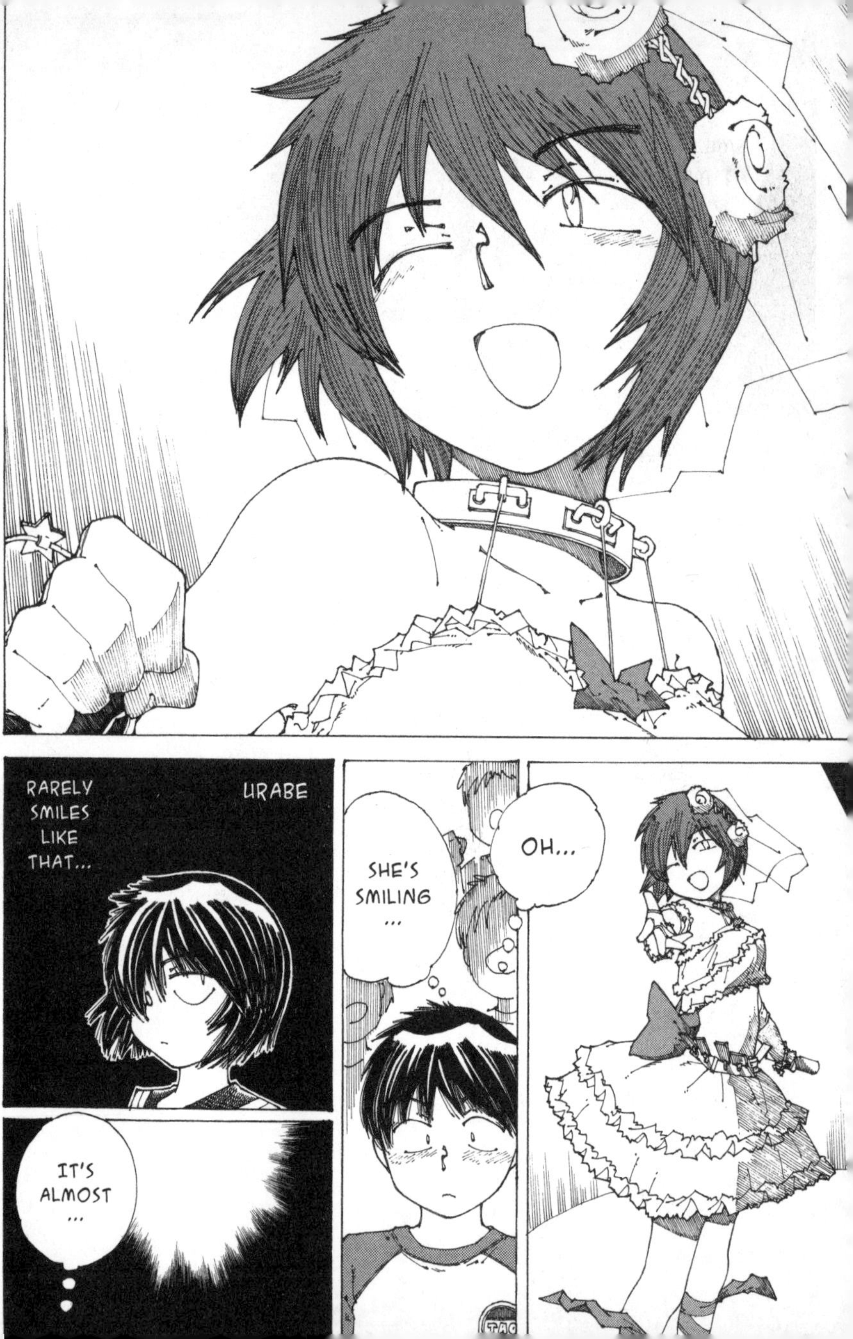
OH...
SHE'S SMILING ...
URABE
RARELY SMILES LIKE THAT...
IT'S ALMOST ...

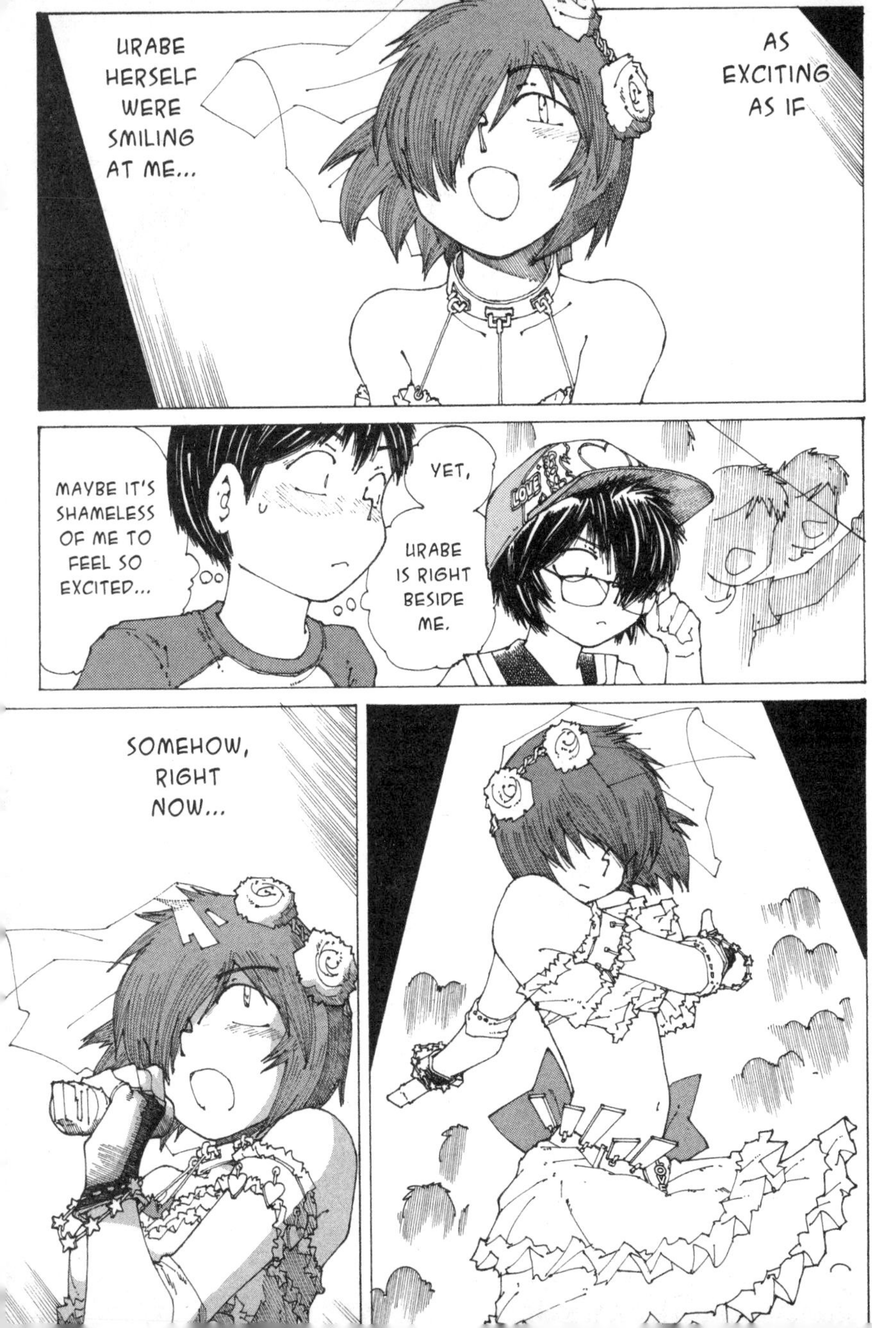
AS EXCITING AS IF
URABE HERSELF WERE SMILING AT ME...
YET,
URABE IS RIGHT BESIDE ME.
MAYBE IT'S SHAMELESS OF ME TO FEEL SO EXCITED...
SOMEHOW, RIGHT NOW...

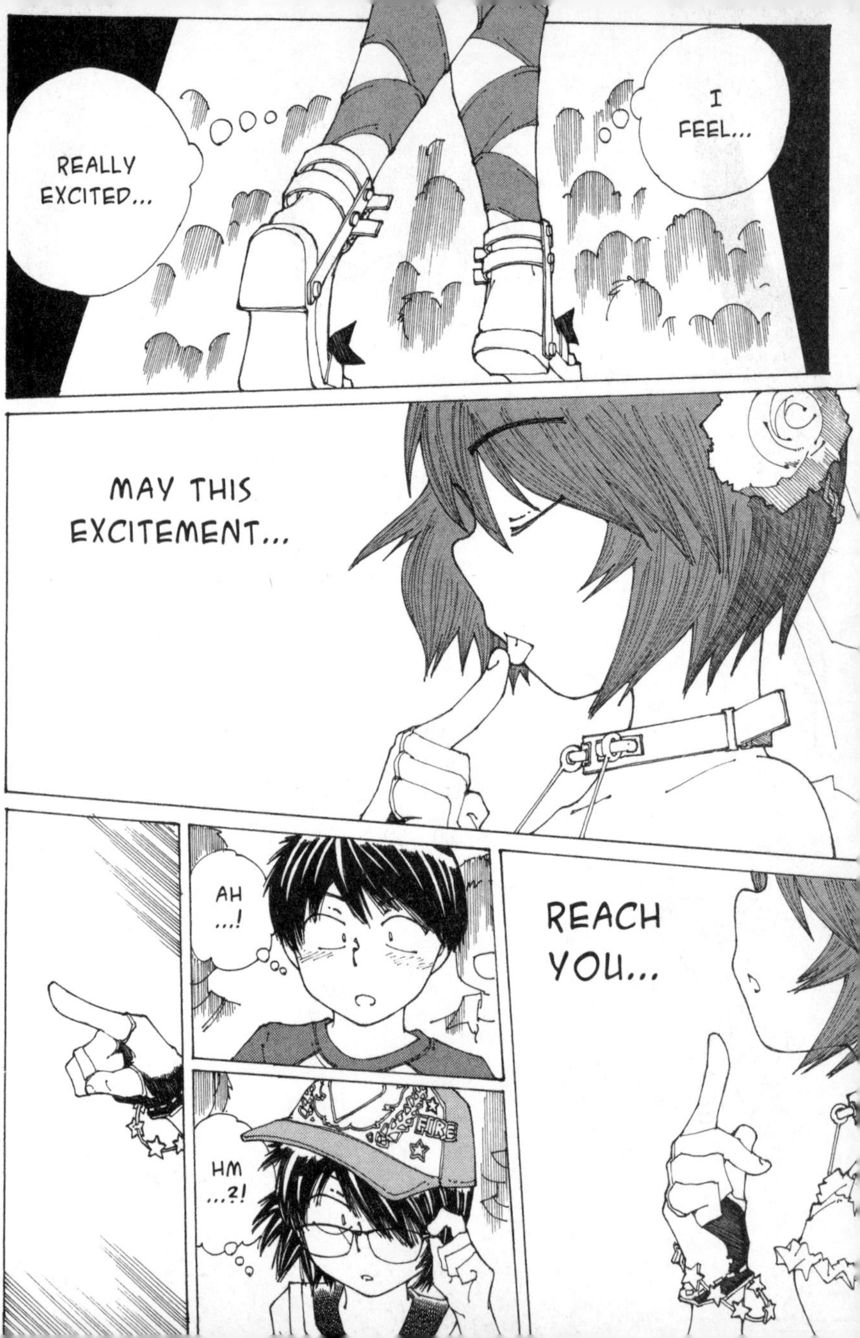
I FEEL...
REALLY EXCITED...
MAY THIS EXCITEMENT...
REACH YOU...
AH ...!
HM ...?!

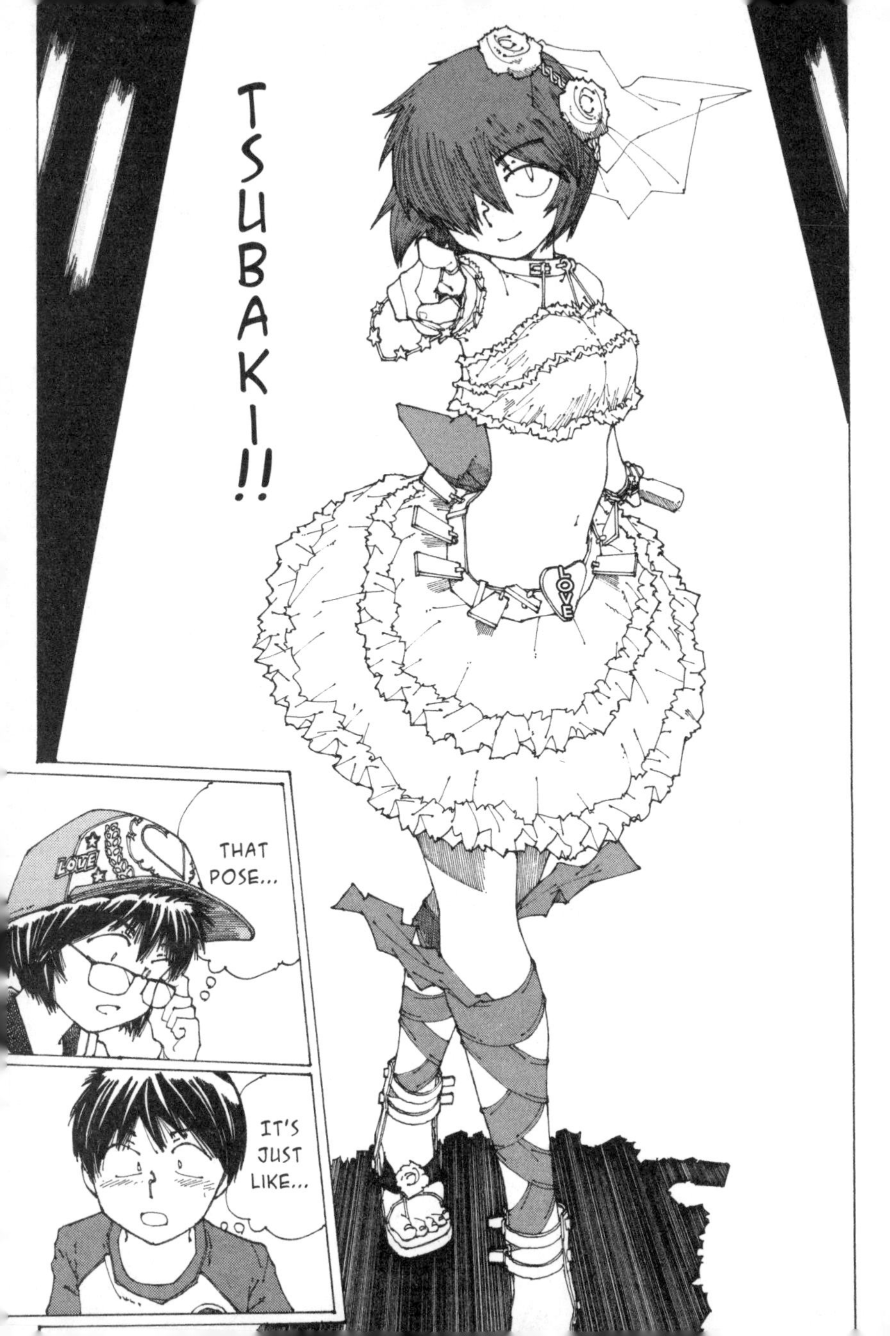
TSUBAKI!!
LOVE
LOVE
THAT POSE...
IT'S JUST LIKE...

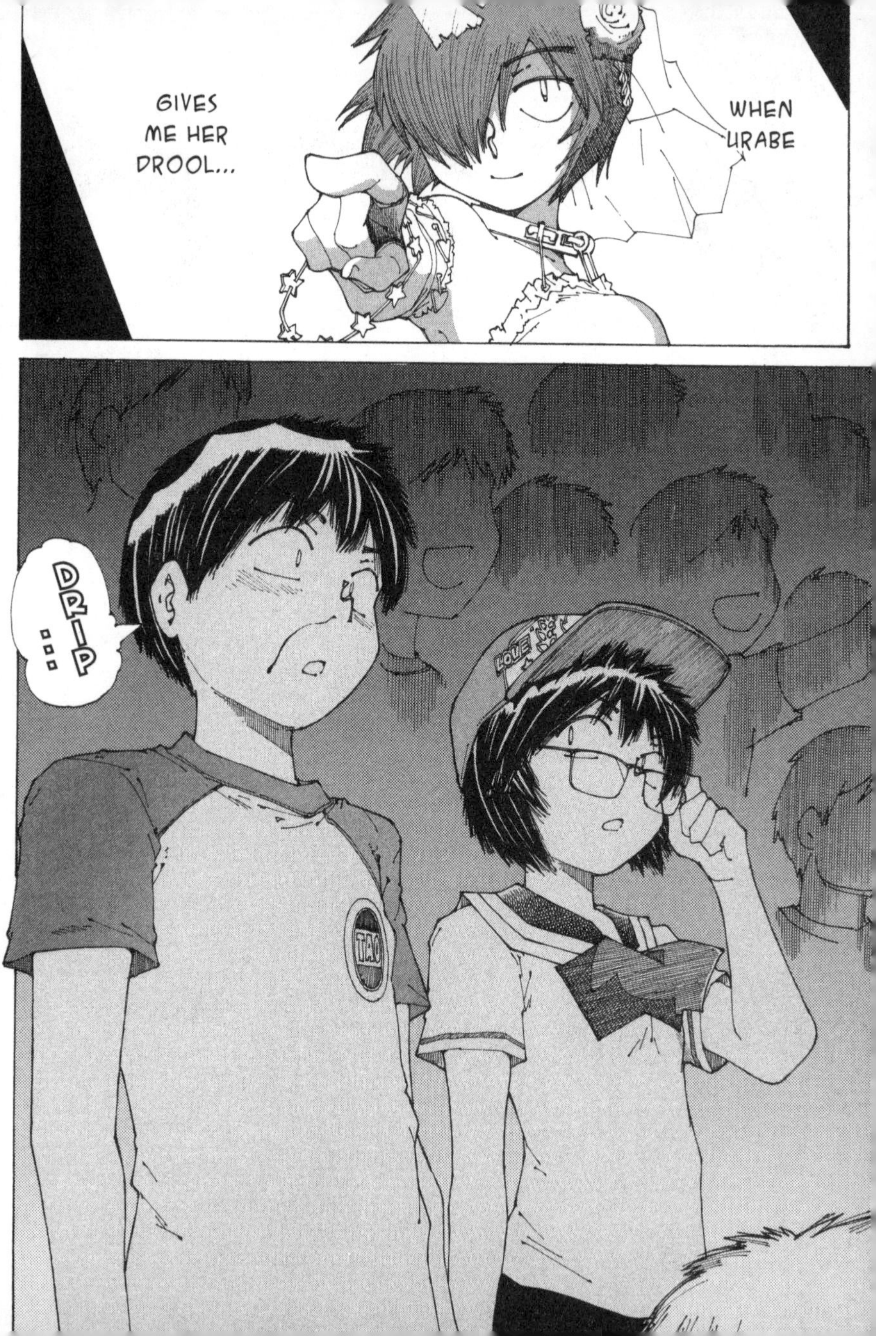
WHEN URABE
GIVES ME HER DROOL...
DRIP...
TAO
LOVE

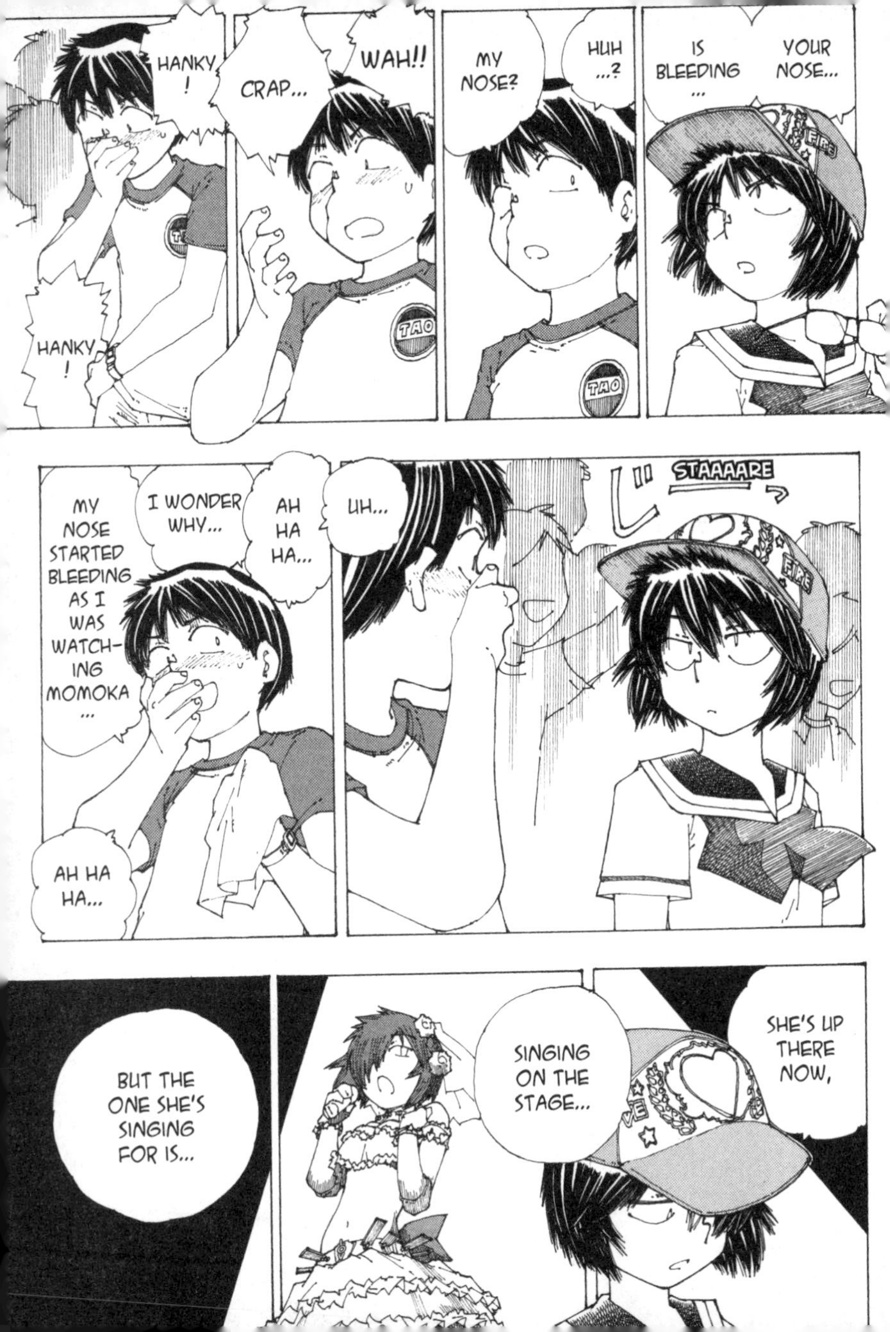
YOUR NOSE...
IS BLEEDING ...
HUH ...?
MY NOSE?
WAH!!
CRAP...
HANKY!
HANKY!
STAAAARE
UH...
AH HA HA...
I WONDER WHY...
MY NOSE STARTED BLEEDING AS I WAS WATCHING MOMOKA ...
AH HA HA...
SHE'S UP THERE NOW,
SINGING ON THE STAGE...
BUT THE ONE SHE'S SINGING FOR IS...

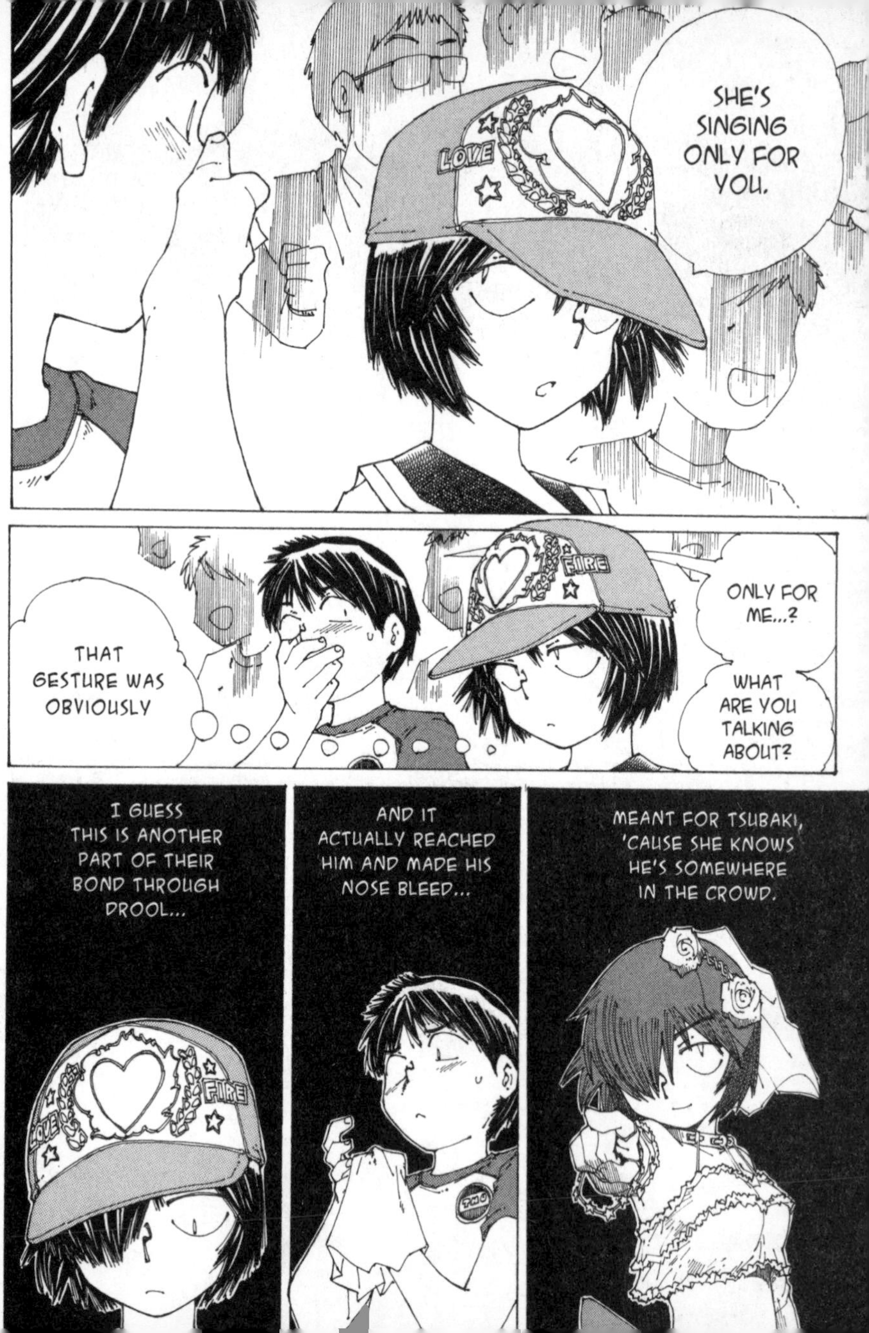
LOVE
SHE'S SINGING ONLY FOR YOU.
FIRE
ONLY FOR ME...?
WHAT ARE YOU TALKING ABOUT?
THAT GESTURE WAS OBVIOUSLY
MEANT FOR TSUBAKI, 'CAUSE SHE KNOWS HE'S SOMEWHERE IN THE CROWD.
AND IT ACTUALLY REACHED HIM AND MADE HIS NOSE BLEED...
I GUESS THIS IS ANOTHER PART OF THEIR BOND THROUGH DROOL...
LOVE
FIRE

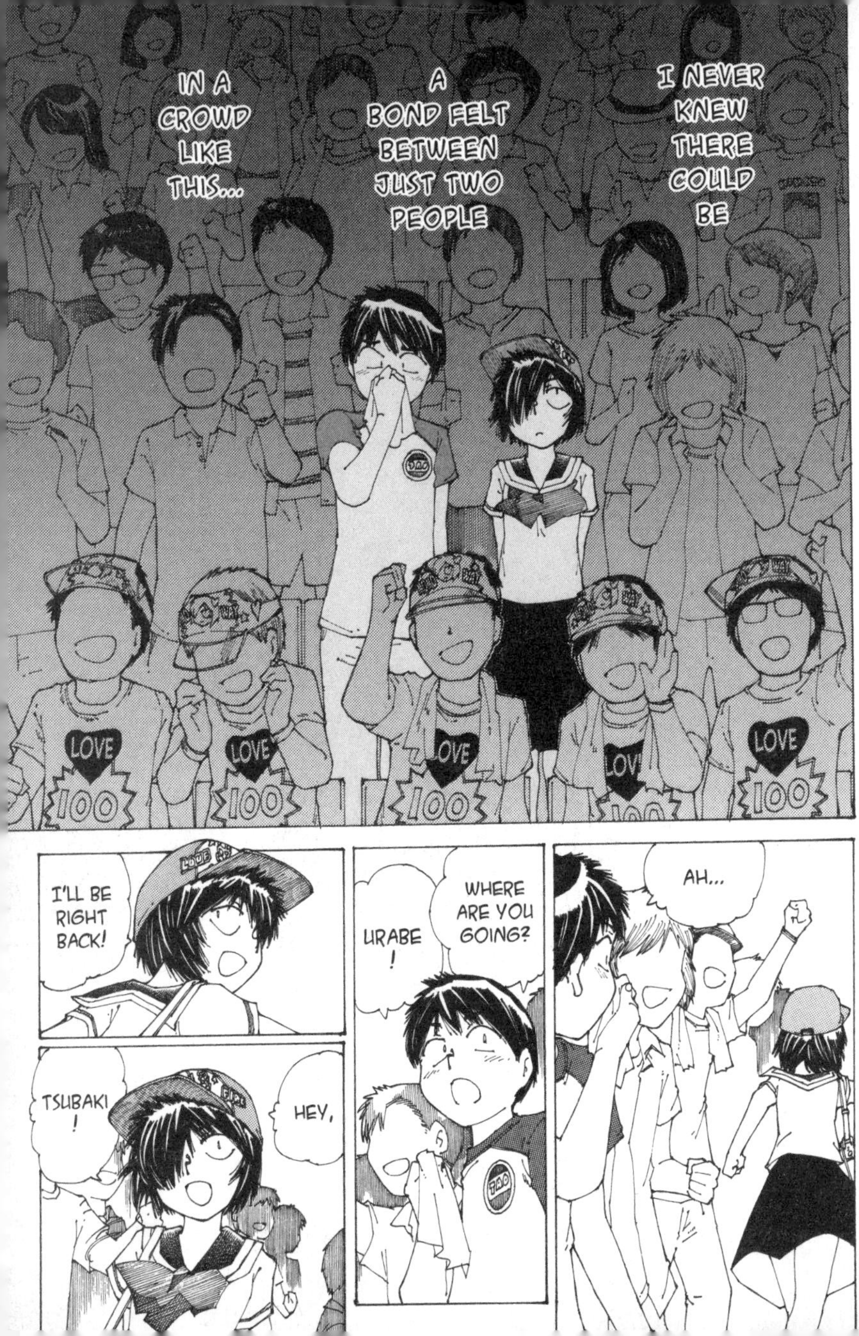
I NEVER KNEW THERE COULD BE
A BOND FELT BETWEEN JUST TWO PEOPLE
IN A CROWD LIKE THIS...
LOVE 100
LOVE 100
LOVE 100
LOVE 100
AH...
WHERE ARE YOU GOING?
URABE!
I'LL BE RIGHT BACK!
HEY,
TSUBAKI!

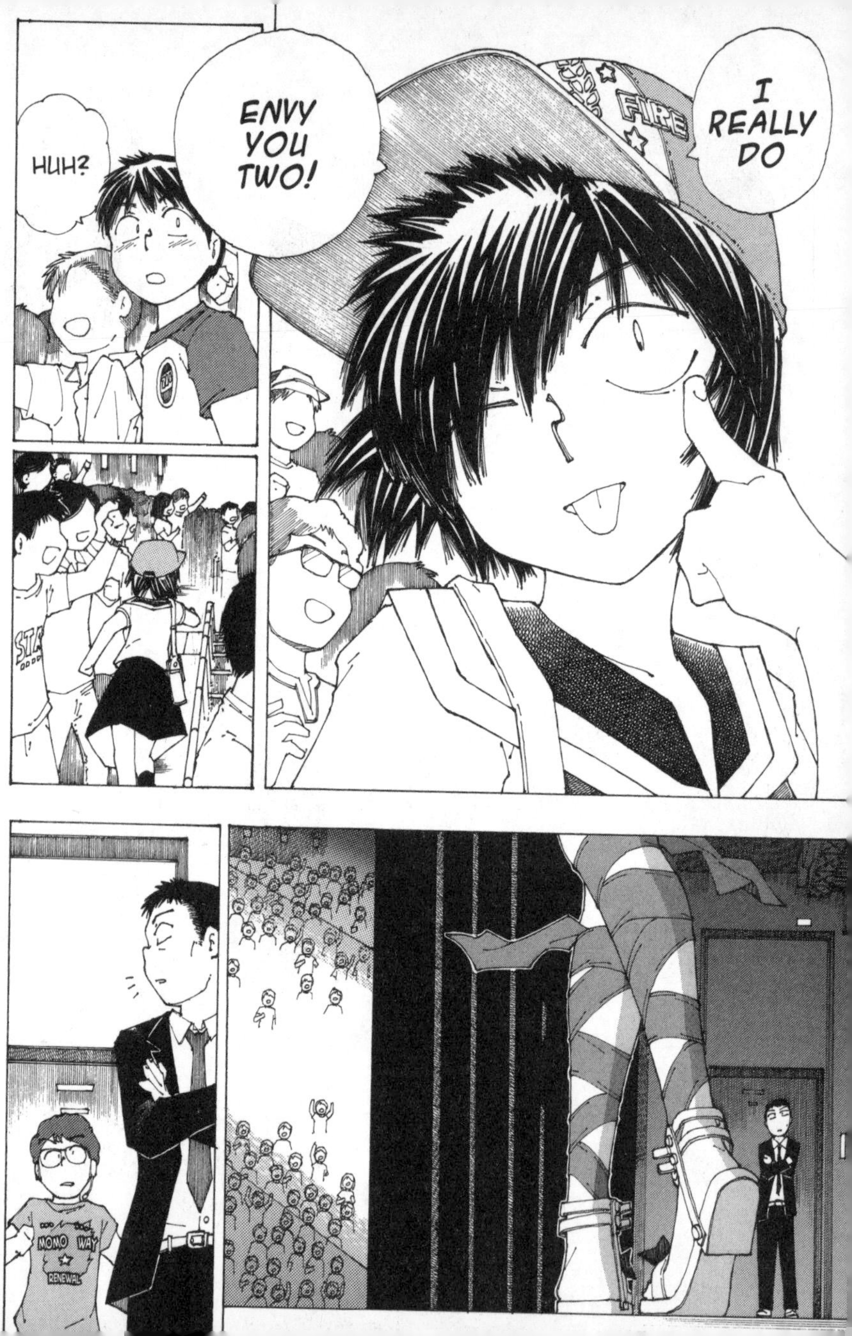
FIRE
I REALLY DO
ENVY YOU TWO!
HUH?
MOMO WAY
RENEWAL

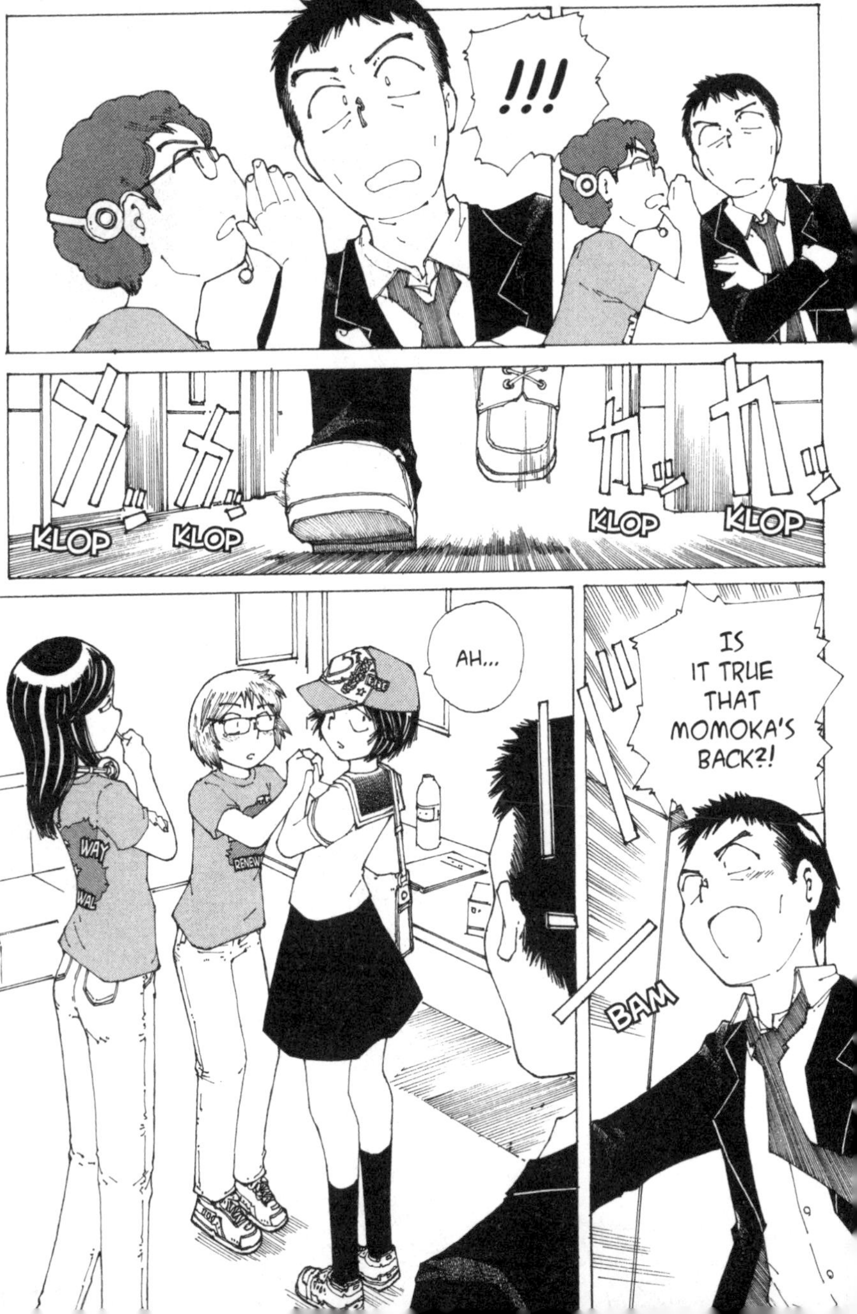
!!!
KLOP
KLOP
KLOP
KLOP
IS IT TRUE THAT MOMOKA'S BACK?!
BAM
AH...
WAY
WAL
RENEW

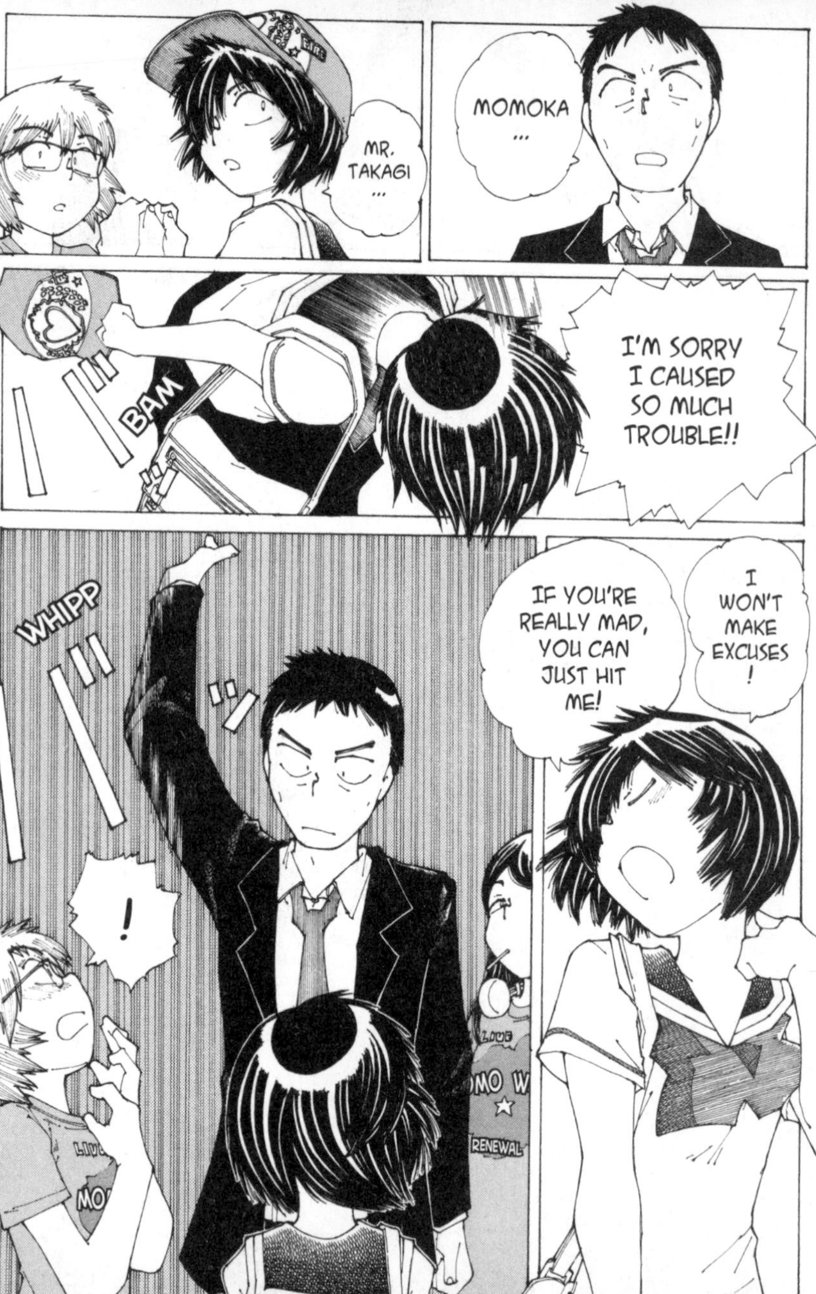
MOMOKA ...
MR. TAKAGI ...
I'M SORRY I CAUSED SO MUCH TROUBLE!!
BAM
I WON'T MAKE EXCUSES!
IF YOU'RE REALLY MAD, YOU CAN JUST HIT ME!
WHIPP
!
LIVE
RENEWAL

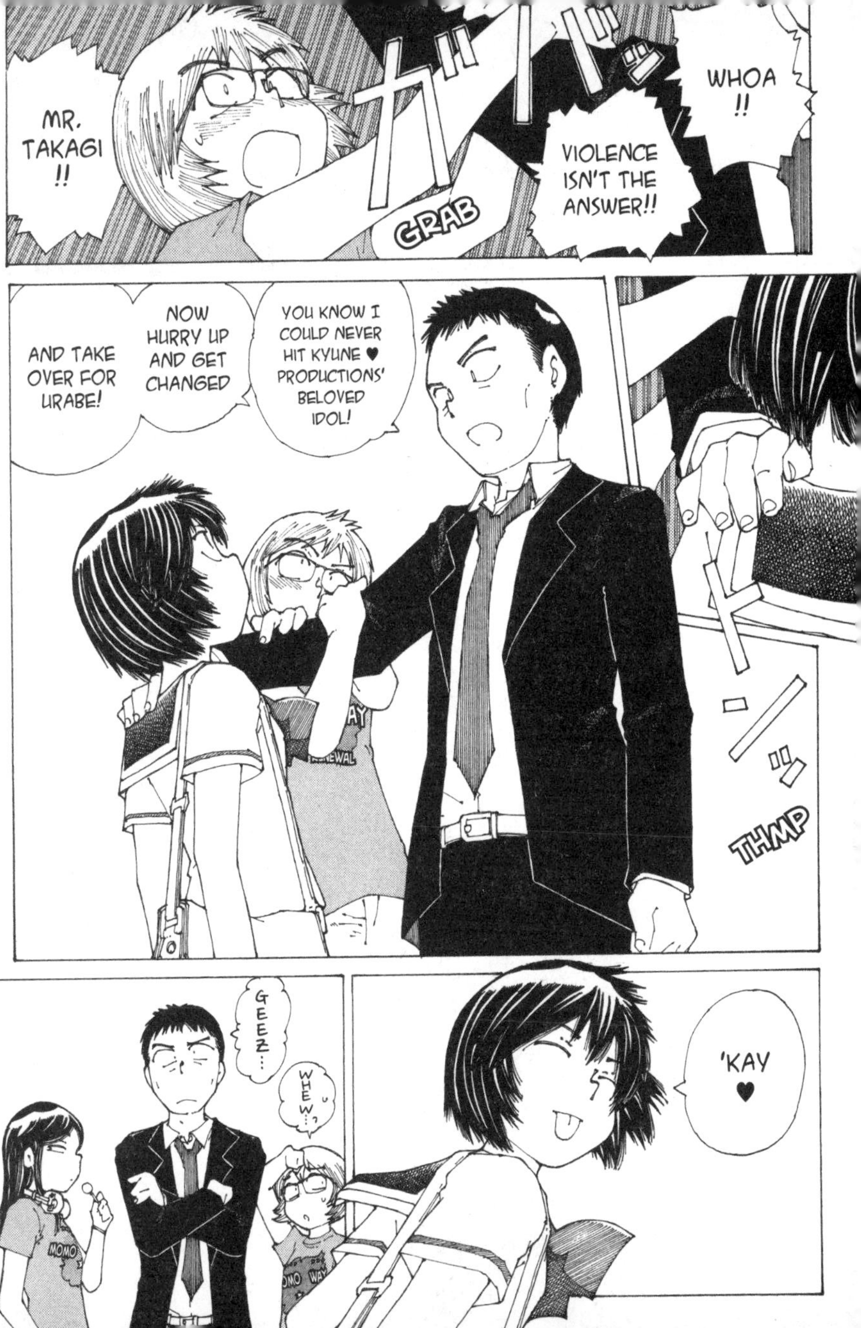
WHOA!!
VIOLENCE ISN'T THE ANSWER!!
GRAB
MR. TAKAGI!!
THMP
YOU KNOW I COULD NEVER HIT KYUNE ♥ PRODUCTIONS' BELOVED IDOL!
NOW HURRY UP AND GET CHANGED
AND TAKE OVER FOR URABE!
'KAY ♥
GEEZ...
WHEW...?

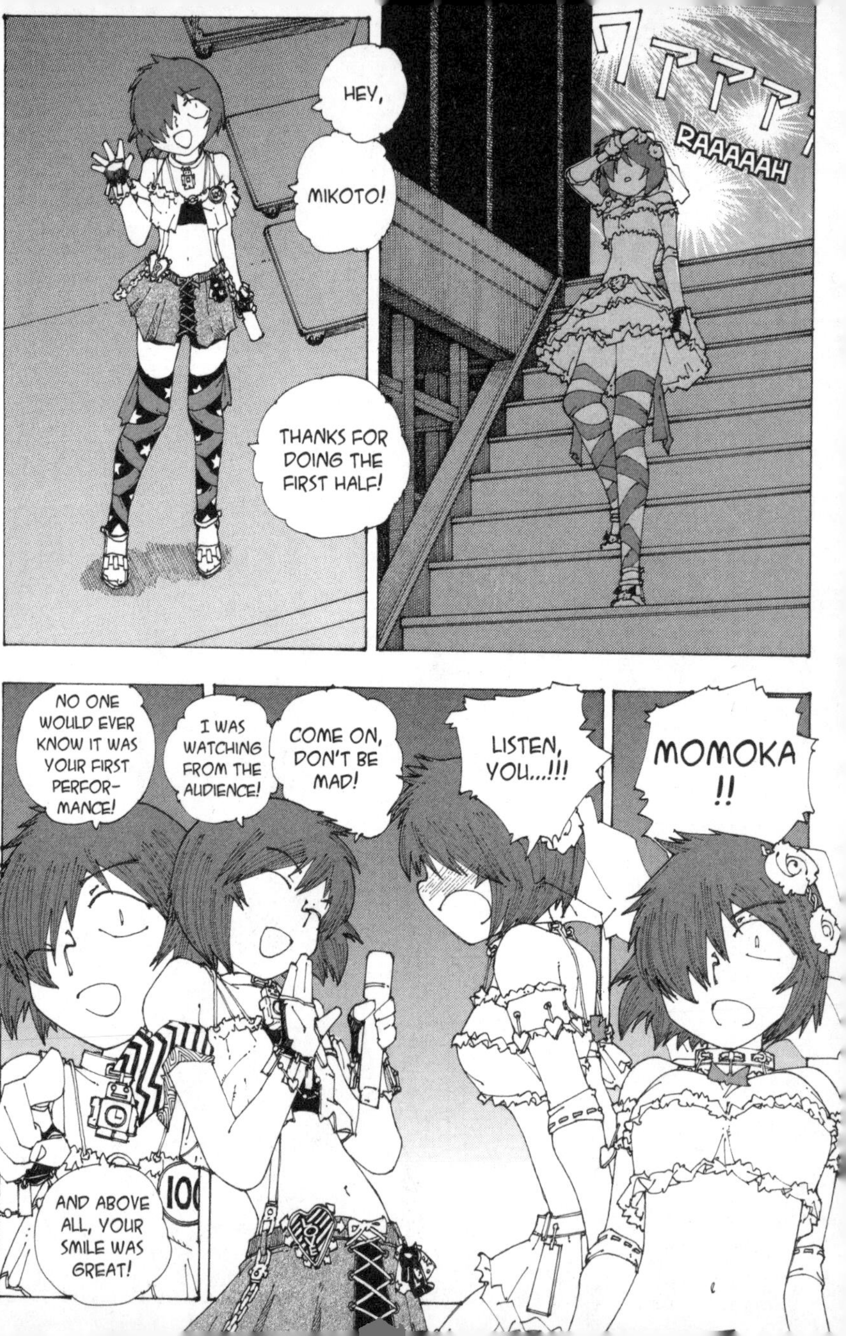
RAAAAAH
HEY,
MIKOTO!
THANKS FOR DOING THE FIRST HALF!
MOMOKA !!
LISTEN, YOU...!!!
COME ON, DON'T BE MAD!
I WAS WATCHING FROM THE AUDIENCE!
NO ONE WOULD EVER KNOW IT WAS YOUR FIRST PERFOR-MANCE!
AND ABOVE ALL, YOUR SMILE WAS GREAT!

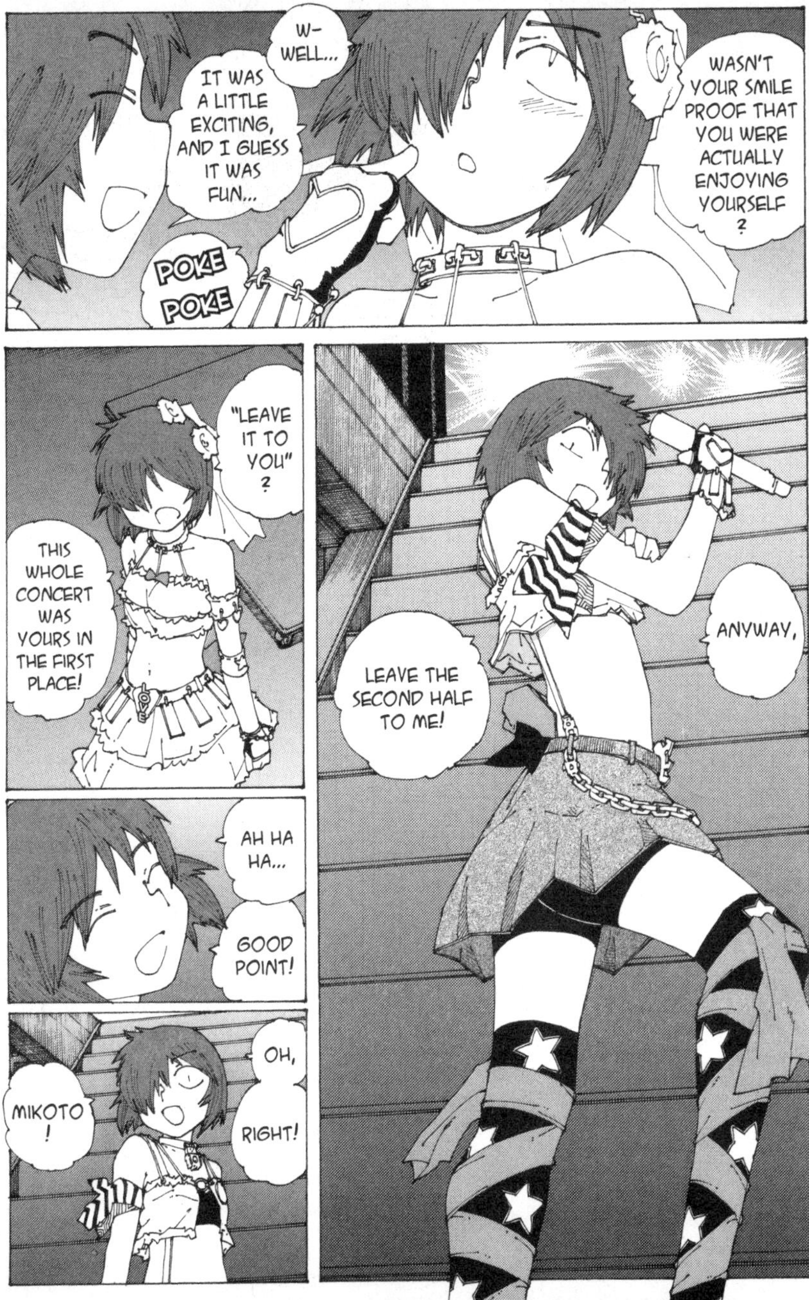
WASN'T YOUR SMILE PROOF THAT YOU WERE ACTUALLY ENJOYING YOURSELF?
W-WELL...
IT WAS A LITTLE EXCITING, AND I GUESS IT WAS FUN...
POKE POKE
ANYWAY,
LEAVE THE SECOND HALF TO ME!
"LEAVE IT TO YOU"?
THIS WHOLE CONCERT WAS YOURS IN THE FIRST PLACE!
AH HA HA...
GOOD POINT!
OH, RIGHT!
MIKOTO!

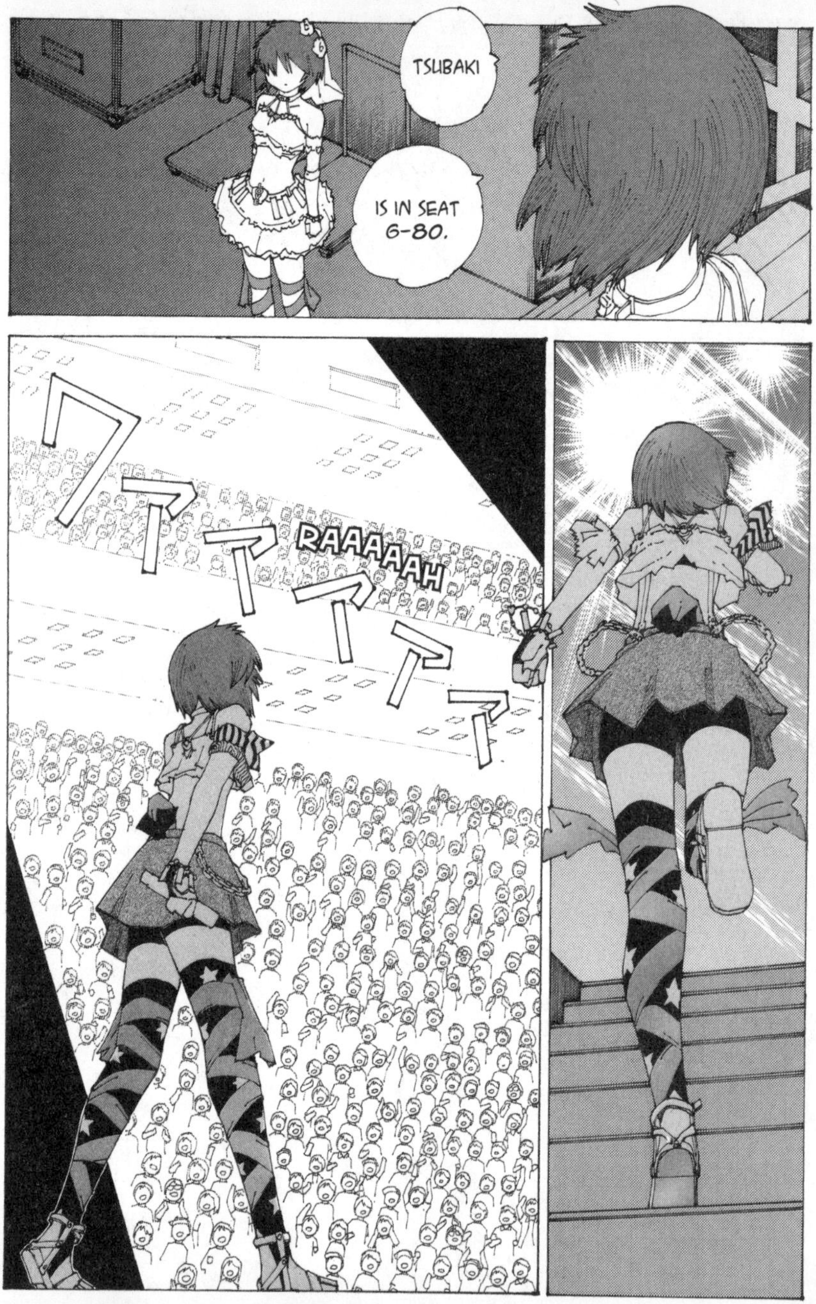
TSUBAKI
IS IN SEAT 6-80.
ワァァァァァ
RAAAAAAH

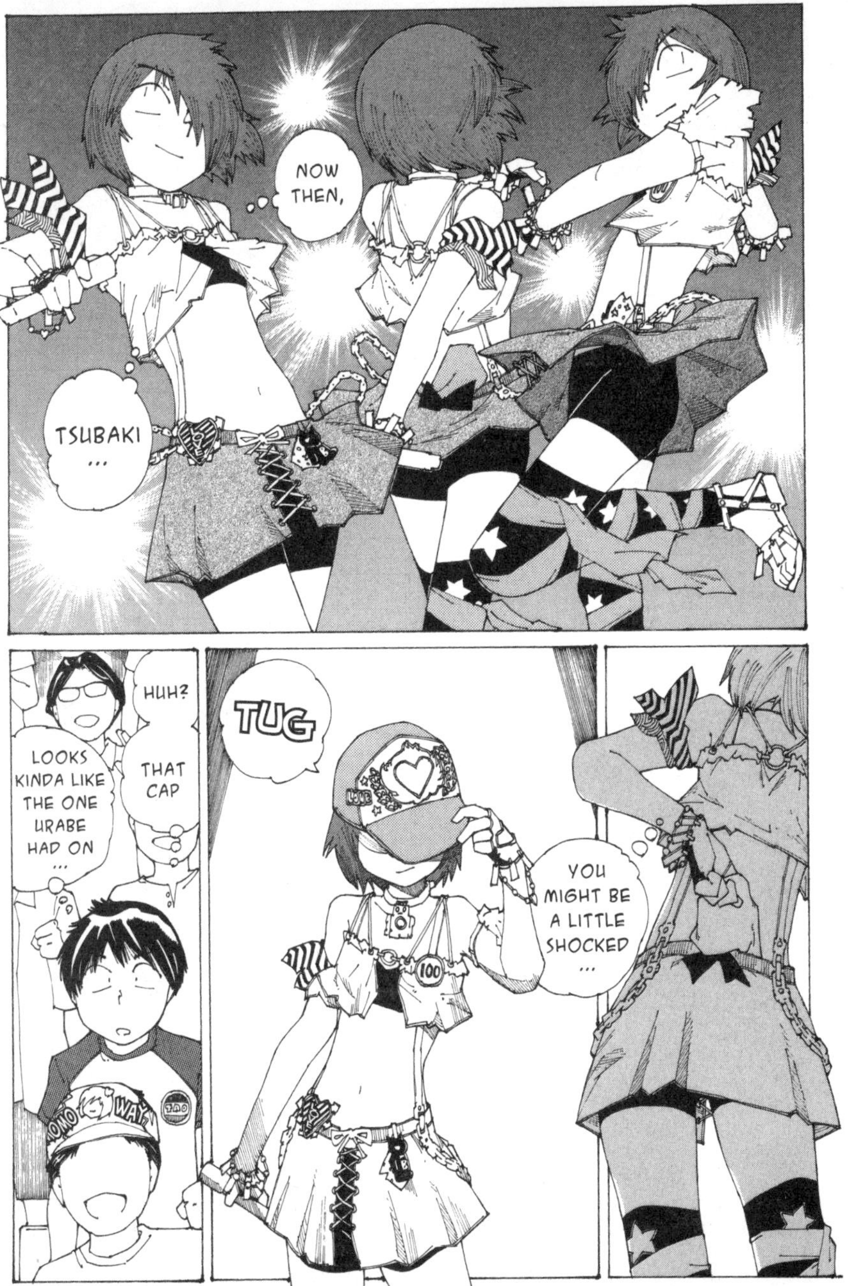
NOW THEN,
TSUBAKI ...
YOU MIGHT BE A LITTLE SHOCKED ...
TUG
HUH?
THAT CAP
LOOKS KINDA LIKE THE ONE URABE HAD ON ...

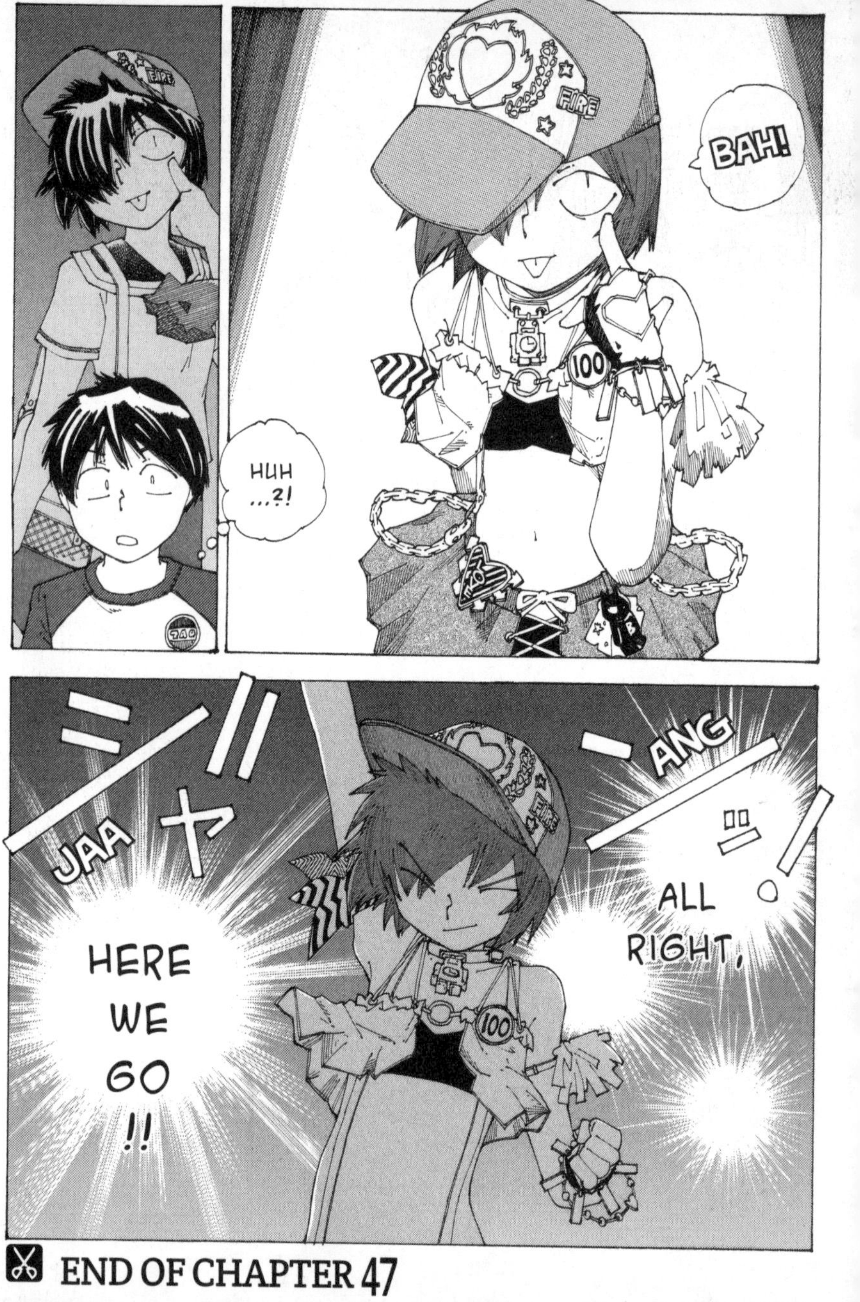
BAH!
HUH ...?!
ANG
ALL RIGHT,
JAA
HERE WE GO !!

END OF CHAPTER 47

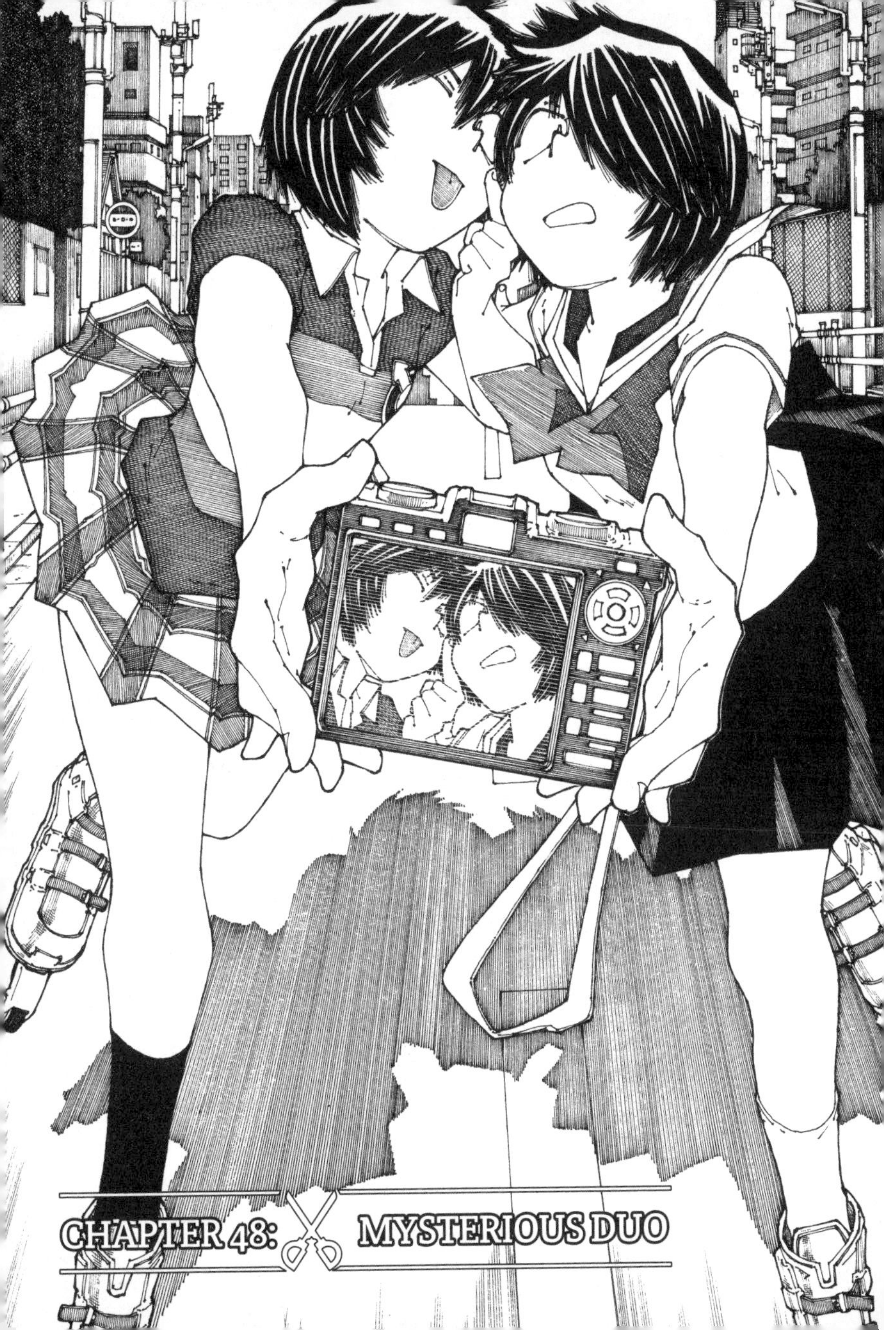

CHAPTER 48: MYSTERIOUS DUO

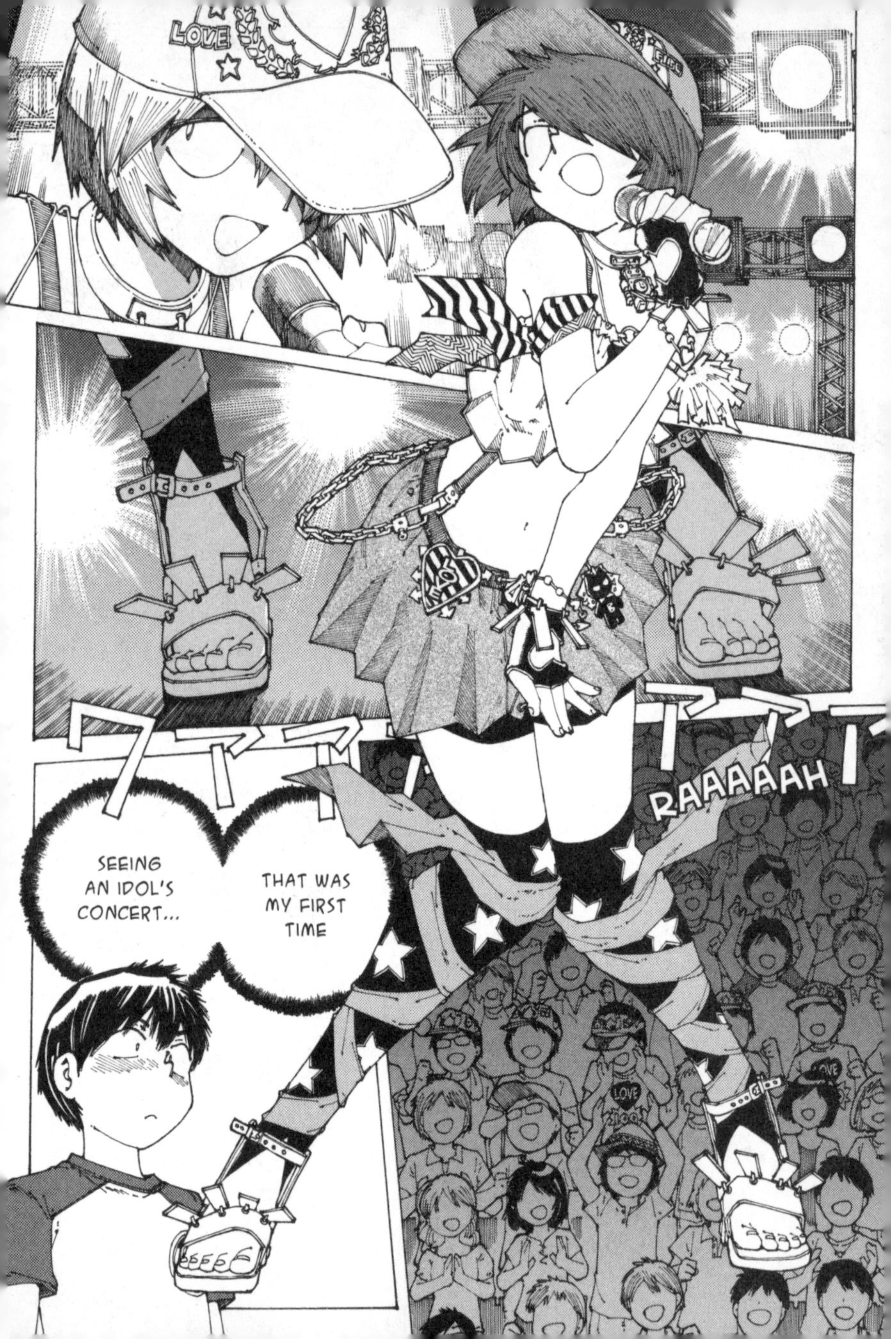
RAAAAAH
SEEING AN IDOL'S CONCERT... THAT WAS MY FIRST TIME

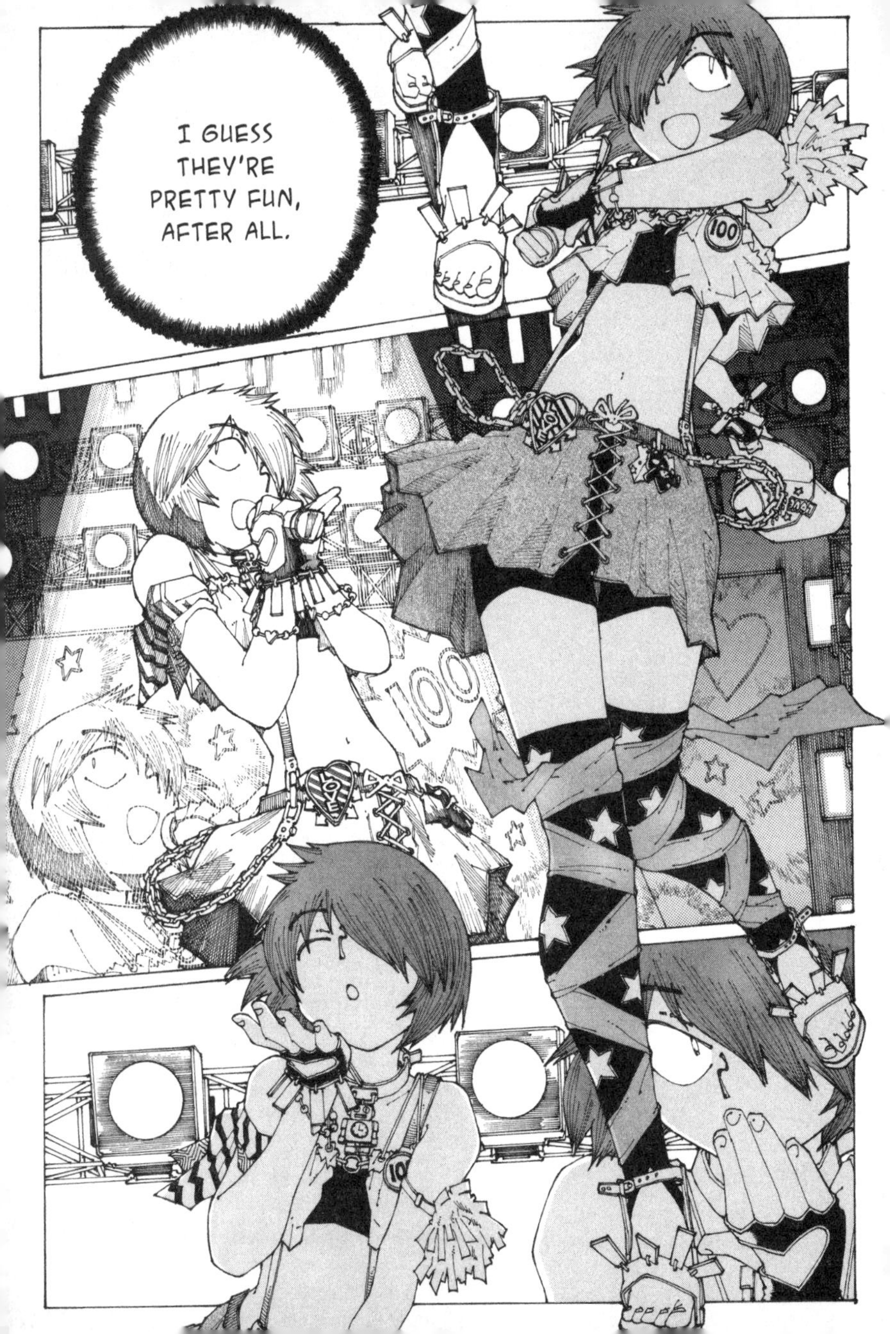
I GUESS THEY'RE PRETTY FUN, AFTER ALL.
100
LOVE
100
LOVE
10

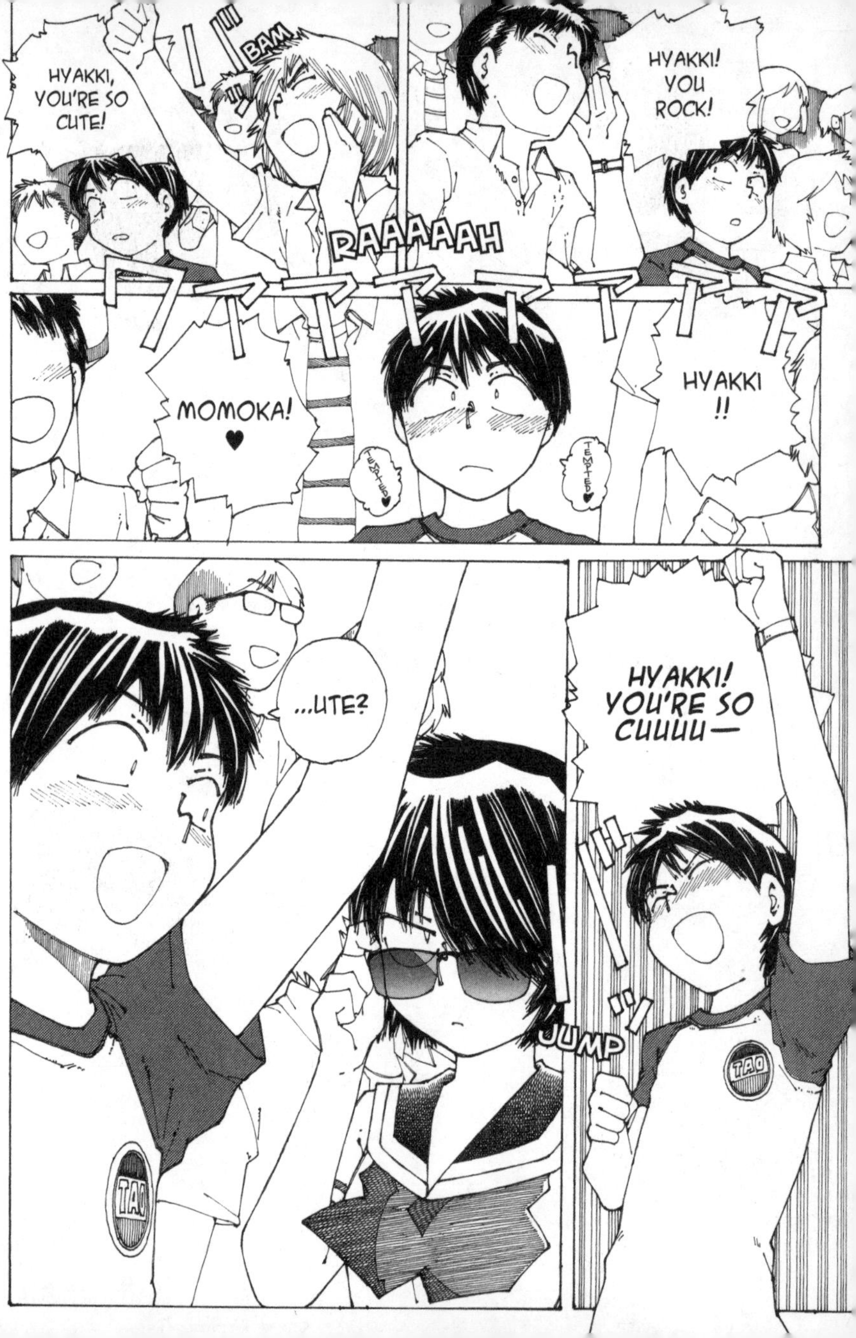
HYAKKI! YOU ROCK!
HYAKKI, YOU'RE SO CUTE!
BAM
RAAAAAAH
HYAKKI !!
TEMPTED♥
TEMPTED♥
MOMOKA! ♥
HYAKKI! YOU'RE SO CUUUU—
JUMP
...UTE?

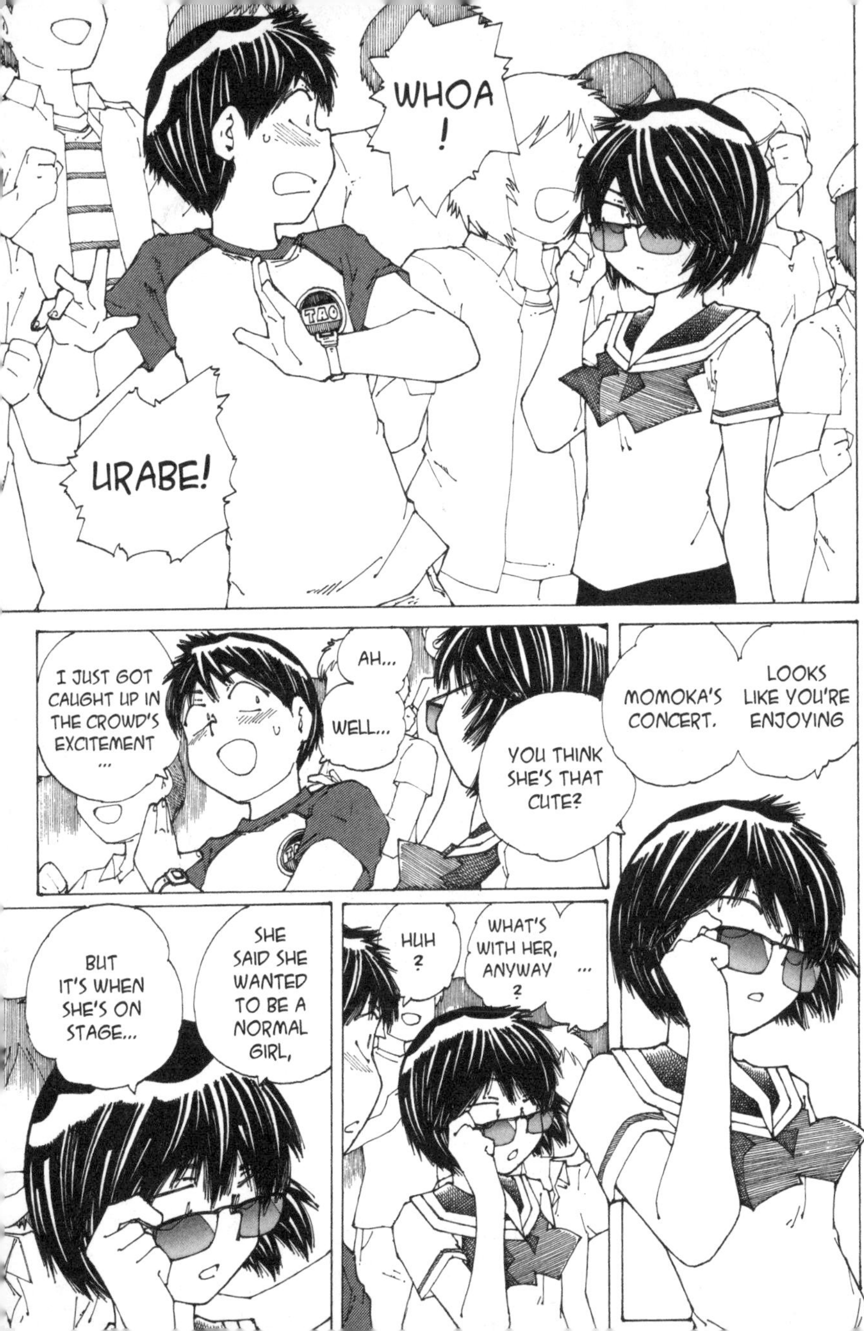
WHOA!
URABE!
LOOKS LIKE YOU'RE ENJOYING MOMOKA'S CONCERT.
YOU THINK SHE'S THAT CUTE?
AH... WELL...
I JUST GOT CAUGHT UP IN THE CROWD'S EXCITEMENT...
WHAT'S WITH HER, ANYWAY? ...
HUH?
SHE SAID SHE WANTED TO BE A NORMAL GIRL,
BUT IT'S WHEN SHE'S ON STAGE...

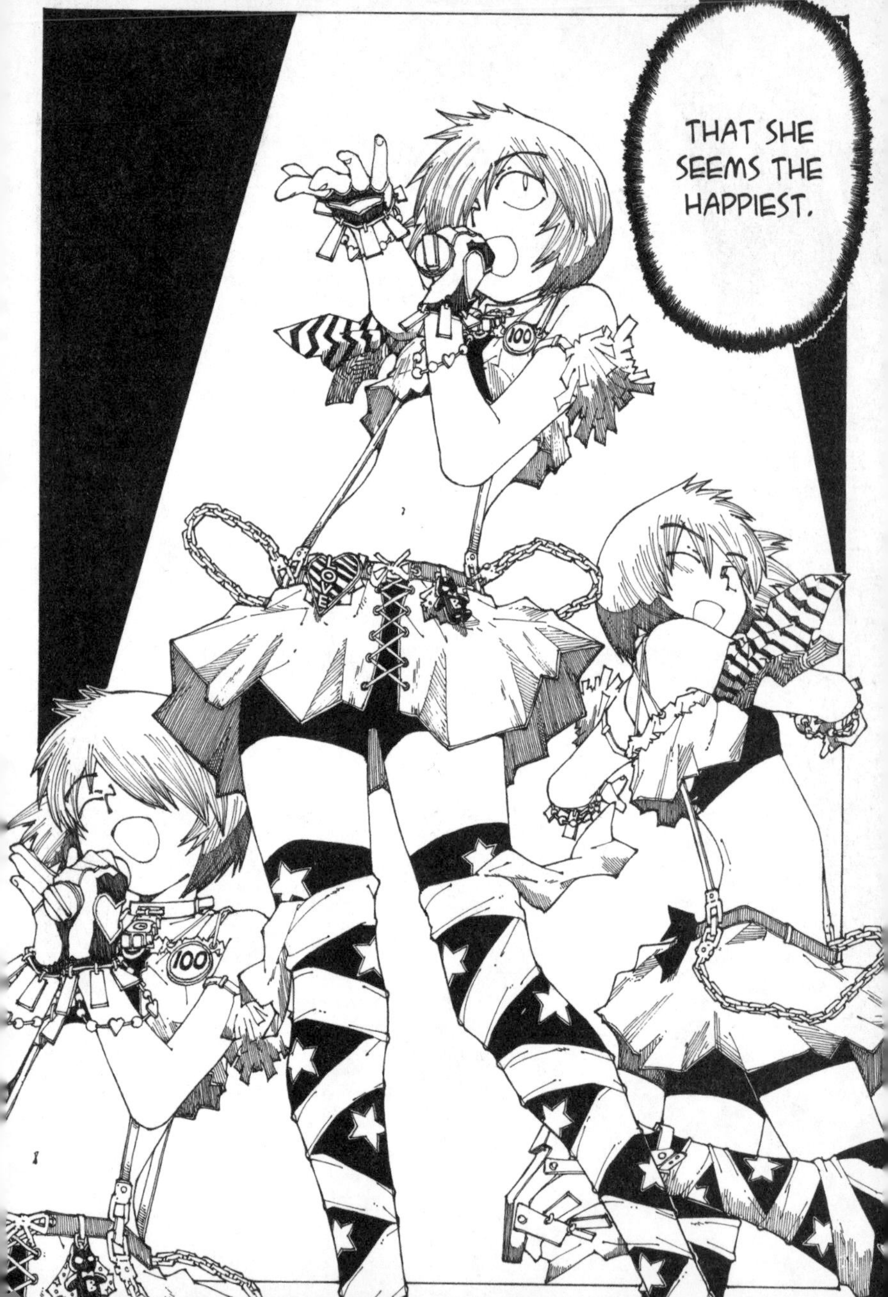
THAT SHE SEEMS THE HAPPIEST.
100
LOVE
100

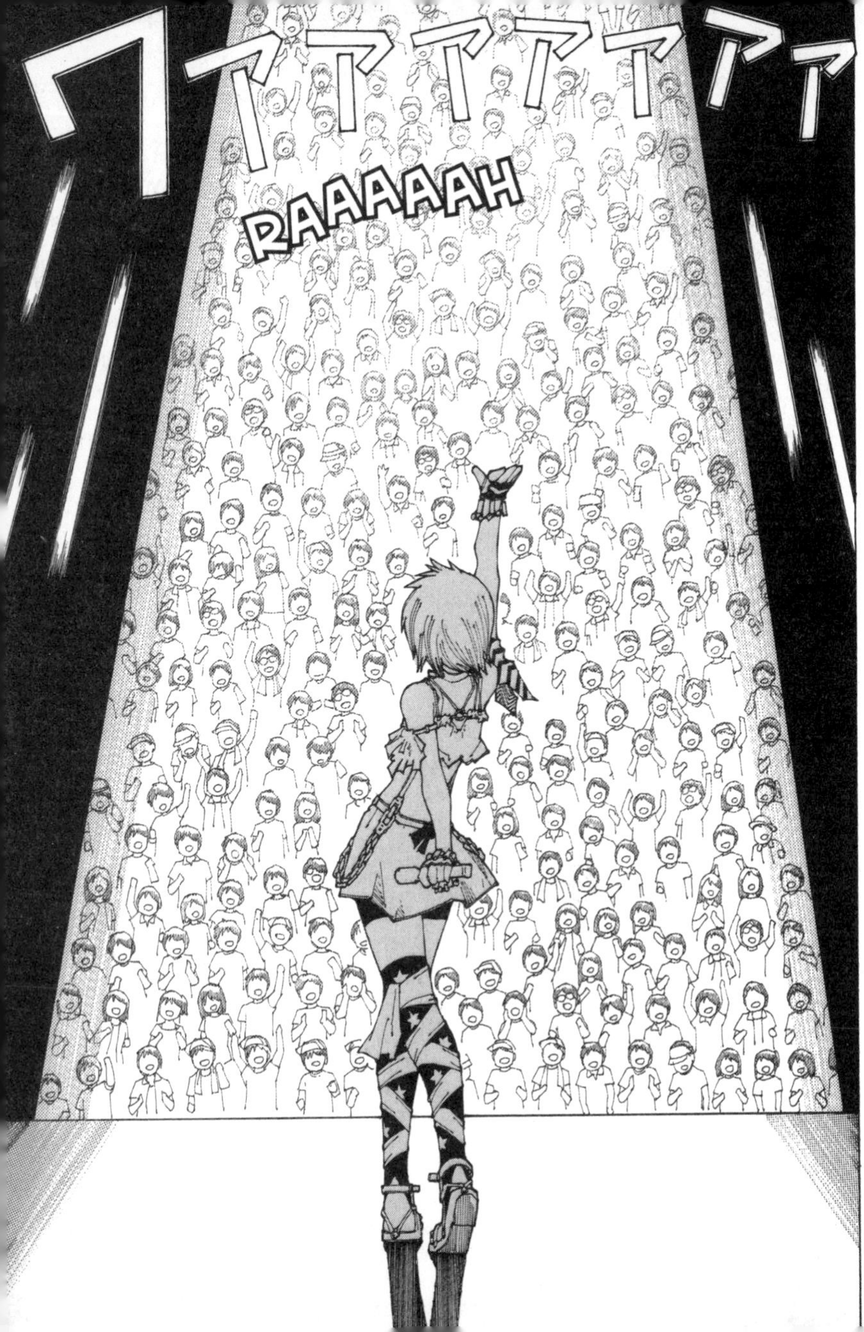
ワァァァァァァ
RAAAAAH

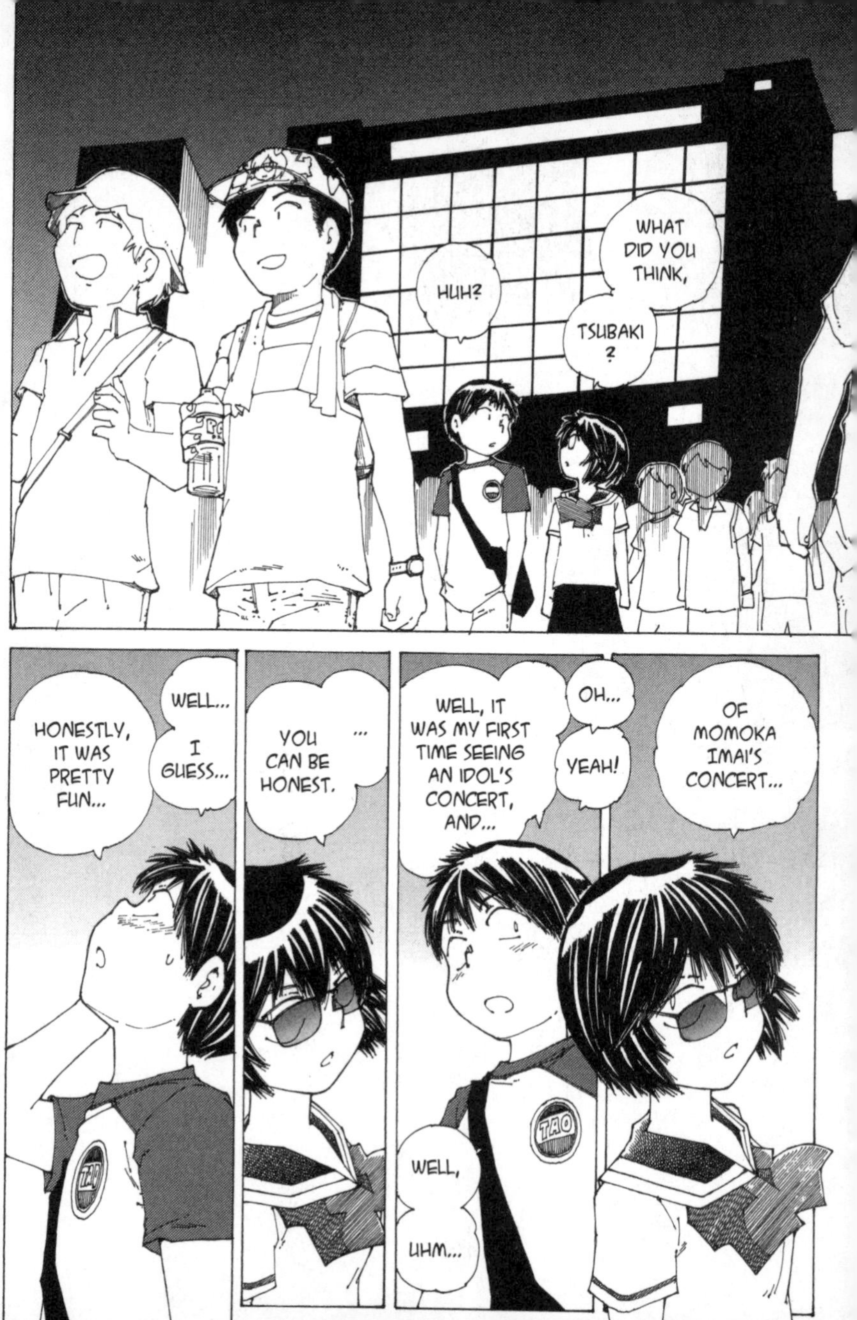
WHAT DID YOU THINK,
TSUBAKI ?
HUH?
OF MOMOKA IMAI'S CONCERT...
OH...
YEAH!
WELL, IT WAS MY FIRST TIME SEEING AN IDOL'S CONCERT, AND...
WELL,
UHM...
...
YOU CAN BE HONEST.
WELL...
I GUESS...
HONESTLY, IT WAS PRETTY FUN...

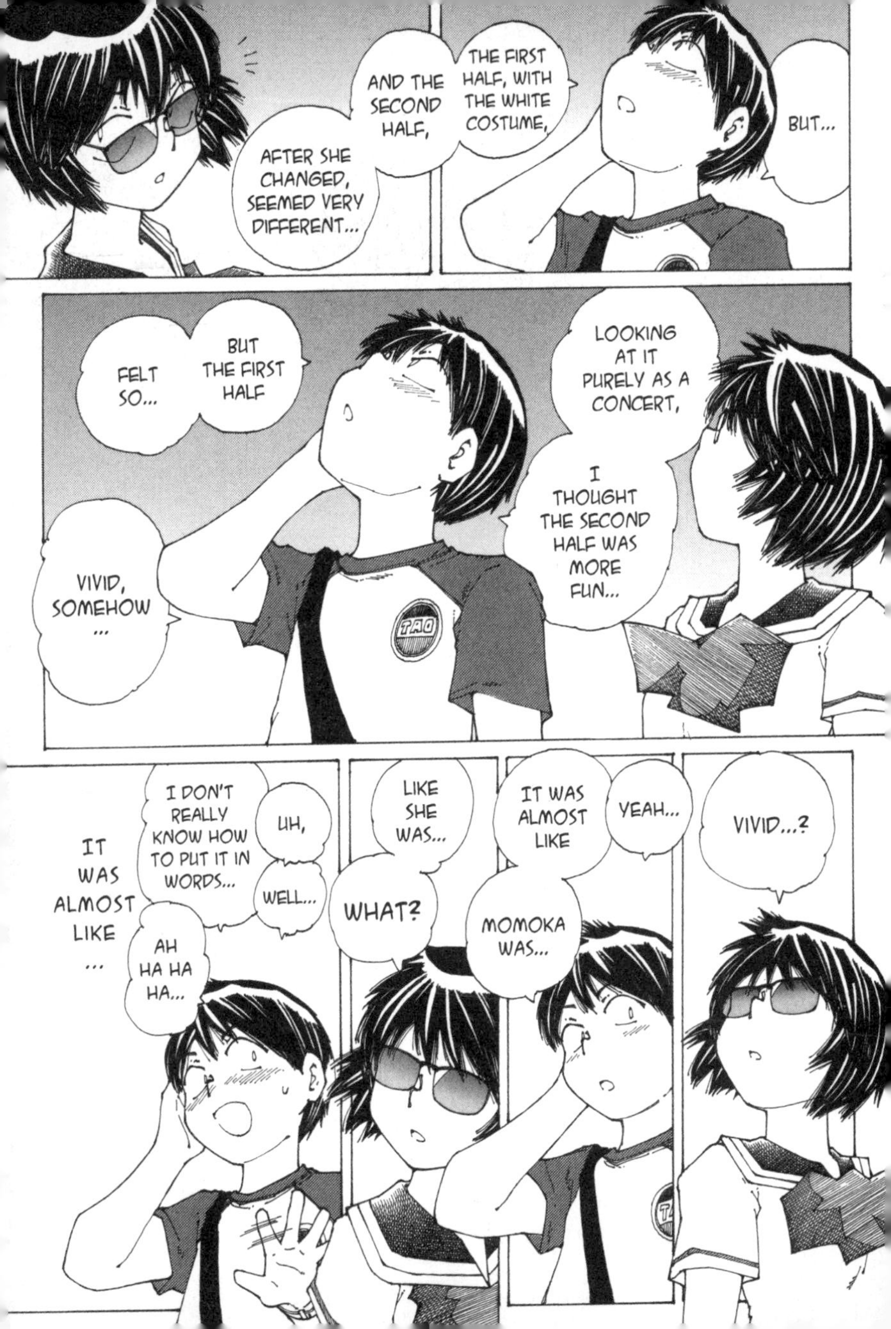
BUT...
THE FIRST HALF, WITH THE WHITE COSTUME,
AND THE SECOND HALF,
AFTER SHE CHANGED, SEEMED VERY DIFFERENT...
LOOKING AT IT PURELY AS A CONCERT,
I THOUGHT THE SECOND HALF WAS MORE FUN...
BUT THE FIRST HALF
FELT SO...
VIVID, SOMEHOW ...
VIVID...?
YEAH...
IT WAS ALMOST LIKE
MOMOKA WAS...
LIKE SHE WAS...
WHAT?
UH,
WELL...
I DON'T REALLY KNOW HOW TO PUT IT IN WORDS...
AH HA HA HA...
IT WAS ALMOST LIKE ...

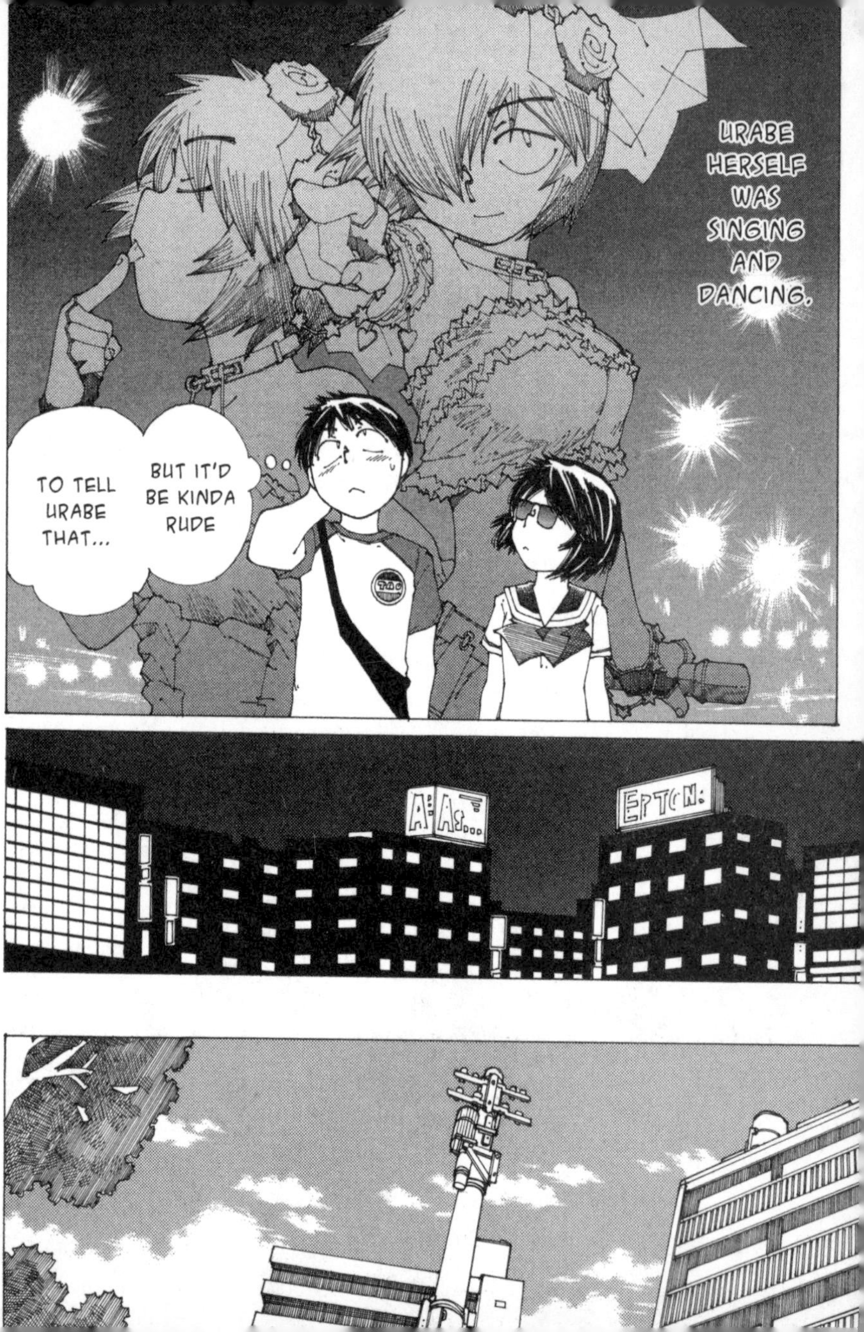
URABE HERSELF WAS SINGING AND DANCING.
BUT IT'D BE KINDA RUDE
TO TELL URABE THAT...

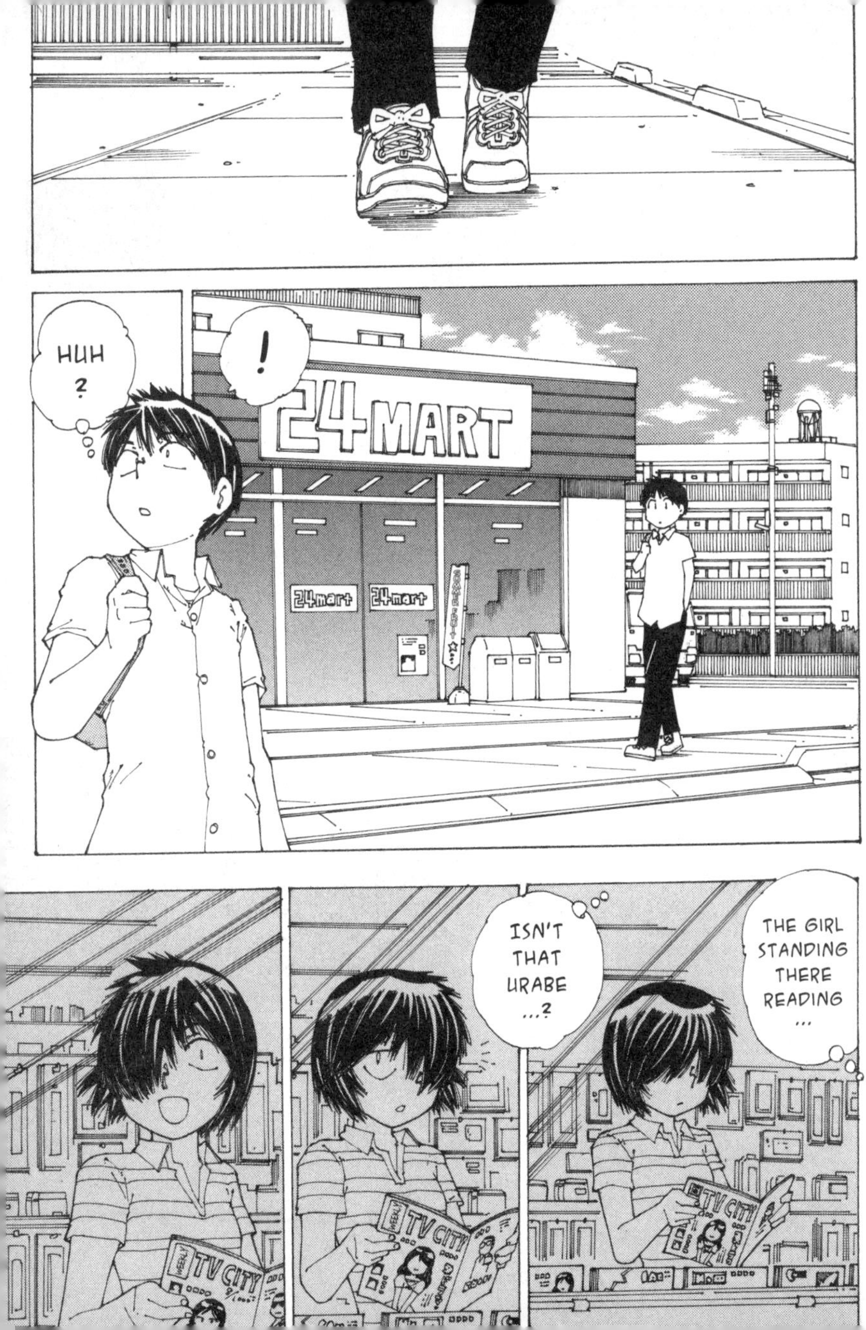
24MART
!
HUH ?
24mart
24mart
THE GIRL STANDING THERE READING ...
ISN'T THAT URABE ...?
TV CITY

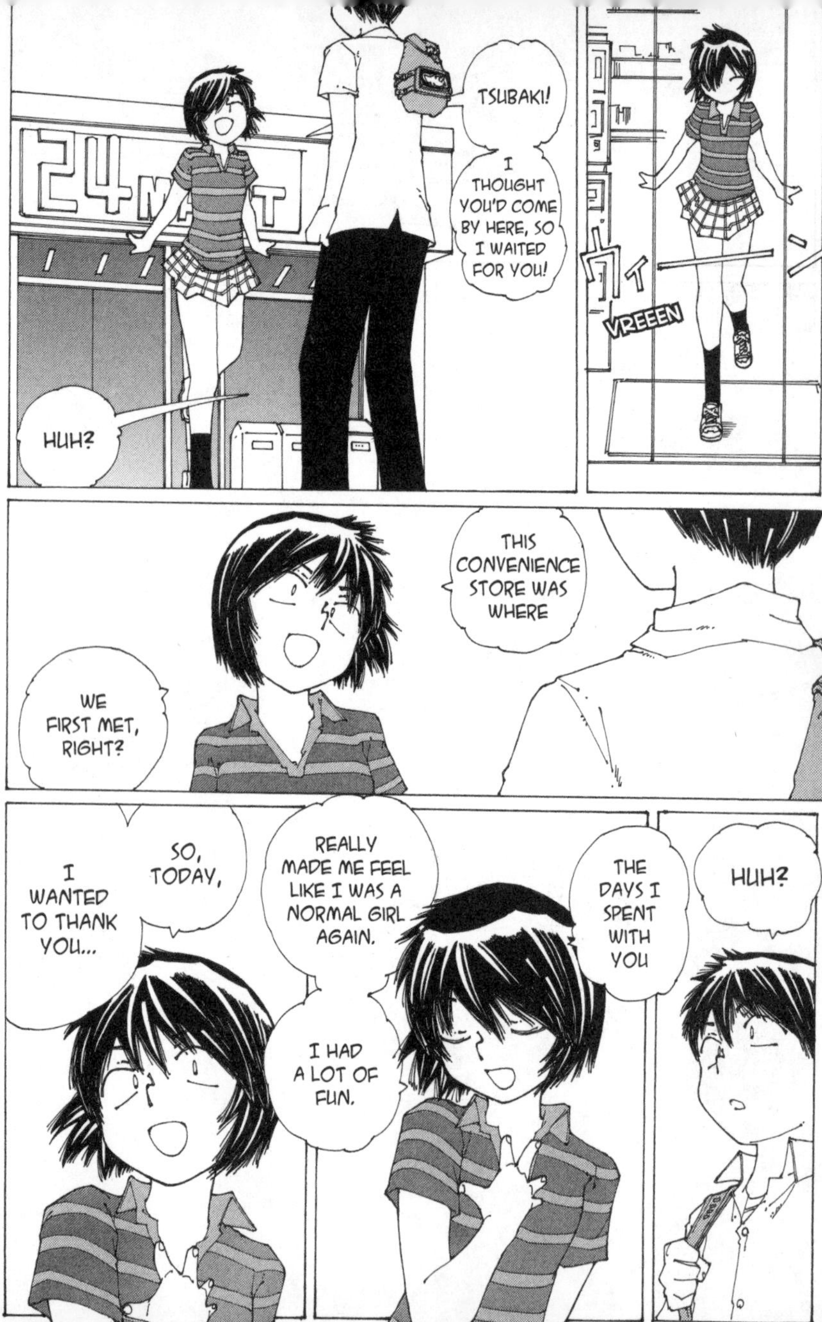
VREEEN
TSUBAKI!
I THOUGHT YOU'D COME BY HERE, SO I WAITED FOR YOU!
HUH?
THIS CONVENIENCE STORE WAS WHERE
WE FIRST MET, RIGHT?
HUH?
THE DAYS I SPENT WITH YOU
REALLY MADE ME FEEL LIKE I WAS A NORMAL GIRL AGAIN.
I HAD A LOT OF FUN.
SO, TODAY,
I WANTED TO THANK YOU...

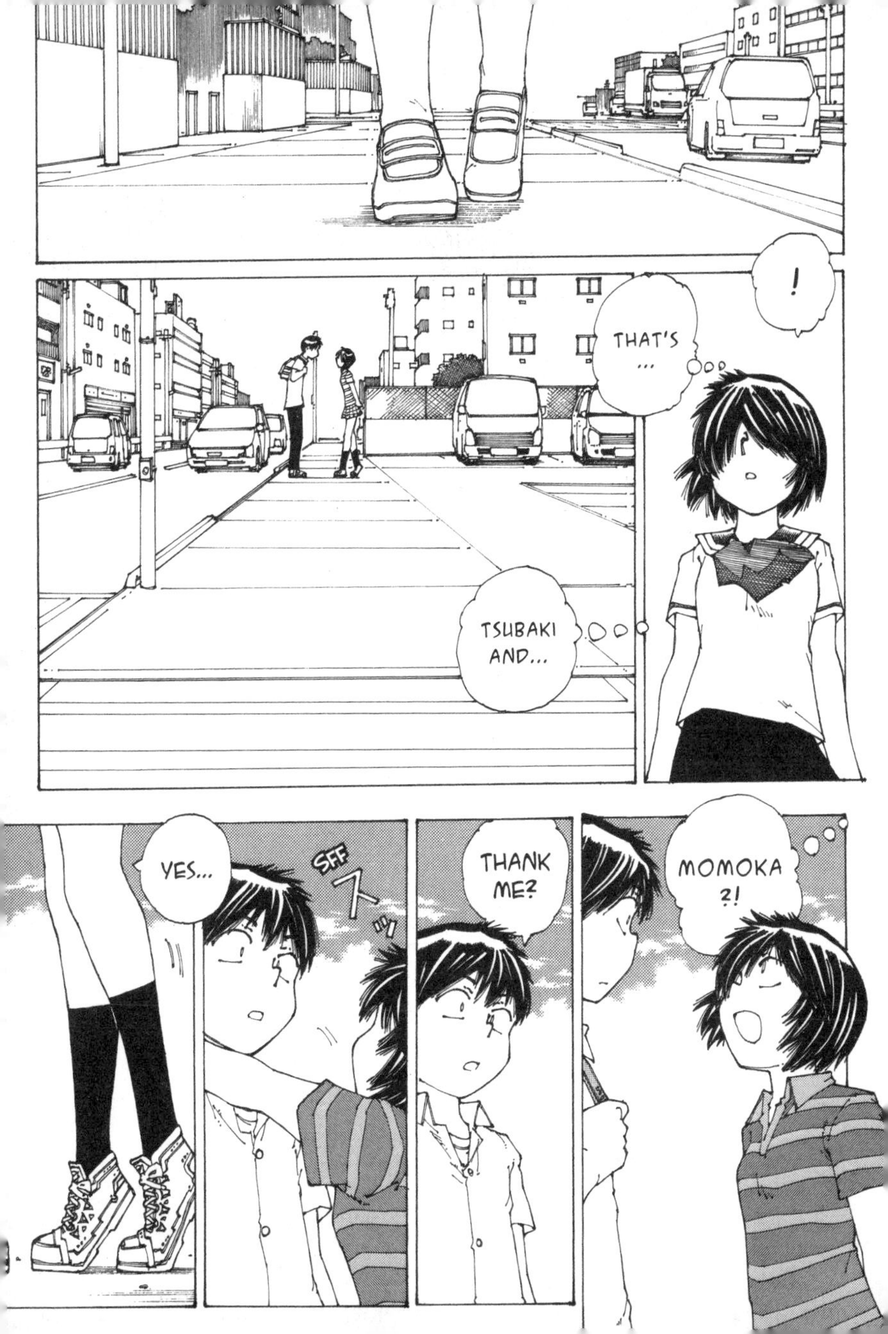
!
THAT'S ...
TSUBAKI AND...
MOMOKA ?!
THANK ME?
SFF
YES...

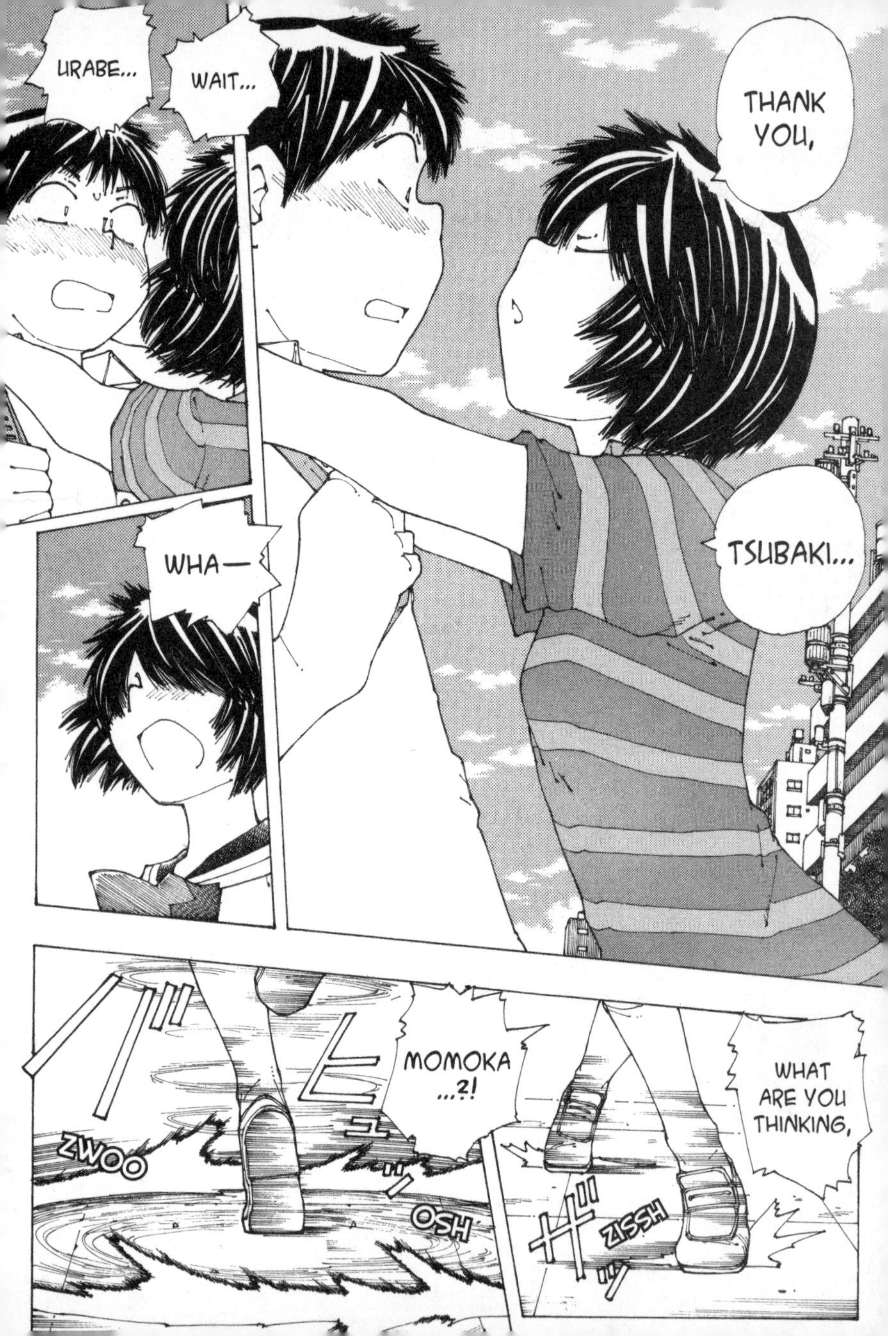
THANK YOU,
TSUBAKI...
WAIT...
URABE...
WHA—
WHAT ARE YOU THINKING,
ZISSH
MOMOKA ...?!
ZWOO
OSH

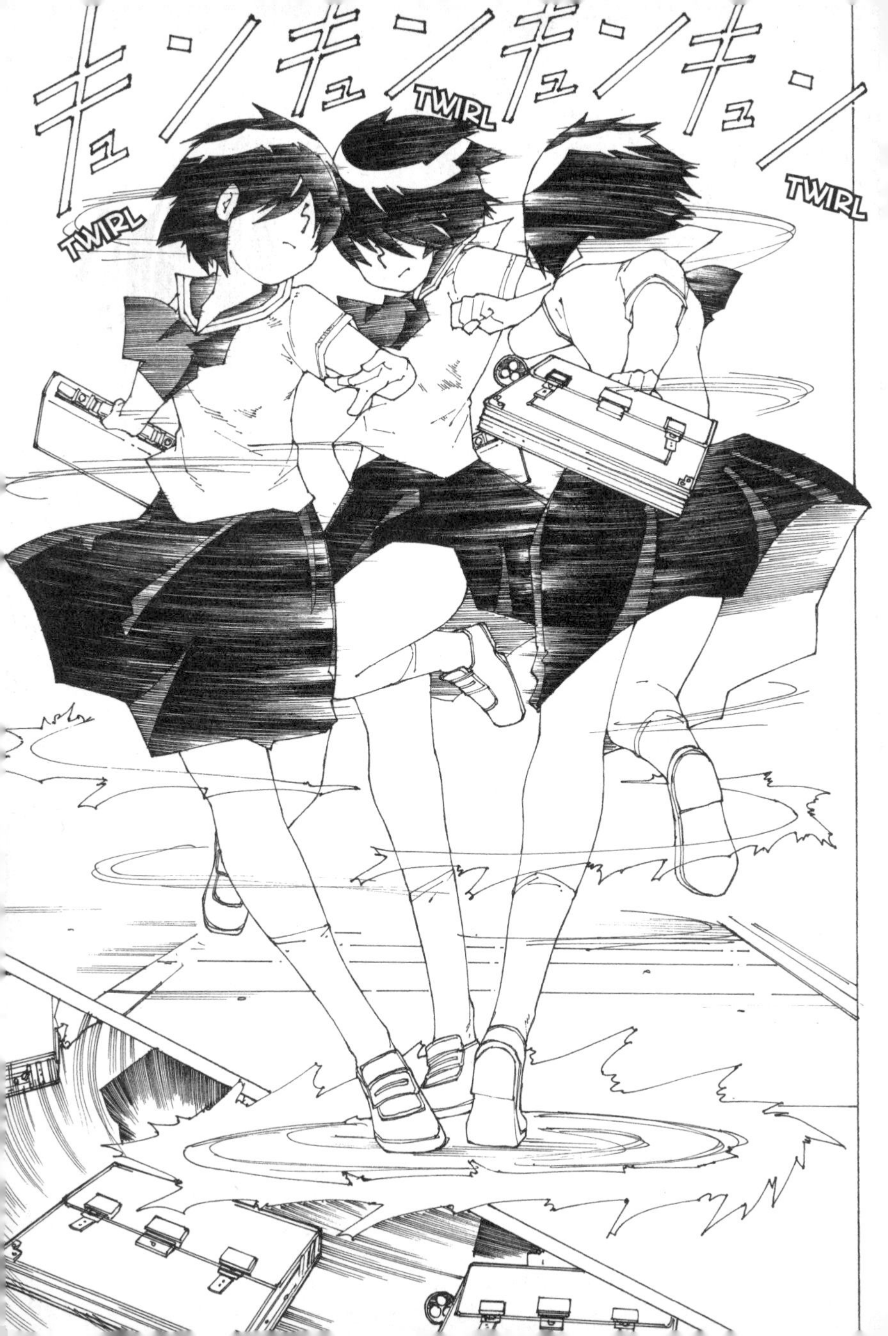
キューンキューンキューンキューン
TWIRL
TWIRL
TWIRL
TWIRL

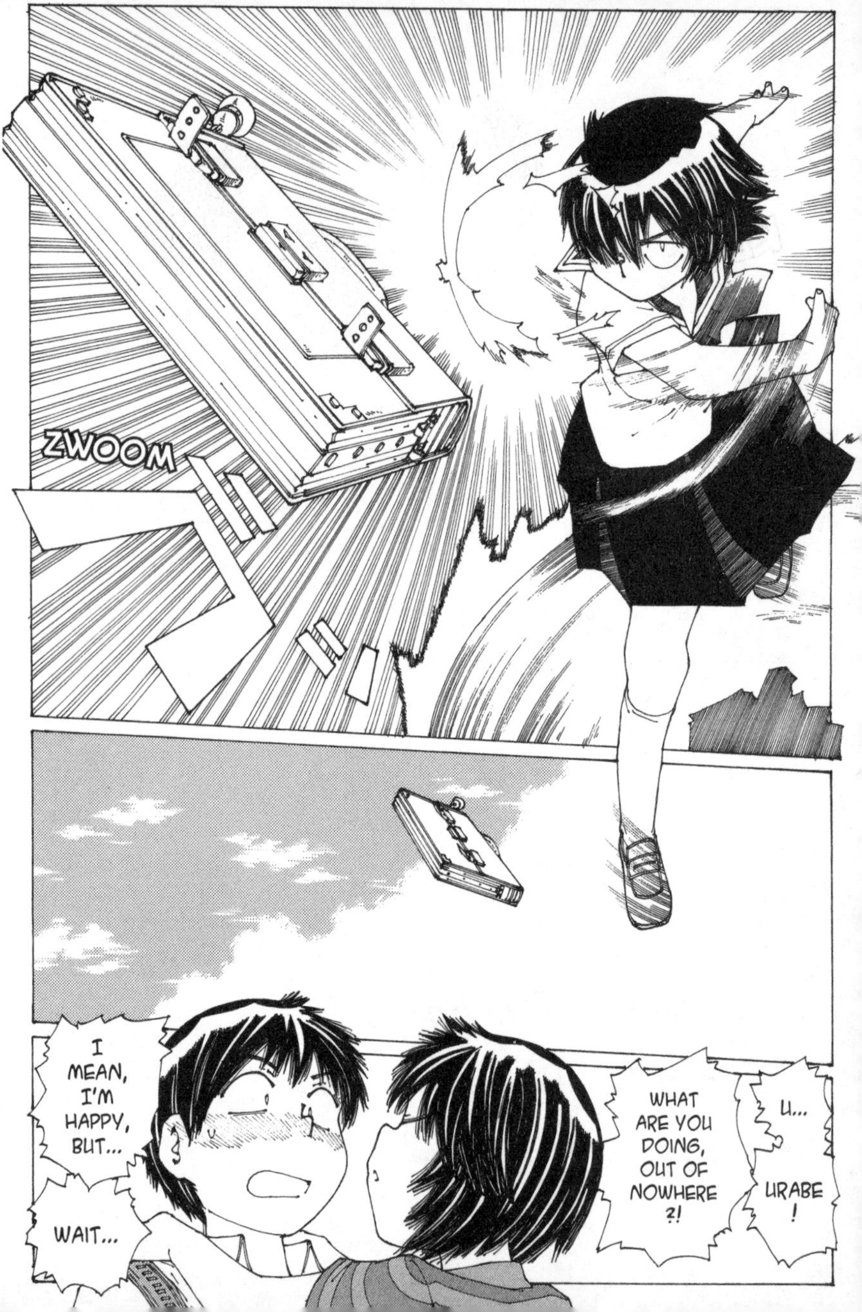
ZWOOM
U... URABE!
WHAT ARE YOU DOING, OUT OF NOWHERE?!
I MEAN, I'M HAPPY, BUT...
WAIT...

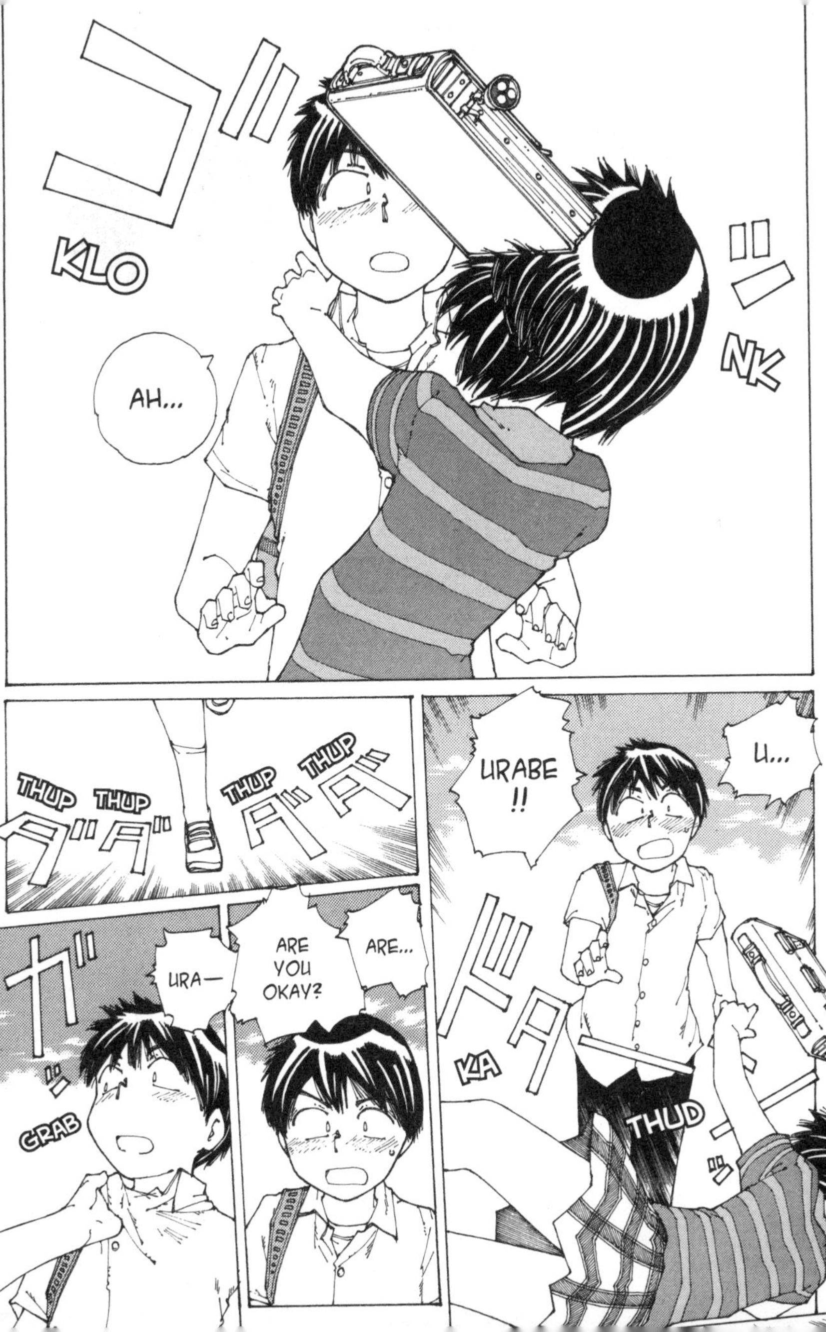
ゴン
KLO
NK
AH...
U...
URABE !!
ドタ
KA
THUD
ダダダダ
THUP THUP
THUP THUP
ARE...
ARE YOU OKAY?
URA—
ガッ
GRAB

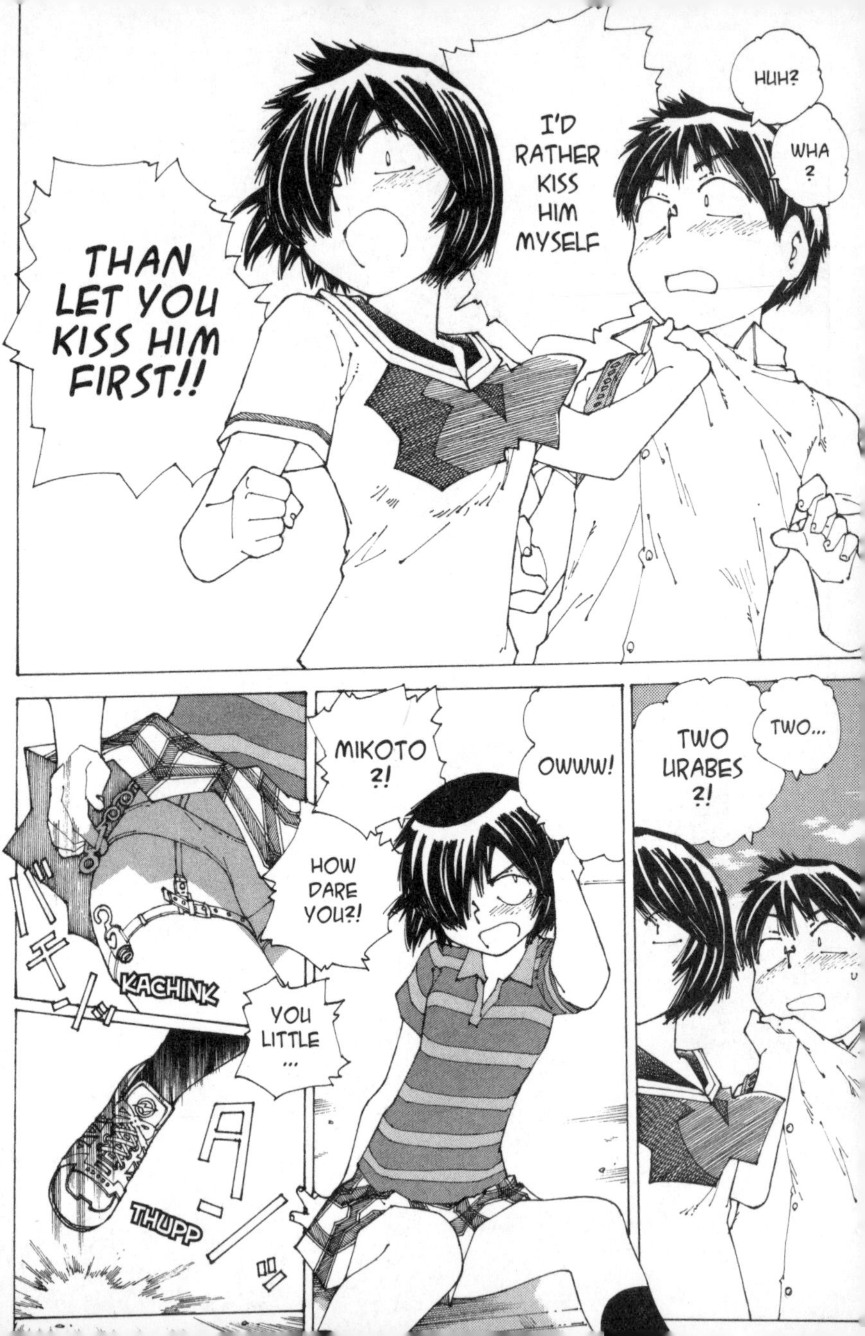
HUH?
WHA ?
I'D RATHER KISS HIM MYSELF
THAN LET YOU KISS HIM FIRST!!
TWO...
TWO URABES ?!
OWWW!
MIKOTO ?!
HOW DARE YOU?!
YOU LITTLE ...
KACHINK
THUPP

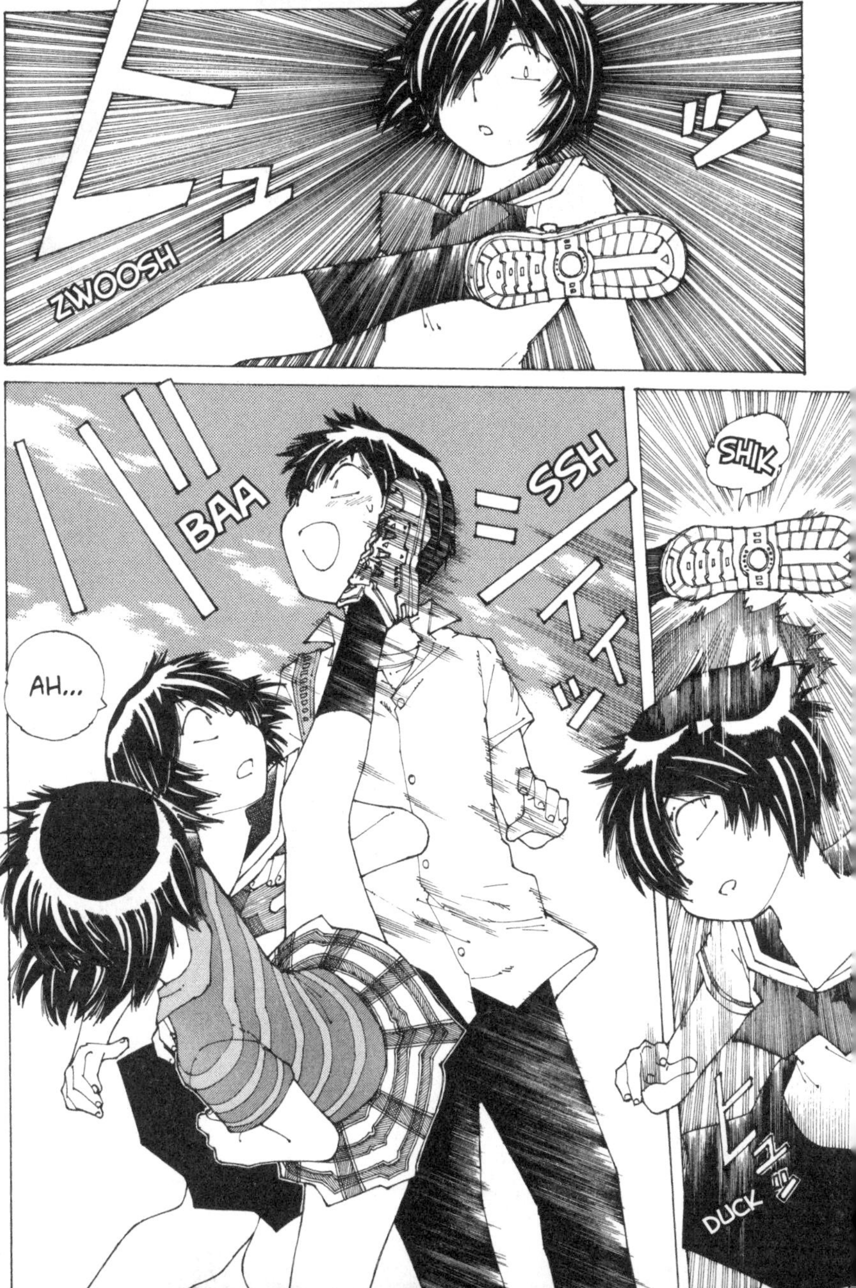
ZWOOSH
SHIK
DUCK
BAA SSH
AH...

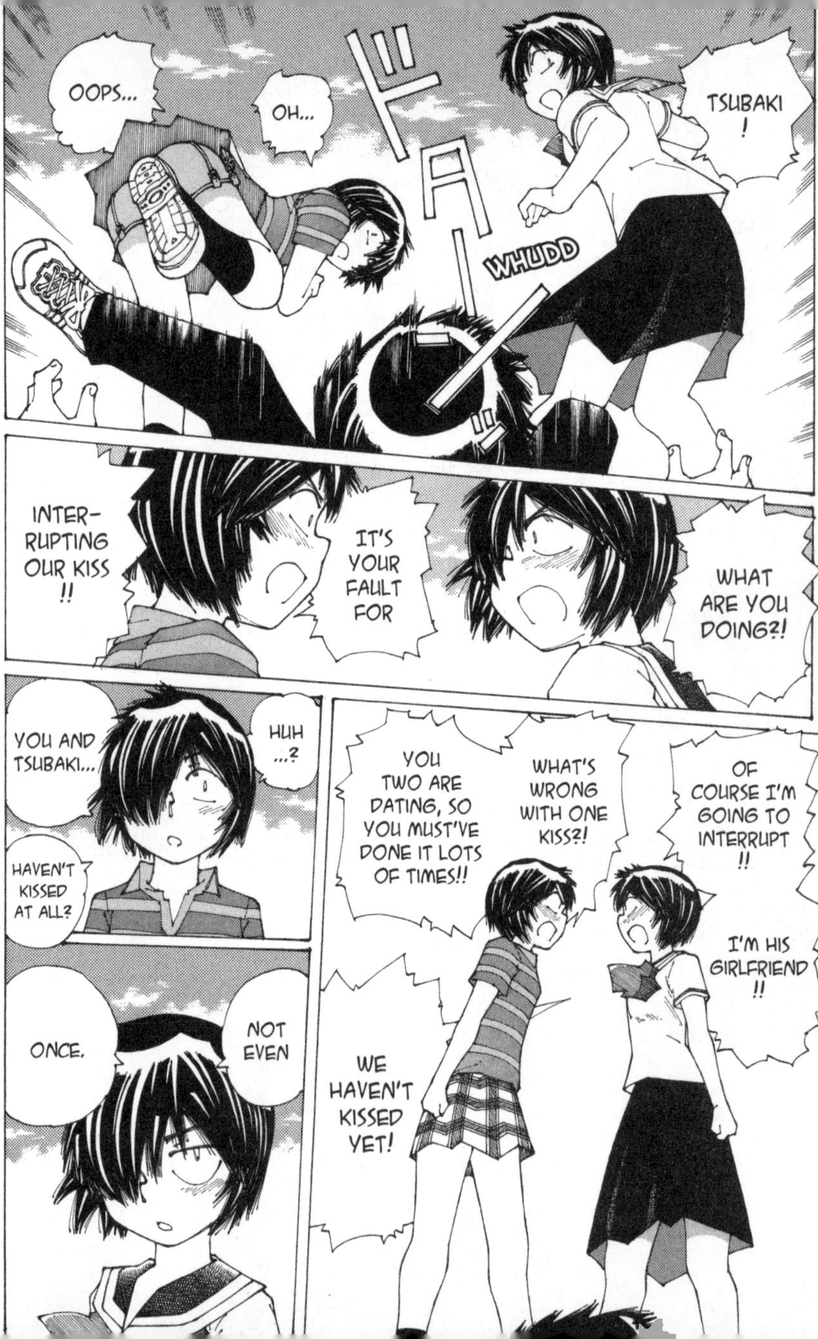
TSUBAKI !
WHUDD
OH...
OOPS...
WHAT ARE YOU DOING?!
IT'S YOUR FAULT FOR
INTERRUPTING OUR KISS !!
OF COURSE I'M GOING TO INTERRUPT !!
WHAT'S WRONG WITH ONE KISS?!
YOU TWO ARE DATING, SO YOU MUST'VE DONE IT LOTS OF TIMES!!
I'M HIS GIRLFRIEND !!
WE HAVEN'T KISSED YET!
HUH ...?
YOU AND TSUBAKI...
HAVEN'T KISSED AT ALL?
NOT EVEN
ONCE.

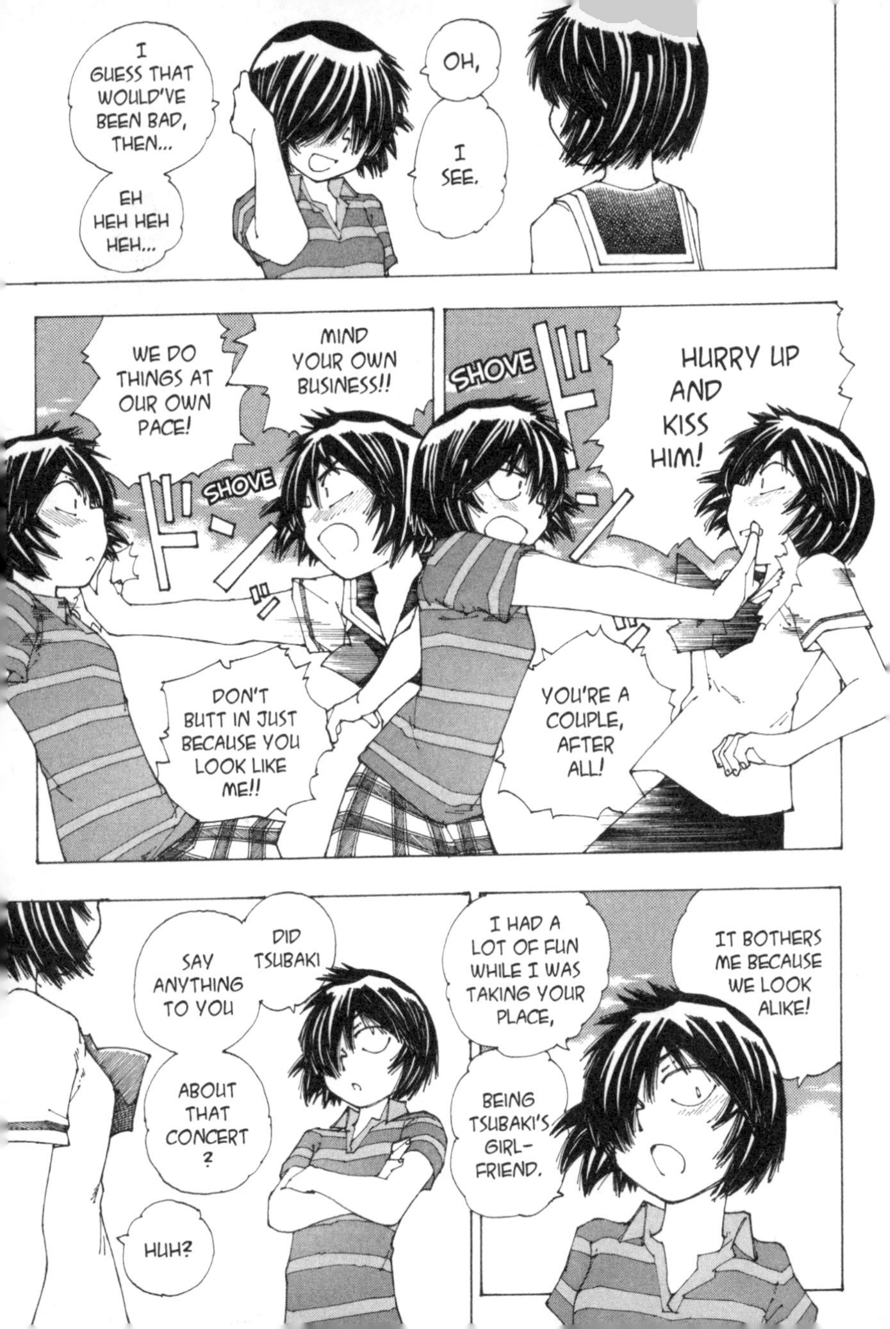
OH, I SEE.
I GUESS THAT WOULD'VE BEEN BAD, THEN...
EH HEH HEH HEH...
SHOVE
HURRY UP AND KISS HIM!
YOU'RE A COUPLE, AFTER ALL!
MIND YOUR OWN BUSINESS!!
WE DO THINGS AT OUR OWN PACE!
SHOVE
DON'T BUTT IN JUST BECAUSE YOU LOOK LIKE ME!!
IT BOTHERS ME BECAUSE WE LOOK ALIKE!
I HAD A LOT OF FUN WHILE I WAS TAKING YOUR PLACE,
BEING TSUBAKI'S GIRL-FRIEND.
DID TSUBAKI SAY ANYTHING TO YOU
ABOUT THAT CONCERT?
HUH?

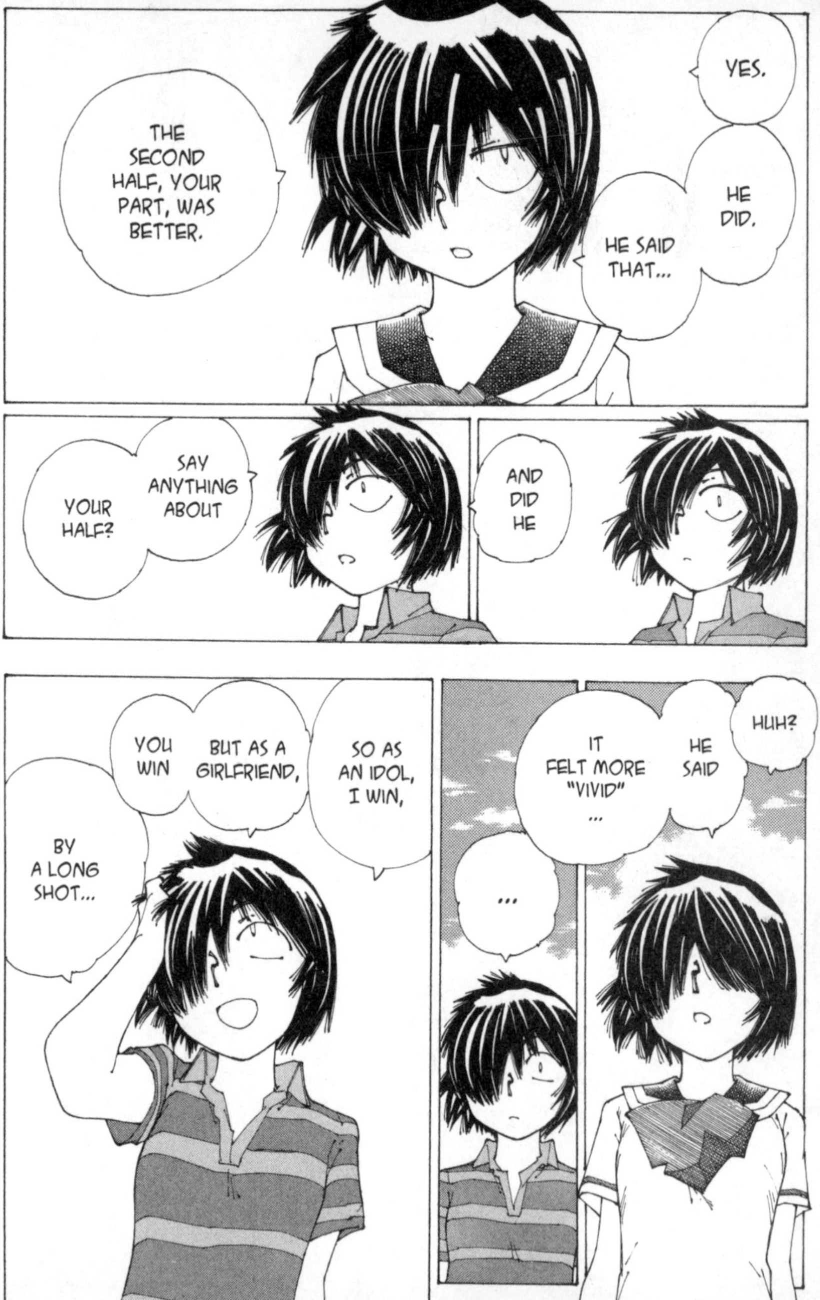
YES.
HE DID.
HE SAID THAT...
THE SECOND HALF, YOUR PART, WAS BETTER.
AND DID HE
SAY ANYTHING ABOUT
YOUR HALF?
HUH?
HE SAID
IT FELT MORE "VIVID" ...
...
SO AS AN IDOL, I WIN,
BUT AS A GIRLFRIEND,
YOU WIN
BY A LONG SHOT...

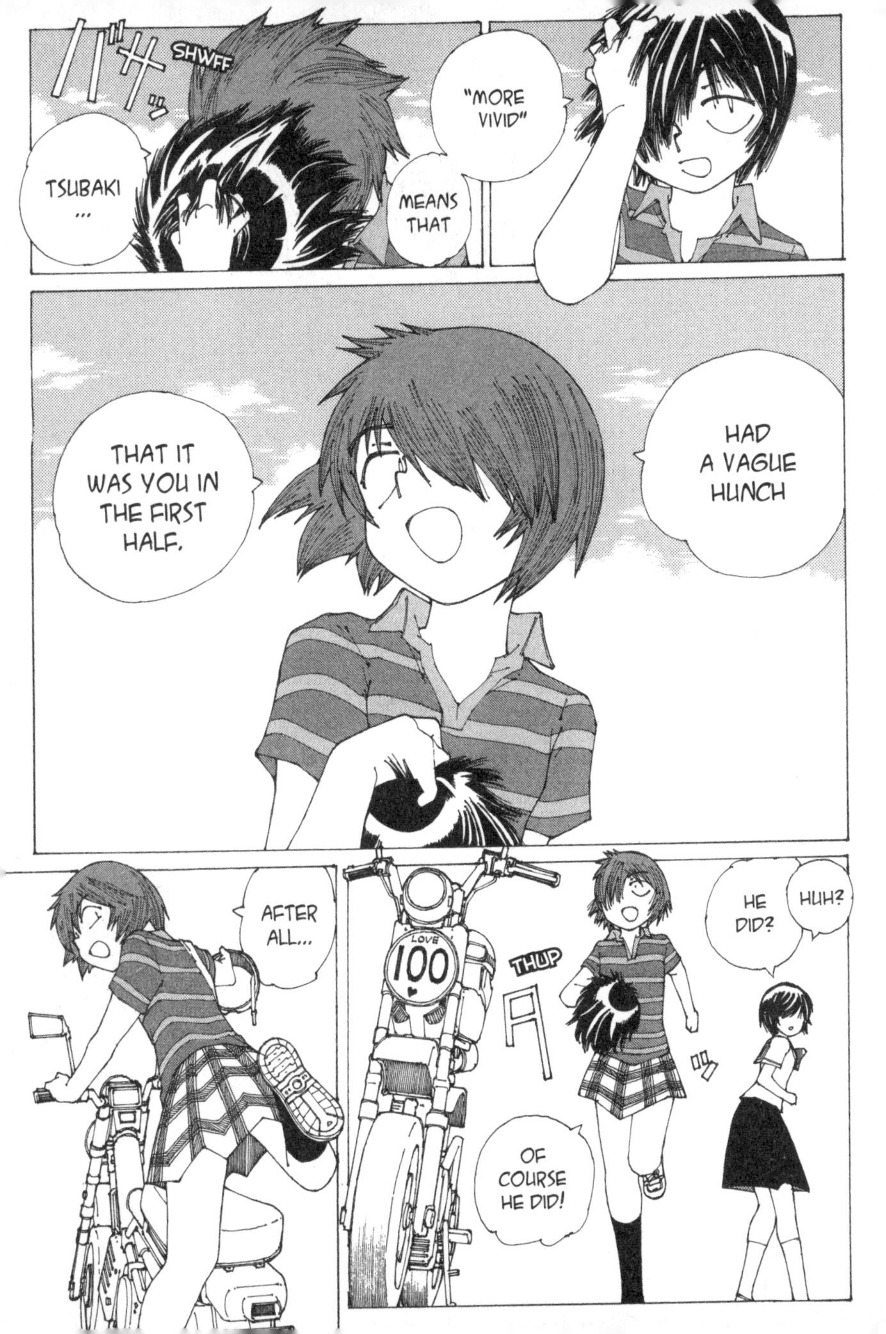
"MORE VIVID"
MEANS THAT
SHWFF
TSUBAKI ...
HAD A VAGUE HUNCH
THAT IT WAS YOU IN THE FIRST HALF.
HUH?
HE DID?
THUP
OF COURSE HE DID!
LOVE 100
AFTER ALL...

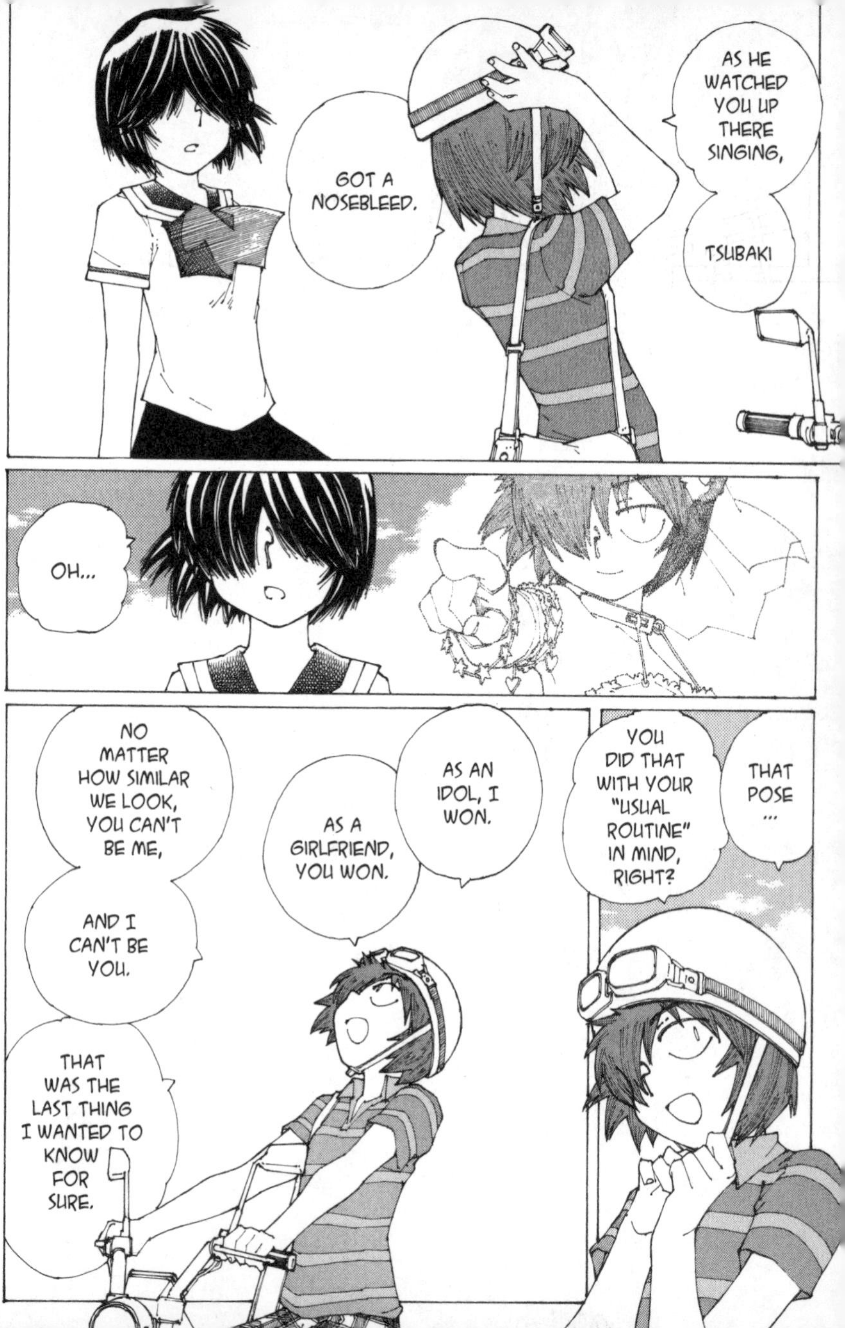
AS HE WATCHED YOU UP THERE SINGING,
TSUBAKI
GOT A NOSEBLEED.
OH...
THAT POSE ...
YOU DID THAT WITH YOUR "USUAL ROUTINE" IN MIND, RIGHT?
AS AN IDOL, I WON.
AS A GIRLFRIEND, YOU WON.
NO MATTER HOW SIMILAR WE LOOK, YOU CAN'T BE ME,
AND I CAN'T BE YOU.
THAT WAS THE LAST THING I WANTED TO KNOW FOR SURE.

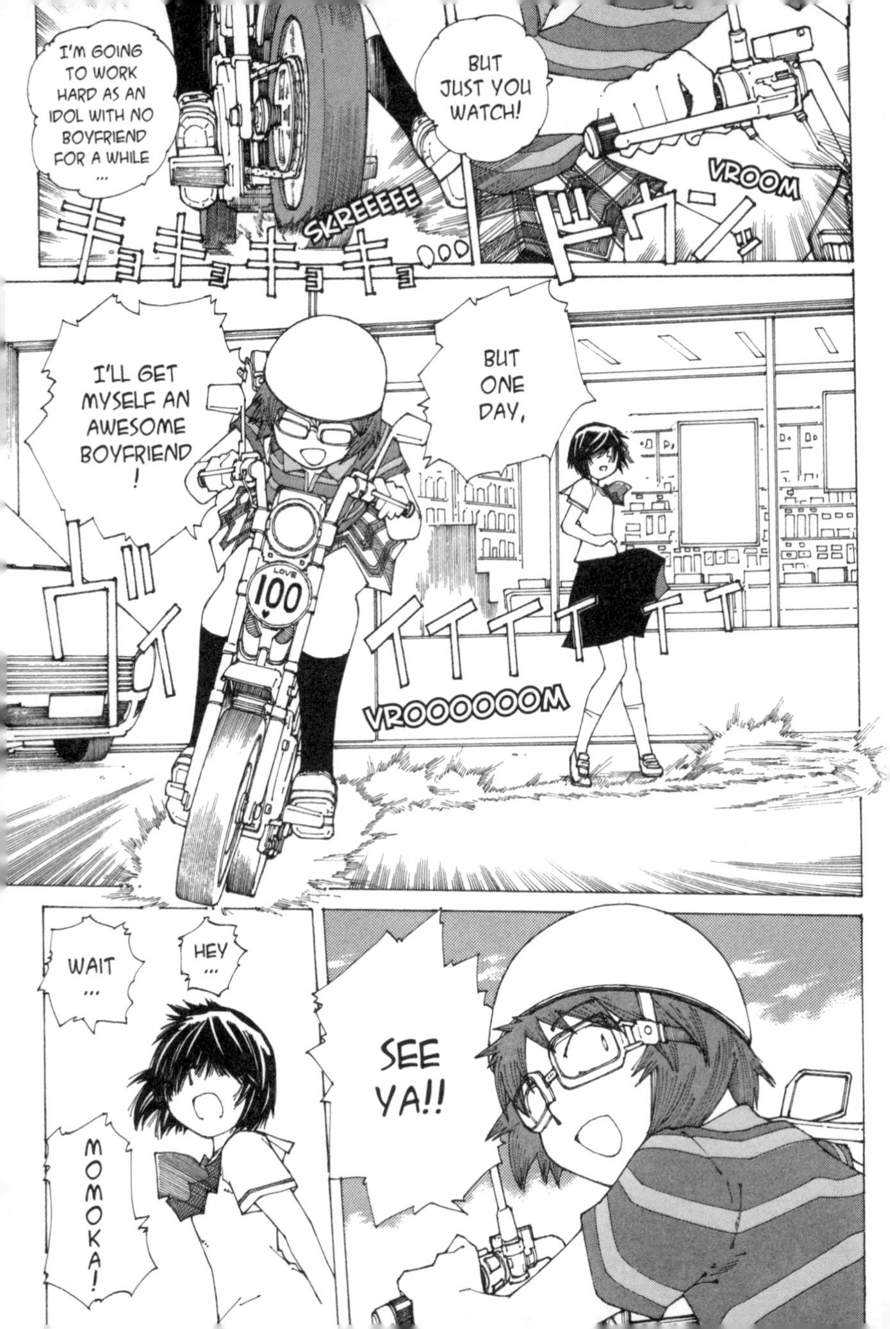
VROOM
BUT JUST YOU WATCH!
I'M GOING TO WORK HARD AS AN IDOL WITH NO BOYFRIEND FOR A WHILE ...
SKREEEEE
BUT ONE DAY,
I'LL GET MYSELF AN AWESOME BOYFRIEND!
VROOOOOOOM
SEE YA!!
HEY ...
WAIT ...
MOMOKA!

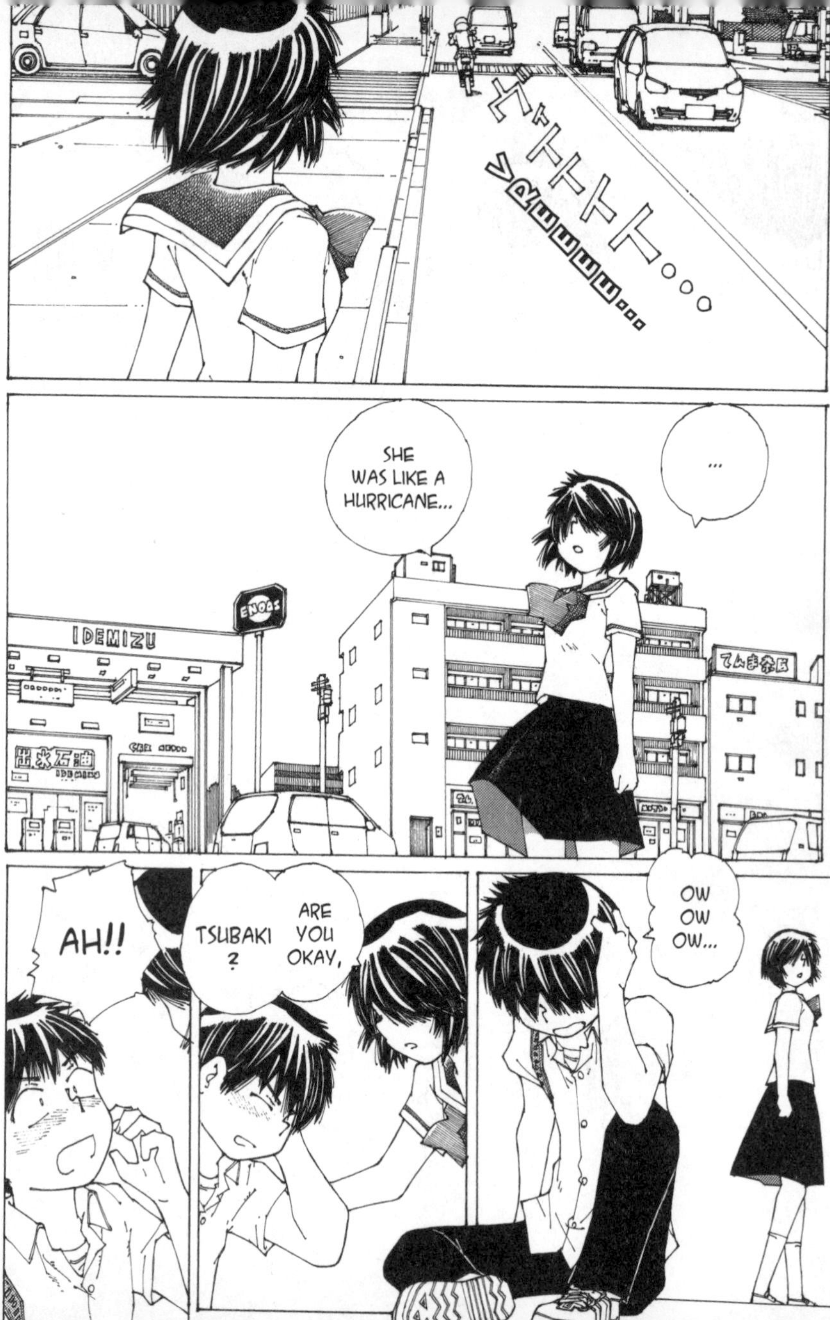

ヴィトトトト。。。
VREEEE...
...
SHE WAS LIKE A HURRICANE...
IDEMIZU
出水石油
OW OW OW...
ARE YOU OKAY, TSUBAKI?
AH!!

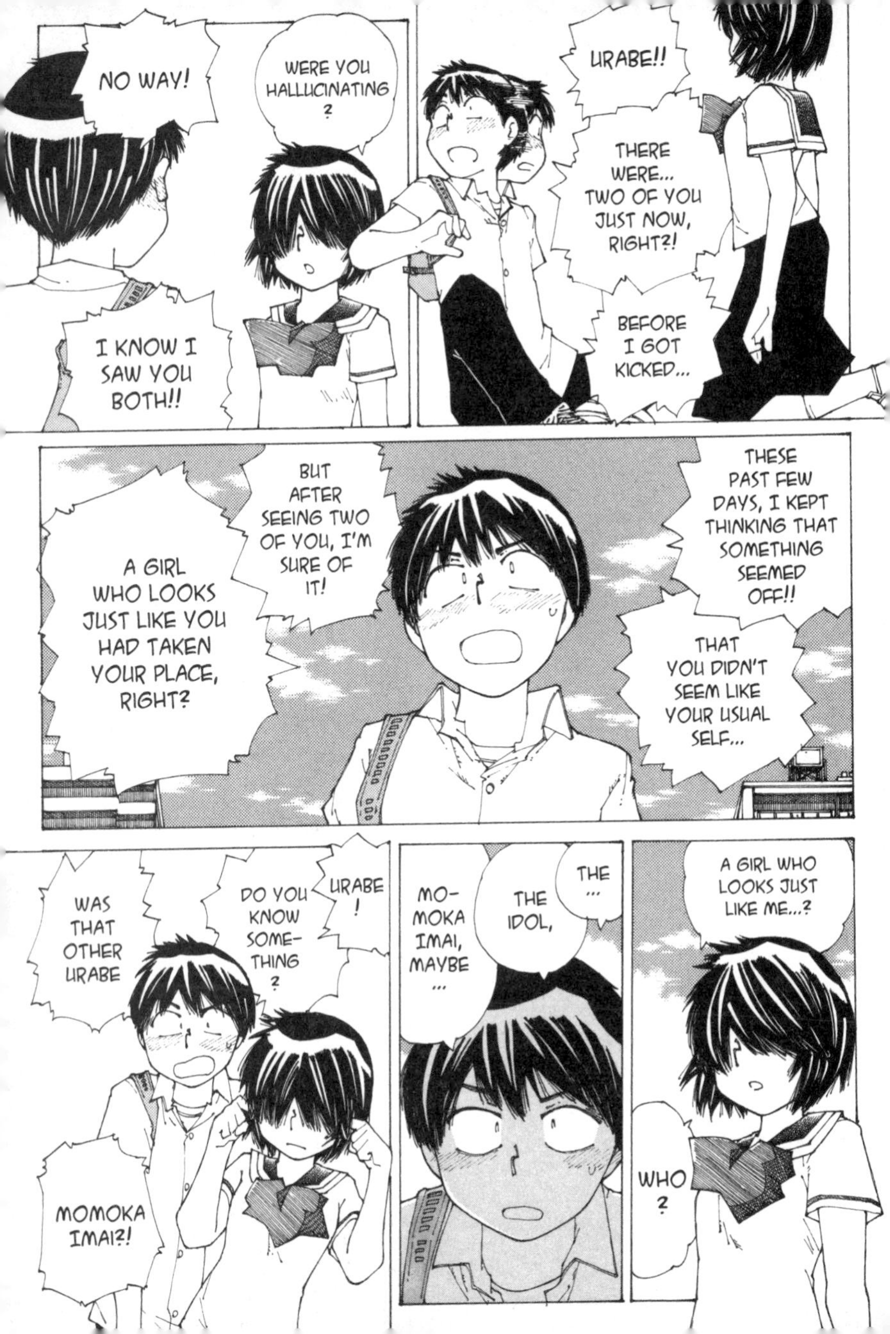
URABE!!
THERE WERE... TWO OF YOU JUST NOW, RIGHT?!
BEFORE I GOT KICKED...
WERE YOU HALLUCINATING?
NO WAY!
I KNOW I SAW YOU BOTH!!
THESE PAST FEW DAYS, I KEPT THINKING THAT SOMETHING SEEMED OFF!!
THAT YOU DIDN'T SEEM LIKE YOUR USUAL SELF...
BUT AFTER SEEING TWO OF YOU, I'M SURE OF IT!
A GIRL WHO LOOKS JUST LIKE YOU HAD TAKEN YOUR PLACE, RIGHT?
A GIRL WHO LOOKS JUST LIKE ME...?
WHO?
THE...
THE IDOL,
MO-MOKA IMAI, MAYBE...
URABE!
DO YOU KNOW SOMETHING?
WAS THAT OTHER URABE
MOMOKA IMAI?!

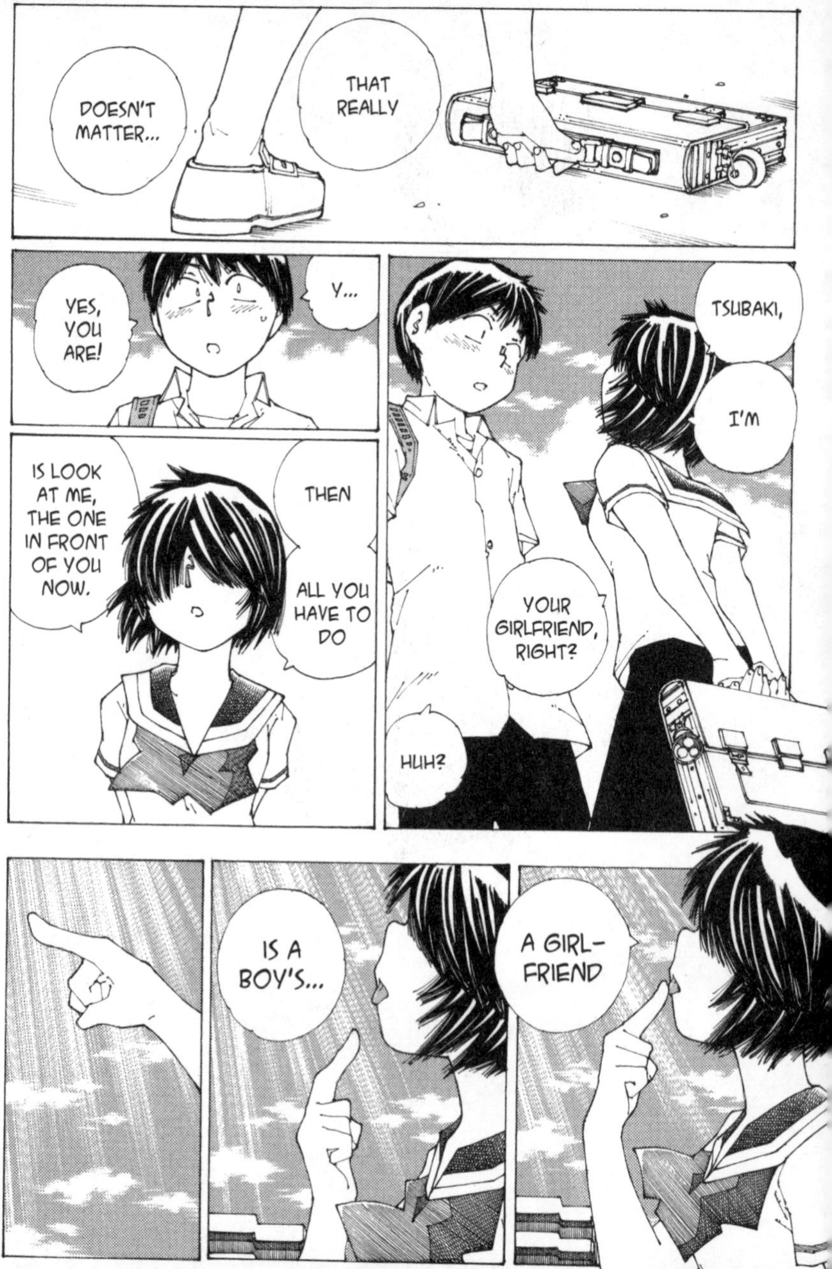
THAT REALLY
DOESN'T MATTER...
TSUBAKI,
I'M
YOUR GIRLFRIEND, RIGHT?
HUH?
Y...
YES, YOU ARE!
THEN
ALL YOU HAVE TO DO
IS LOOK AT ME, THE ONE IN FRONT OF YOU NOW.
A GIRL-FRIEND
IS A BOY'S...

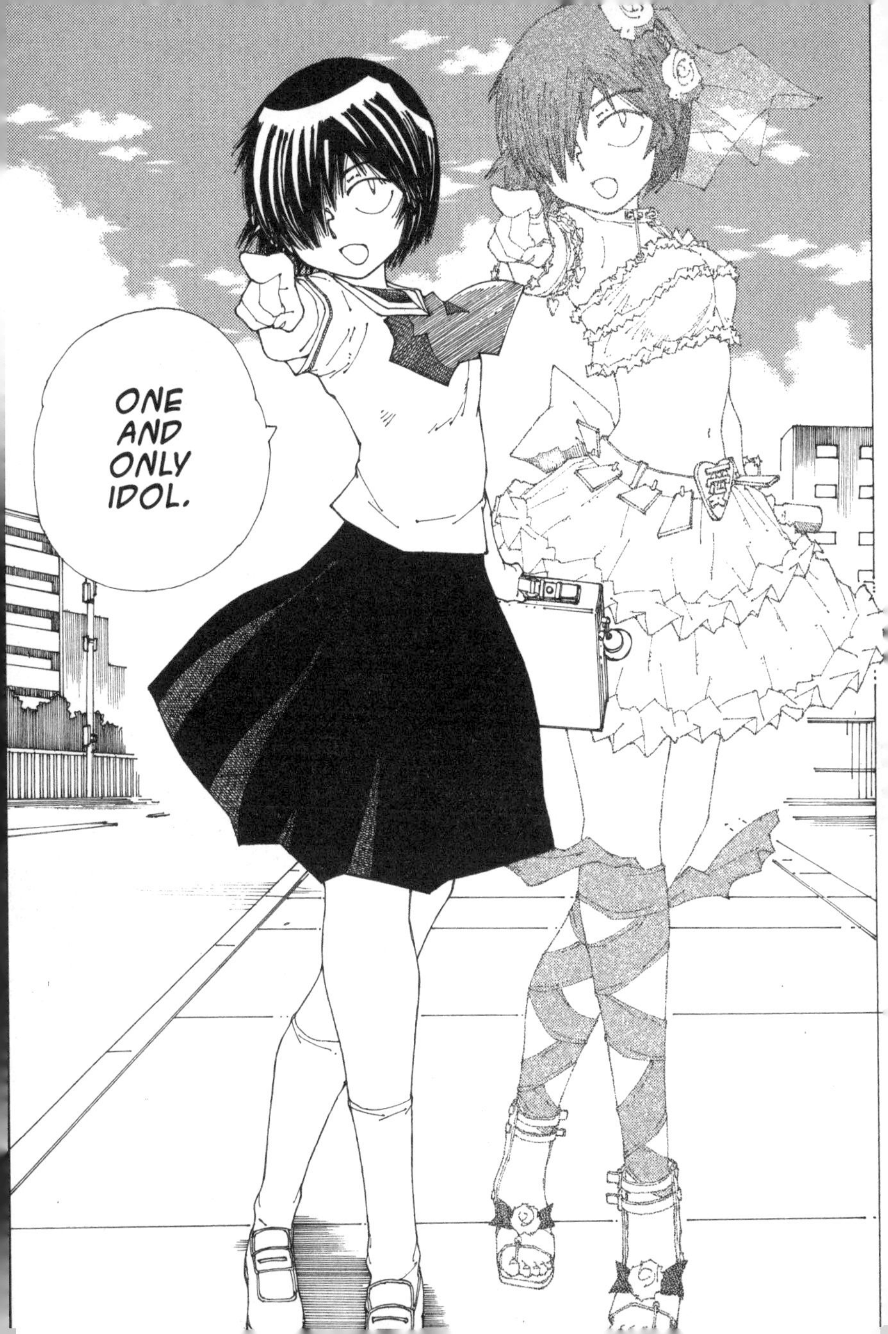
ONE AND ONLY IDOL.

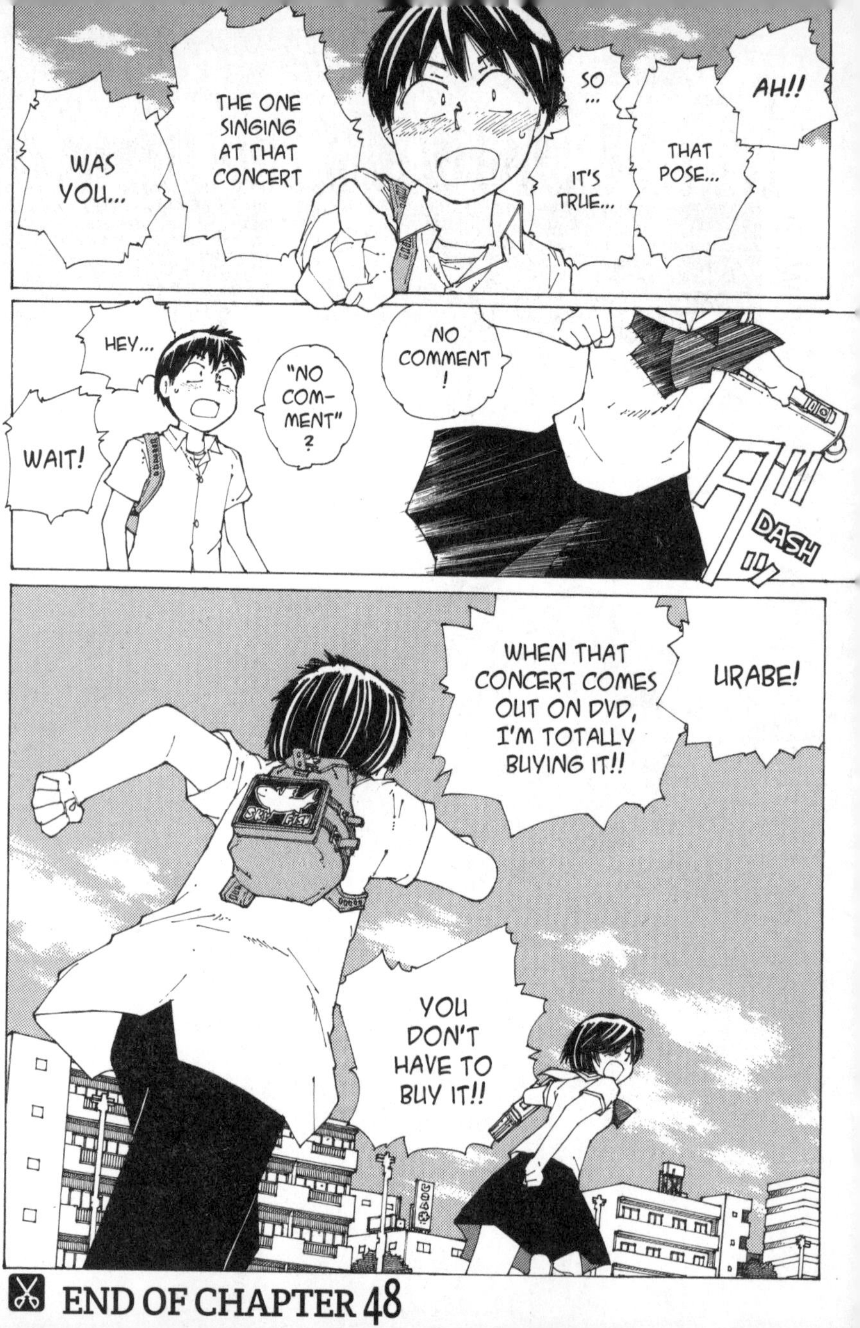
AH!!
THAT POSE...
SO ...
IT'S TRUE...
THE ONE SINGING AT THAT CONCERT
WAS YOU...
NO COMMENT !
DASH
"NO COMMENT" ?
HEY...
WAIT!
URABE!
WHEN THAT CONCERT COMES OUT ON DVD, I'M TOTALLY BUYING IT!!
YOU DON'T HAVE TO BUY IT!!

END OF CHAPTER 48

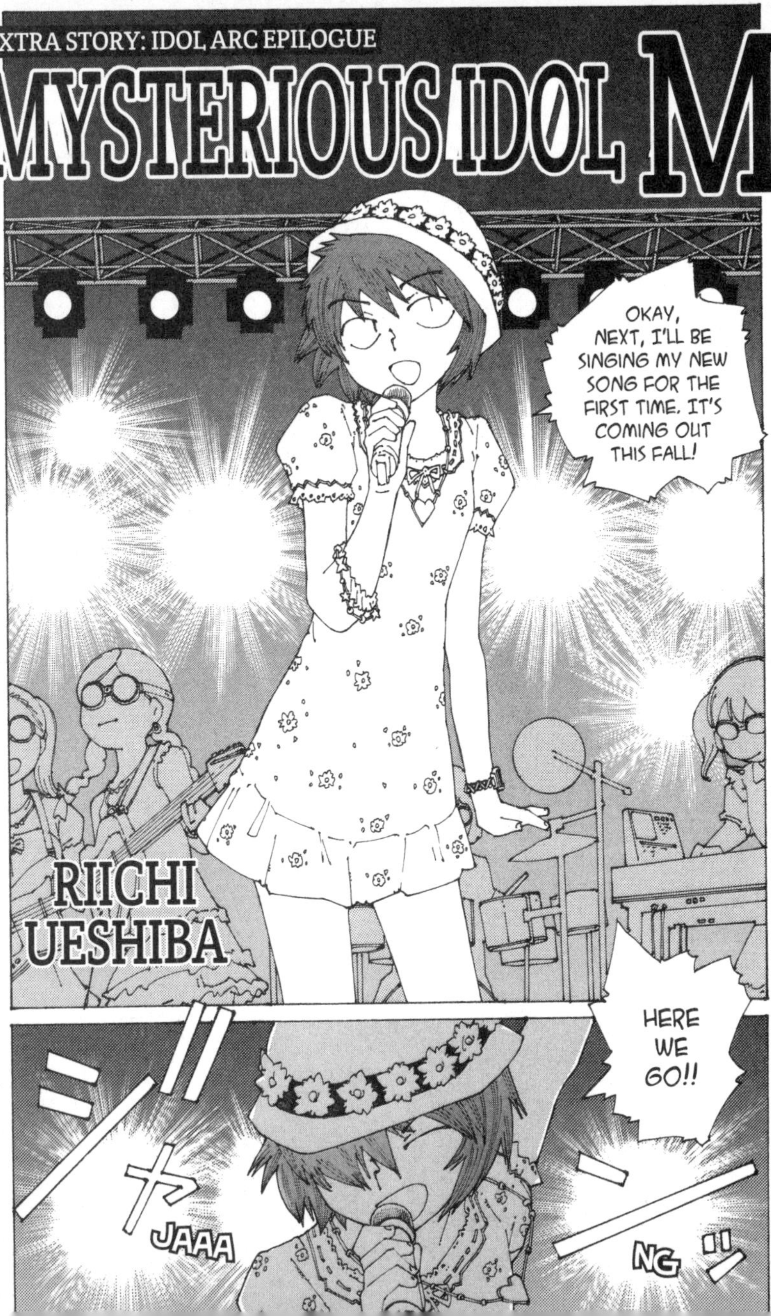
EXTRA STORY: IDOL ARC EPILOGUE
MYSTERIOUS IDOL M
OKAY, NEXT, I'LL BE SINGING MY NEW SONG FOR THE FIRST TIME. IT'S COMING OUT THIS FALL!
RIICHI UESHIBA
HERE WE GO!!
NG
JAAA

MOMOKA PLANS TO CONCENTRATE ONLY ON BEING AN IDOL FOR NOW...?!

The Latest from the Author

Riichi Ueshiba

RECENTLY, I'VE BEEN LISTENING TO A COLLECTION OF THEME SONGS FROM NHK TAIGA DRAMAS WHILE I WORK. THE HISTORICAL SONGS THAT I PARTICULARLY LIKE ARE "KUNITORI MONOGATARI" AND "KASHIN" BY HIKARU HAYASHI. BOTH OF THE DRAMAS HAPPENED TO BE BASED ON STORIES BY RYOTARO SHIBA.

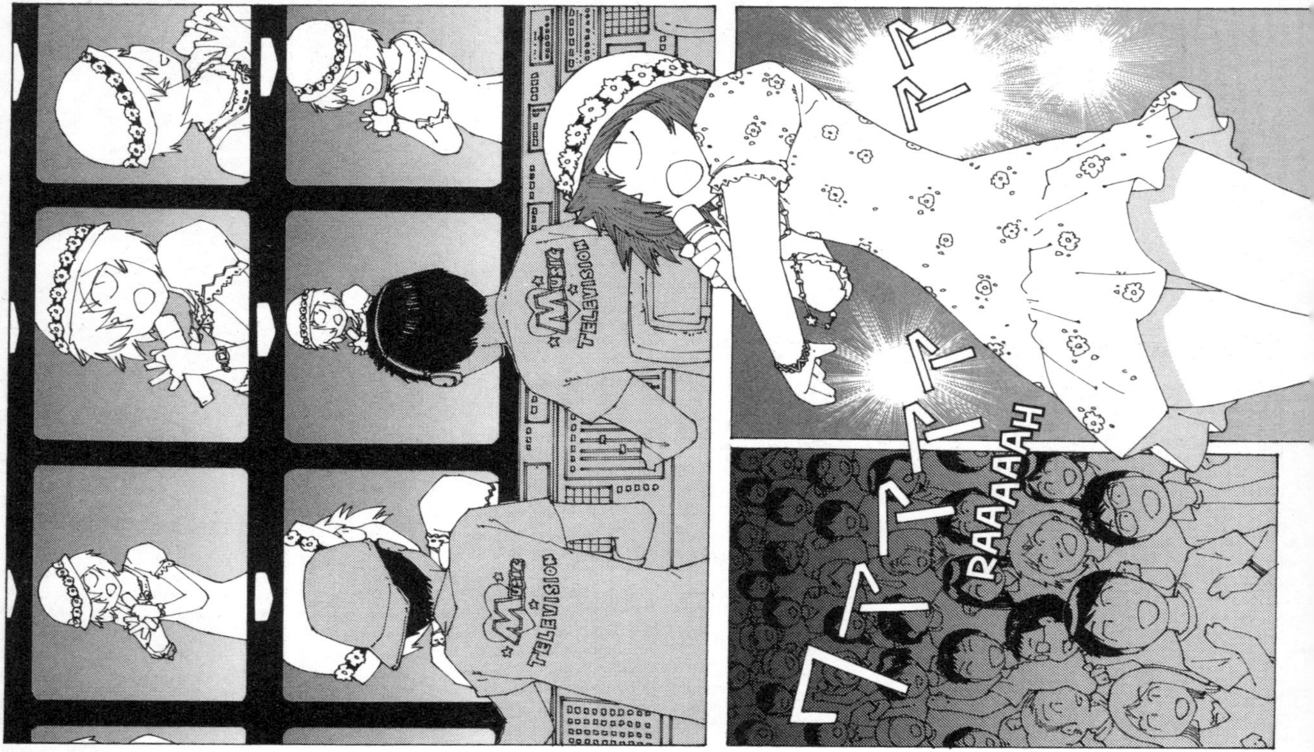
ワアアアアア
RAAAAAAH

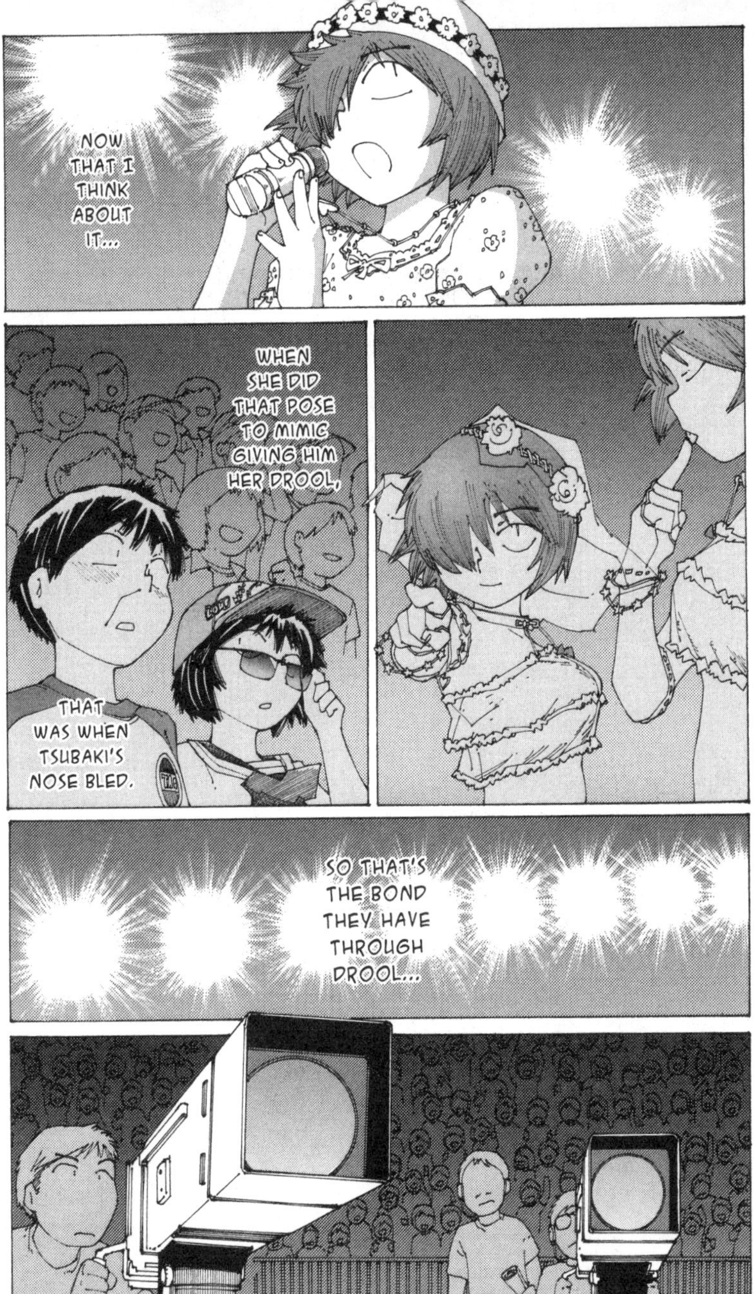
NOW THAT I THINK ABOUT IT...
WHEN SHE DID THAT POSE TO MIMIC GIVING HIM HER DROOL,
THAT WAS WHEN TSUBAKI'S NOSE BLED.
SO THAT'S THE BOND THEY HAVE THROUGH DROOL...

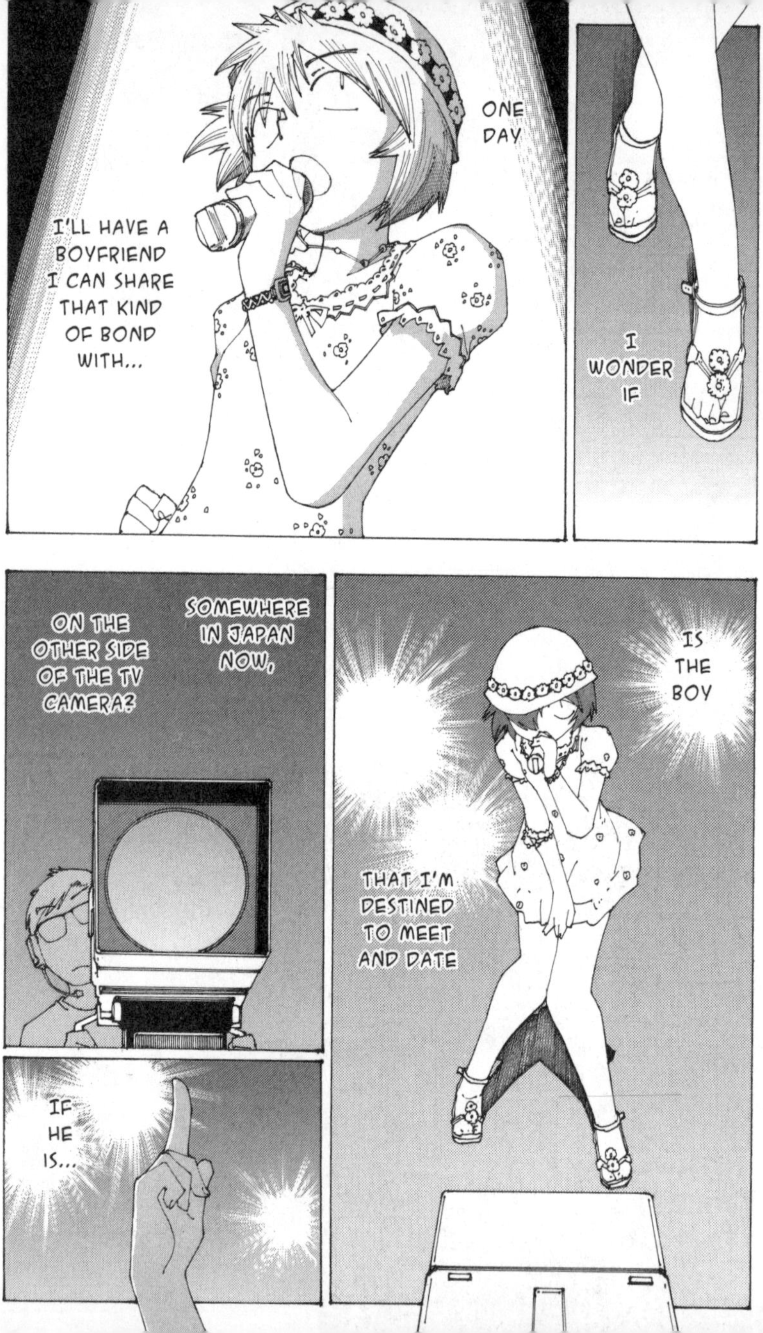
I WONDER IF
ONE DAY
I'LL HAVE A BOYFRIEND I CAN SHARE THAT KIND OF BOND WITH...
IS THE BOY
THAT I'M DESTINED TO MEET AND DATE
SOMEWHERE IN JAPAN NOW,
ON THE OTHER SIDE OF THE TV CAMERA?
IF HE IS...

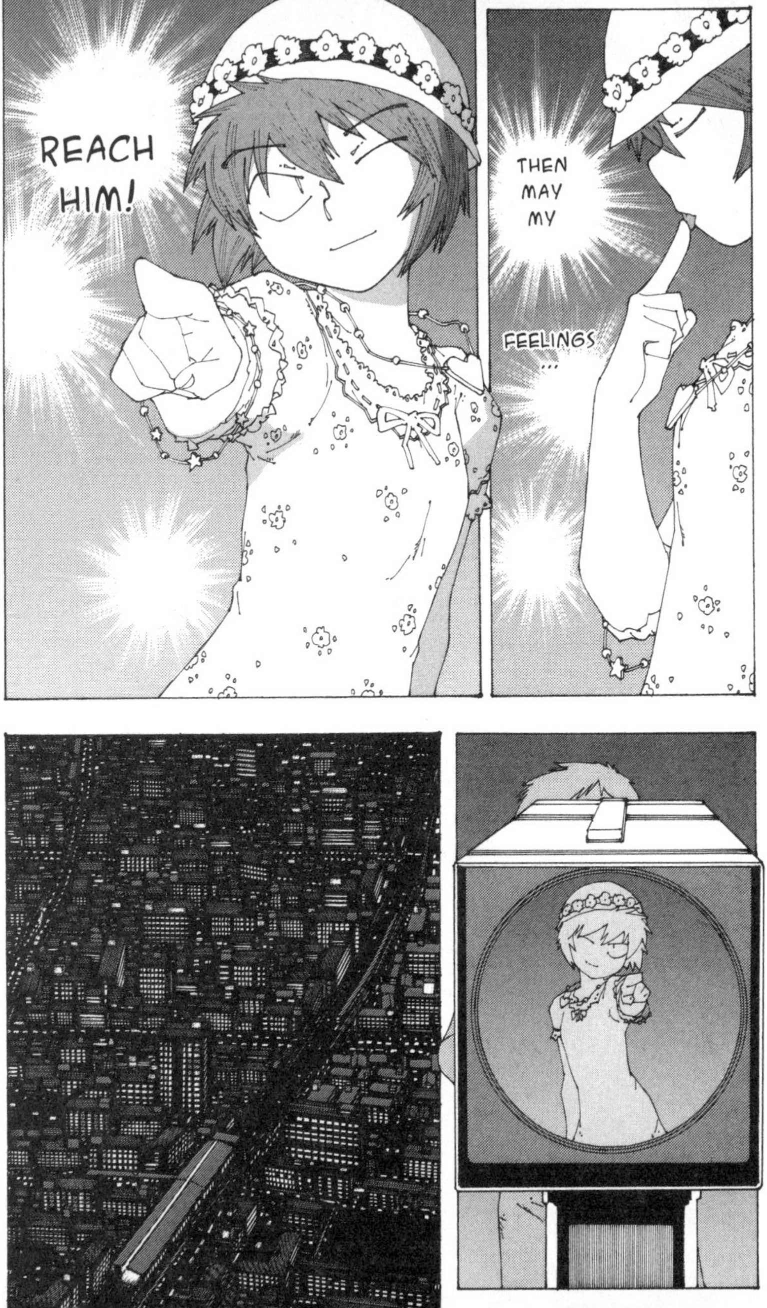
THEN MAY MY
FEELINGS...
REACH HIM!

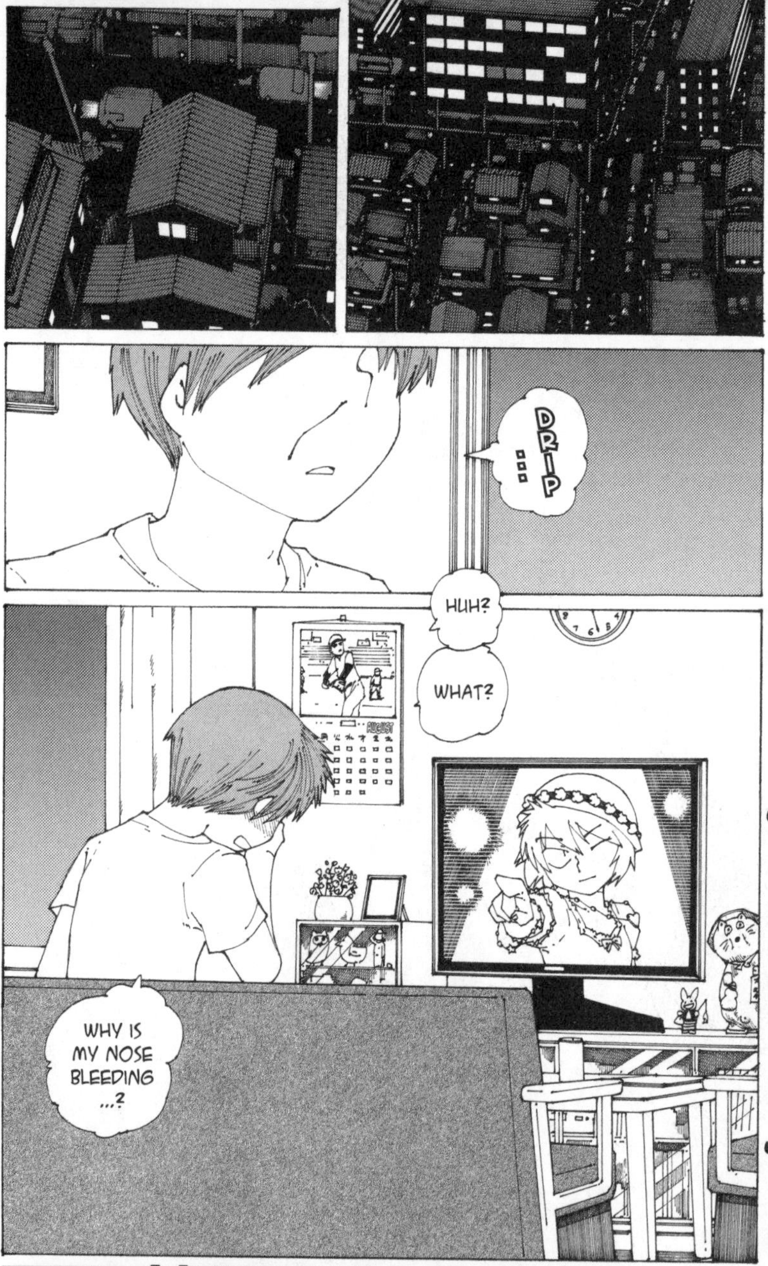
DRIP...
HUH?
WHAT?
AUGUST
WHY IS MY NOSE BLEEDING...?

A bond connects you, no matter where you are.

MYSTERIOUS IDOL M | END OF EXTRA STORY | NEXT TIME, UENO AND OKA HAVE A STRANGE RULE?!

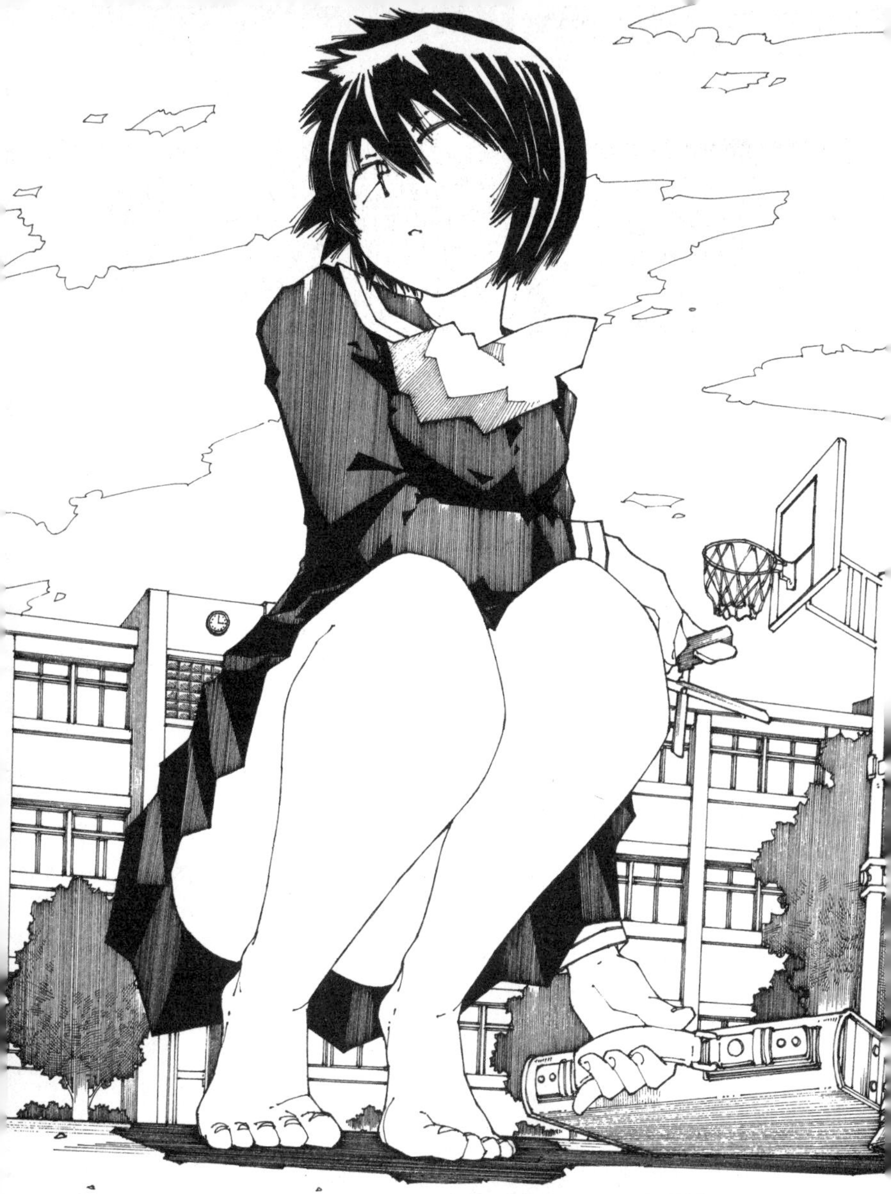

CHAPTER 49: MYSTERIOUS CARNIVORE GIRL (PART 1)

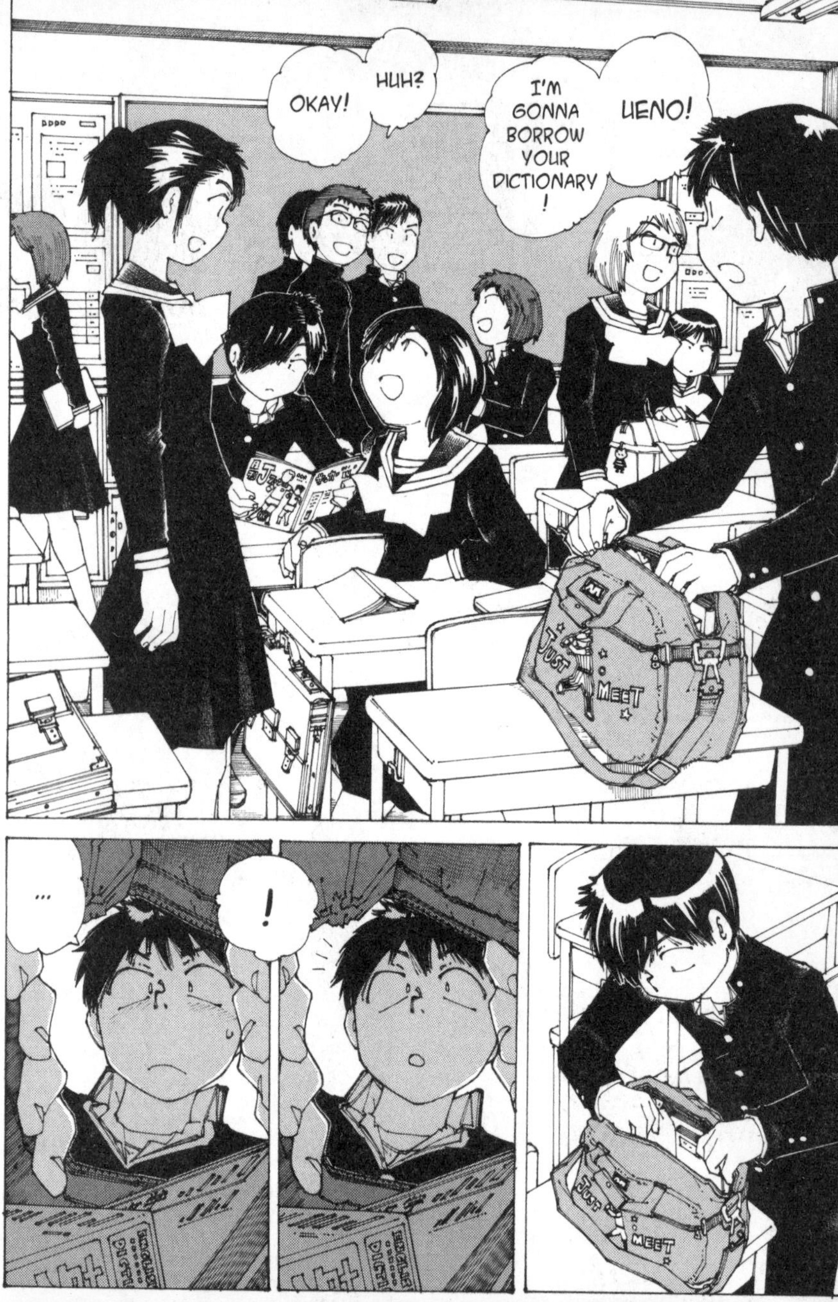
UENO!
I'M GONNA BORROW YOUR DICTIONARY!
HUH?
OKAY!
!
...

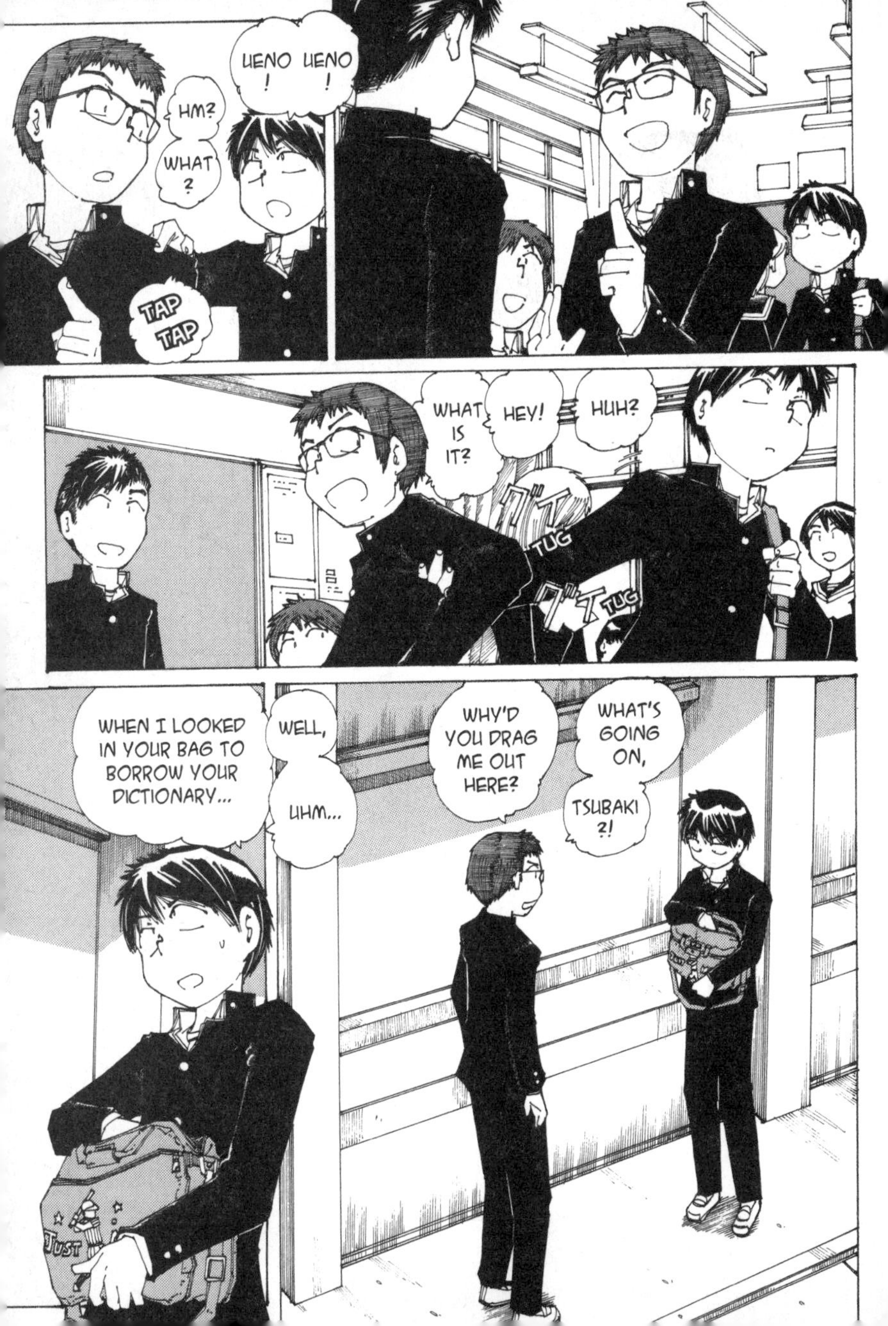
UENO !
UENO !
HM?
WHAT ?
TAP TAP
HUH?
HEY!
WHAT IS IT?
TUG
TUG
WHAT'S GOING ON,
TSUBAKI ?!
WHY'D YOU DRAG ME OUT HERE?
WELL,
UHM...
WHEN I LOOKED IN YOUR BAG TO BORROW YOUR DICTIONARY...
JUST

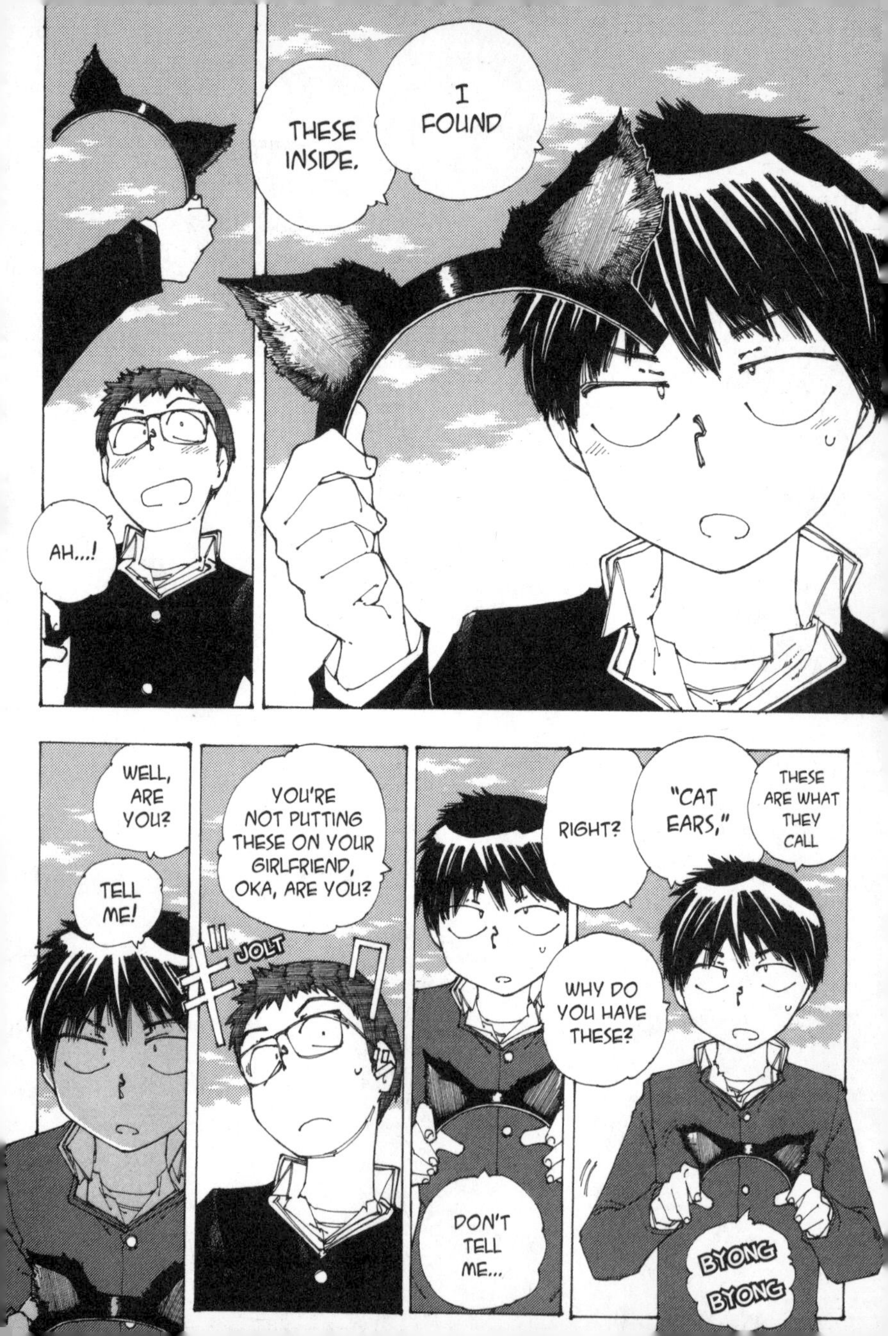
I FOUND
THESE INSIDE.
AH...!
THESE ARE WHAT THEY CALL
"CAT EARS,"
RIGHT?
WHY DO YOU HAVE THESE?
DON'T TELL ME...
BYONG BYONG
YOU'RE NOT PUTTING THESE ON YOUR GIRLFRIEND, OKA, ARE YOU?
JOLT
WELL, ARE YOU?
TELL ME!

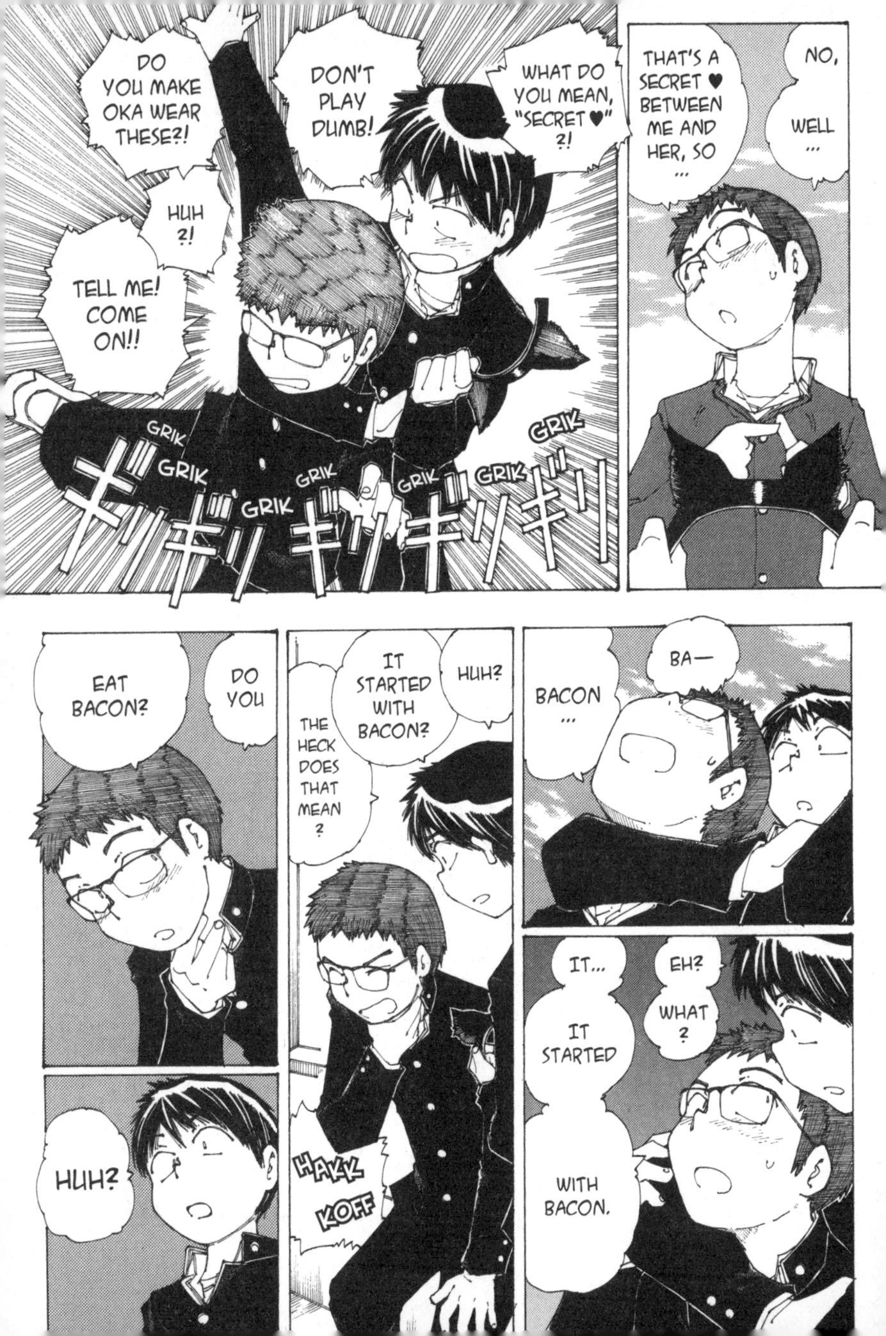
NO, WELL ...
THAT'S A SECRET ♥ BETWEEN ME AND HER, SO ...
WHAT DO YOU MEAN, "SECRET ♥" ?!
DON'T PLAY DUMB!
DO YOU MAKE OKA WEAR THESE?!
HUH ?!
TELL ME! COME ON!!
GRIK
GRIK
GRIK
GRIK
GRIK
GRIK
GRIK
ギリギリ ギリギリ ギリ
BA—
BACON ...
EH?
WHAT ?
IT...
IT STARTED
WITH BACON.
HUH?
IT STARTED WITH BACON?
THE HECK DOES THAT MEAN ?
HAKK
KOFF
DO YOU
EAT BACON?
HUH?

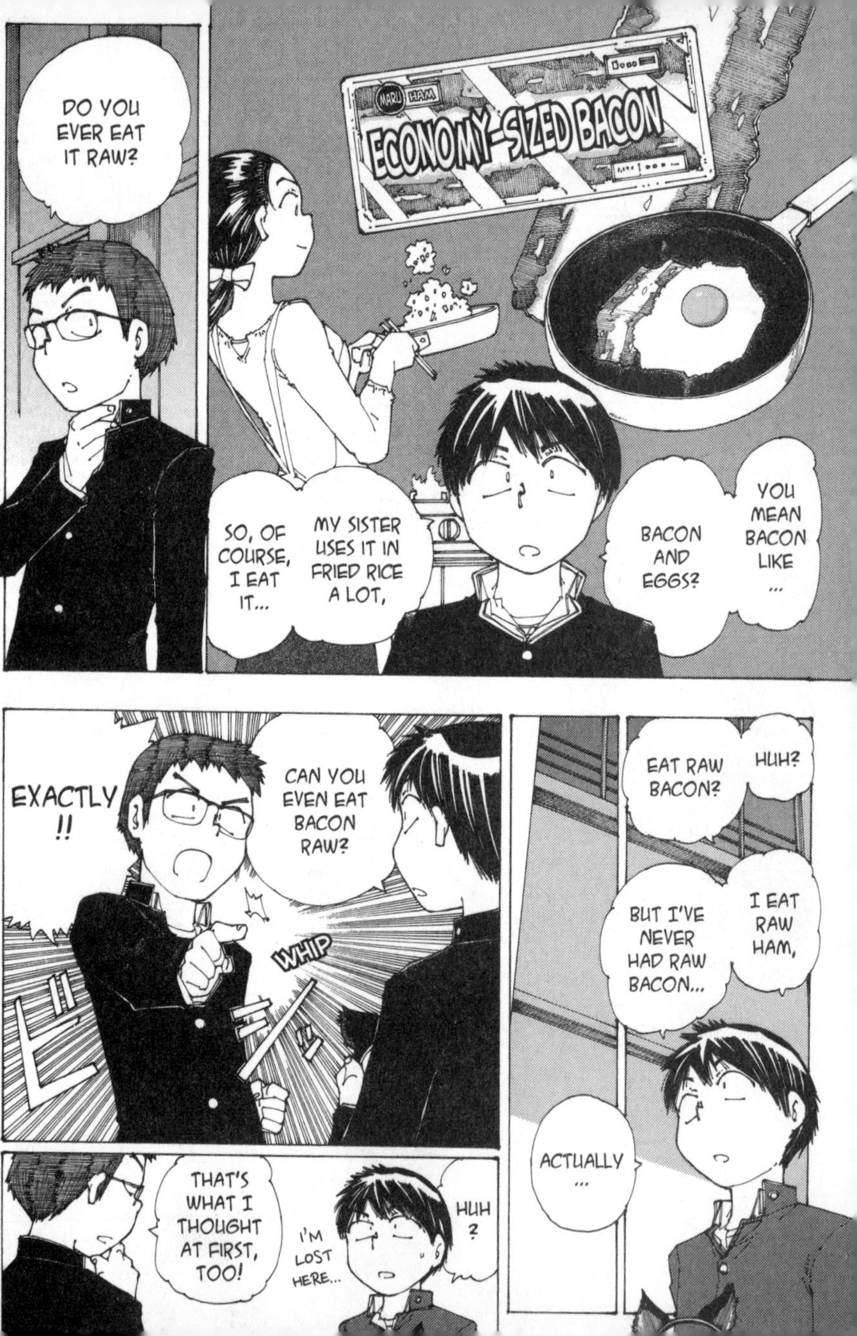
MARU HAM
ECONOMY-SIZED BACON
YOU MEAN BACON LIKE ...
BACON AND EGGS?
MY SISTER USES IT IN FRIED RICE A LOT,
SO, OF COURSE, I EAT IT...
DO YOU EVER EAT IT RAW?
HUH?
EAT RAW BACON?
I EAT RAW HAM,
BUT I'VE NEVER HAD RAW BACON...
ACTUALLY ...
CAN YOU EVEN EAT BACON RAW?
EXACTLY !!
WHIP
HUH ?
I'M LOST HERE...
THAT'S WHAT I THOUGHT AT FIRST, TOO!

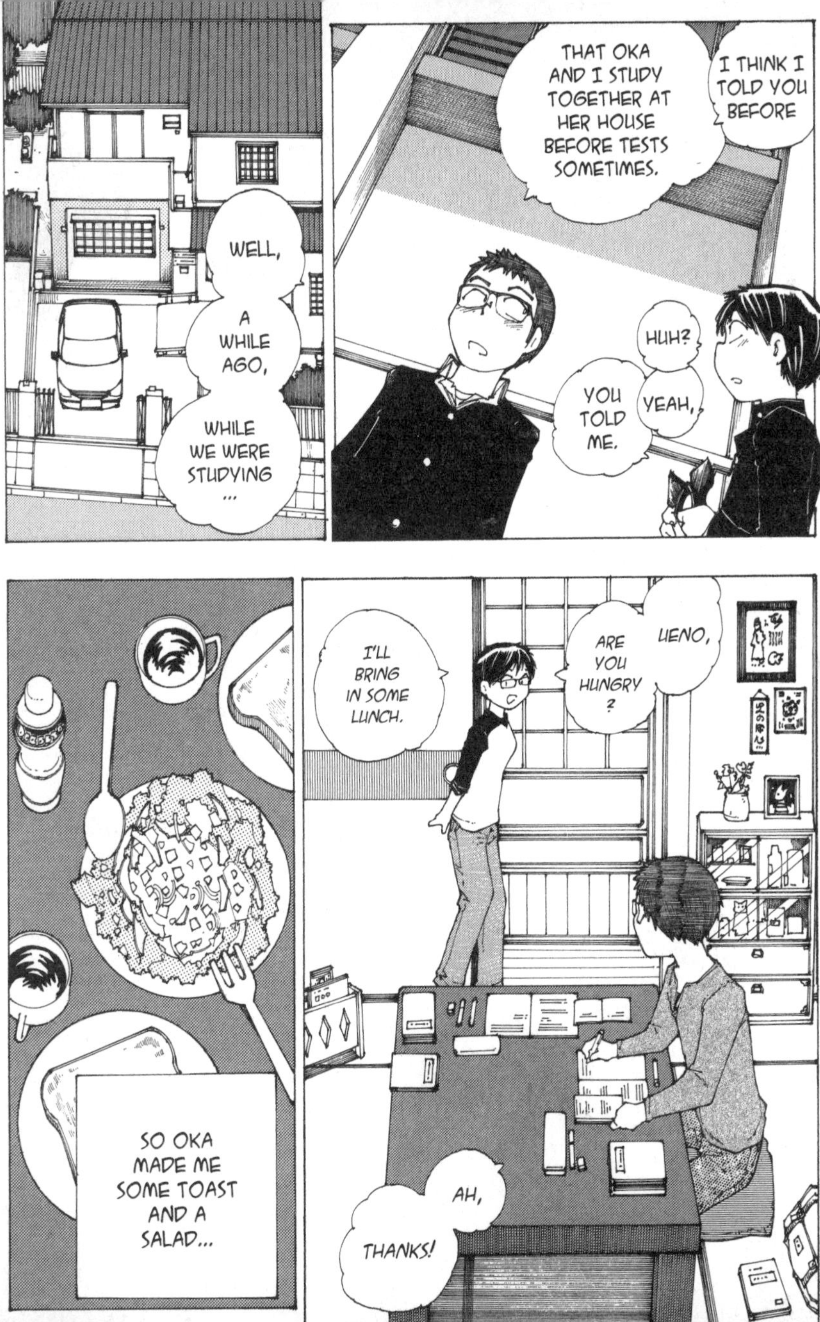
I THINK I TOLD YOU BEFORE
THAT OKA AND I STUDY TOGETHER AT HER HOUSE BEFORE TESTS SOMETIMES.
HUH?
YEAH,
YOU TOLD ME.
WELL,
A WHILE AGO,
WHILE WE WERE STUDYING ...
UENO,
ARE YOU HUNGRY ?
I'LL BRING IN SOME LUNCH.
AH,
THANKS!
SO OKA MADE ME SOME TOAST AND A SALAD...

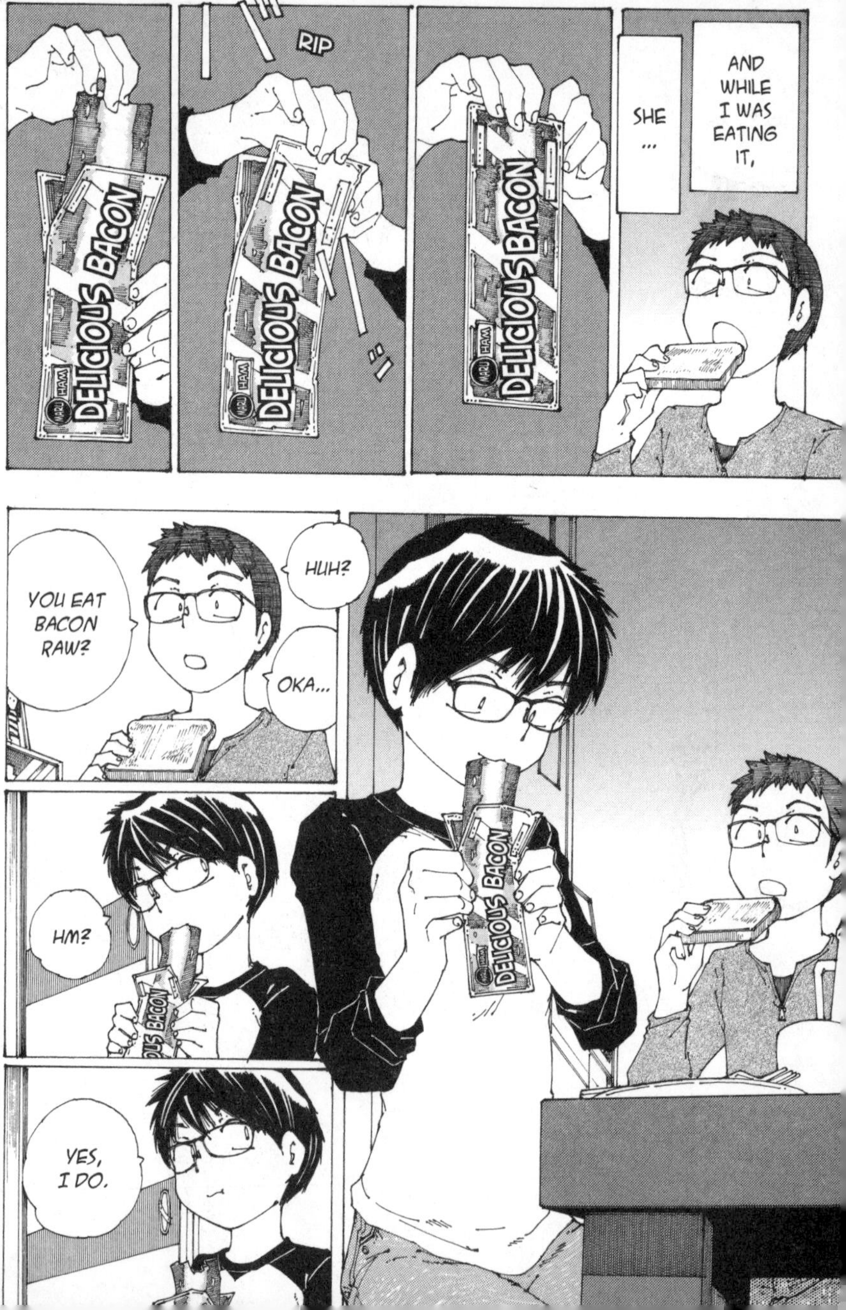
AND WHILE I WAS EATING IT,
SHE ...
MARU HAM
DELICIOUS BACON
RIP
MARU HAM
DELICIOUS BACON
MARU HAM
DELICIOUS BACON
DELICIOUS BACON
HUH?
YOU EAT BACON RAW?
OKA...
HM?
YES, I DO.

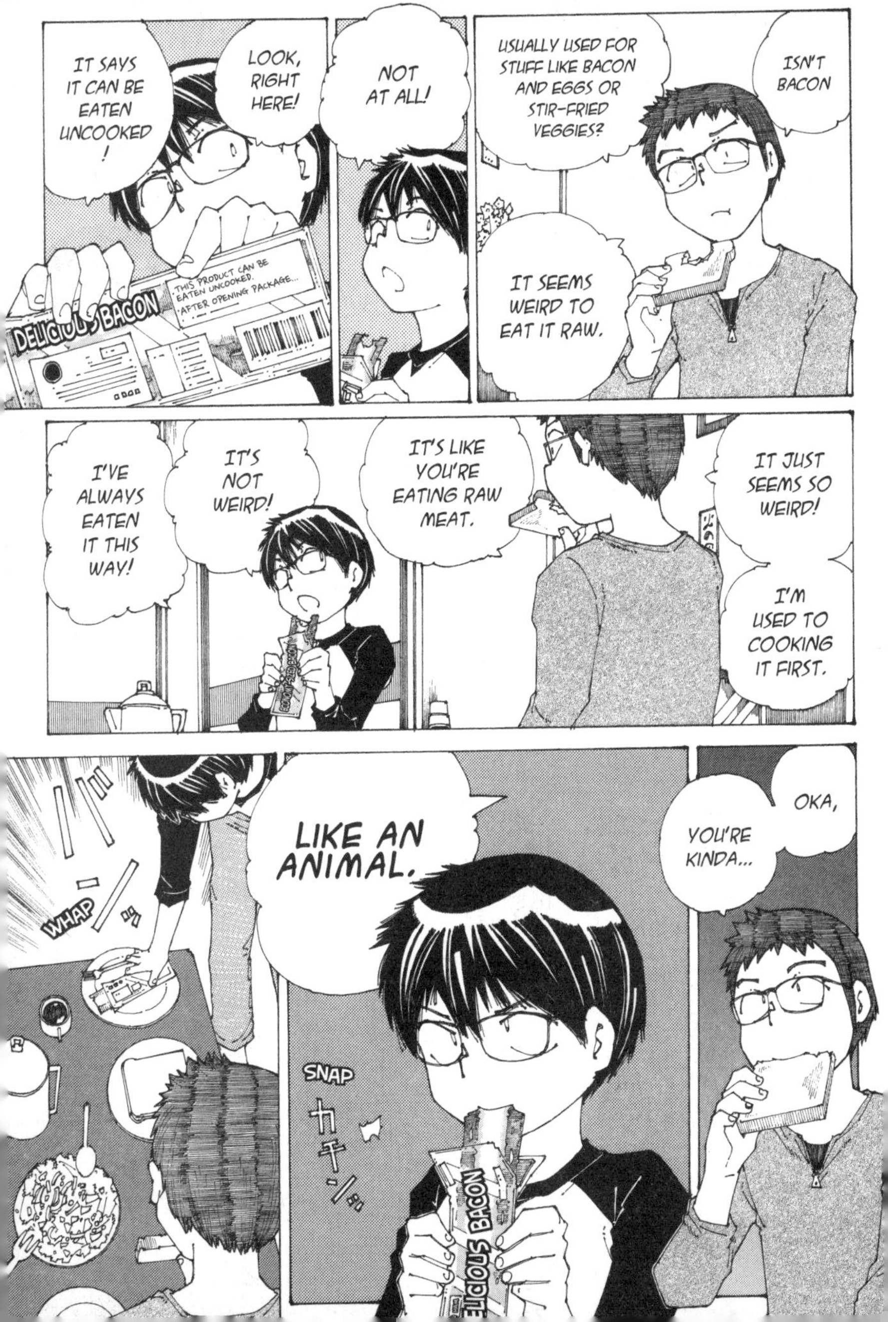
ISN'T BACON
USUALLY USED FOR STUFF LIKE BACON AND EGGS OR STIR-FRIED VEGGIES?
IT SEEMS WEIRD TO EAT IT RAW.
NOT AT ALL!
LOOK, RIGHT HERE!
IT SAYS IT CAN BE EATEN UNCOOKED!
DELICIOUS BACON
·THIS PRODUCT CAN BE EATEN UNCOOKED.
·AFTER OPENING PACKAGE...
IT JUST SEEMS SO WEIRD!
I'M USED TO COOKING IT FIRST.
IT'S LIKE YOU'RE EATING RAW MEAT.
IT'S NOT WEIRD!
I'VE ALWAYS EATEN IT THIS WAY!
OKA,
YOU'RE KINDA...
LIKE AN ANIMAL.
SNAP
DELICIOUS BACON
WHAP

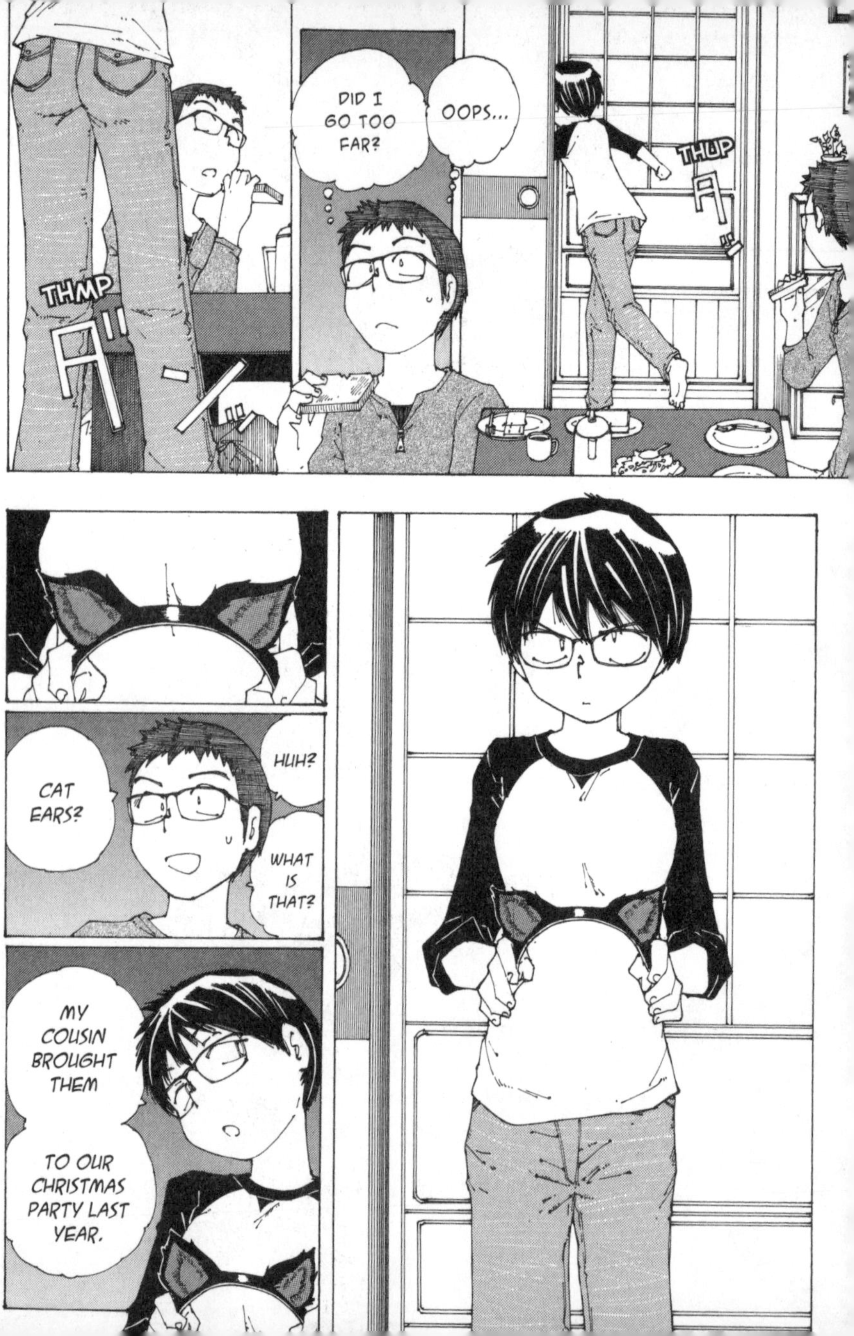
THUP
OOPS...
DID I GO TOO FAR?
THMP
HUH?
WHAT IS THAT?
CAT EARS?
MY COUSIN BROUGHT THEM
TO OUR CHRISTMAS PARTY LAST YEAR.

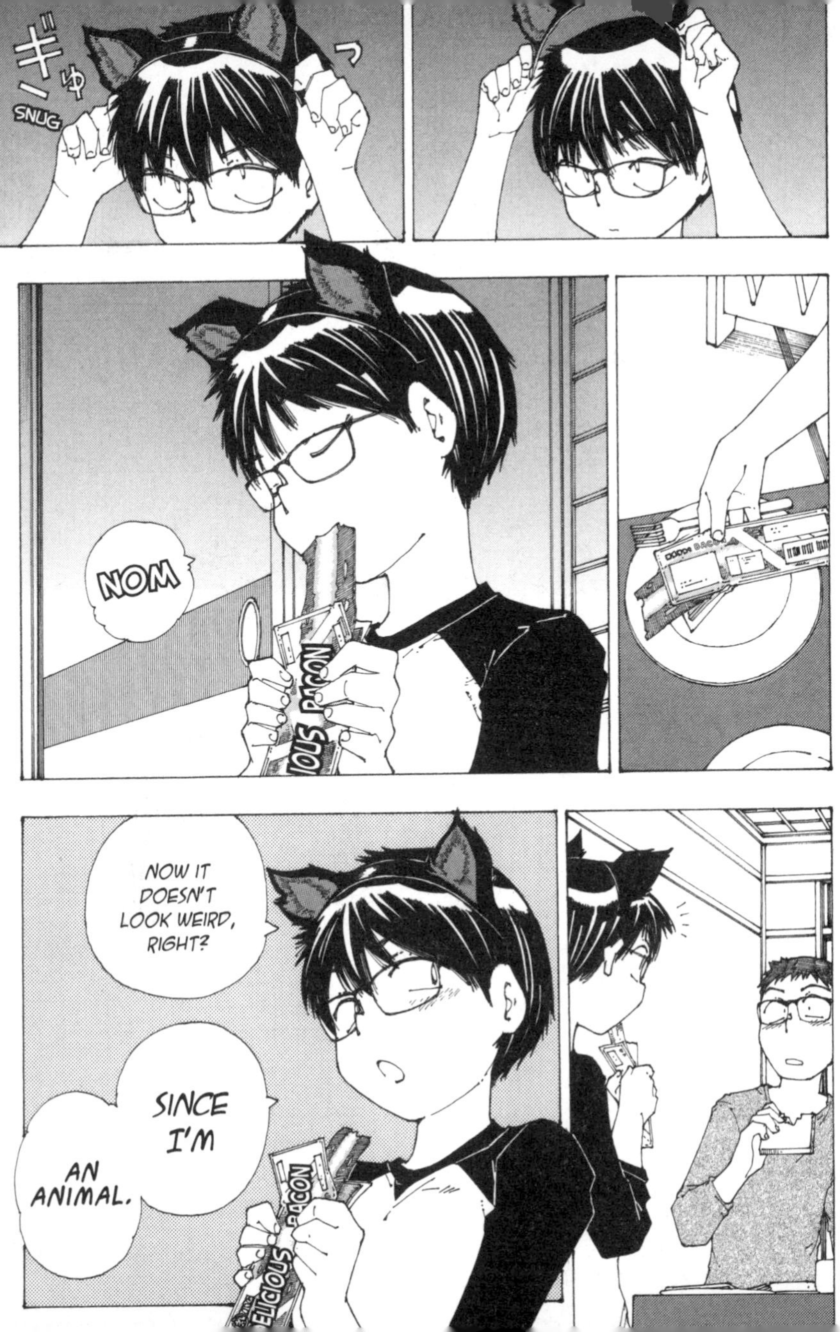

ギゅーっ
SNUG
NOM
NOW IT DOESN'T LOOK WEIRD, RIGHT?
SINCE I'M
AN ANIMAL.

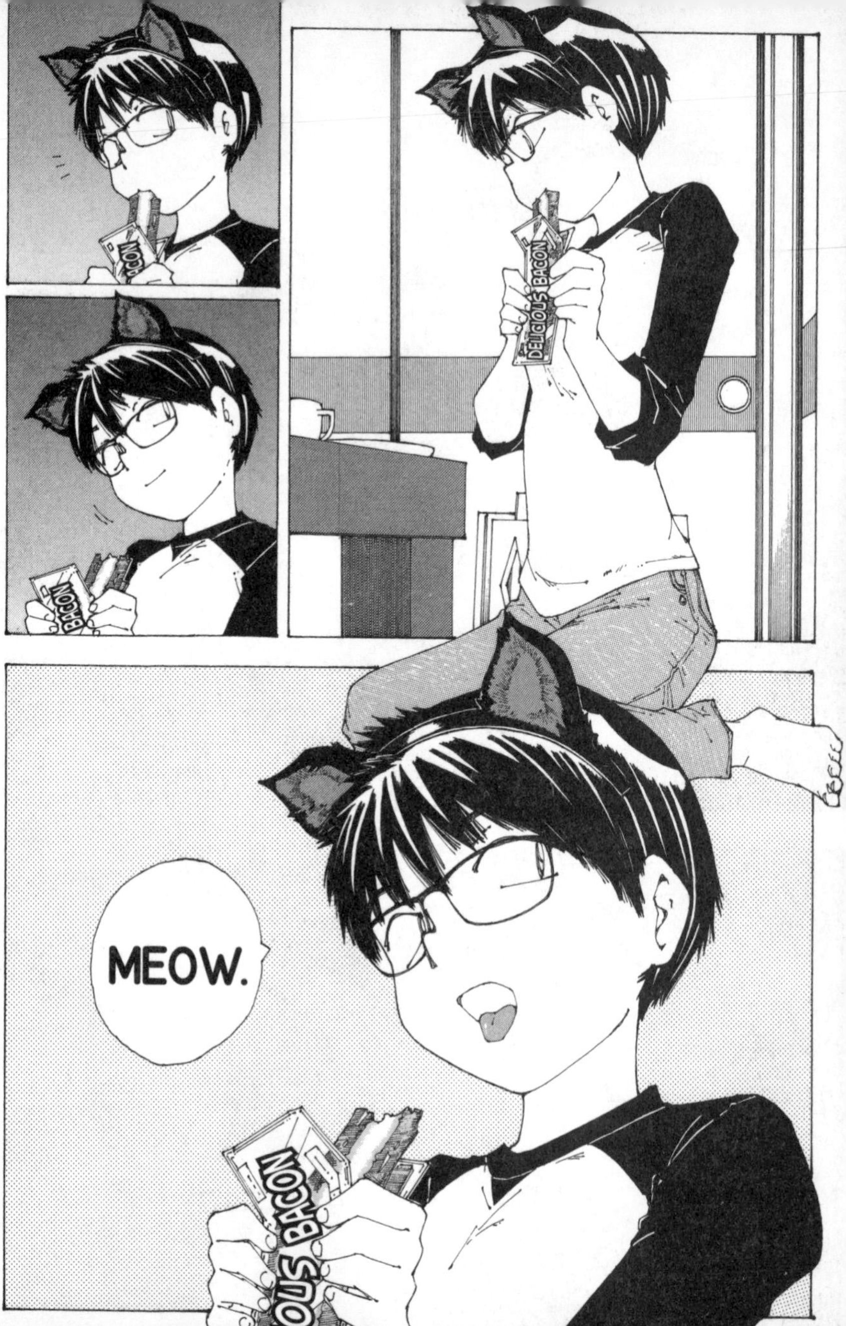
DELICIOUS BACON
BACON
BACON
MEOW.
OUS BACON

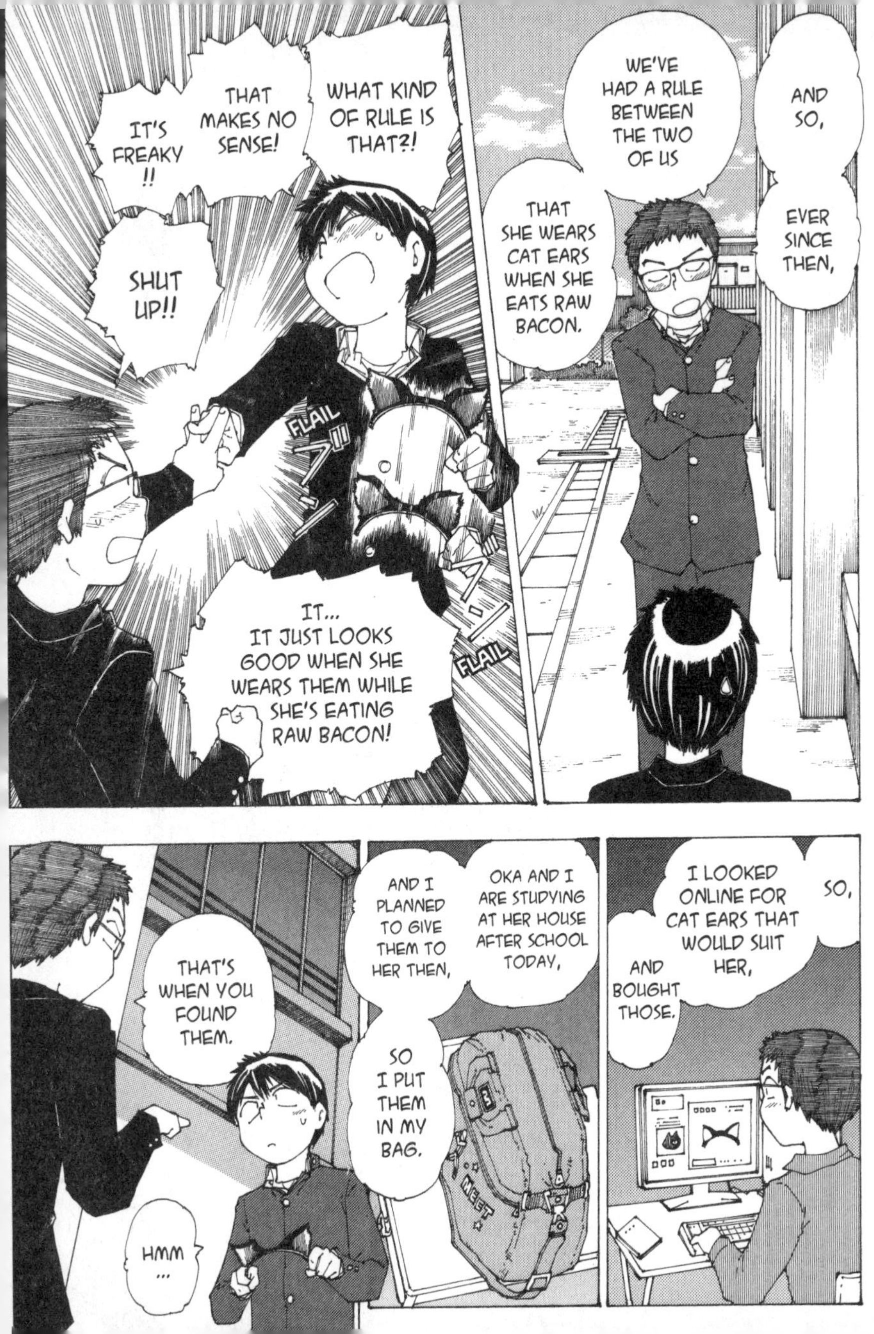
AND SO,
WE'VE HAD A RULE BETWEEN THE TWO OF US
EVER SINCE THEN,
THAT SHE WEARS CAT EARS WHEN SHE EATS RAW BACON.
WHAT KIND OF RULE IS THAT?!
THAT MAKES NO SENSE!
IT'S FREAKY!!
SHUT UP!!
FLAIL
IT... IT JUST LOOKS GOOD WHEN SHE WEARS THEM WHILE SHE'S EATING RAW BACON!
FLAIL
SO,
I LOOKED ONLINE FOR CAT EARS THAT WOULD SUIT HER,
AND BOUGHT THOSE.
OKA AND I ARE STUDYING AT HER HOUSE AFTER SCHOOL TODAY,
AND I PLANNED TO GIVE THEM TO HER THEN,
SO I PUT THEM IN MY BAG.
MEET
THAT'S WHEN YOU FOUND THEM.
HMM ...

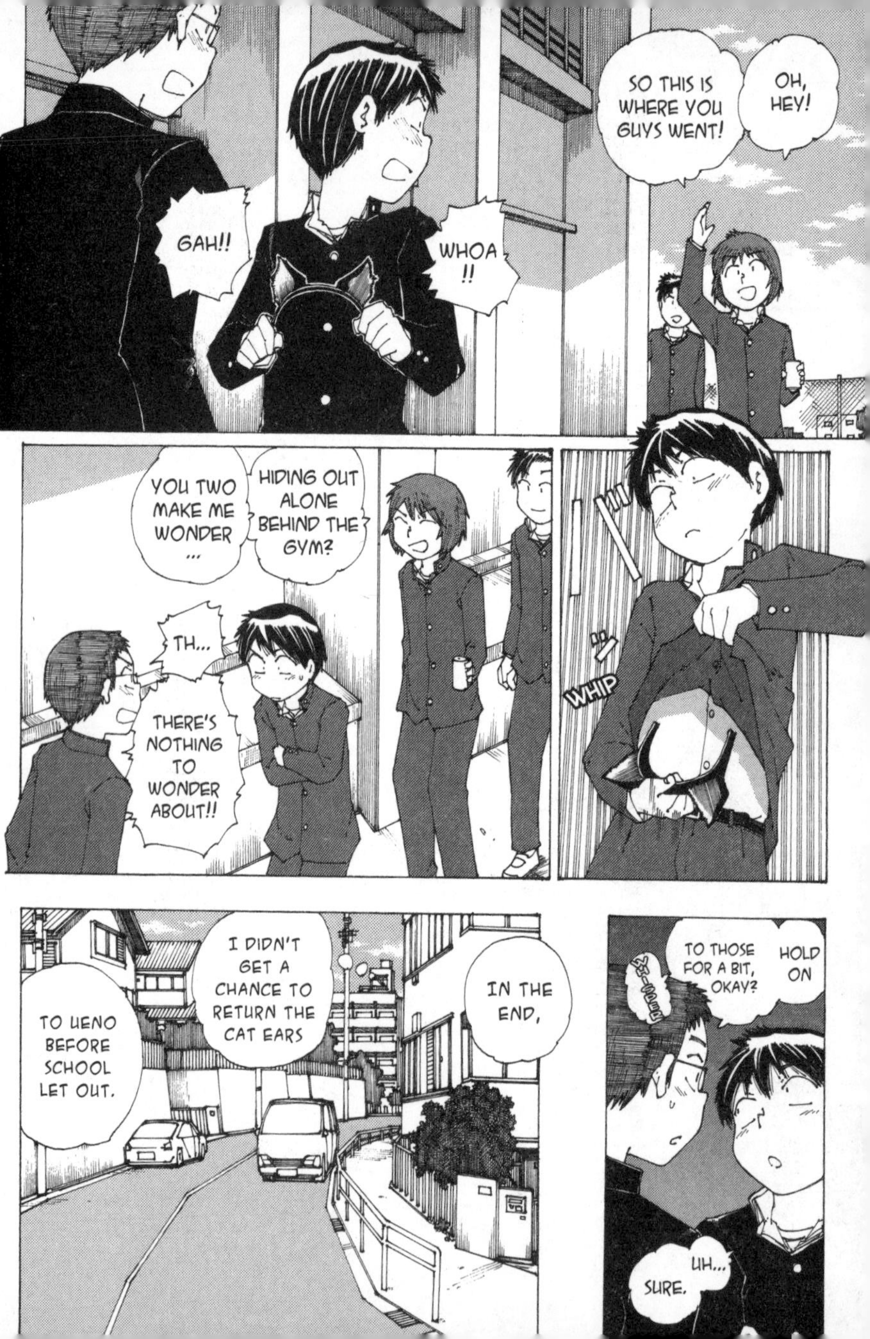
OH, HEY!
SO THIS IS WHERE YOU GUYS WENT!
WHOA !!
GAH!!
WHIP
HIDING OUT ALONE BEHIND THE GYM?
YOU TWO MAKE ME WONDER ...
TH...
THERE'S NOTHING TO WONDER ABOUT!!
HOLD ON
TO THOSE FOR A BIT, OKAY?
UH... SURE.
IN THE END,
I DIDN'T GET A CHANCE TO RETURN THE CAT EARS
TO UENO BEFORE SCHOOL LET OUT.

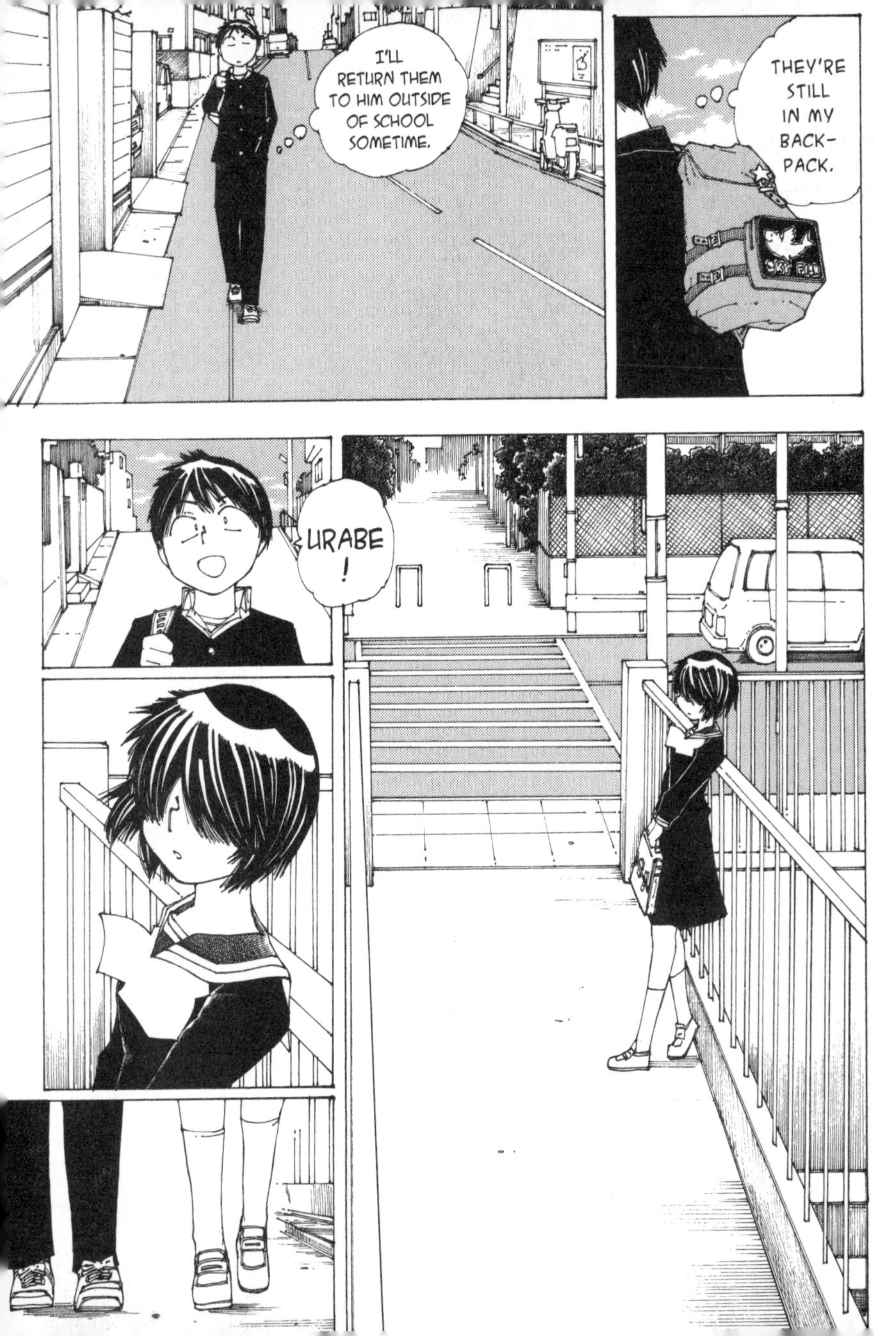
THEY'RE STILL IN MY BACK-PACK.
I'LL RETURN THEM TO HIM OUTSIDE OF SCHOOL SOMETIME.
URABE!

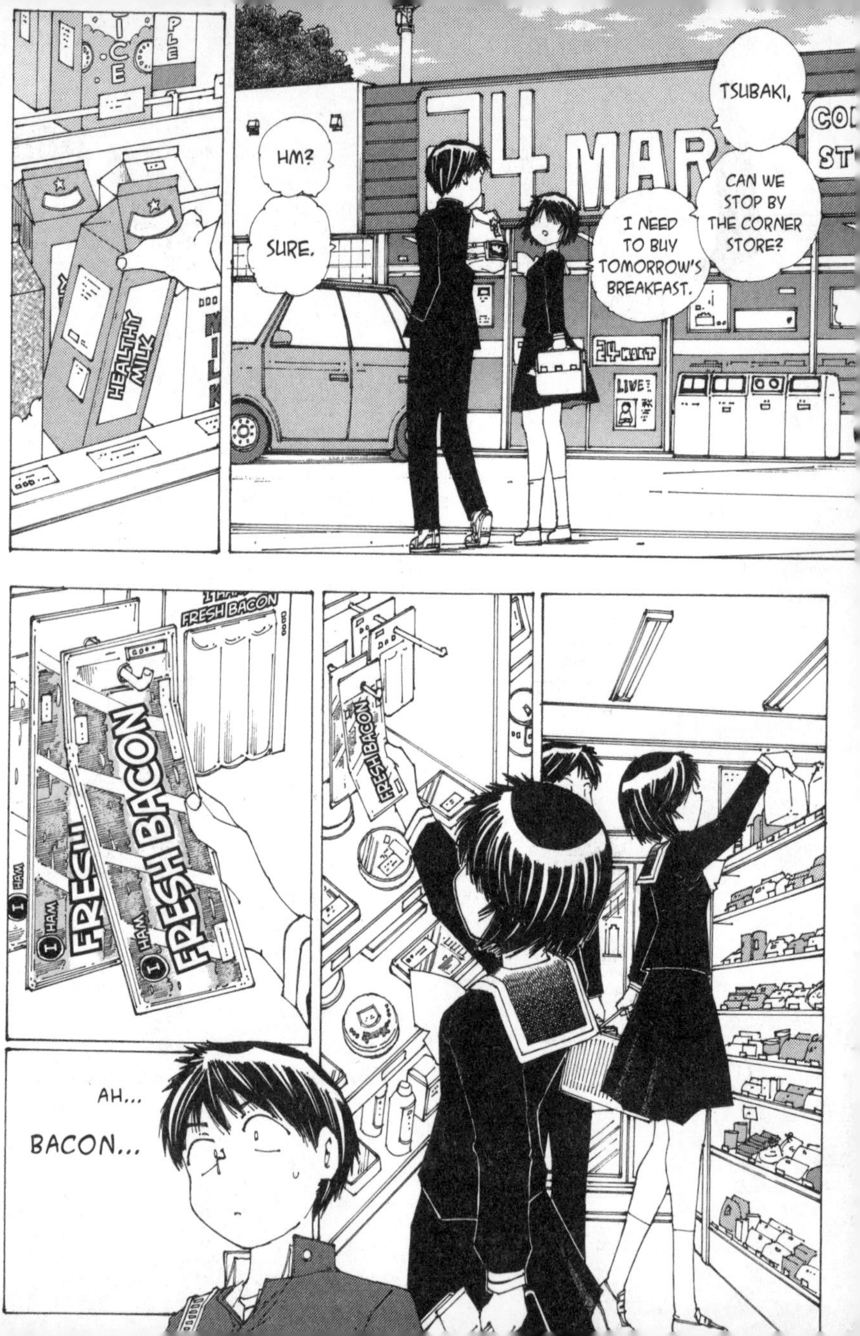
24 MAR
TSUBAKI,
CAN WE STOP BY THE CORNER STORE?
I NEED TO BUY TOMORROW'S BREAKFAST.
HM?
SURE.
24 MART
LIVE!
HEALTHY MILK
FRESH BACON
I HAM
FRESH BACON
FRESH BACON
I HAM
FRESH
I HAM
AH...
BACON...

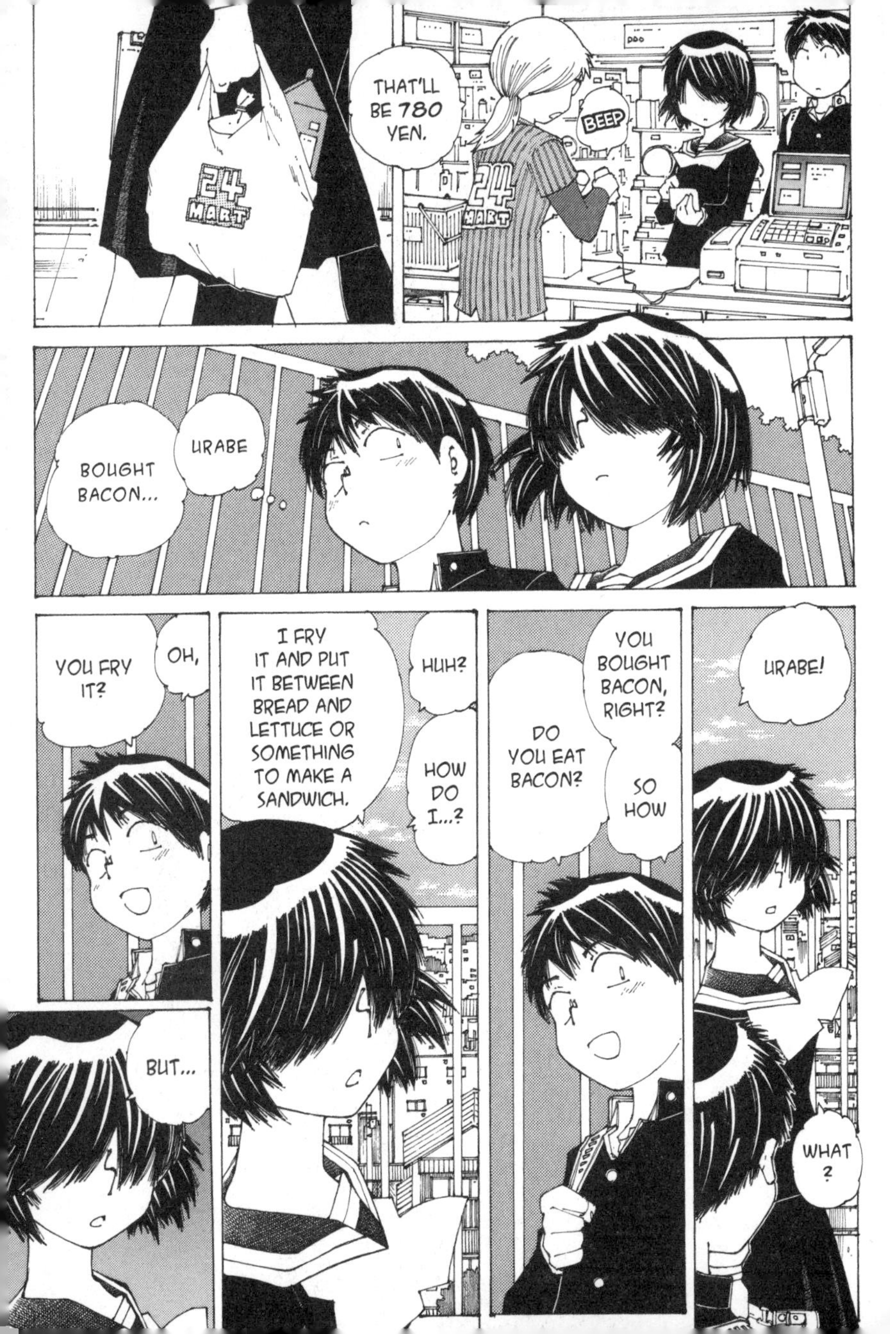
BEEP
THAT'LL BE 780 YEN.
URABE
BOUGHT BACON...
URABE!
WHAT?
YOU BOUGHT BACON, RIGHT?
SO HOW
DO YOU EAT BACON?
HUH?
HOW DO I...?
I FRY IT AND PUT IT BETWEEN BREAD AND LETTUCE OR SOMETHING TO MAKE A SANDWICH.
OH,
YOU FRY IT?
BUT...

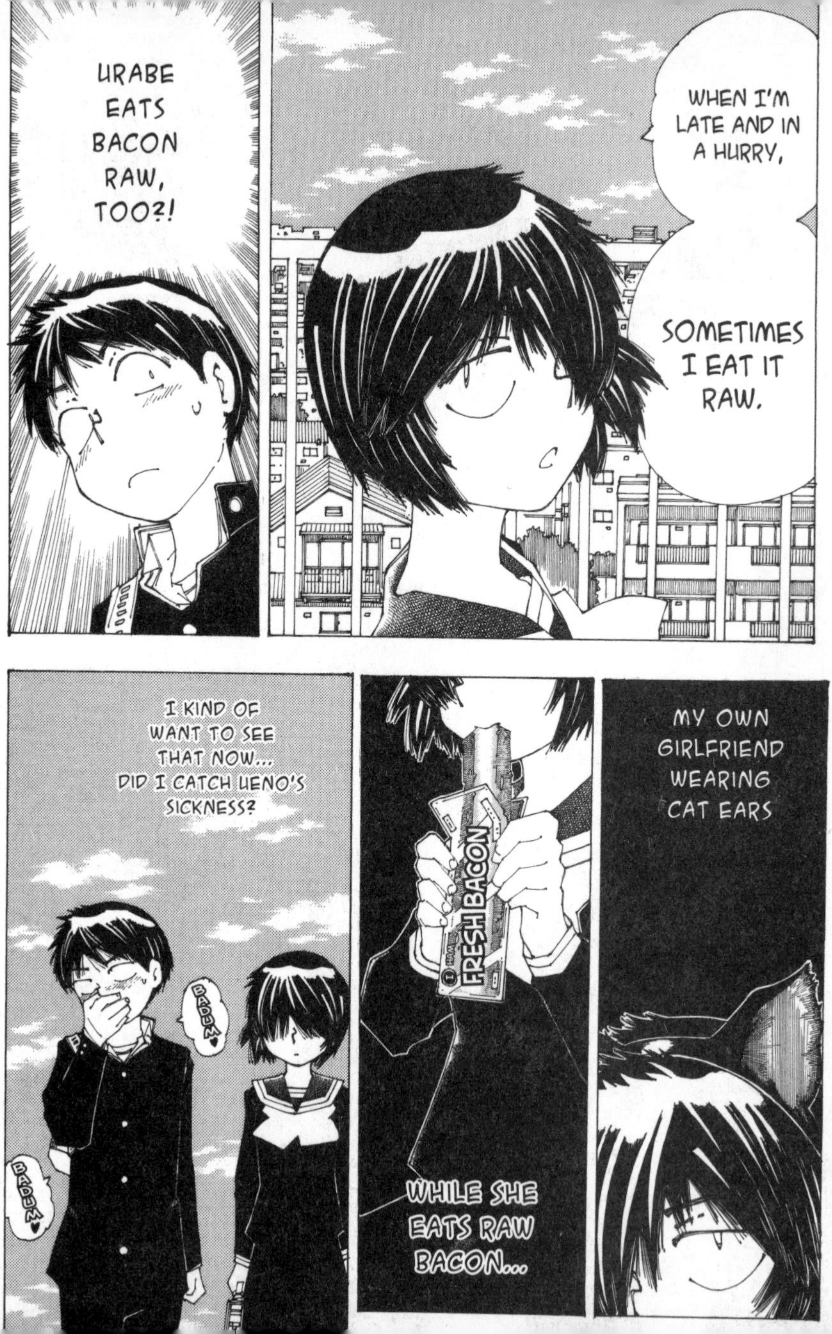
WHEN I'M LATE AND IN A HURRY,
SOMETIMES I EAT IT RAW.
URABE EATS BACON RAW, TOO?!
MY OWN GIRLFRIEND WEARING CAT EARS
FRESH BACON
HAM
WHILE SHE EATS RAW BACON...
I KIND OF WANT TO SEE THAT NOW... DID I CATCH UENO'S SICKNESS?
BADUM♥
BADUM♥

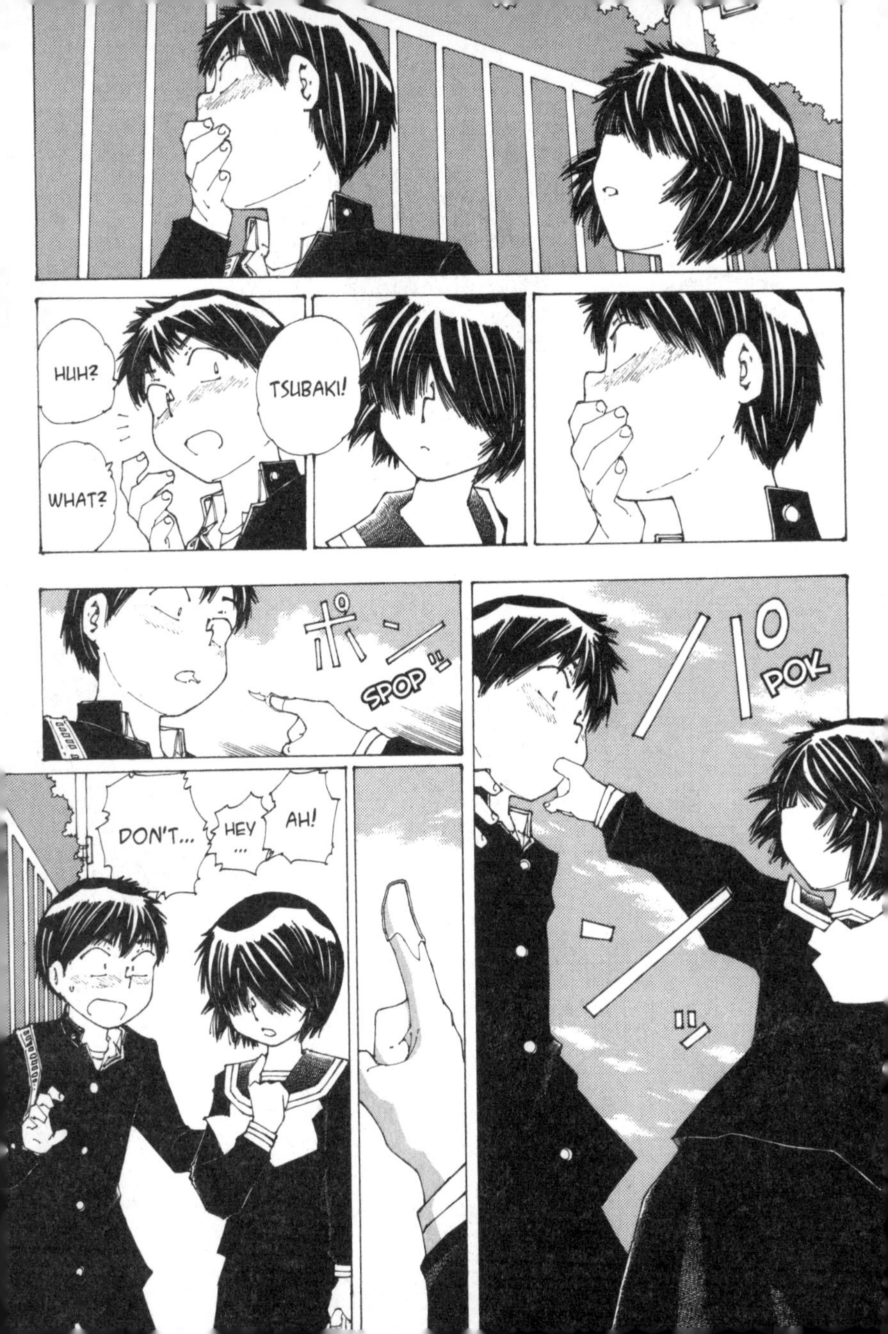
TSUBAKI!
HUH?
WHAT?
ポン
POK
ポーン
SPOP
AH!
HEY ...
DON'T...

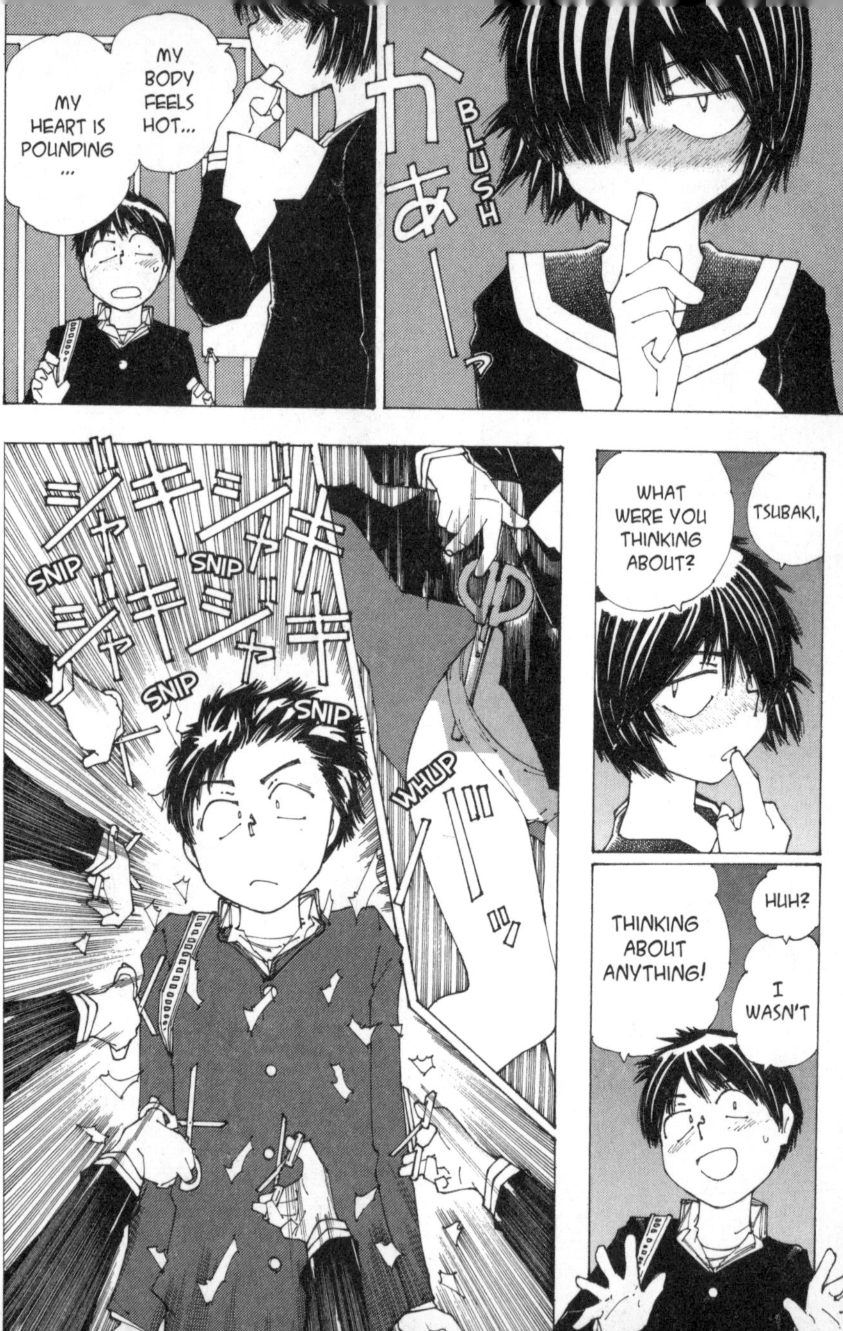
わぁーっ
BLUSH
MY BODY FEELS HOT...
MY HEART IS POUNDING ...
TSUBAKI,
WHAT WERE YOU THINKING ABOUT?
HUH?
I WASN'T
THINKING ABOUT ANYTHING!
SNIP
SNIP
SNIP
SNIP
WHUP

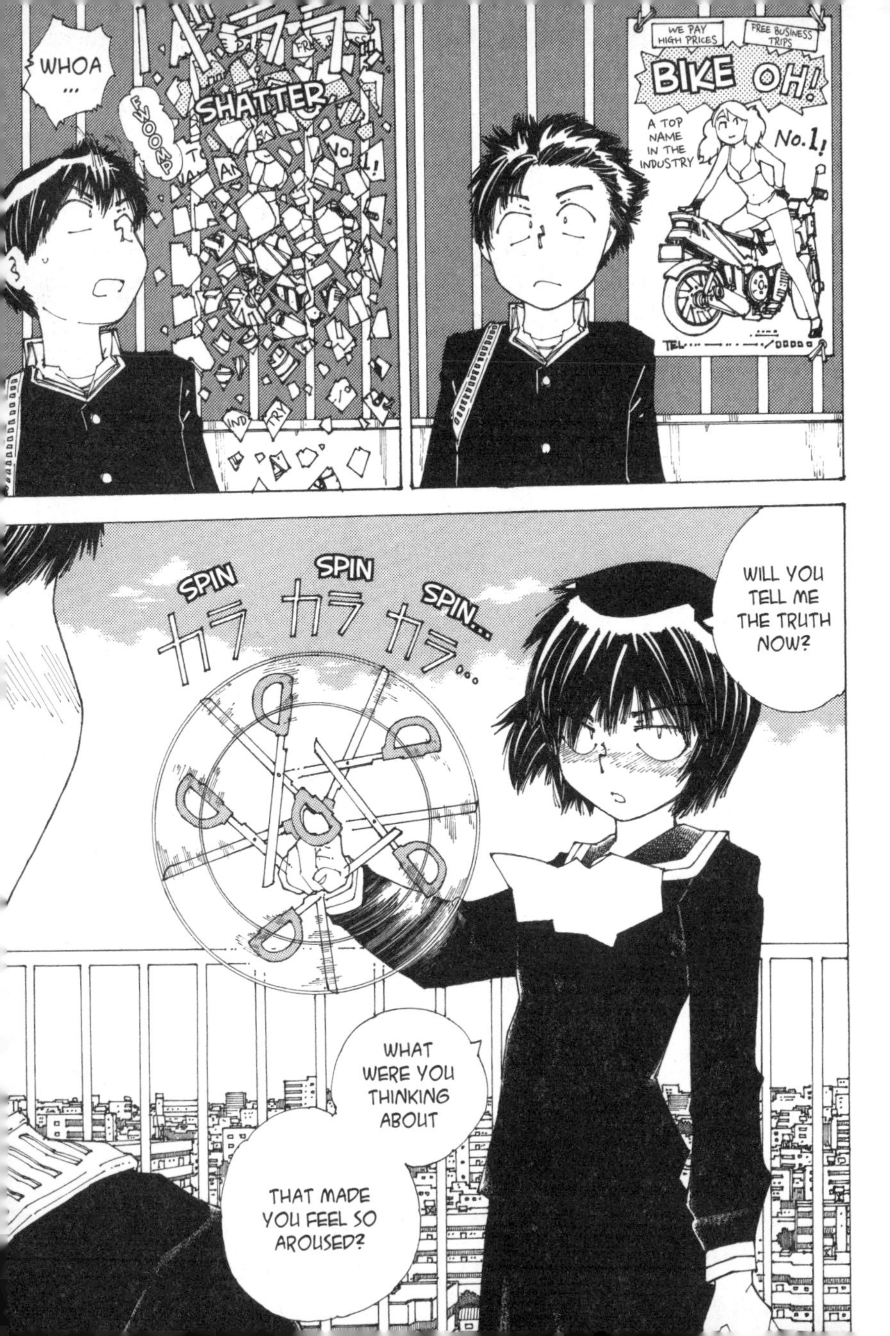
WE PAY HIGH PRICES
FREE BUSINESS TRIPS
BIKE OH!
A TOP NAME IN THE INDUSTRY
No.1!
SHATTER
FWOOMP
WHOA ...
WILL YOU TELL ME THE TRUTH NOW?
SPIN SPIN SPIN...
カラ カラ カラ...
WHAT WERE YOU THINKING ABOUT
THAT MADE YOU FEEL SO AROUSED?

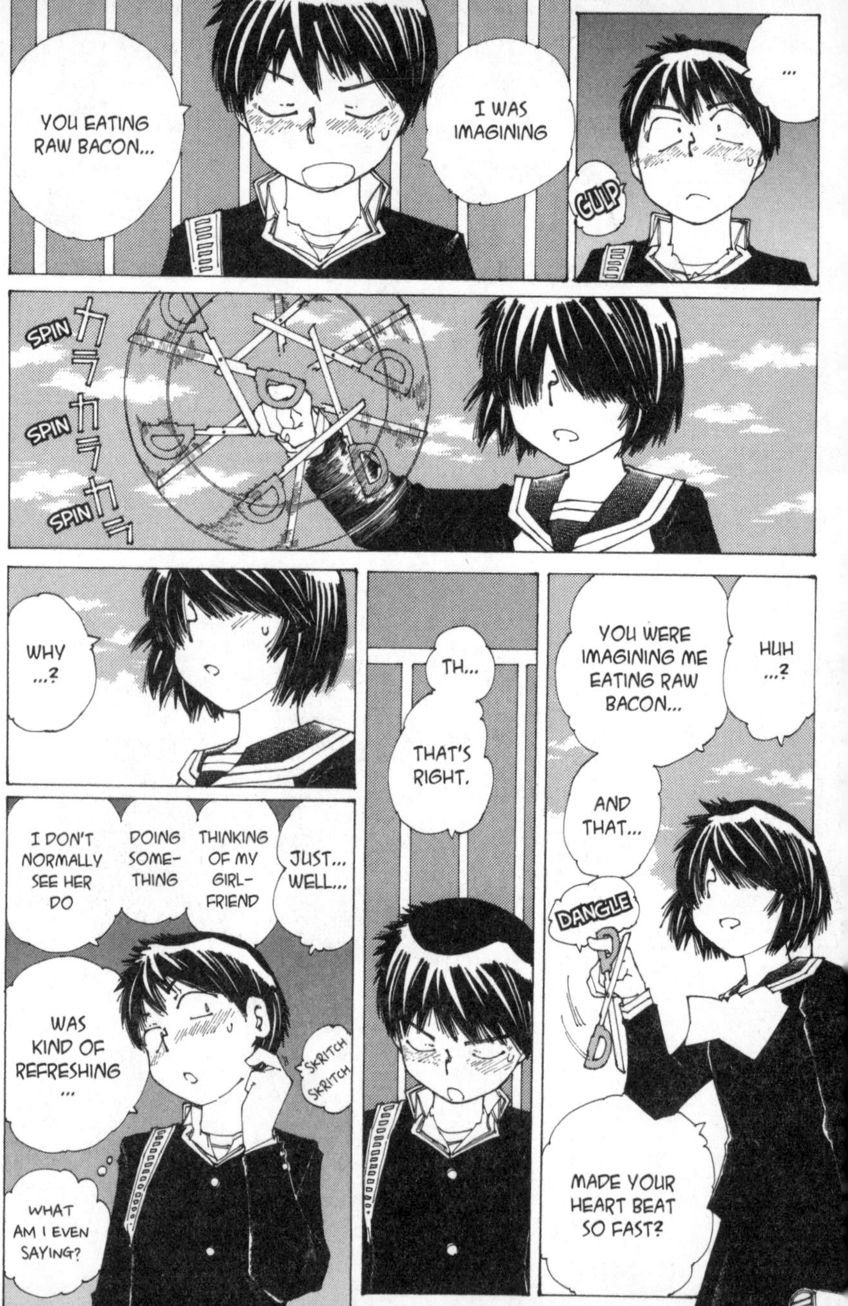
...
GULP
I WAS IMAGINING
YOU EATING RAW BACON...
SPIN SPIN SPIN
HUH ...?
YOU WERE IMAGINING ME EATING RAW BACON...
AND THAT...
DANGLE
MADE YOUR HEART BEAT SO FAST?
TH...
THAT'S RIGHT.
WHY ...?
JUST... WELL...
THINKING OF MY GIRL-FRIEND
DOING SOME-THING
I DON'T NORMALLY SEE HER DO
WAS KIND OF REFRESHING ...
SKRITCH SKRITCH
WHAT AM I EVEN SAYING?

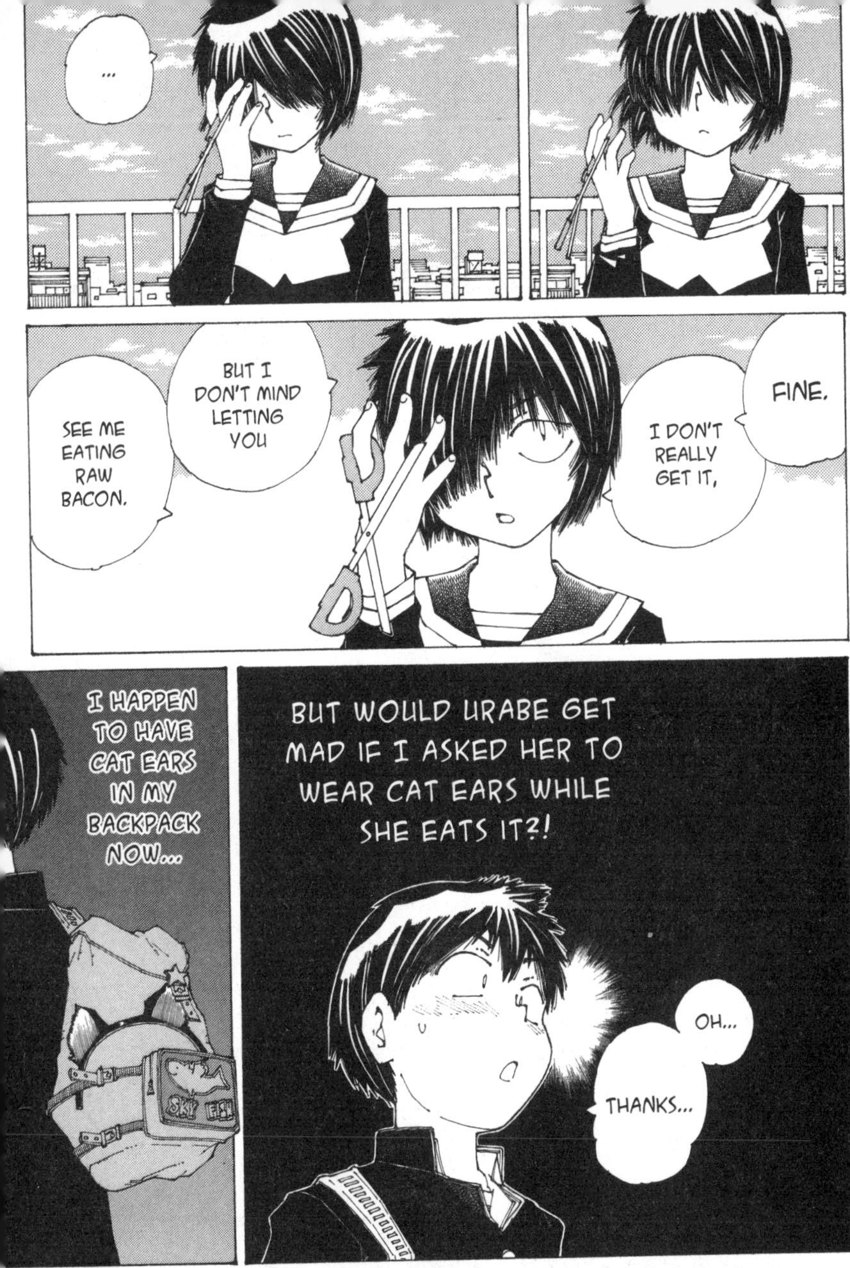
...
FINE.
I DON'T REALLY GET IT,
BUT I DON'T MIND LETTING YOU
SEE ME EATING RAW BACON.
BUT WOULD URABE GET MAD IF I ASKED HER TO WEAR CAT EARS WHILE SHE EATS IT?!
OH...
THANKS...
I HAPPEN TO HAVE CAT EARS IN MY BACKPACK NOW...

END OF CHAPTER 49

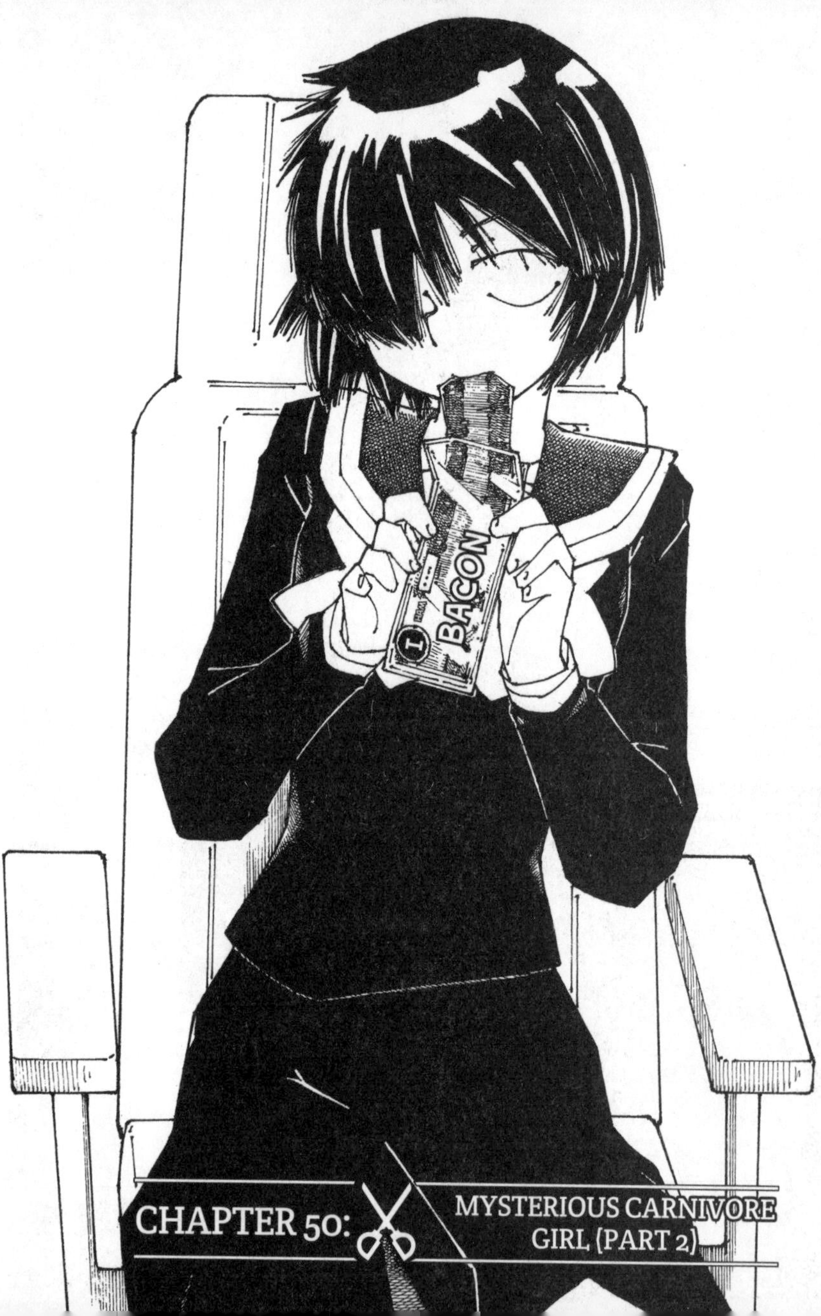
BACON

CHAPTER 50: MYSTERIOUS CARNIVORE GIRL (PART 2)

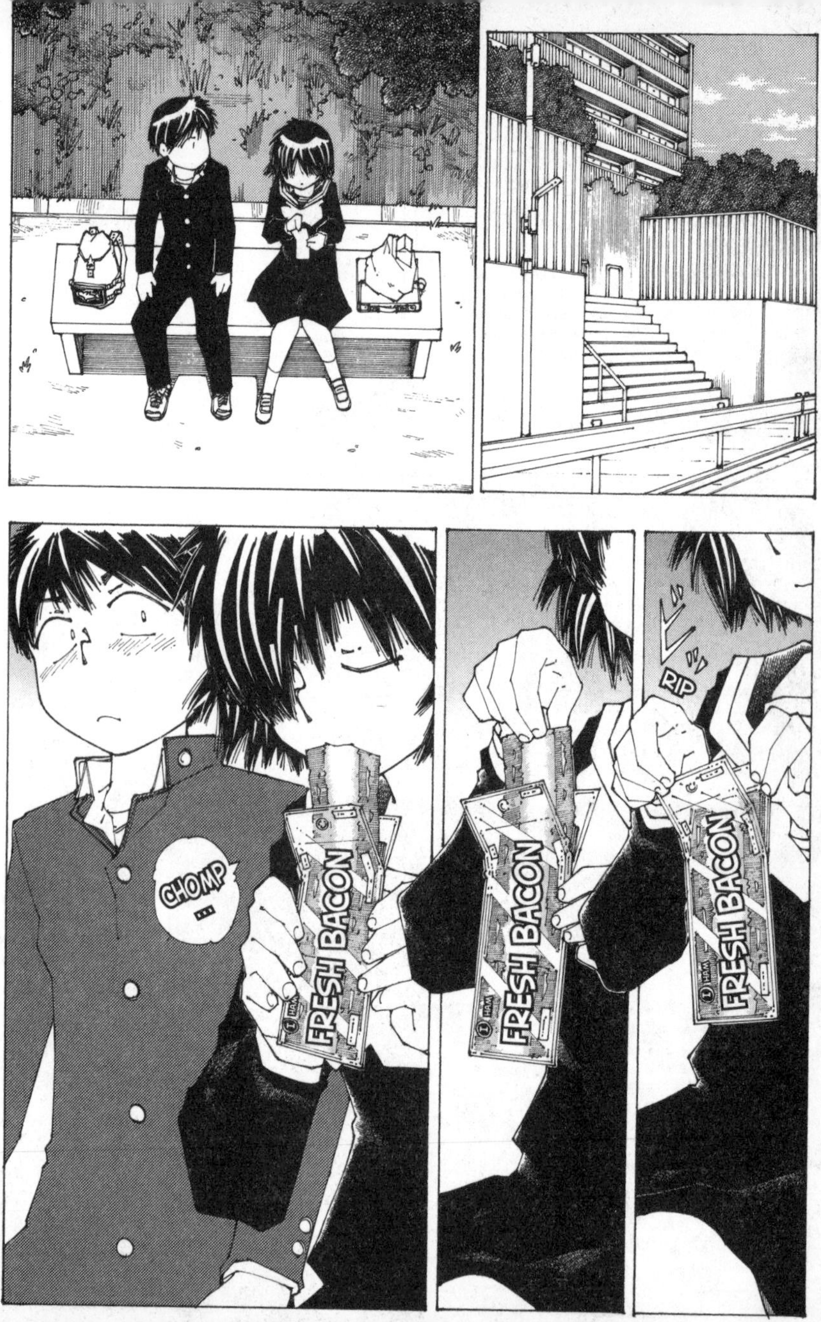
RIP
HAM
FRESH BACON
HAM
FRESH BACON
CHOMP
...
HAM
FRESH BACON

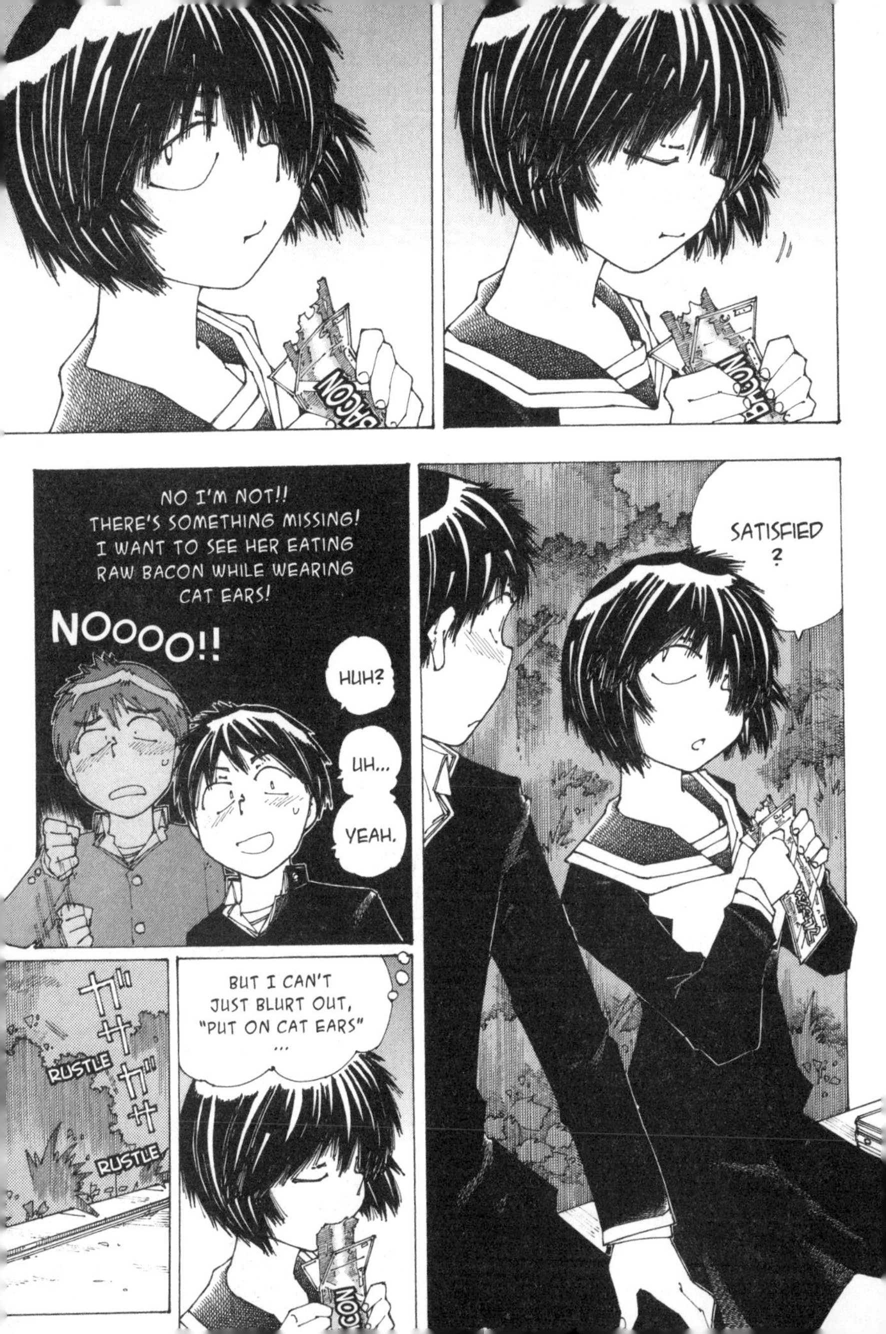
SATISFIED?
NO I'M NOT!! THERE'S SOMETHING MISSING! I WANT TO SEE HER EATING RAW BACON WHILE WEARING CAT EARS!
NOOOO!!
HUH?
UH...
YEAH.
BUT I CAN'T JUST BLURT OUT, "PUT ON CAT EARS" ...
ガサ
RUSTLE
ガサ
RUSTLE

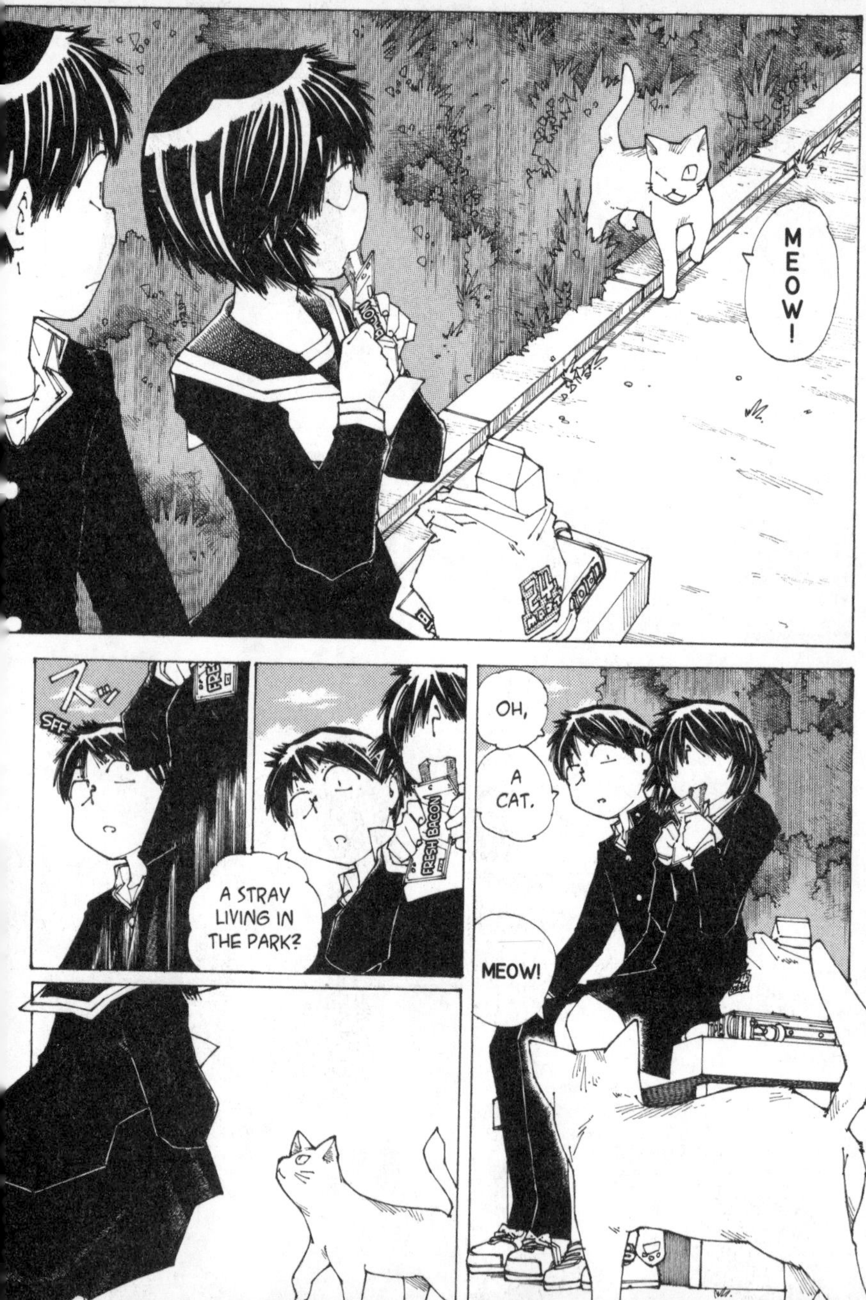
MEOW!
OH,
A CAT.
MEOW!
A STRAY LIVING IN THE PARK?
SFF

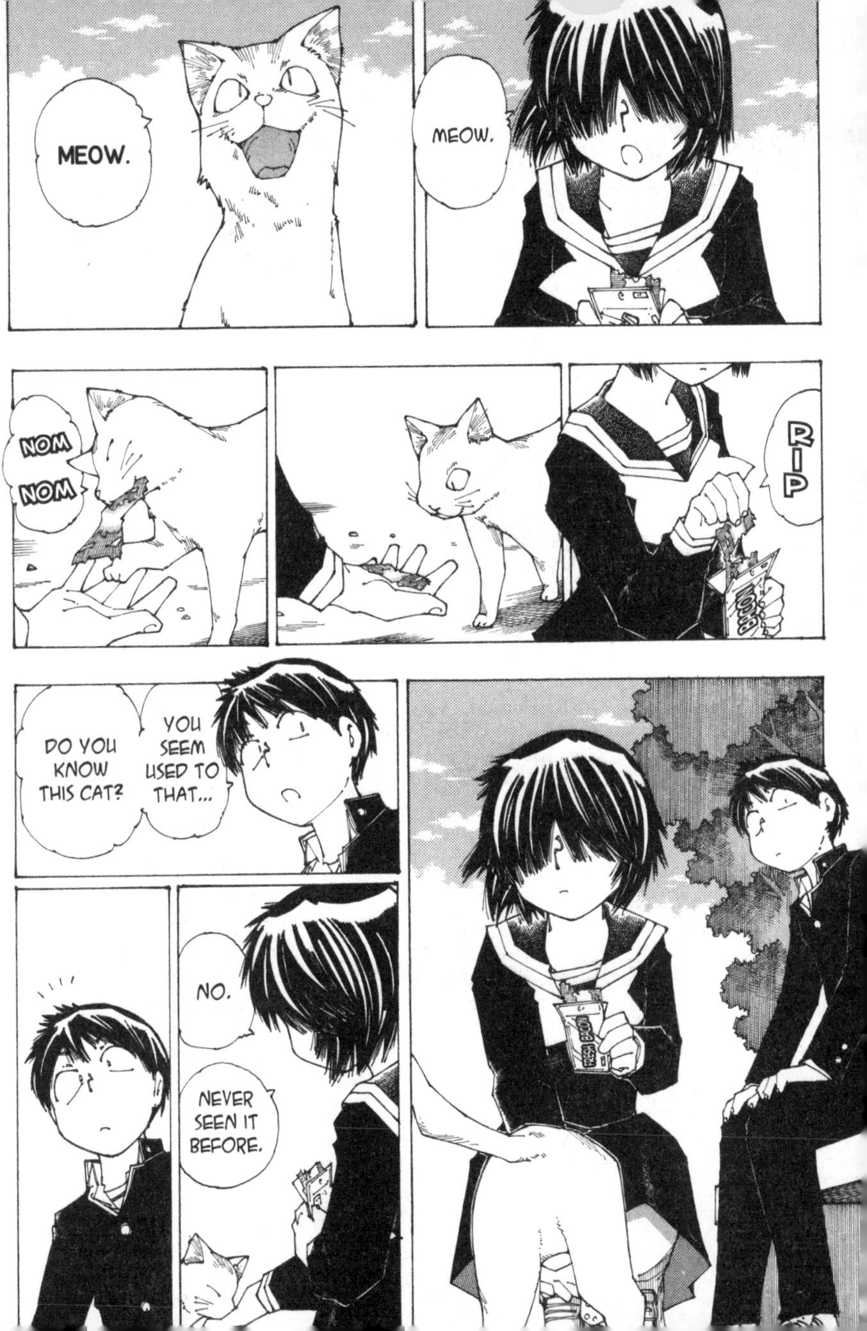

MEOW.
MEOW.
RIP
BACON
NOM NOM
FRESH BACON
YOU SEEM USED TO THAT...
DO YOU KNOW THIS CAT?
NO.
NEVER SEEN IT BEFORE.

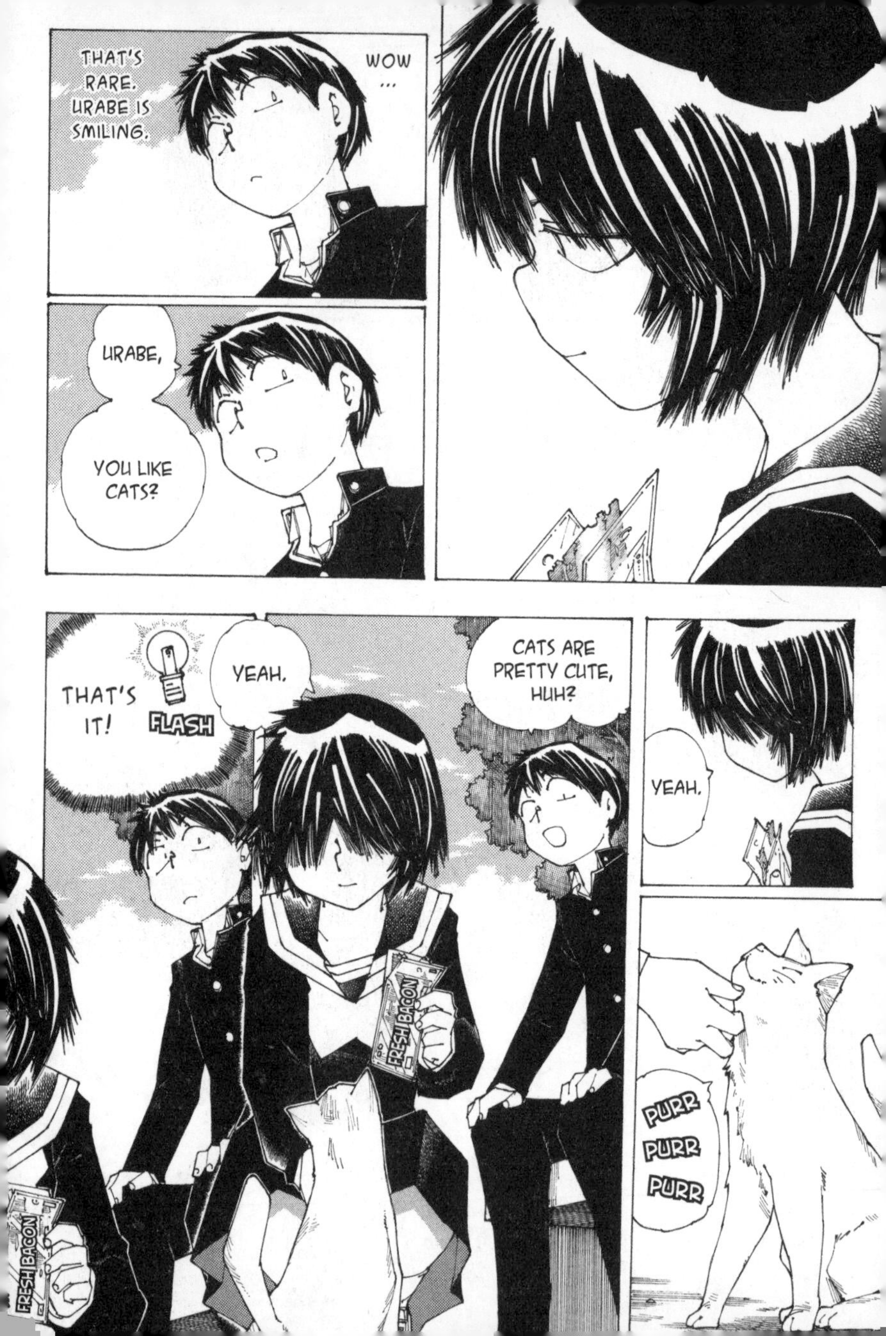
WOW ...
THAT'S RARE. URABE IS SMILING.
URABE,
YOU LIKE CATS?
YEAH.
PURR
PURR
PURR
CATS ARE PRETTY CUTE, HUH?
YEAH.
FLASH
THAT'S IT!
FRESH BACON
FRESH BACON

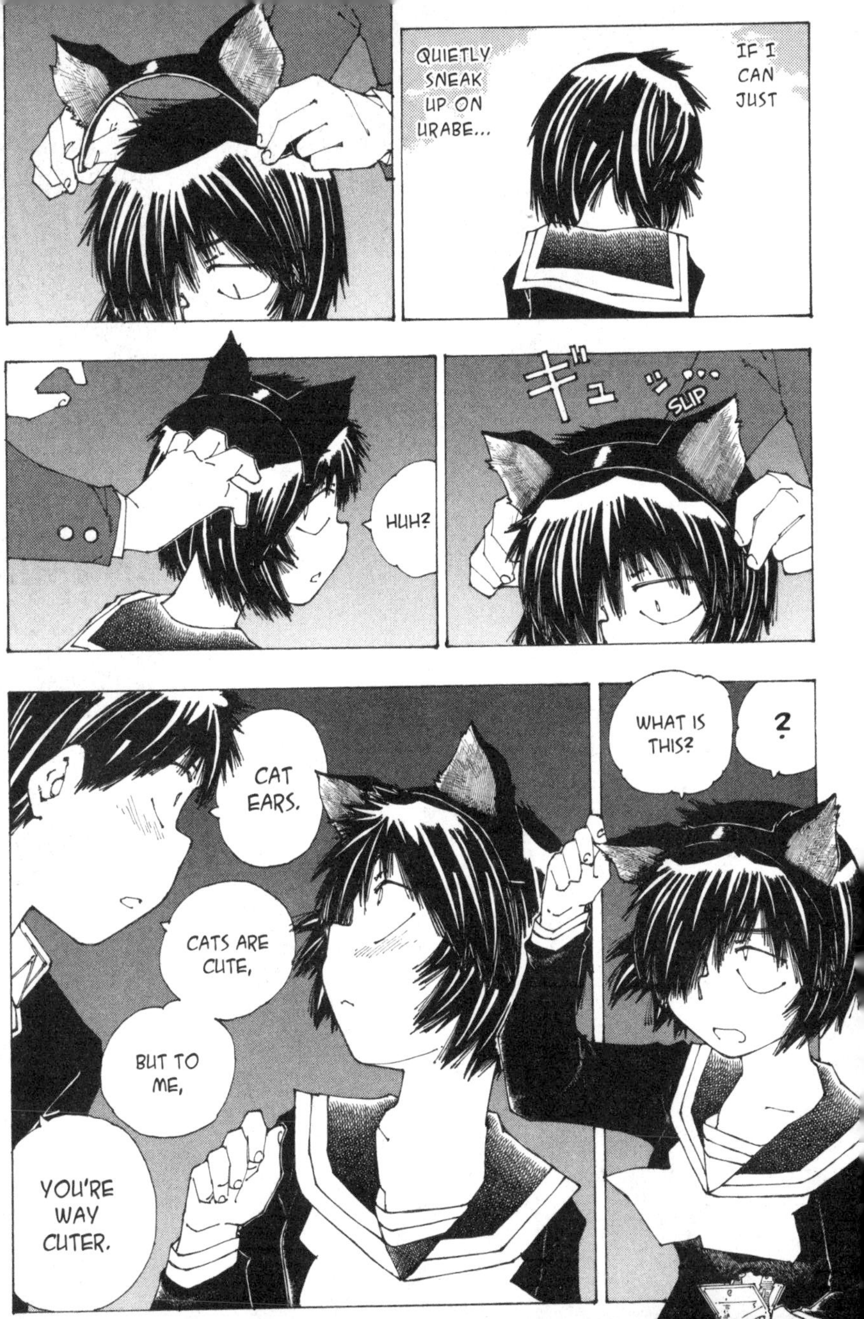
IF I CAN JUST
QUIETLY SNEAK UP ON URABE...
ギュッ
SLIP
HUH?
?
WHAT IS THIS?
CAT EARS.
CATS ARE CUTE,
BUT TO ME,
YOU'RE WAY CUTER.

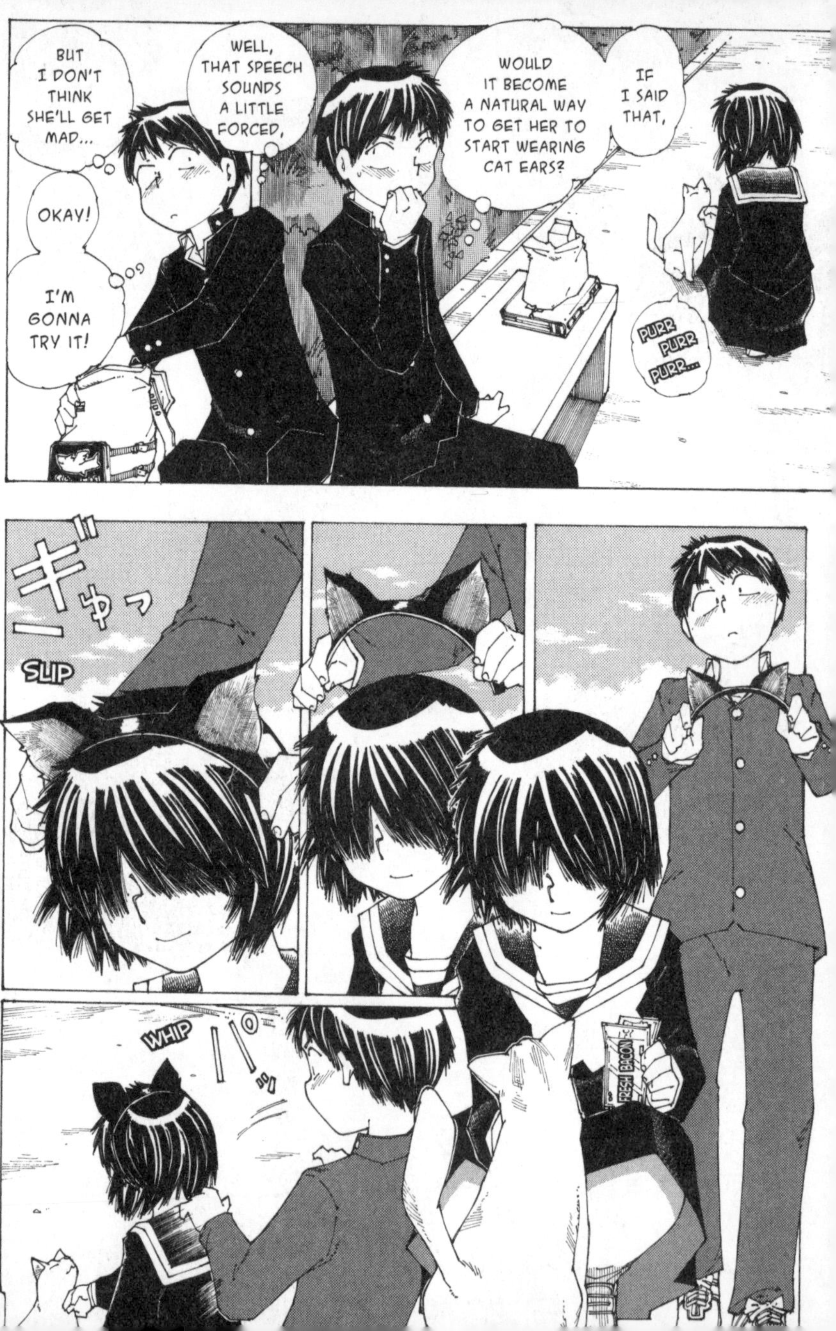
IF I SAID THAT,
WOULD IT BECOME A NATURAL WAY TO GET HER TO START WEARING CAT EARS?
WELL, THAT SPEECH SOUNDS A LITTLE FORCED,
BUT I DON'T THINK SHE'LL GET MAD...
PURR PURR PURR...
OKAY!
I'M GONNA TRY IT!
ギゅっ
SLIP
FRESH BACON
WHIP

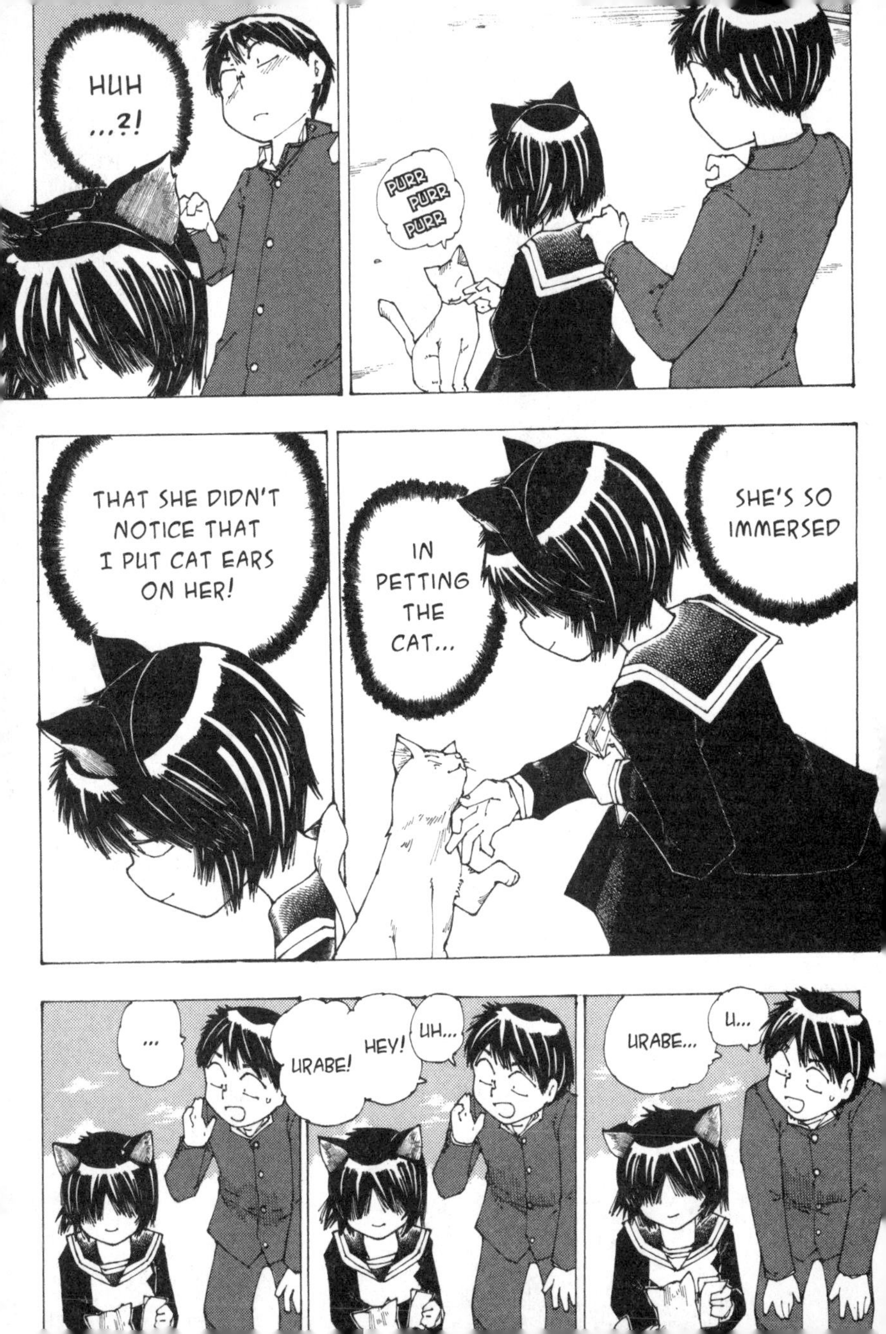
PURR PURR PURR
HUH ...?!
SHE'S SO IMMERSED
IN PETTING THE CAT...
THAT SHE DIDN'T NOTICE THAT I PUT CAT EARS ON HER!
U...
URABE...
UH...
HEY!
URABE!
...

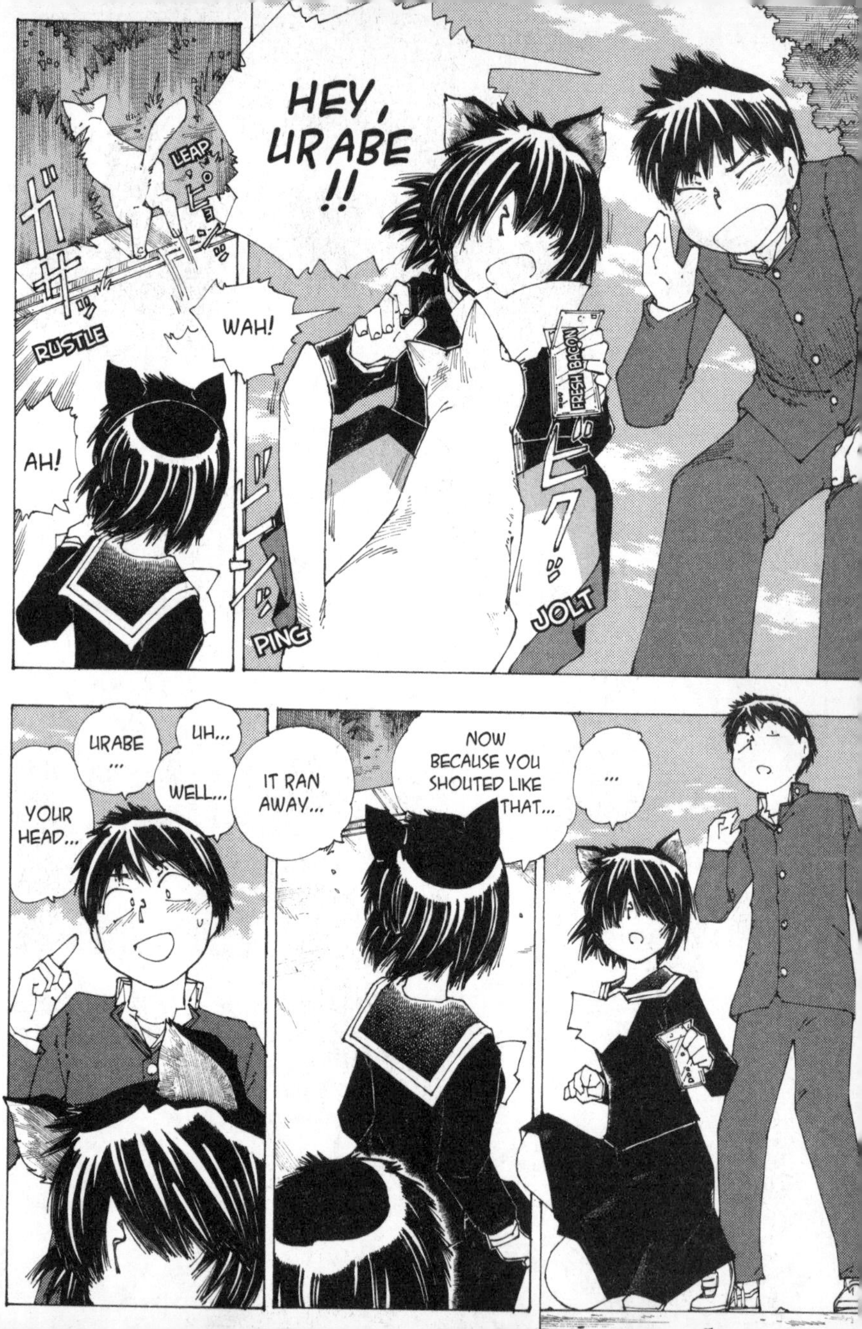
HEY, URABE!!
WAH!
FRESH BACON
JOLT
PING
LEAP
RUSTLE
AH!
...
NOW BECAUSE YOU SHOUTED LIKE THAT...
IT RAN AWAY...
UH... WELL...
URABE...
YOUR HEAD...

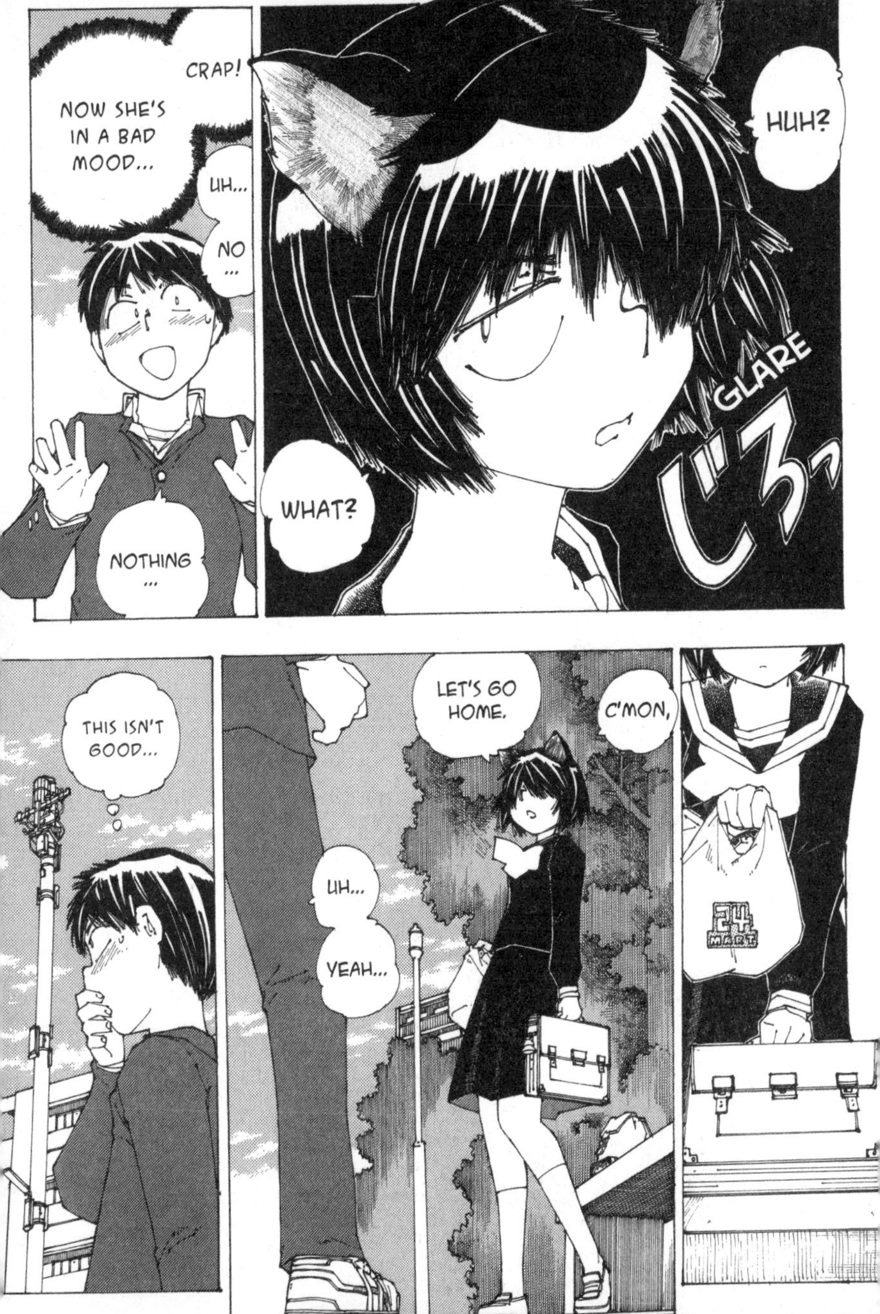
HUH?
GLARE
じろっ
WHAT?
CRAP!
NOW SHE'S IN A BAD MOOD...
UH...
NO ...
NOTHING ...
24 MART
C'MON,
LET'S GO HOME.
UH...
YEAH...
THIS ISN'T GOOD...

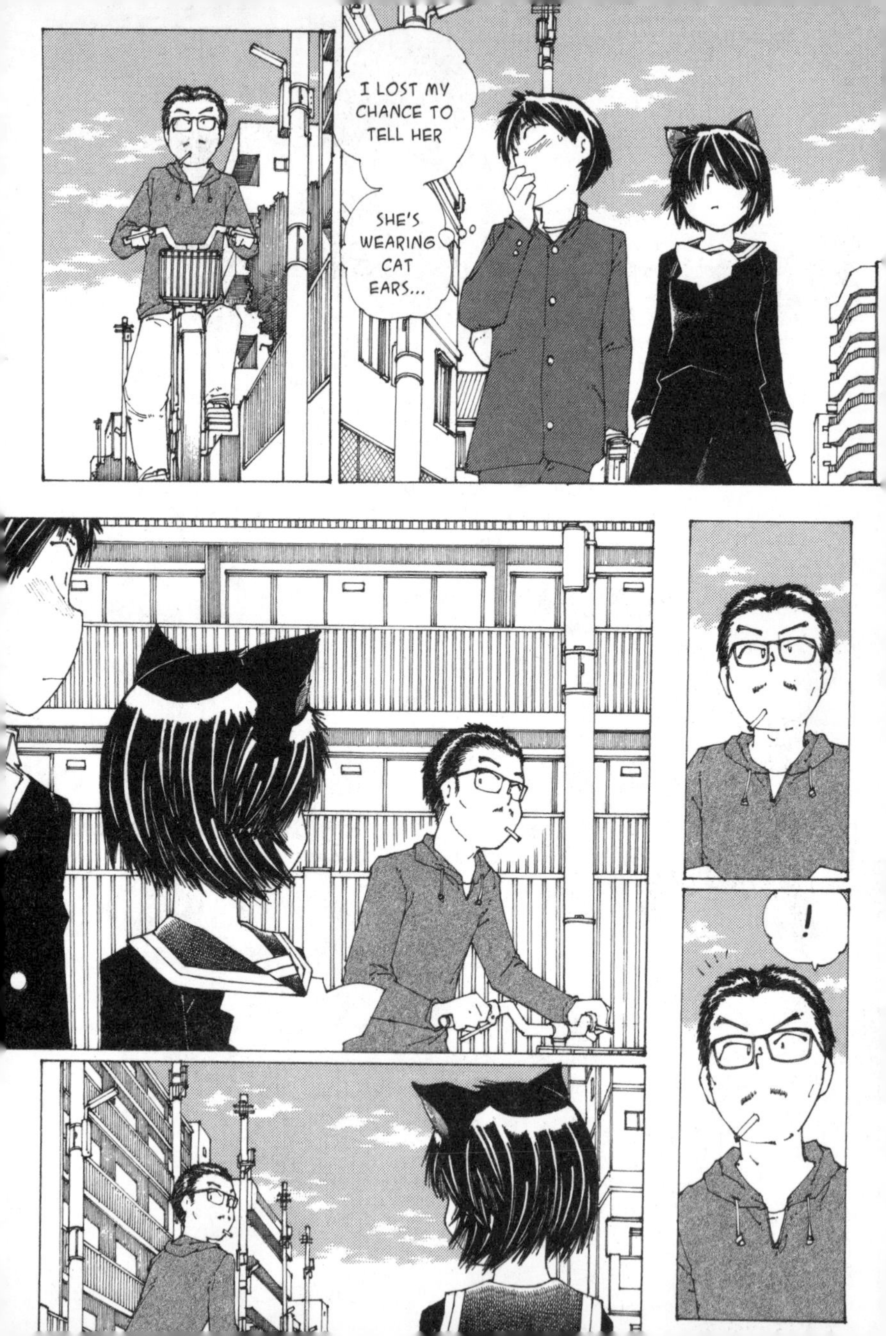
I LOST MY CHANCE TO TELL HER
SHE'S WEARING CAT EARS...
!

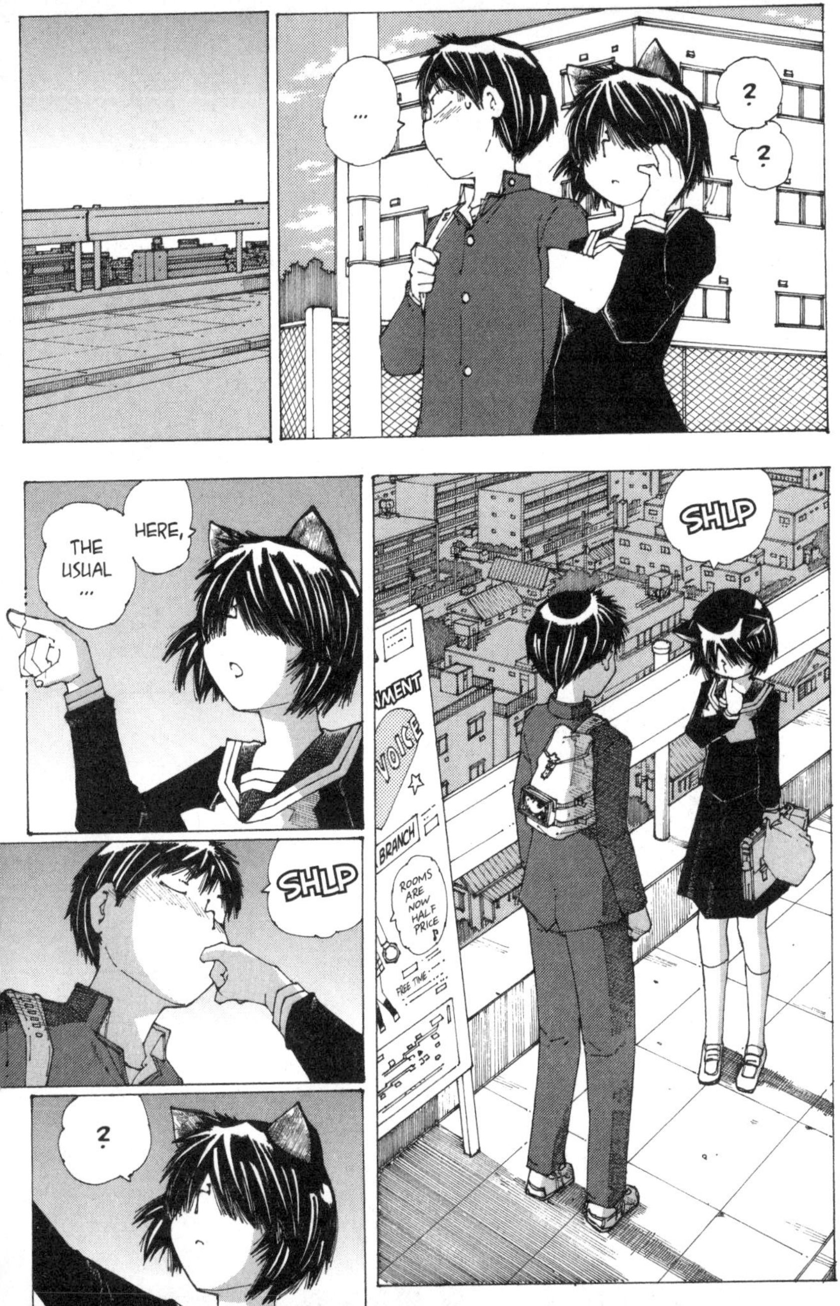
?
?
...
SHLP
VOICE
BRANCH
ROOMS ARE NOW HALF PRICE
FREE TIME
HERE, THE USUAL ...
SHLP
?

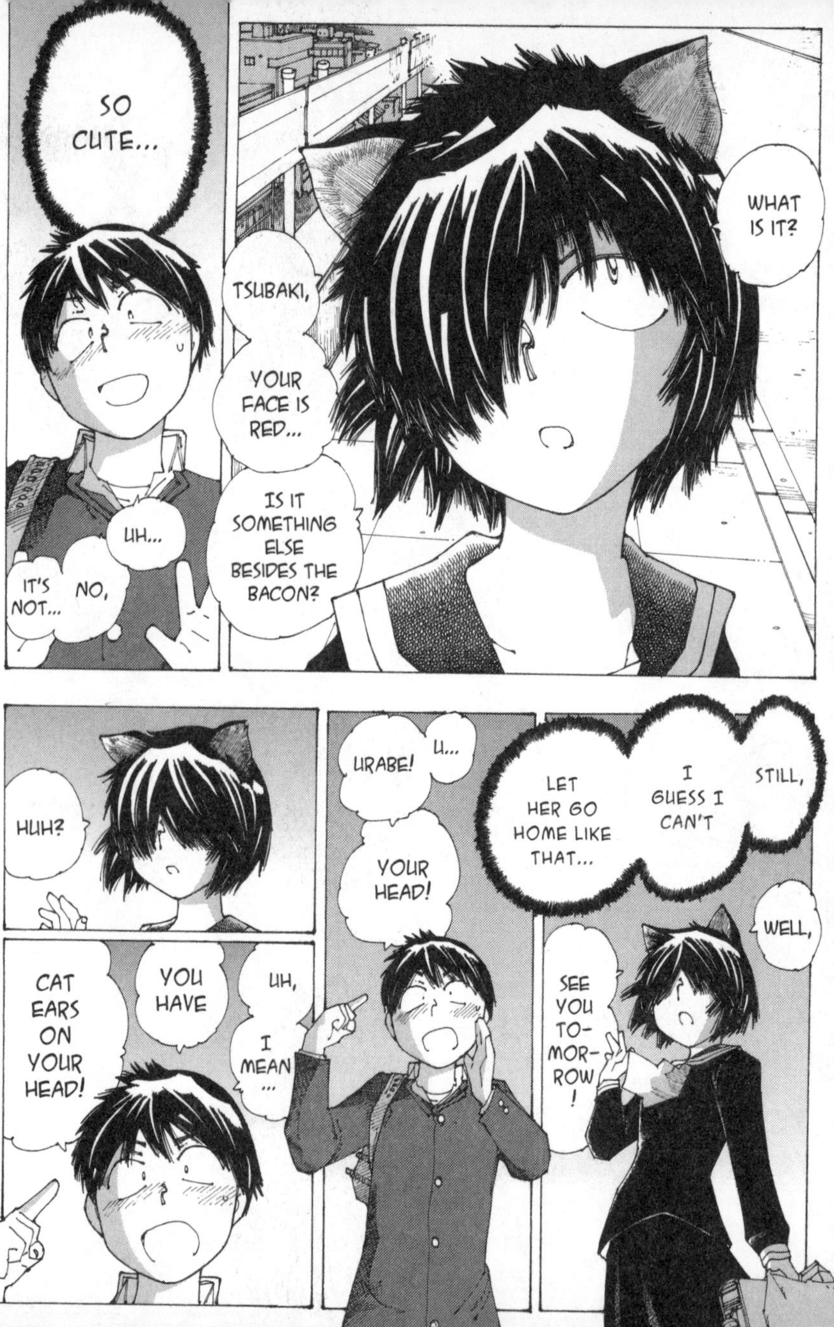
WHAT IS IT?
TSUBAKI,
YOUR FACE IS RED...
IS IT SOMETHING ELSE BESIDES THE BACON?
SO CUTE...
UH...
NO,
IT'S NOT...
STILL,
I GUESS I CAN'T
LET HER GO HOME LIKE THAT...
WELL,
SEE YOU TO-MOR-ROW!
U...
URABE!
YOUR HEAD!
HUH?
UH,
I MEAN...
YOU HAVE
CAT EARS ON YOUR HEAD!

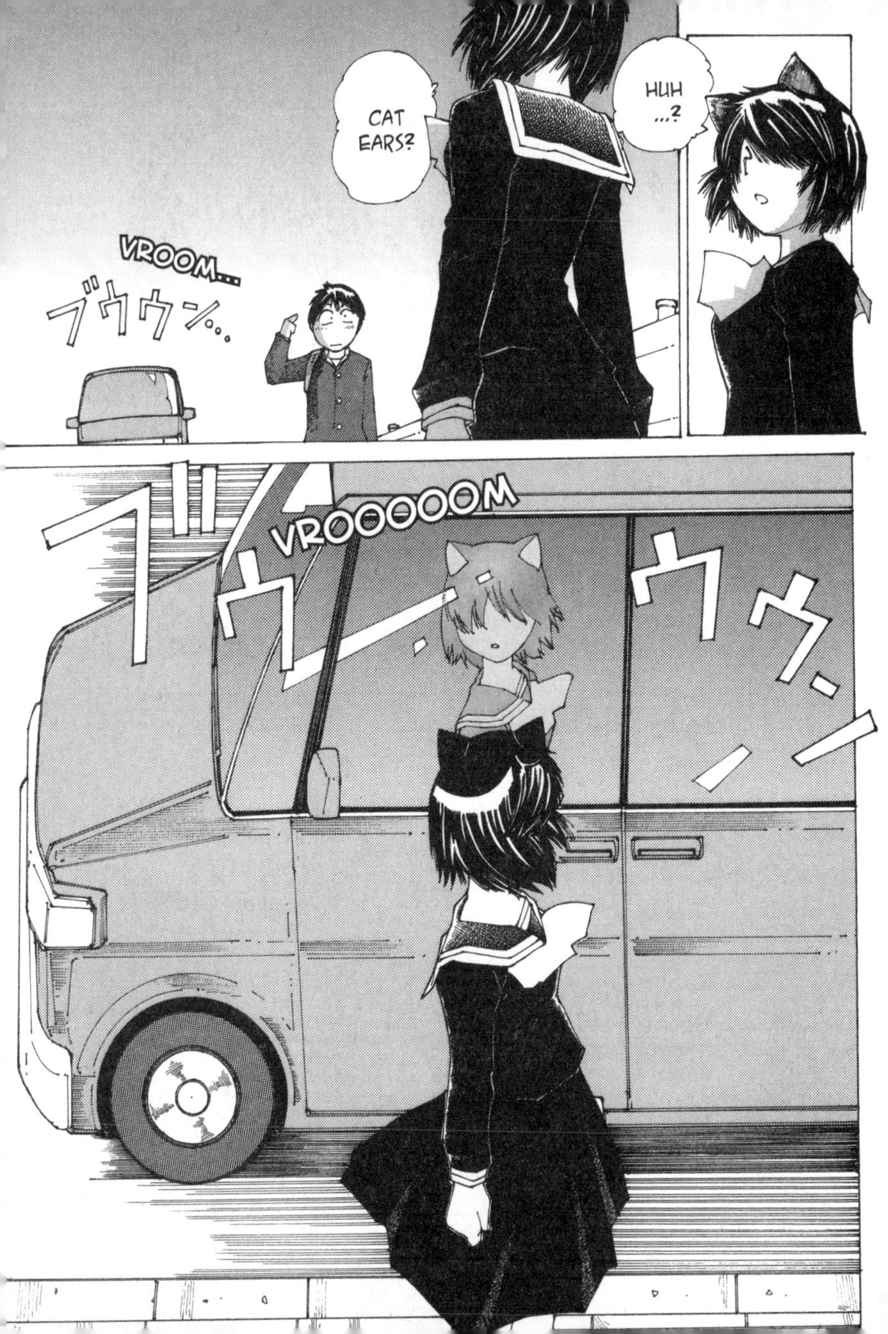
HUH ...?
CAT EARS?
VROOM...
ブウウン...
ブウーウウーン
VROOOOOOM

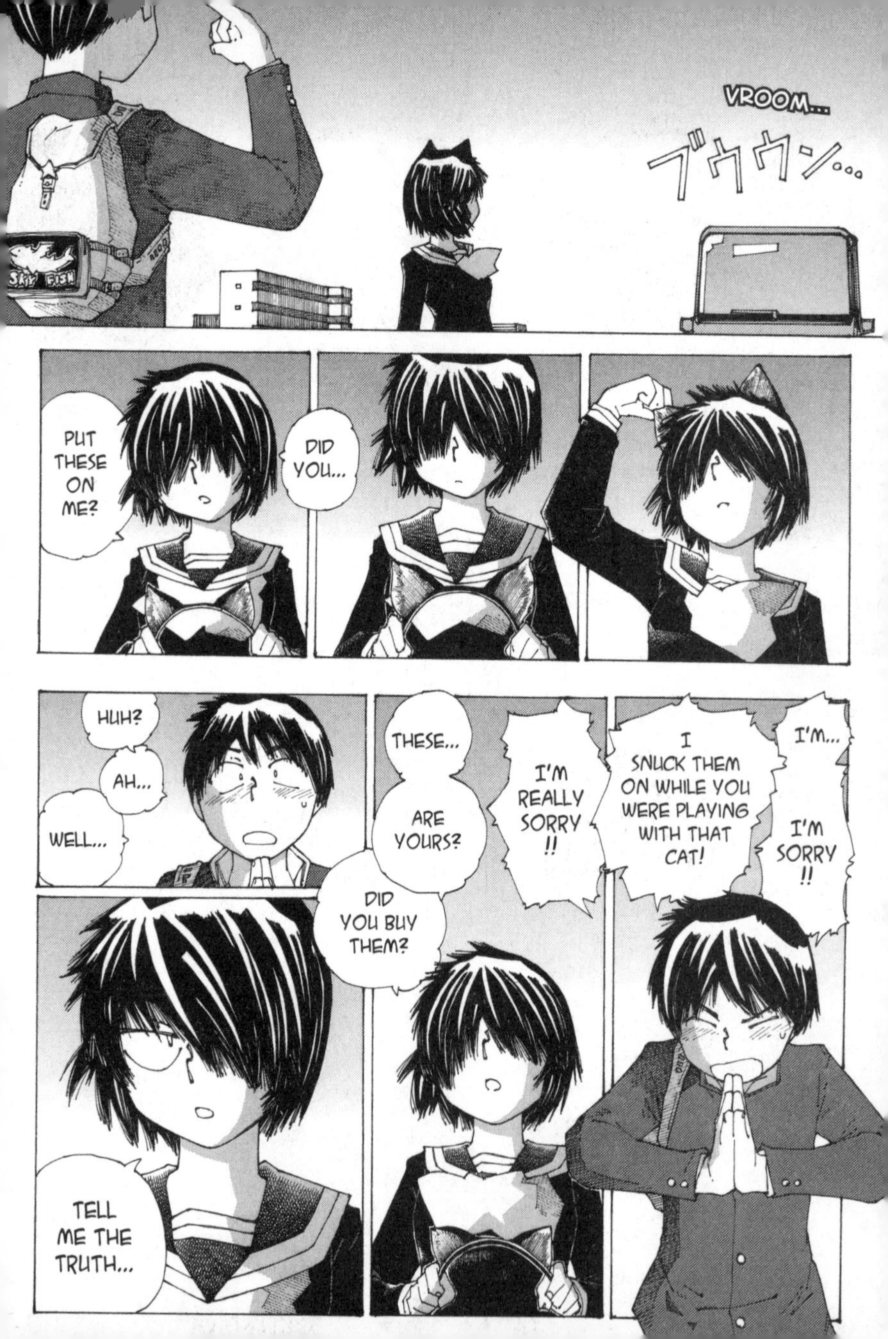
VROOM...
ブウウン…
DID YOU...
PUT THESE ON ME?
I'M...
I'M SORRY!!
I SNUCK THEM ON WHILE YOU WERE PLAYING WITH THAT CAT!
I'M REALLY SORRY!!
THESE...
ARE YOURS?
DID YOU BUY THEM?
HUH?
AH...
WELL...
TELL ME THE TRUTH...

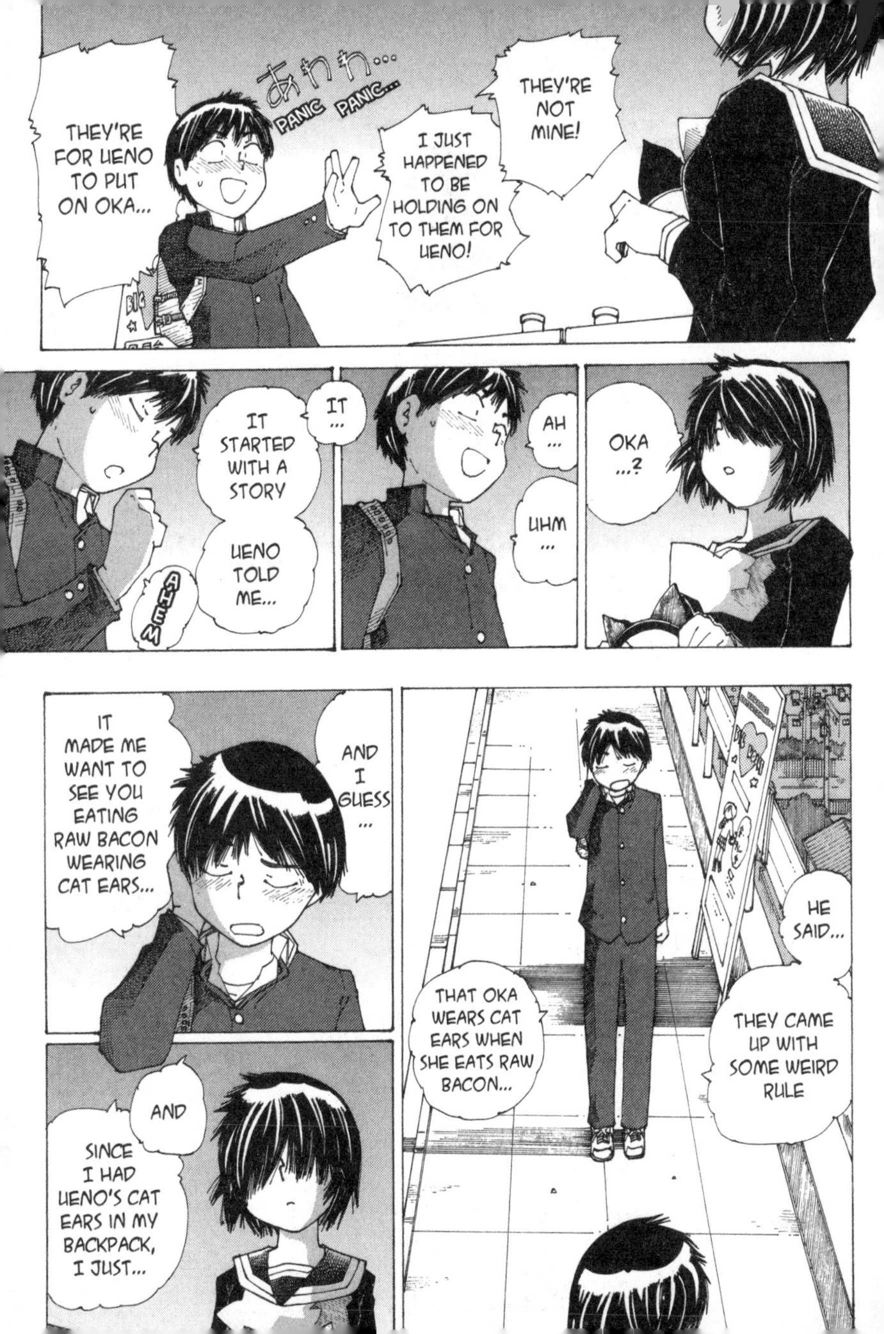
THEY'RE NOT MINE!
I JUST HAPPENED TO BE HOLDING ON TO THEM FOR UENO!
あれれ…
PANIC PANIC...
THEY'RE FOR UENO TO PUT ON OKA...
OKA ...?
AH ...
UHM ...
IT ...
IT STARTED WITH A STORY
UENO TOLD ME...
AHEM
HE SAID...
THAT OKA WEARS CAT EARS WHEN SHE EATS RAW BACON...
THEY CAME UP WITH SOME WEIRD RULE
AND I GUESS ...
IT MADE ME WANT TO SEE YOU EATING RAW BACON WEARING CAT EARS...
AND
SINCE I HAD UENO'S CAT EARS IN MY BACKPACK, I JUST...

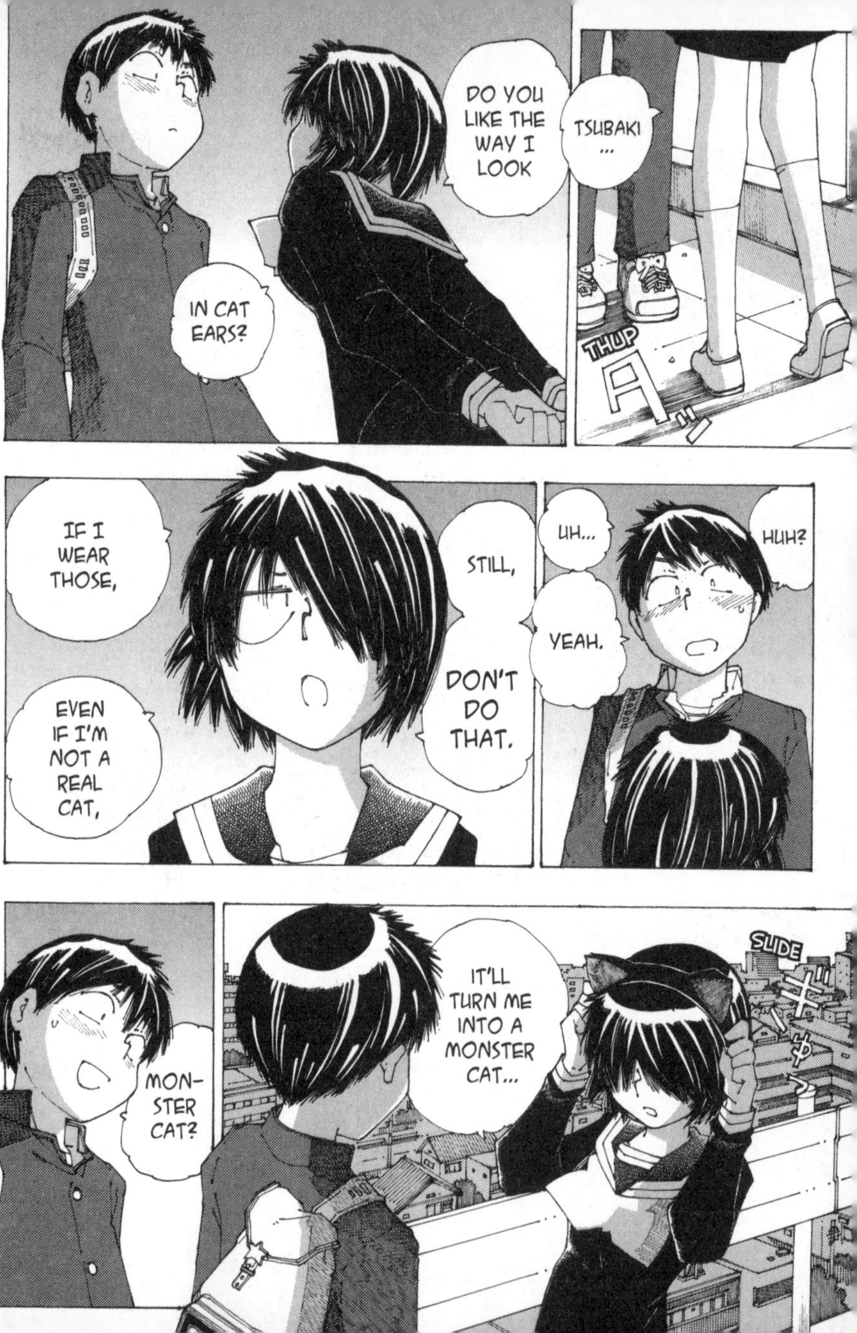
TSUBAKI ...
THUP
DO YOU LIKE THE WAY I LOOK
IN CAT EARS?
HUH?
UH...
YEAH.
STILL,
DON'T DO THAT.
IF I WEAR THOSE,
EVEN IF I'M NOT A REAL CAT,
SLIDE
IT'LL TURN ME INTO A MONSTER CAT...
MON-STER CAT?

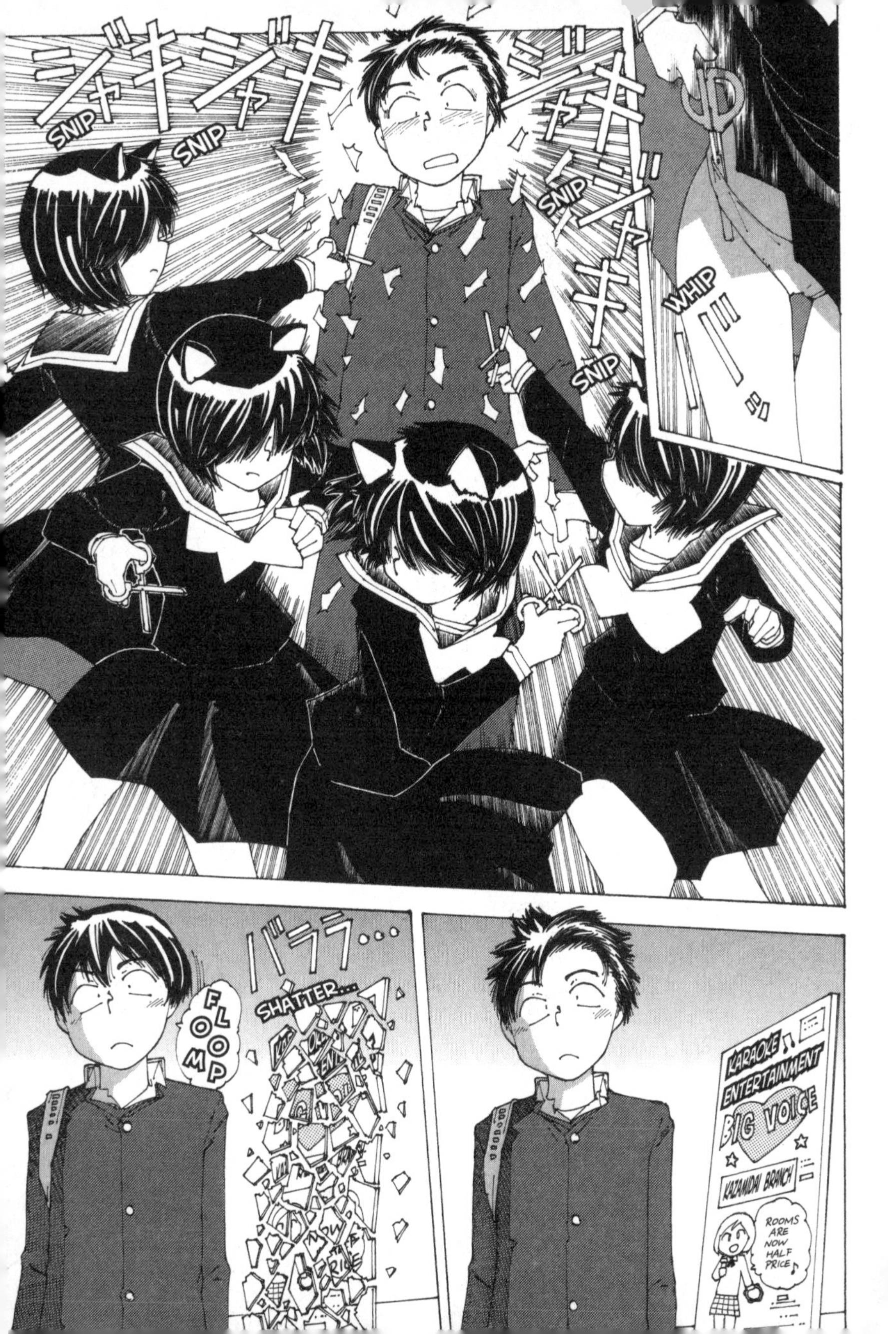

WHIP
SNIP
SNIP
SNIP
SNIP
ROOMS ARE NOW HALF PRICE
KARAOKE ENTERTAINMENT
BIG VOICE
KAZAMIDAI BRANCH
バララ…
SHATTER...
FLOOMP

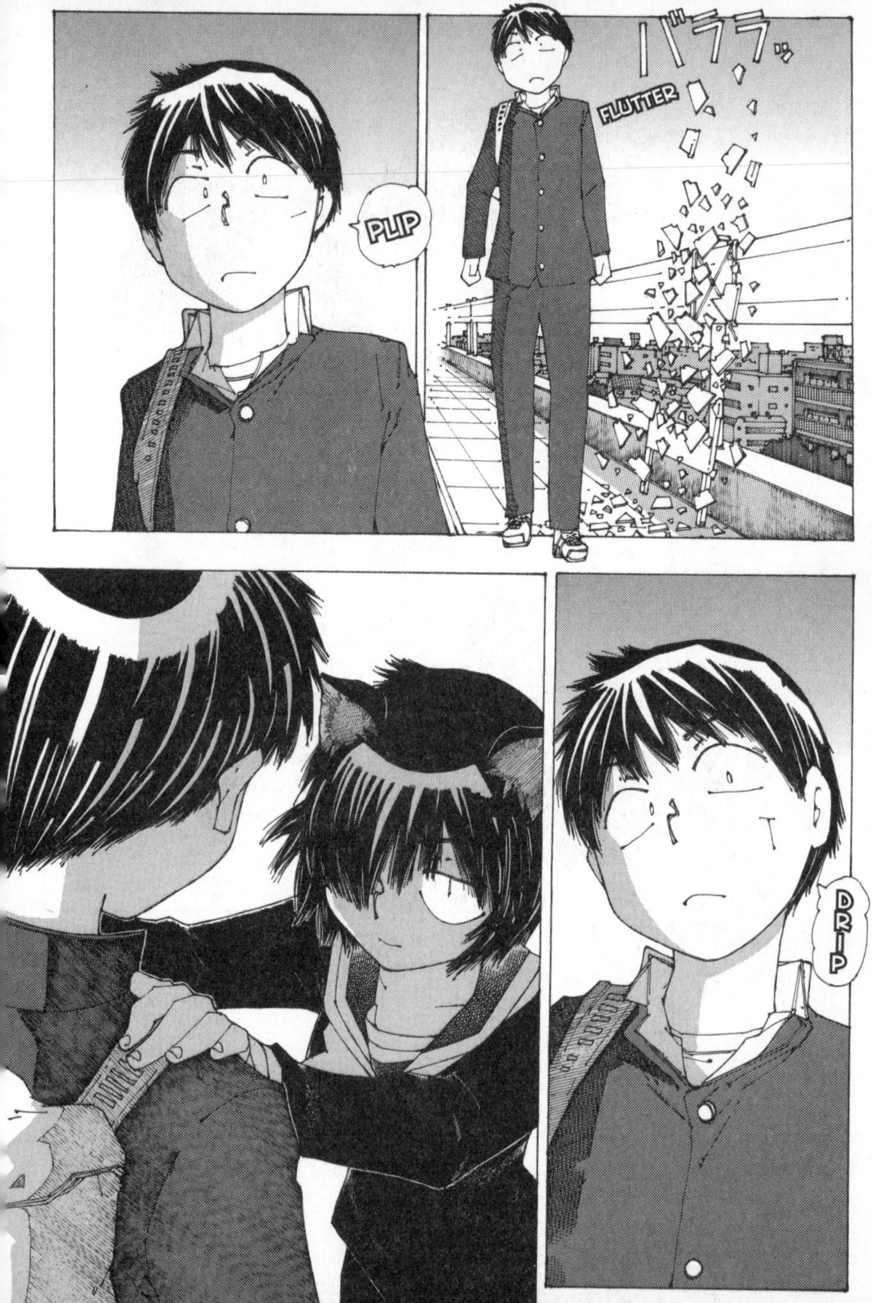
バララッ
FLUTTER
PLIP
DRIP

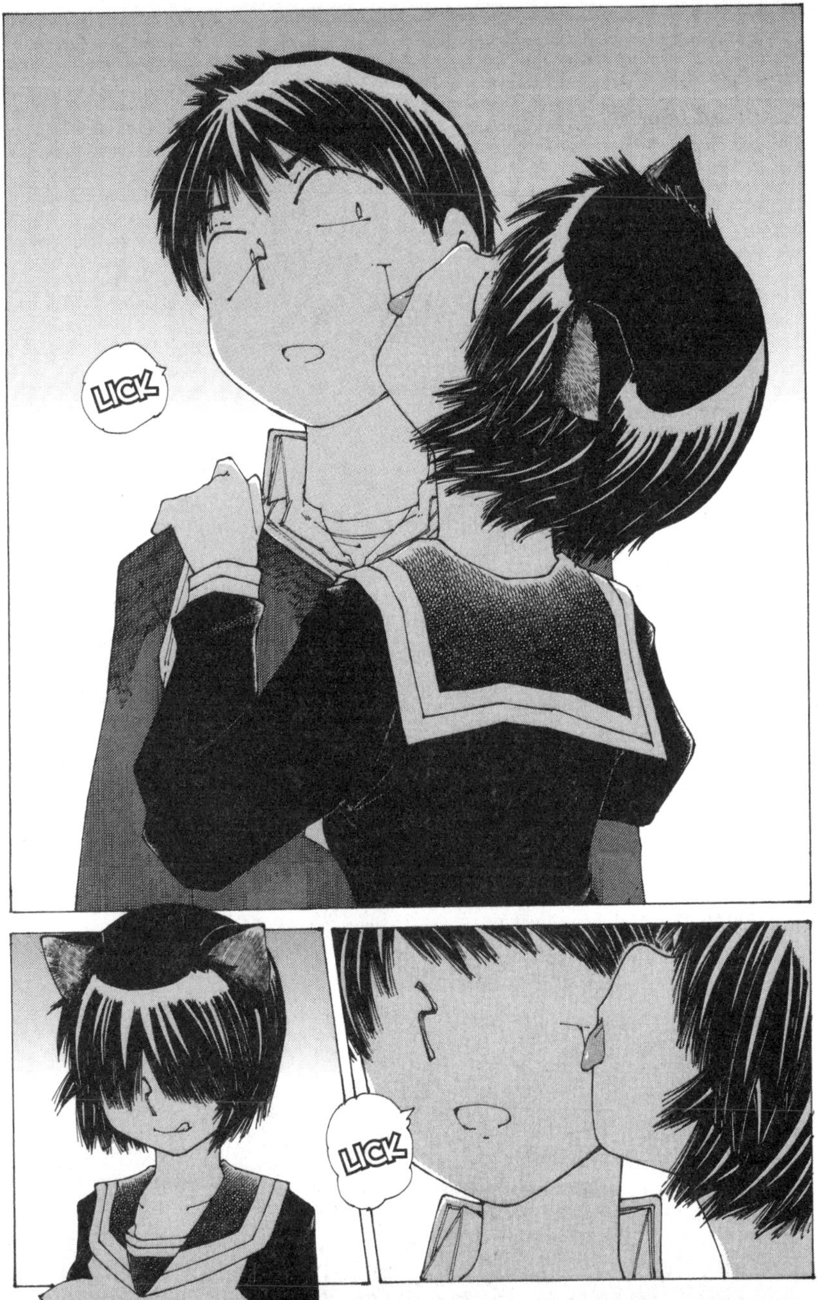
LICK
LICK

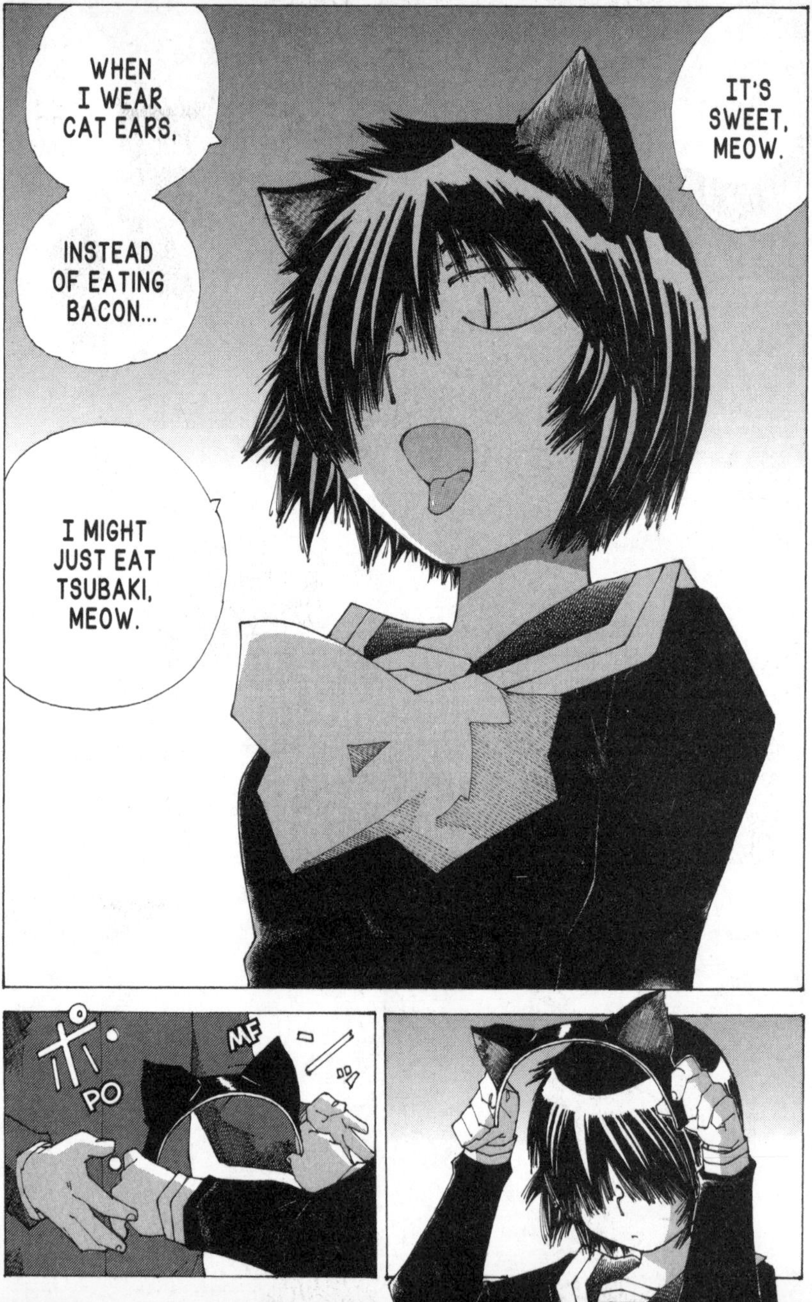
IT'S SWEET, MEOW.
WHEN I WEAR CAT EARS,
INSTEAD OF EATING BACON...
I MIGHT JUST EAT TSUBAKI, MEOW.
MF
PO

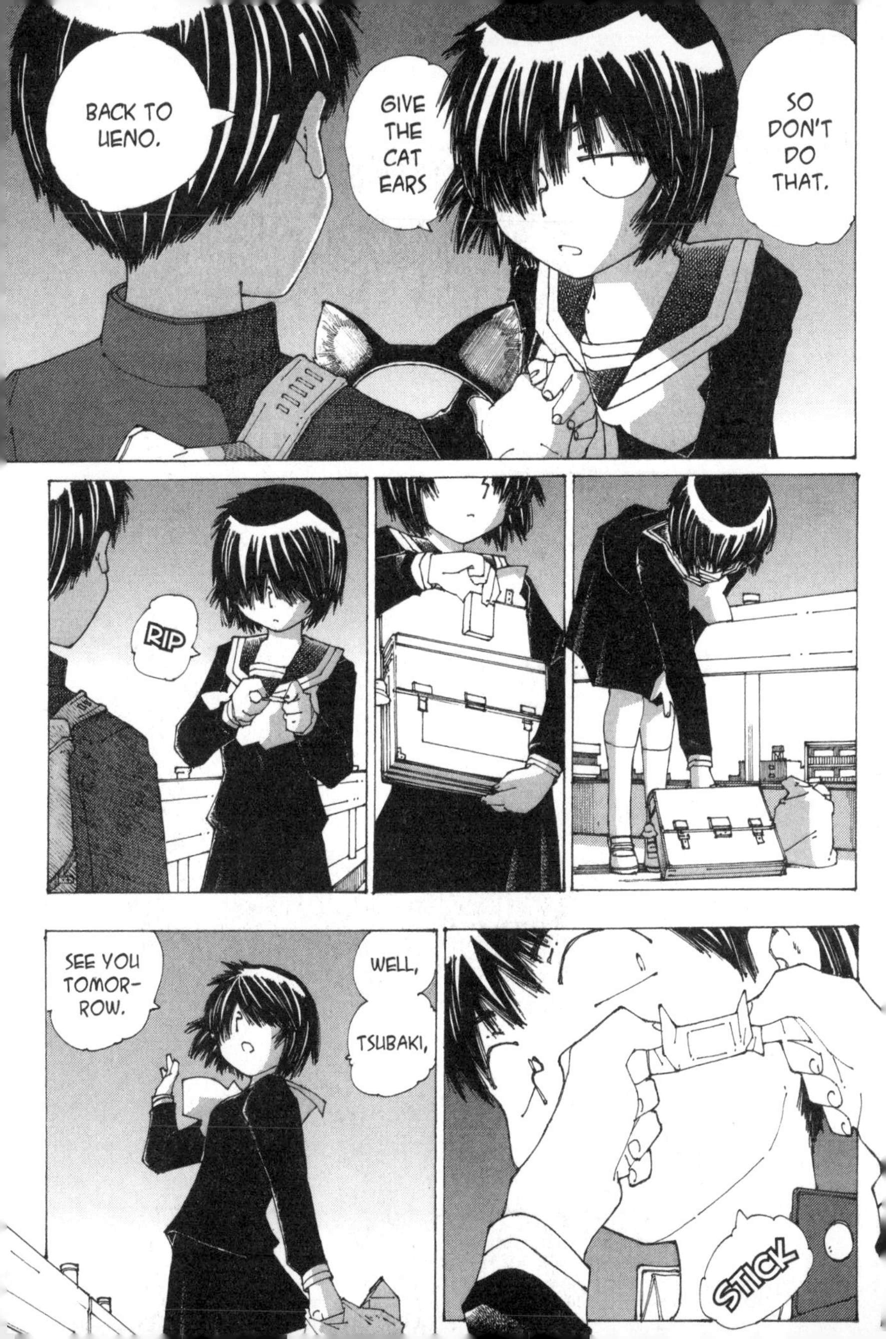
SO DON'T DO THAT.
GIVE THE CAT EARS
BACK TO UENO.
RIP
STICK
WELL,
TSUBAKI,
SEE YOU TOMOR-ROW.

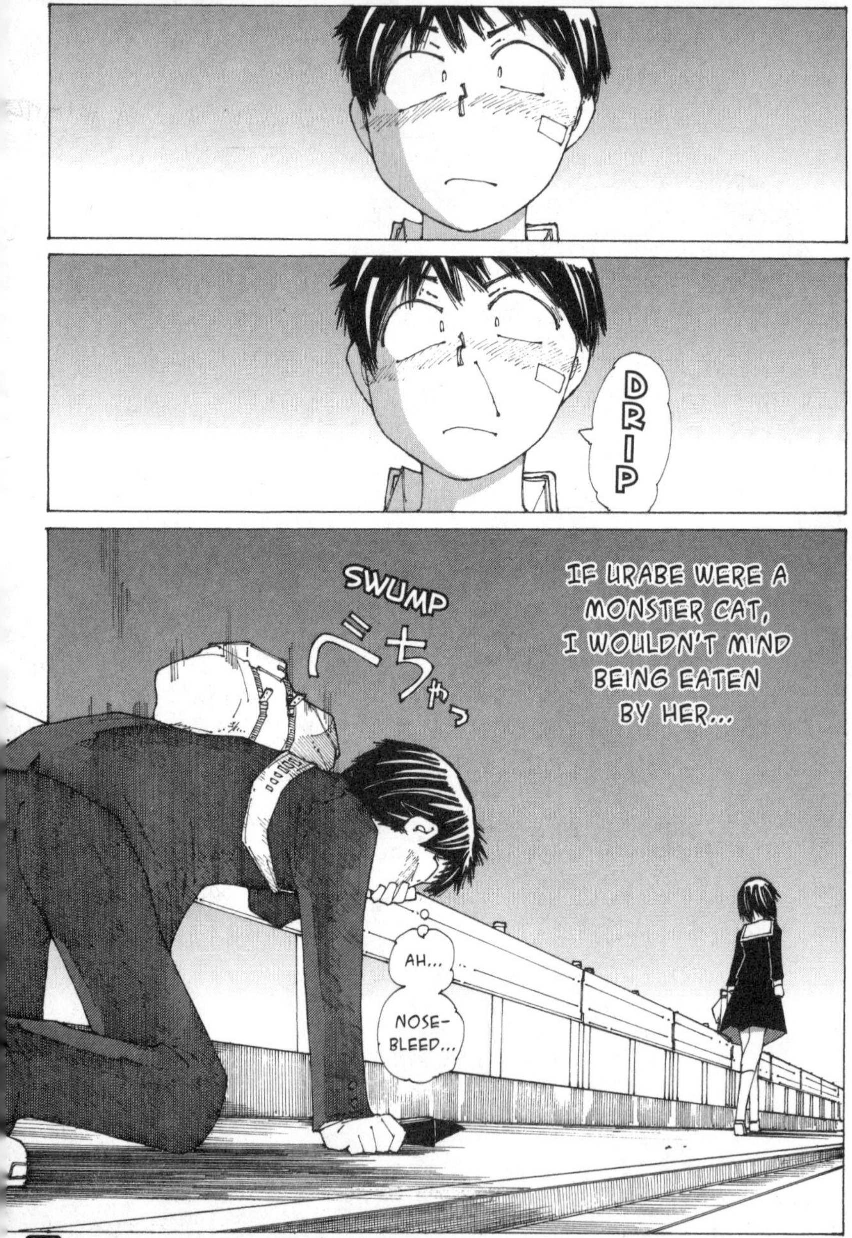
DRIP
IF URABE WERE A MONSTER CAT, I WOULDN'T MIND BEING EATEN BY HER...
SWUMP
べちゃっ
AH...
NOSE-BLEED...

END OF CHAPTER 50

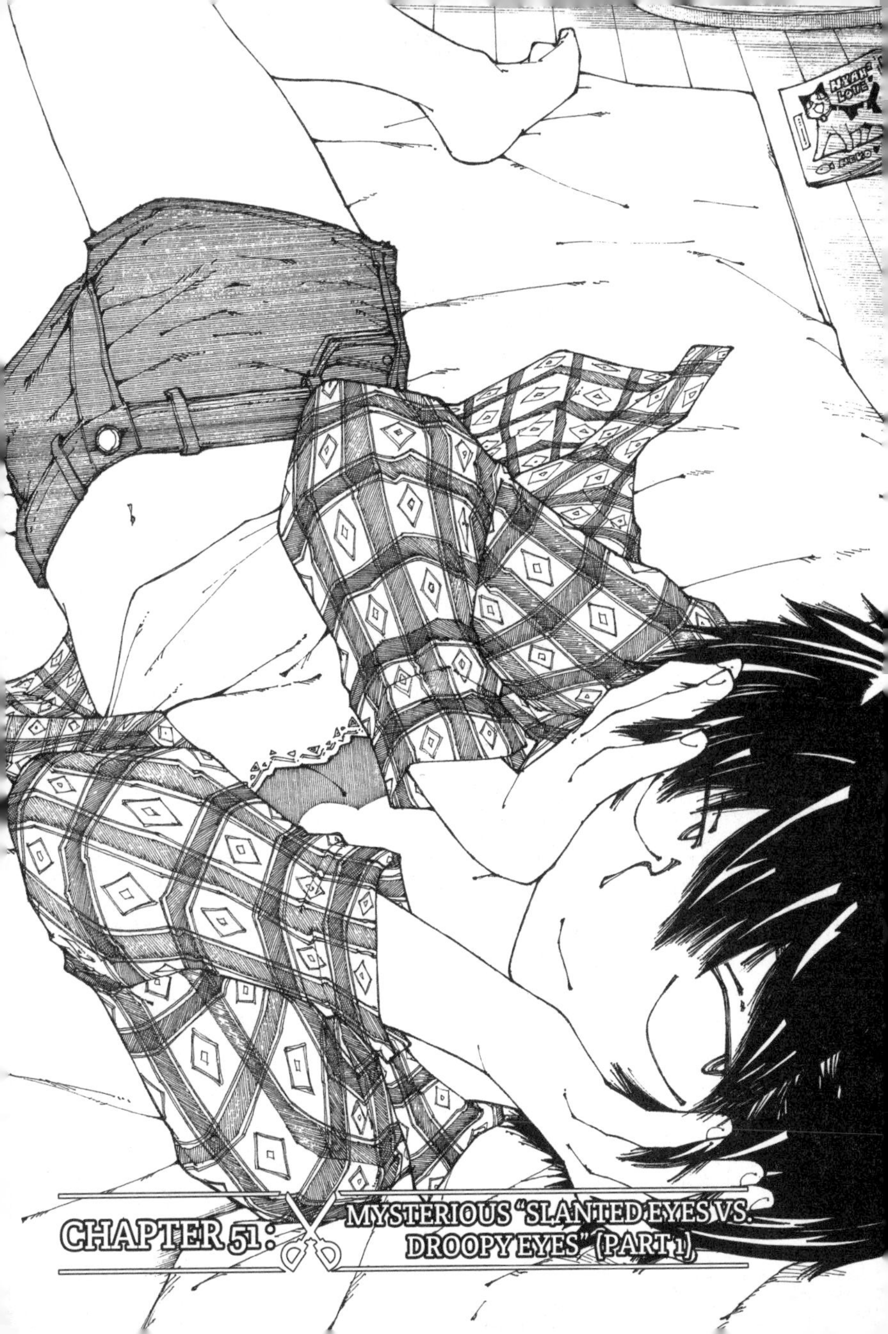

CHAPTER 51: MYSTERIOUS "SLANTED EYES VS. DROOPY EYES" (PART 1)

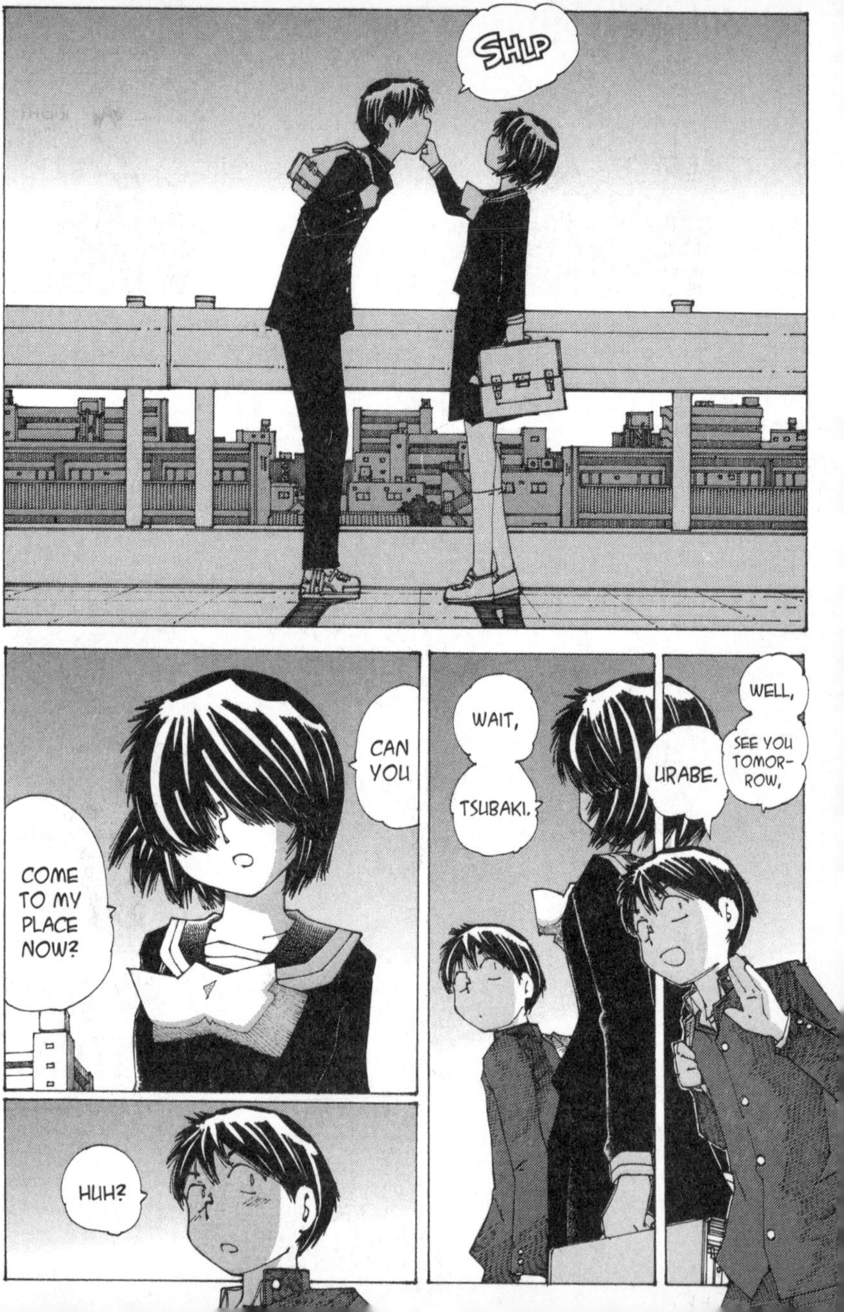
SHLP
WELL,
SEE YOU TOMOR-ROW,
URABE.
WAIT,
TSUBAKI.
CAN YOU
COME TO MY PLACE NOW?
HUH?

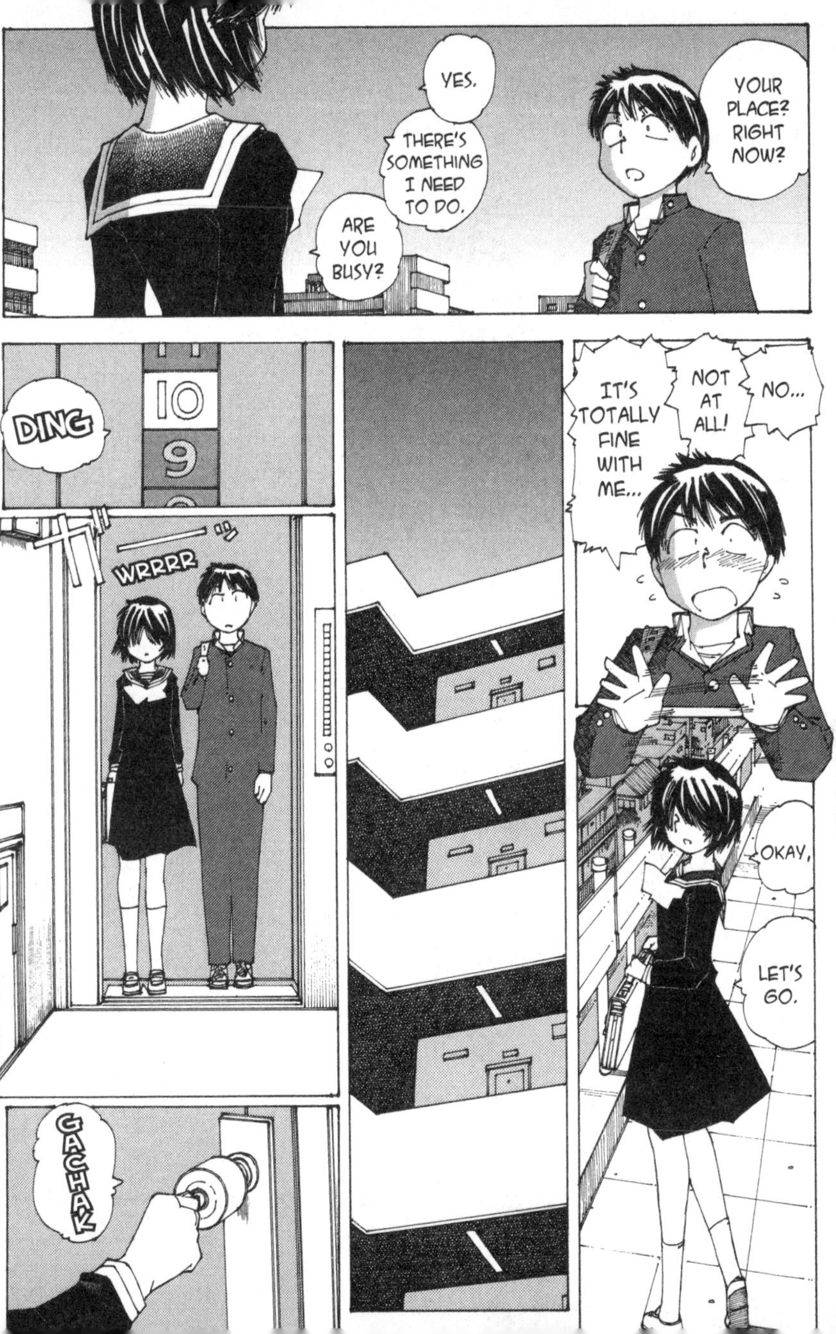
YOUR PLACE? RIGHT NOW?
YES.
THERE'S SOMETHING I NEED TO DO.
ARE YOU BUSY?
NO...
NOT AT ALL!
IT'S TOTALLY FINE WITH ME...
OKAY,
LET'S GO.
DING
10
9
WRRRR
GACHAK

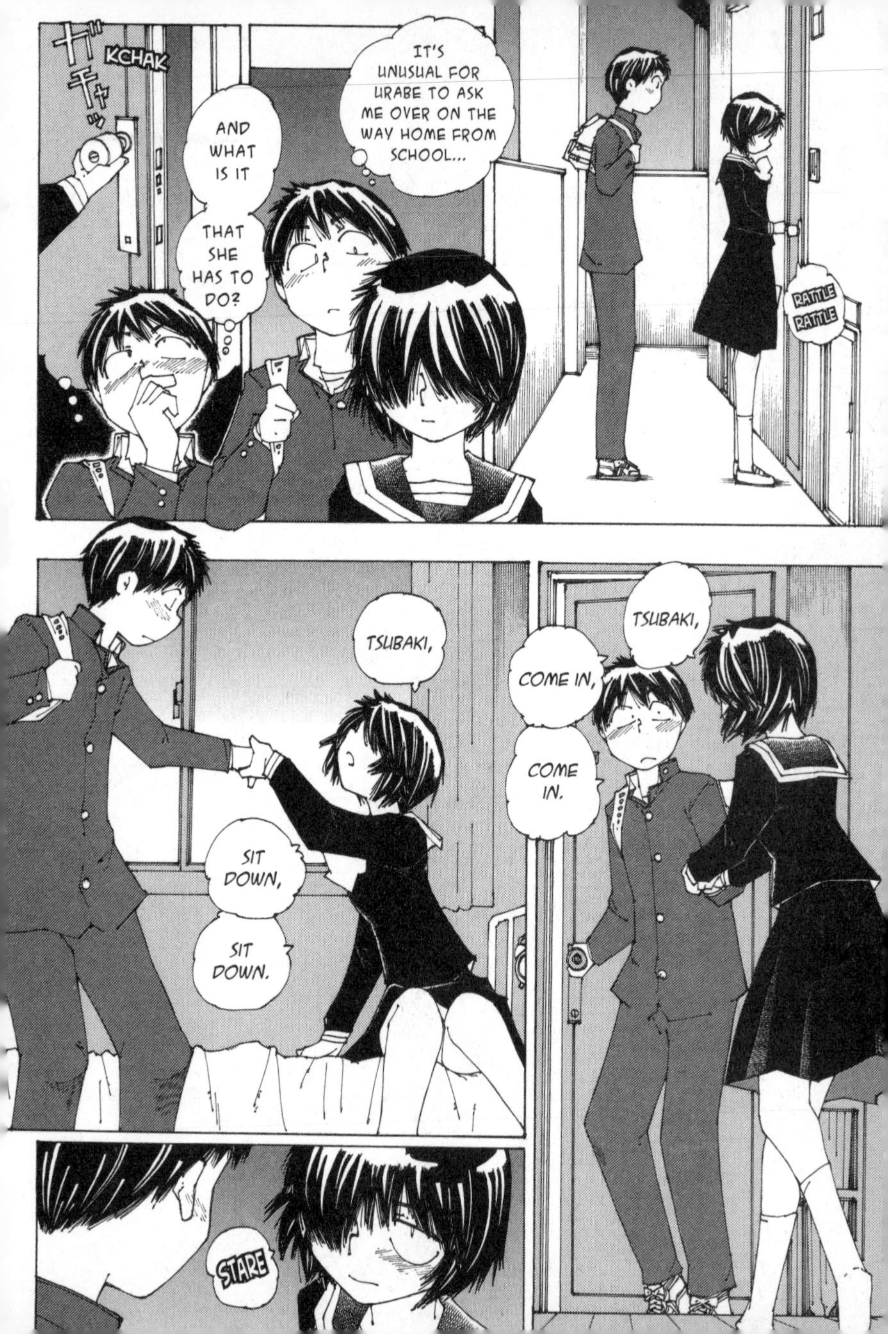
RATTLE RATTLE
IT'S UNUSUAL FOR URABE TO ASK ME OVER ON THE WAY HOME FROM SCHOOL...
AND WHAT IS IT
THAT SHE HAS TO DO?
ガチャッ
KCHAK
TSUBAKI,
COME IN,
COME IN.
TSUBAKI,
SIT DOWN,
SIT DOWN.
STARE

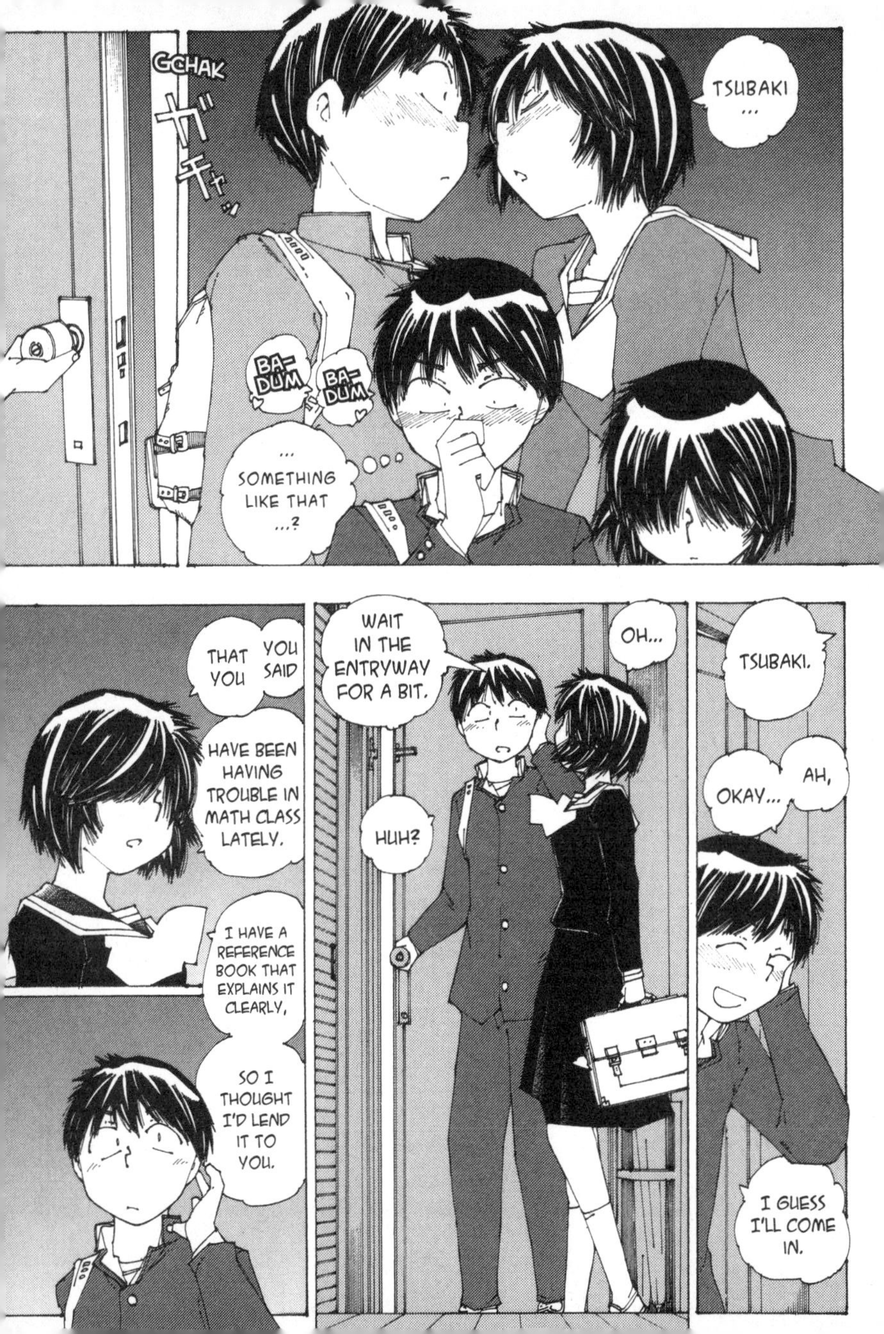
TSUBAKI ...
GCHAK
ガチャッ
BA-DUM
BA-DUM
... SOMETHING LIKE THAT ...?
TSUBAKI.
AH, OKAY...
I GUESS I'LL COME IN.
OH...
WAIT IN THE ENTRYWAY FOR A BIT.
HUH?
YOU SAID THAT YOU
HAVE BEEN HAVING TROUBLE IN MATH CLASS LATELY.
I HAVE A REFERENCE BOOK THAT EXPLAINS IT CLEARLY,
SO I THOUGHT I'D LEND IT TO YOU.

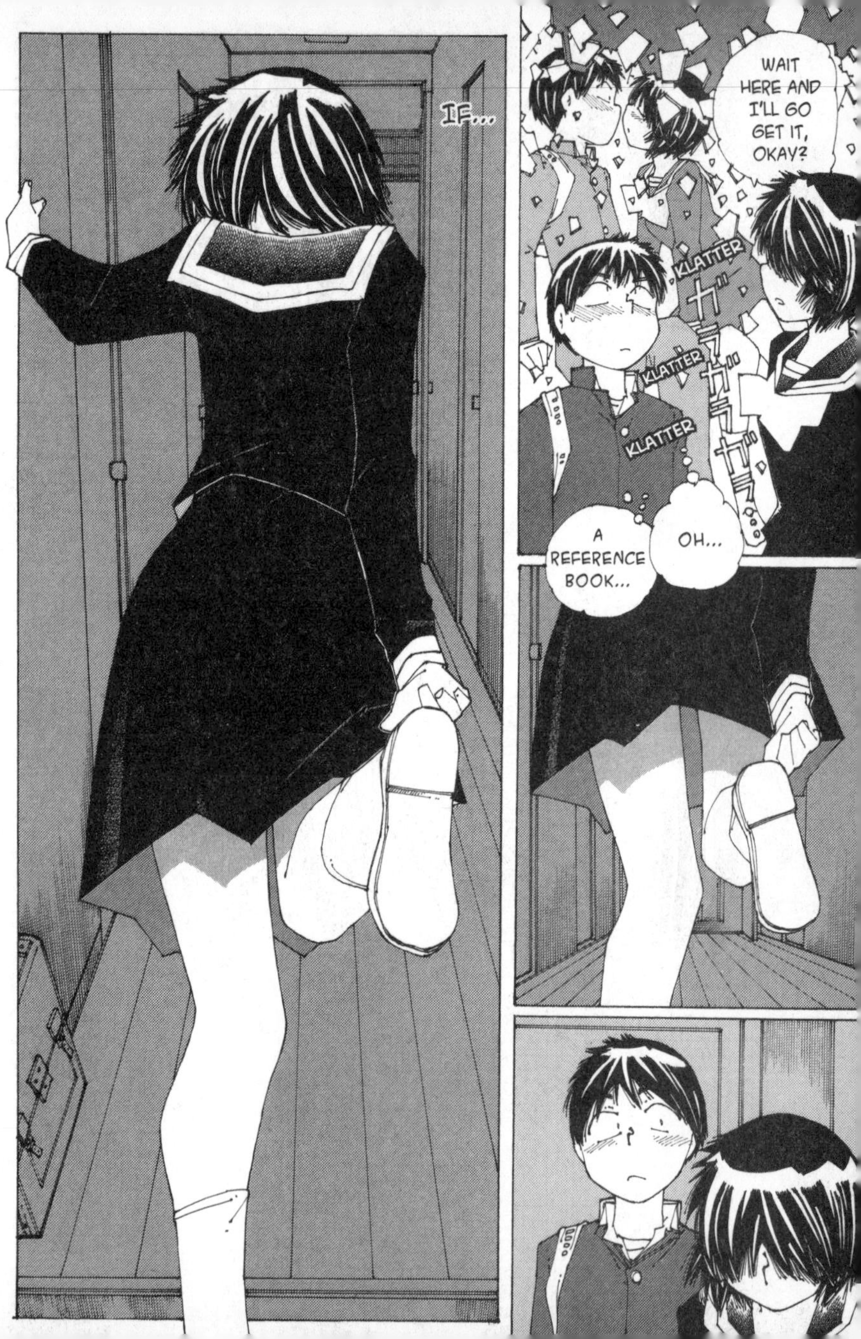
WAIT HERE AND I'LL GO GET IT, OKAY?
KLATTER
KLATTER
KLATTER
ガラガラガラ
OH...
A REFERENCE BOOK...
IF...

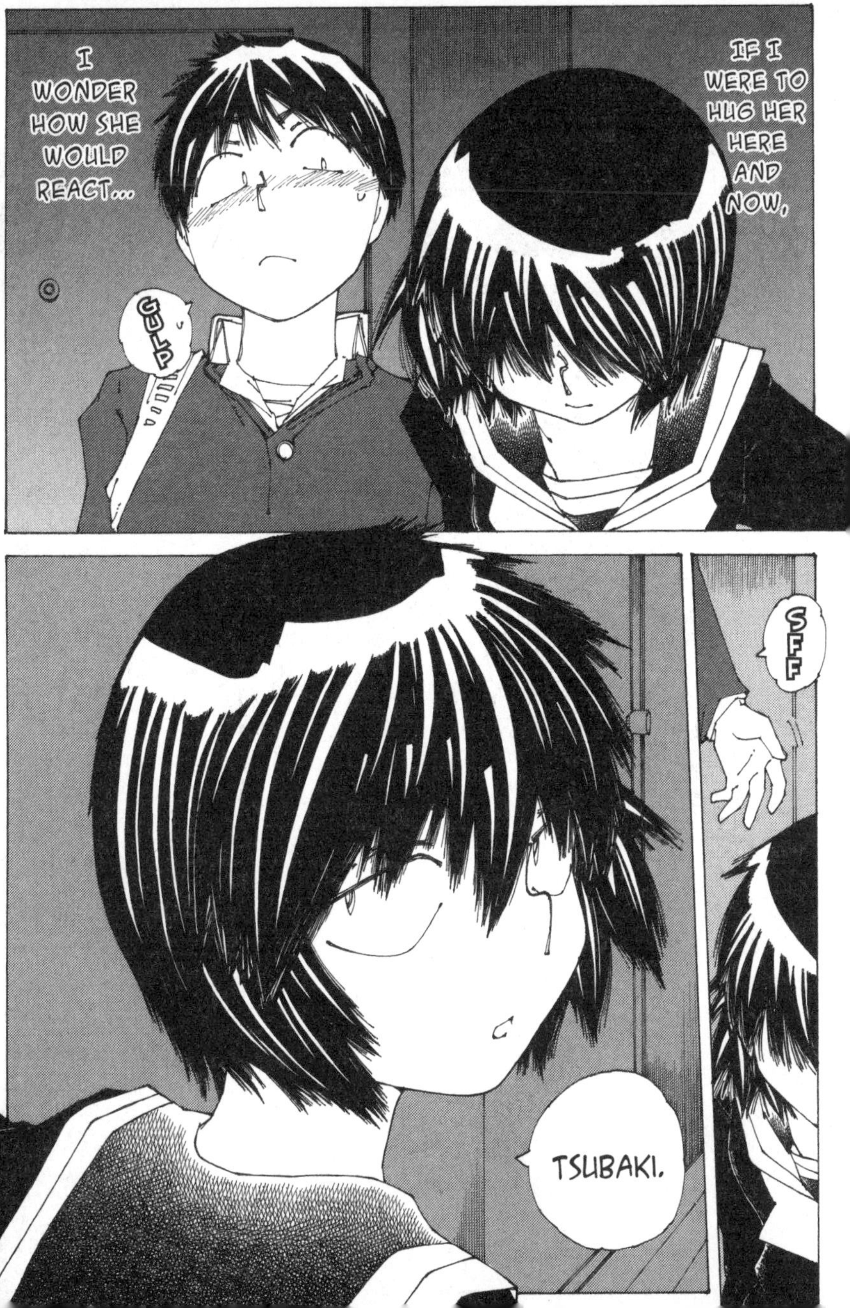
IF I WERE TO HUG HER HERE AND NOW,
I WONDER HOW SHE WOULD REACT...
GULP
SFF
TSUBAKI.

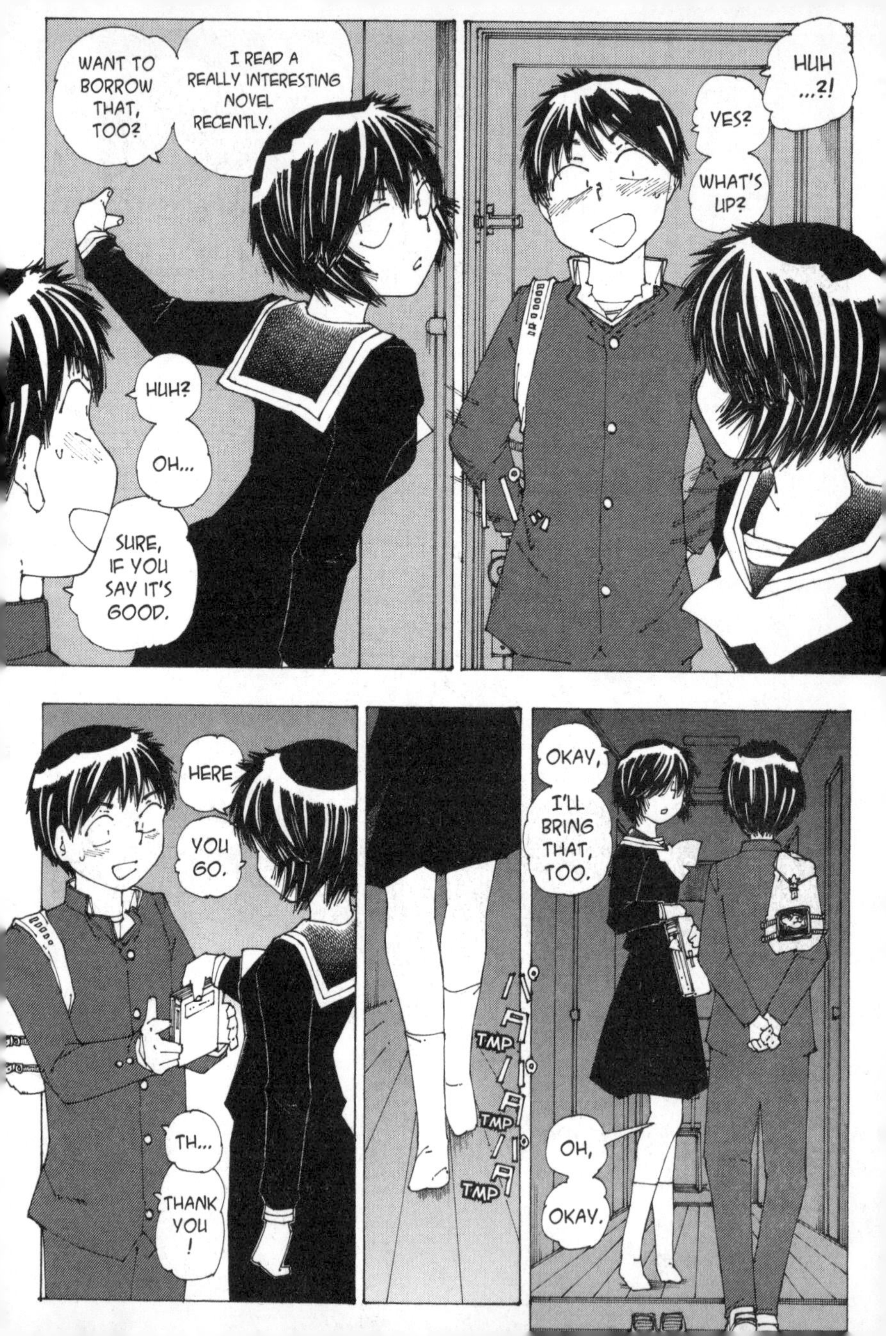
HUH ...?!
YES?
WHAT'S UP?
I READ A REALLY INTERESTING NOVEL RECENTLY.
WANT TO BORROW THAT, TOO?
HUH?
OH...
SURE, IF YOU SAY IT'S GOOD.
OKAY,
I'LL BRING THAT, TOO.
OH,
OKAY.
TMP
TMP
TMP
HERE
YOU GO.
TH...
THANK YOU!

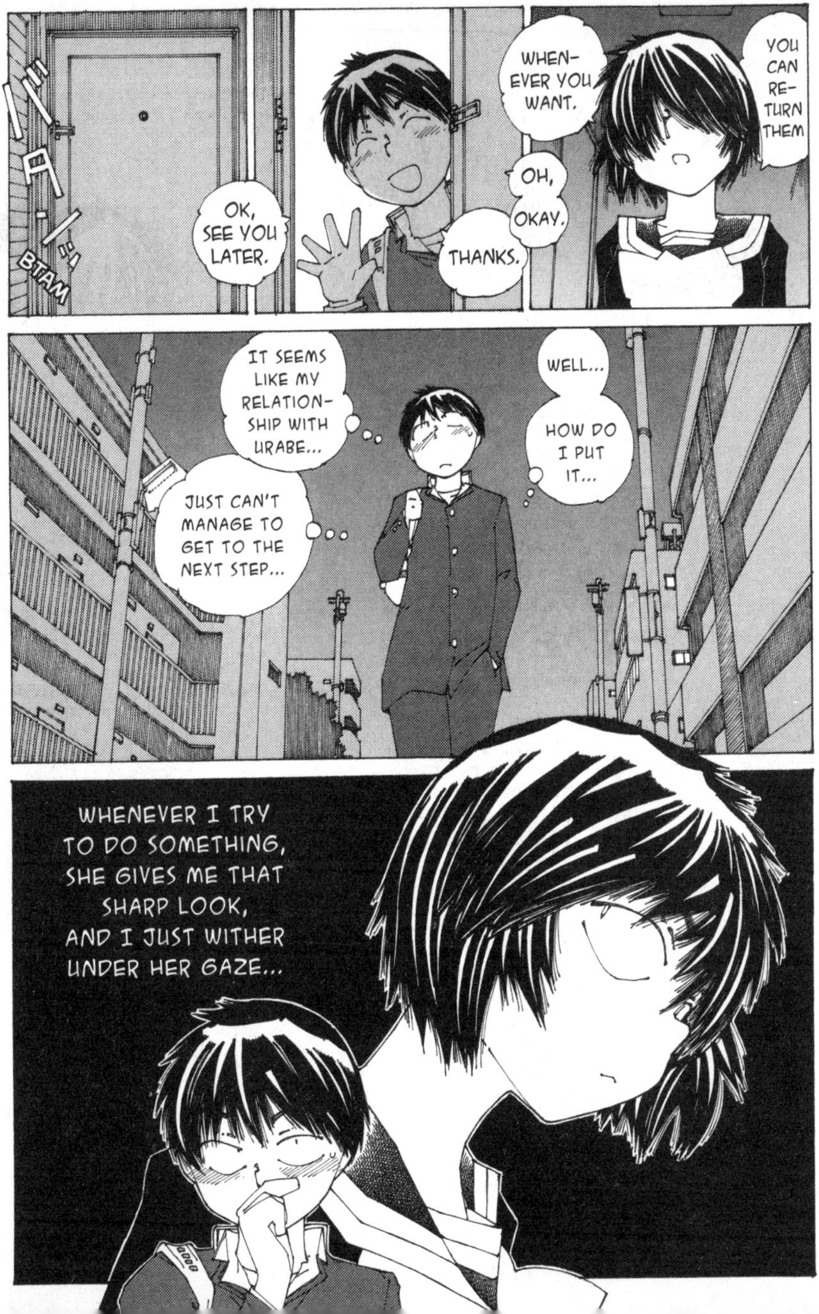
YOU CAN RE-TURN THEM
WHEN-EVER YOU WANT.
OH, OKAY.
THANKS.
OK, SEE YOU LATER.
BTAM
WELL...
HOW DO I PUT IT...
IT SEEMS LIKE MY RELATION-SHIP WITH URABE...
JUST CAN'T MANAGE TO GET TO THE NEXT STEP...
WHENEVER I TRY TO DO SOMETHING, SHE GIVES ME THAT SHARP LOOK, AND I JUST WITHER UNDER HER GAZE...

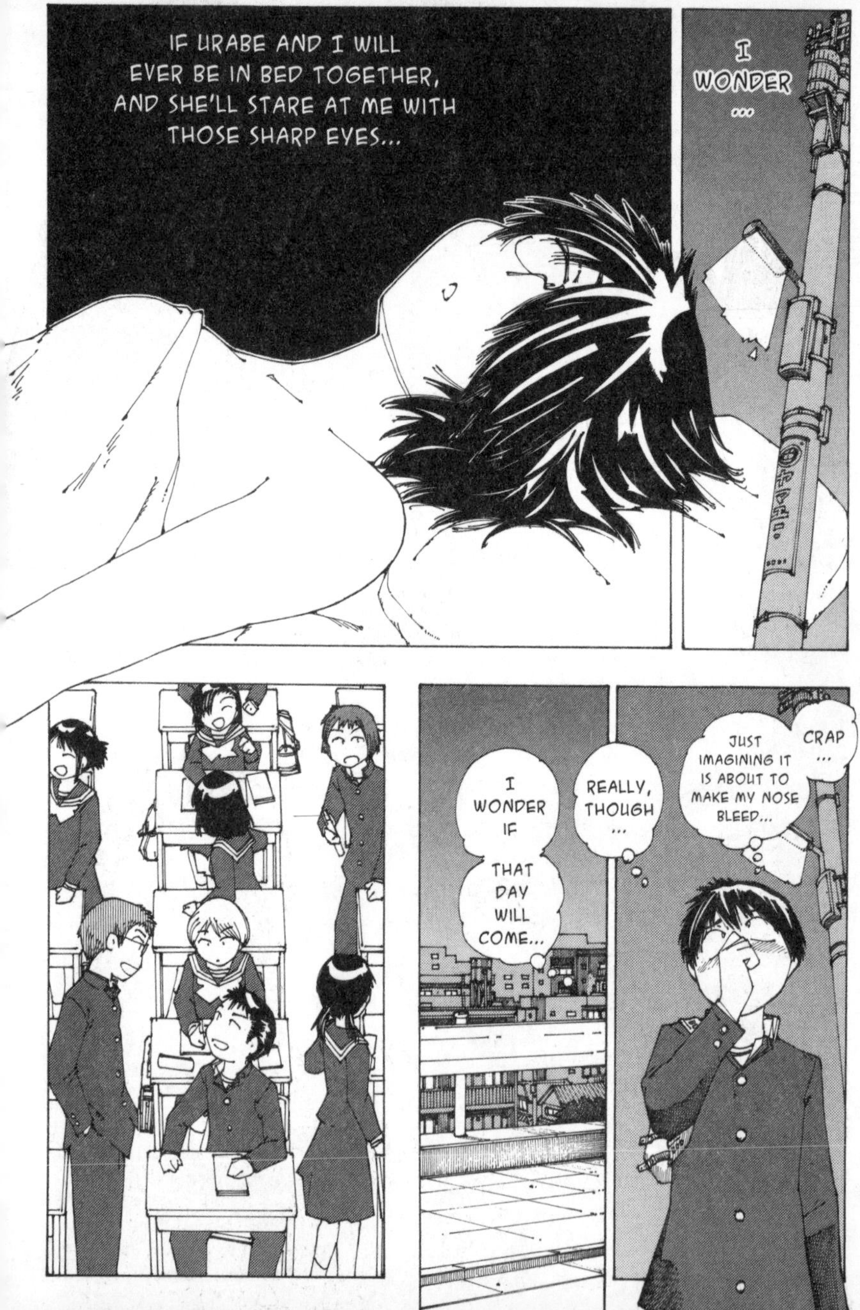
I WONDER ...
IF URABE AND I WILL EVER BE IN BED TOGETHER, AND SHE'LL STARE AT ME WITH THOSE SHARP EYES...
CRAP ...
JUST IMAGINING IT IS ABOUT TO MAKE MY NOSE BLEED...
REALLY, THOUGH ...
I WONDER IF THAT DAY WILL COME...

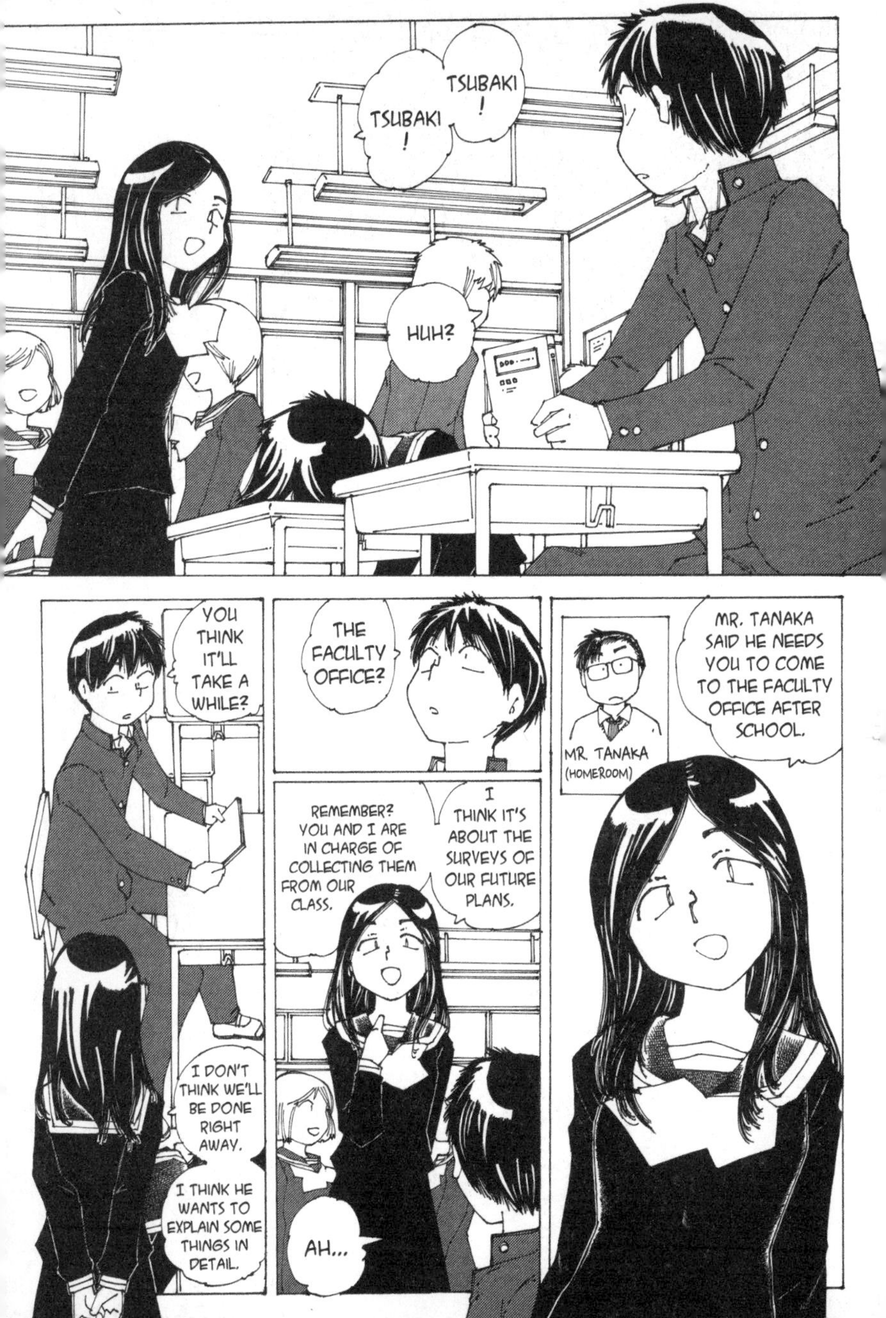
TSUBAKI!
TSUBAKI!
HUH?
MR. TANAKA SAID HE NEEDS YOU TO COME TO THE FACULTY OFFICE AFTER SCHOOL.
MR. TANAKA (HOMEROOM)
THE FACULTY OFFICE?
I THINK IT'S ABOUT THE SURVEYS OF OUR FUTURE PLANS.
REMEMBER? YOU AND I ARE IN CHARGE OF COLLECTING THEM FROM OUR CLASS.
AH...
YOU THINK IT'LL TAKE A WHILE?
I DON'T THINK WE'LL BE DONE RIGHT AWAY.
I THINK HE WANTS TO EXPLAIN SOME THINGS IN DETAIL.

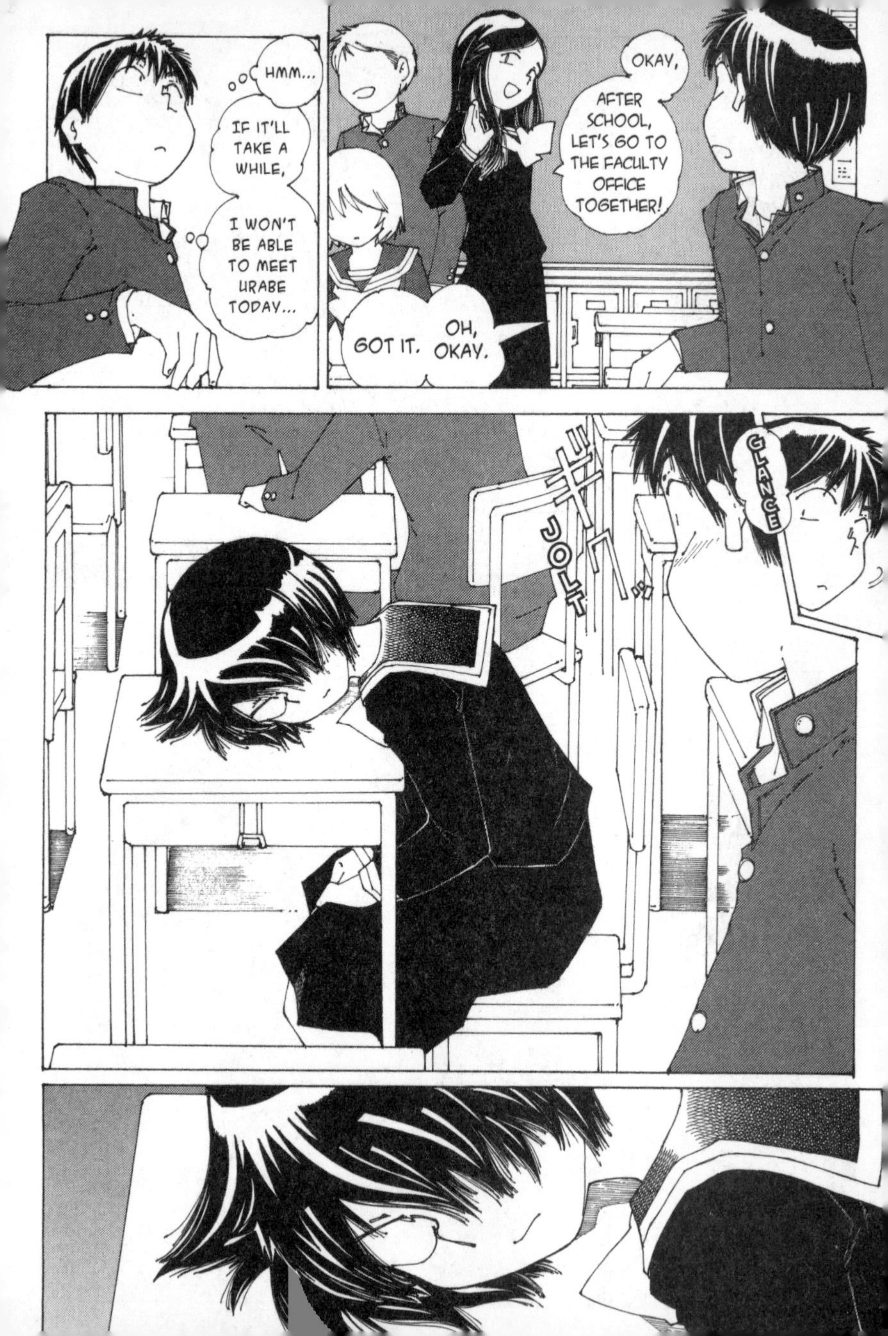
OKAY,
AFTER SCHOOL, LET'S GO TO THE FACULTY OFFICE TOGETHER!
OH, OKAY.
GOT IT.
HMM...
IF IT'LL TAKE A WHILE,
I WON'T BE ABLE TO MEET URABE TODAY...
GLANCE
JOLT

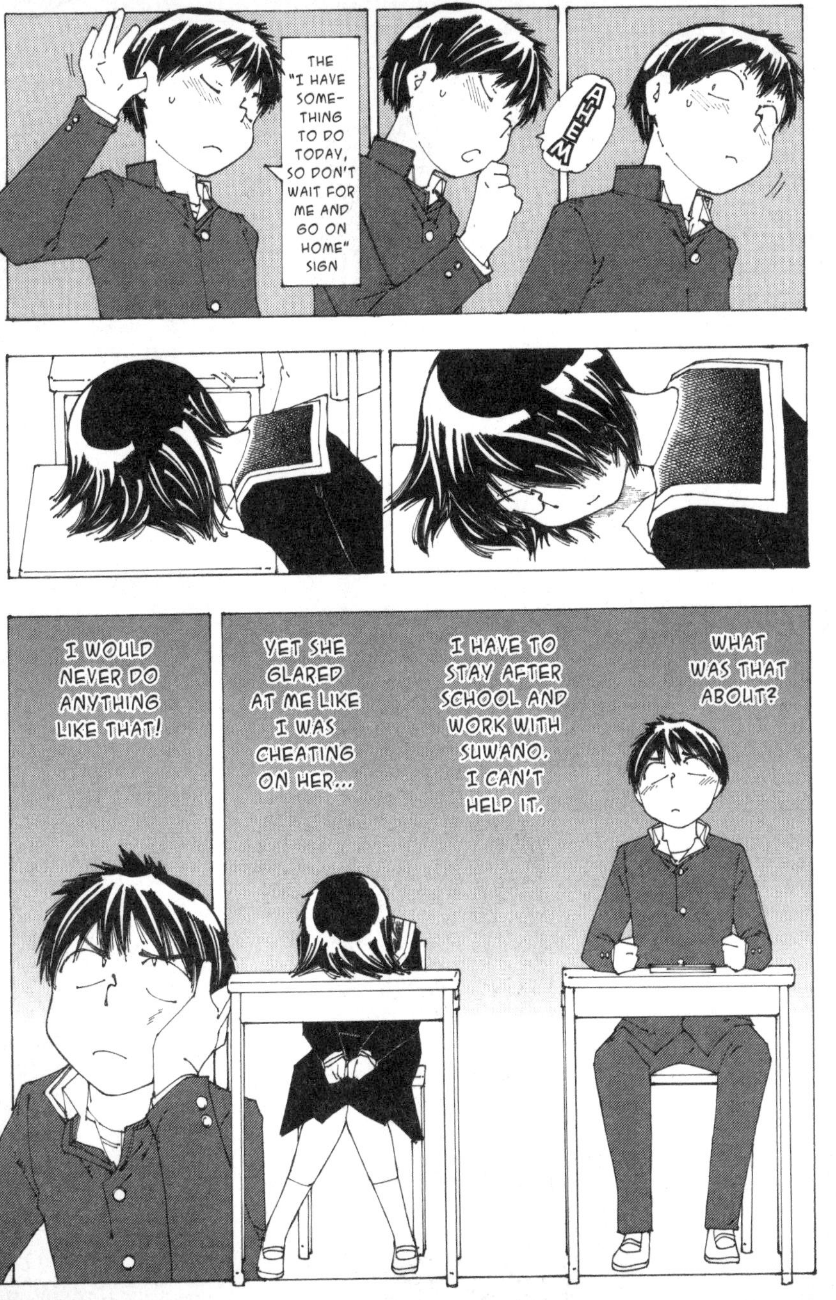
AHEM
THE "I HAVE SOMETHING TO DO TODAY, SO DON'T WAIT FOR ME AND GO ON HOME" SIGN
WHAT WAS THAT ABOUT?
I HAVE TO STAY AFTER SCHOOL AND WORK WITH SUWANO. I CAN'T HELP IT.
YET SHE GLARED AT ME LIKE I WAS CHEATING ON HER...
I WOULD NEVER DO ANYTHING LIKE THAT!

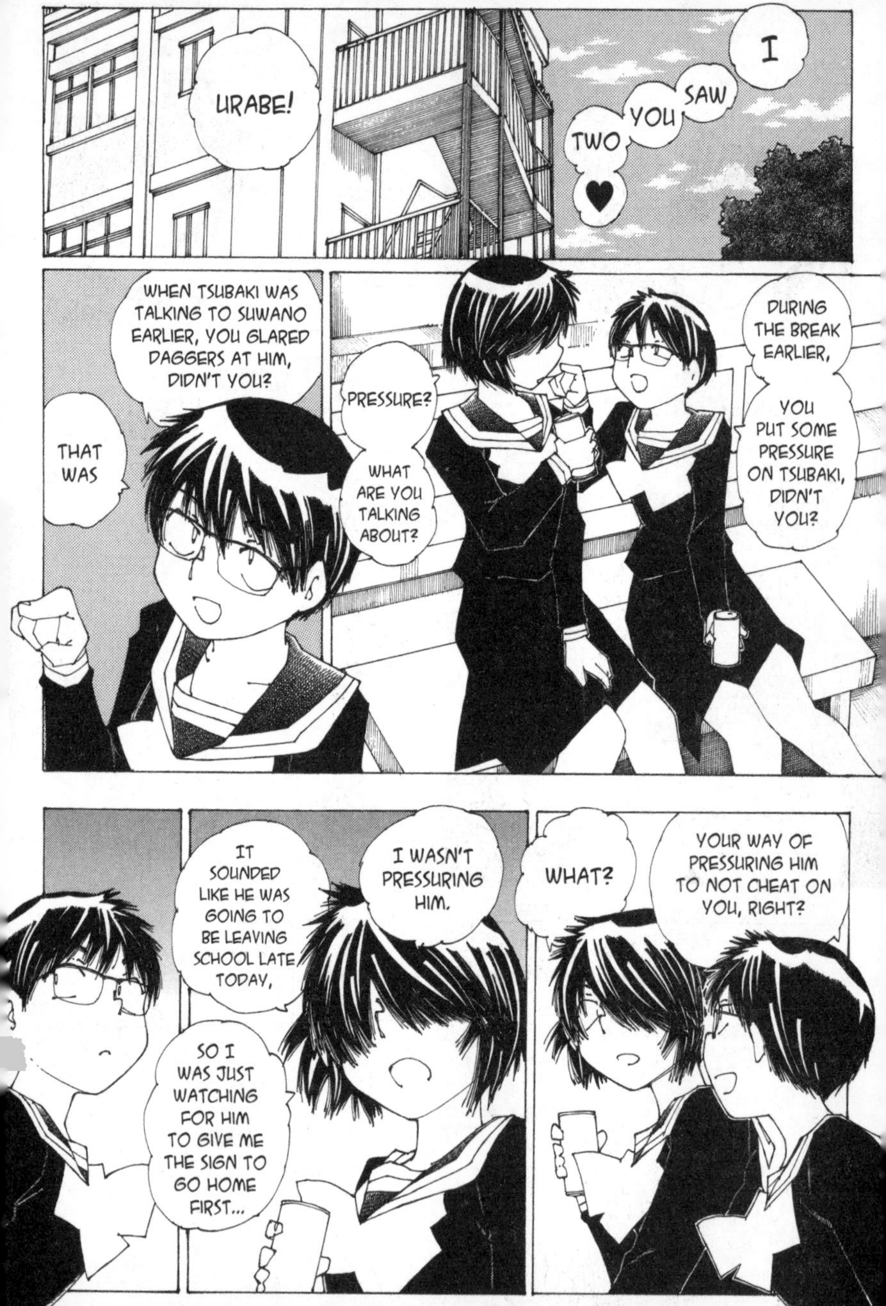
I SAW YOU TWO ♥
URABE!
DURING THE BREAK EARLIER,
YOU PUT SOME PRESSURE ON TSUBAKI, DIDN'T YOU?
PRESSURE?
WHAT ARE YOU TALKING ABOUT?
WHEN TSUBAKI WAS TALKING TO SUWANO EARLIER, YOU GLARED DAGGERS AT HIM, DIDN'T YOU?
THAT WAS
YOUR WAY OF PRESSURING HIM TO NOT CHEAT ON YOU, RIGHT?
WHAT?
I WASN'T PRESSURING HIM.
IT SOUNDED LIKE HE WAS GOING TO BE LEAVING SCHOOL LATE TODAY,
SO I WAS JUST WATCHING FOR HIM TO GIVE ME THE SIGN TO GO HOME FIRST...

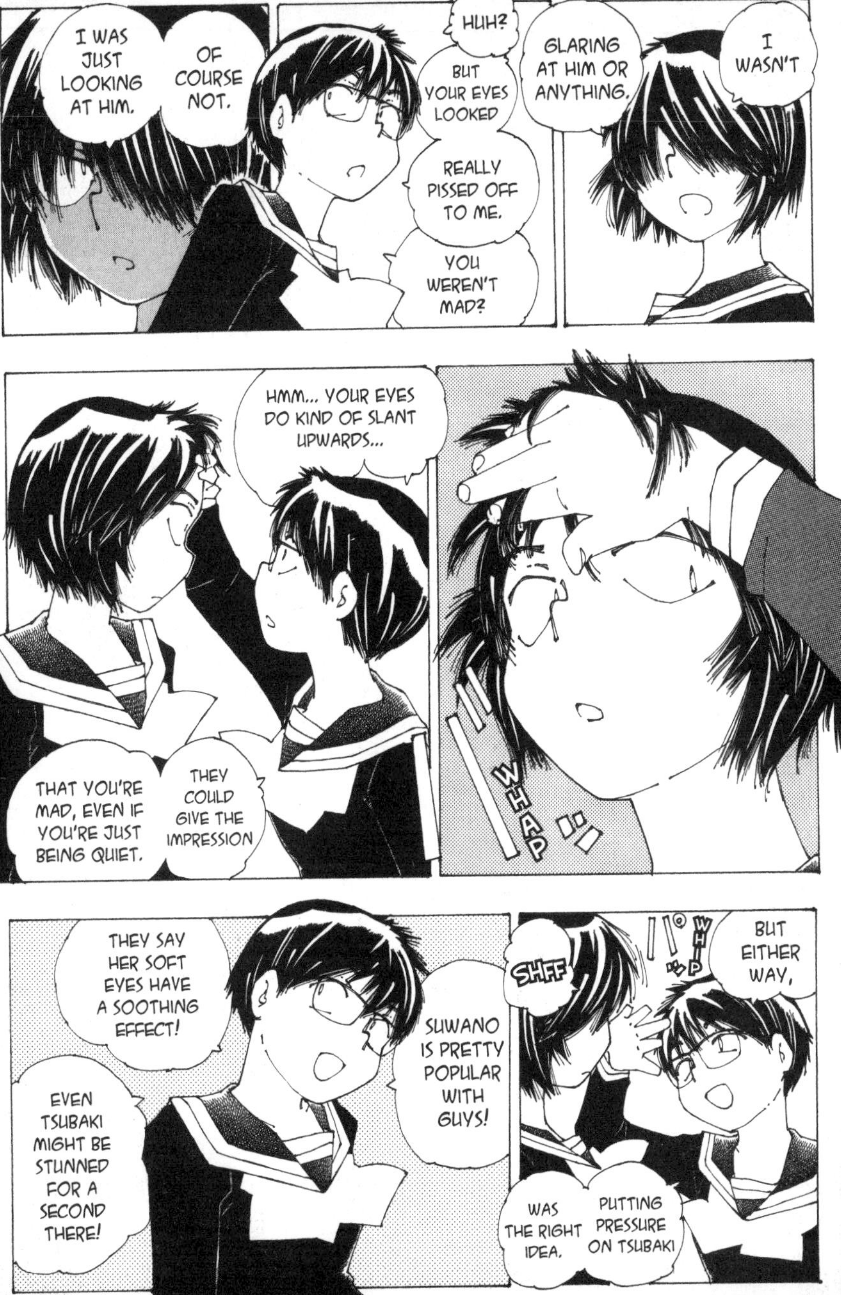

I WASN'T
GLARING AT HIM OR ANYTHING.
HUH?
BUT YOUR EYES LOOKED
REALLY PISSED OFF TO ME.
YOU WEREN'T MAD?
OF COURSE NOT.
I WAS JUST LOOKING AT HIM.
WHAP
HMM... YOUR EYES DO KIND OF SLANT UPWARDS...
THEY COULD GIVE THE IMPRESSION
THAT YOU'RE MAD, EVEN IF YOU'RE JUST BEING QUIET.
BUT EITHER WAY,
WHIP
SHFF
PUTTING PRESSURE ON TSUBAKI
WAS THE RIGHT IDEA.
SUWANO IS PRETTY POPULAR WITH GUYS!
THEY SAY HER SOFT EYES HAVE A SOOTHING EFFECT!
EVEN TSUBAKI MIGHT BE STUNNED FOR A SECOND THERE!

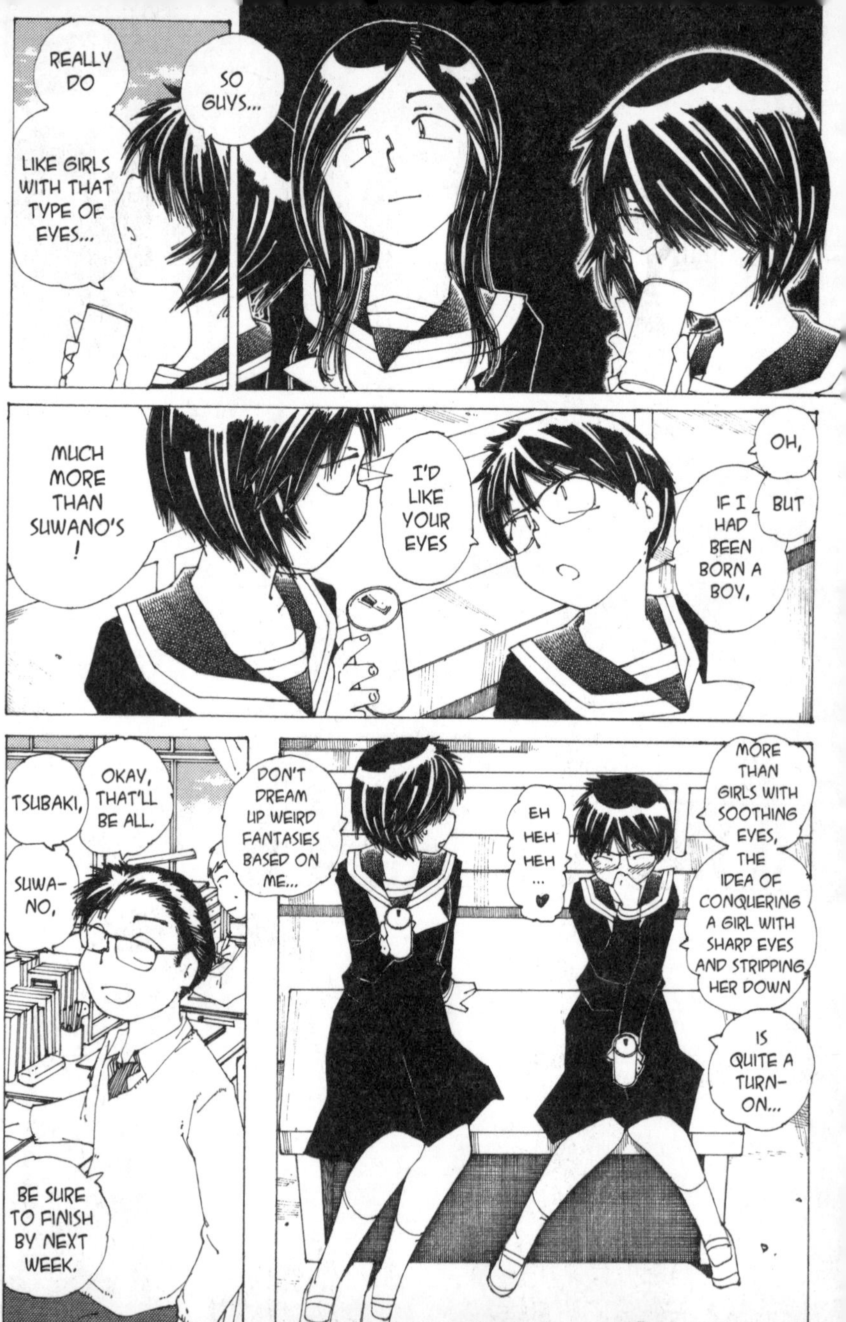

SO GUYS...
REALLY DO
LIKE GIRLS WITH THAT TYPE OF EYES...
OH,
BUT
IF I HAD BEEN BORN A BOY,
I'D LIKE YOUR EYES
MUCH MORE THAN SUWANO'S!
MORE THAN GIRLS WITH SOOTHING EYES,
THE IDEA OF CONQUERING A GIRL WITH SHARP EYES AND STRIPPING HER DOWN
IS QUITE A TURN-ON...
EH HEH HEH ... ♥
DON'T DREAM UP WEIRD FANTASIES BASED ON ME...
OKAY, THAT'LL BE ALL.
TSUBAKI,
SUWA-NO,
BE SURE TO FINISH BY NEXT WEEK.

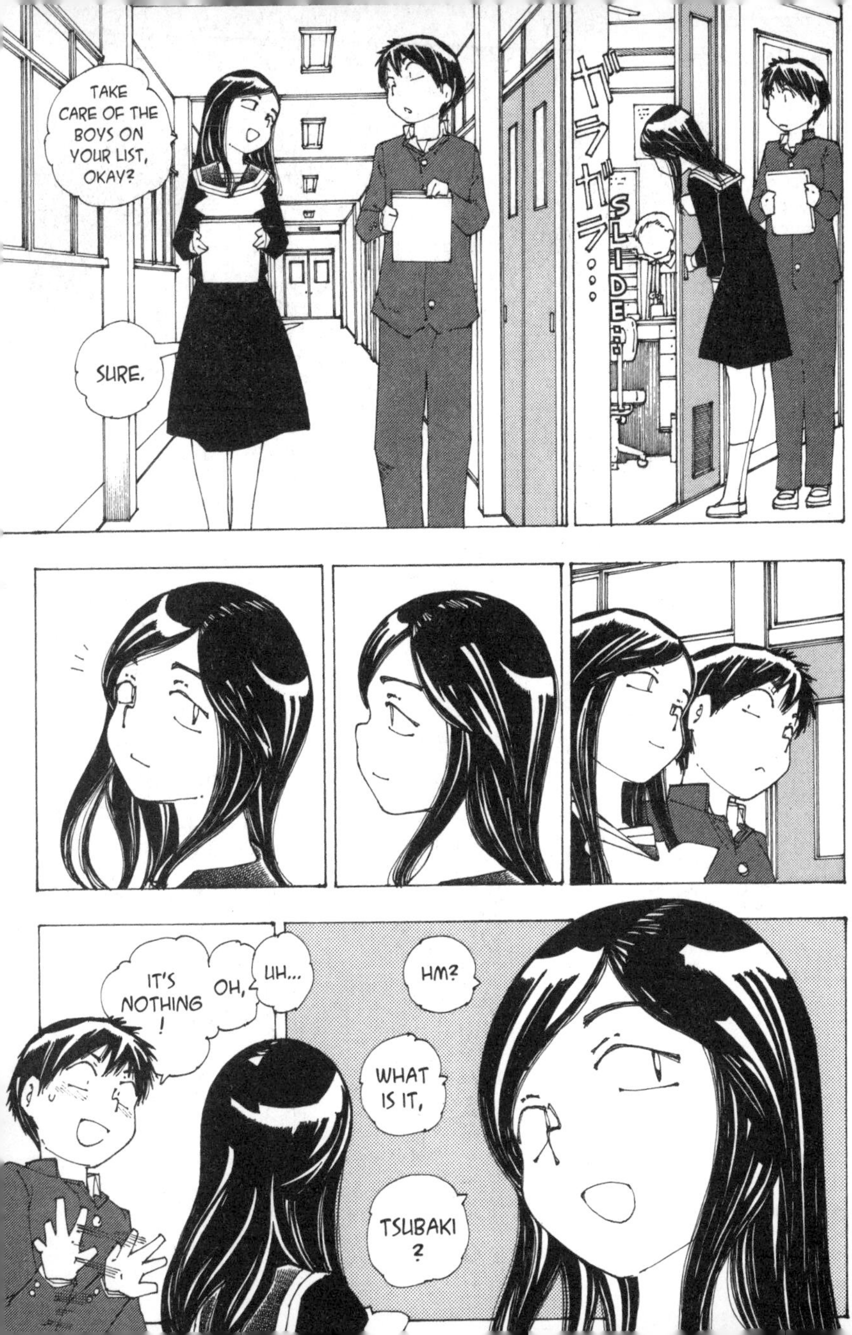
ガラガラ…
SLIDE…
TAKE CARE OF THE BOYS ON YOUR LIST, OKAY?
SURE.
HM?
WHAT IS IT,
TSUBAKI?
UH…
OH,
IT'S NOTHING!

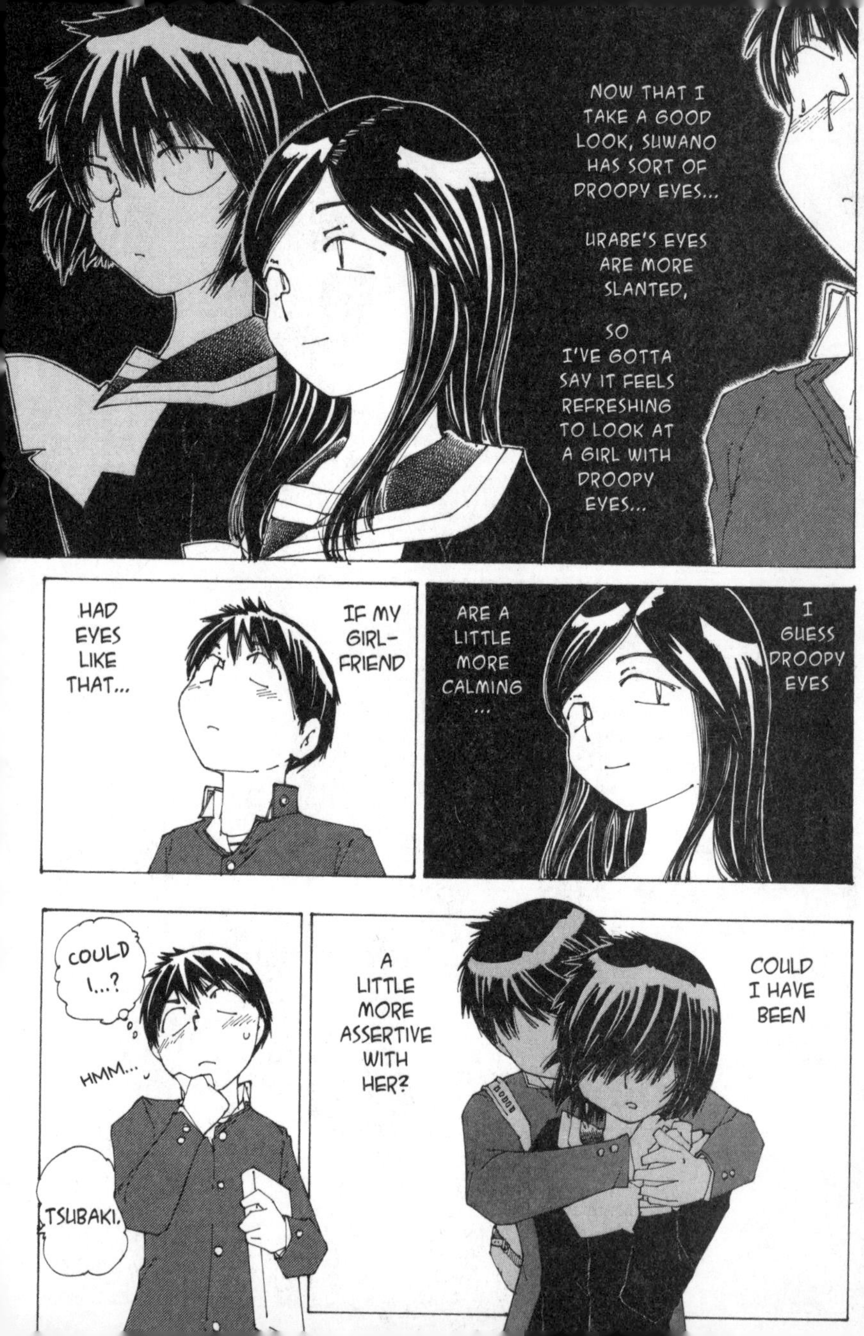
NOW THAT I TAKE A GOOD LOOK, SUWANO HAS SORT OF DROOPY EYES...
URABE'S EYES ARE MORE SLANTED,
SO I'VE GOTTA SAY IT FEELS REFRESHING TO LOOK AT A GIRL WITH DROOPY EYES...
I GUESS DROOPY EYES
ARE A LITTLE MORE CALMING ...
IF MY GIRL-FRIEND
HAD EYES LIKE THAT...
COULD I HAVE BEEN
A LITTLE MORE ASSERTIVE WITH HER?
COULD I...?
HMM...
TSUBAKI.

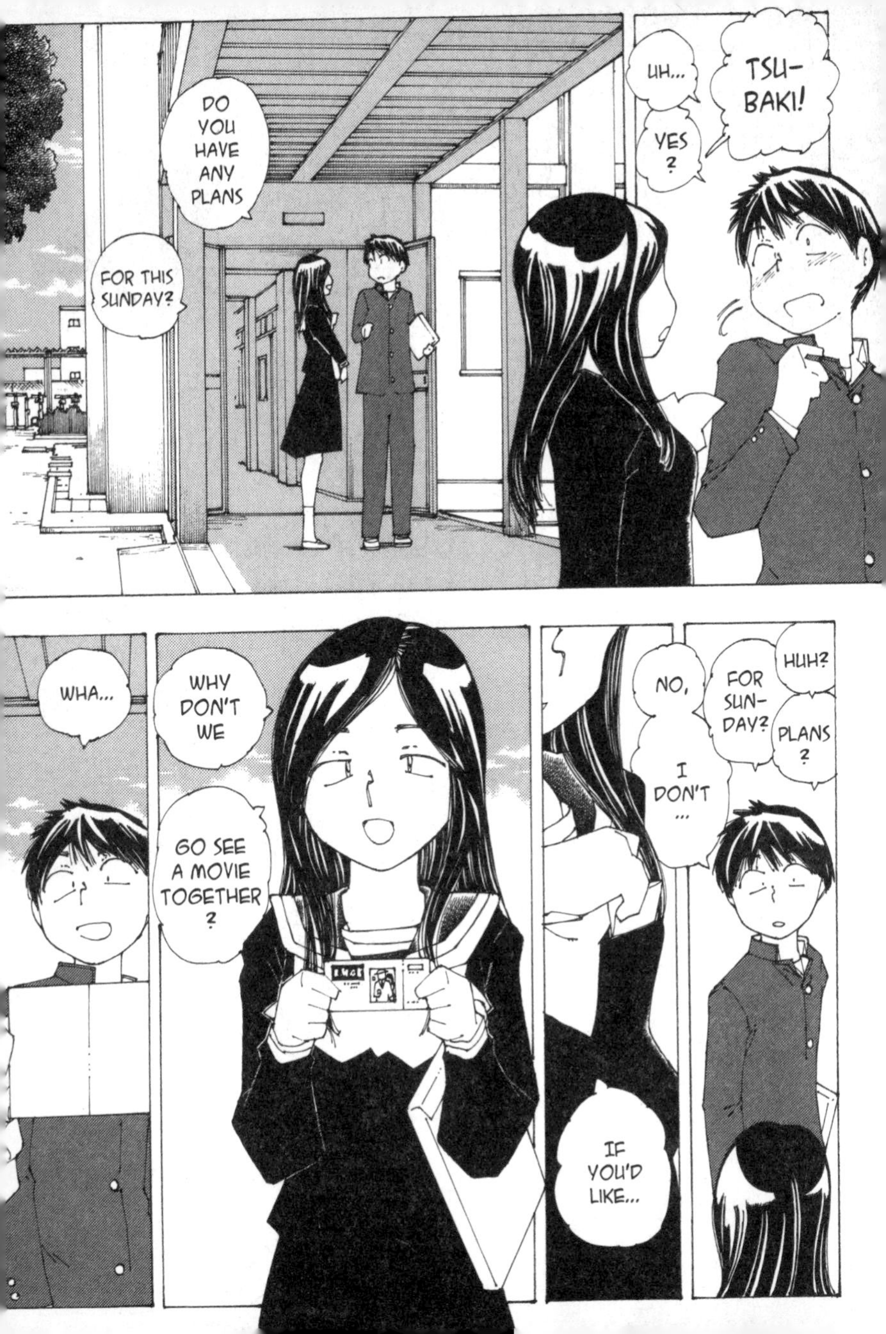
TSU-BAKI!
UH... YES?
DO YOU HAVE ANY PLANS
FOR THIS SUNDAY?
HUH?
PLANS?
FOR SUN-DAY?
NO, I DON'T ...
IF YOU'D LIKE...
WHY DON'T WE
GO SEE A MOVIE TOGETHER?
WHA...

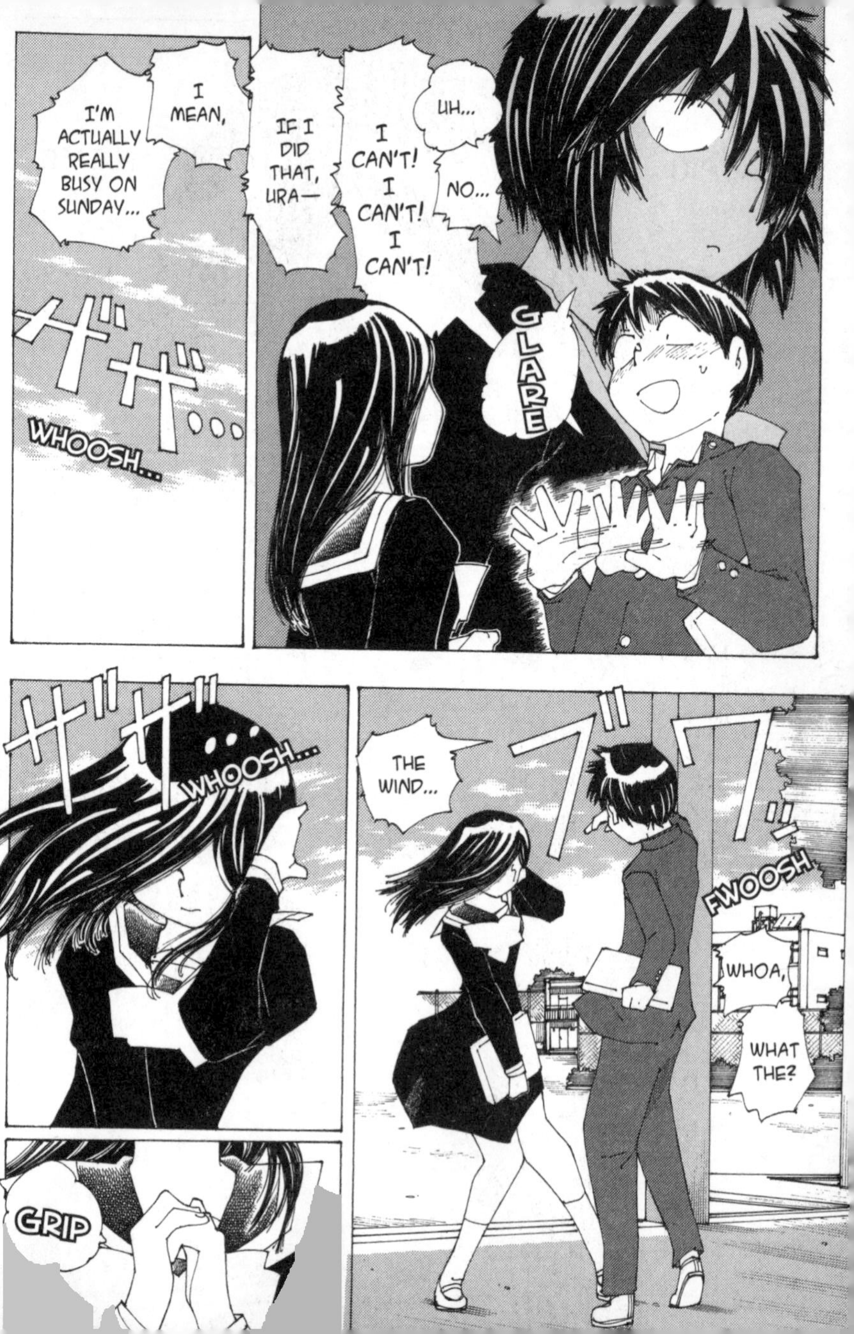
UH...
NO...
I CAN'T! I CAN'T! I CAN'T!
IF I DID THAT, URA—
GLARE
I MEAN,
I'M ACTUALLY REALLY BUSY ON SUNDAY...
ザザ…
WHOOSH...
ブワッ
THE WIND...
FWOOSH
WHOA,
WHAT THE?
ザザ…
WHOOSH...
GRIP

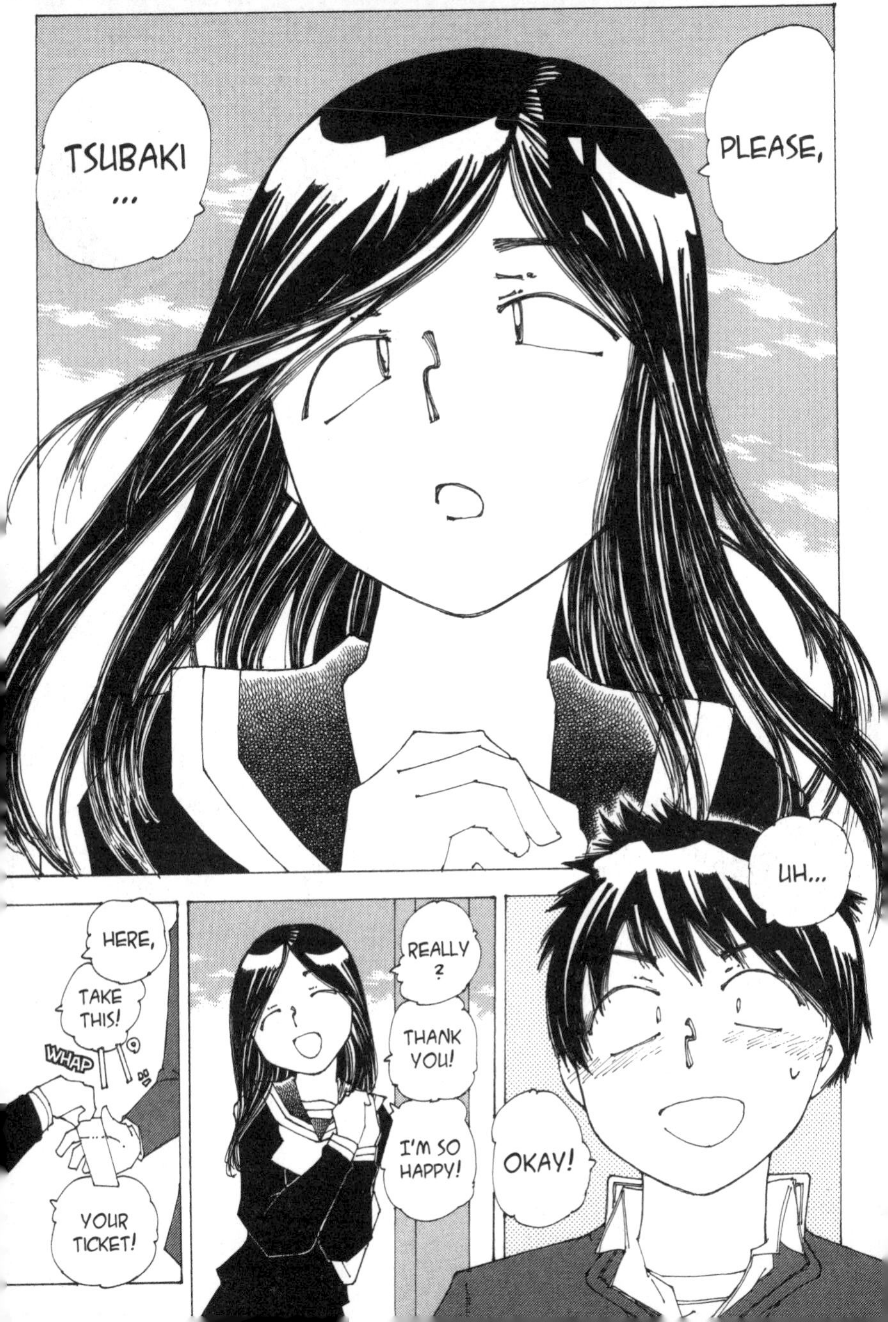
PLEASE,
TSUBAKI ...
UH...
OKAY!
REALLY?
THANK YOU!
I'M SO HAPPY!
HERE,
TAKE THIS!
WHAP
YOUR TICKET!

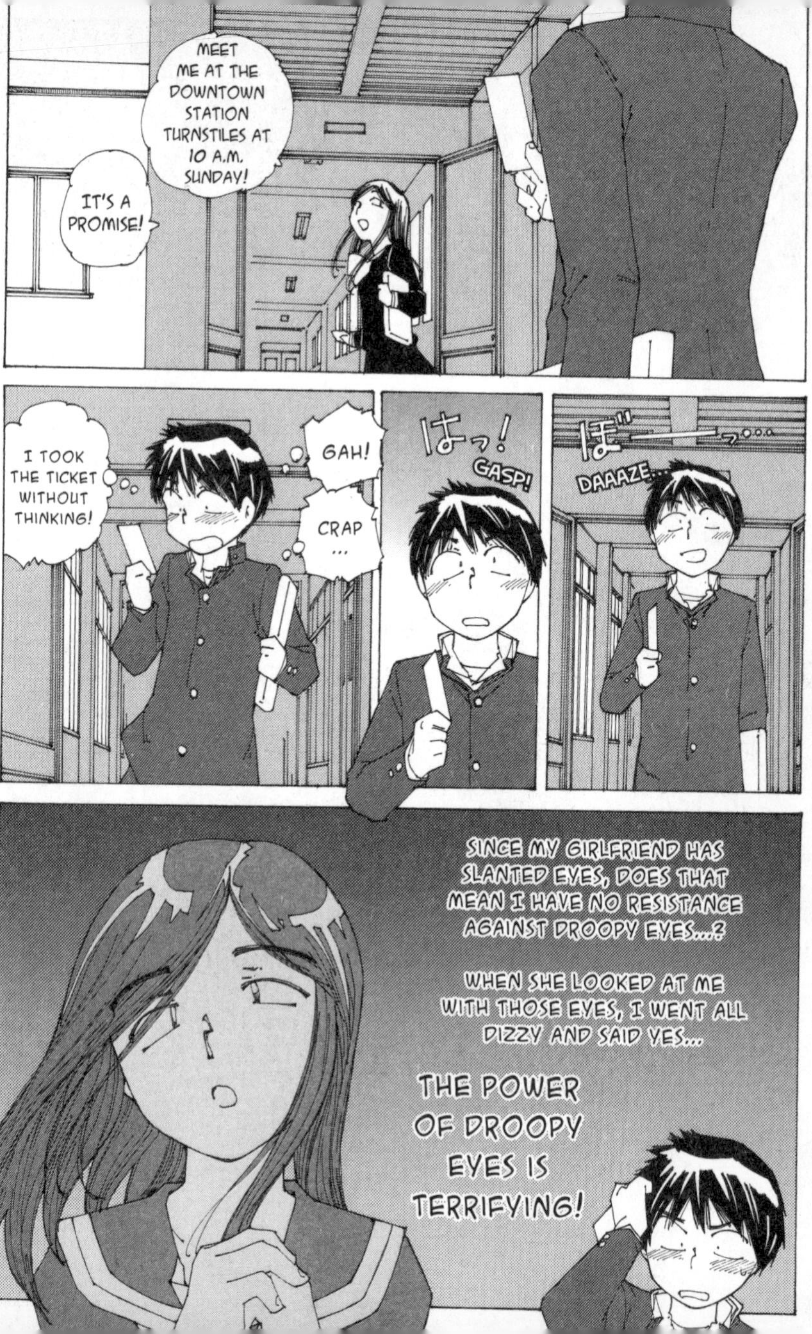
MEET ME AT THE DOWNTOWN STATION TURNSTILES AT 10 A.M. SUNDAY!
IT'S A PROMISE!
ぼーーっ
DAAAZE...
はっ!
GASP!
GAH!
CRAP...
I TOOK THE TICKET WITHOUT THINKING!
SINCE MY GIRLFRIEND HAS SLANTED EYES, DOES THAT MEAN I HAVE NO RESISTANCE AGAINST DROOPY EYES...?
WHEN SHE LOOKED AT ME WITH THOSE EYES, I WENT ALL DIZZY AND SAID YES...
THE POWER OF DROOPY EYES IS TERRIFYING!

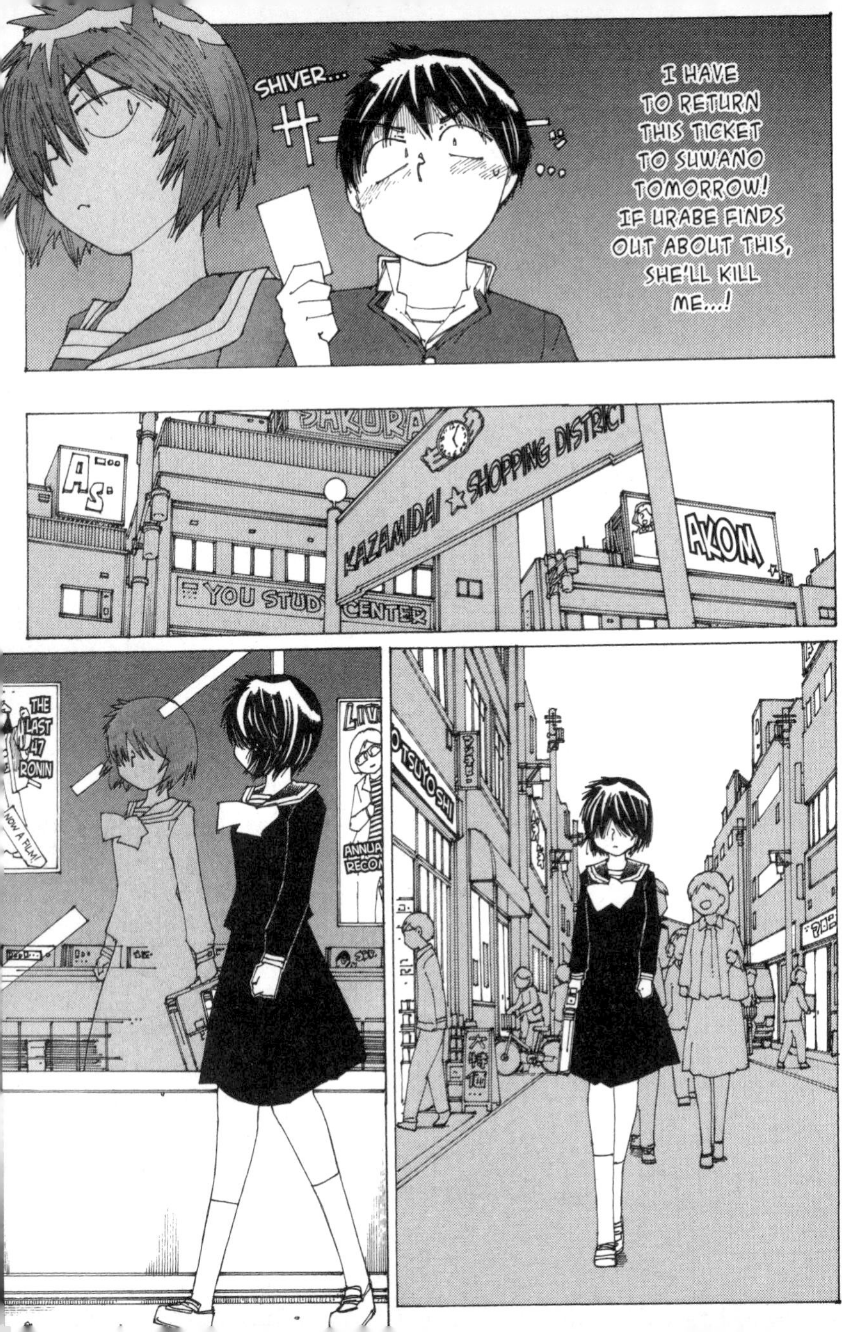

I HAVE TO RETURN THIS TICKET TO SUWANO TOMORROW! IF URABE FINDS OUT ABOUT THIS, SHE'LL KILL ME...!
SHIVER...
KAZAMIDAI ☆ SHOPPING DISTRICT
AKOM
YOU STUDY CENTER
OTSUYOSHI
THE LAST 47 RONIN
NOW A FILM!

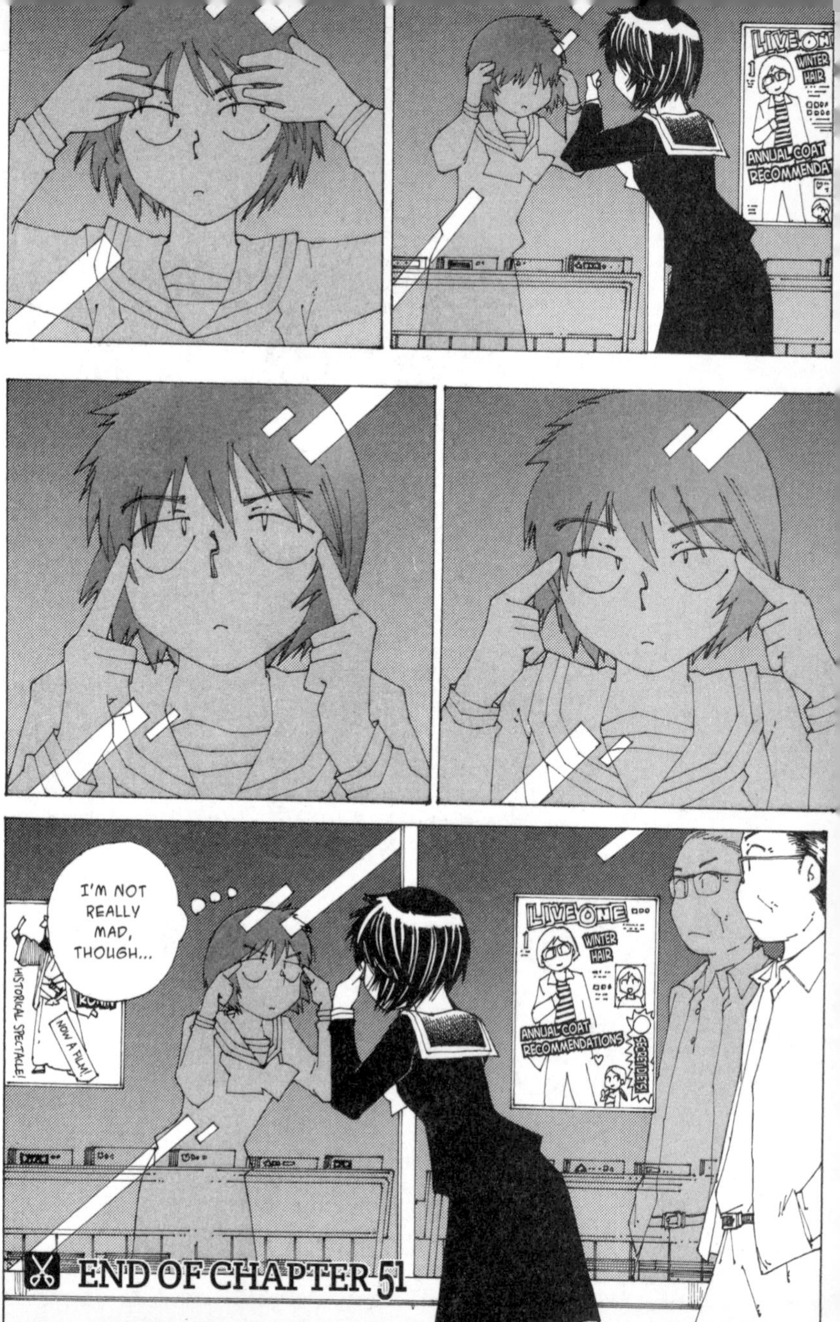
LIVE ONE
WINTER HAIR
ANNUAL COAT RECOMMENDAT
I'M NOT REALLY MAD, THOUGH...
LIVE ONE
WINTER HAIR
ANNUAL COAT RECOMMENDATIONS
HISTORICAL SPECTACLE!
NOW A FILM!
END OF CHAPTER 51

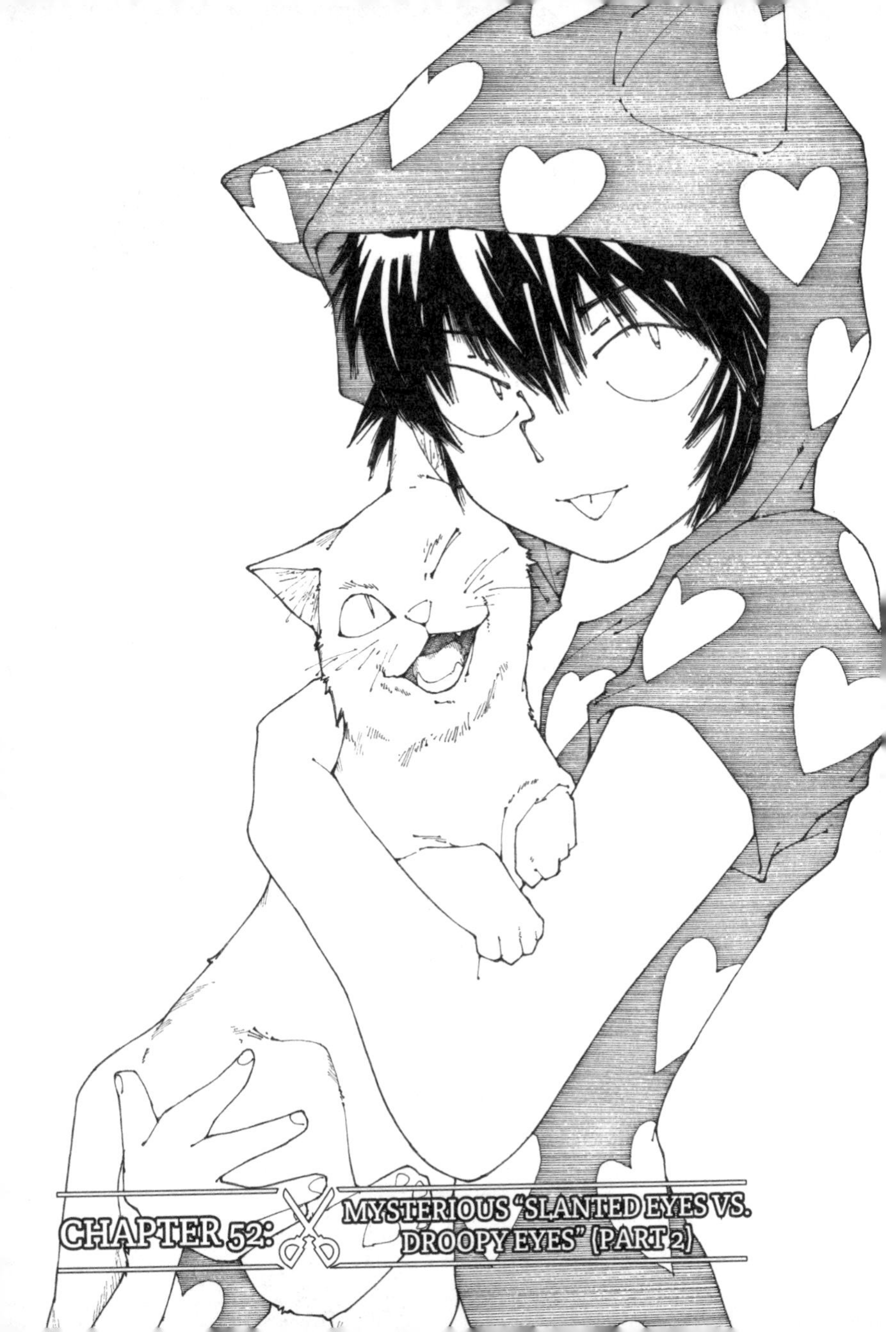

CHAPTER 52: MYSTERIOUS "SLANTED EYES VS. DROOPY EYES" (PART 2)

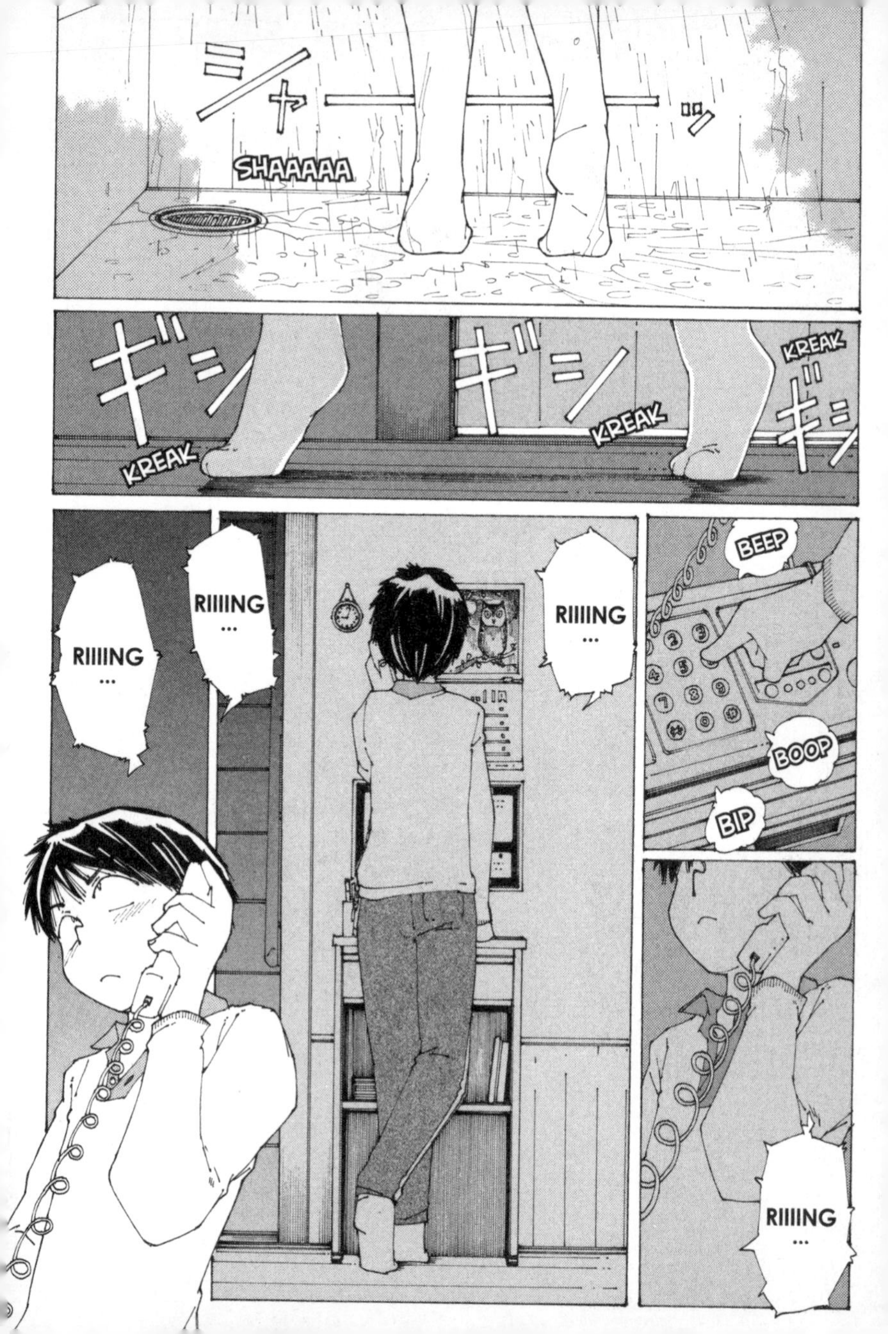

ジャーッ
SHAAAAA
KREAK
ギシ
KREAK
ギシ
KREAK
ギシ
BEEP
BOOP
BIP
RIIIING …
RIIIING …
RIIIING …
RIIIING …

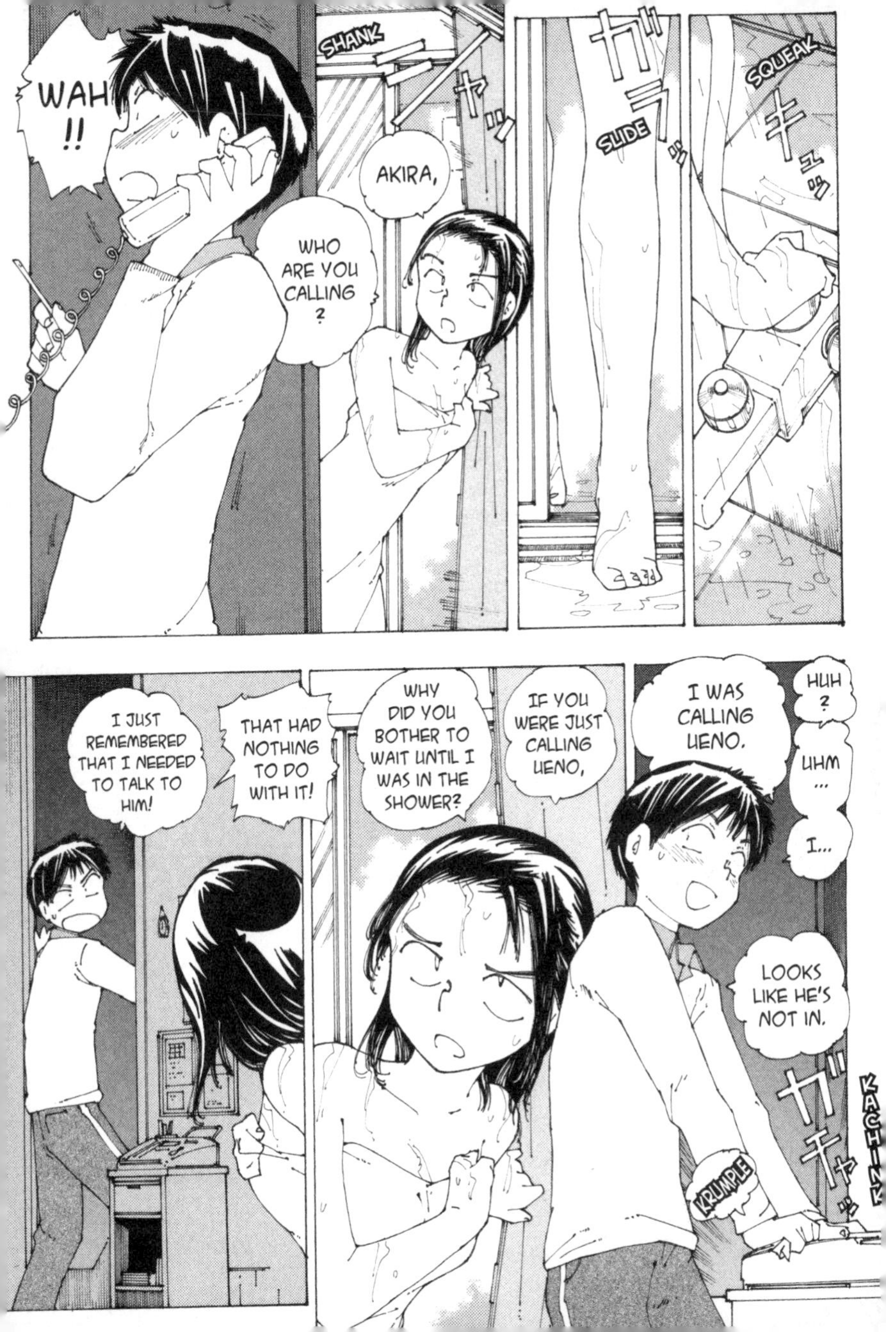
SQUEAK
SLIDE
SHANK
AKIRA,
WHO ARE YOU CALLING?
WAH!!
HUH?
UHM...
I...
I WAS CALLING UENO.
LOOKS LIKE HE'S NOT IN.
KACHINK
KRUMPLE
IF YOU WERE JUST CALLING UENO,
WHY DID YOU BOTHER TO WAIT UNTIL I WAS IN THE SHOWER?
THAT HAD NOTHING TO DO WITH IT!
I JUST REMEMBERED THAT I NEEDED TO TALK TO HIM!

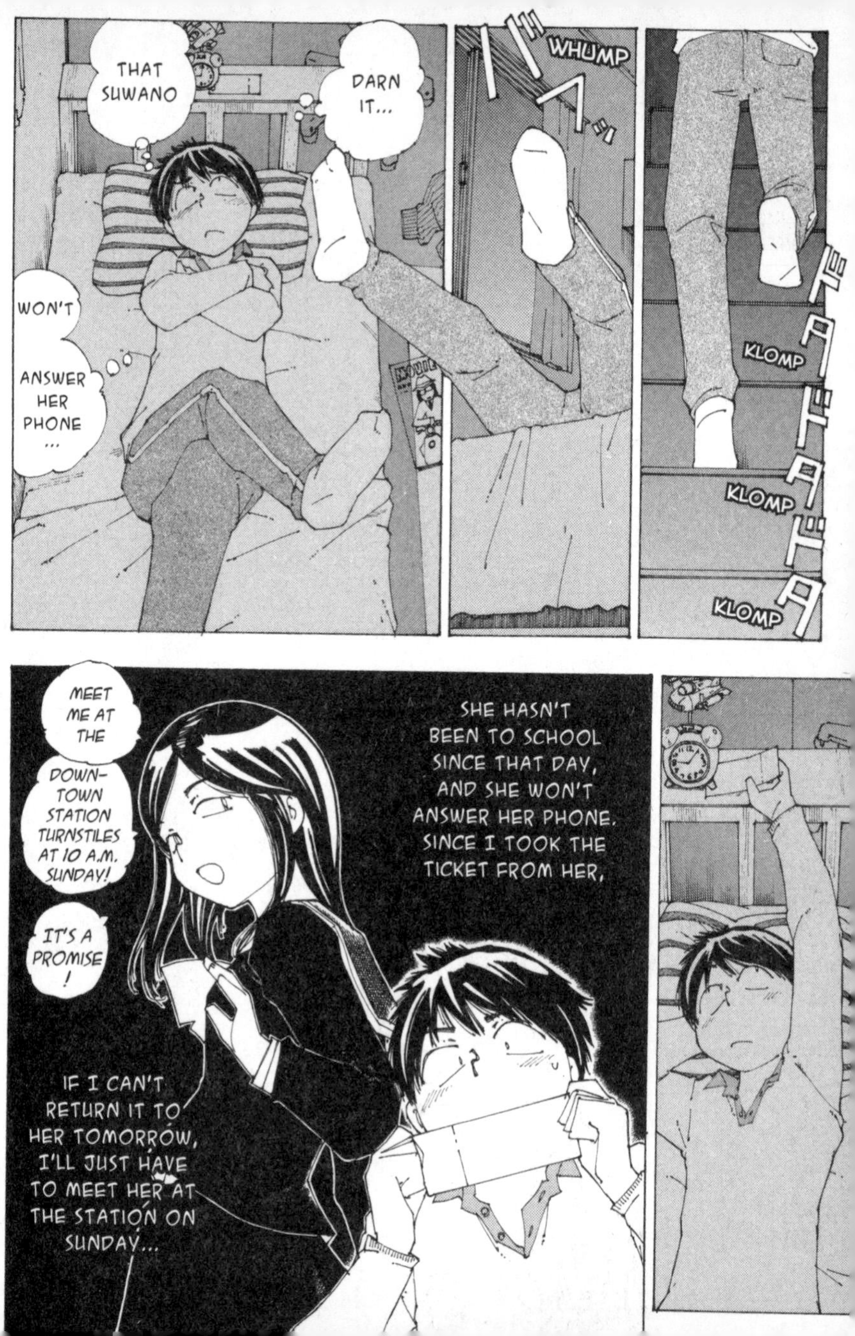
KLOMP
KLOMP
KLOMP
WHUMP
DARN IT...
THAT SUWANO
WON'T ANSWER HER PHONE...
SHE HASN'T BEEN TO SCHOOL SINCE THAT DAY, AND SHE WON'T ANSWER HER PHONE. SINCE I TOOK THE TICKET FROM HER,
MEET ME AT THE DOWN-TOWN STATION TURNSTILES AT 10 A.M. SUNDAY!
IT'S A PROMISE!
IF I CAN'T RETURN IT TO HER TOMORROW, I'LL JUST HAVE TO MEET HER AT THE STATION ON SUNDAY...

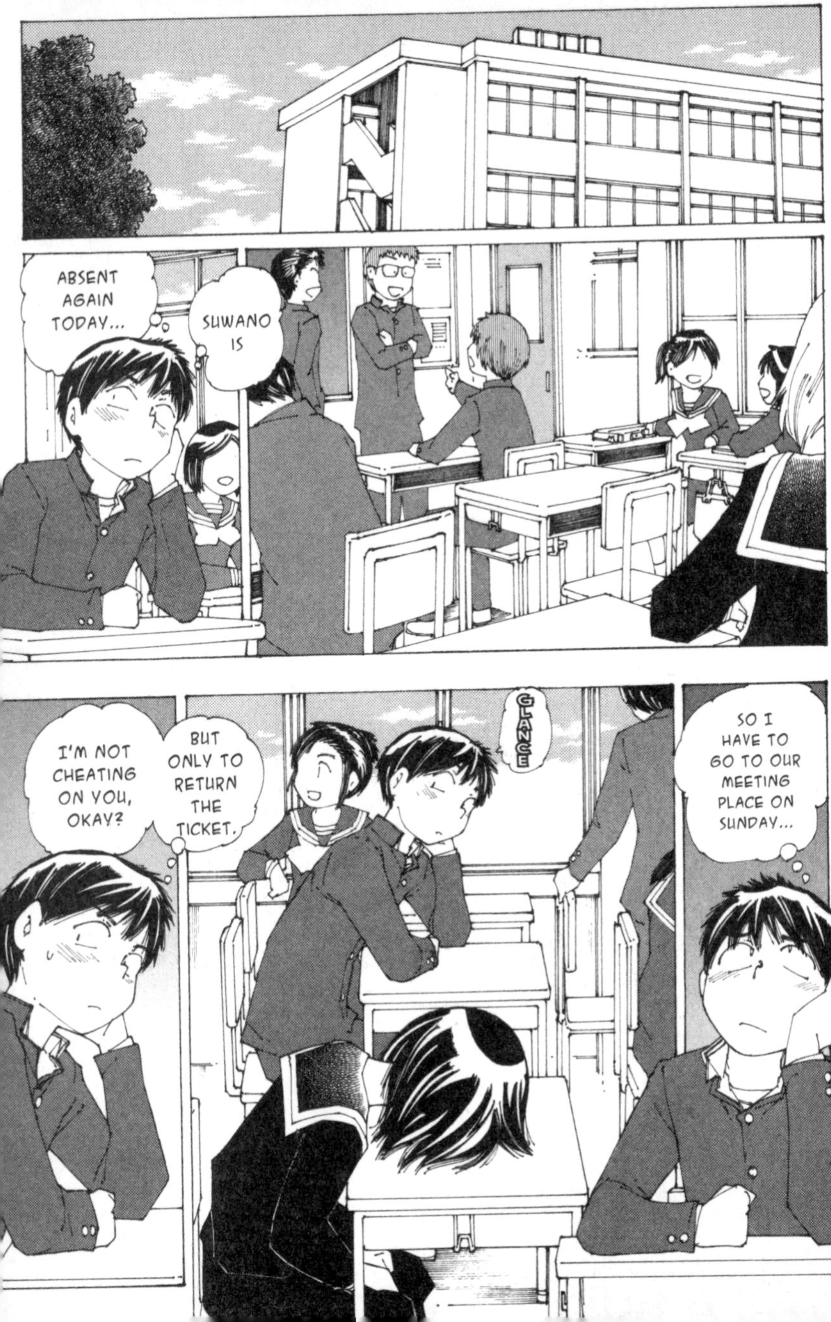
SUWANO IS
ABSENT AGAIN TODAY...
SO I HAVE TO GO TO OUR MEETING PLACE ON SUNDAY...
GLANCE
BUT ONLY TO RETURN THE TICKET.
I'M NOT CHEATING ON YOU, OKAY?

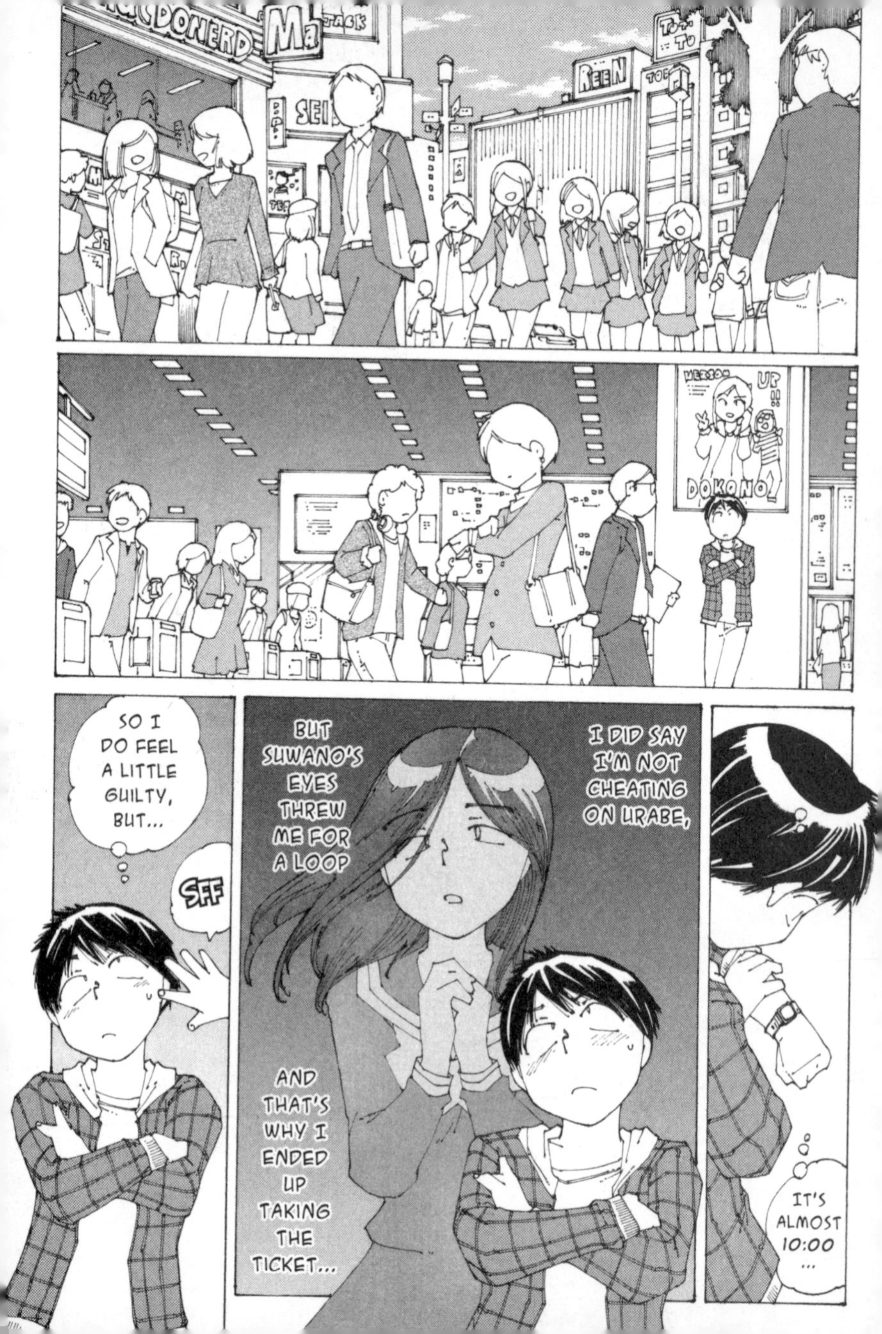
IT'S ALMOST 10:00 ...
I DID SAY I'M NOT CHEATING ON URABE,
BUT SUWANO'S EYES THREW ME FOR A LOOP
AND THAT'S WHY I ENDED UP TAKING THE TICKET...
SO I DO FEEL A LITTLE GUILTY, BUT...
SFF

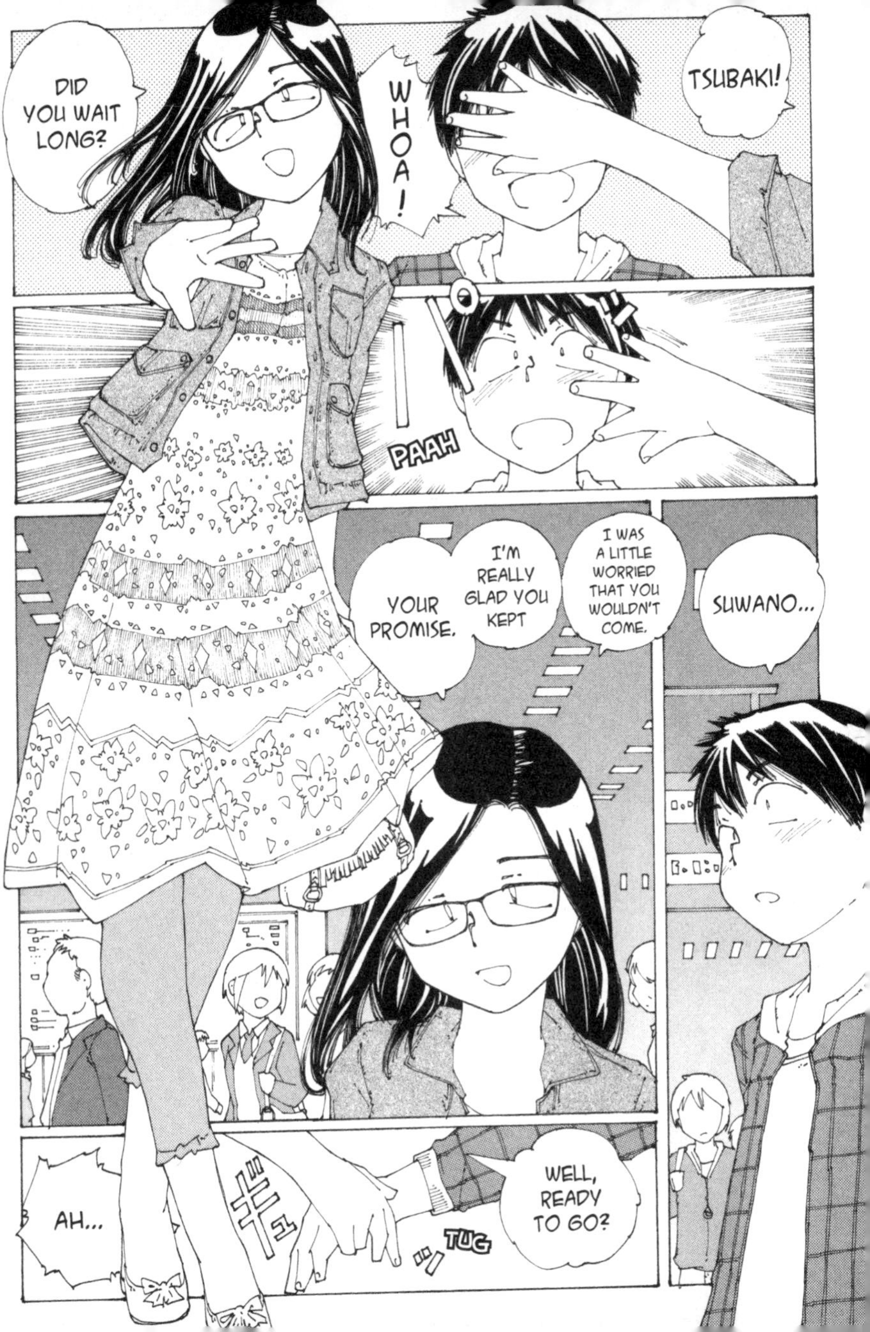
TSUBAKI!
WHOA!
DID YOU WAIT LONG?
PAAH
SUWANO...
I WAS A LITTLE WORRIED THAT YOU WOULDN'T COME.
I'M REALLY GLAD YOU KEPT YOUR PROMISE.
WELL, READY TO GO?
TUG
AH...

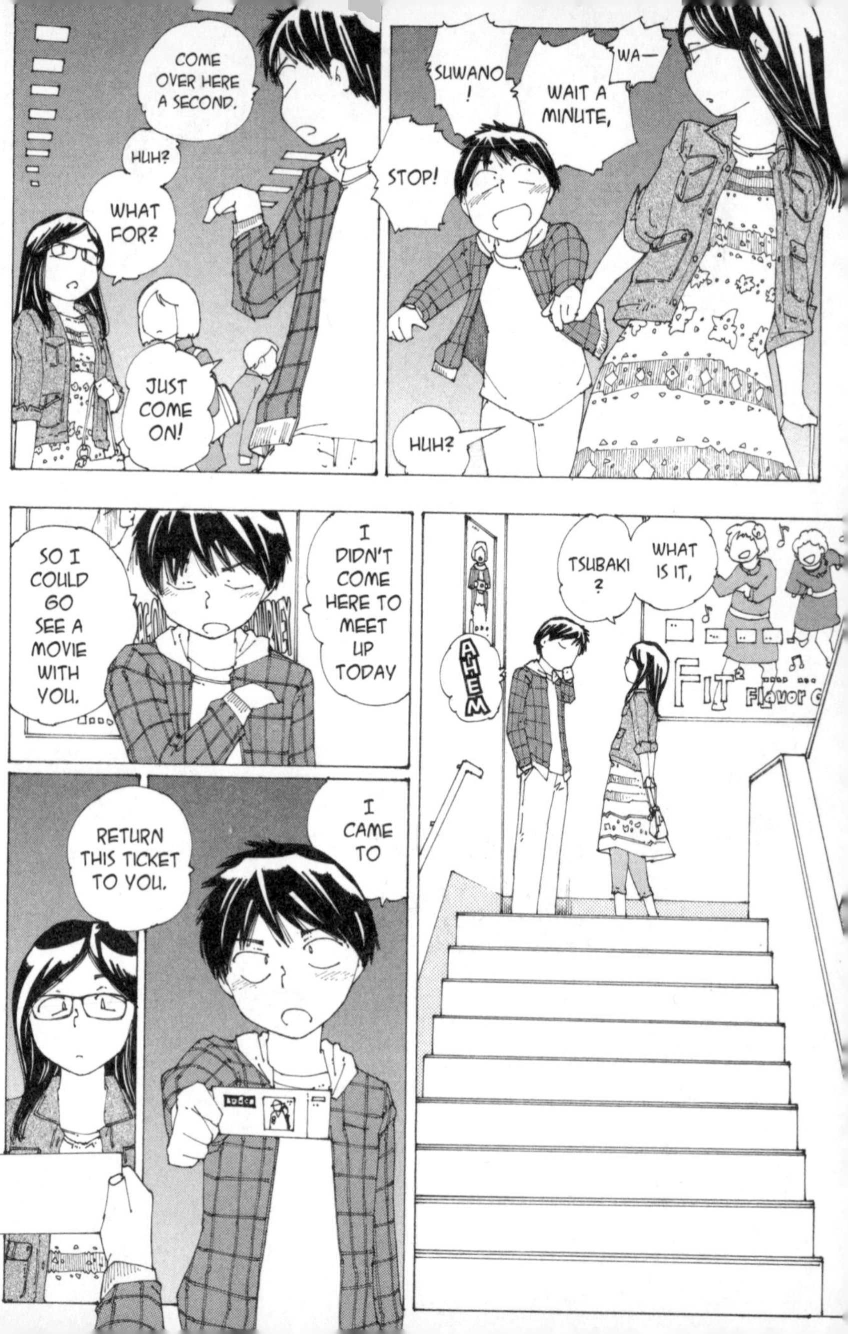
WA—
WAIT A MINUTE,
SUWANO !
STOP!
HUH?
COME OVER HERE A SECOND.
HUH?
WHAT FOR?
JUST COME ON!
WHAT IS IT,
TSUBAKI ?
AHEM
I DIDN'T COME HERE TO MEET UP TODAY
SO I COULD GO SEE A MOVIE WITH YOU.
I CAME TO
RETURN THIS TICKET TO YOU.

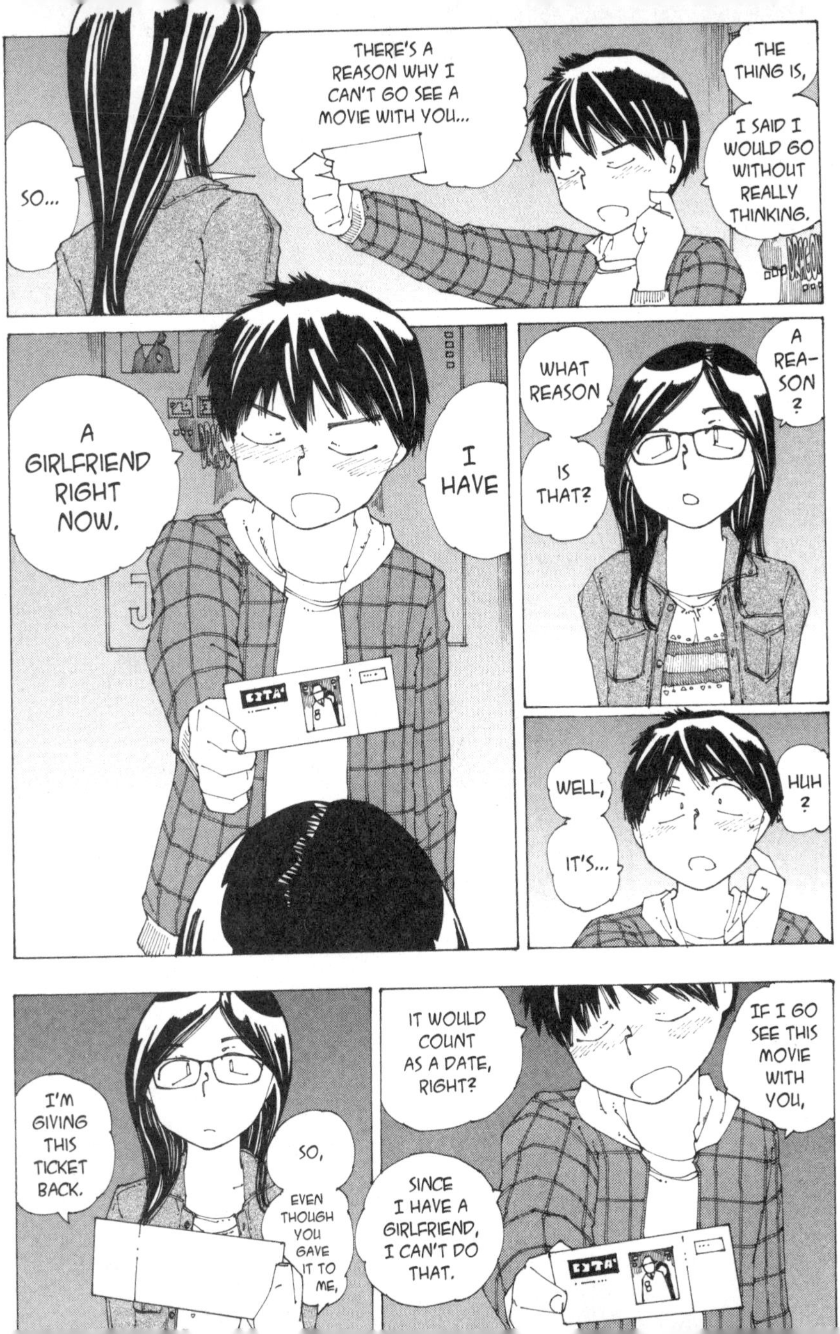
THE THING IS,
I SAID I WOULD GO WITHOUT REALLY THINKING.
THERE'S A REASON WHY I CAN'T GO SEE A MOVIE WITH YOU...
SO...
A REA-SON?
WHAT REASON
IS THAT?
HUH?
WELL,
IT'S...
I HAVE
A GIRLFRIEND RIGHT NOW.
IF I GO SEE THIS MOVIE WITH YOU,
IT WOULD COUNT AS A DATE, RIGHT?
SINCE I HAVE A GIRLFRIEND, I CAN'T DO THAT.
SO,
EVEN THOUGH YOU GAVE IT TO ME,
I'M GIVING THIS TICKET BACK.

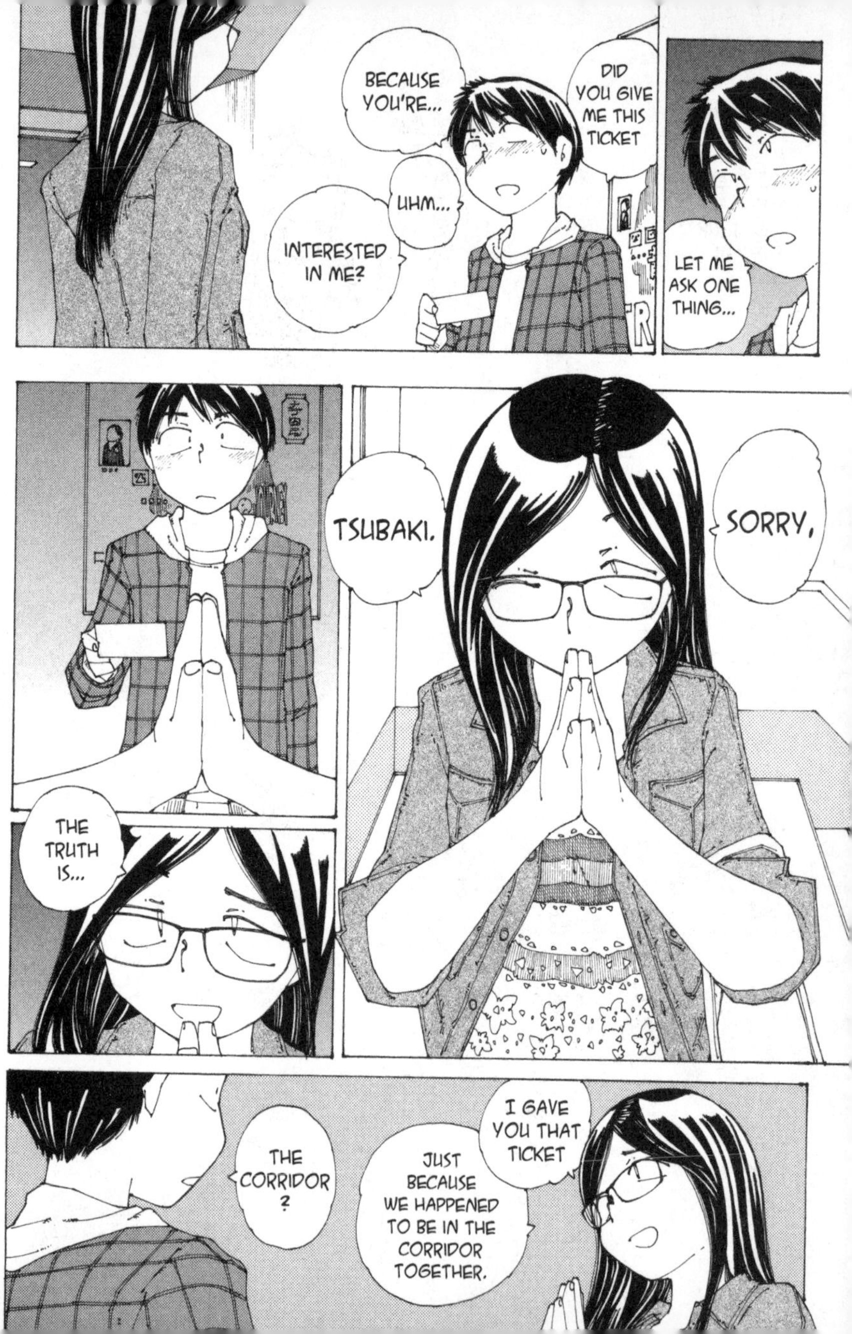
LET ME ASK ONE THING...
DID YOU GIVE ME THIS TICKET
BECAUSE YOU'RE...
UHM...
INTERESTED IN ME?
SORRY,
TSUBAKI.
THE TRUTH IS...
I GAVE YOU THAT TICKET
JUST BECAUSE WE HAPPENED TO BE IN THE CORRIDOR TOGETHER.
THE CORRIDOR?

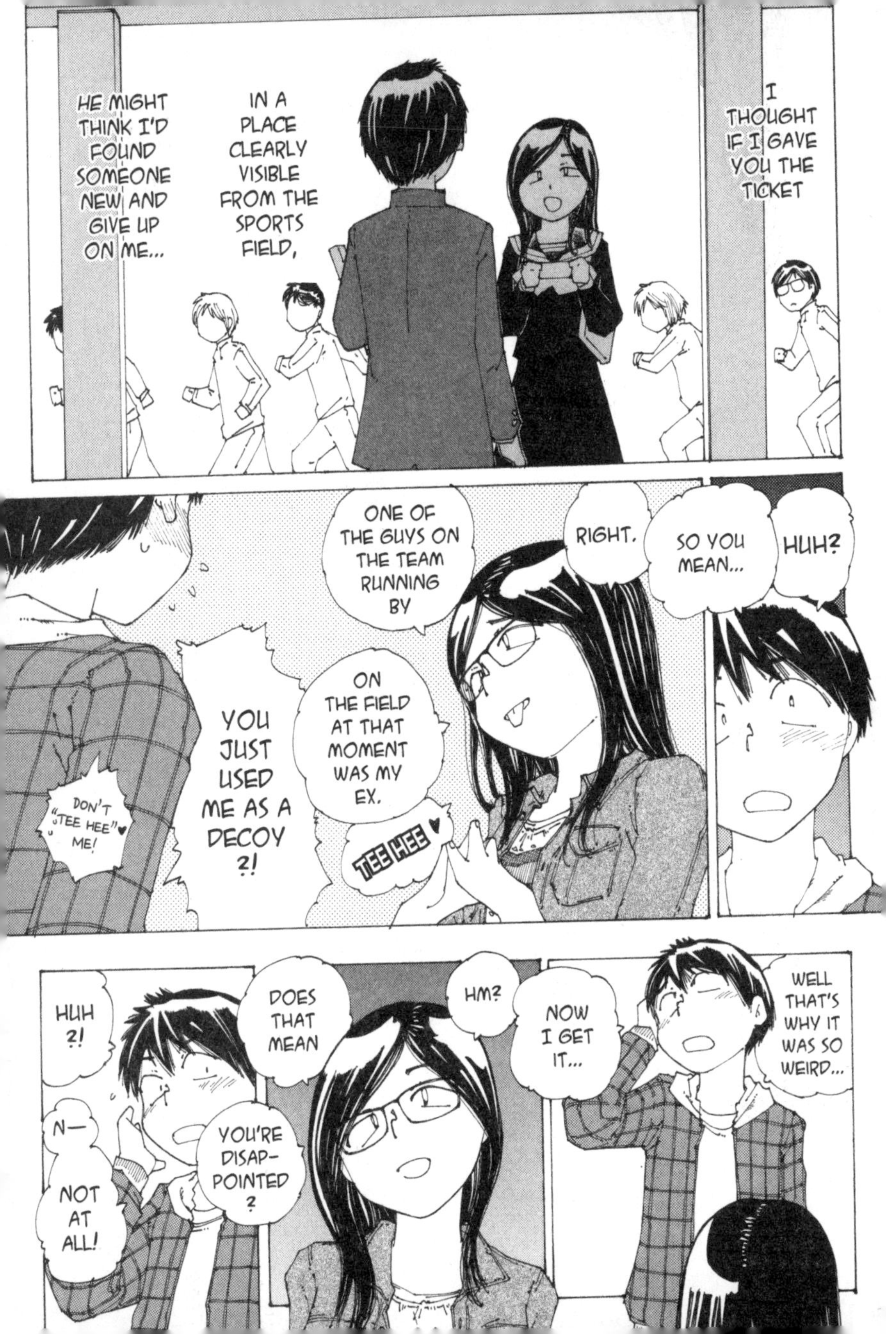
I THOUGHT IF I GAVE YOU THE TICKET
IN A PLACE CLEARLY VISIBLE FROM THE SPORTS FIELD,
HE MIGHT THINK I'D FOUND SOMEONE NEW AND GIVE UP ON ME...
HUH?
SO YOU MEAN...
RIGHT.
ONE OF THE GUYS ON THE TEAM RUNNING BY
ON THE FIELD AT THAT MOMENT WAS MY EX.
TEE HEE ♥
YOU JUST USED ME AS A DECOY ?!
DON'T "TEE HEE"♥ ME!
WELL THAT'S WHY IT WAS SO WEIRD...
NOW I GET IT...
HM?
DOES THAT MEAN
YOU'RE DISAP-POINTED ?
HUH ?!
N—
NOT AT ALL!

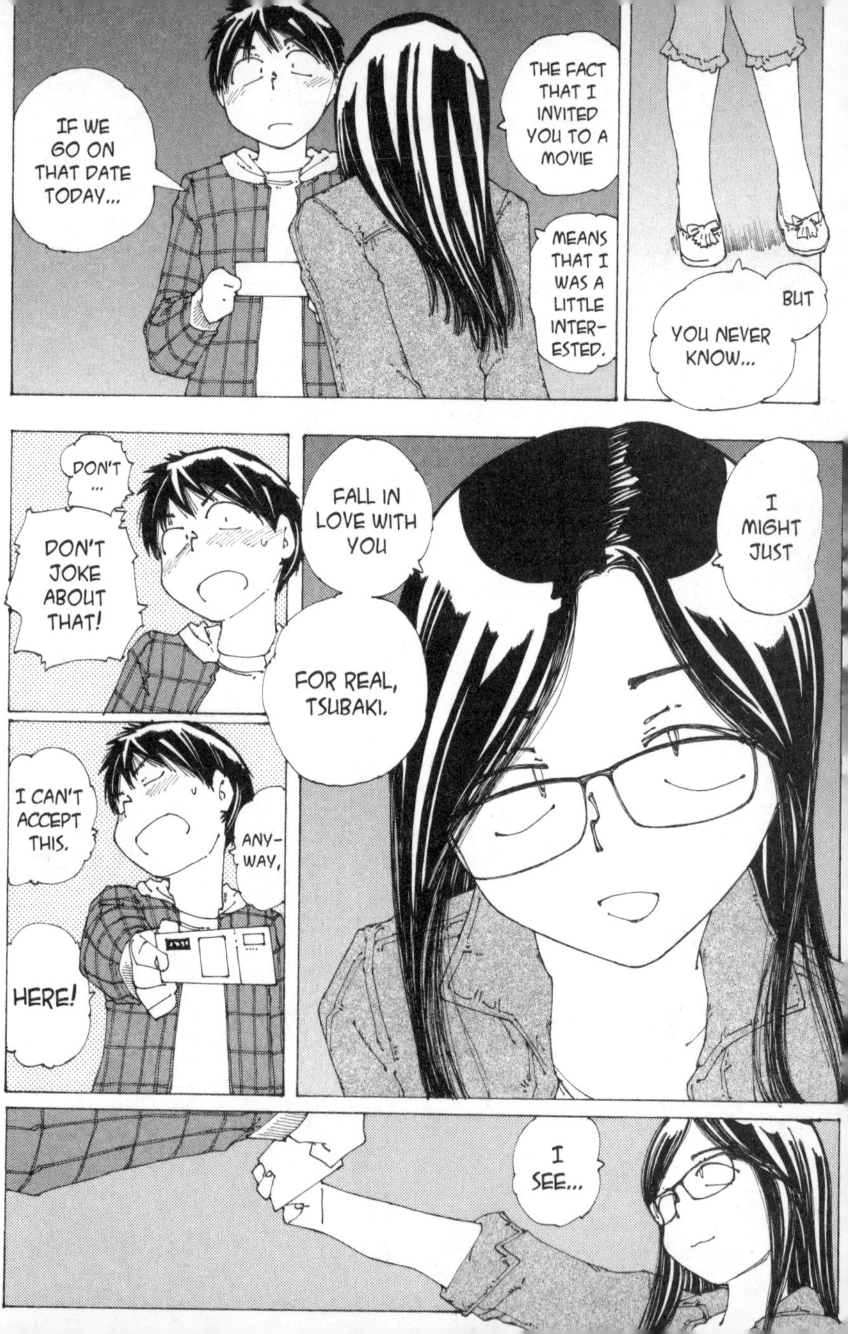
BUT
YOU NEVER KNOW...
THE FACT THAT I INVITED YOU TO A MOVIE
MEANS THAT I WAS A LITTLE INTER-ESTED.
IF WE GO ON THAT DATE TODAY...
I MIGHT JUST
FALL IN LOVE WITH YOU
FOR REAL, TSUBAKI.
DON'T ...
DON'T JOKE ABOUT THAT!
ANY-WAY,
I CAN'T ACCEPT THIS.
HERE!
I SEE...

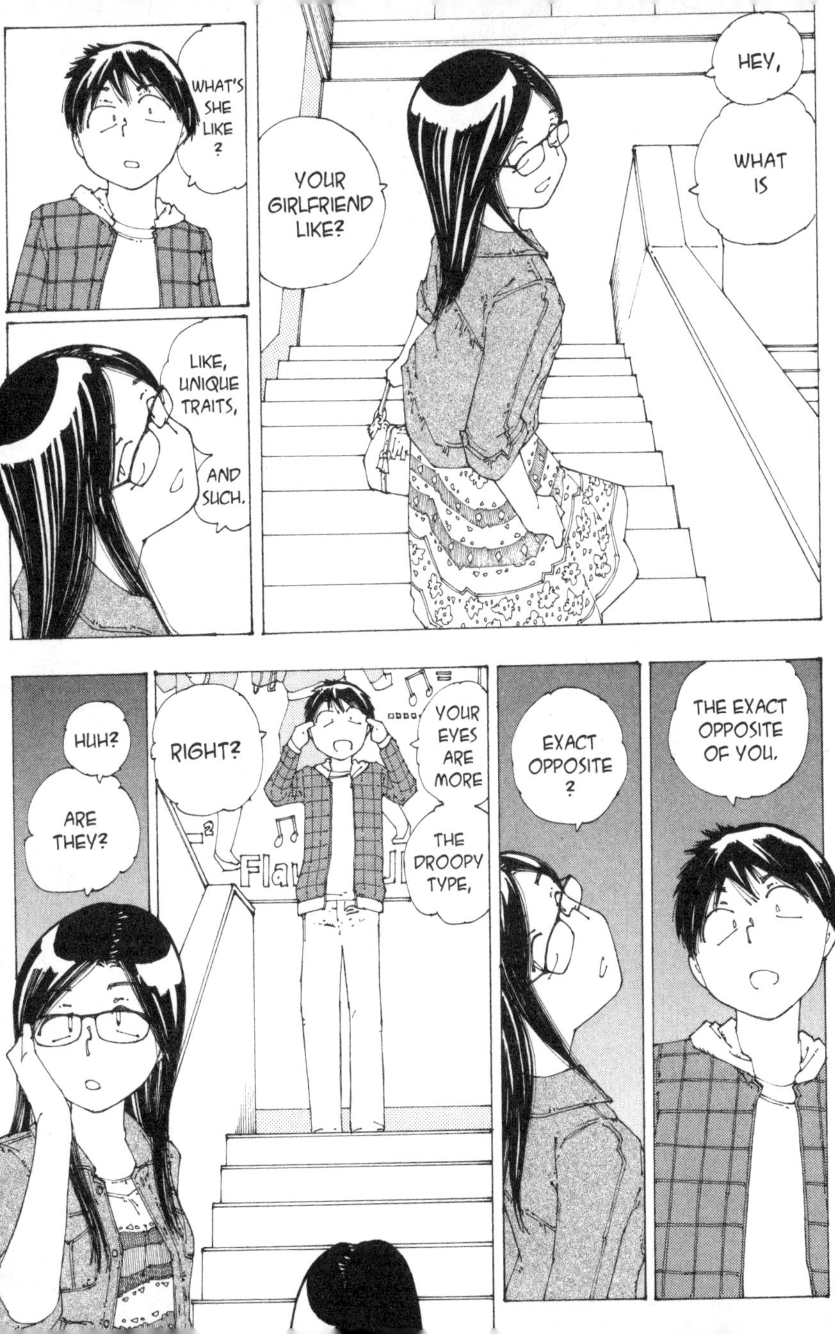
HEY,
WHAT IS
YOUR GIRLFRIEND LIKE?
WHAT'S SHE LIKE?
LIKE, UNIQUE TRAITS,
AND SUCH.
THE EXACT OPPOSITE OF YOU.
EXACT OPPOSITE?
YOUR EYES ARE MORE
THE DROOPY TYPE,
RIGHT?
HUH?
ARE THEY?

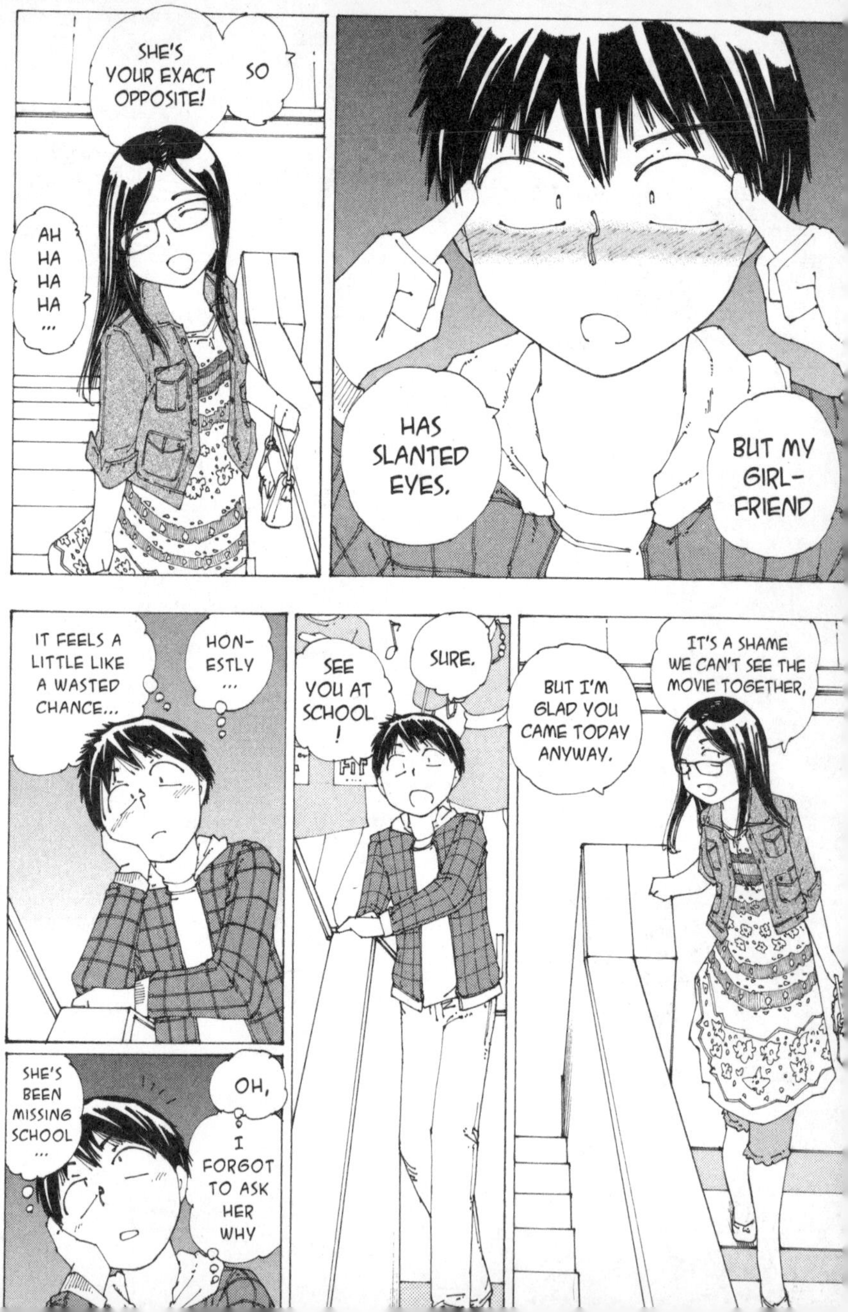
BUT MY GIRL-FRIEND
HAS SLANTED EYES.
SO
SHE'S YOUR EXACT OPPOSITE!
AH HA HA HA ...
IT'S A SHAME WE CAN'T SEE THE MOVIE TOGETHER,
BUT I'M GLAD YOU CAME TODAY ANYWAY.
SURE.
SEE YOU AT SCHOOL!
HON-ESTLY ...
IT FEELS A LITTLE LIKE A WASTED CHANCE...
OH,
I FORGOT TO ASK HER WHY
SHE'S BEEN MISSING SCHOOL ...

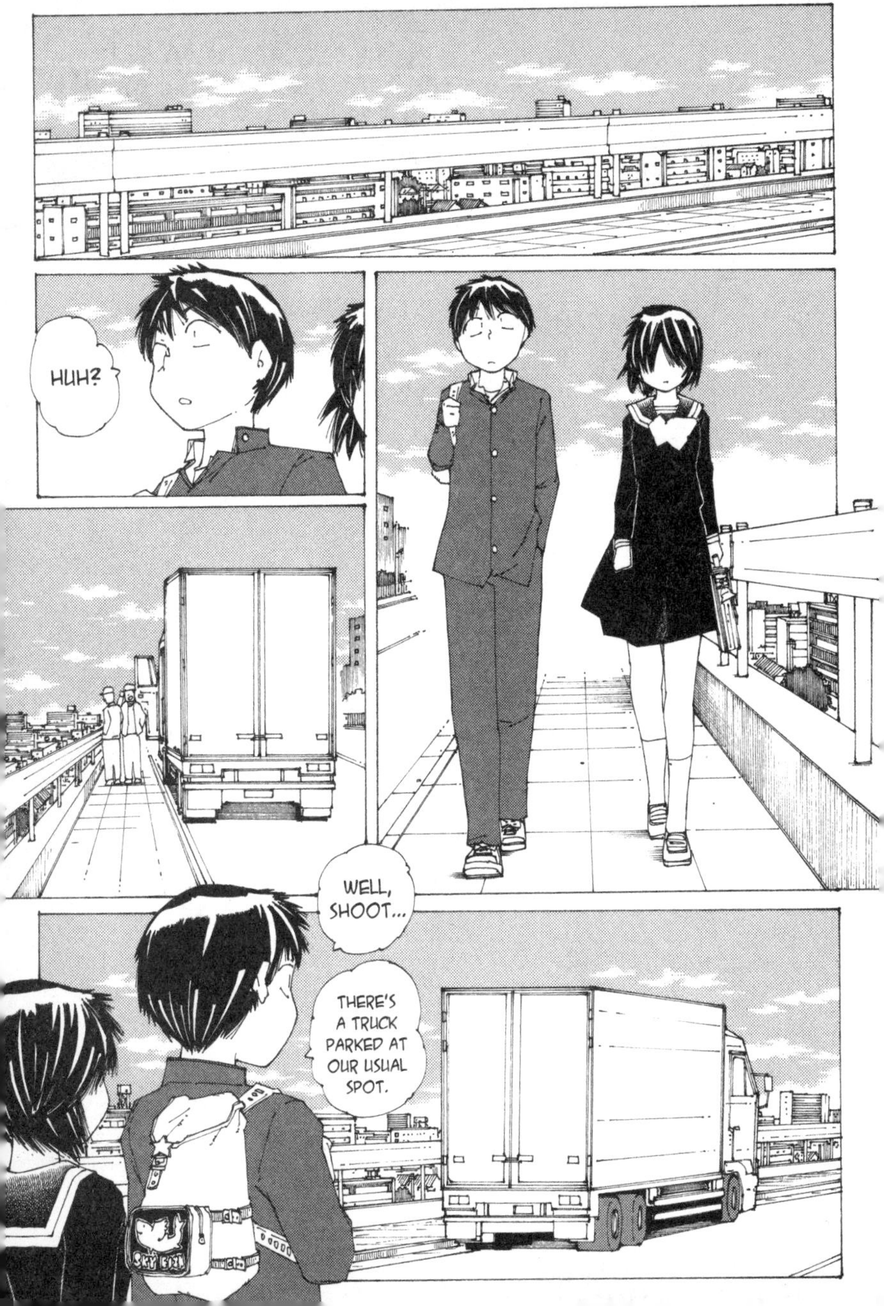
HUH?
WELL, SHOOT...
THERE'S A TRUCK PARKED AT OUR USUAL SPOT.

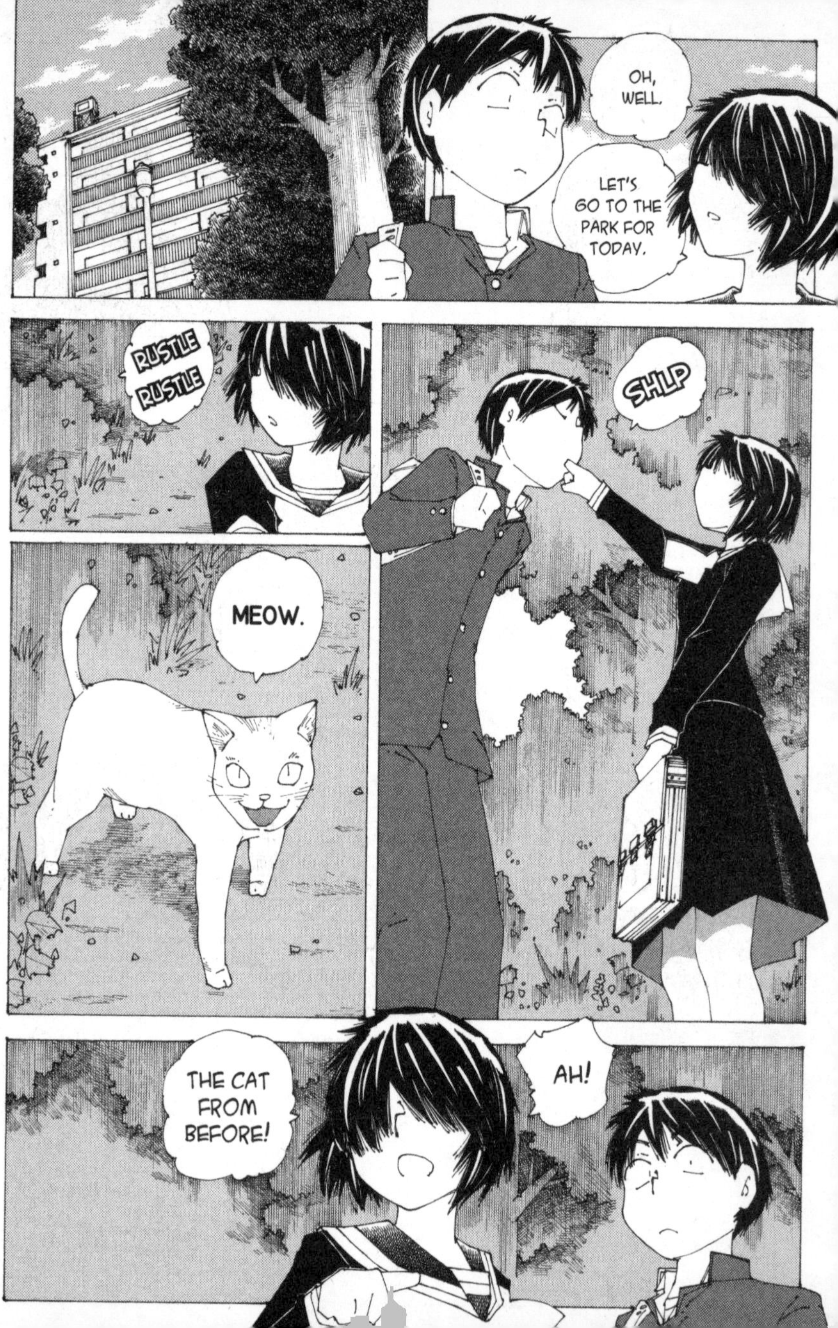
OH, WELL.
LET'S GO TO THE PARK FOR TODAY.
SHLP
RUSTLE RUSTLE
MEOW.
AH!
THE CAT FROM BEFORE!

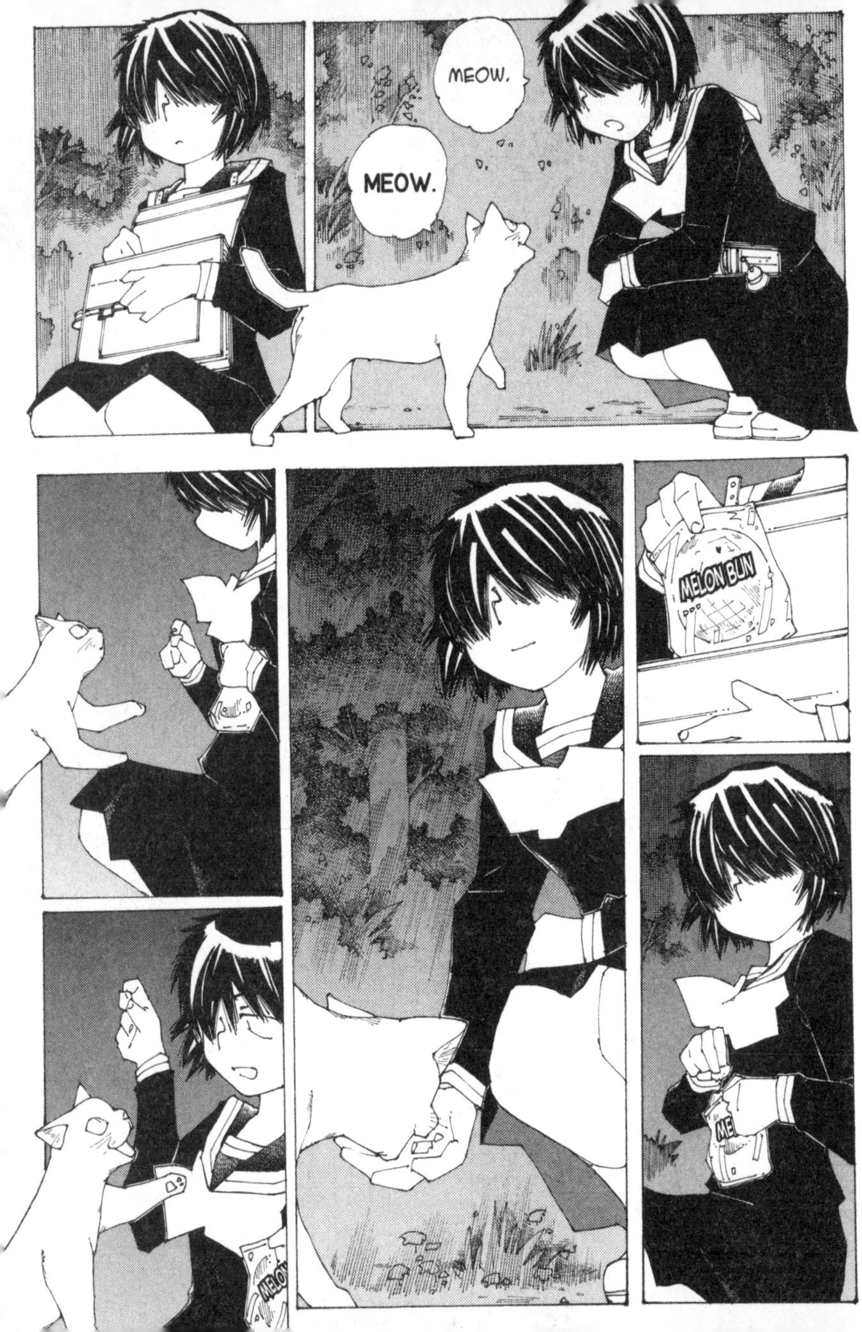

MEOW.
MEOW.
MELON BUN

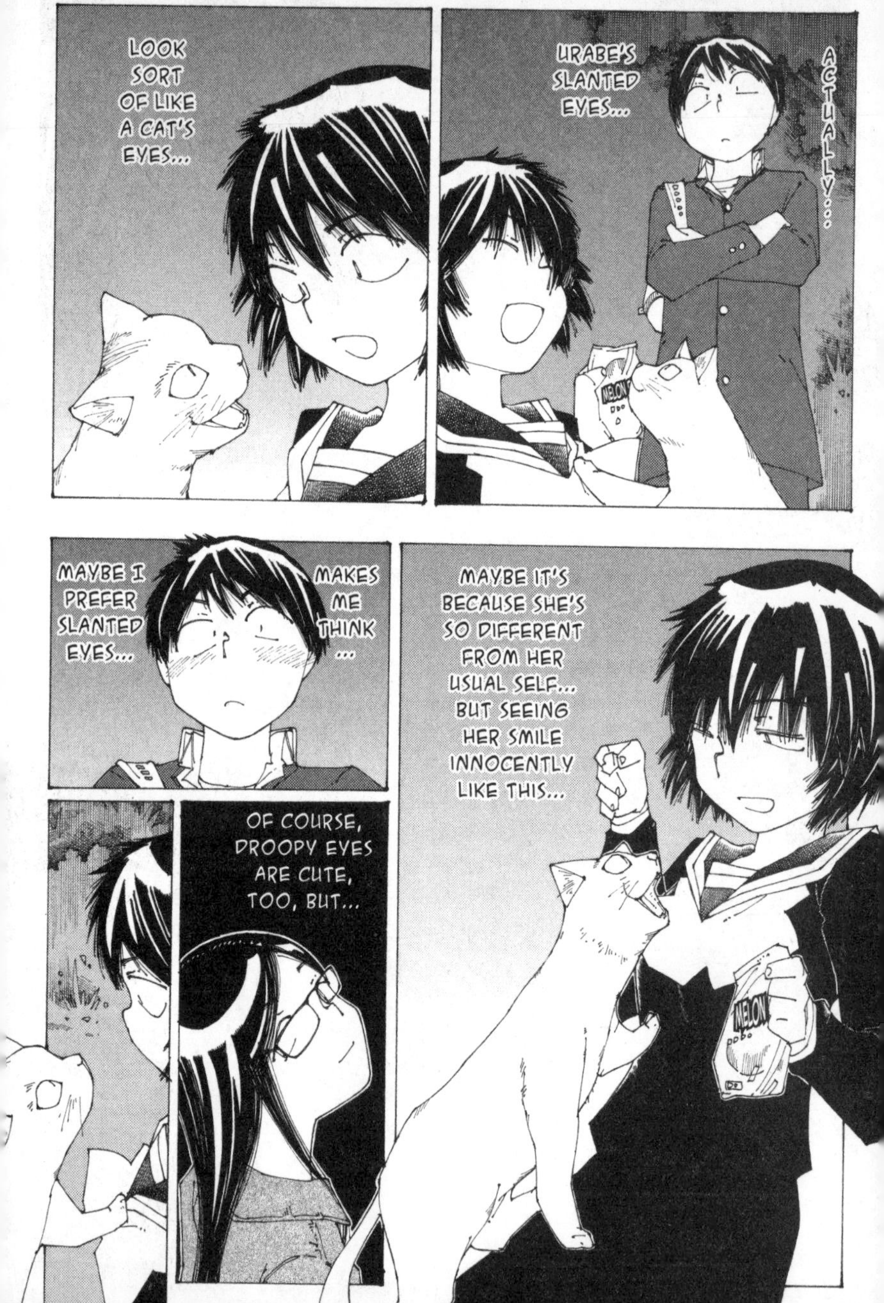
ACTUALLY...
URABE'S SLANTED EYES...
LOOK SORT OF LIKE A CAT'S EYES...
MAYBE IT'S BECAUSE SHE'S SO DIFFERENT FROM HER USUAL SELF... BUT SEEING HER SMILE INNOCENTLY LIKE THIS...
MAKES ME THINK ...
MAYBE I PREFER SLANTED EYES...
OF COURSE, DROOPY EYES ARE CUTE, TOO, BUT...
MELON
MELON

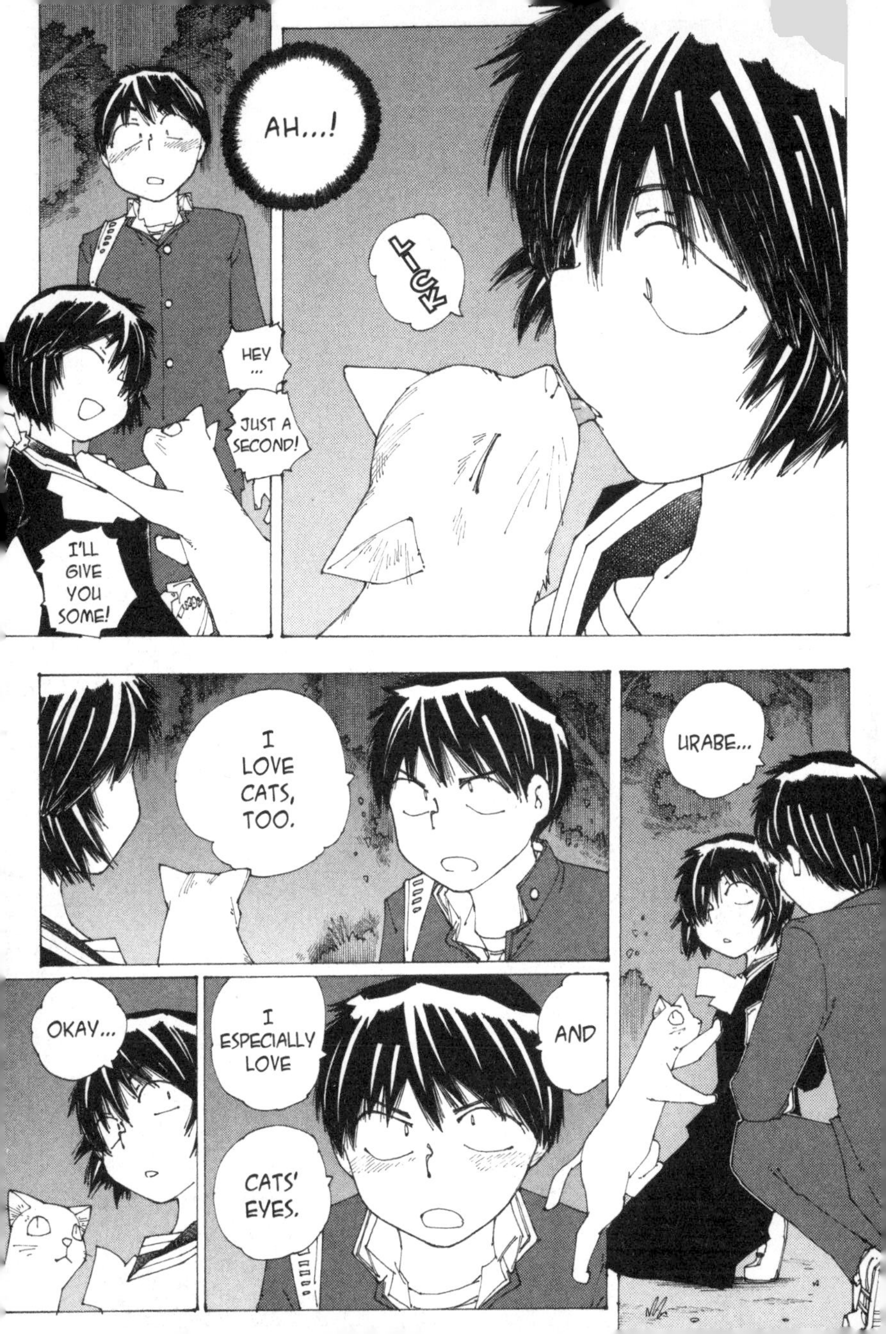
AH...!
LICK
HEY ...
JUST A SECOND!
I'LL GIVE YOU SOME!
URABE...
I LOVE CATS, TOO.
AND
I ESPECIALLY LOVE
CATS' EYES.
OKAY...

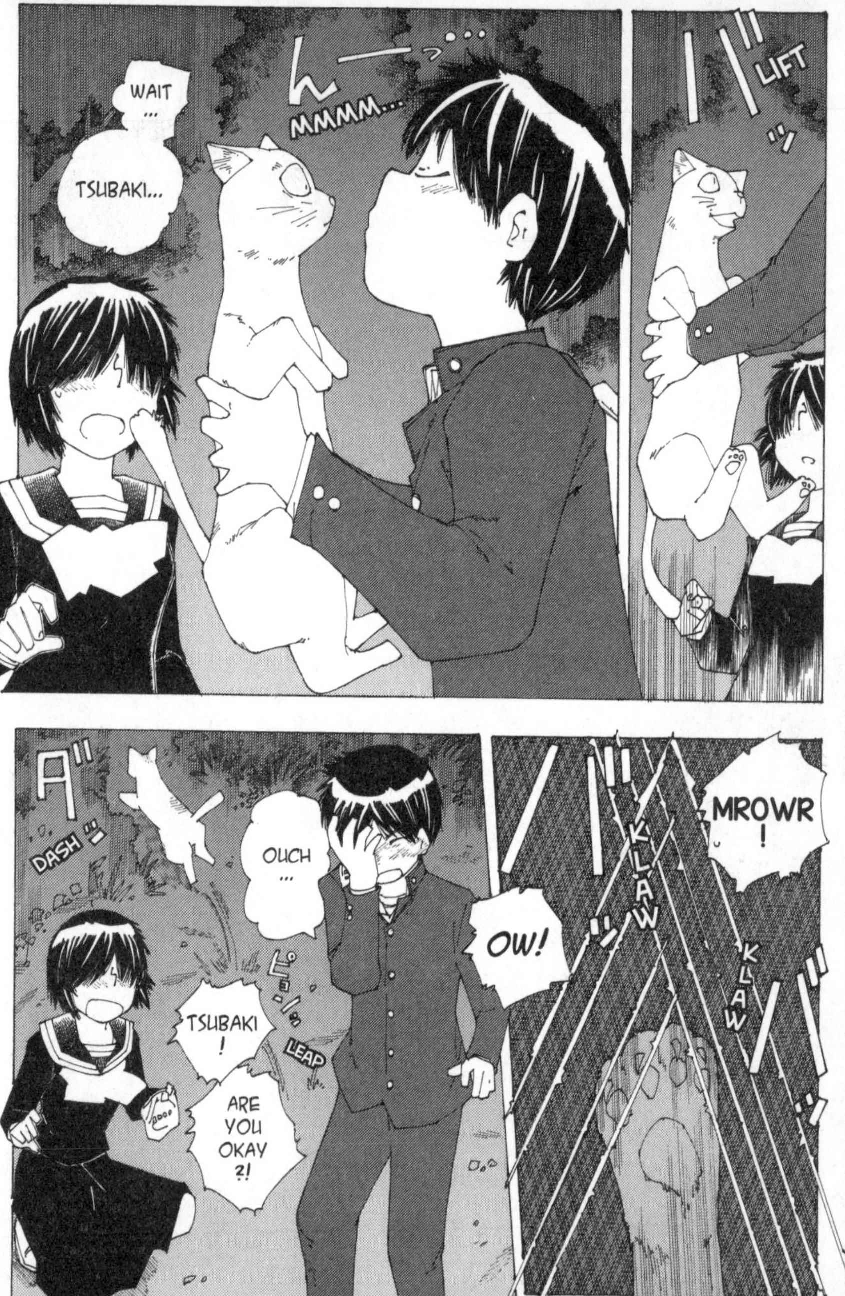

LIFT
MMMM...
WAIT ...
TSUBAKI...
MROWR !
KLAW
KLAW
OUCH ...
OW!
DASH
TSUBAKI !
LEAP
ARE YOU OKAY ?!

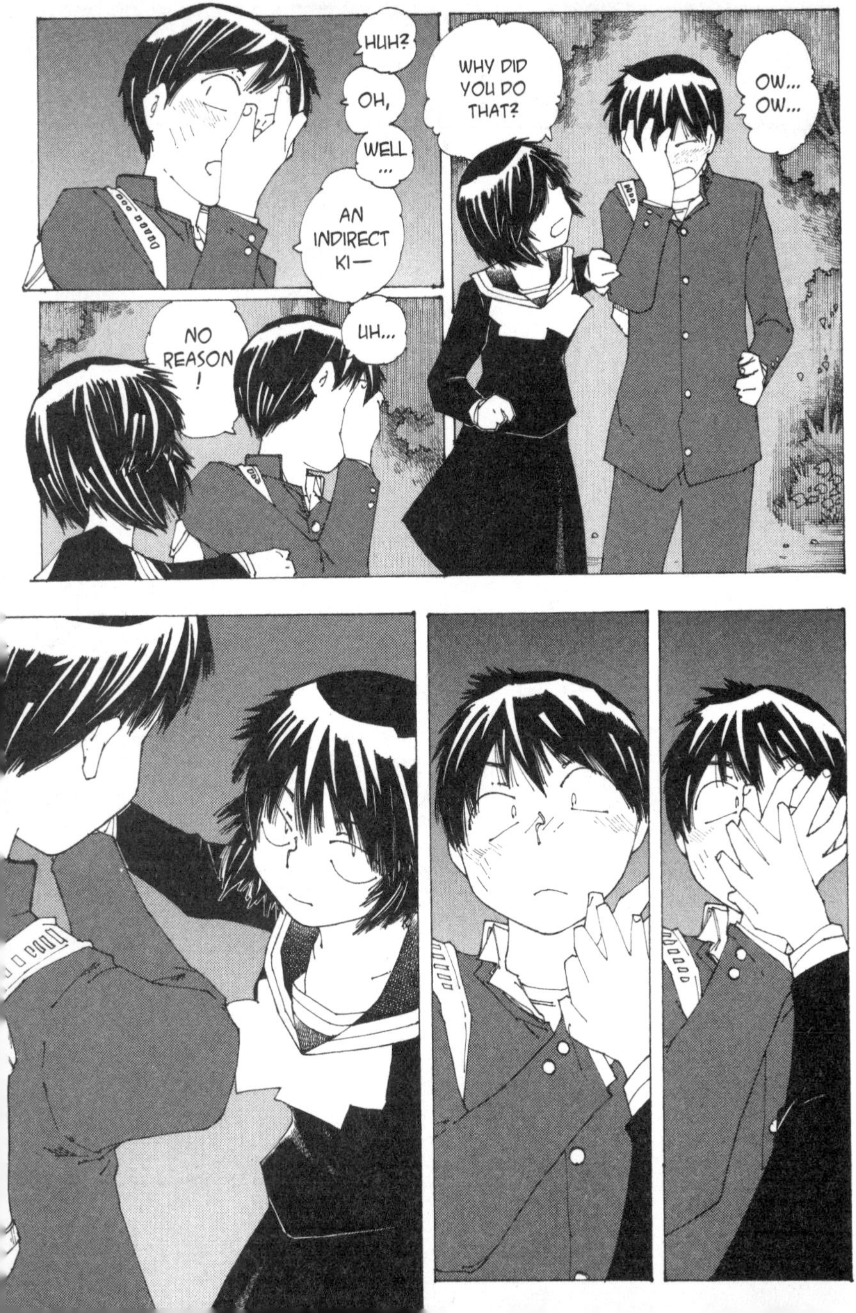
OW... OW...
WHY DID YOU DO THAT?
HUH?
OH,
WELL ...
AN INDIRECT KI—
UH...
NO REASON !

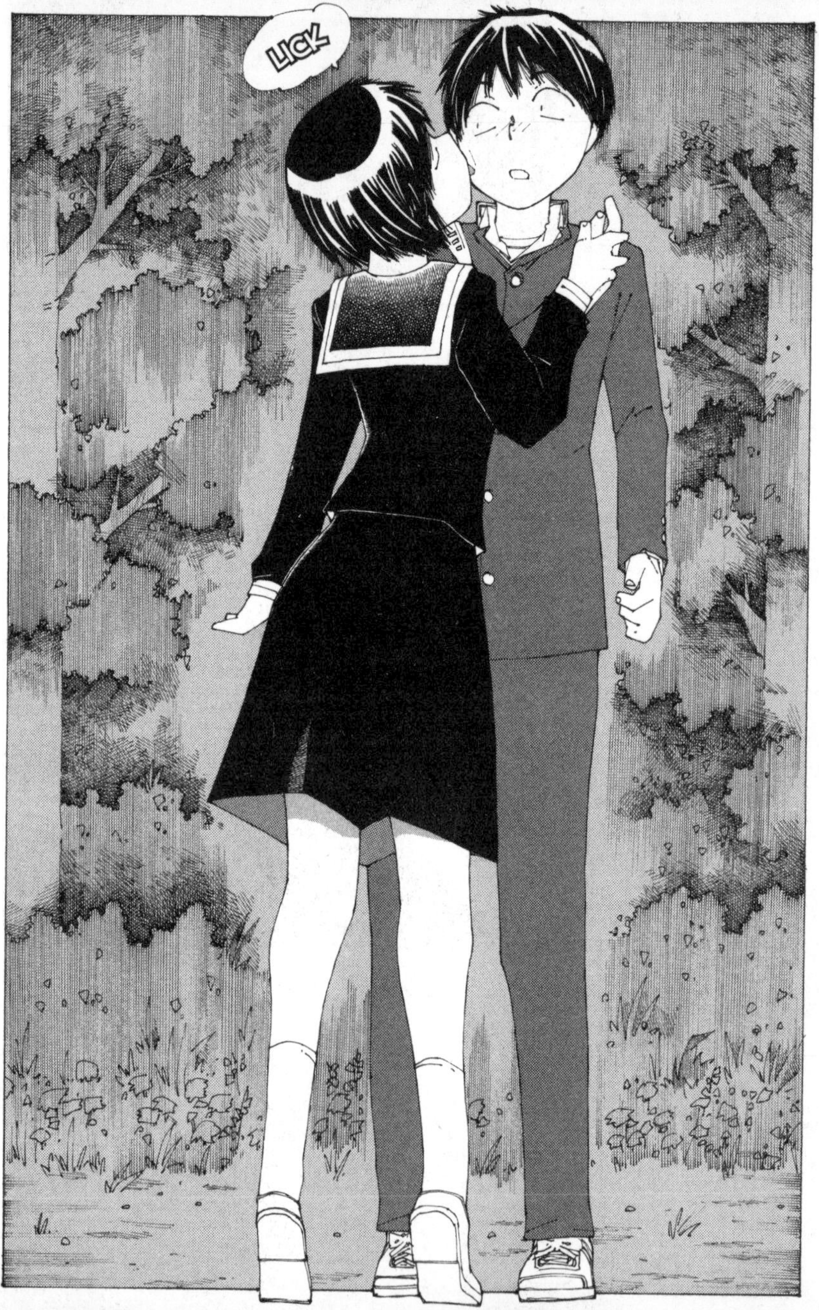
LICK

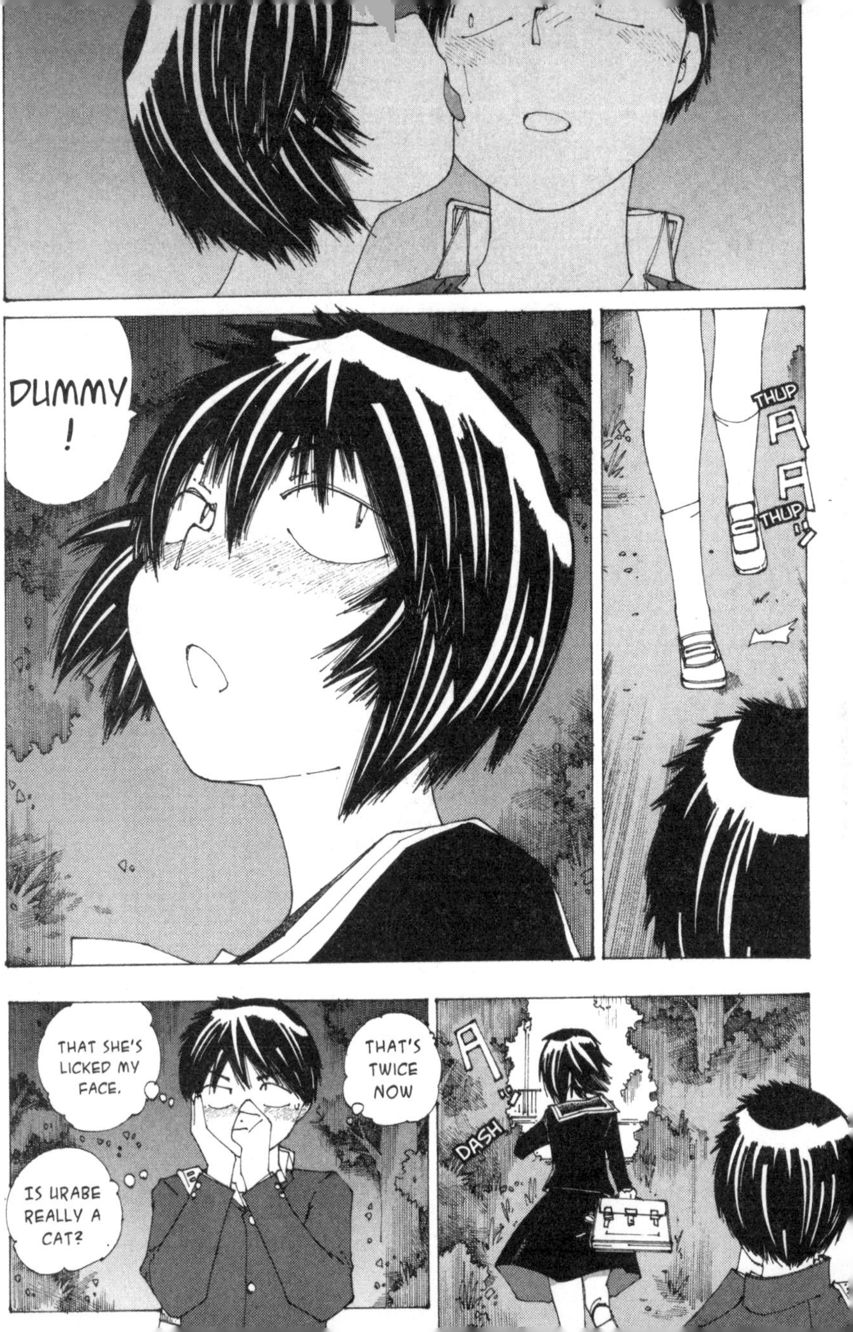
THUP
THUP
DUMMY!
DASH
THAT'S TWICE NOW
THAT SHE'S LICKED MY FACE.
IS URABE REALLY A CAT?

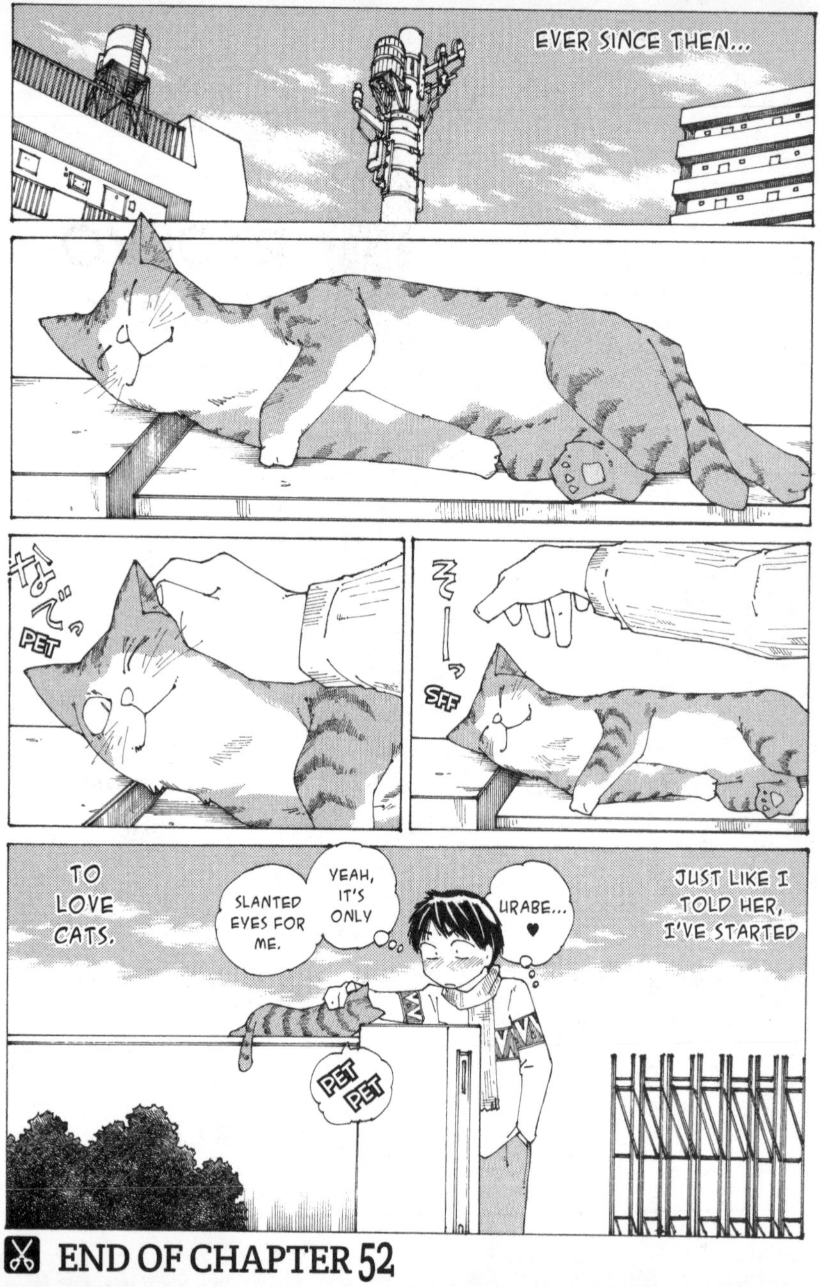
EVER SINCE THEN...
そーっ
SFF
なでっ
PET
JUST LIKE I TOLD HER, I'VE STARTED
URABE... ♥
YEAH, IT'S ONLY
SLANTED EYES FOR ME.
TO LOVE CATS.
PET PET

END OF CHAPTER 52

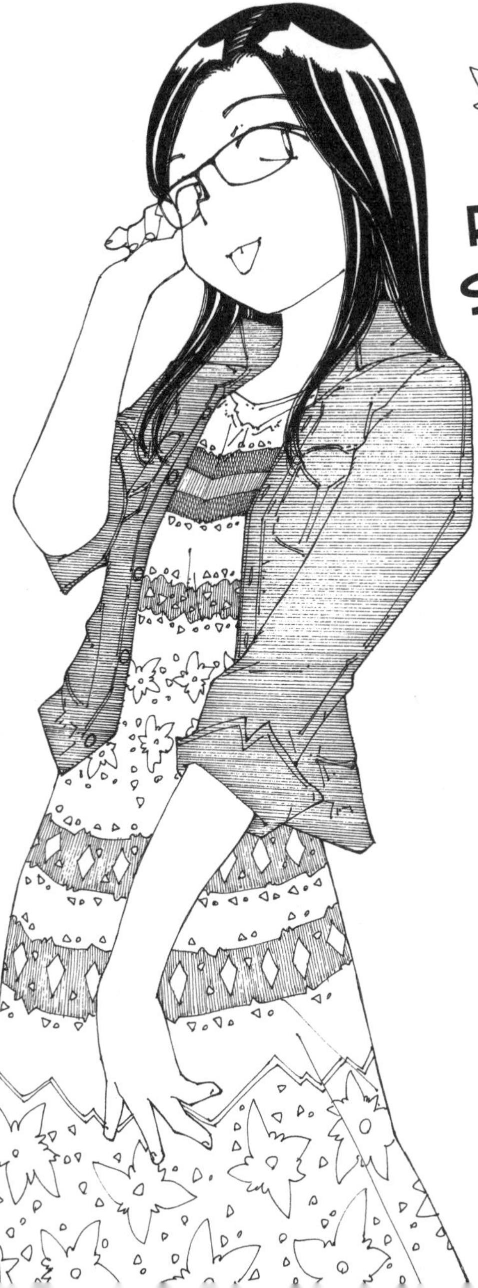

NEW CHARACTER

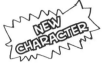

RYOUKO SUWANO (17)

SHE DOESN'T WEAR GLASSES AT SCHOOL, BUT SHE WEARS THEM ON HER OWN TIME.

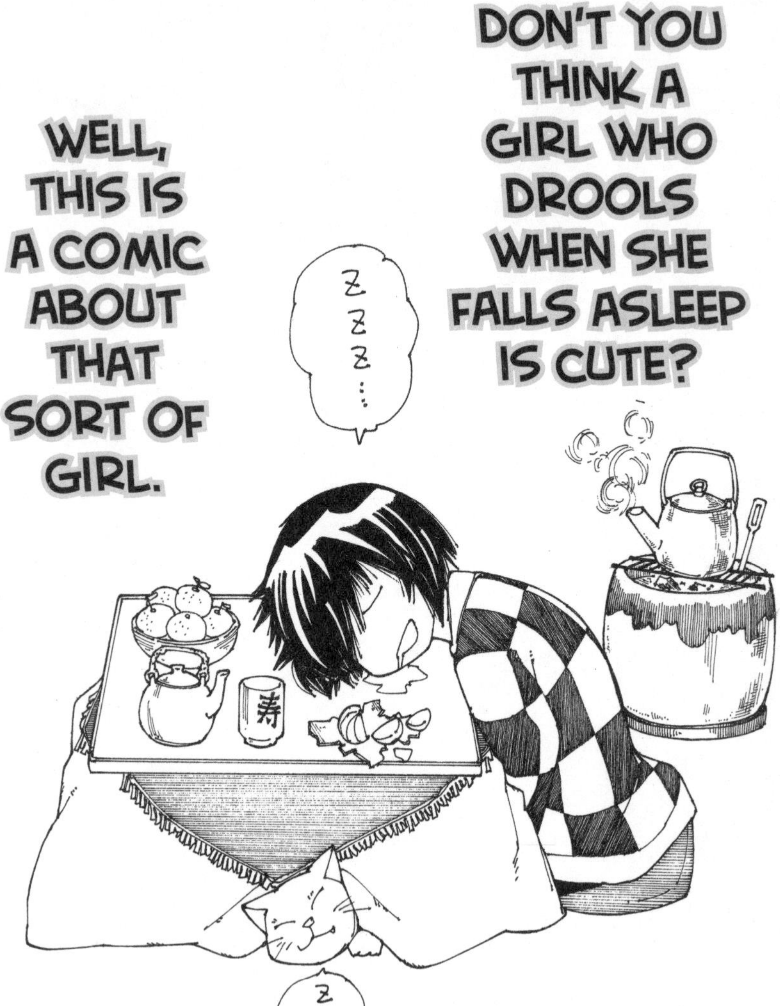
DON'T YOU THINK A GIRL WHO DROOLS WHEN SHE FALLS ASLEEP IS CUTE?
WELL, THIS IS A COMIC ABOUT THAT SORT OF GIRL.
Z Z Z...
Z Z Z...

MYSTERIOUS GIRLFRIEND X

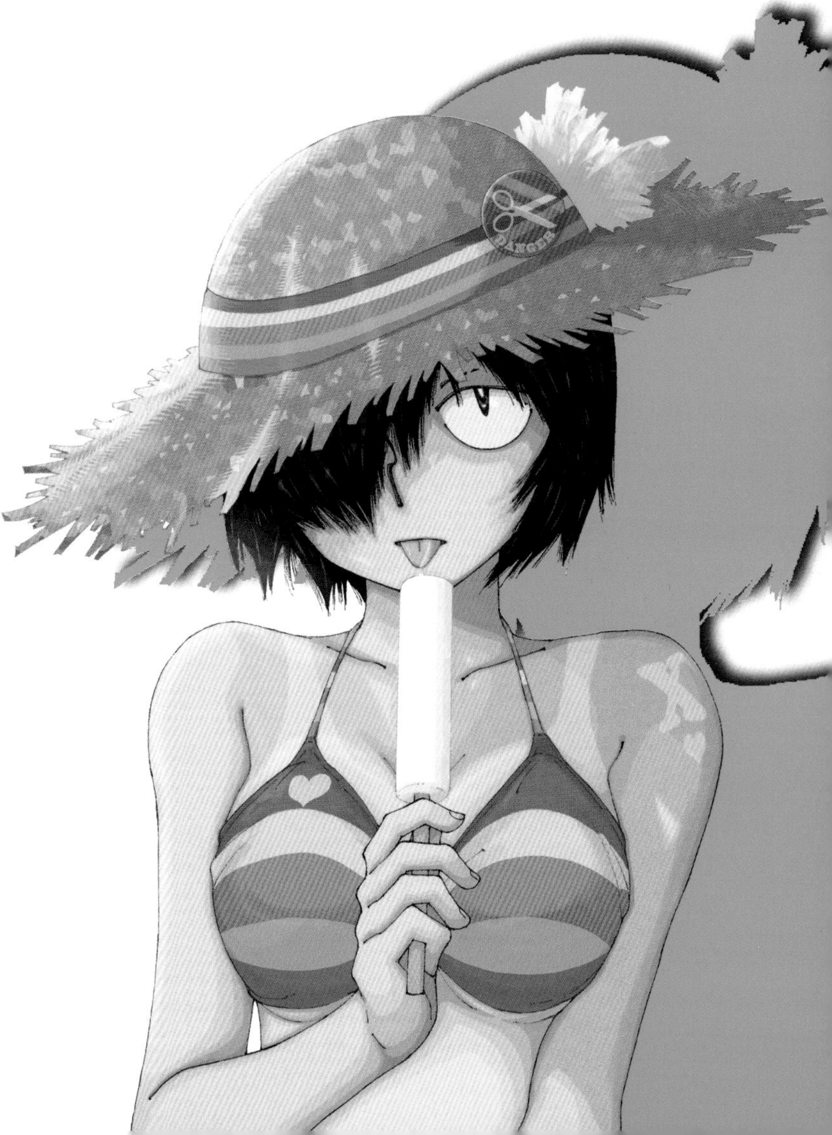
DANGER

VERTICAL COMICS

MYSTERIOUS GIRLFRIEND X

RIICHI UESHIBA

MYSTERIOUS GIRLFRIEND X

Ayuko Oka (17)

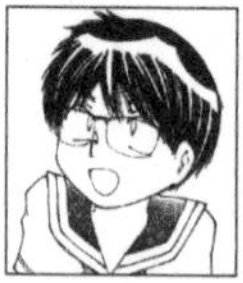

At 4'8", she's very small, but her figure is well-developed and quite gorgeous. She is Ueno's girlfriend. She often toys with Urabe through her impish personality. Like Tsubaki, she is responsive to Urabe's drool.

Kouhei Ueno (17)

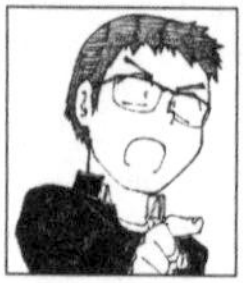

Tsubaki's best friend. He's been going out with their classmate, Oka, since they were sophomores. Ueno's fond way of talking about Oka frequently influences Tsubaki's ideas about relationships.

Youko Tsubaki (24)

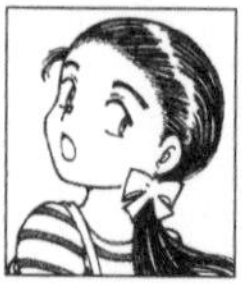

Akira's sister, seven years his senior. She handles all the housework in place of their mother, who died when they were young. Akira is highly indebted to her.

Ryouko Suwano (17)

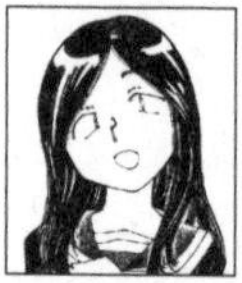

Tsubaki's classmate who shares his class duties. Her drooping eyes are her most charming feature. She knows Tsubaki has a girlfriend, though she doesn't know that it's Urabe.

Characters

Mikoto Urabe (17)

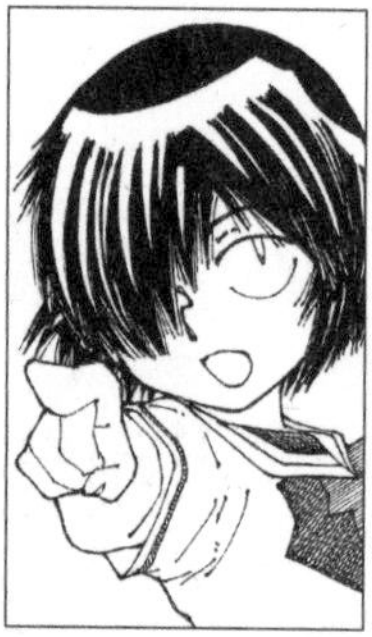

A transfer student who joined Tsubaki's class. She can convey her own feelings through her drool, as well as pick up on Tsubaki's feelings through his. She's antisocial and everything she says and does is mysterious, but her ideas about love are very pure. Her hobby is using scissors, which she can use to cut up anything.

Akira Tsubaki (17)

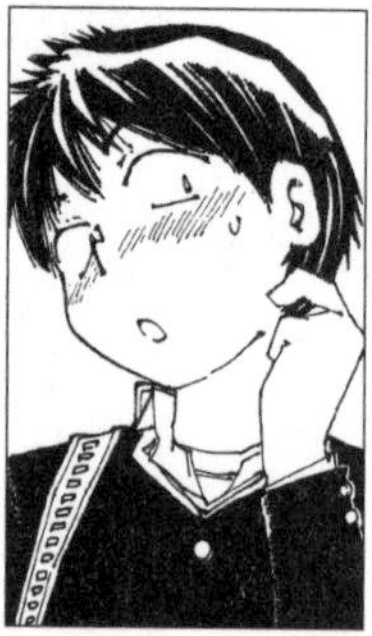

The protagonist of the story. His bizarre relationship with Urabe began after he licked her drool one day. He is as interested in girls as any boy his age, but Urabe takes the lead in their relationship and Tsubaki can't seem to initiate any progress between them.

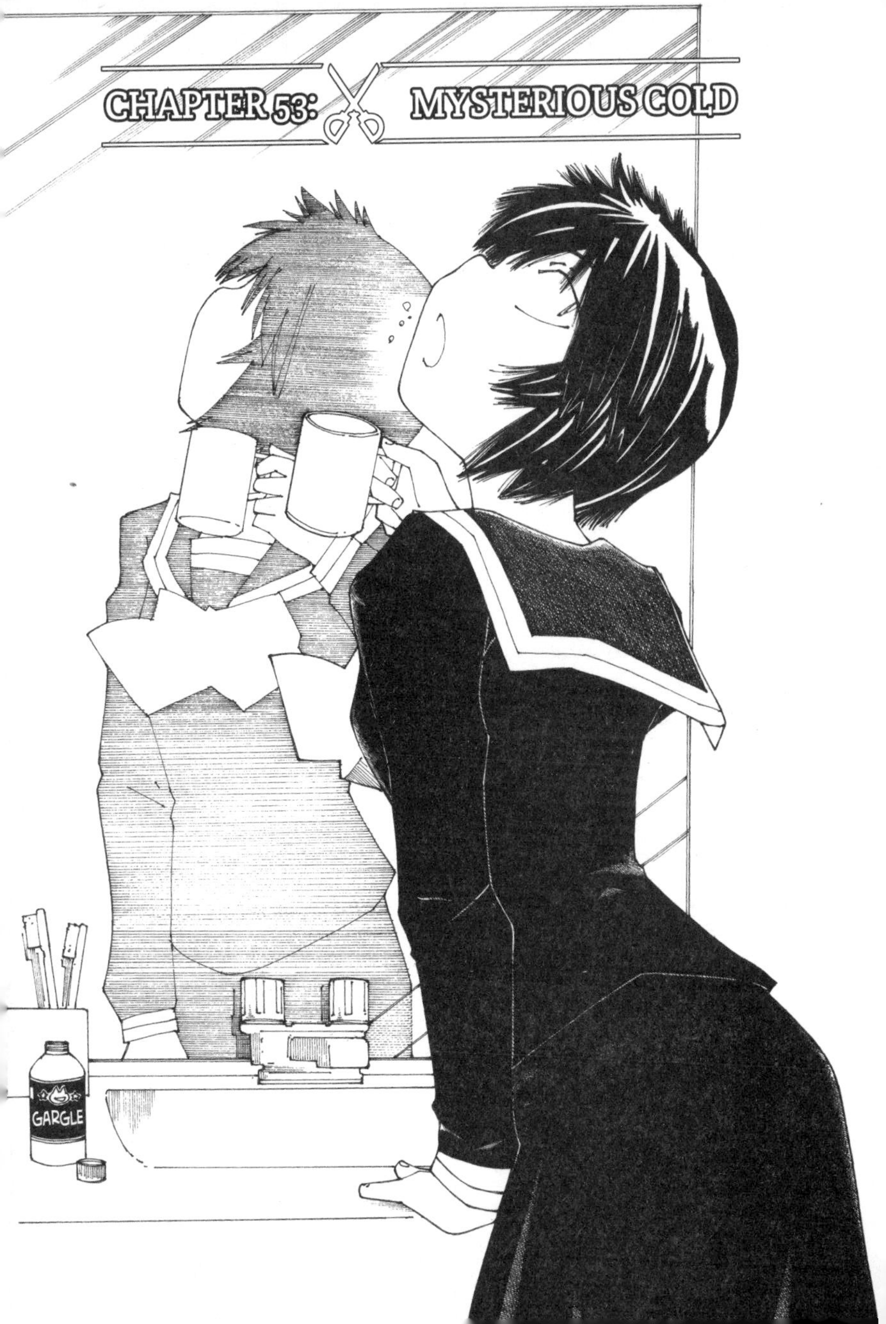
CHAPTER 53: MYSTERIOUS COLD
GARGLE

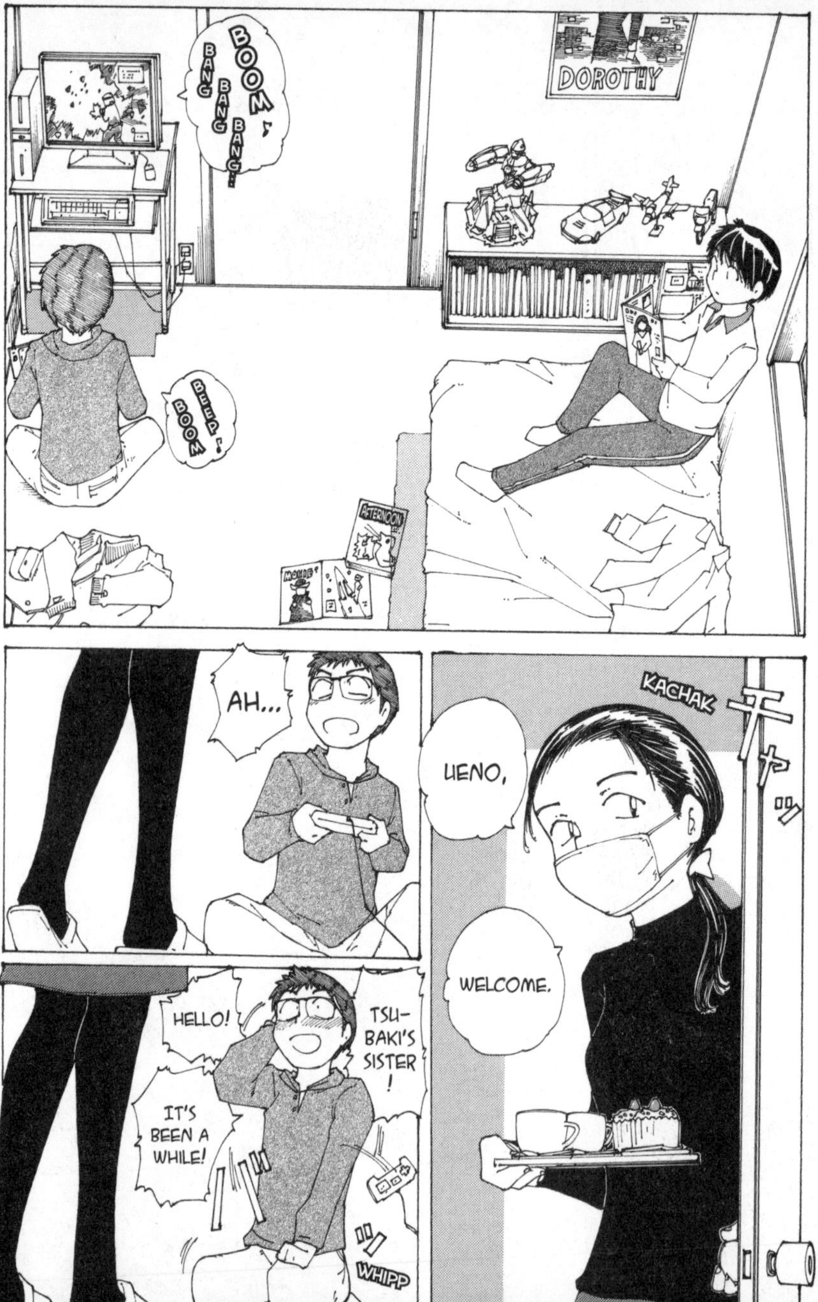
DOROTHY
BOOM BANG BANG BANG...
BEEP BOOM
AFTERNOON
KACHAK
チャッ
UENO,
WELCOME.
AH...
TSU-BAKI'S SISTER!
HELLO!
IT'S BEEN A WHILE!
WHIPP

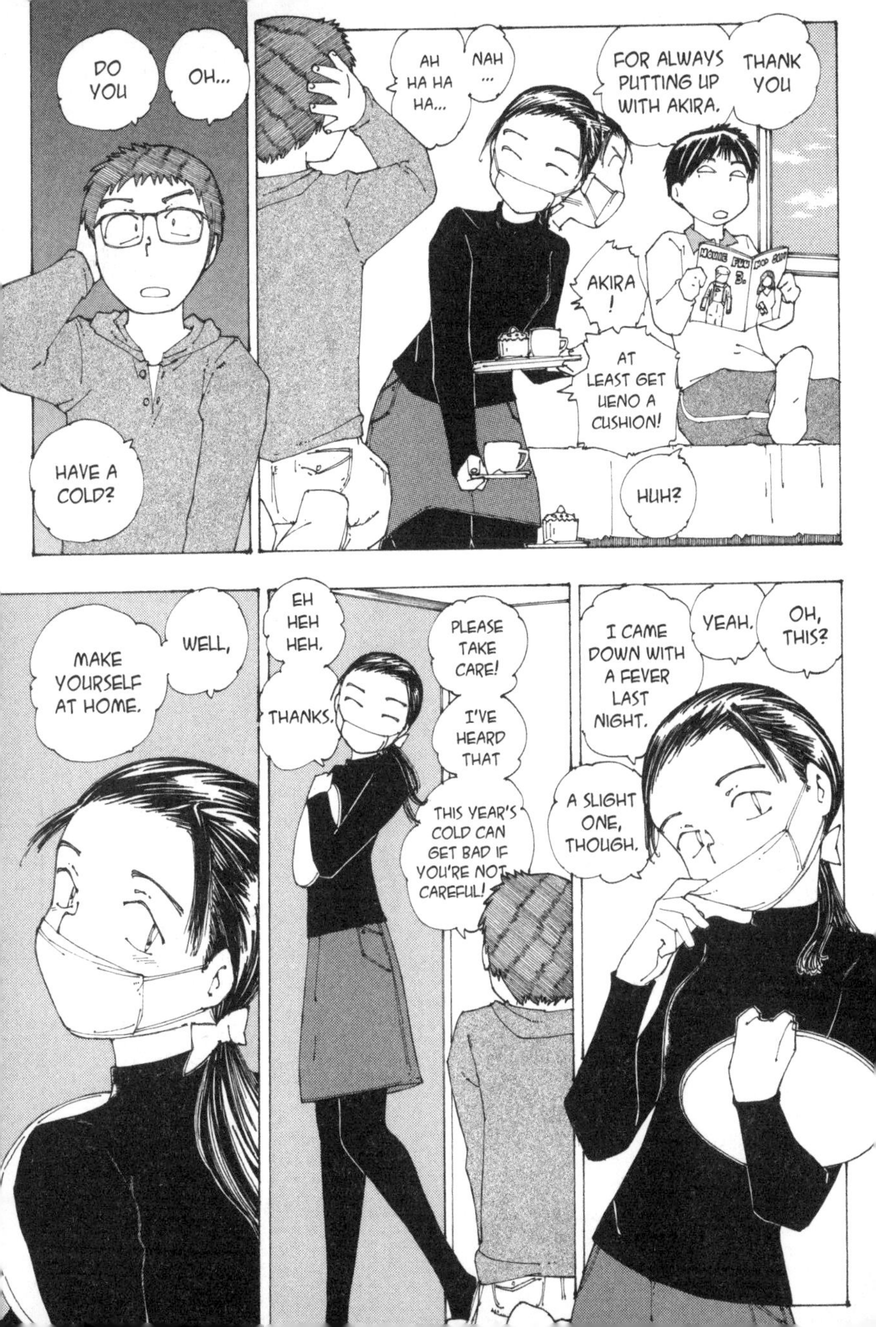
THANK YOU
FOR ALWAYS PUTTING UP WITH AKIRA.
NAH...
AH HA HA HA...
AKIRA!
AT LEAST GET UENO A CUSHION!
HUH?
OH...
DO YOU
HAVE A COLD?
OH, THIS?
YEAH.
I CAME DOWN WITH A FEVER LAST NIGHT.
A SLIGHT ONE, THOUGH.
PLEASE TAKE CARE!
I'VE HEARD THAT
THIS YEAR'S COLD CAN GET BAD IF YOU'RE NOT CAREFUL!
EH HEH HEH.
THANKS.
WELL,
MAKE YOURSELF AT HOME.

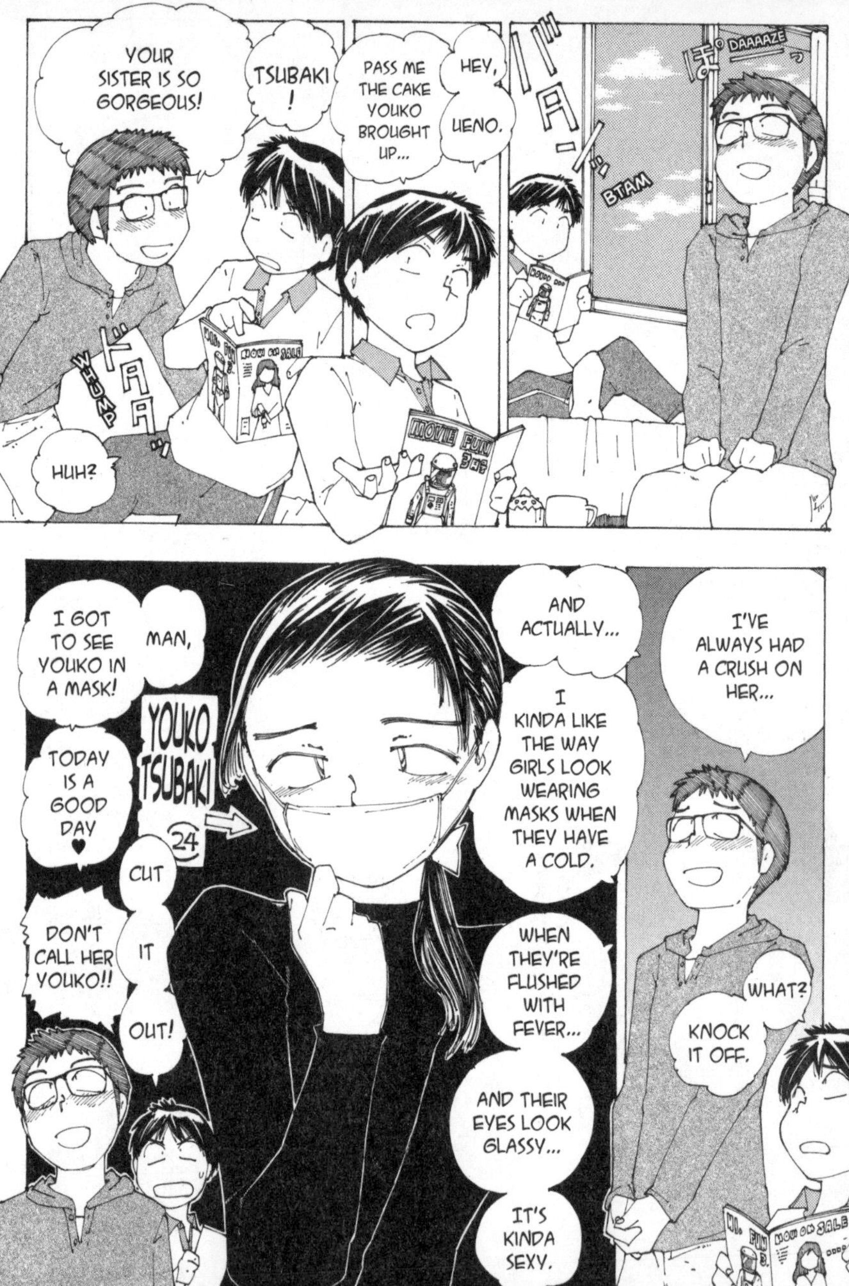

DAAAAAZE
BTAM
HEY, UENO.
PASS ME THE CAKE YOUKO BROUGHT UP...
TSUBAKI!
YOUR SISTER IS SO GORGEOUS!
MOVIE FUN
NOW ON SALE
WHUMP
HUH?
I'VE ALWAYS HAD A CRUSH ON HER...
WHAT?
KNOCK IT OFF.
AND ACTUALLY...
I KINDA LIKE THE WAY GIRLS LOOK WEARING MASKS WHEN THEY HAVE A COLD.
WHEN THEY'RE FLUSHED WITH FEVER...
AND THEIR EYES LOOK GLASSY...
IT'S KINDA SEXY.
YOUKO TSUBAKI
24
MAN,
I GOT TO SEE YOUKO IN A MASK!
TODAY IS A GOOD DAY ♥
CUT IT OUT!
DON'T CALL HER YOUKO!!

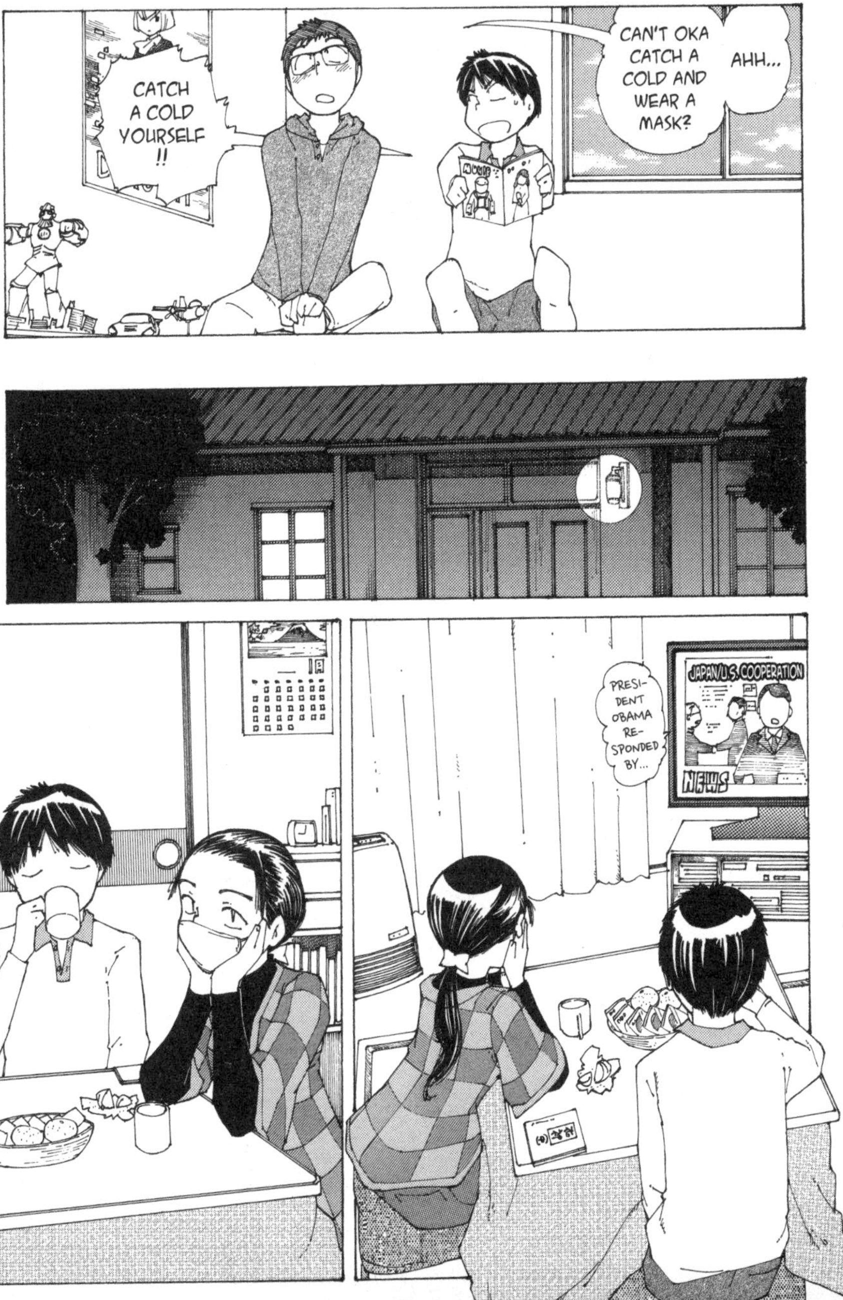
AHH...
CAN'T OKA CATCH A COLD AND WEAR A MASK?
CATCH A COLD YOURSELF !!
JAPAN/U.S. COOPERATION
NEWS
PRESIDENT OBAMA RESPONDED BY...

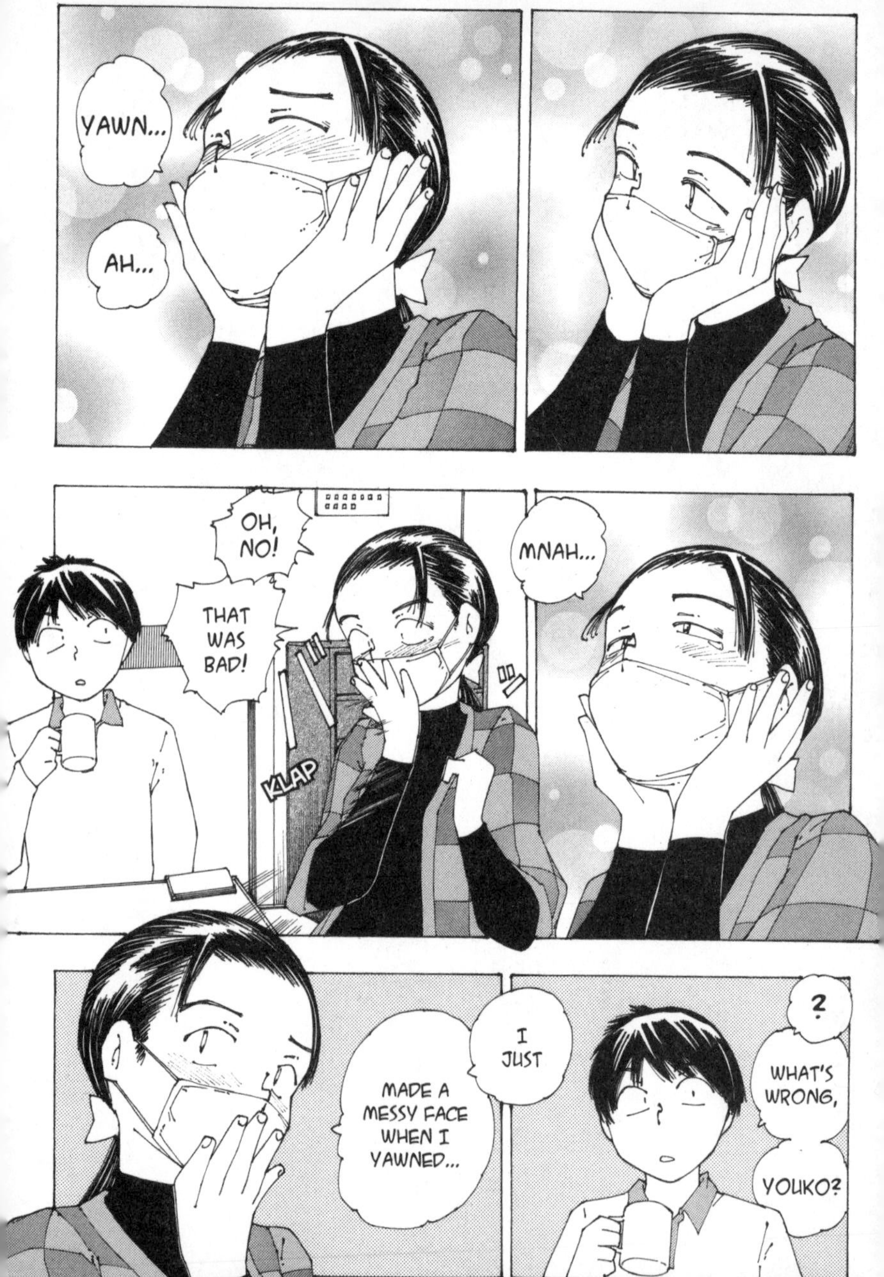
YAWN...
AH...
MNAH...
OH, NO!
THAT WAS BAD!
KLAP
?
WHAT'S WRONG,
YOUKO?
I JUST
MADE A MESSY FACE WHEN I YAWNED...

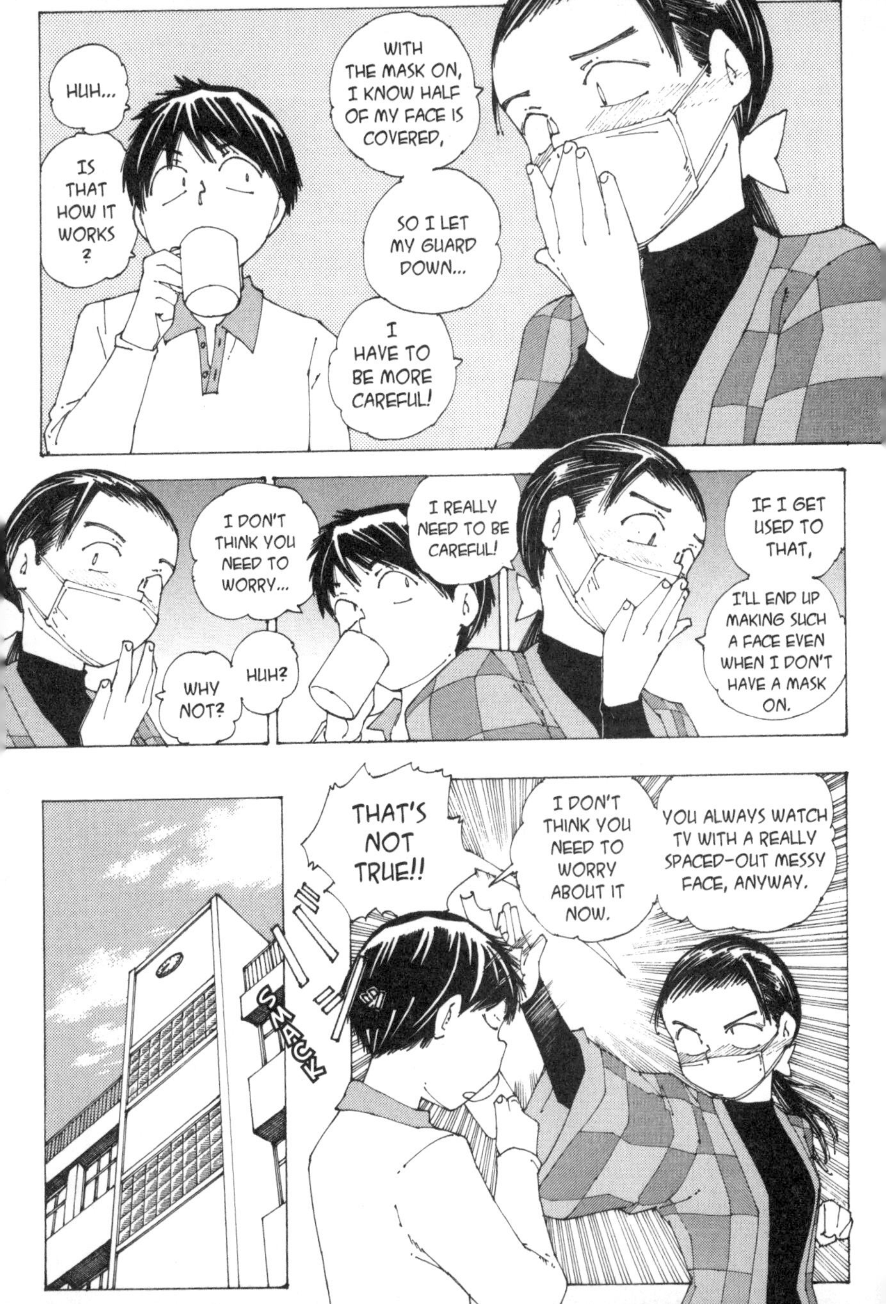
WITH THE MASK ON, I KNOW HALF OF MY FACE IS COVERED,
SO I LET MY GUARD DOWN...
I HAVE TO BE MORE CAREFUL!
HUH...
IS THAT HOW IT WORKS?
I REALLY NEED TO BE CAREFUL!
IF I GET USED TO THAT,
I'LL END UP MAKING SUCH A FACE EVEN WHEN I DON'T HAVE A MASK ON.
I DON'T THINK YOU NEED TO WORRY...
HUH?
WHY NOT?
I DON'T THINK YOU NEED TO WORRY ABOUT IT NOW.
YOU ALWAYS WATCH TV WITH A REALLY SPACED-OUT MESSY FACE, ANYWAY.
THAT'S NOT TRUE!!
SMACK

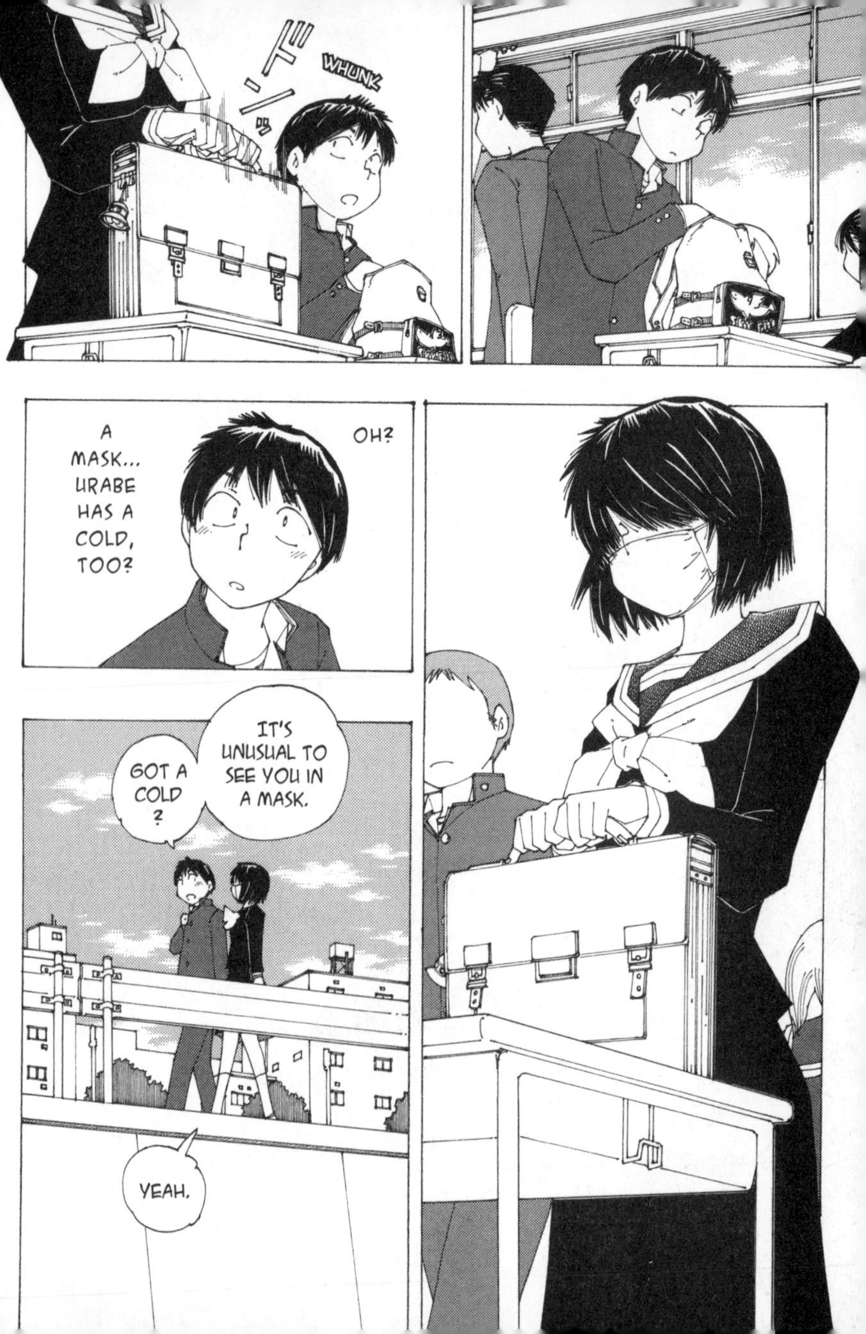
WHUNK
OH?
A MASK... URABE HAS A COLD, TOO?
IT'S UNUSUAL TO SEE YOU IN A MASK.
GOT A COLD?
YEAH.

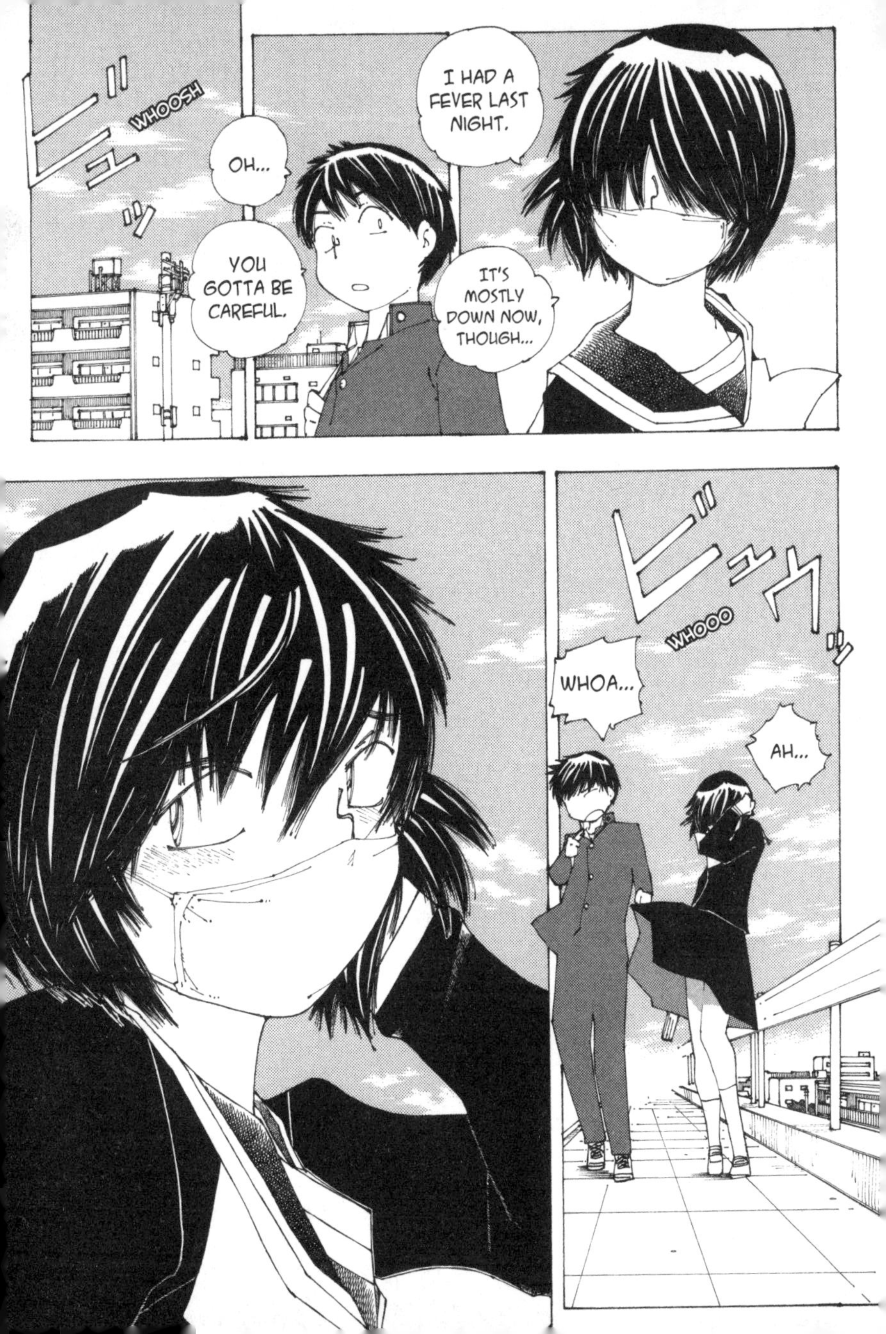
I HAD A FEVER LAST NIGHT.
OH...
IT'S MOSTLY DOWN NOW, THOUGH...
YOU GOTTA BE CAREFUL.
WHOOSH
WHOOO
WHOA...
AH...

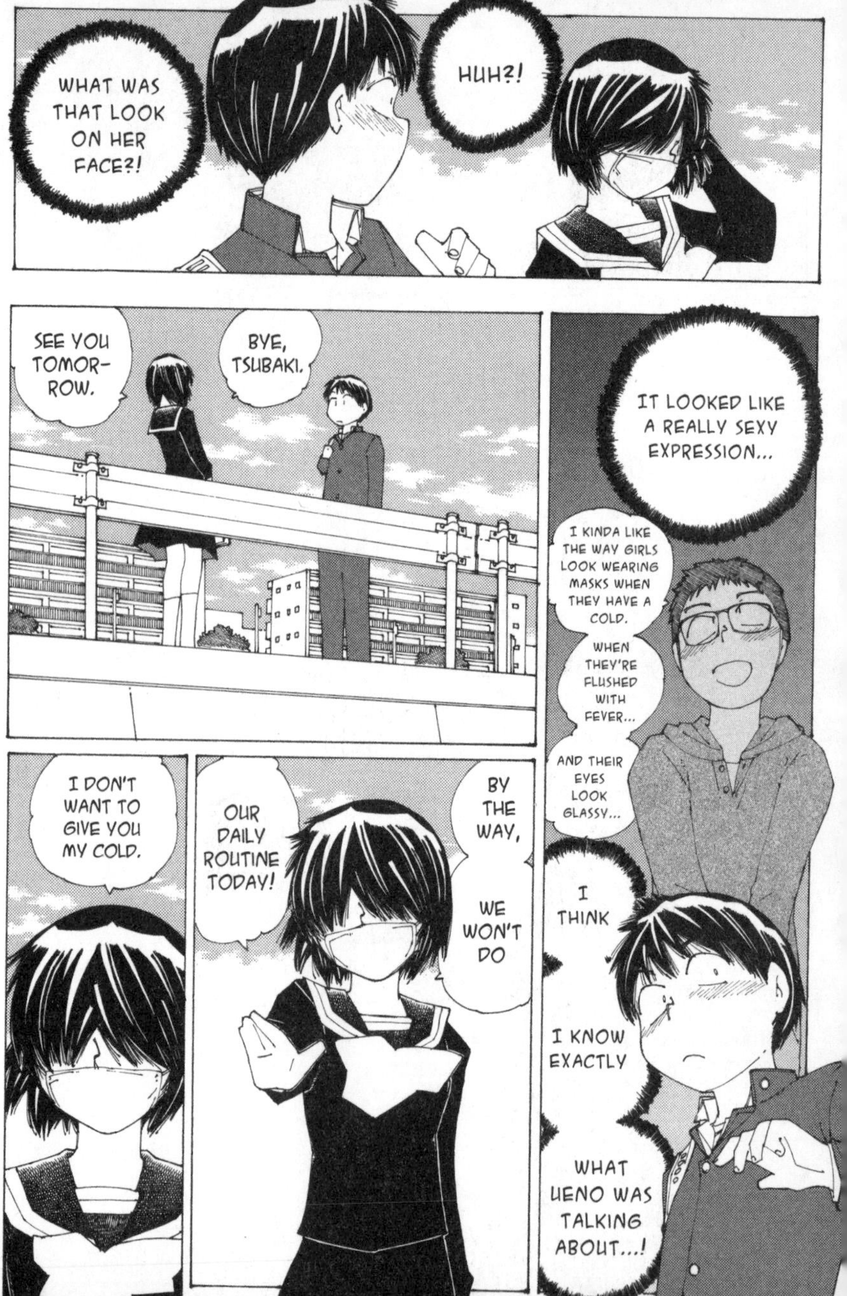
HUH?!
WHAT WAS THAT LOOK ON HER FACE?!
IT LOOKED LIKE A REALLY SEXY EXPRESSION...
I KINDA LIKE THE WAY GIRLS LOOK WEARING MASKS WHEN THEY HAVE A COLD.
WHEN THEY'RE FLUSHED WITH FEVER...
AND THEIR EYES LOOK GLASSY...
I THINK
I KNOW EXACTLY
WHAT UENO WAS TALKING ABOUT...!
BYE, TSUBAKI.
SEE YOU TOMOR-ROW.
BY THE WAY,
WE WON'T DO
OUR DAILY ROUTINE TODAY!
I DON'T WANT TO GIVE YOU MY COLD.

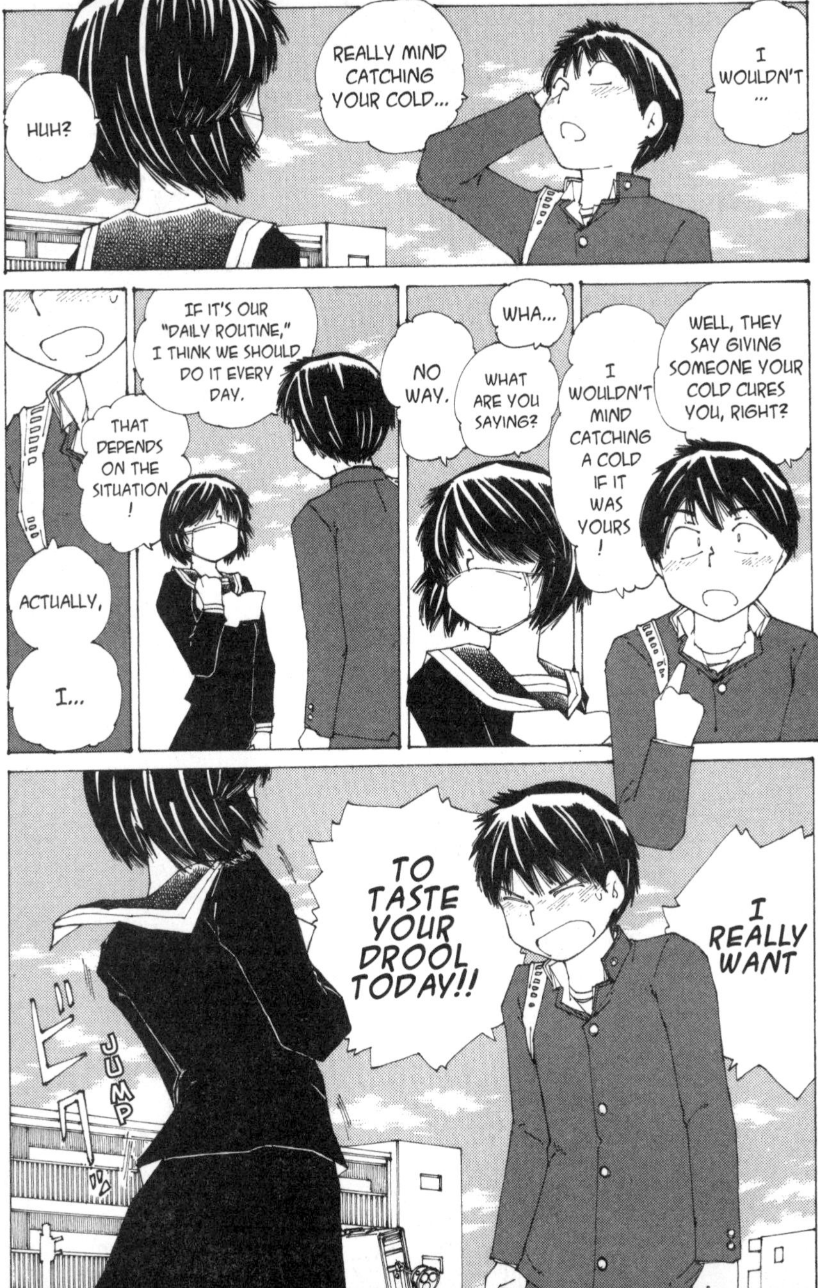
I WOULDN'T ...
REALLY MIND CATCHING YOUR COLD...
HUH?
WELL, THEY SAY GIVING SOMEONE YOUR COLD CURES YOU, RIGHT?
I WOULDN'T MIND CATCHING A COLD IF IT WAS YOURS!
WHA...
WHAT ARE YOU SAYING?
NO WAY.
IF IT'S OUR "DAILY ROUTINE," I THINK WE SHOULD DO IT EVERY DAY.
THAT DEPENDS ON THE SITUATION!
ACTUALLY,
I...
I REALLY WANT
TO TASTE YOUR DROOL TODAY!!
JUMP

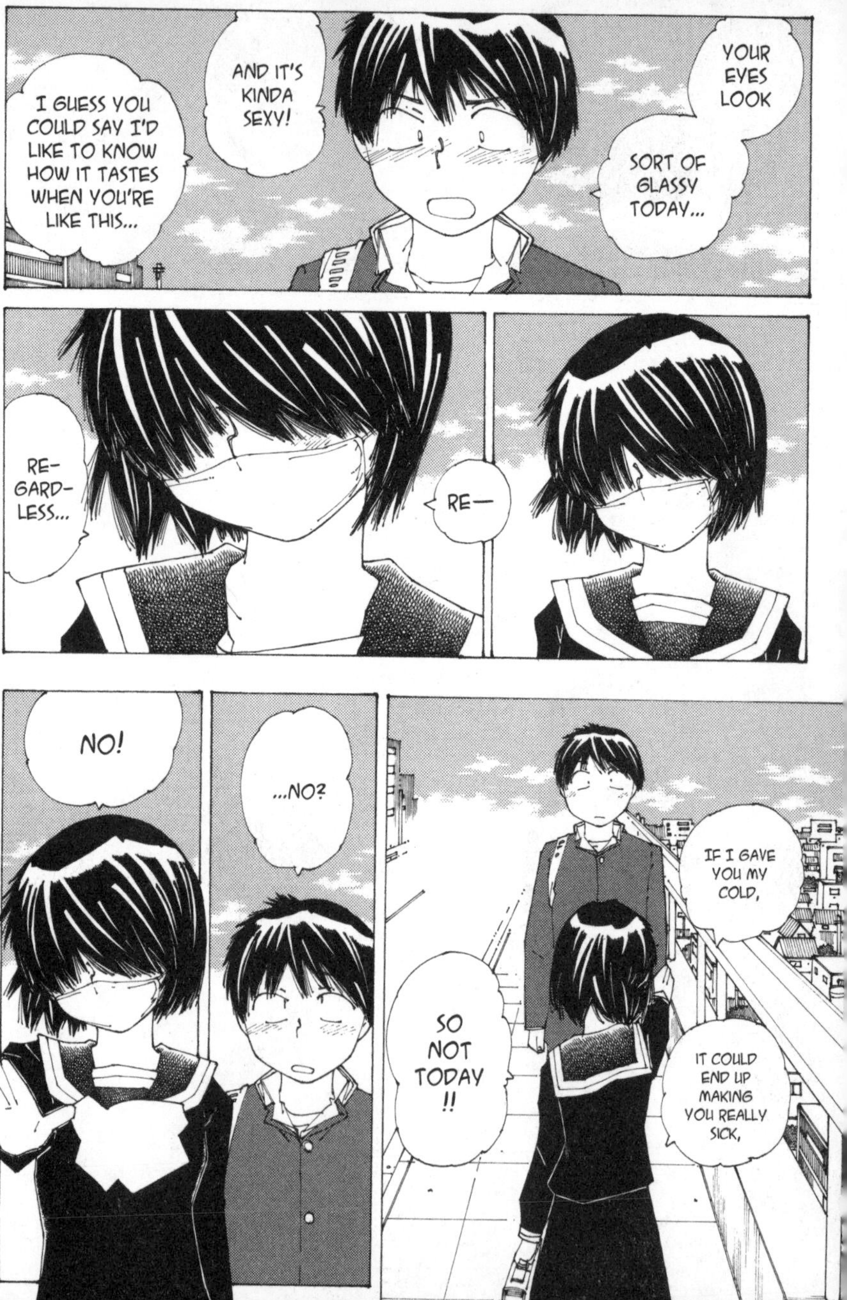
YOUR EYES LOOK
SORT OF GLASSY TODAY...
AND IT'S KINDA SEXY!
I GUESS YOU COULD SAY I'D LIKE TO KNOW HOW IT TASTES WHEN YOU'RE LIKE THIS...
RE—
RE-GARD-LESS...
IF I GAVE YOU MY COLD,
IT COULD END UP MAKING YOU REALLY SICK,
SO NOT TODAY !!
...NO?
NO!

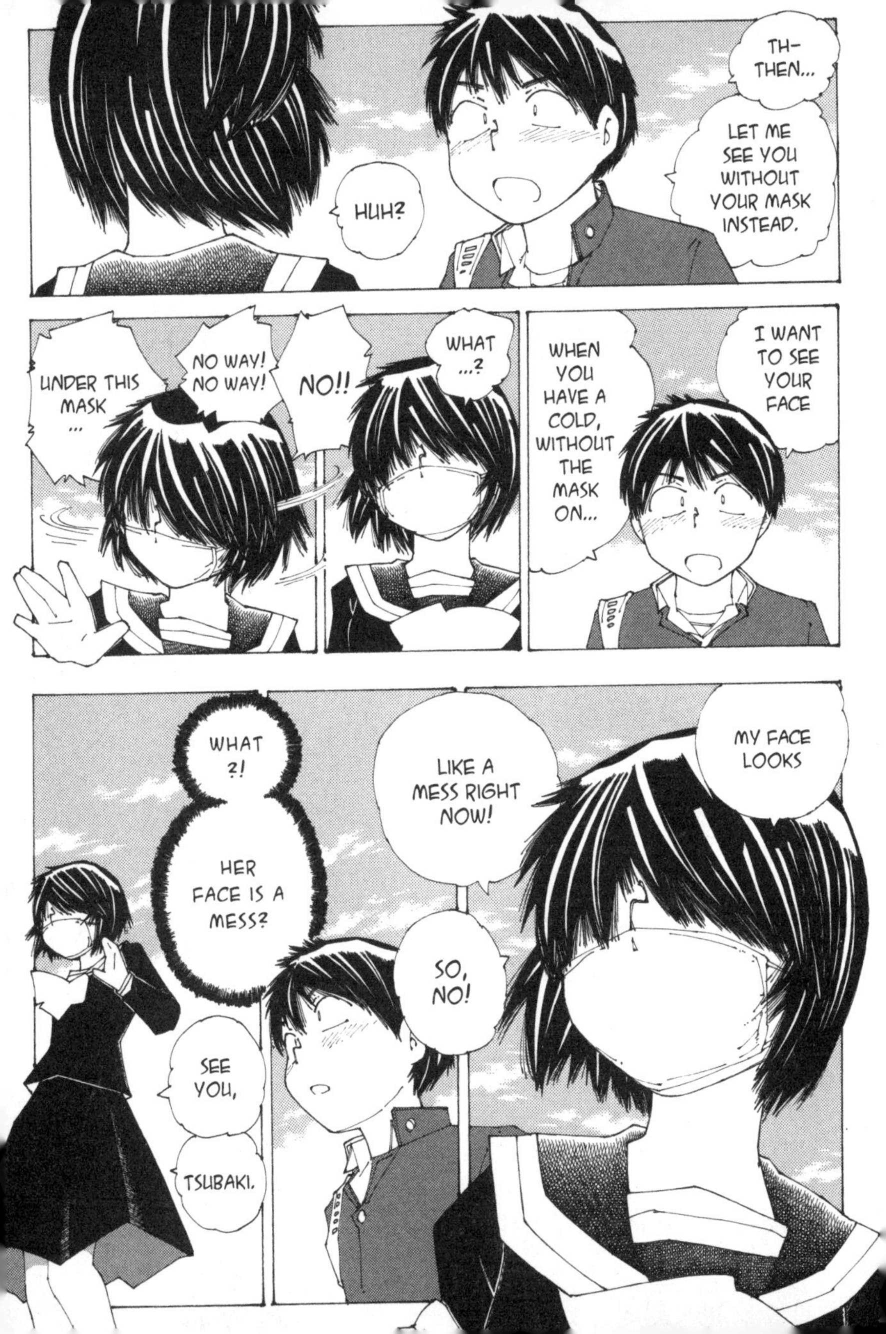
TH-THEN...
LET ME SEE YOU WITHOUT YOUR MASK INSTEAD.
HUH?
I WANT TO SEE YOUR FACE
WHEN YOU HAVE A COLD, WITHOUT THE MASK ON...
WHAT ...?
NO!!
NO WAY! NO WAY!
UNDER THIS MASK ...
MY FACE LOOKS
LIKE A MESS RIGHT NOW!
SO, NO!
WHAT ?!
HER FACE IS A MESS?
SEE YOU,
TSUBAKI.

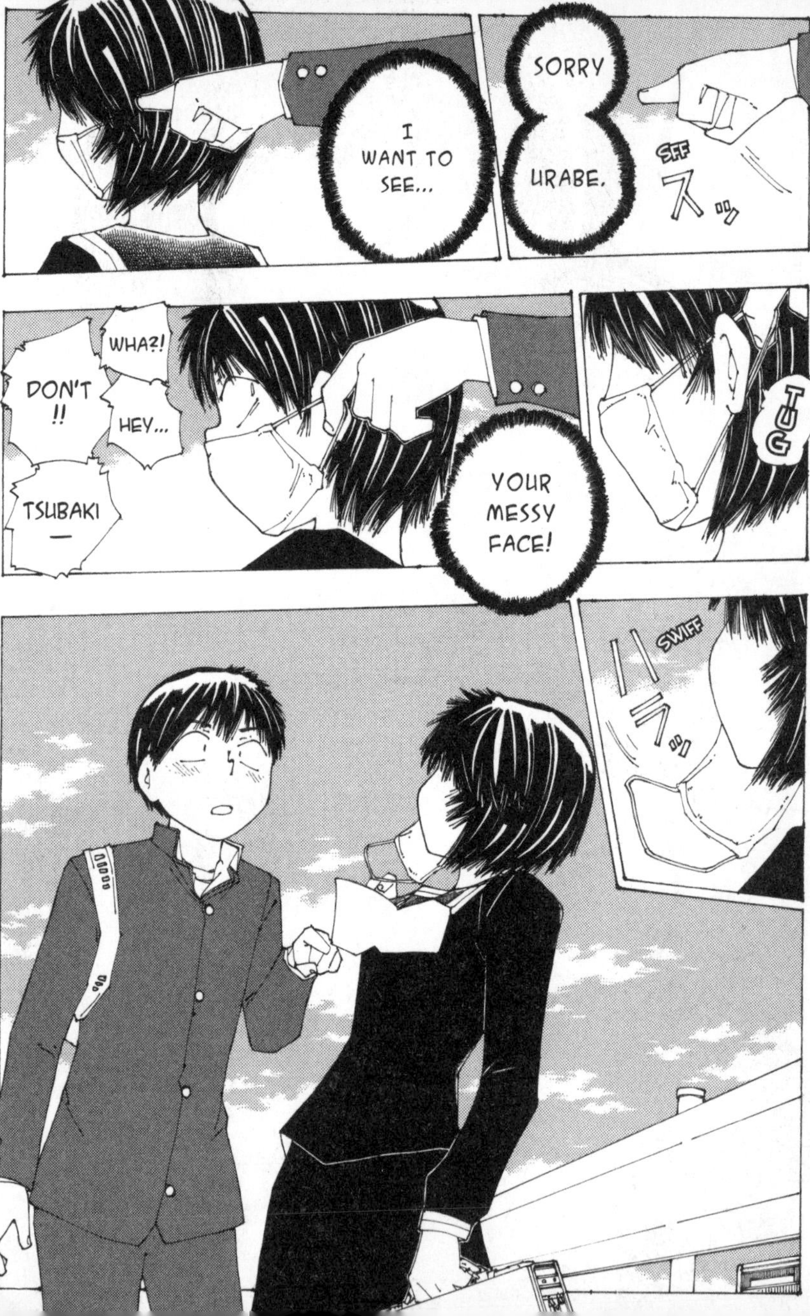
SORRY URABE.
SFF
スッ
I WANT TO SEE...
TUG
YOUR MESSY FACE!
WHA?!
HEY...
DON'T !!
TSUBAKI —
SWIFF
ハラッ

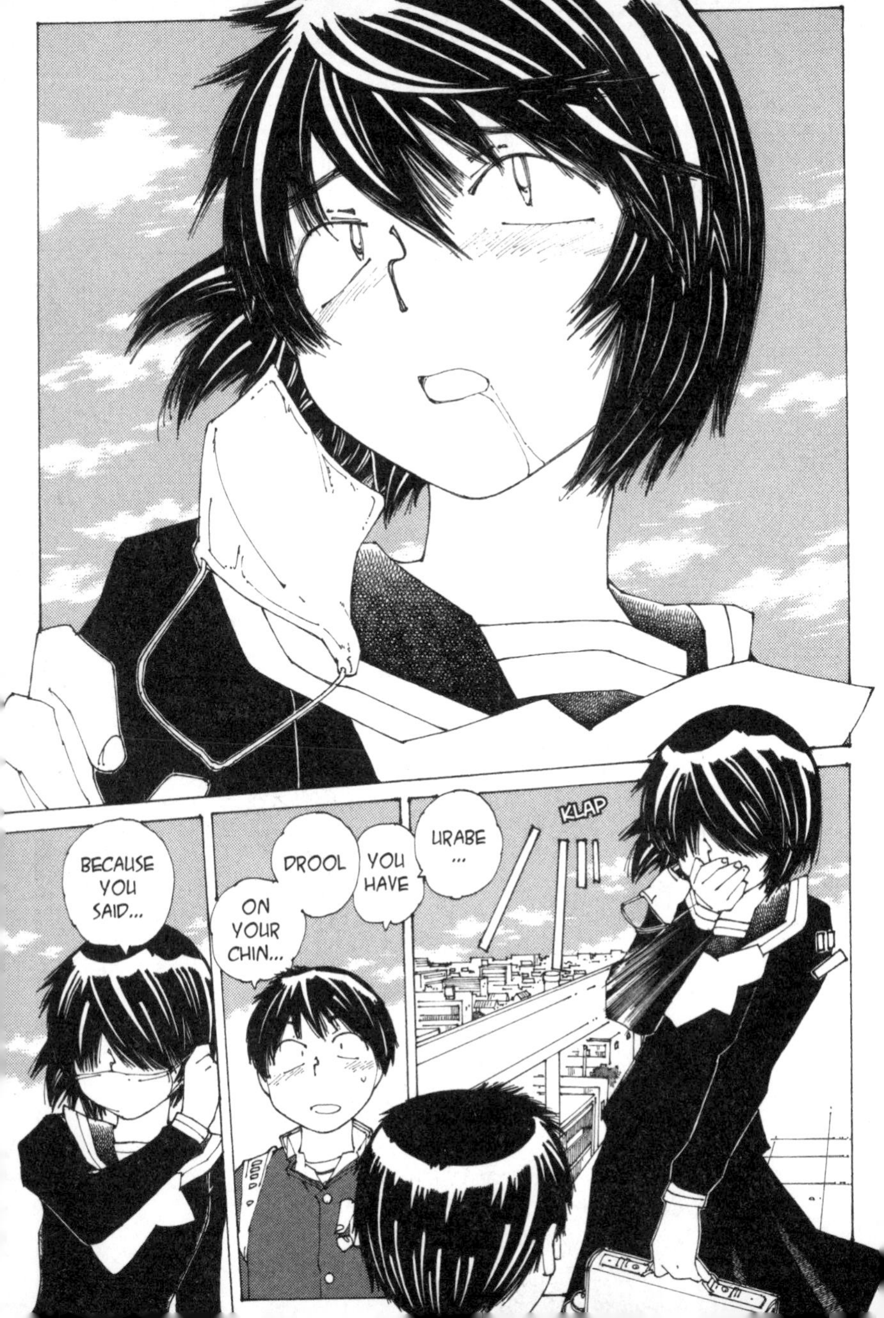
KLAP
URABE ...
YOU HAVE
DROOL
ON YOUR CHIN...
BECAUSE YOU SAID...

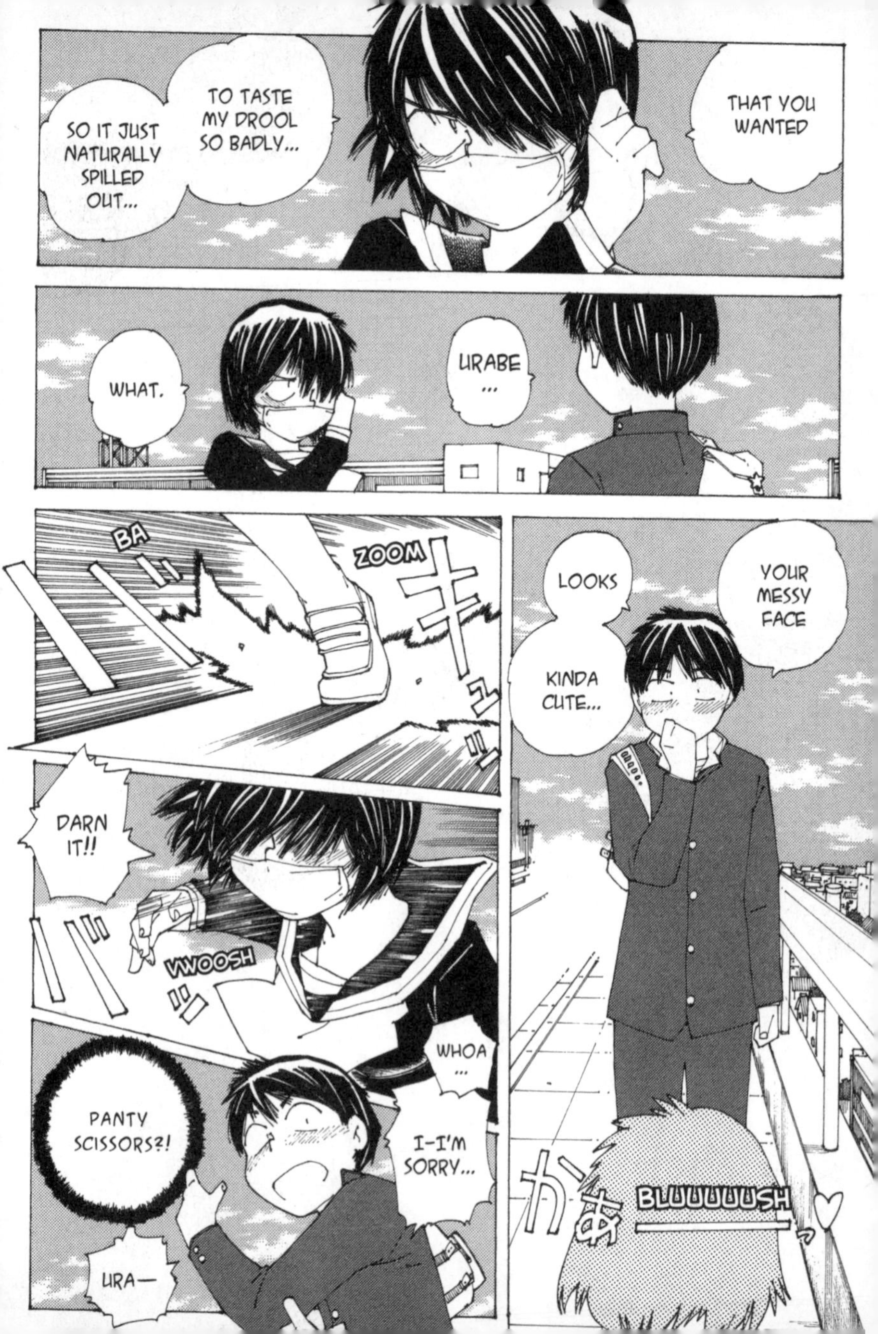
THAT YOU WANTED
TO TASTE MY DROOL SO BADLY...
SO IT JUST NATURALLY SPILLED OUT...
URABE ...
WHAT.
YOUR MESSY FACE
LOOKS KINDA CUTE...
BLUUUUUSH
ZOOM
BA
DARN IT!!
VWOOSH
WHOA ...
I-I'M SORRY...
PANTY SCISSORS?!
URA—

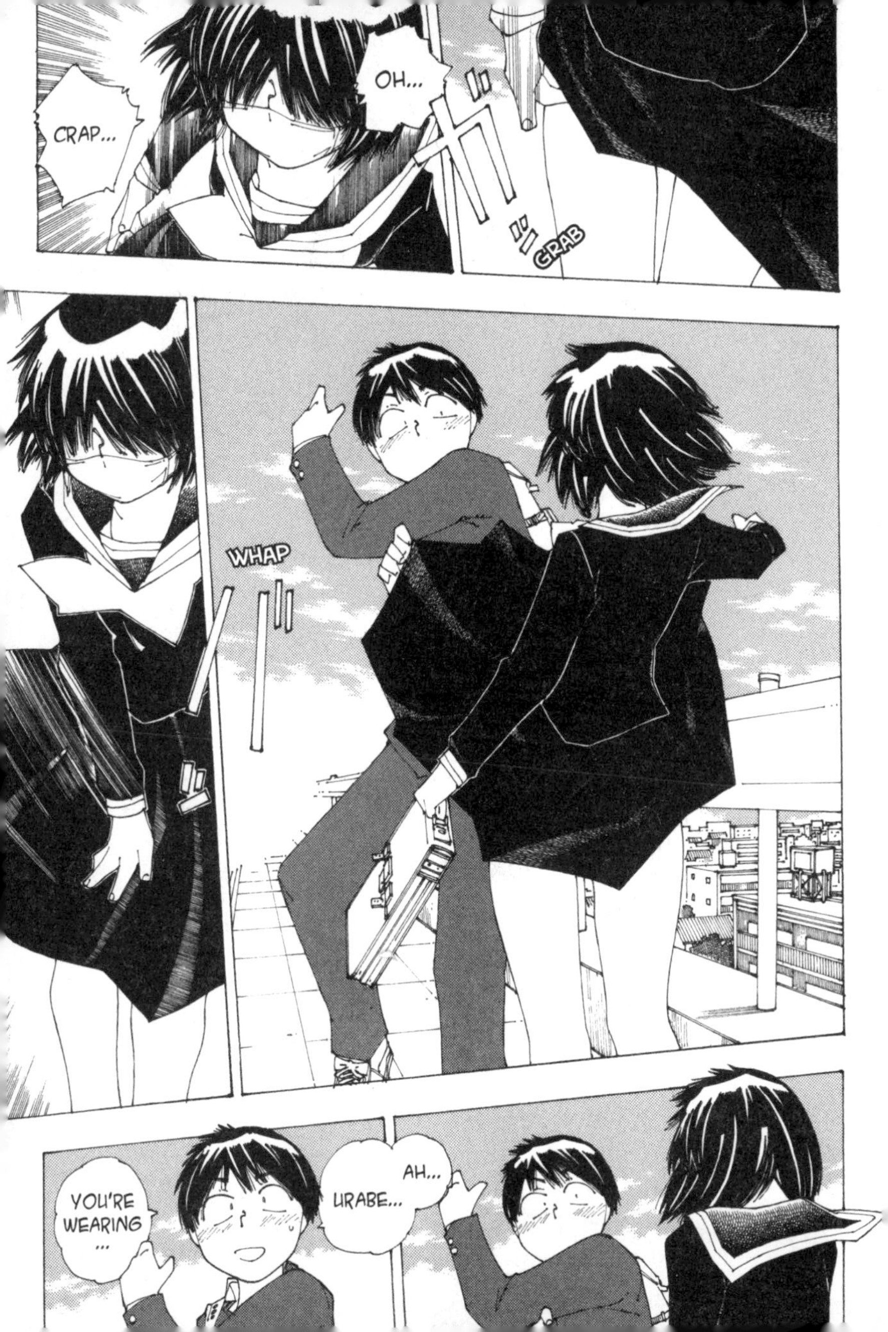
OH...
GRAB
CRAP...
WHAP
AH... URABE...
YOU'RE WEARING ...

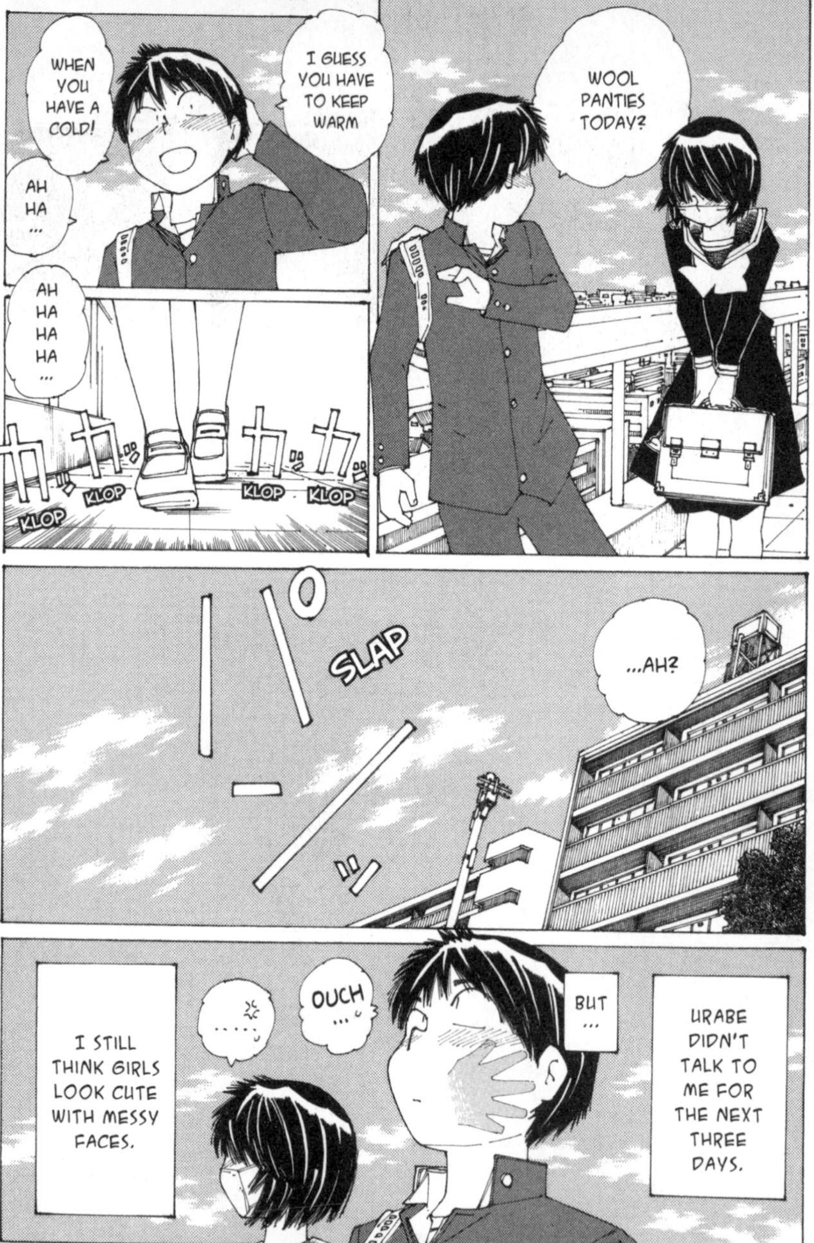
WOOL PANTIES TODAY?
I GUESS YOU HAVE TO KEEP WARM
WHEN YOU HAVE A COLD!
AH HA ...
AH HA HA HA ...
KLOP KLOP
KLOP KLOP
...AH?
SLAP
URABE DIDN'T TALK TO ME FOR THE NEXT THREE DAYS.
BUT ...
OUCH ...
...
I STILL THINK GIRLS LOOK CUTE WITH MESSY FACES.

END OF CHAPTER 53

CHAPTER 54: MYSTERIOUS MAN'S DREAM

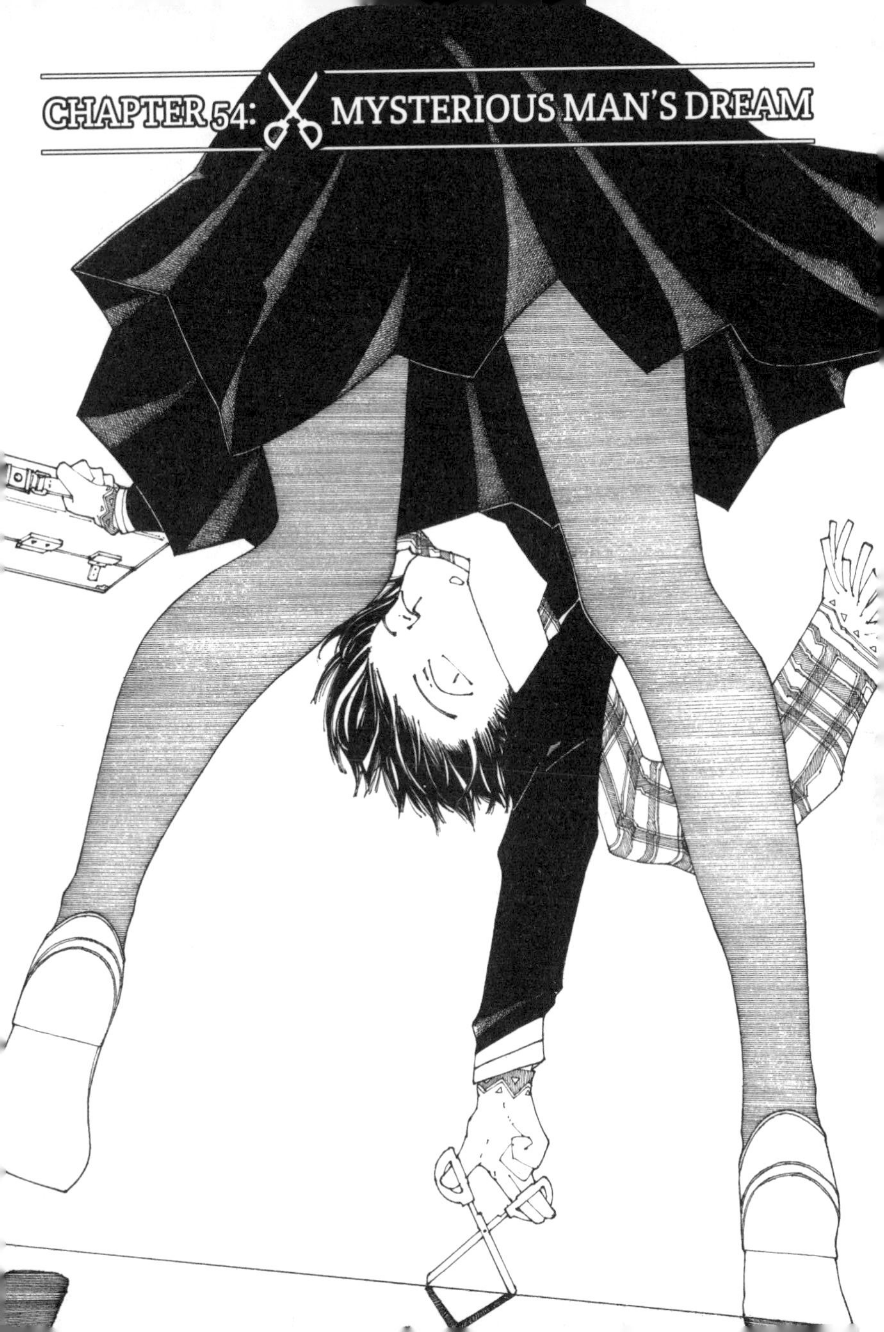

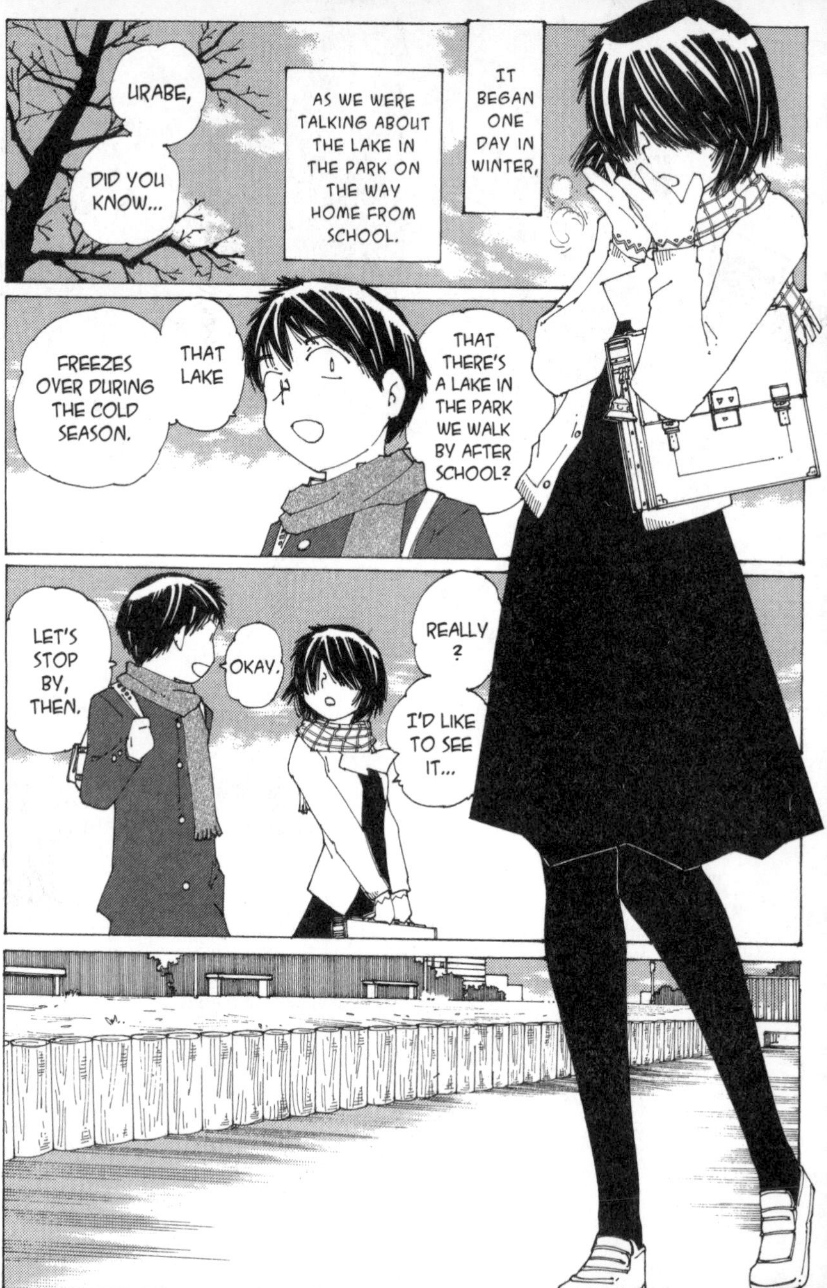
IT BEGAN ONE DAY IN WINTER,
AS WE WERE TALKING ABOUT THE LAKE IN THE PARK ON THE WAY HOME FROM SCHOOL.
URABE,
DID YOU KNOW...
THAT THERE'S A LAKE IN THE PARK WE WALK BY AFTER SCHOOL?
THAT LAKE
FREEZES OVER DURING THE COLD SEASON.
REALLY?
I'D LIKE TO SEE IT...
LET'S STOP BY, THEN.
OKAY.

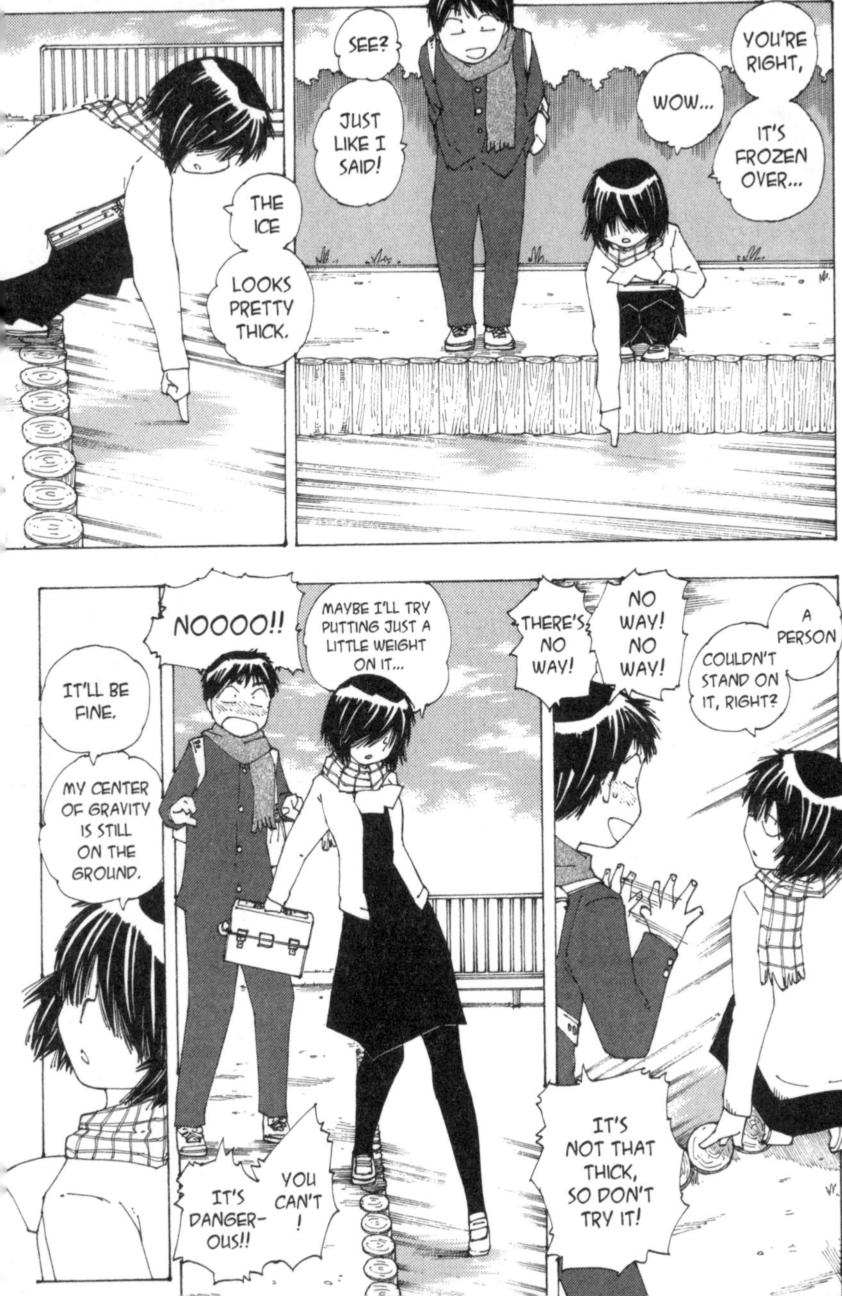
YOU'RE RIGHT,
IT'S FROZEN OVER...
WOW...
SEE?
JUST LIKE I SAID!
THE ICE
LOOKS PRETTY THICK.
A PERSON COULDN'T STAND ON IT, RIGHT?
NO WAY! NO WAY!
THERE'S NO WAY!
IT'S NOT THAT THICK, SO DON'T TRY IT!
MAYBE I'LL TRY PUTTING JUST A LITTLE WEIGHT ON IT...
NOOOO!!
YOU CAN'T!
IT'S DANGER-OUS!!
IT'LL BE FINE.
MY CENTER OF GRAVITY IS STILL ON THE GROUND.

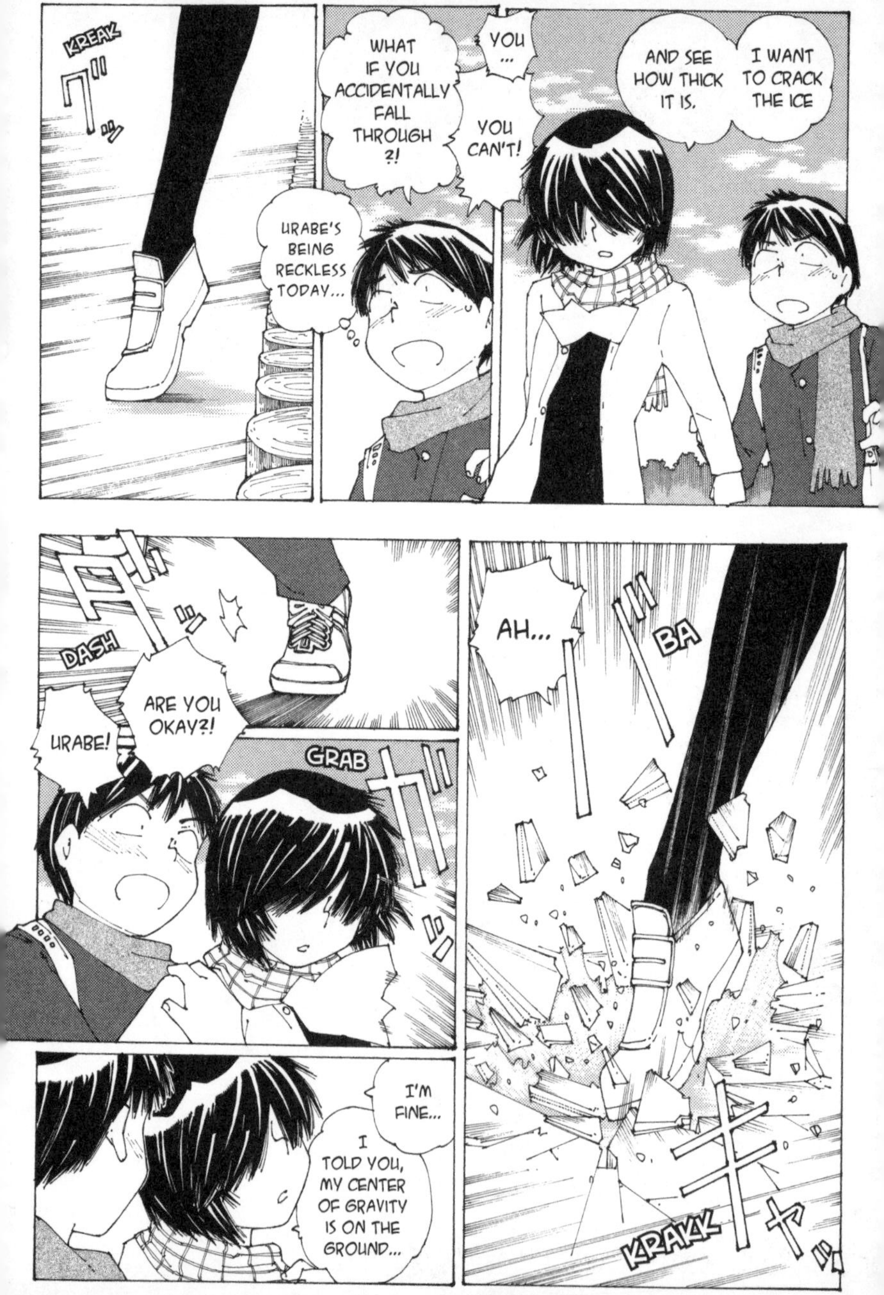
I WANT TO CRACK THE ICE
AND SEE HOW THICK IT IS.
YOU ...
YOU CAN'T!
WHAT IF YOU ACCIDENTALLY FALL THROUGH ?!
URABE'S BEING RECKLESS TODAY...
KREAK
AH...
BA
KRAKK
DASH
ARE YOU OKAY?!
URABE!
GRAB
I'M FINE...
I TOLD YOU, MY CENTER OF GRAVITY IS ON THE GROUND...

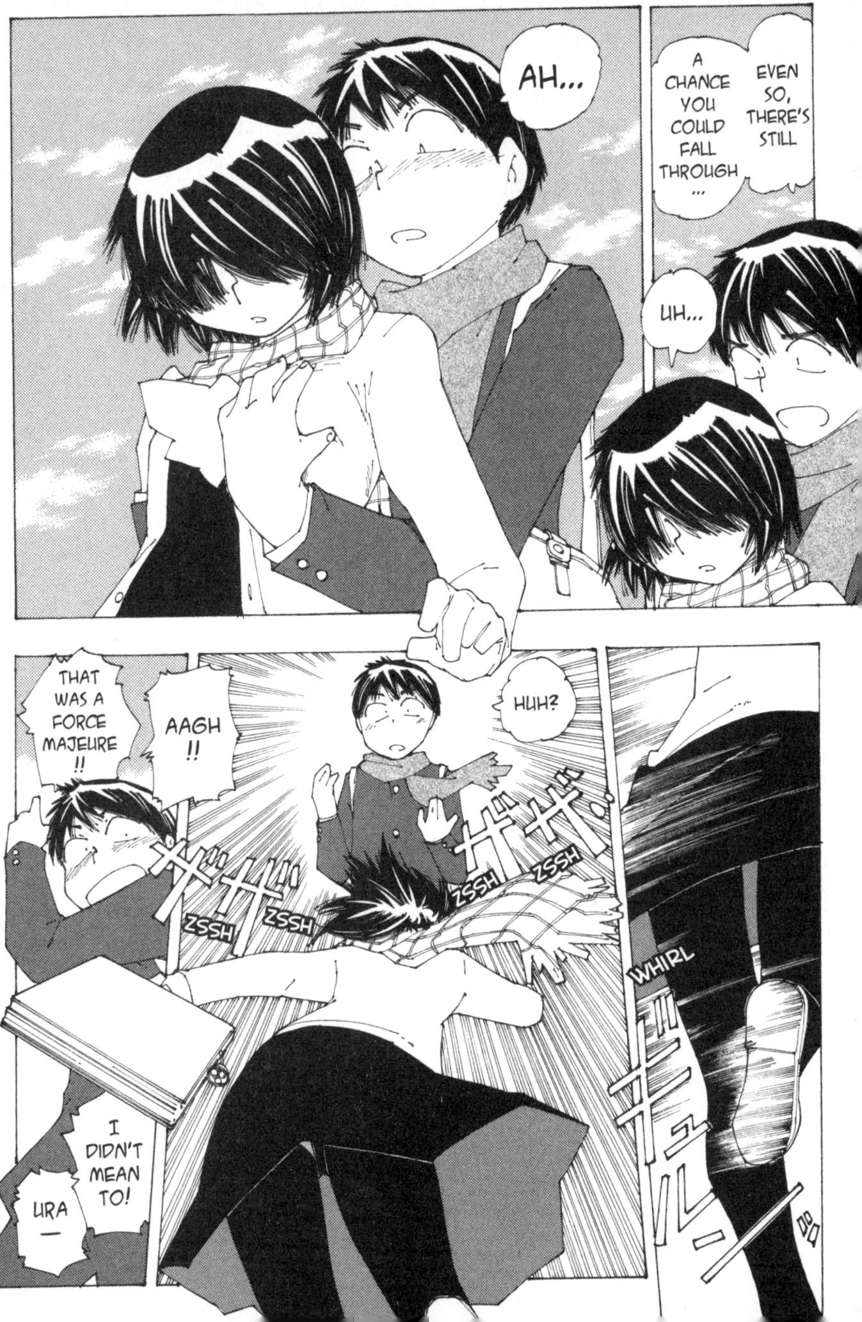
EVEN SO, THERE'S STILL
A CHANCE YOU COULD FALL THROUGH ...
UH...
AH...
WHIRL
HUH?
ZSSH
ZSSH
ZSSH
ZSSH
AAGH !!
THAT WAS A FORCE MAJEURE !!
I DIDN'T MEAN TO!
URA —

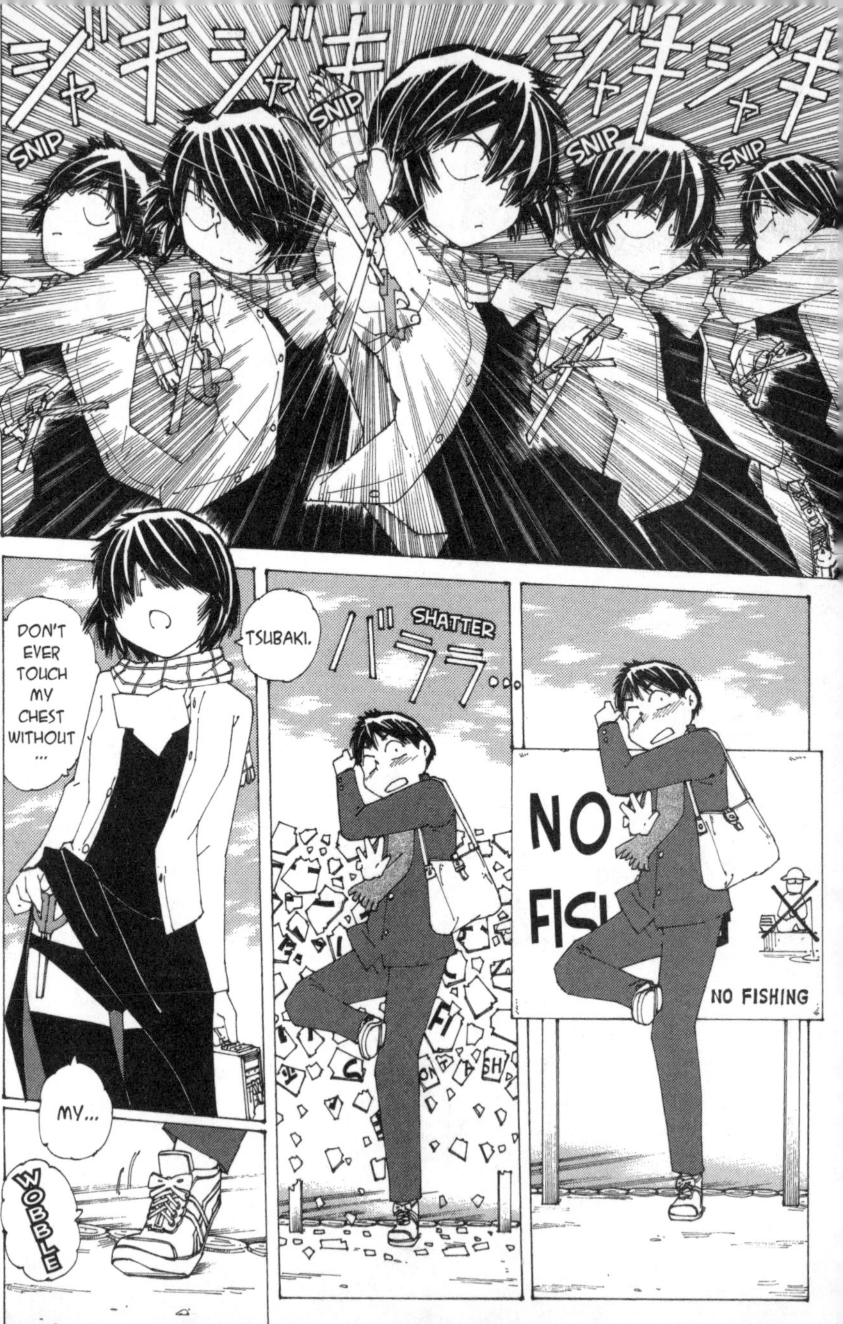
ジャキジャキ
SNIP
SNIP
ジャキジャキ
SNIP
SNIP
NO FISH
NO FISHING
バラララ…
SHATTER
TSUBAKI.
DON'T EVER TOUCH MY CHEST WITHOUT ...
MY...
WOBBLE

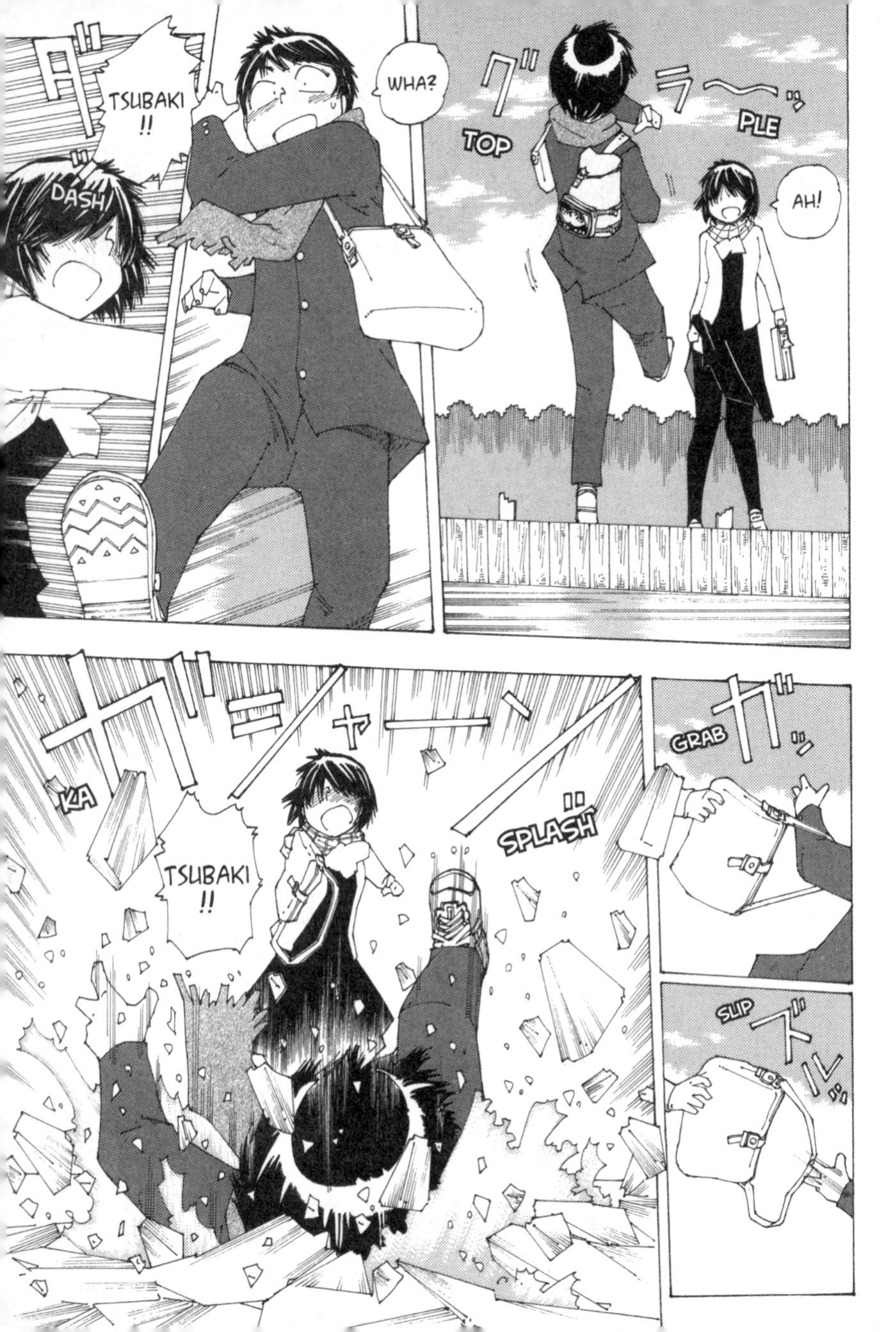
PLE
TOP
AH!
WHA?
TSUBAKI !!
DASH
GRAB
SLIP
SPLASH
TSUBAKI !!
KA

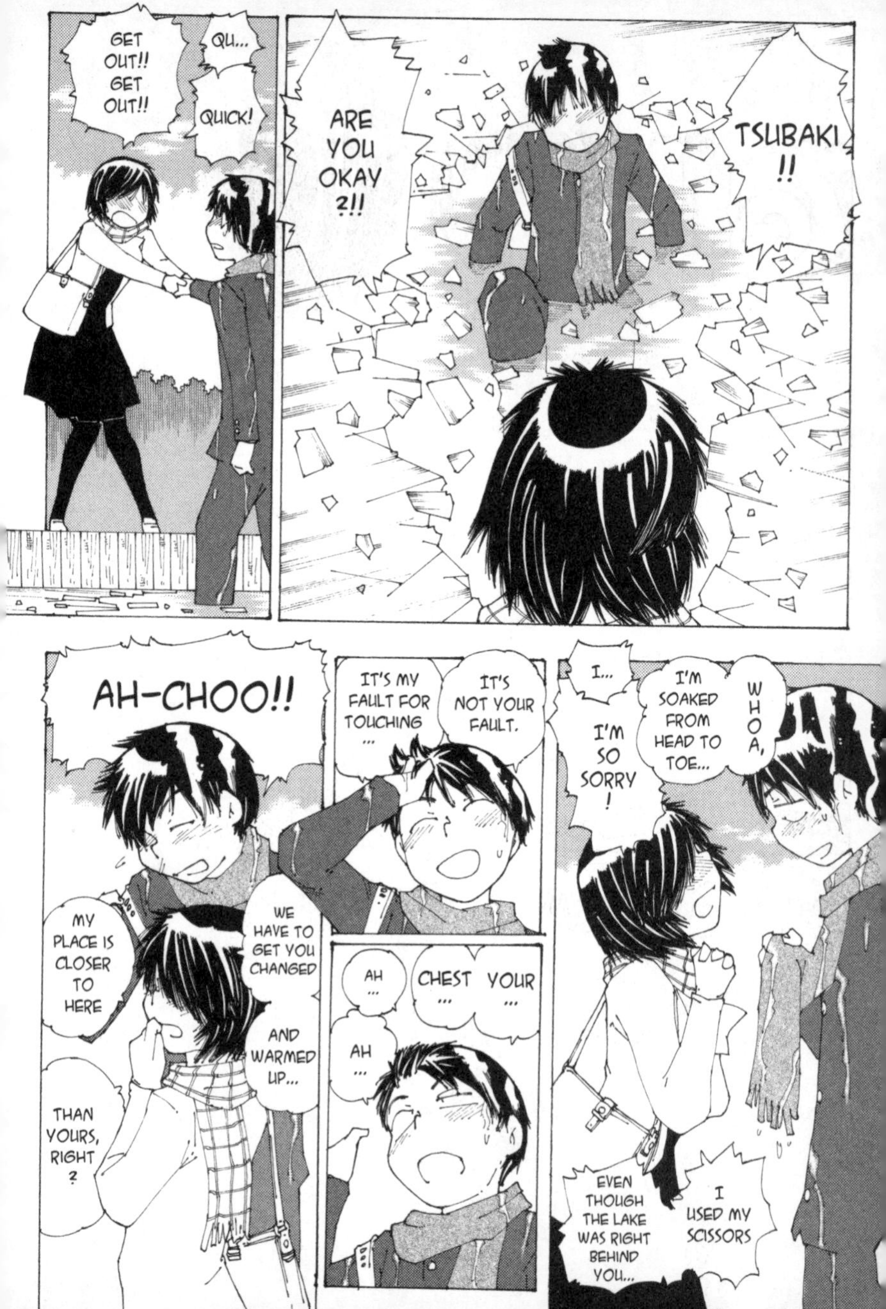
TSUBAKI!!
ARE YOU OKAY?!!
QU...
QUICK!
GET OUT!! GET OUT!!
WHOA,
I'M SOAKED FROM HEAD TO TOE...
I...
I'M SO SORRY!
I USED MY SCISSORS
EVEN THOUGH THE LAKE WAS RIGHT BEHIND YOU...
IT'S NOT YOUR FAULT.
IT'S MY FAULT FOR TOUCHING ...
YOUR ...
CHEST ...
AH ...
AH ...
AH-CHOO!!
WE HAVE TO GET YOU CHANGED
AND WARMED UP...
MY PLACE IS CLOSER TO HERE
THAN YOURS, RIGHT?

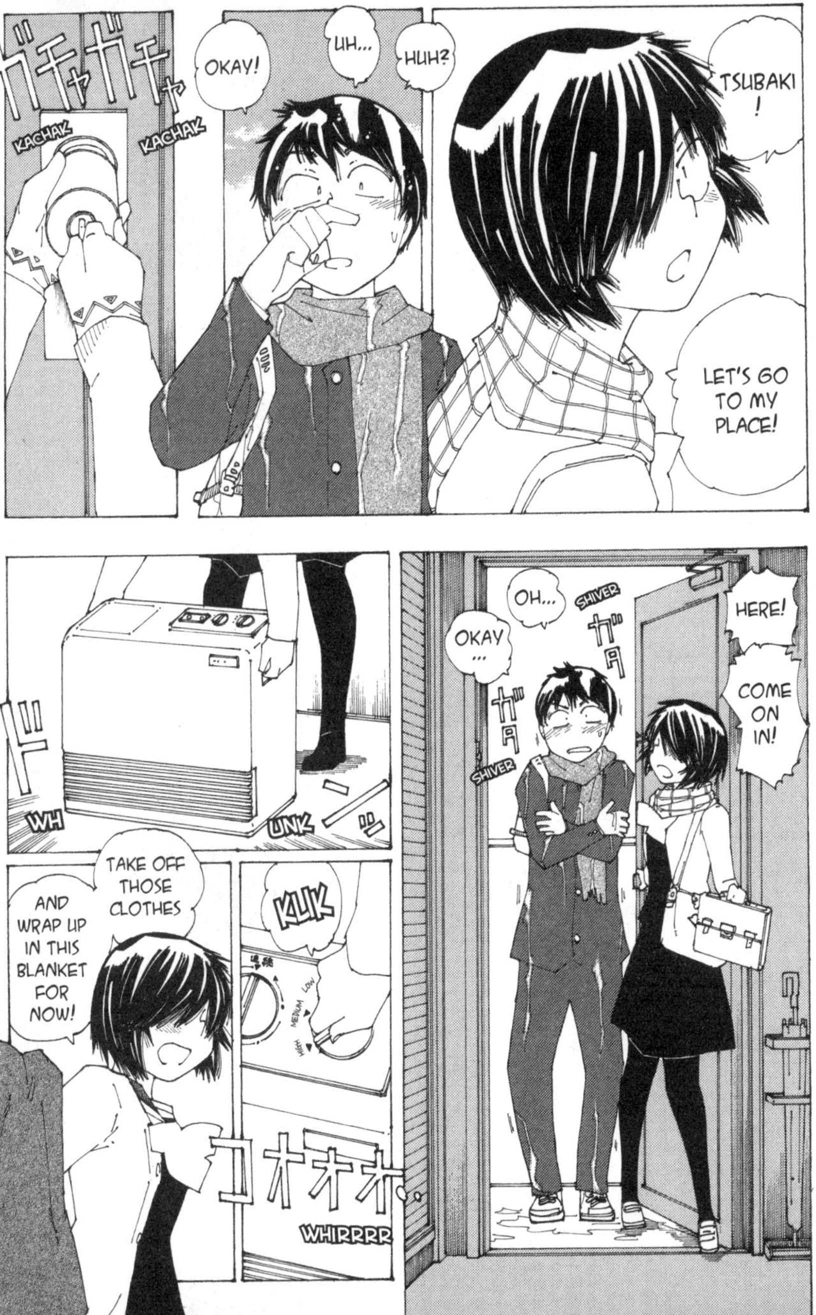
TSUBAKI!
LET'S GO TO MY PLACE!
HUH?
UH...
OKAY!
ガチャガチャ
KACHAK
KACHAK
HERE!
COME ON IN!
OH...
OKAY...
ガタ
SHIVER
ガタ
SHIVER
ドン
WH
UNK
KLIK
HIGH
MEDIUM
LOW
TAKE OFF THOSE CLOTHES
AND WRAP UP IN THIS BLANKET FOR NOW!
コオオオ...
WHIRRRR

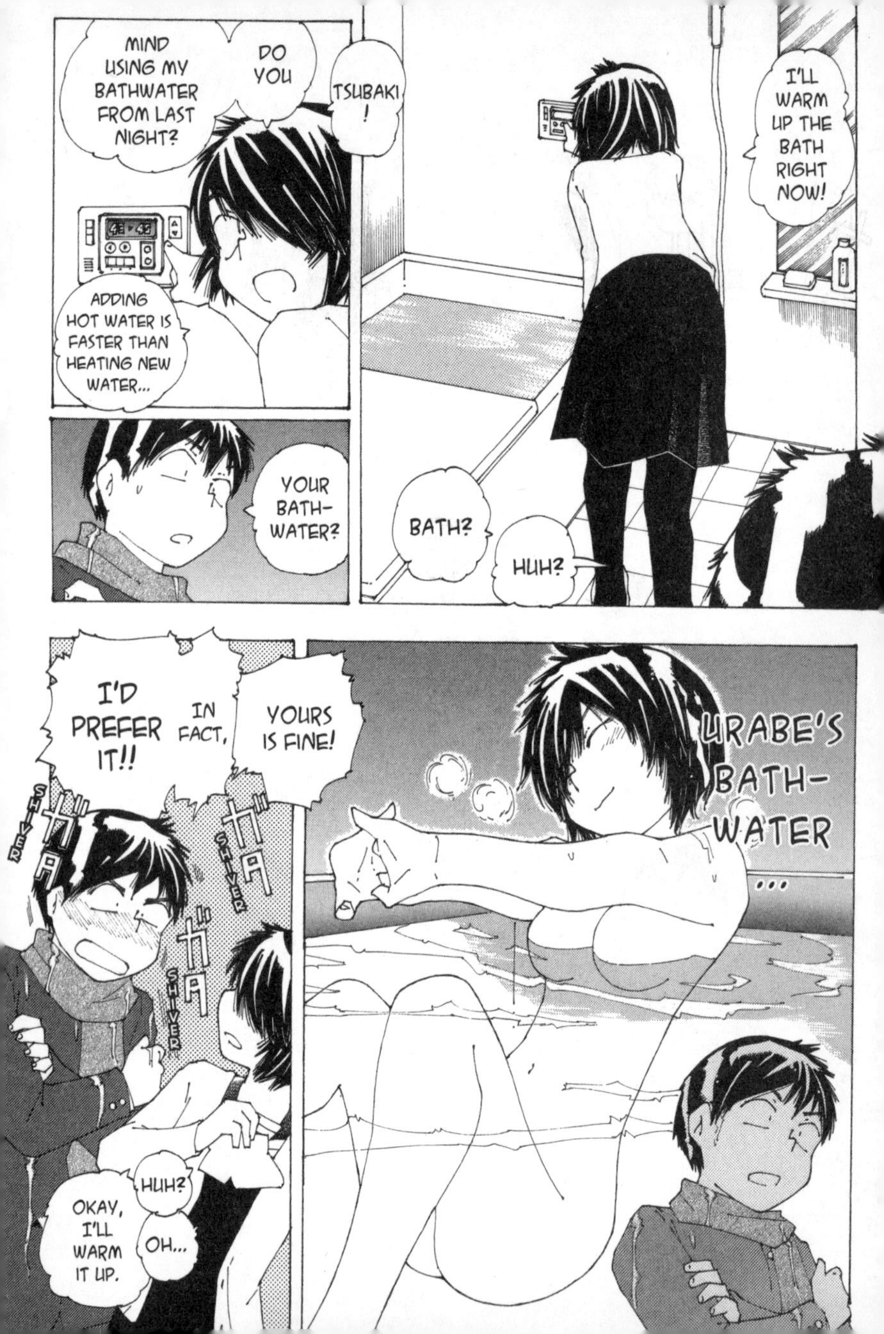
I'LL WARM UP THE BATH RIGHT NOW!
HUH?
BATH?
TSUBAKI!
DO YOU
MIND USING MY BATHWATER FROM LAST NIGHT?
ADDING HOT WATER IS FASTER THAN HEATING NEW WATER...
YOUR BATH-WATER?
URABE'S BATH-WATER...
YOURS IS FINE!
IN FACT,
I'D PREFER IT!!
SHIVER
SHIVER
SHIVER
HUH?
OH...
OKAY, I'LL WARM IT UP.

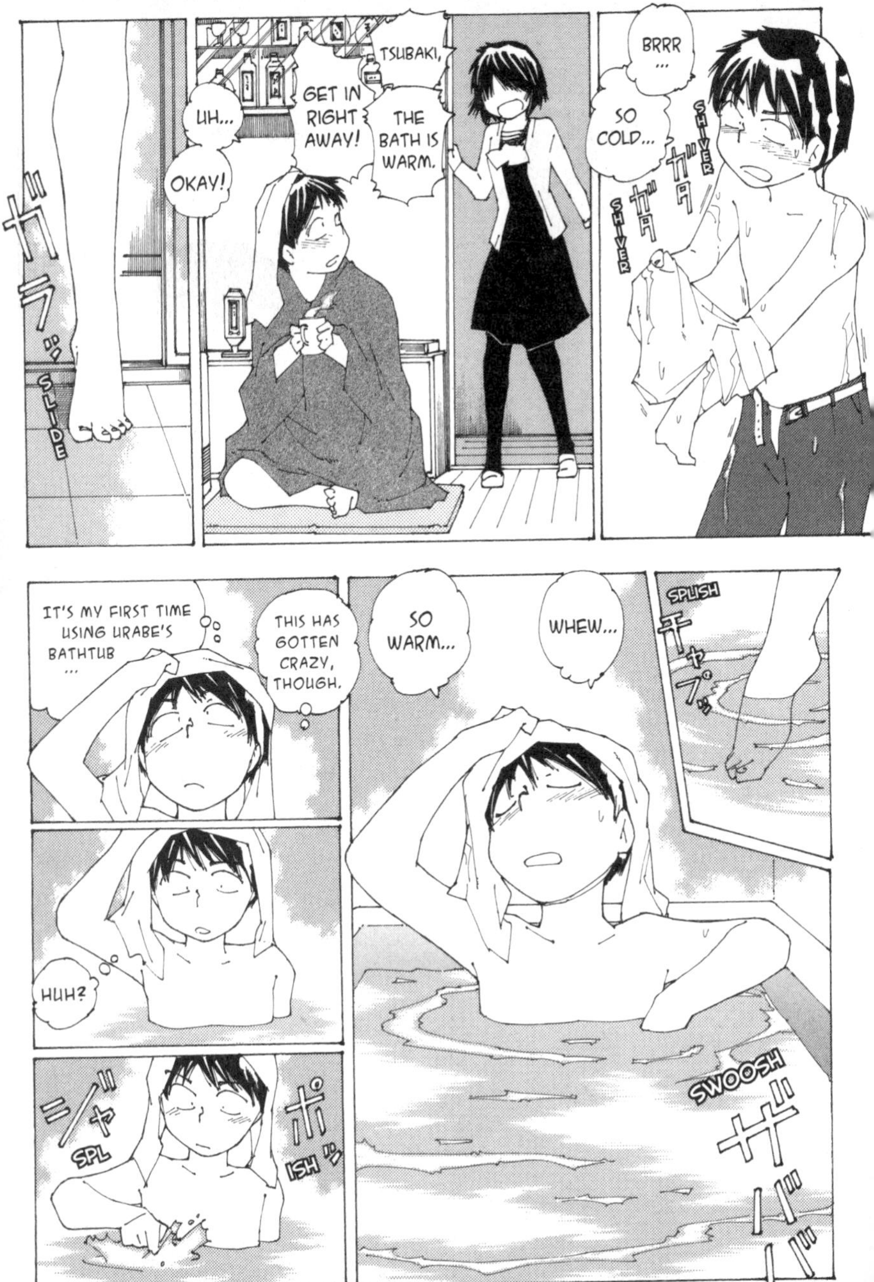
BRRR ...
SO COLD...
SHIVER
SHIVER
TSUBAKI,
THE BATH IS WARM.
GET IN RIGHT AWAY!
UH...
OKAY!
SLIDE
SPLUSH
WHEW...
SO WARM...
SWOOSH
THIS HAS GOTTEN CRAZY, THOUGH.
IT'S MY FIRST TIME USING URABE'S BATHTUB ...
HUH?
SPL
ISH

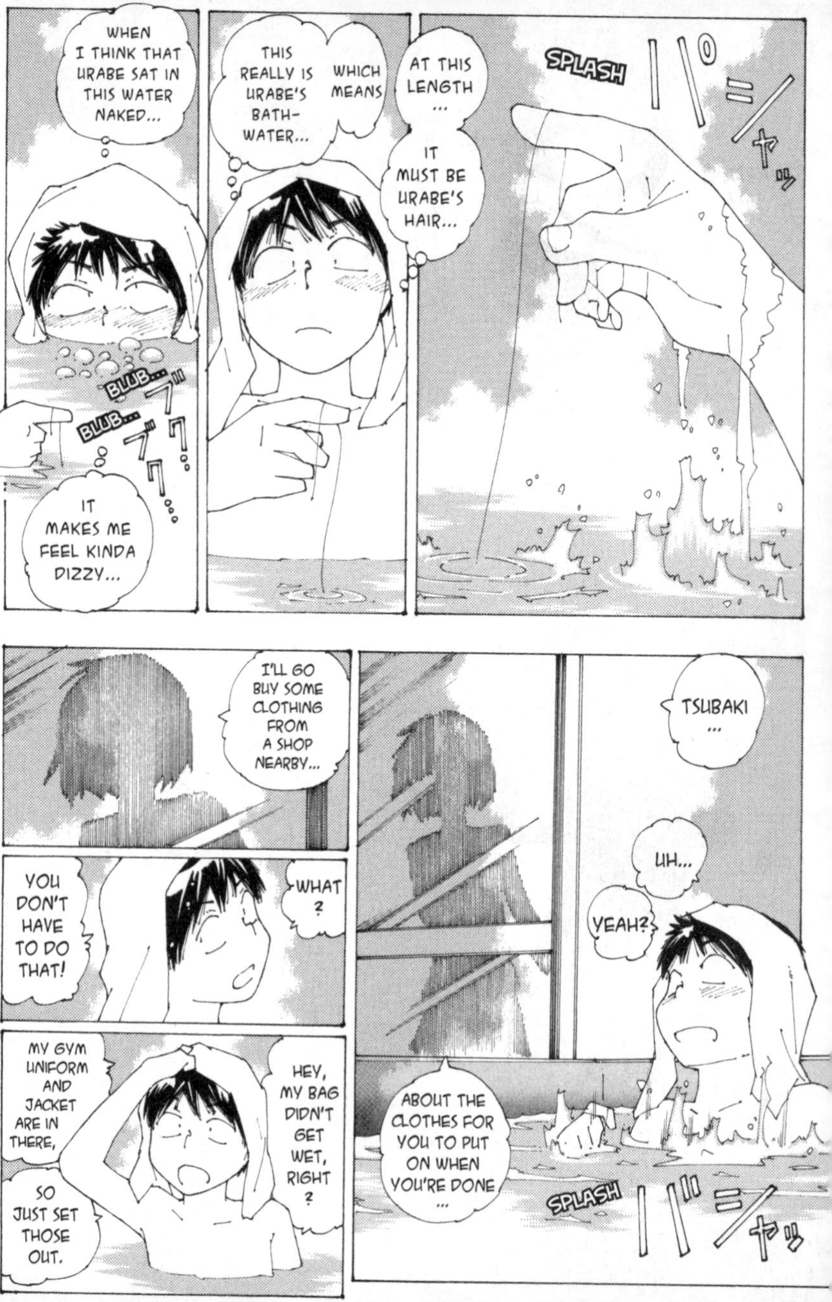
SPLASH
AT THIS LENGTH ...
IT MUST BE URABE'S HAIR...
WHICH MEANS
THIS REALLY IS URABE'S BATH-WATER...
WHEN I THINK THAT URABE SAT IN THIS WATER NAKED...
BLUB...
BLUB...
IT MAKES ME FEEL KINDA DIZZY...
TSUBAKI ...
UH...
YEAH?
ABOUT THE CLOTHES FOR YOU TO PUT ON WHEN YOU'RE DONE ...
SPLASH
I'LL GO BUY SOME CLOTHING FROM A SHOP NEARBY...
WHAT ?
YOU DON'T HAVE TO DO THAT!
HEY, MY BAG DIDN'T GET WET, RIGHT ?
MY GYM UNIFORM AND JACKET ARE IN THERE,
SO JUST SET THOSE OUT.

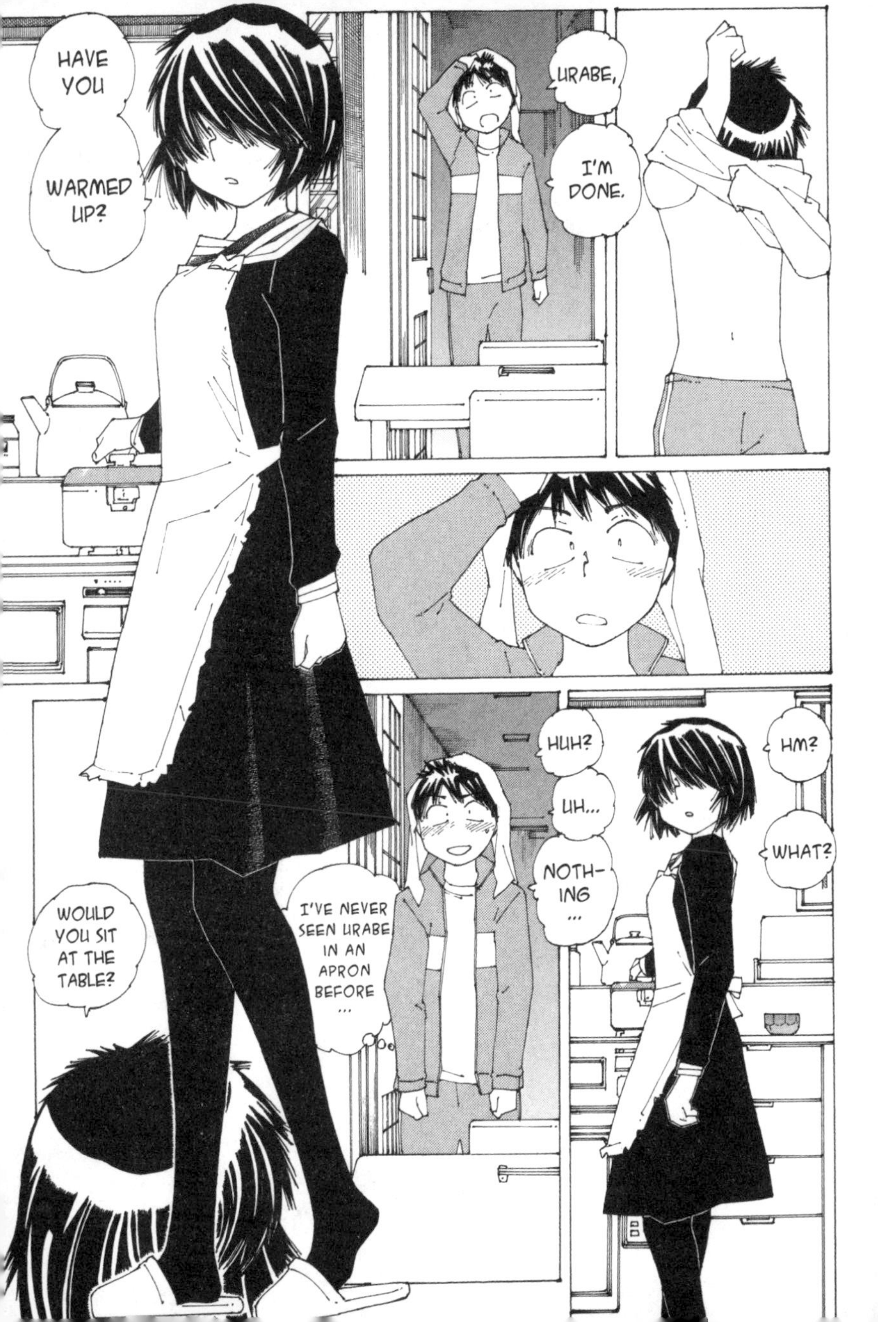
URABE,
I'M DONE.
HM?
HUH?
UH...
WHAT?
NOTH-ING ...
I'VE NEVER SEEN URABE IN AN APRON BEFORE ...
HAVE YOU WARMED UP?
WOULD YOU SIT AT THE TABLE?

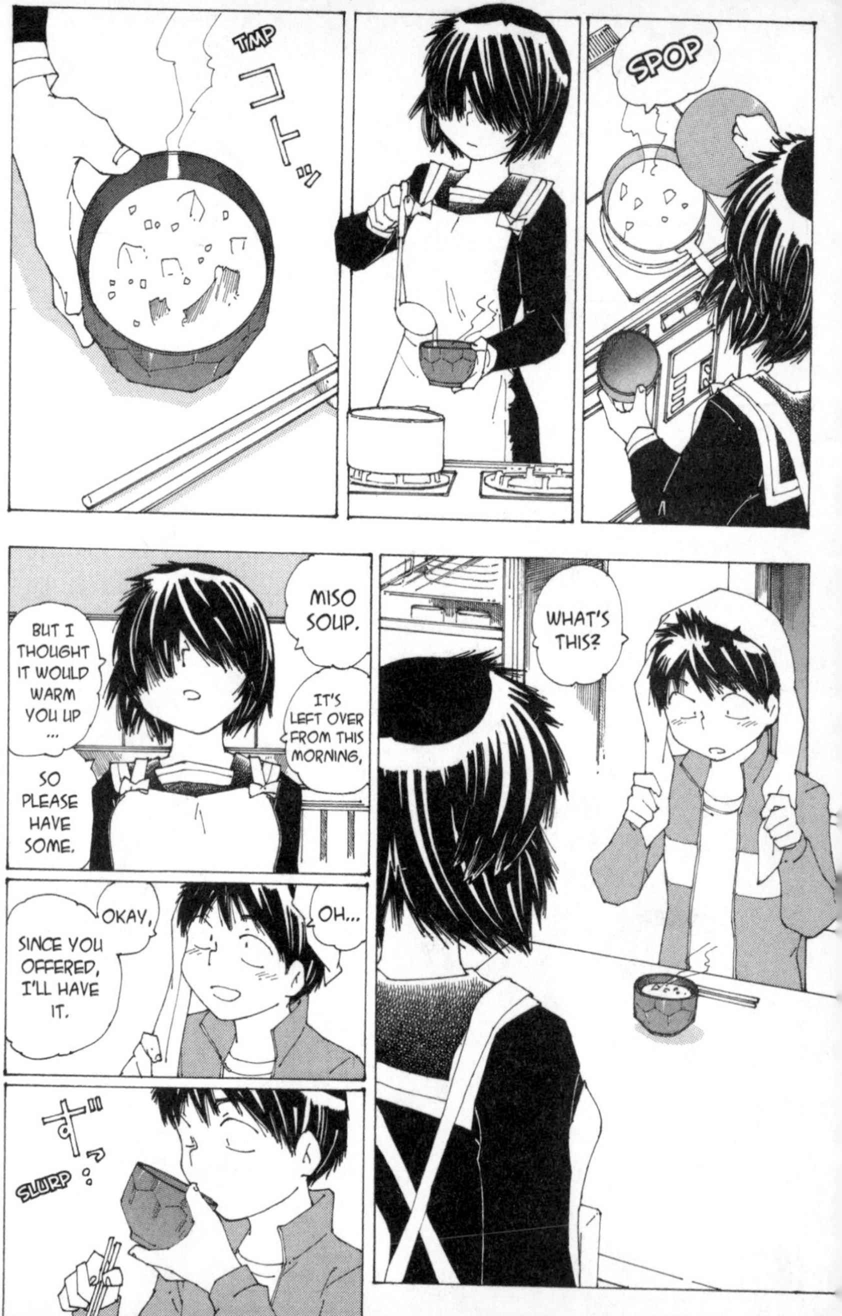
SPOP
TMP
コトッ
WHAT'S THIS?
MISO SOUP.
IT'S LEFT OVER FROM THIS MORNING,
BUT I THOUGHT IT WOULD WARM YOU UP...
SO PLEASE HAVE SOME.
OH...
OKAY,
SINCE YOU OFFERED, I'LL HAVE IT.
ずずっ
SLURP

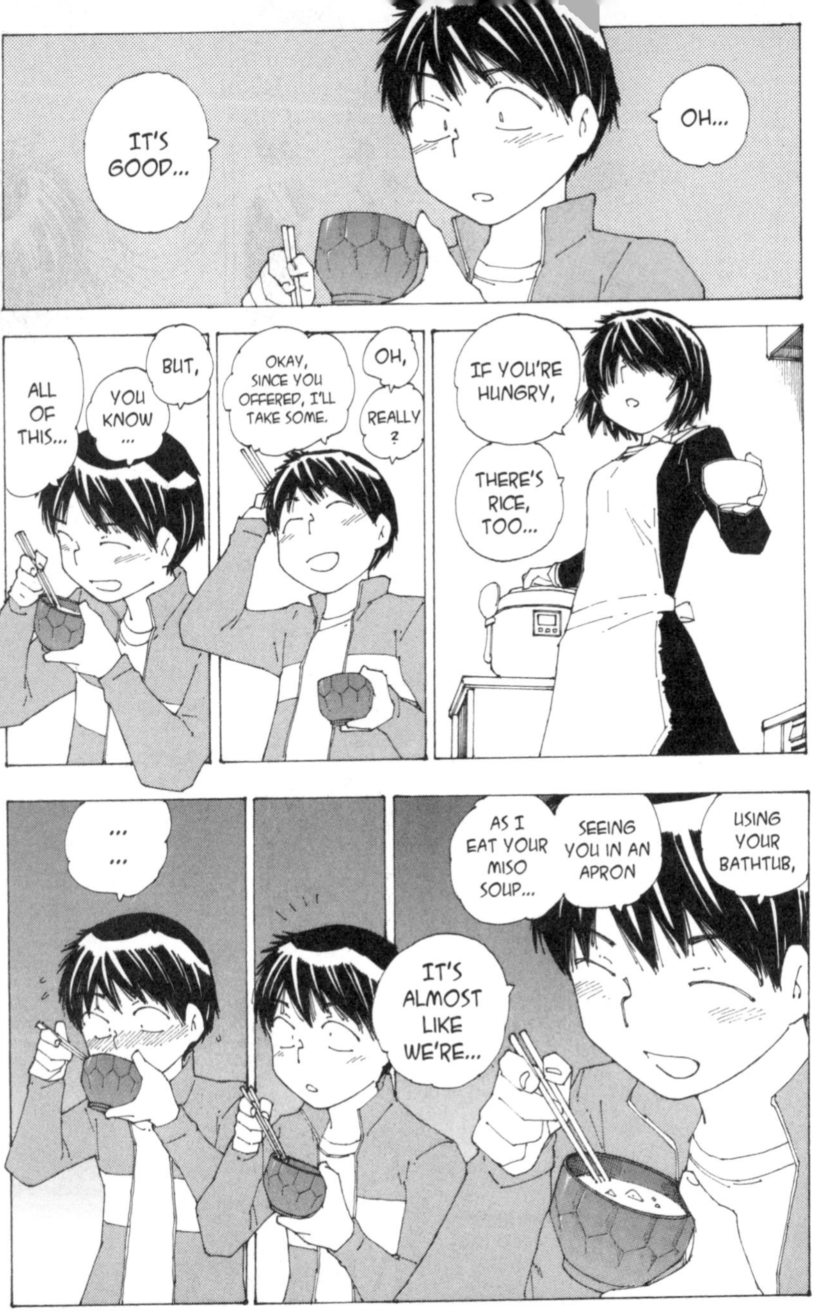
OH...
IT'S GOOD...
IF YOU'RE HUNGRY,
THERE'S RICE, TOO...
OH,
REALLY?
OKAY, SINCE YOU OFFERED, I'LL TAKE SOME.
BUT,
YOU KNOW ...
ALL OF THIS...
USING YOUR BATHTUB,
SEEING YOU IN AN APRON
AS I EAT YOUR MISO SOUP...
IT'S ALMOST LIKE WE'RE...
... ...

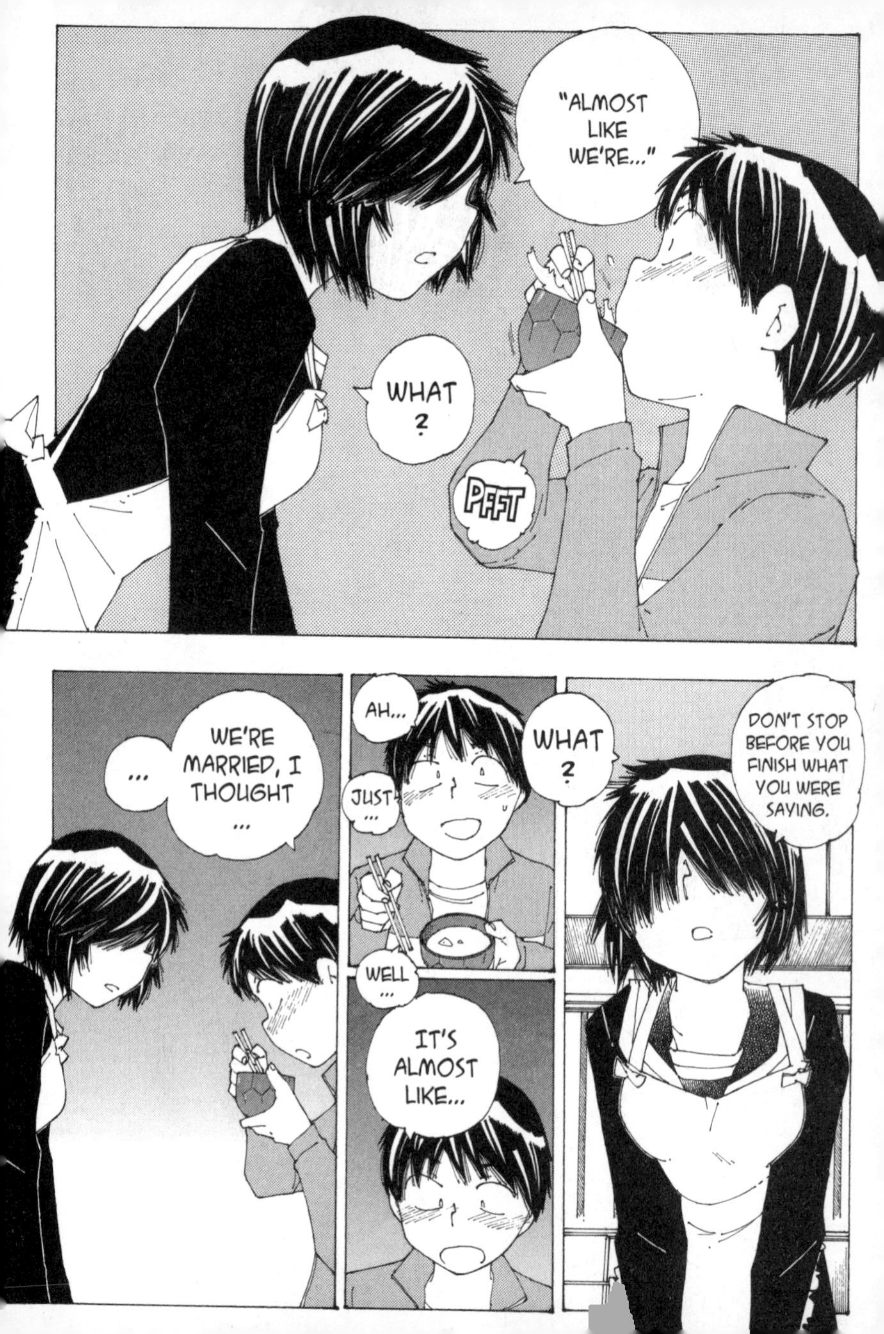
"ALMOST LIKE WE'RE..."
WHAT?
PFFT
DON'T STOP BEFORE YOU FINISH WHAT YOU WERE SAYING.
WHAT?
AH...
JUST...
WELL...
IT'S ALMOST LIKE...
WE'RE MARRIED, I THOUGHT...
...

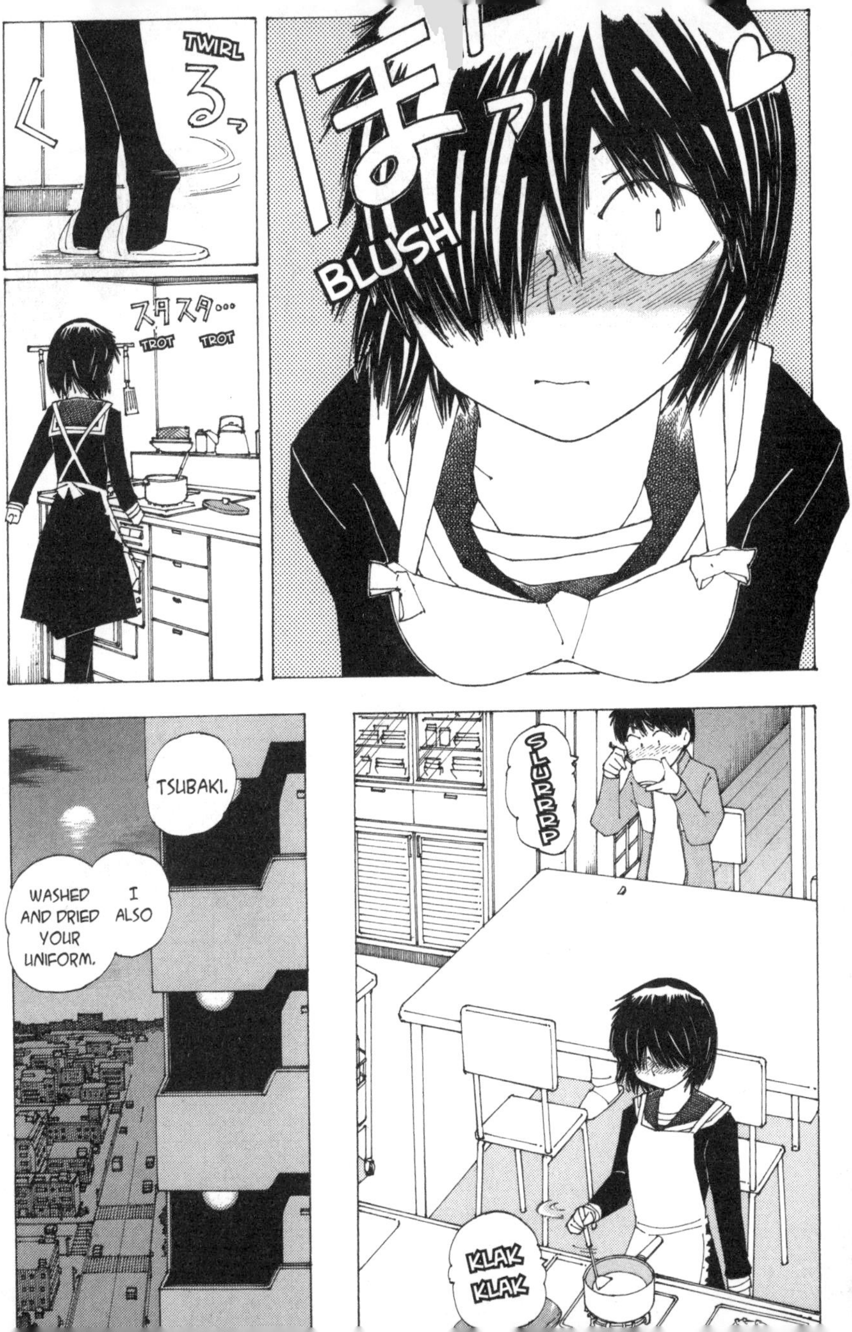
ほァ
BLUSH
くるっ
TWIRL
スタスタ…
TROT TROT
SLURRRP
KLAK KLAK
TSUBAKI.
I ALSO WASHED AND DRIED YOUR UNIFORM.

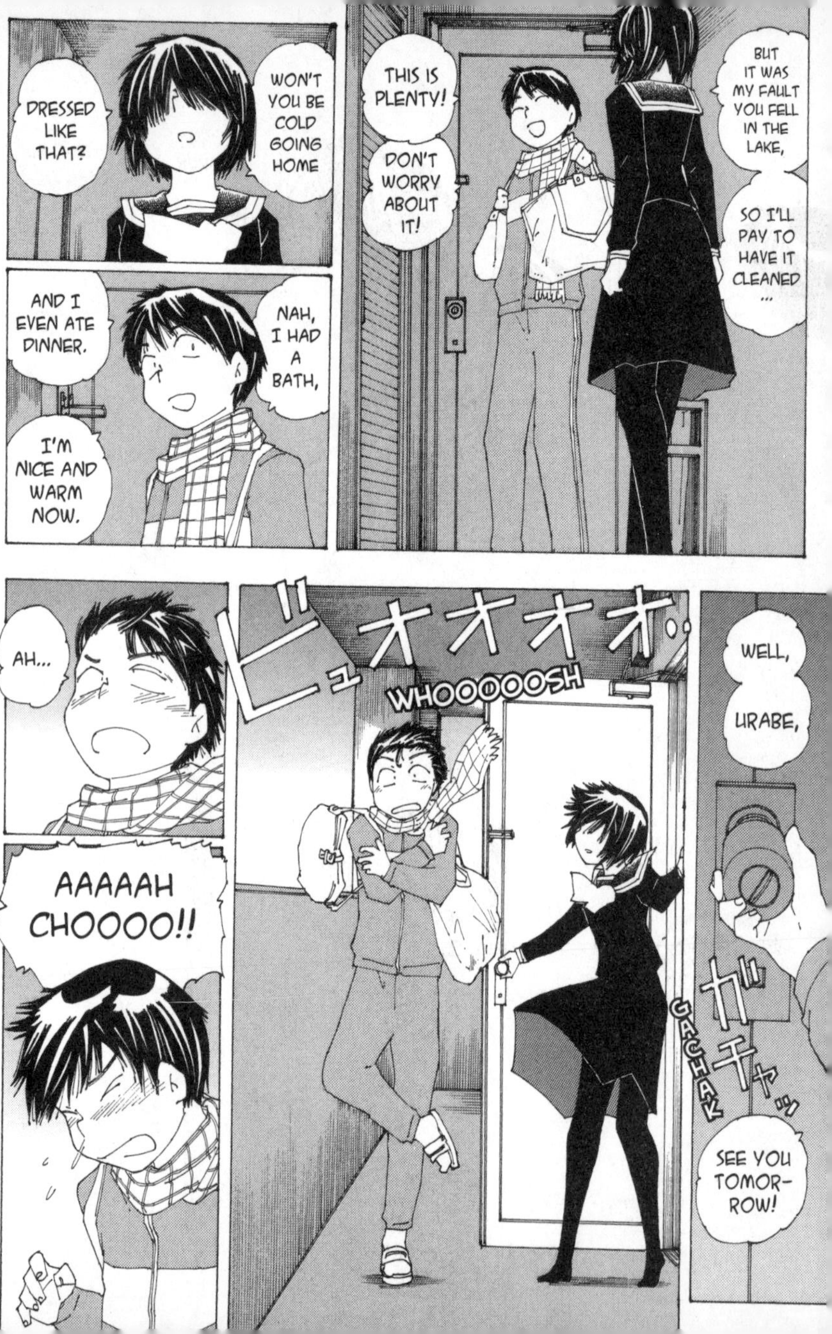
BUT IT WAS MY FAULT YOU FELL IN THE LAKE,
SO I'LL PAY TO HAVE IT CLEANED ...
THIS IS PLENTY!
DON'T WORRY ABOUT IT!
WON'T YOU BE COLD GOING HOME
DRESSED LIKE THAT?
NAH, I HAD A BATH,
AND I EVEN ATE DINNER.
I'M NICE AND WARM NOW.
WELL,
URABE,
ガチャッ
GACHAK
SEE YOU TOMOR-ROW!
ビュオオオオオ
WHOOOOOOSH
AH...
AAAAAH CHOOOO!!

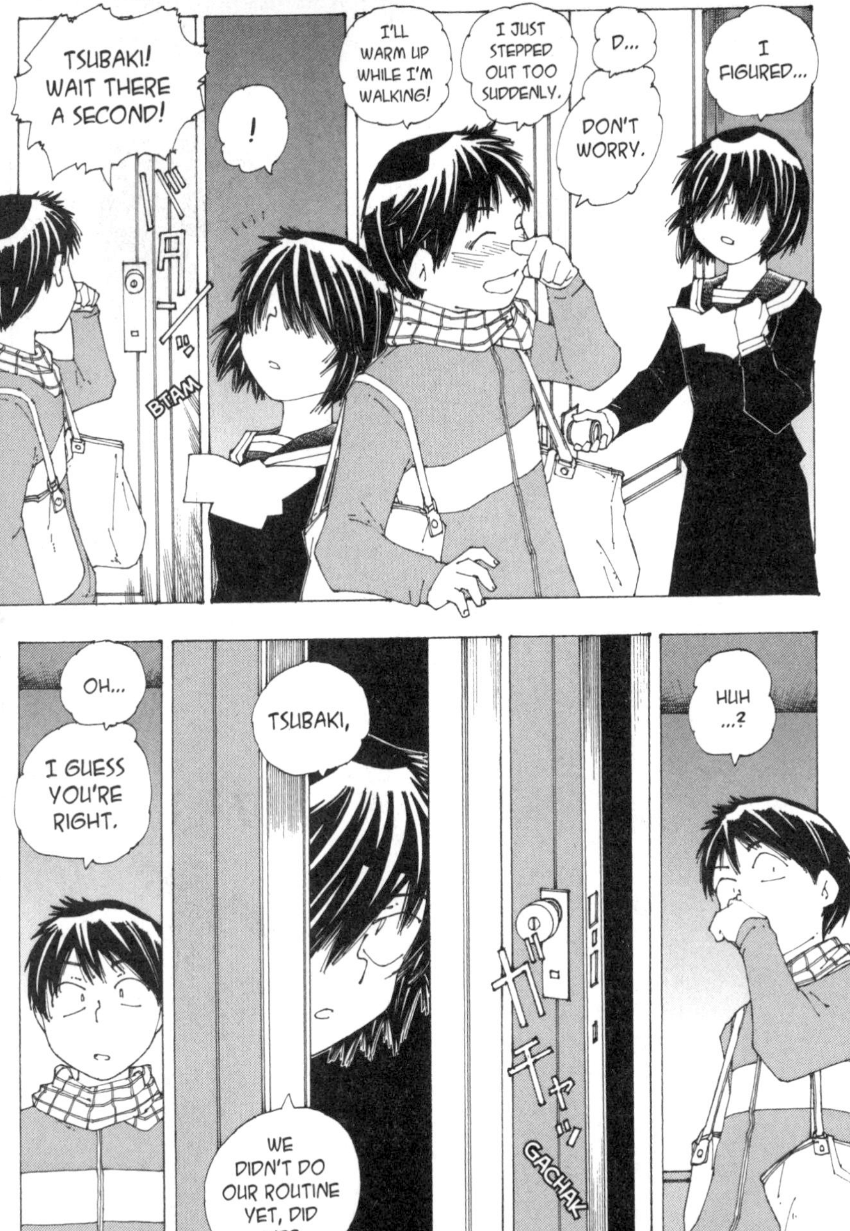
I FIGURED...
D...
DON'T WORRY.
I JUST STEPPED OUT TOO SUDDENLY.
I'LL WARM UP WHILE I'M WALKING!
!
TSUBAKI! WAIT THERE A SECOND!
BTAM
HUH ...?
GACHAK
TSUBAKI,
WE DIDN'T DO OUR ROUTINE YET, DID WE?
OH...
I GUESS YOU'RE RIGHT.

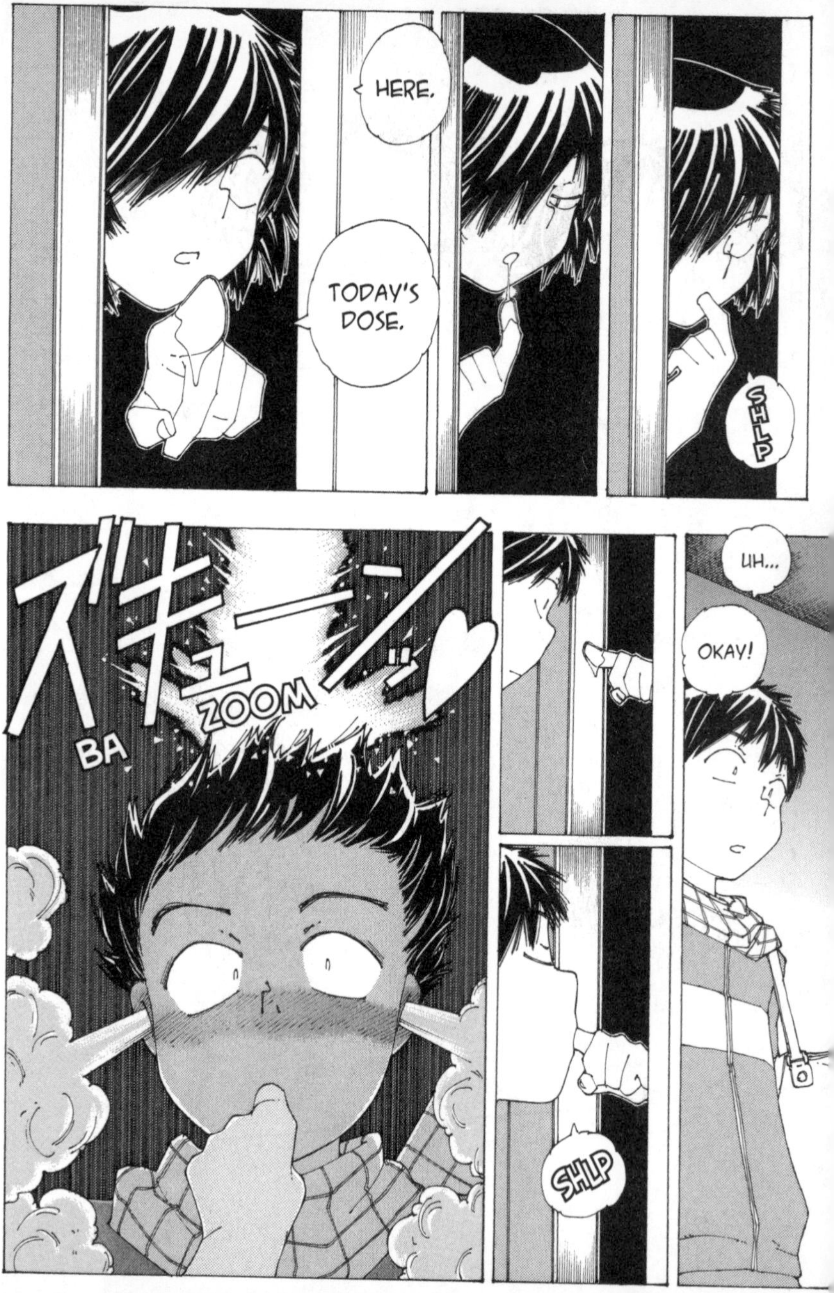
SHLP
HERE.
TODAY'S DOSE.
UH...
OKAY!
SHLP
ズキューン
BA
ZOOM

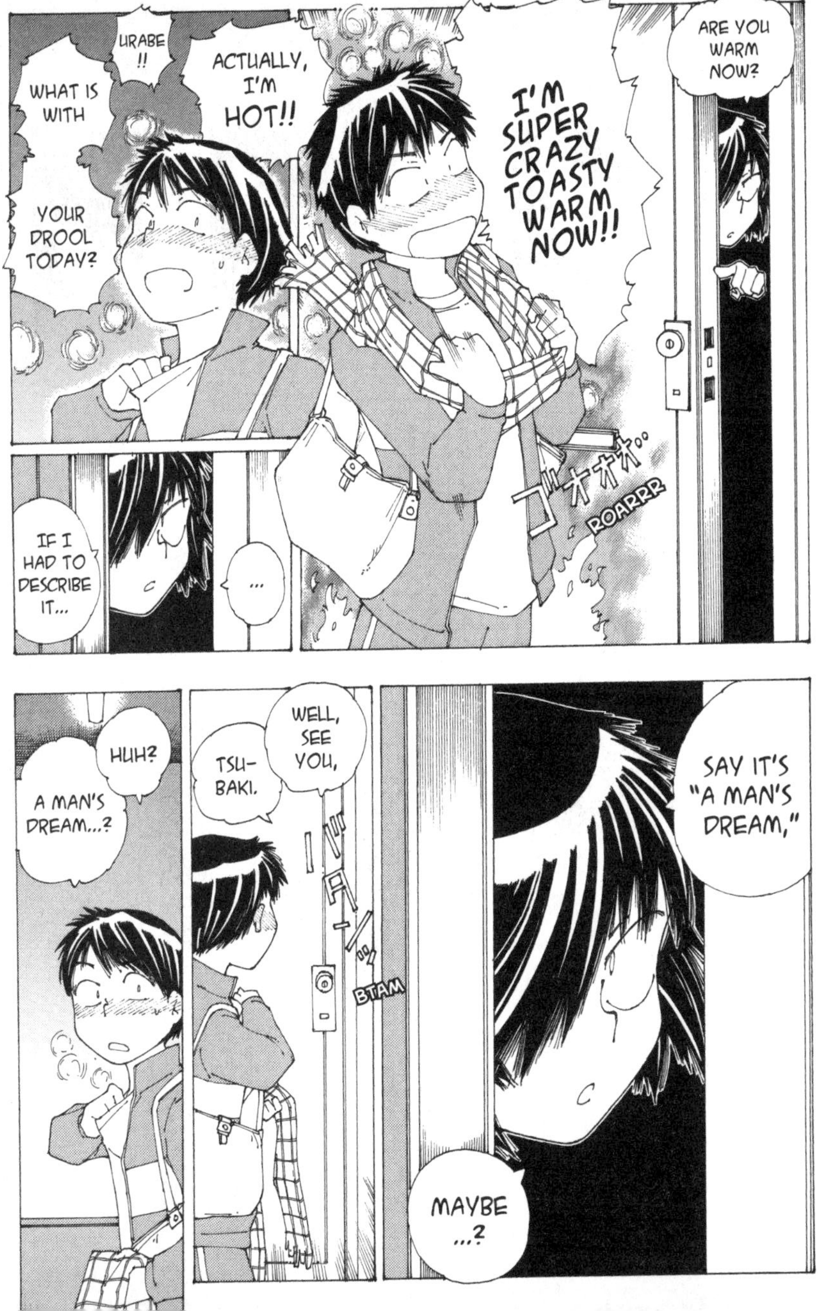
ARE YOU WARM NOW?
I'M SUPER CRAZY TOASTY WARM NOW!!
ACTUALLY, I'M HOT!!
URABE !!
WHAT IS WITH YOUR DROOL TODAY?
ROARRR
...
IF I HAD TO DESCRIBE IT...
SAY IT'S "A MAN'S DREAM,"
MAYBE ...?
WELL, SEE YOU,
TSU-BAKI.
BTAM
HUH?
A MAN'S DREAM...?

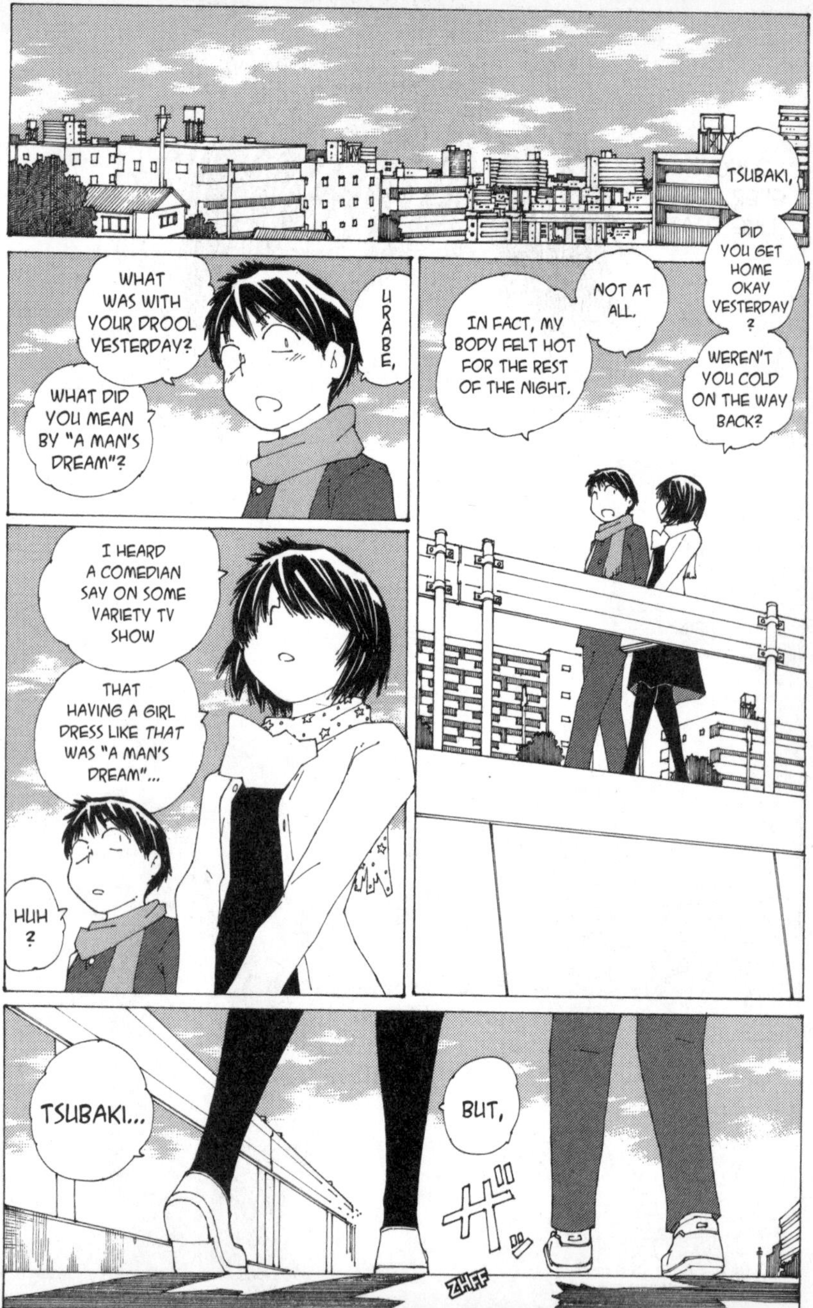
TSUBAKI,
DID YOU GET HOME OKAY YESTERDAY?
WEREN'T YOU COLD ON THE WAY BACK?
NOT AT ALL.
IN FACT, MY BODY FELT HOT FOR THE REST OF THE NIGHT.
URABE,
WHAT WAS WITH YOUR DROOL YESTERDAY?
WHAT DID YOU MEAN BY "A MAN'S DREAM"?
I HEARD A COMEDIAN SAY ON SOME VARIETY TV SHOW
THAT HAVING A GIRL DRESS LIKE *THAT* WAS "A MAN'S DREAM"...
HUH?
BUT,
TSUBAKI...
ZHFF

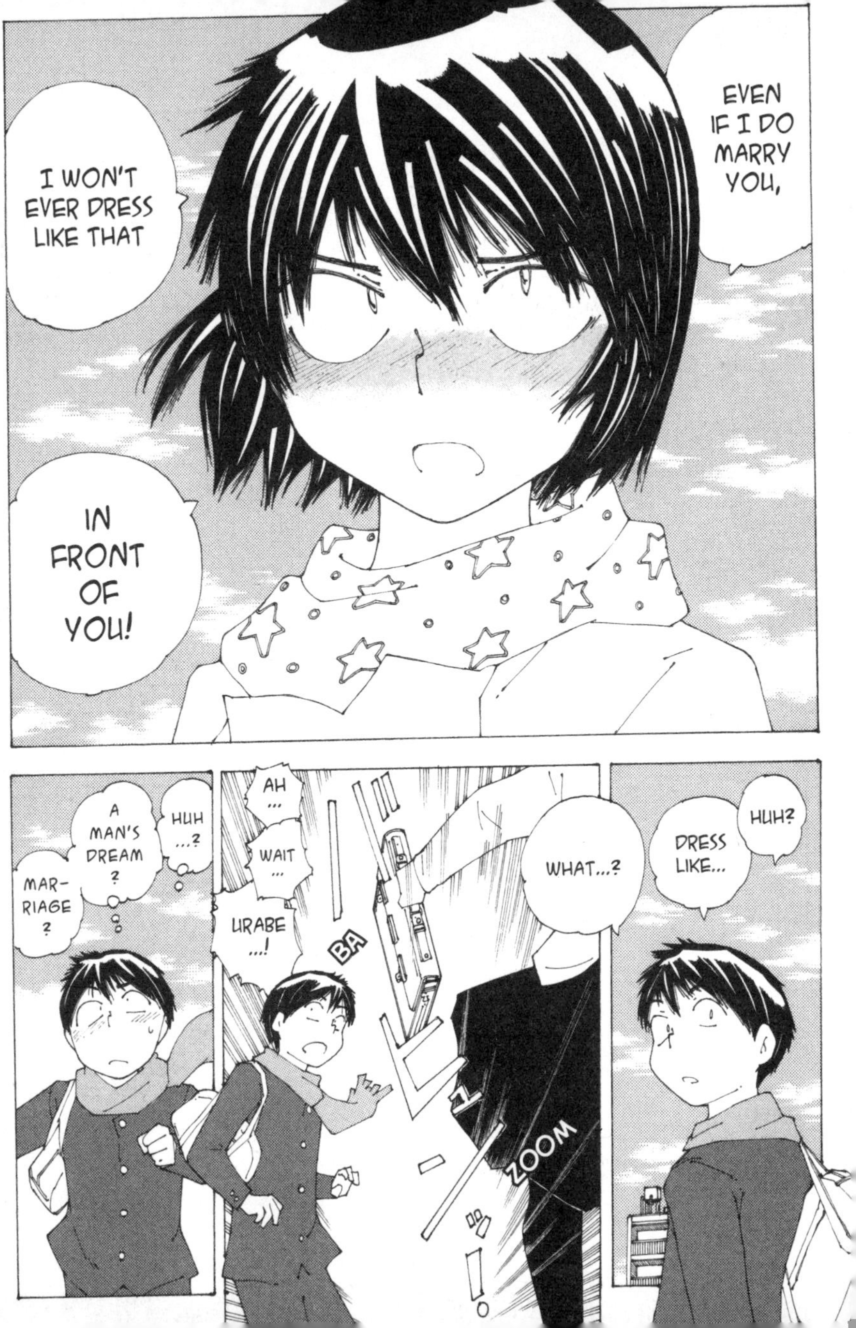

EVEN IF I DO MARRY YOU,
I WON'T EVER DRESS LIKE THAT
IN FRONT OF YOU!
HUH?
DRESS LIKE...
WHAT...?
AH...
WAIT...
URABE...!
BA
ZOOM
HUH...?
A MAN'S DREAM?
MAR-RIAGE?

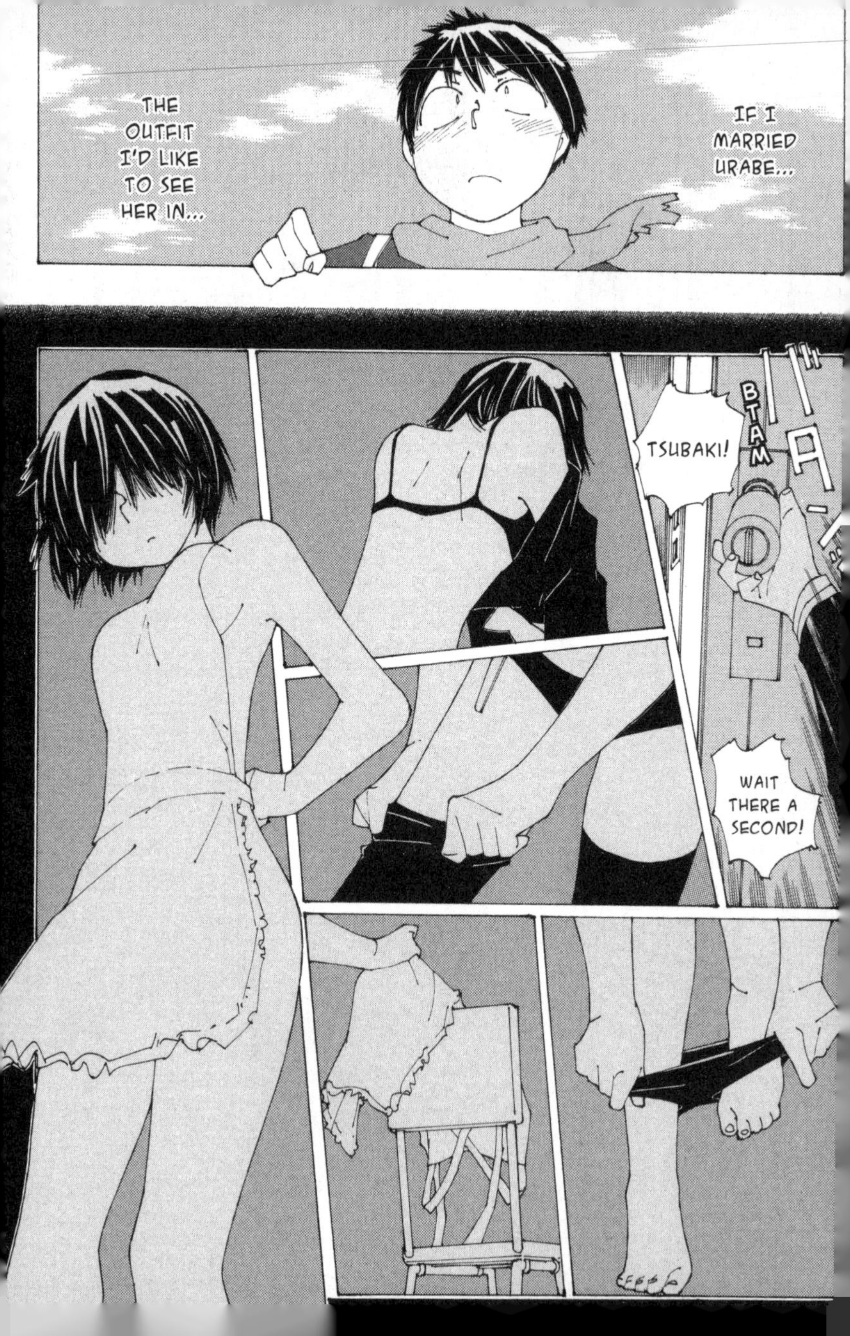
IF I MARRIED URABE...
THE OUTFIT I'D LIKE TO SEE HER IN...
BTAM
TSUBAKI!
WAIT THERE A SECOND!

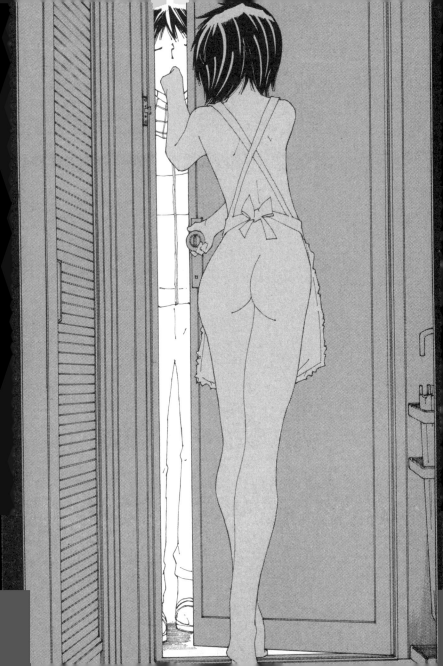

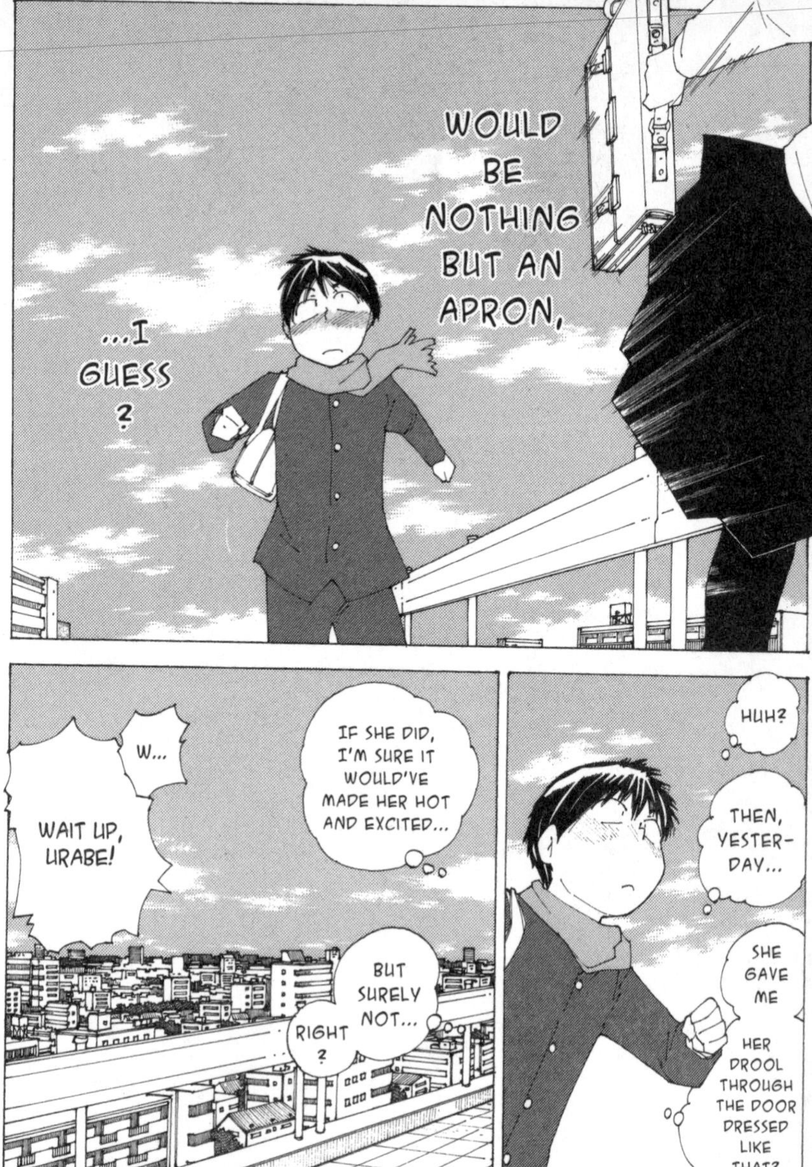

WOULD BE NOTHING BUT AN APRON,
...I GUESS?
HUH?
THEN, YESTER-DAY...
SHE GAVE ME HER DROOL THROUGH THE DOOR DRESSED LIKE THAT?
IF SHE DID, I'M SURE IT WOULD'VE MADE HER HOT AND EXCITED...
BUT SURELY NOT...
RIGHT?
W...
WAIT UP, URABE!

END OF CHAPTER 54

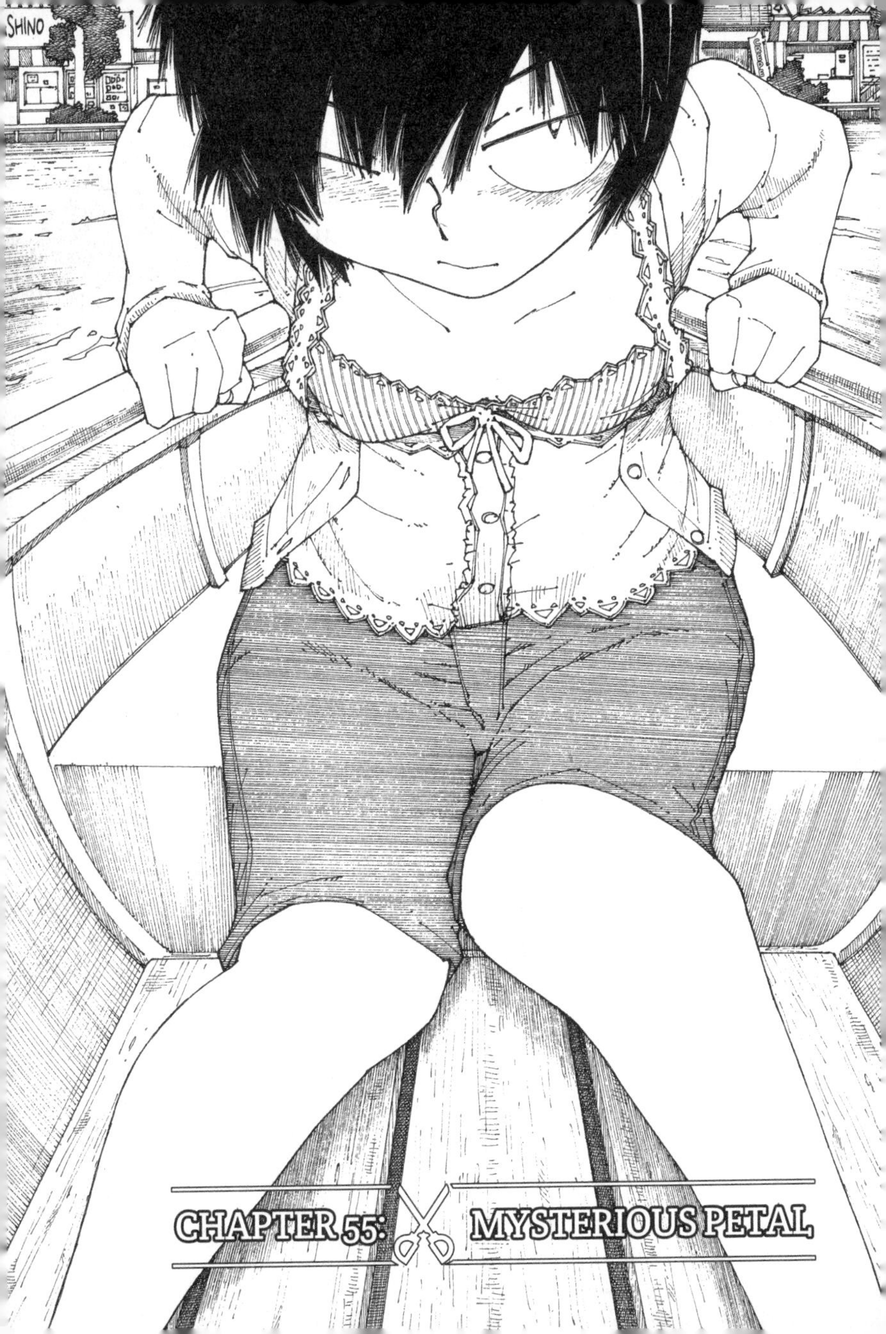
SHINO
CHAPTER 55: MYSTERIOUS PETAL

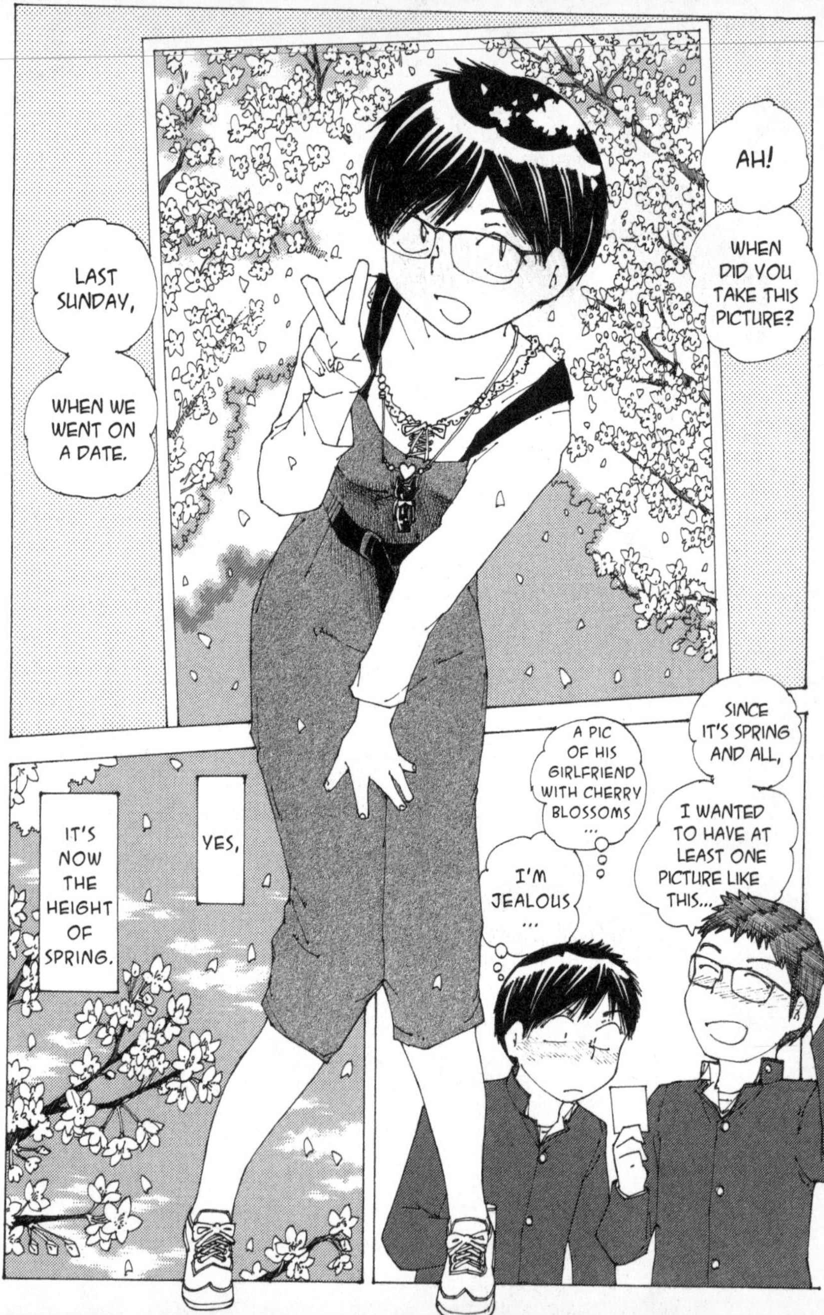
AH!
WHEN DID YOU TAKE THIS PICTURE?
LAST SUNDAY,
WHEN WE WENT ON A DATE.
SINCE IT'S SPRING AND ALL,
I WANTED TO HAVE AT LEAST ONE PICTURE LIKE THIS...
A PIC OF HIS GIRLFRIEND WITH CHERRY BLOSSOMS ...
I'M JEALOUS ...
YES,
IT'S NOW THE HEIGHT OF SPRING.

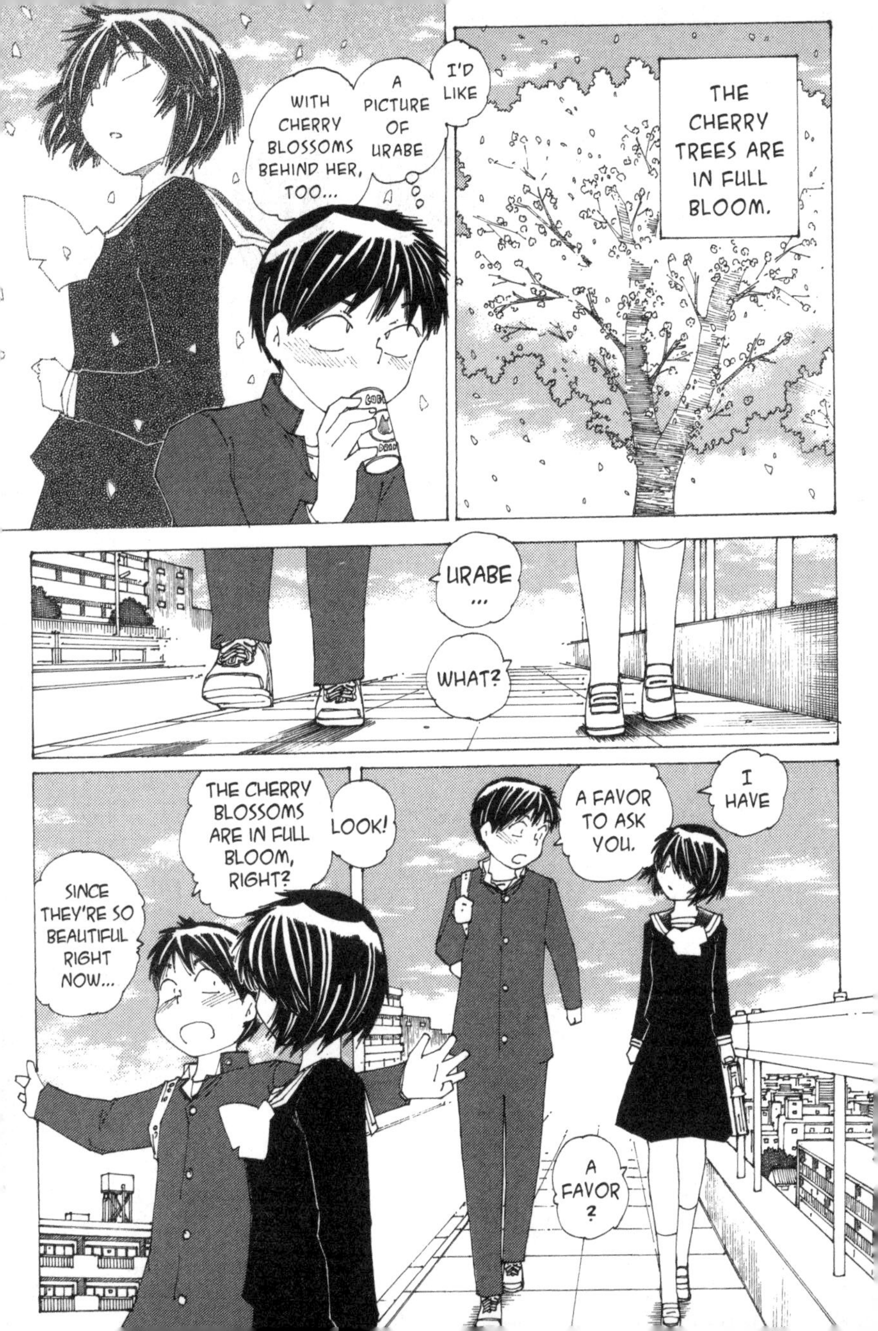
THE CHERRY TREES ARE IN FULL BLOOM.
I'D LIKE
A PICTURE OF URABE
WITH CHERRY BLOSSOMS BEHIND HER, TOO...
URABE ...
WHAT?
I HAVE
A FAVOR TO ASK YOU.
A FAVOR ?
LOOK!
THE CHERRY BLOSSOMS ARE IN FULL BLOOM, RIGHT?
SINCE THEY'RE SO BEAUTIFUL RIGHT NOW...

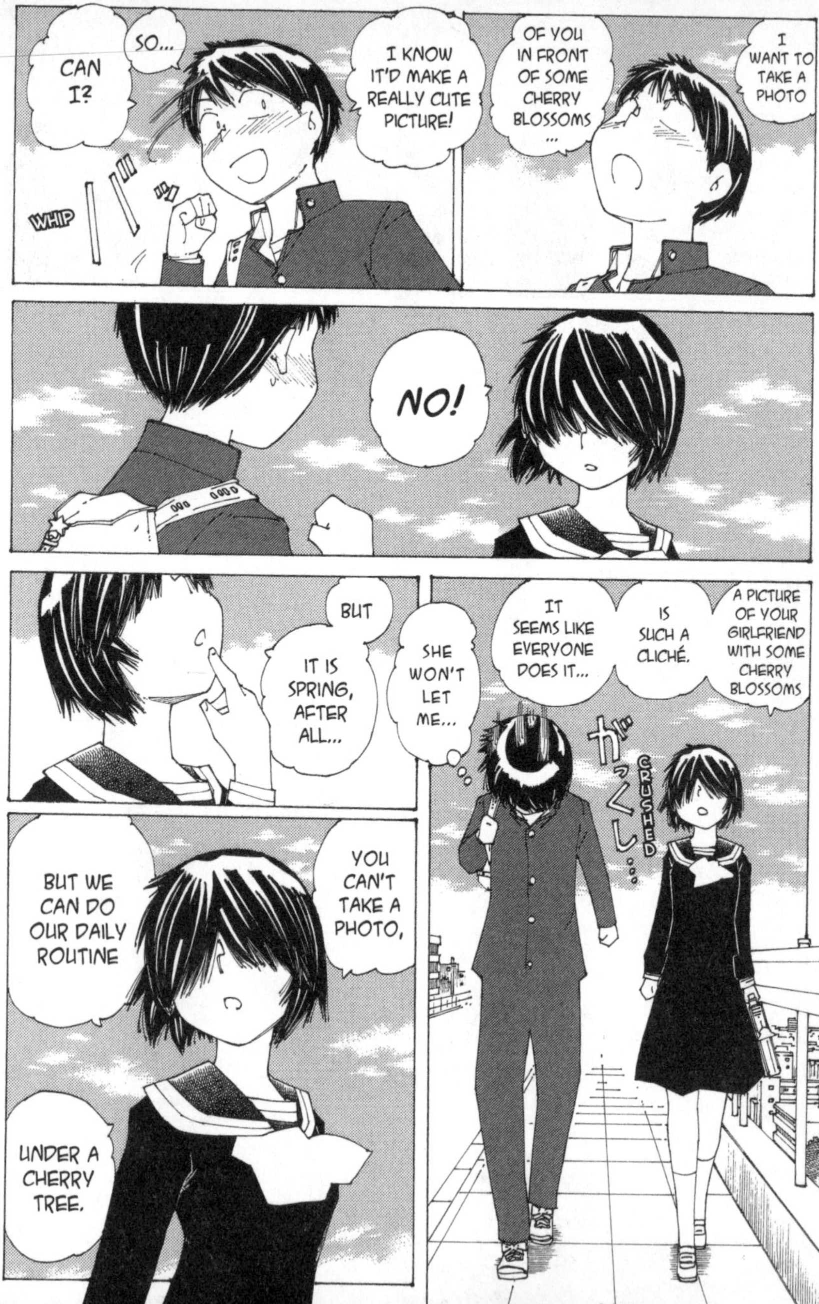
I WANT TO TAKE A PHOTO
OF YOU IN FRONT OF SOME CHERRY BLOSSOMS ...
I KNOW IT'D MAKE A REALLY CUTE PICTURE!
SO...
CAN I?
WHIP
NO!
A PICTURE OF YOUR GIRLFRIEND WITH SOME CHERRY BLOSSOMS
IS SUCH A CLICHÉ.
IT SEEMS LIKE EVERYONE DOES IT...
がっくし...
CRUSHED
SHE WON'T LET ME...
BUT
IT IS SPRING, AFTER ALL...
YOU CAN'T TAKE A PHOTO,
BUT WE CAN DO OUR DAILY ROUTINE
UNDER A CHERRY TREE.

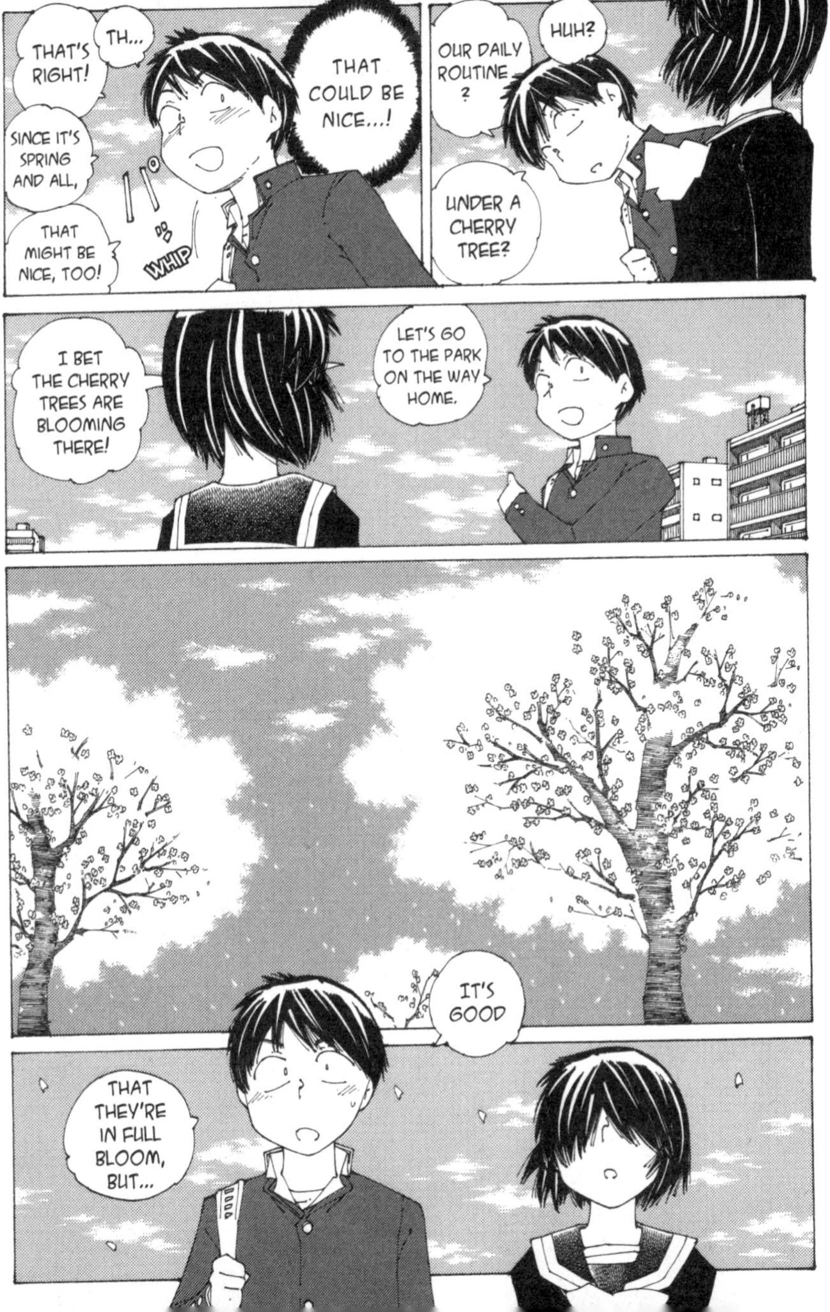
HUH?
OUR DAILY ROUTINE?
UNDER A CHERRY TREE?
THAT COULD BE NICE...!
TH...
THAT'S RIGHT!
SINCE IT'S SPRING AND ALL,
THAT MIGHT BE NICE, TOO!
WHIP
LET'S GO TO THE PARK ON THE WAY HOME.
I BET THE CHERRY TREES ARE BLOOMING THERE!
IT'S GOOD
THAT THEY'RE IN FULL BLOOM, BUT...

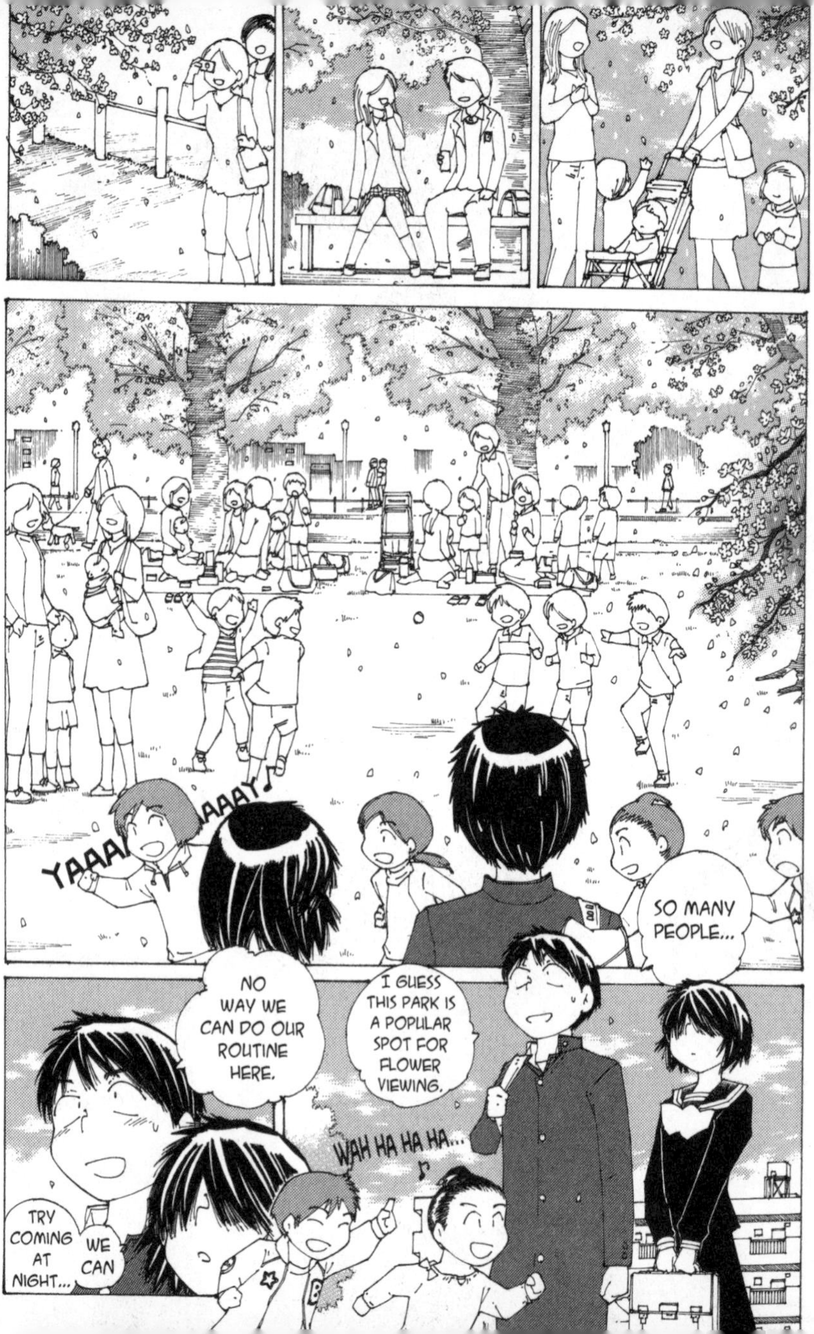
SO MANY PEOPLE...
YAAA AAAAY
I GUESS THIS PARK IS A POPULAR SPOT FOR FLOWER VIEWING.
NO WAY WE CAN DO OUR ROUTINE HERE.
WAH HA HA HA...
WE CAN
TRY COMING AT NIGHT...

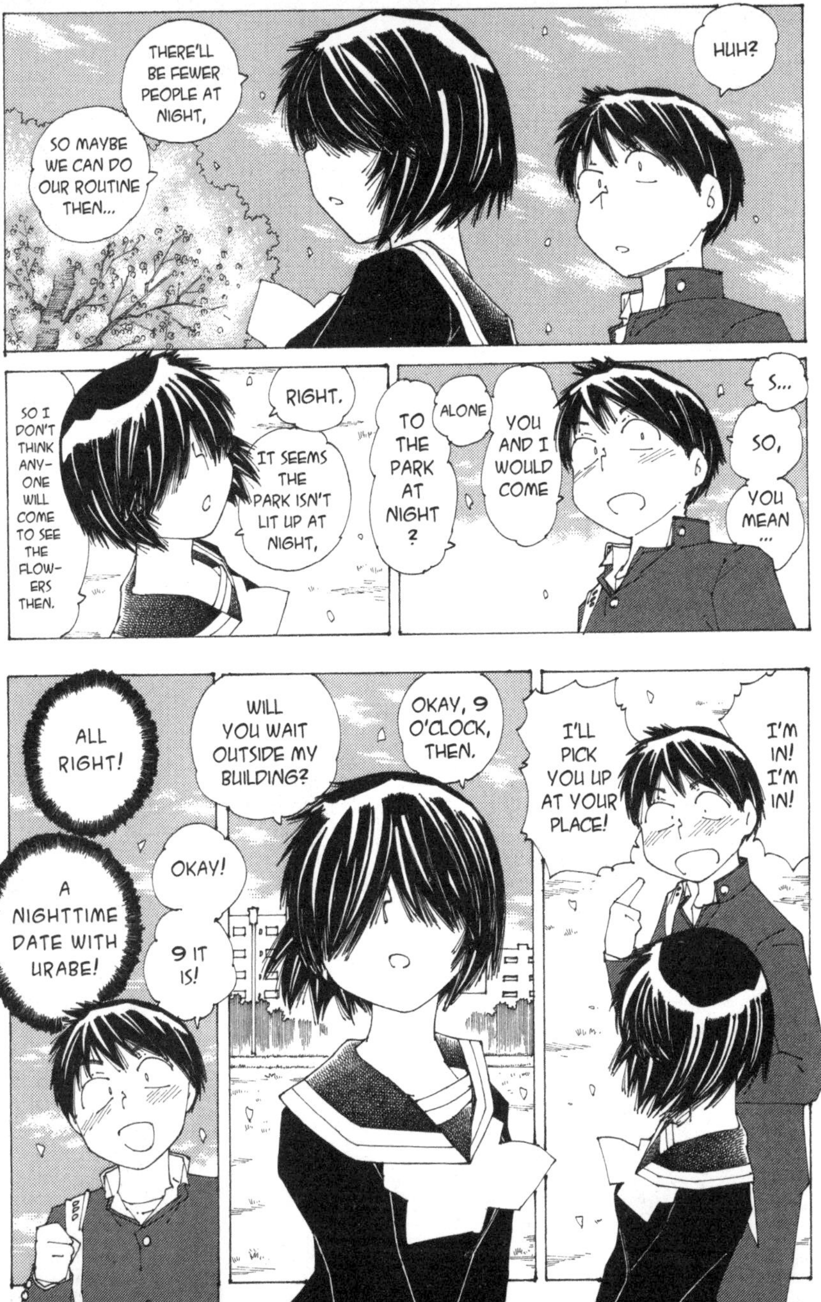
HUH?
THERE'LL BE FEWER PEOPLE AT NIGHT,
SO MAYBE WE CAN DO OUR ROUTINE THEN...
S...
SO,
YOU MEAN...
YOU AND I WOULD COME
ALONE
TO THE PARK AT NIGHT?
RIGHT.
IT SEEMS THE PARK ISN'T LIT UP AT NIGHT,
SO I DON'T THINK ANY-ONE WILL COME TO SEE THE FLOW-ERS THEN.
I'M IN! I'M IN!
I'LL PICK YOU UP AT YOUR PLACE!
OKAY, 9 O'CLOCK, THEN.
WILL YOU WAIT OUTSIDE MY BUILDING?
OKAY!
9 IT IS!
ALL RIGHT!
A NIGHTTIME DATE WITH URABE!

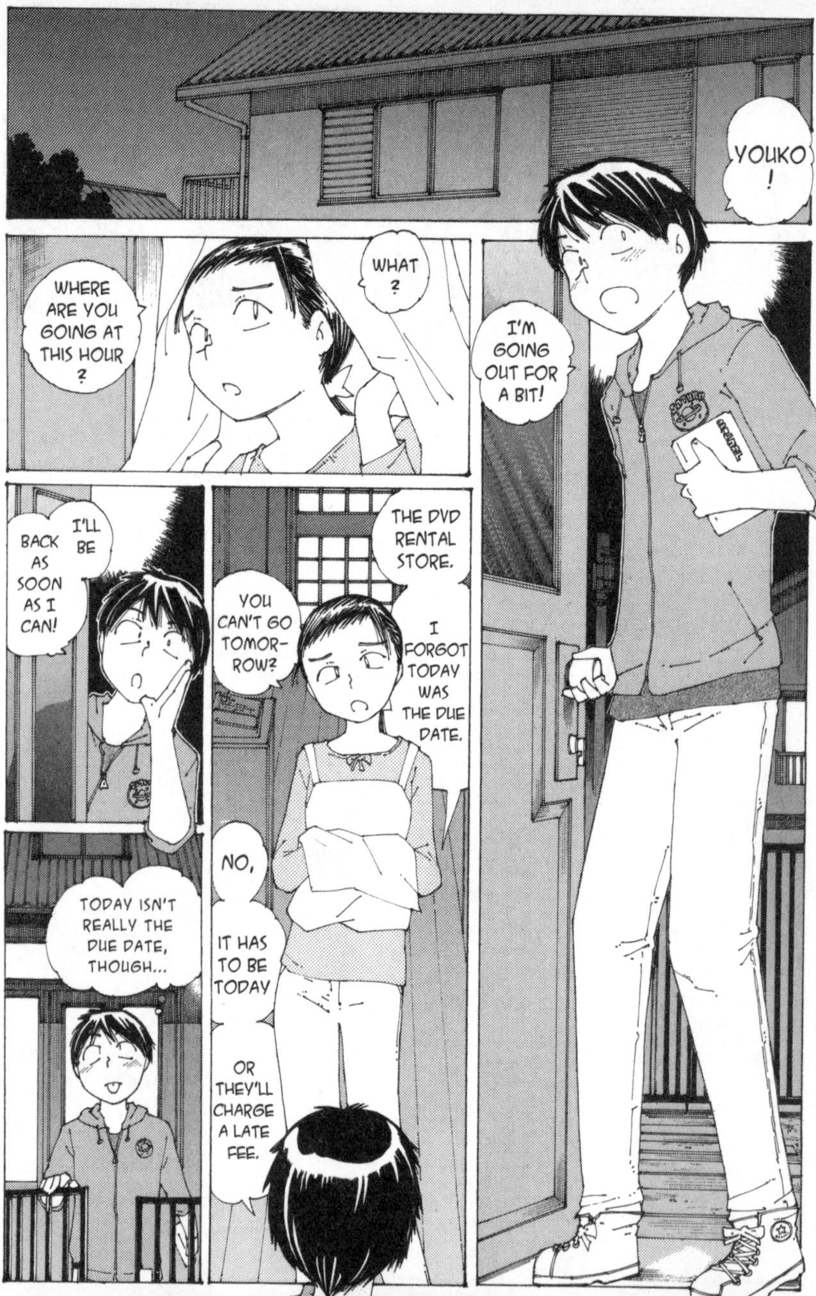
YOUKO!
I'M GOING OUT FOR A BIT!
WHAT?
WHERE ARE YOU GOING AT THIS HOUR?
THE DVD RENTAL STORE.
I FORGOT TODAY WAS THE DUE DATE.
YOU CAN'T GO TOMORROW?
NO,
IT HAS TO BE TODAY
OR THEY'LL CHARGE A LATE FEE.
I'LL BE BACK AS SOON AS I CAN!
TODAY ISN'T REALLY THE DUE DATE, THOUGH...

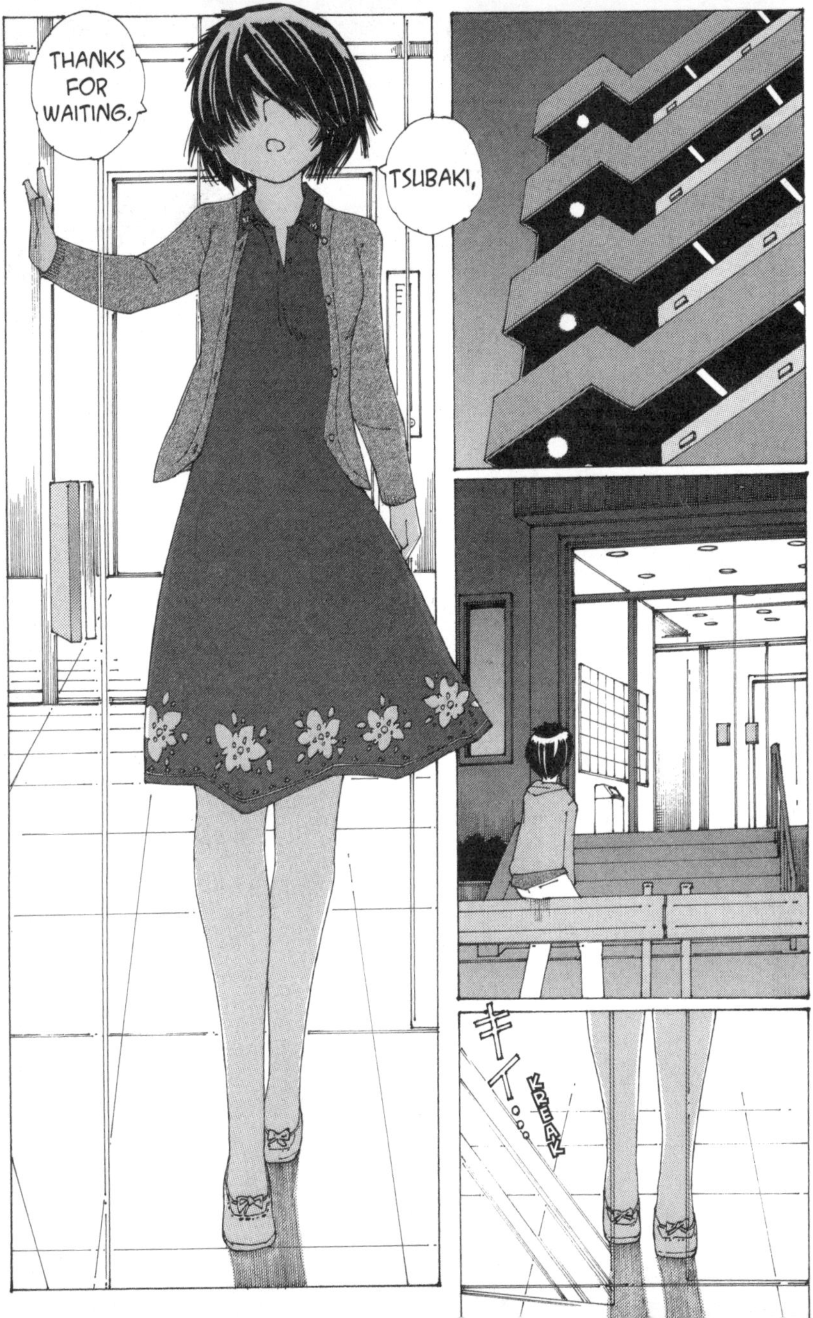
キイ…
KREAK
TSUBAKI,
THANKS FOR WAITING.

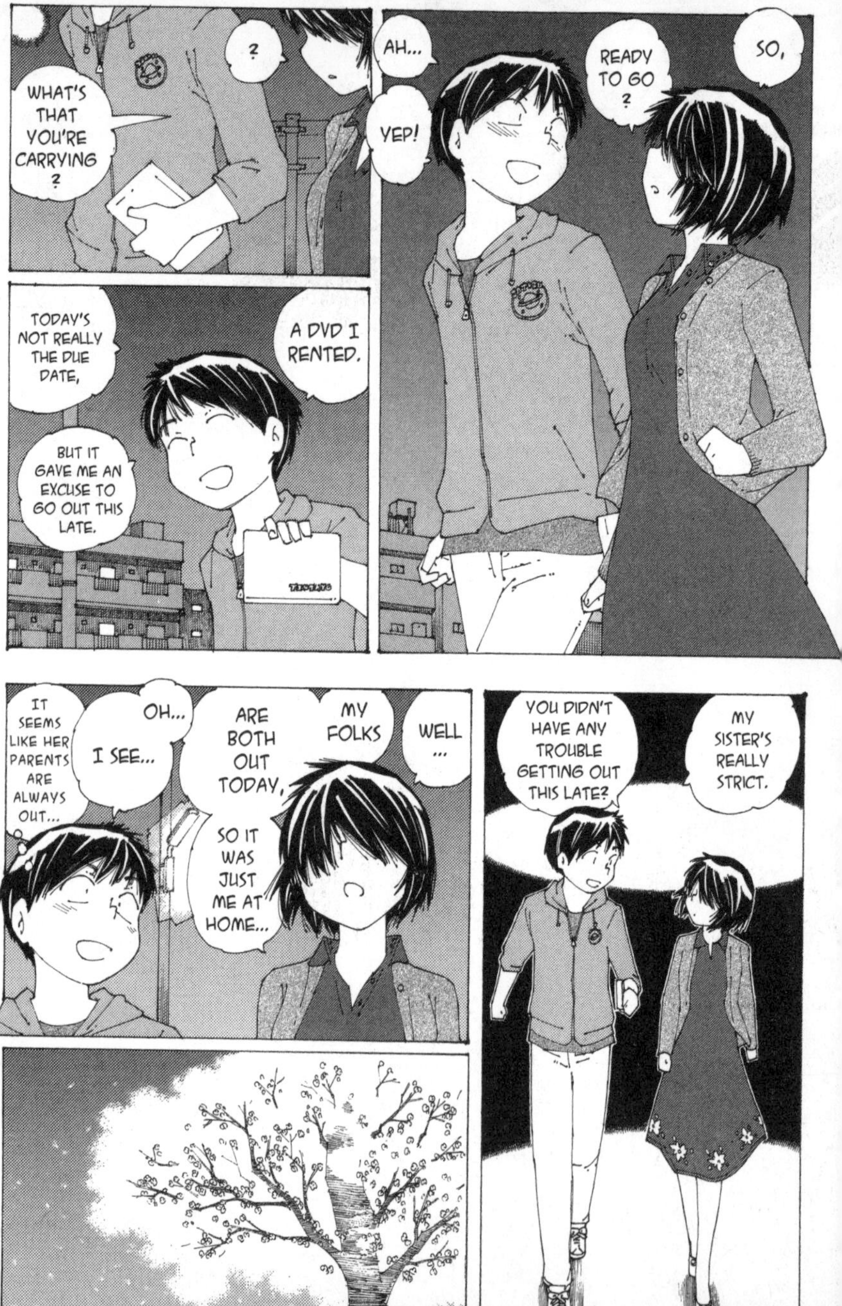
SO,
READY TO GO?
YEP!
AH...
?
WHAT'S THAT YOU'RE CARRYING?
A DVD I RENTED.
TODAY'S NOT REALLY THE DUE DATE,
BUT IT GAVE ME AN EXCUSE TO GO OUT THIS LATE.
YOU DIDN'T HAVE ANY TROUBLE GETTING OUT THIS LATE?
MY SISTER'S REALLY STRICT.
WELL...
MY FOLKS
ARE BOTH OUT TODAY,
SO IT WAS JUST ME AT HOME...
OH... I SEE...
IT SEEMS LIKE HER PARENTS ARE ALWAYS OUT...

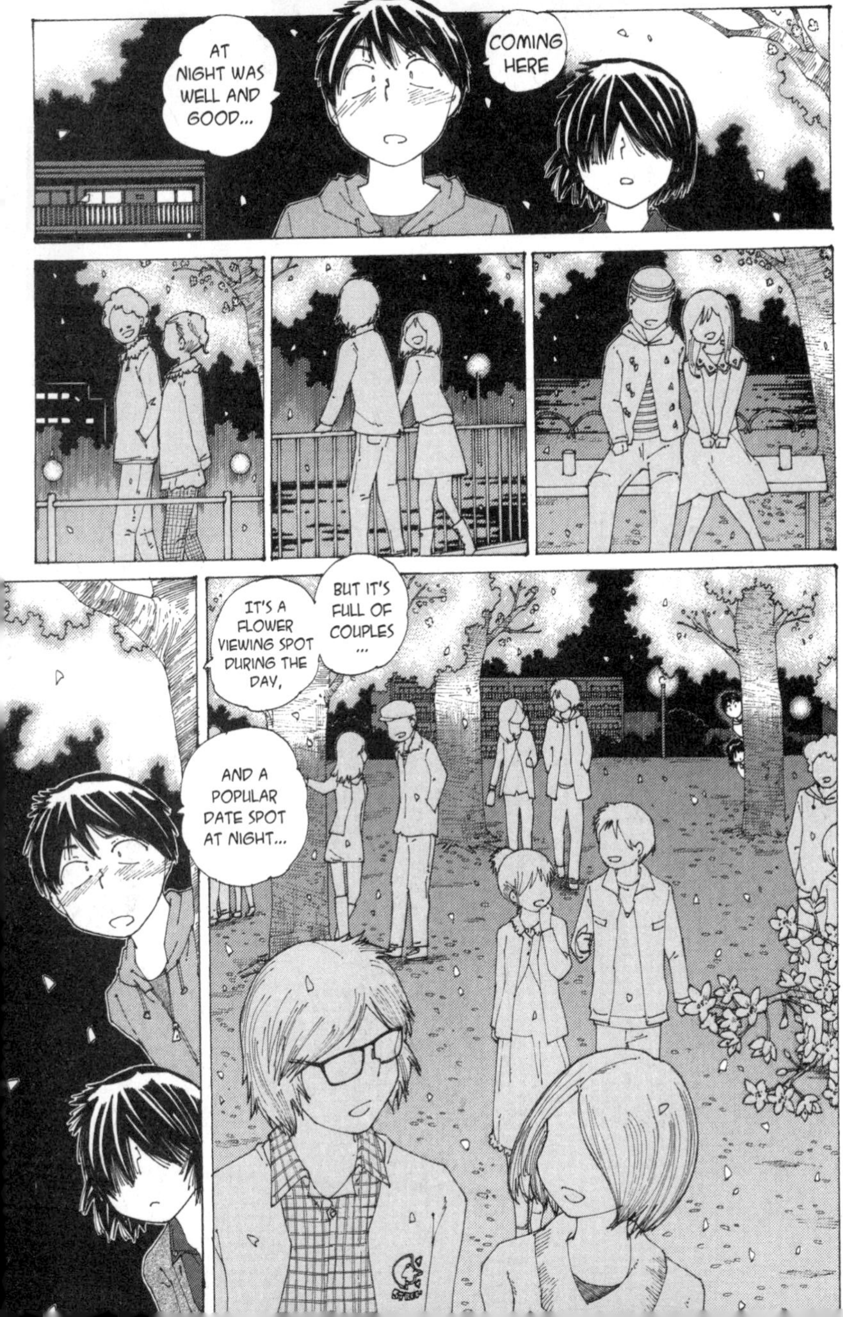
COMING HERE
AT NIGHT WAS WELL AND GOOD...
BUT IT'S FULL OF COUPLES ...
IT'S A FLOWER VIEWING SPOT DURING THE DAY,
AND A POPULAR DATE SPOT AT NIGHT...

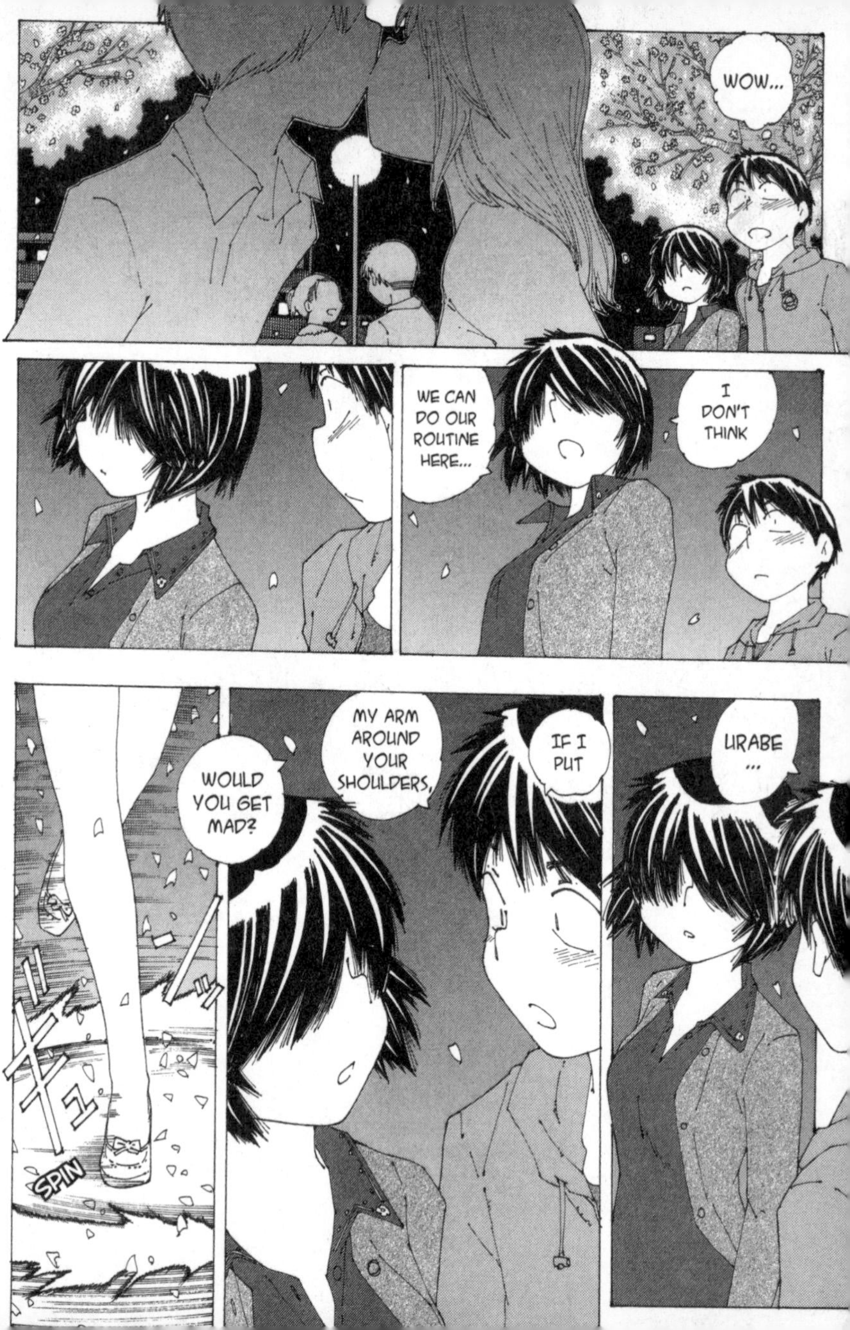
WOW...
I DON'T THINK
WE CAN DO OUR ROUTINE HERE...
URABE ...
IF I PUT
MY ARM AROUND YOUR SHOULDERS,
WOULD YOU GET MAD?
SPIN

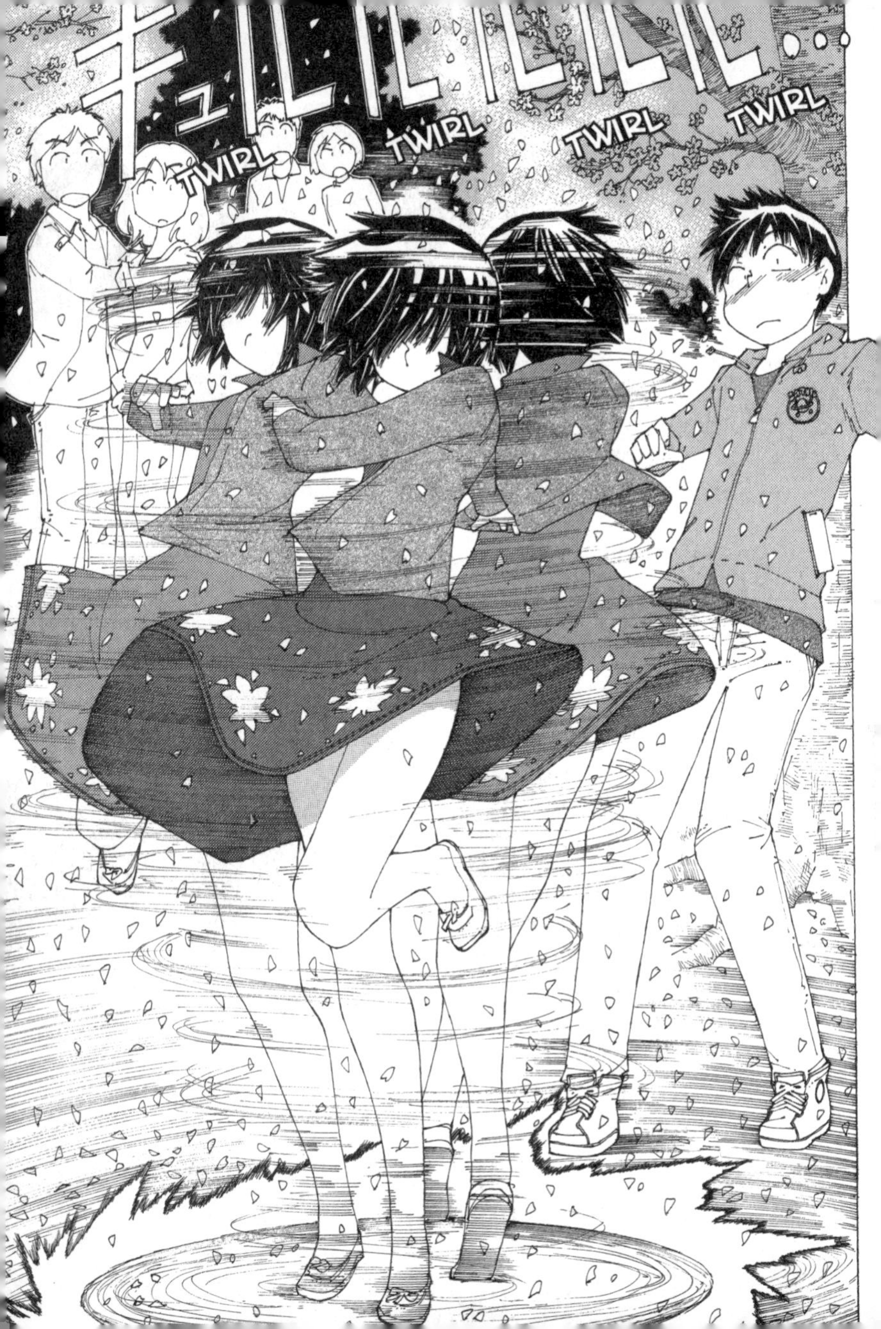
キュルルル ルルル...
TWIRL
TWIRL
TWIRL
TWIRL

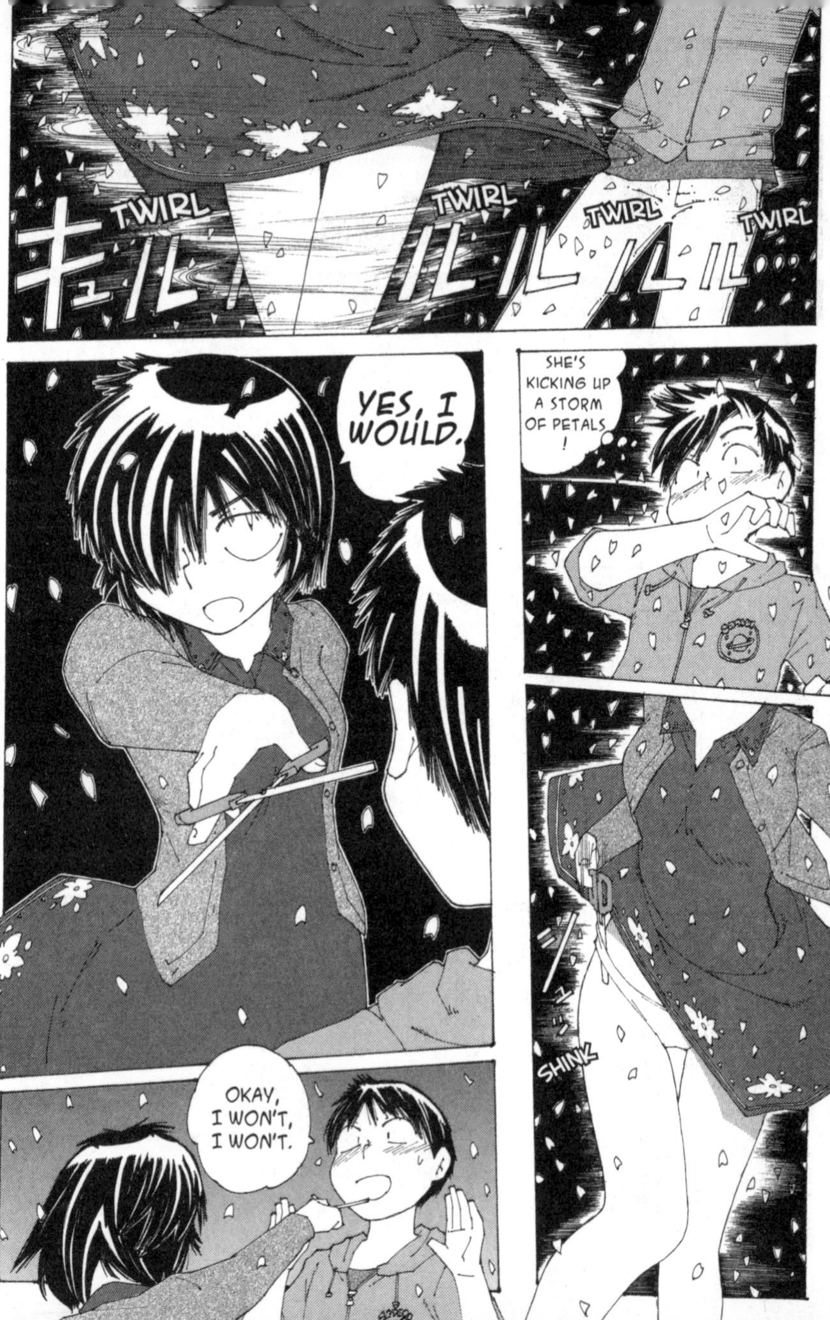
キュルルルル…
TWIRL
TWIRL
TWIRL
TWIRL
SHE'S KICKING UP A STORM OF PETALS!
SHINK
YES, I WOULD.
OKAY, I WON'T, I WON'T.

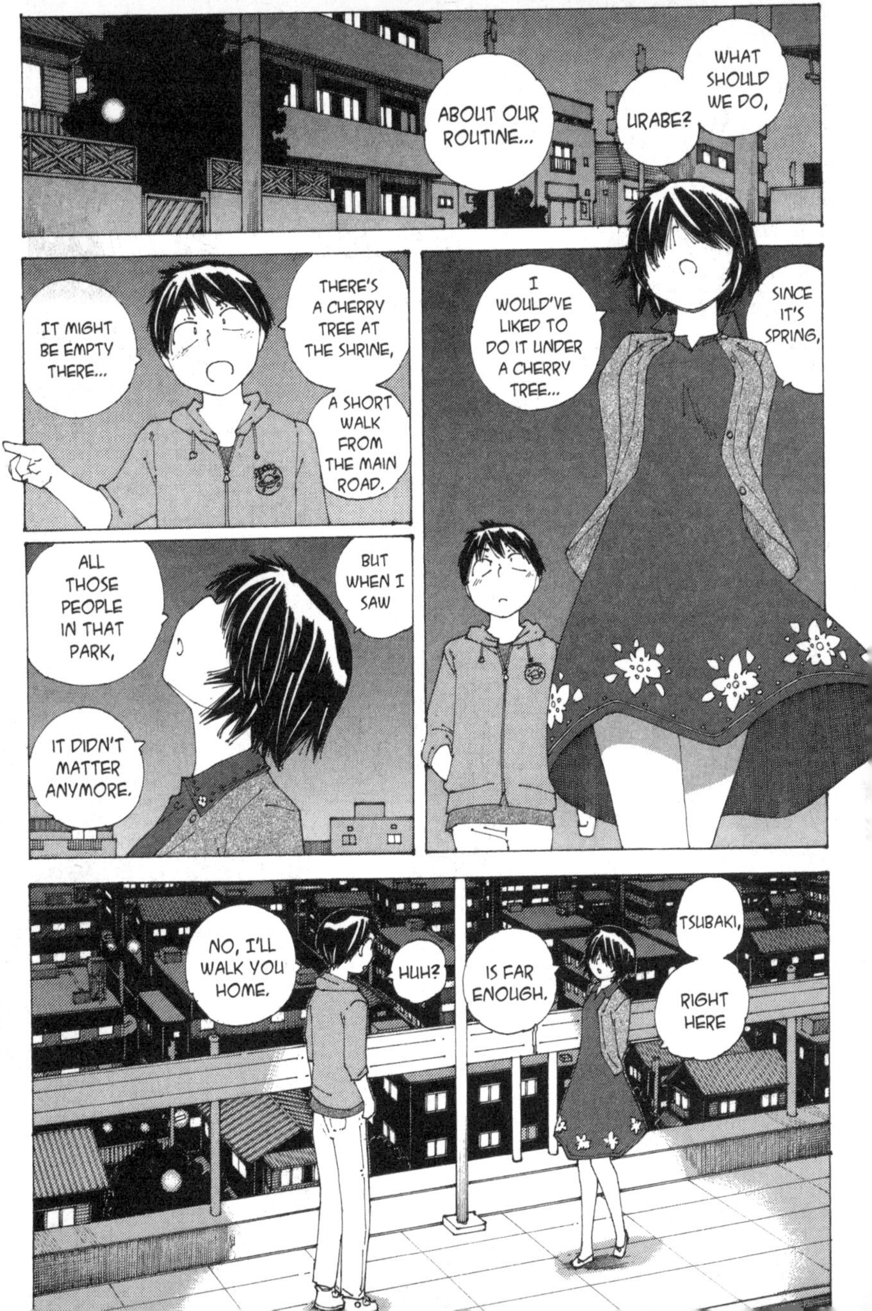
WHAT SHOULD WE DO,
URABE?
ABOUT OUR ROUTINE...
SINCE IT'S SPRING,
I WOULD'VE LIKED TO DO IT UNDER A CHERRY TREE...
THERE'S A CHERRY TREE AT THE SHRINE,
A SHORT WALK FROM THE MAIN ROAD.
IT MIGHT BE EMPTY THERE...
BUT WHEN I SAW
ALL THOSE PEOPLE IN THAT PARK,
IT DIDN'T MATTER ANYMORE.
TSUBAKI,
RIGHT HERE
IS FAR ENOUGH.
HUH?
NO, I'LL WALK YOU HOME.

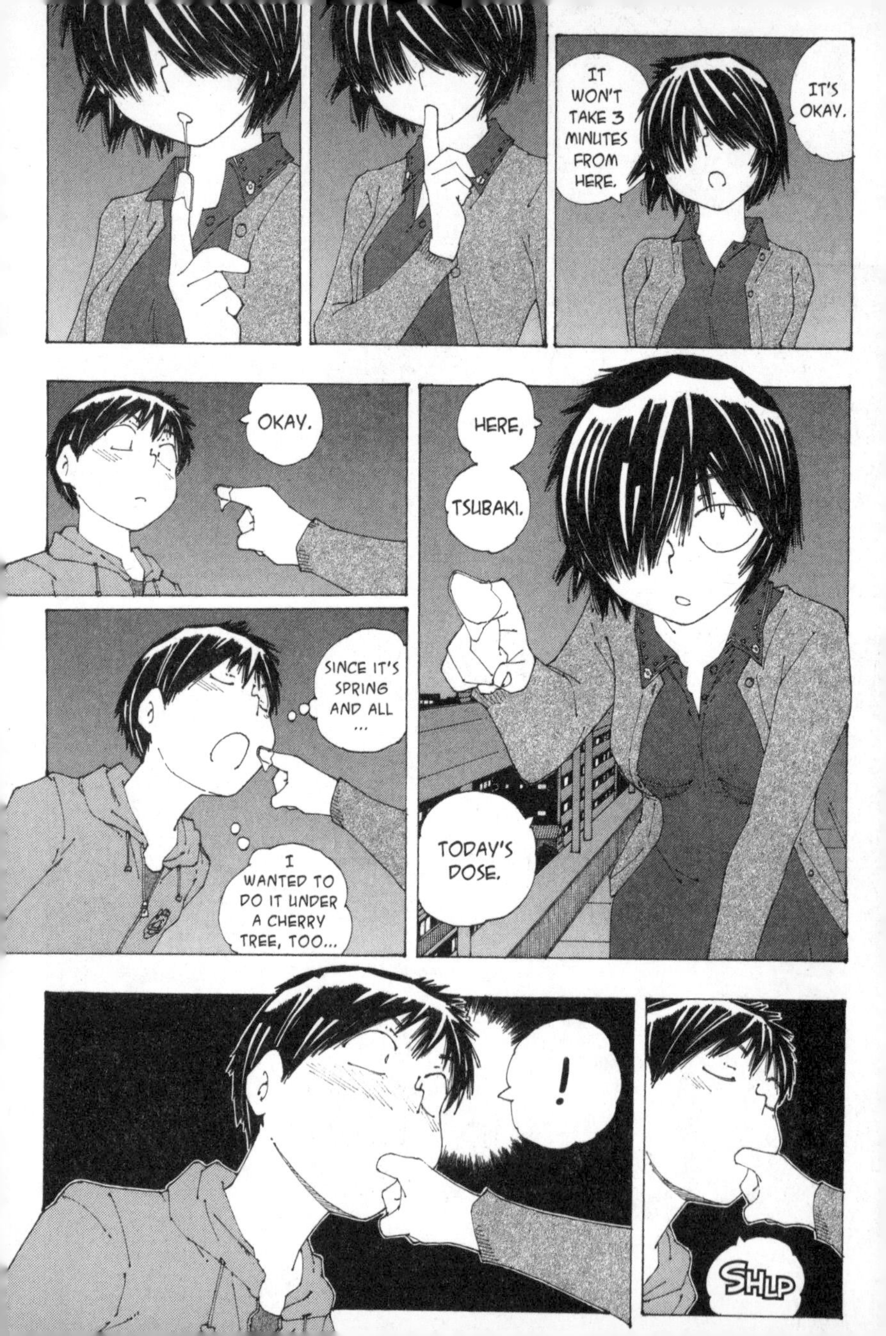
IT'S OKAY.
IT WON'T TAKE 3 MINUTES FROM HERE.
HERE,
TSUBAKI.
TODAY'S DOSE.
OKAY.
SINCE IT'S SPRING AND ALL ...
I WANTED TO DO IT UNDER A CHERRY TREE, TOO...
SHLP
!

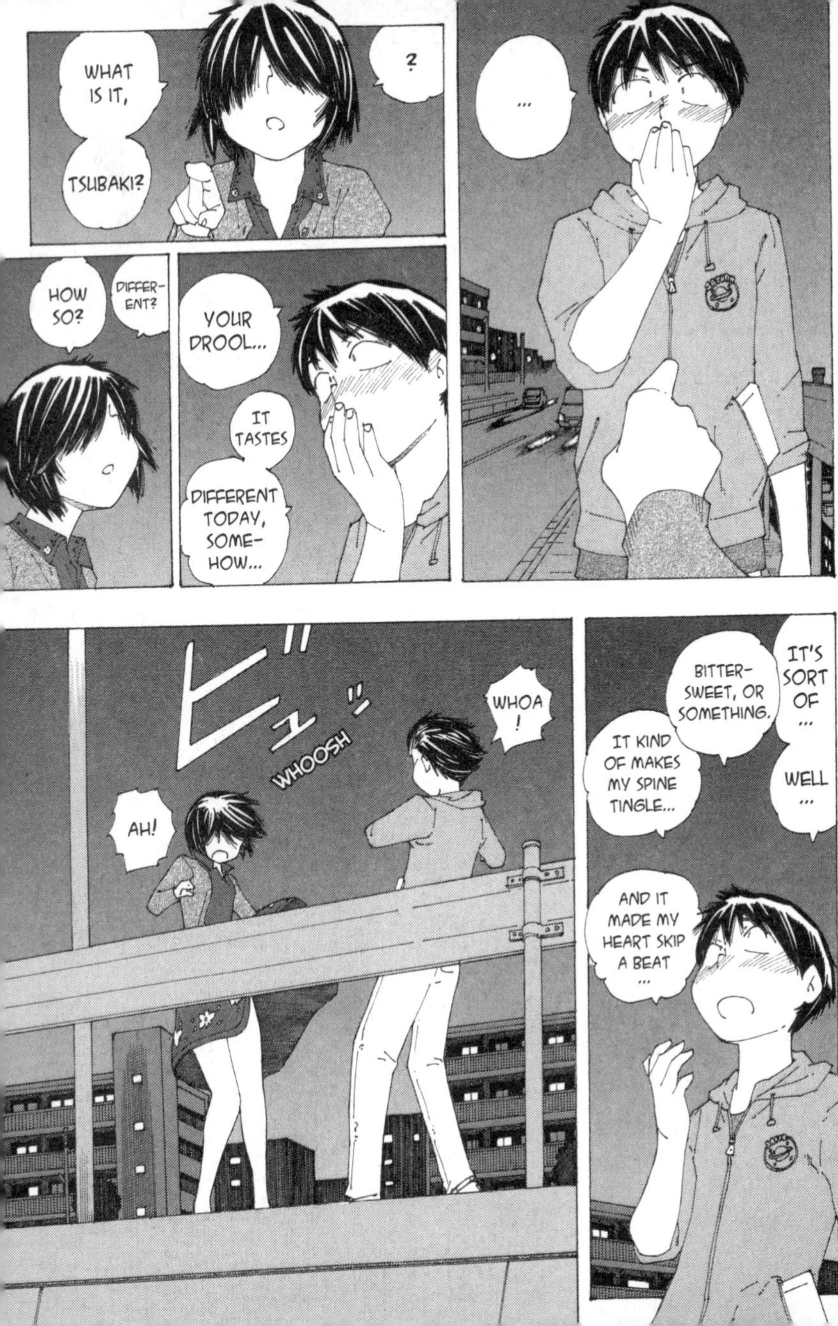

...
?
WHAT IS IT,
TSUBAKI?
YOUR DROOL...
IT TASTES
DIFFERENT TODAY, SOME-HOW...
DIFFER-ENT?
HOW SO?
IT'S SORT OF ...
WELL ...
BITTER-SWEET, OR SOMETHING.
IT KIND OF MAKES MY SPINE TINGLE...
AND IT MADE MY HEART SKIP A BEAT ...
WHOA !
ヒュ"
WHOOSH
AH!

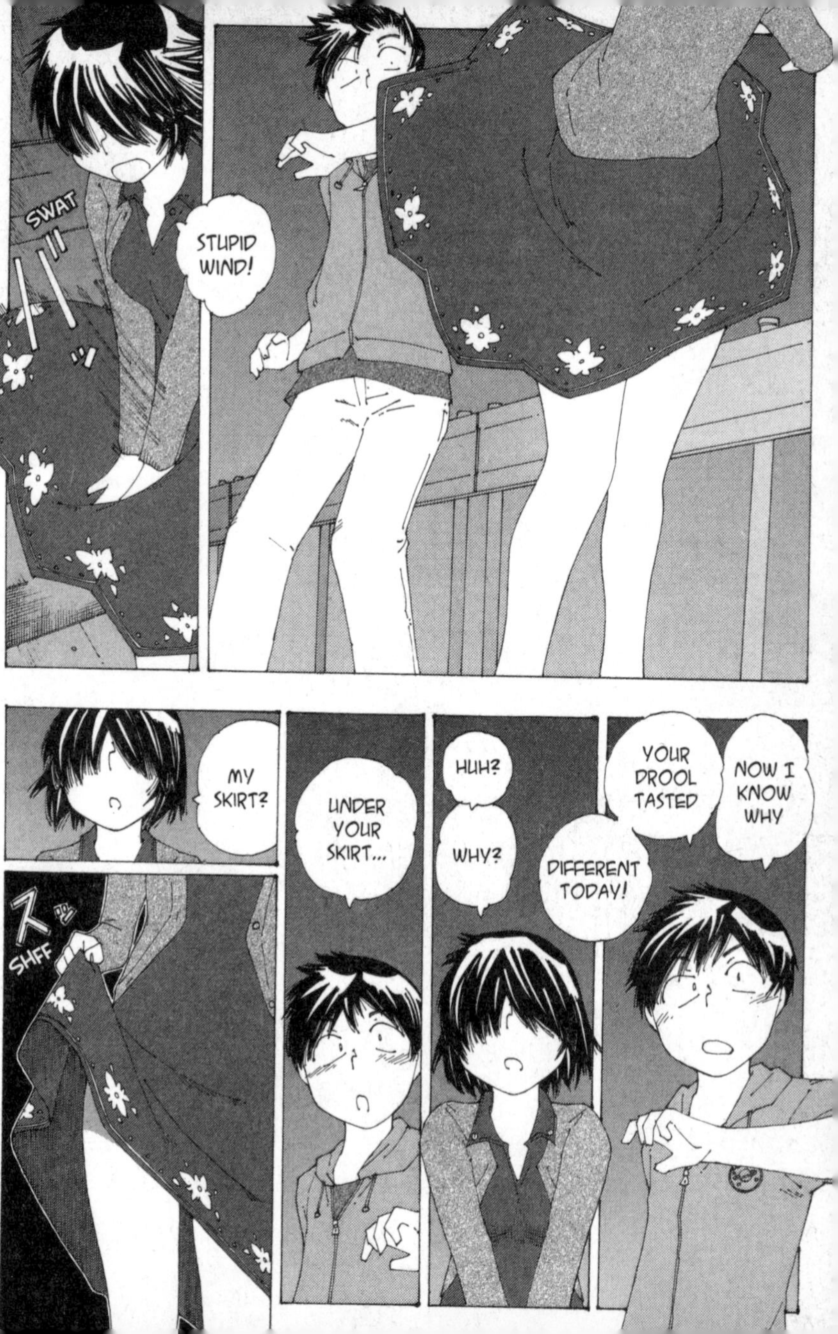
STUPID WIND!
SWAT
NOW I KNOW WHY
YOUR DROOL TASTED
DIFFERENT TODAY!
HUH?
WHY?
UNDER YOUR SKIRT...
MY SKIRT?
SHFF

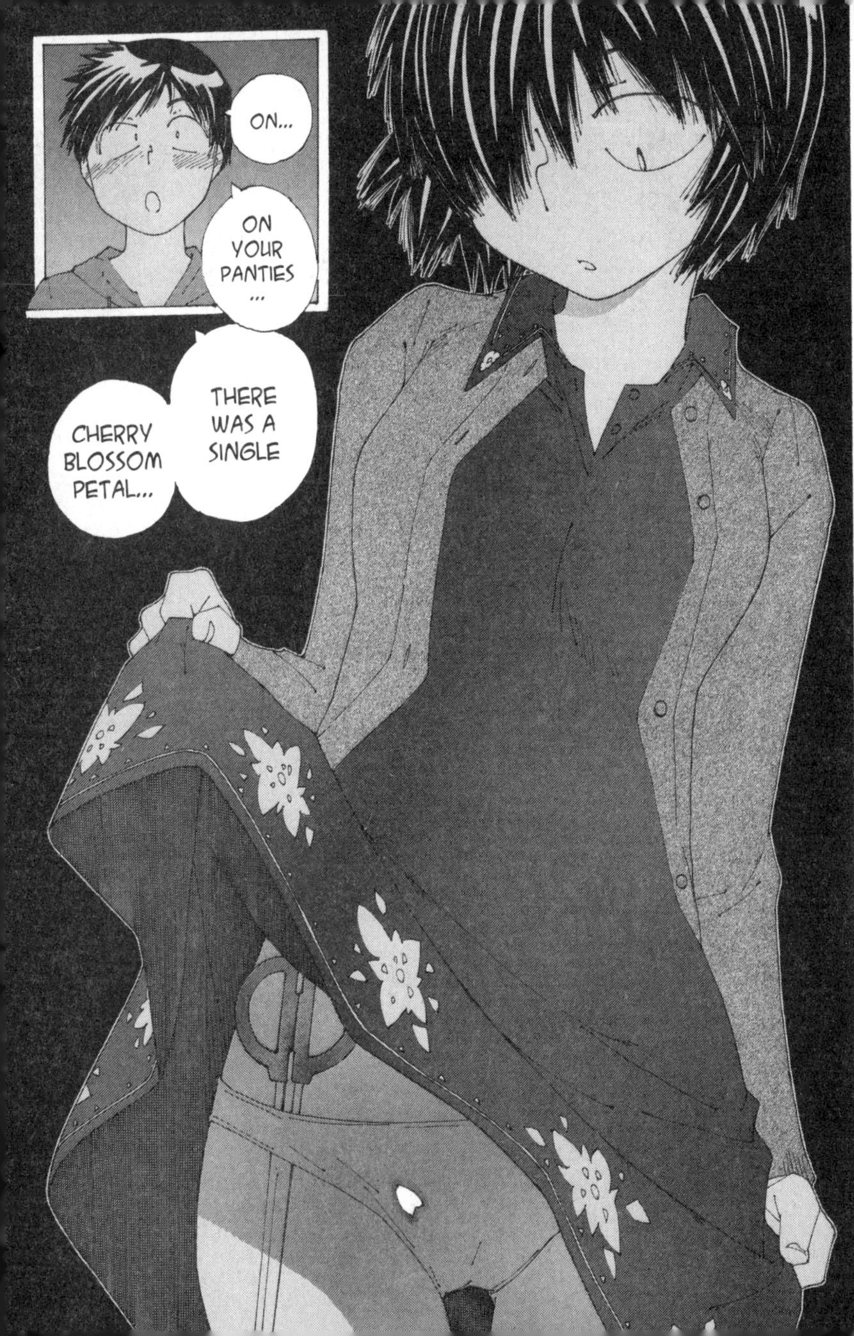
ON...
ON YOUR PANTIES ...
THERE WAS A SINGLE
CHERRY BLOSSOM PETAL...

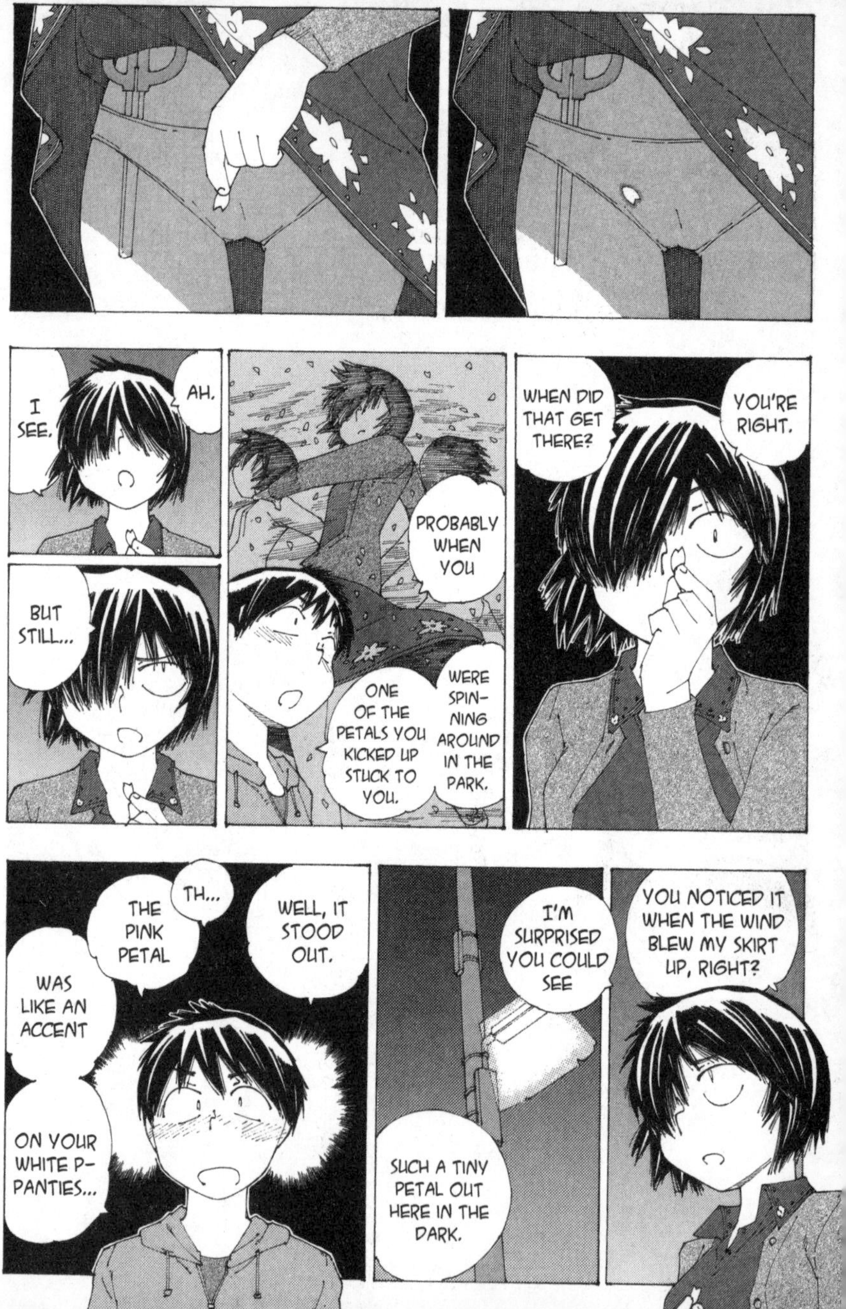
YOU'RE RIGHT.
WHEN DID THAT GET THERE?
PROBABLY WHEN YOU
WERE SPINNING AROUND IN THE PARK,
ONE OF THE PETALS YOU KICKED UP STUCK TO YOU.
AH.
I SEE.
BUT STILL...
YOU NOTICED IT WHEN THE WIND BLEW MY SKIRT UP, RIGHT?
I'M SURPRISED YOU COULD SEE
SUCH A TINY PETAL OUT HERE IN THE DARK.
WELL, IT STOOD OUT.
TH...
THE PINK PETAL
WAS LIKE AN ACCENT
ON YOUR WHITE P-PANTIES...

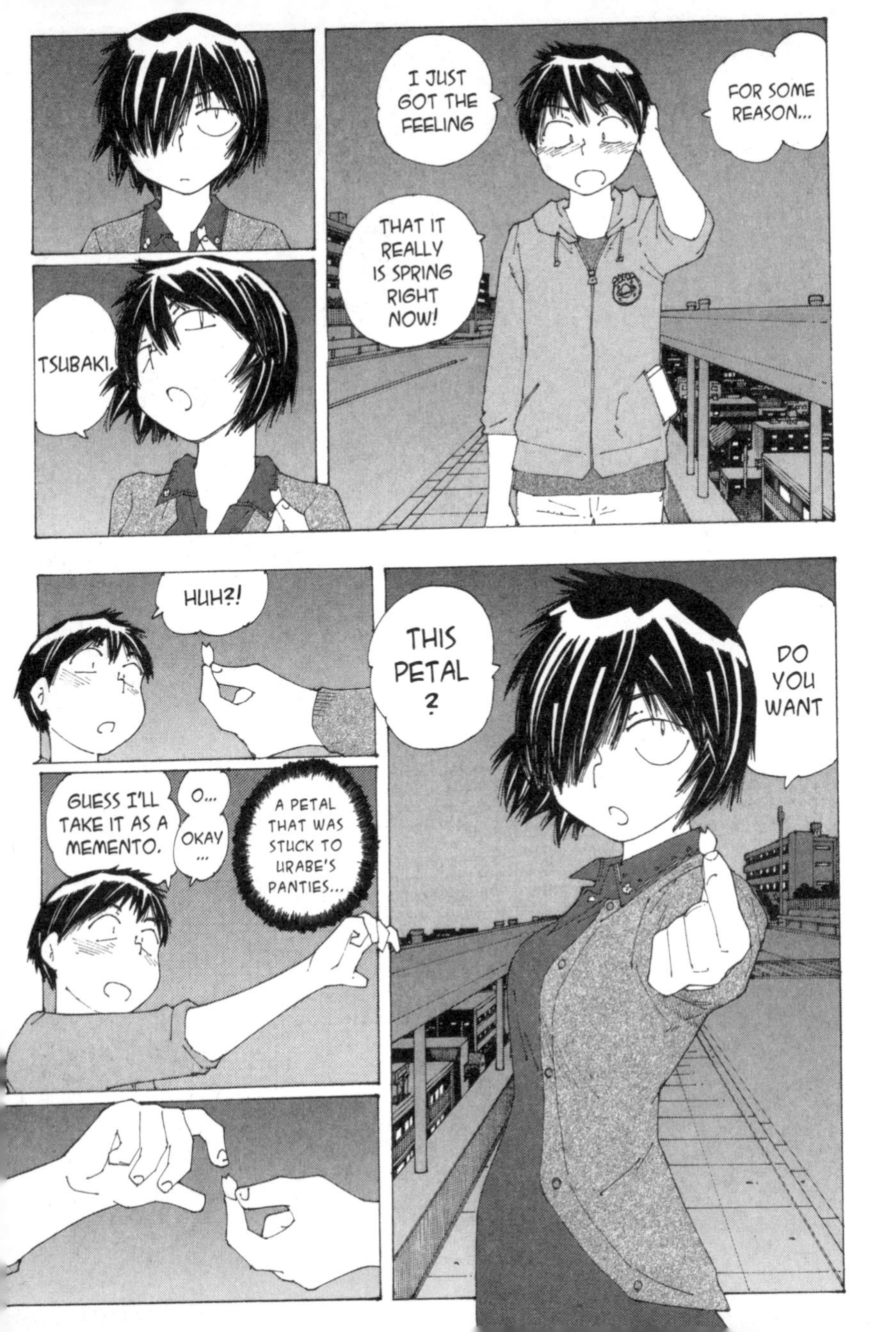
FOR SOME REASON...
I JUST GOT THE FEELING
THAT IT REALLY IS SPRING RIGHT NOW!
TSUBAKI.
DO YOU WANT
THIS PETAL ?
HUH?!
A PETAL THAT WAS STUCK TO URABE'S PANTIES...
O... OKAY...
GUESS I'LL TAKE IT AS A MEMENTO.

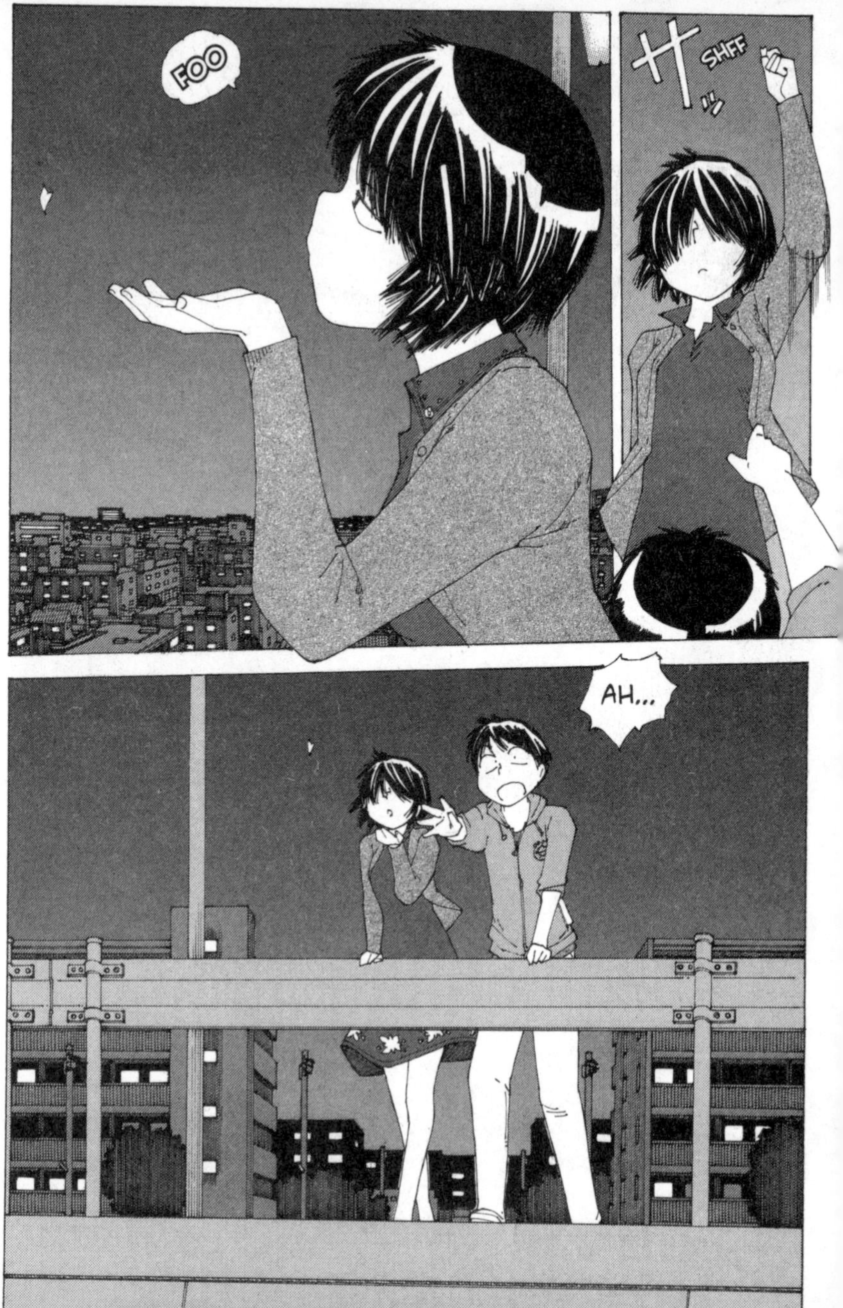
SHFF
FOO
AH...

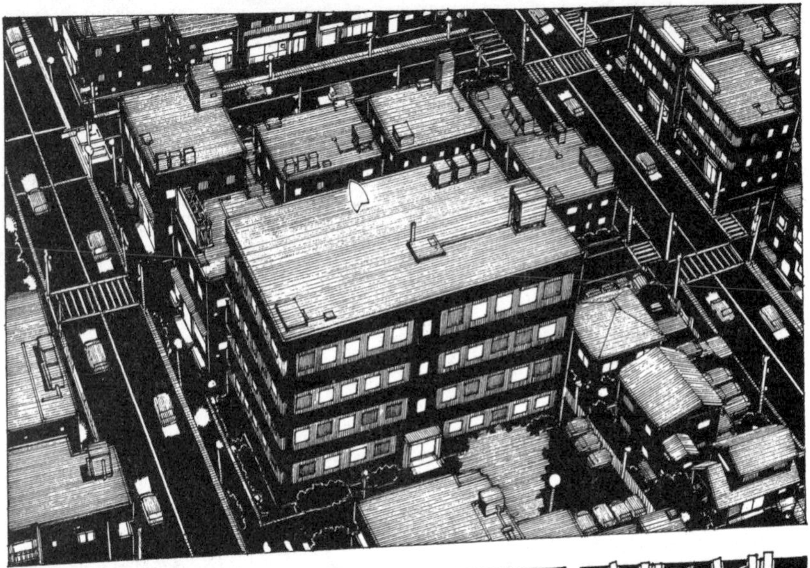

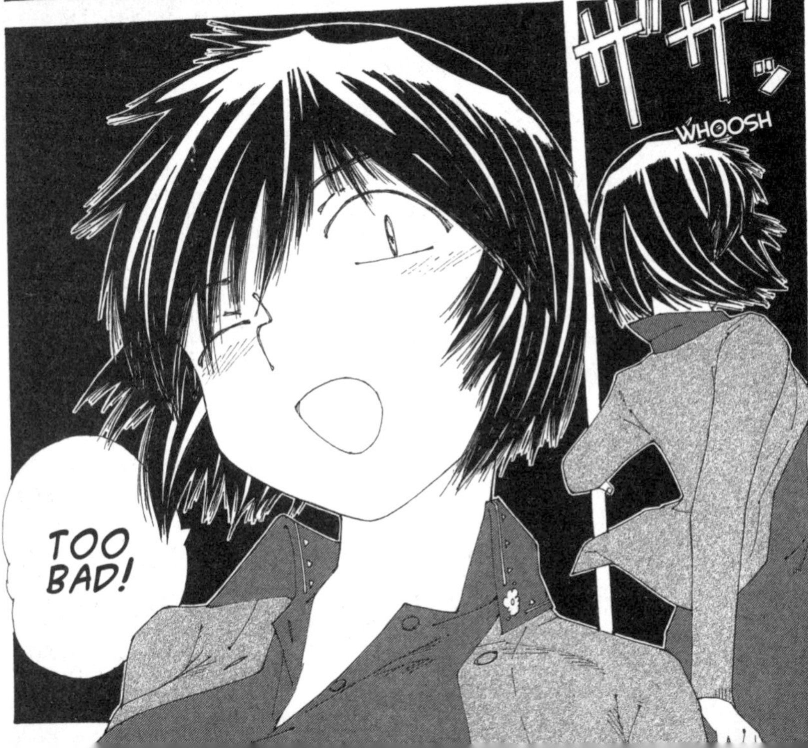
ザザッ
WHOOSH
TOO BAD!

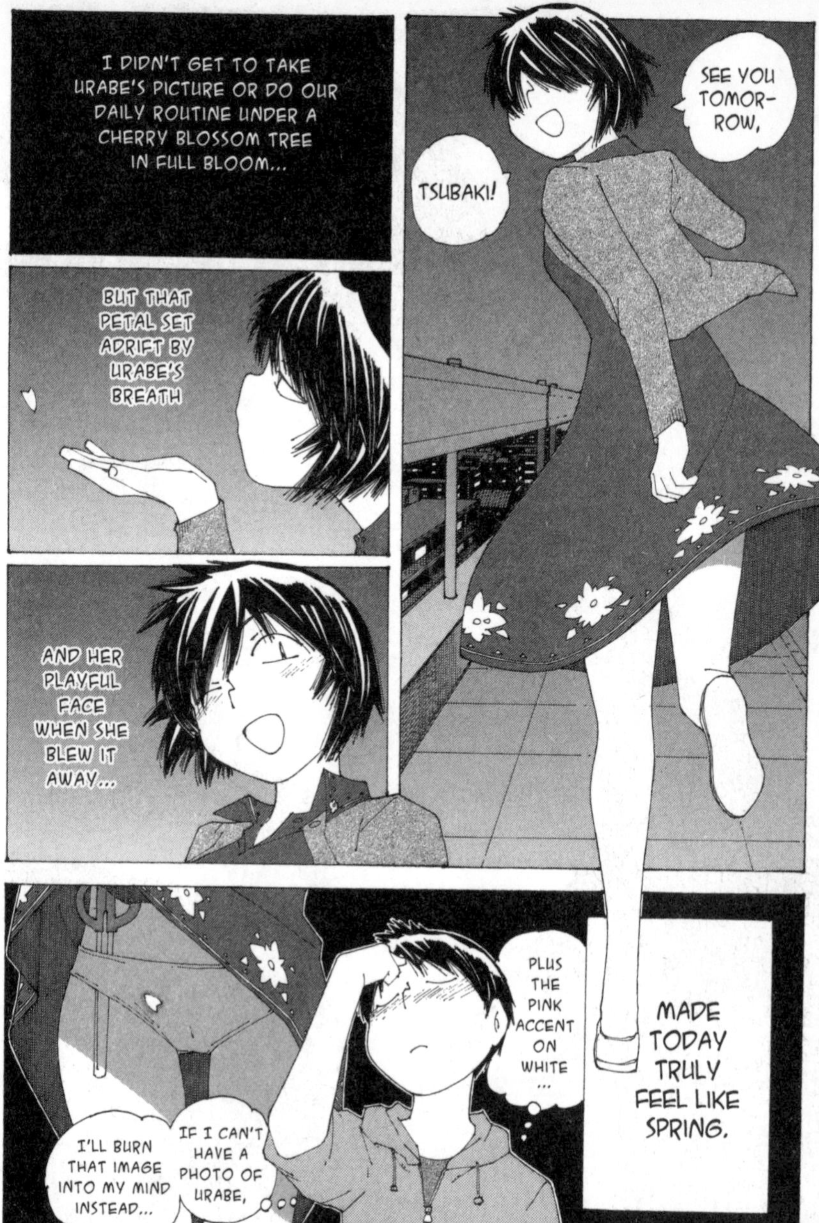
SEE YOU TOMOR-ROW,
TSUBAKI!
I DIDN'T GET TO TAKE URABE'S PICTURE OR DO OUR DAILY ROUTINE UNDER A CHERRY BLOSSOM TREE IN FULL BLOOM...
BUT THAT PETAL SET ADRIFT BY URABE'S BREATH
AND HER PLAYFUL FACE WHEN SHE BLEW IT AWAY...
MADE TODAY TRULY FEEL LIKE SPRING.
PLUS THE PINK ACCENT ON WHITE ...
IF I CAN'T HAVE A PHOTO OF URABE,
I'LL BURN THAT IMAGE INTO MY MIND INSTEAD...

END OF CHAPTER 55

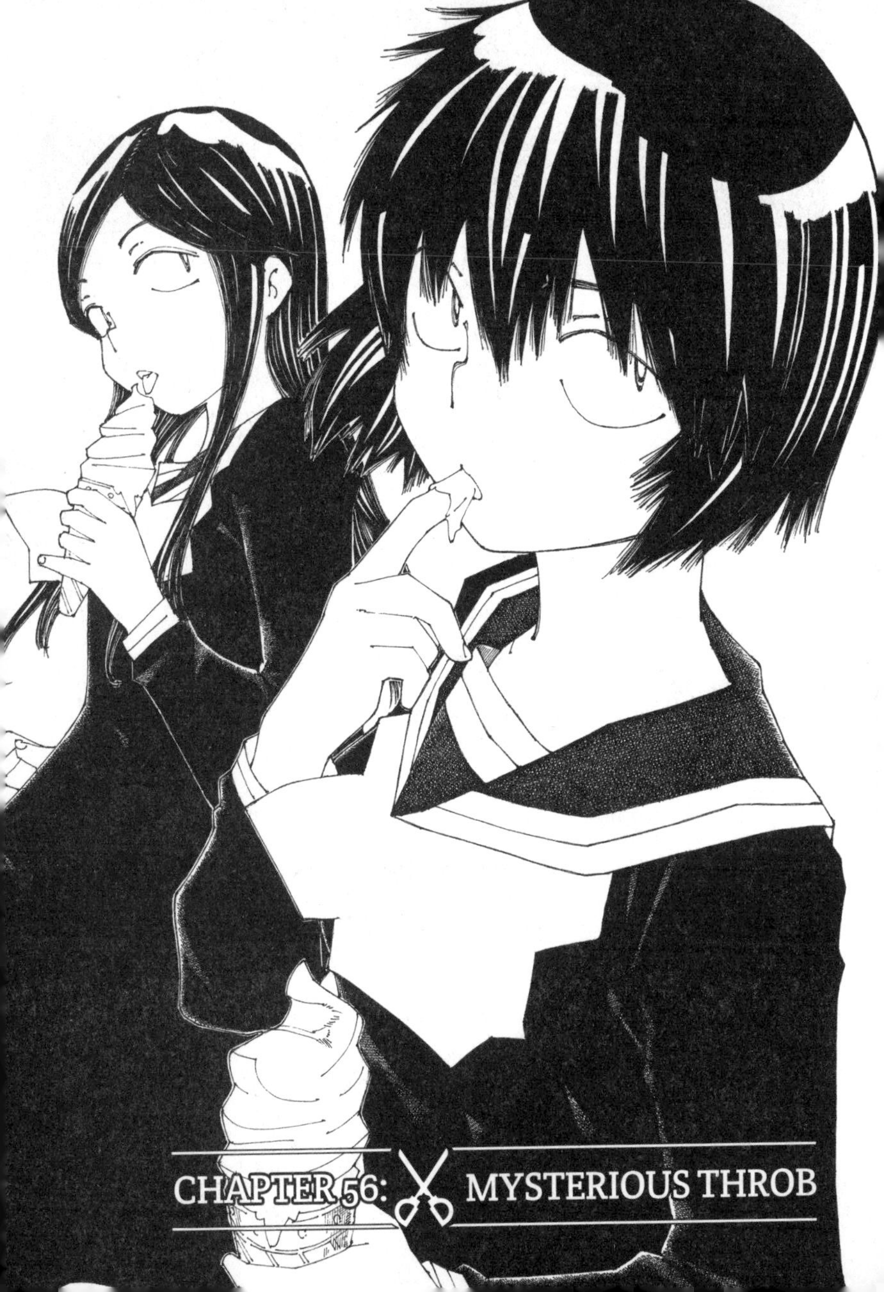
CHAPTER 56: MYSTERIOUS THROB

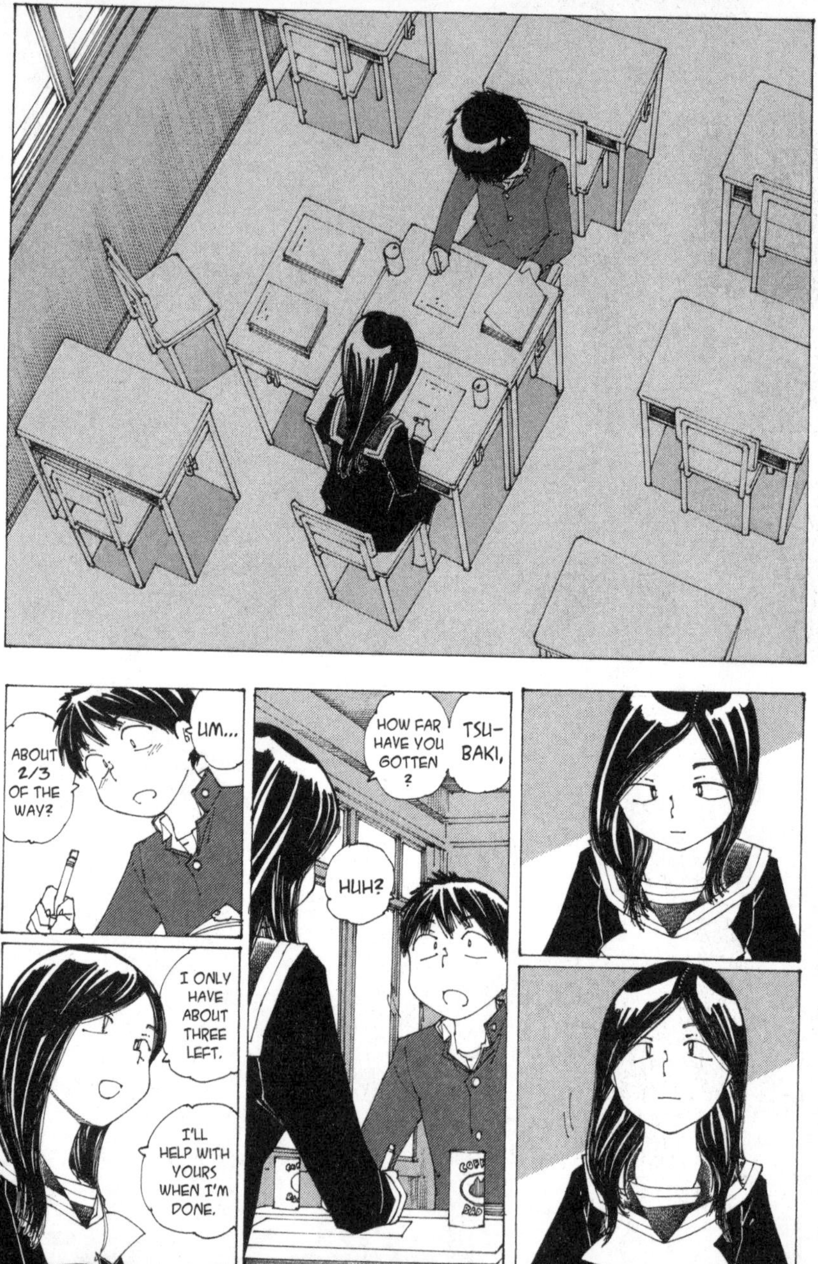
TSU-BAKI,
HOW FAR HAVE YOU GOTTEN?
HUH?
UM...
ABOUT 2/3 OF THE WAY?
I ONLY HAVE ABOUT THREE LEFT.
I'LL HELP WITH YOURS WHEN I'M DONE.

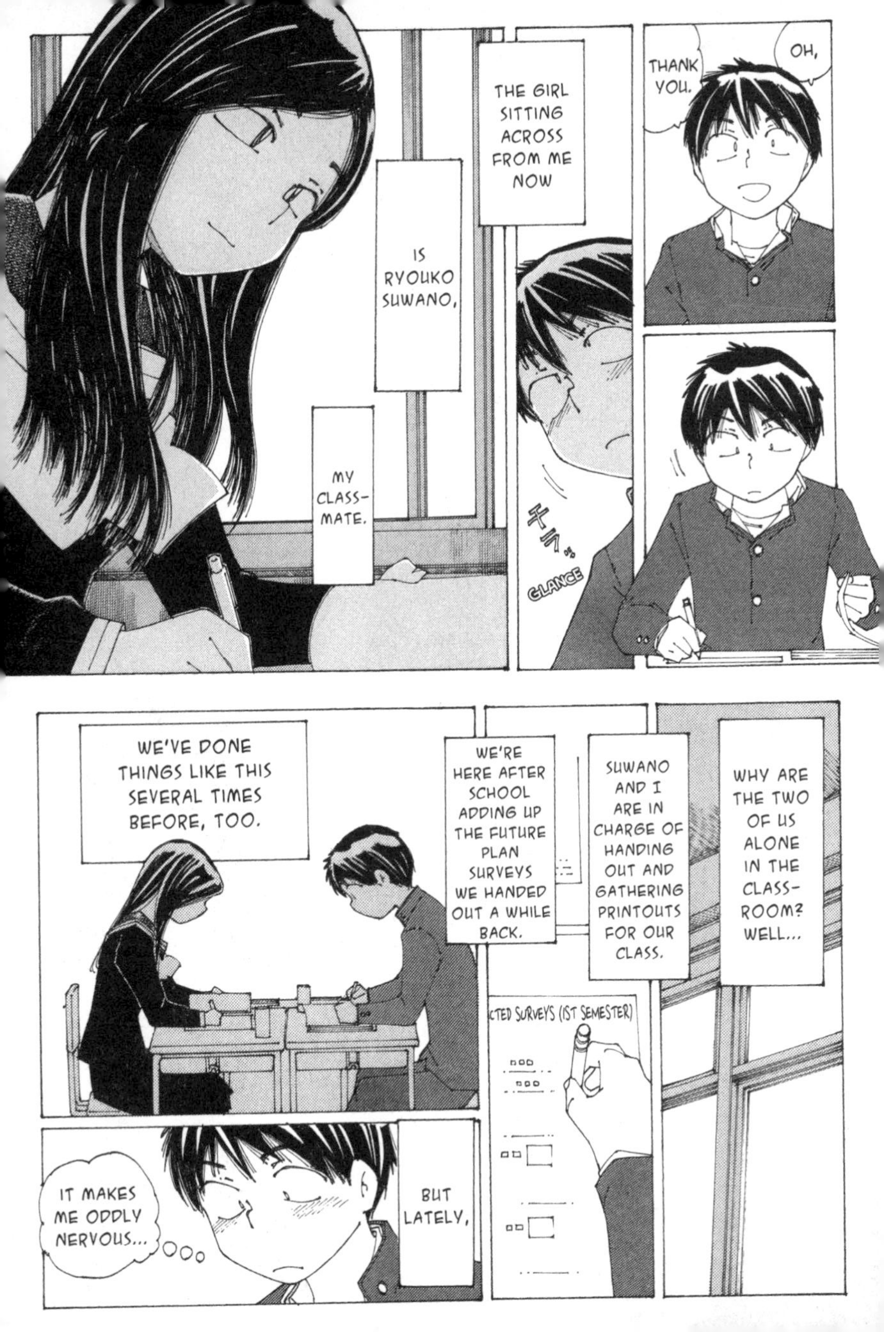
OH,
THANK YOU.
THE GIRL SITTING ACROSS FROM ME NOW
GLANCE
IS RYOUKO SUWANO,
MY CLASS-MATE.
WHY ARE THE TWO OF US ALONE IN THE CLASS-ROOM? WELL...
SUWANO AND I ARE IN CHARGE OF HANDING OUT AND GATHERING PRINTOUTS FOR OUR CLASS.
WE'RE HERE AFTER SCHOOL ADDING UP THE FUTURE PLAN SURVEYS WE HANDED OUT A WHILE BACK.
CTED SURVEYS (1ST SEMESTER)
WE'VE DONE THINGS LIKE THIS SEVERAL TIMES BEFORE, TOO.
BUT LATELY,
IT MAKES ME ODDLY NERVOUS...

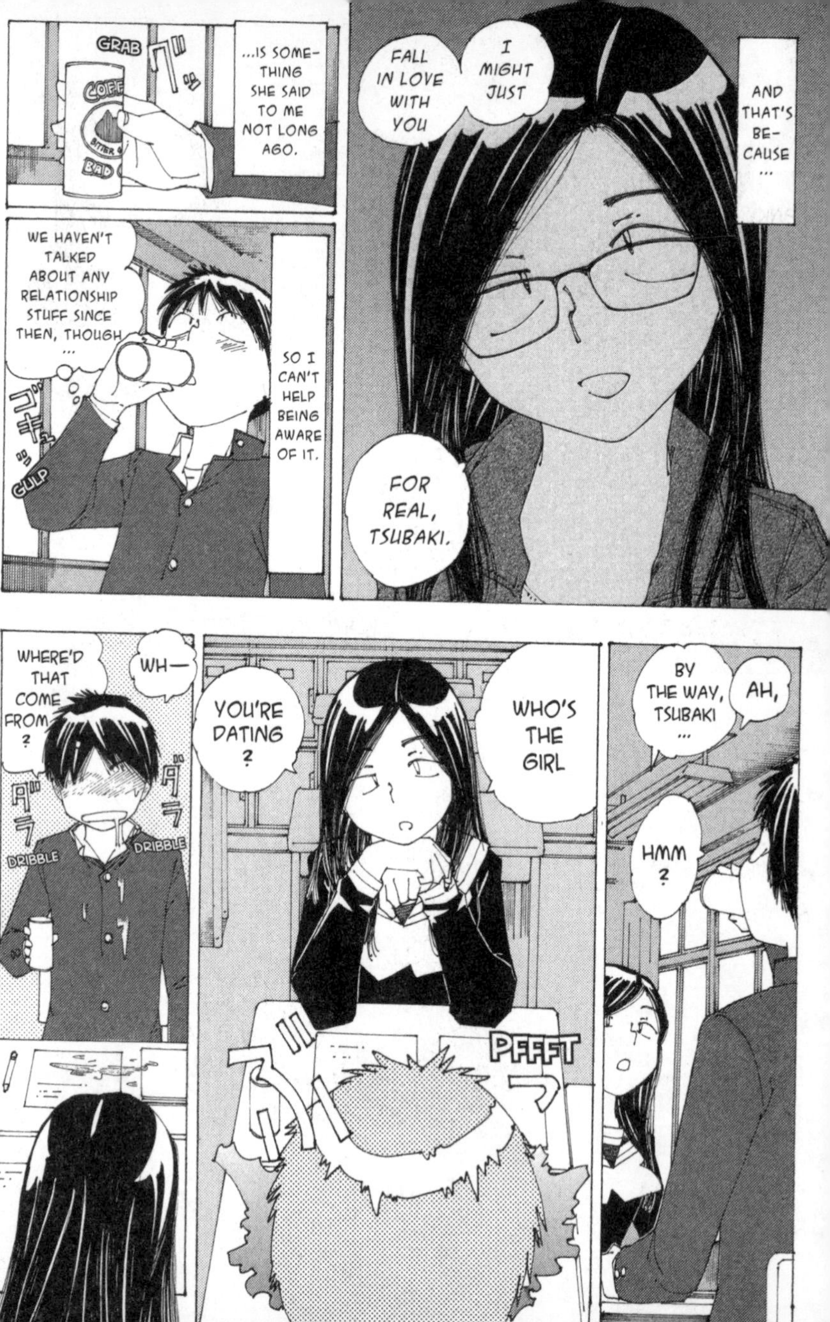
AND THAT'S BE- CAUSE ...
I MIGHT JUST
FALL IN LOVE WITH YOU
FOR REAL, TSUBAKI.
GRAB
...IS SOME- THING SHE SAID TO ME NOT LONG AGO.
WE HAVEN'T TALKED ABOUT ANY RELATIONSHIP STUFF SINCE THEN, THOUGH ...
SO I CAN'T HELP BEING AWARE OF IT.
GULP
AH,
BY THE WAY, TSUBAKI ...
HMM ?
WHO'S THE GIRL
YOU'RE DATING ?
PFFFT
WH—
WHERE'D THAT COME FROM ?
DRIBBLE
DRIBBLE

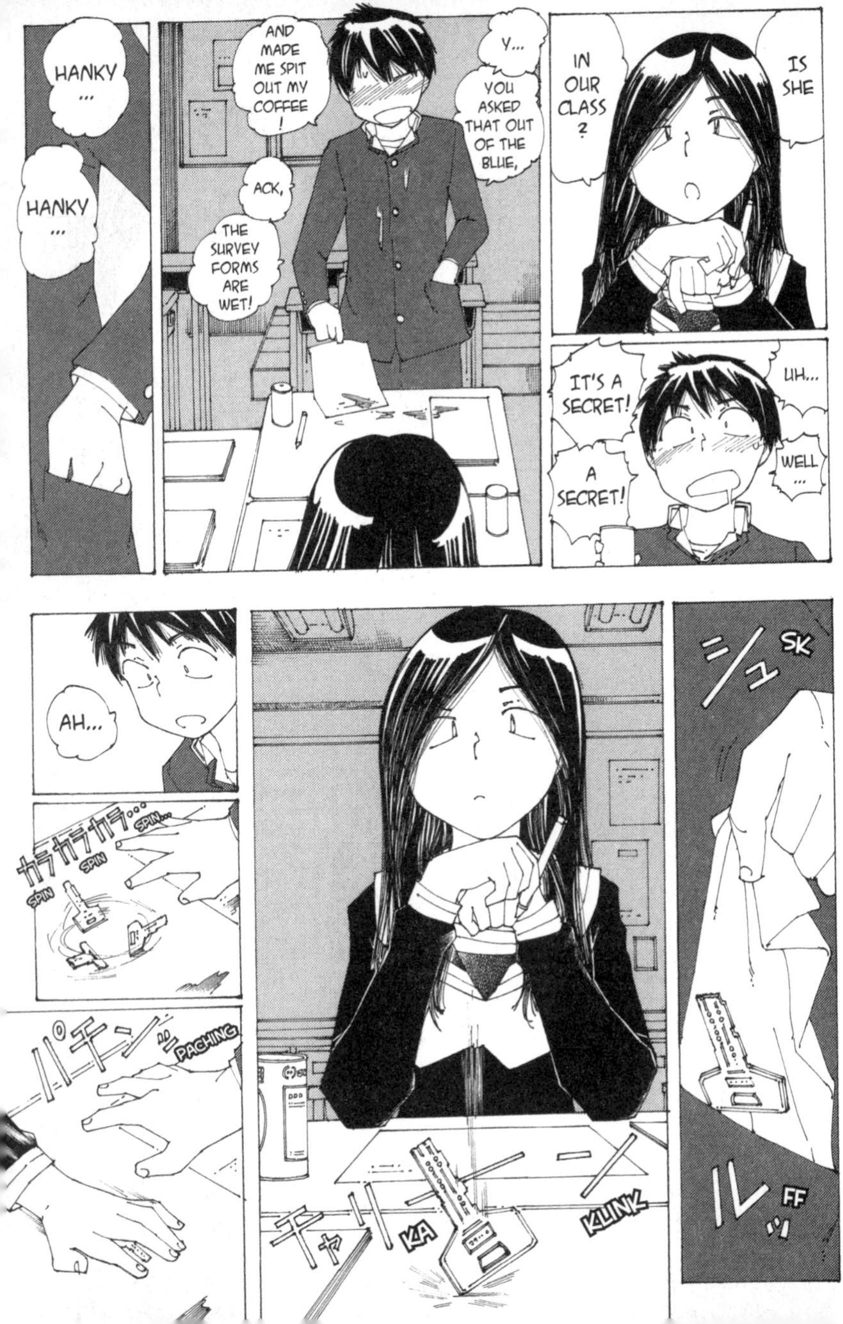

IS SHE
IN OUR CLASS?
UH...
IT'S A SECRET!
WELL...
A SECRET!
Y...
YOU ASKED THAT OUT OF THE BLUE,
AND MADE ME SPIT OUT MY COFFEE!
ACK,
THE SURVEY FORMS ARE WET!
HANKY...
HANKY...
シュ SK
ルッ FF
KLUNK
KA
AH...
カラカラカラ...
SPIN...
SPIN
SPIN
パチン PACHING

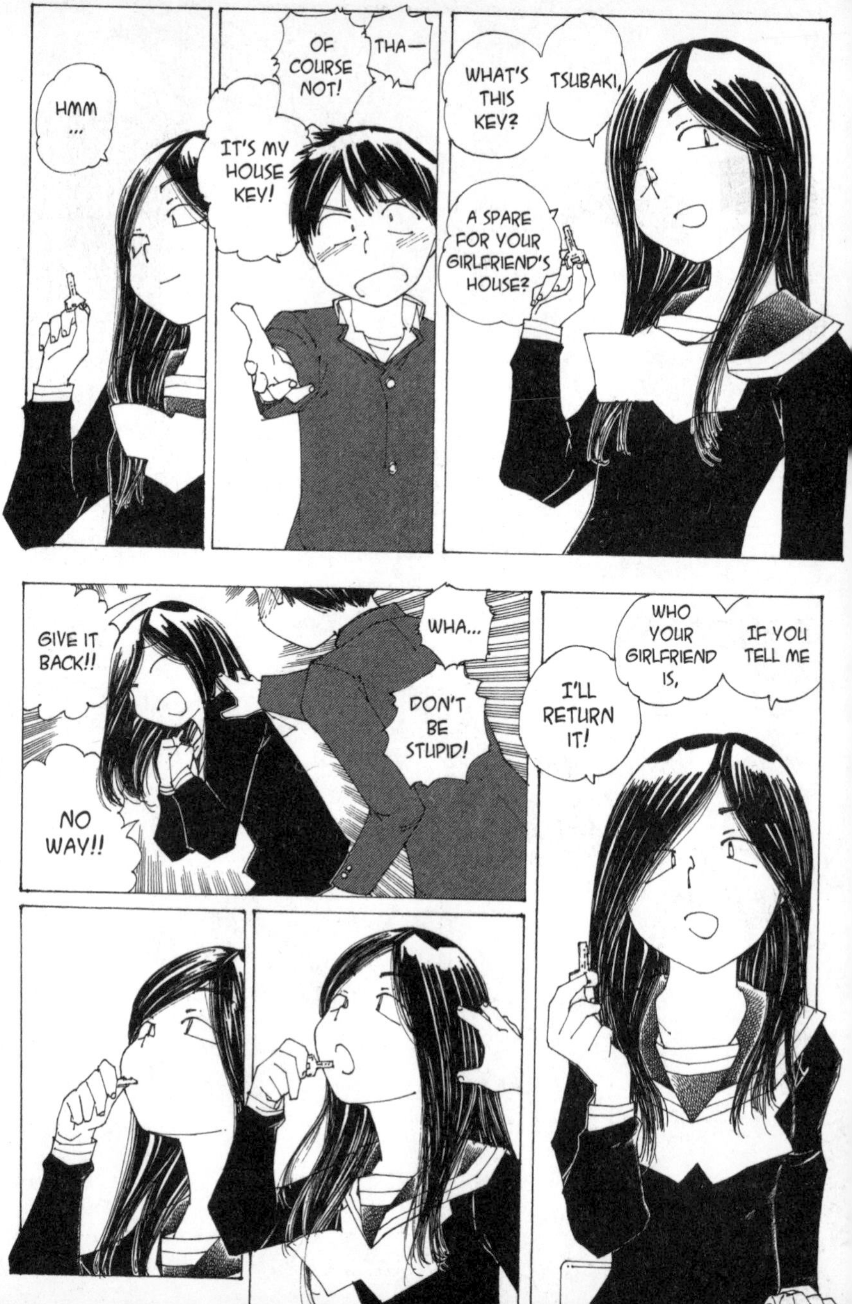
TSUBAKI,
WHAT'S THIS KEY?
A SPARE FOR YOUR GIRLFRIEND'S HOUSE?
THA—
OF COURSE NOT!
IT'S MY HOUSE KEY!
HMM ...
IF YOU TELL ME
WHO YOUR GIRLFRIEND IS,
I'LL RETURN IT!
WHA...
DON'T BE STUPID!
GIVE IT BACK!!
NO WAY!!

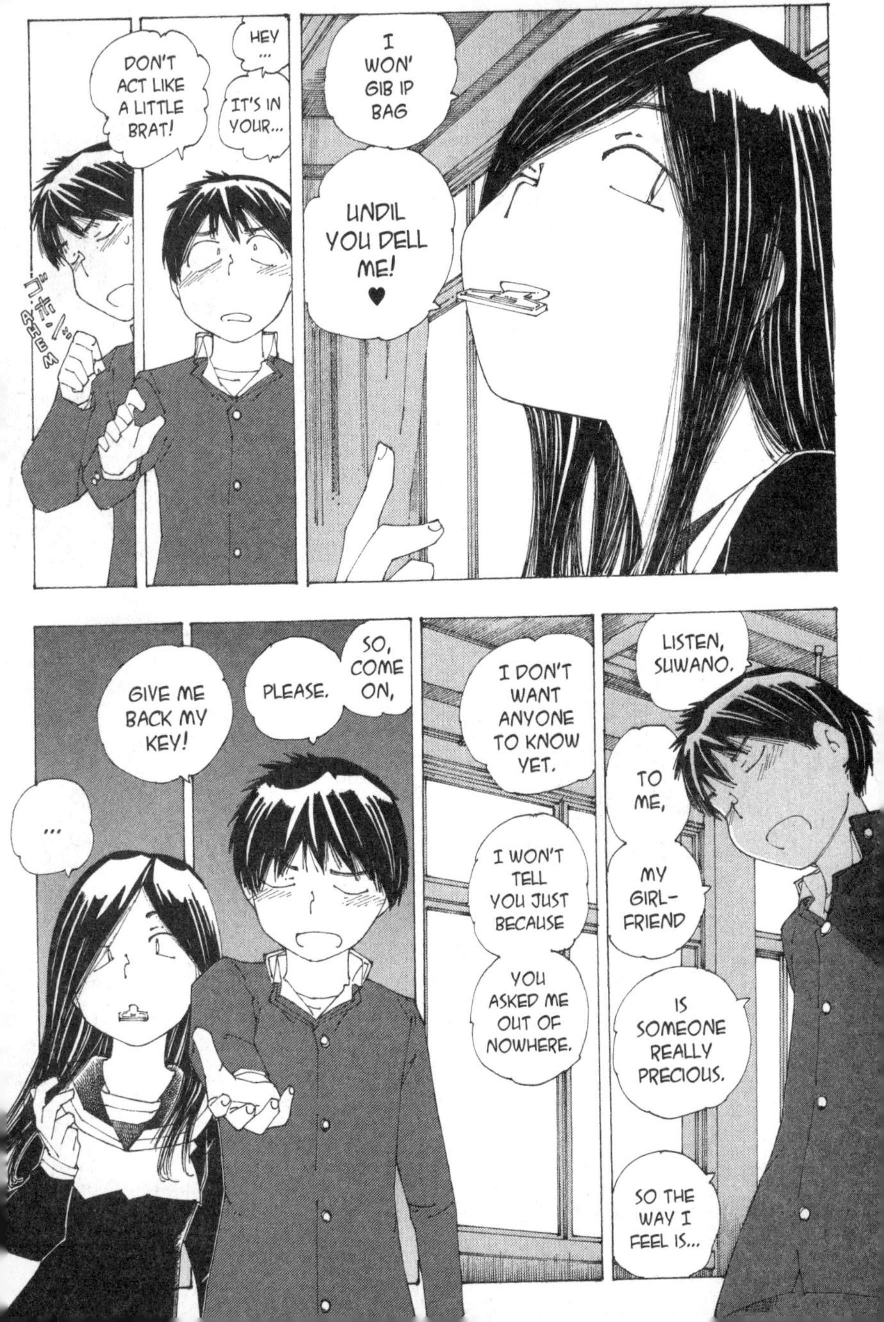
I WON' GIB IP BAG
UNDIL YOU DELL ME! ♥
HEY ...
IT'S IN YOUR...
DON'T ACT LIKE A LITTLE BRAT!
ゴホッ
AHEM
LISTEN, SUWANO.
TO ME,
MY GIRL-FRIEND
IS SOMEONE REALLY PRECIOUS.
SO THE WAY I FEEL IS...
I DON'T WANT ANYONE TO KNOW YET.
I WON'T TELL YOU JUST BECAUSE
YOU ASKED ME OUT OF NOWHERE.
SO, COME ON,
PLEASE.
GIVE ME BACK MY KEY!
...

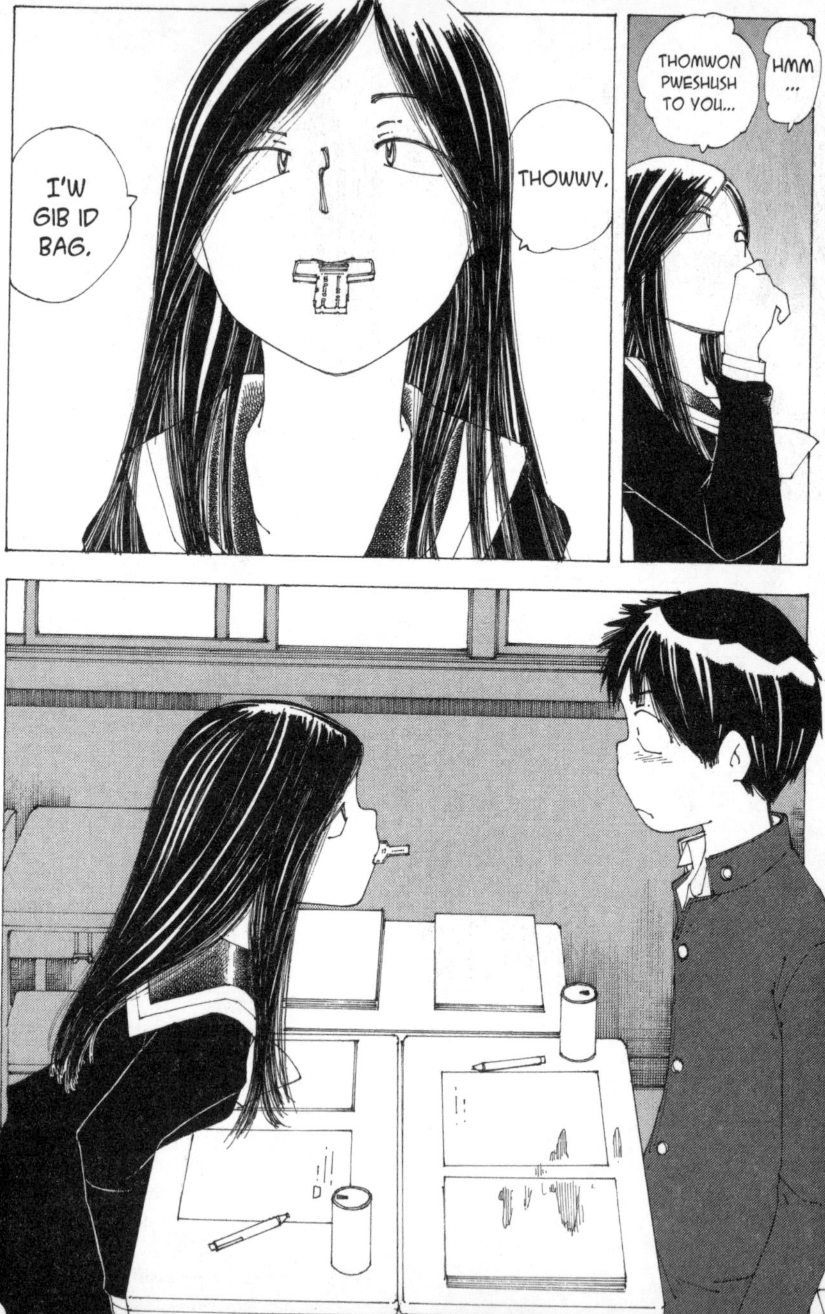
HMM ...
THOMWON PWESHUSH TO YOU...
THOWWY.
I'W GIB ID BAG.

TUG

TAGE ID.

BRUSH

TUG
TUG

I CAN'T TAKE IT IF YOU'RE BITING IT!

HEY...

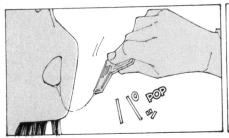

POP

AH...

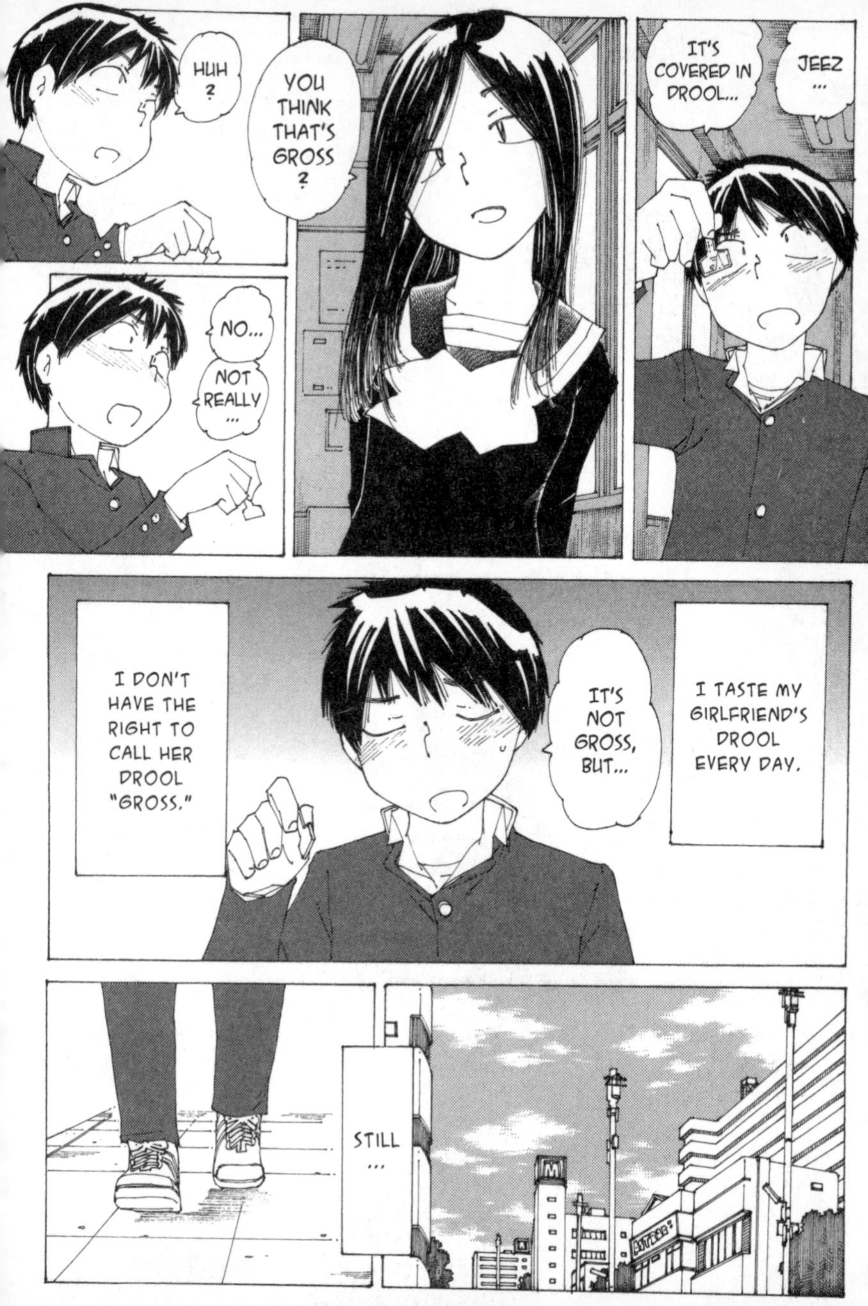
JEEZ...
IT'S COVERED IN DROOL...
YOU THINK THAT'S GROSS?
HUH?
NO...
NOT REALLY...
I TASTE MY GIRLFRIEND'S DROOL EVERY DAY.
IT'S NOT GROSS, BUT...
I DON'T HAVE THE RIGHT TO CALL HER DROOL "GROSS."
STILL...

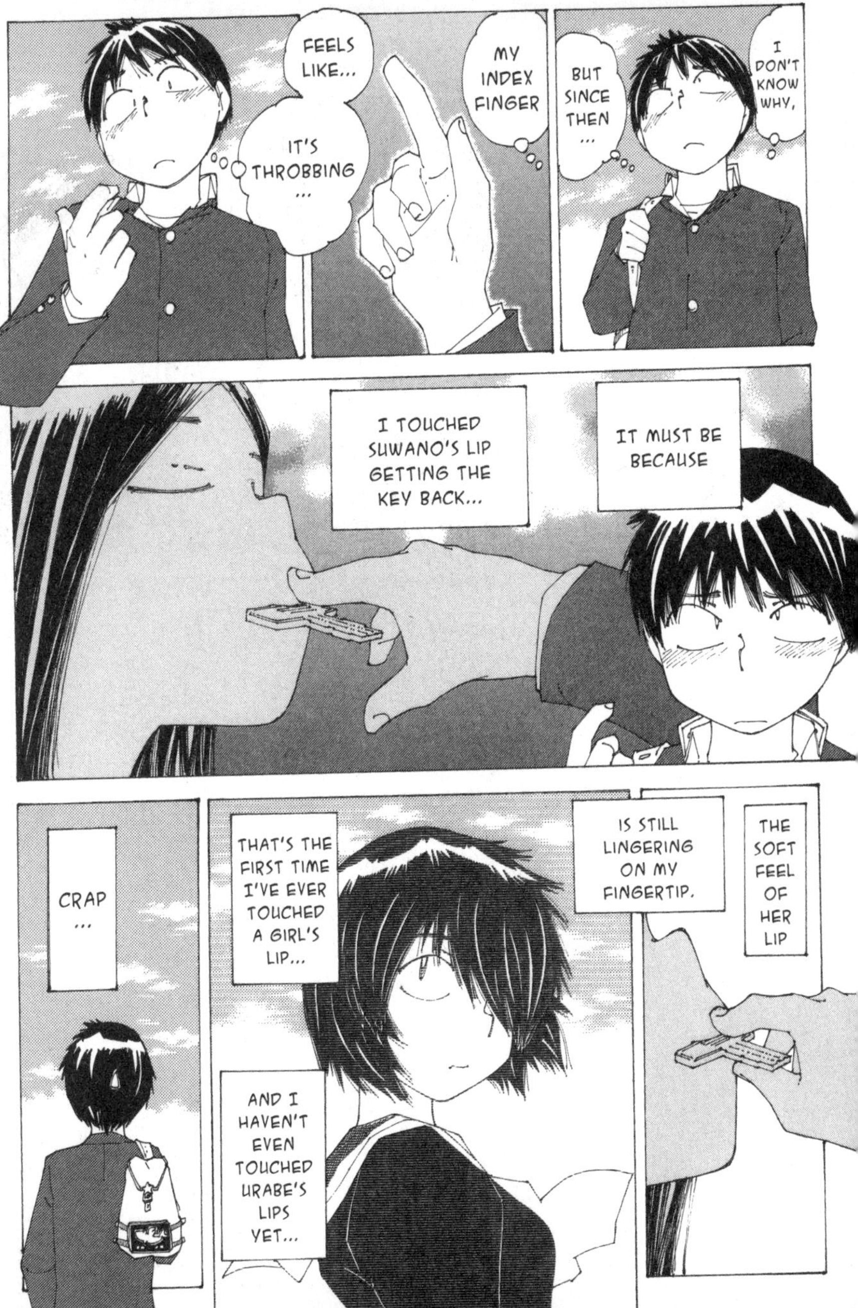
I DON'T KNOW WHY,
BUT SINCE THEN ...
MY INDEX FINGER
FEELS LIKE...
IT'S THROBBING ...
IT MUST BE BECAUSE
I TOUCHED SUWANO'S LIP GETTING THE KEY BACK...
THE SOFT FEEL OF HER LIP
IS STILL LINGERING ON MY FINGERTIP.
THAT'S THE FIRST TIME I'VE EVER TOUCHED A GIRL'S LIP...
AND I HAVEN'T EVEN TOUCHED URABE'S LIPS YET...
CRAP ...

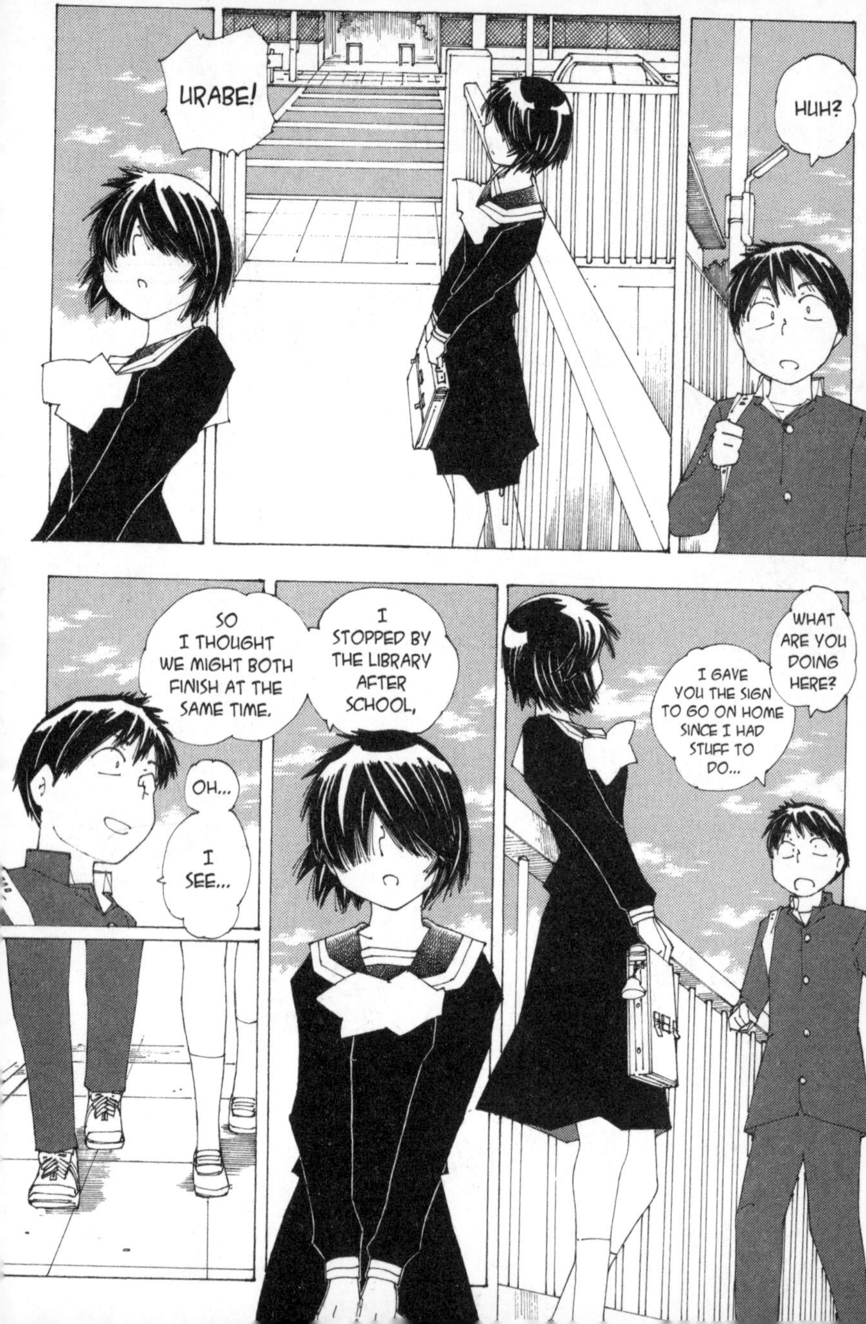
HUH?
URABE!
WHAT ARE YOU DOING HERE?
I GAVE YOU THE SIGN TO GO ON HOME SINCE I HAD STUFF TO DO...
I STOPPED BY THE LIBRARY AFTER SCHOOL,
SO I THOUGHT WE MIGHT BOTH FINISH AT THE SAME TIME.
OH...
I SEE...

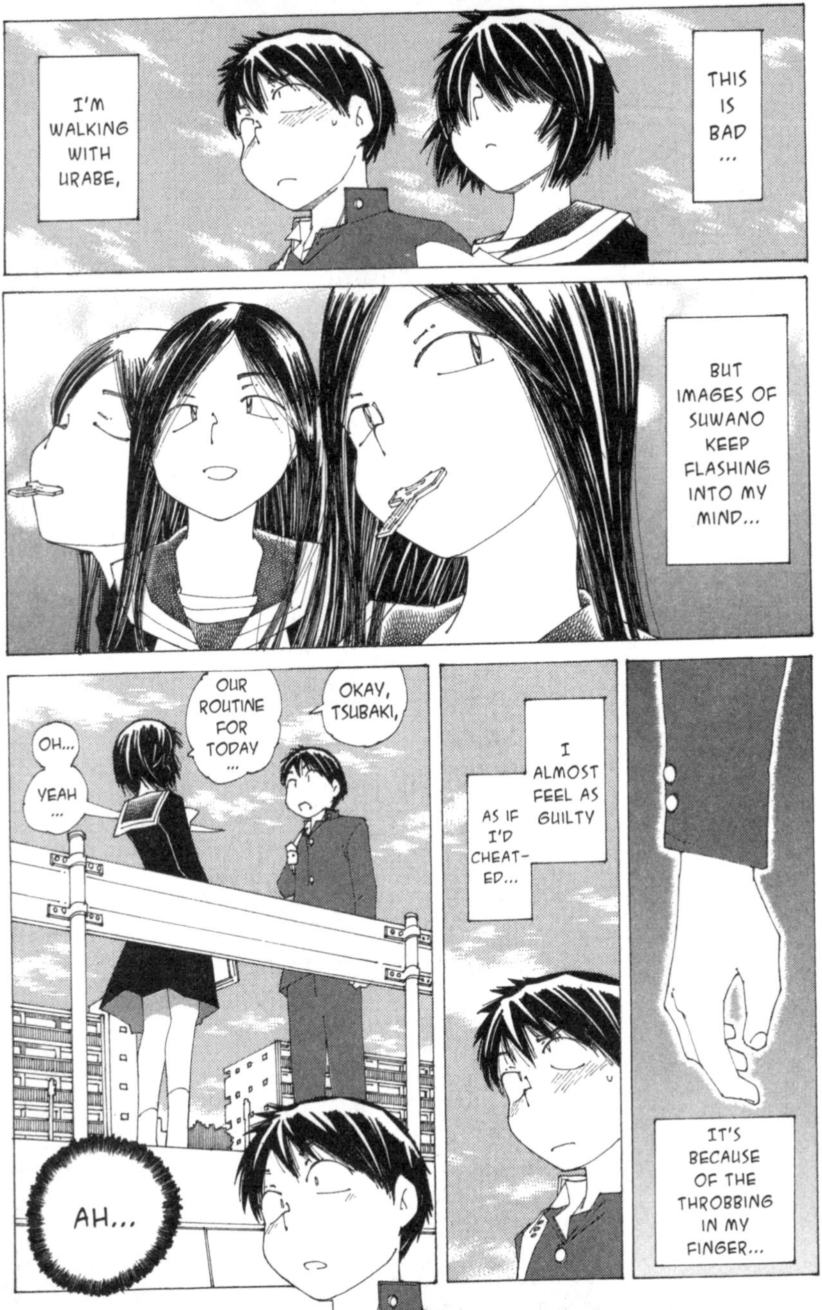
THIS IS BAD ...
I'M WALKING WITH URABE,
BUT IMAGES OF SUWANO KEEP FLASHING INTO MY MIND...
IT'S BECAUSE OF THE THROBBING IN MY FINGER...
I ALMOST FEEL AS GUILTY
AS IF I'D CHEAT-ED...
OKAY, TSUBAKI,
OUR ROUTINE FOR TODAY ...
OH...
YEAH ...
AH...

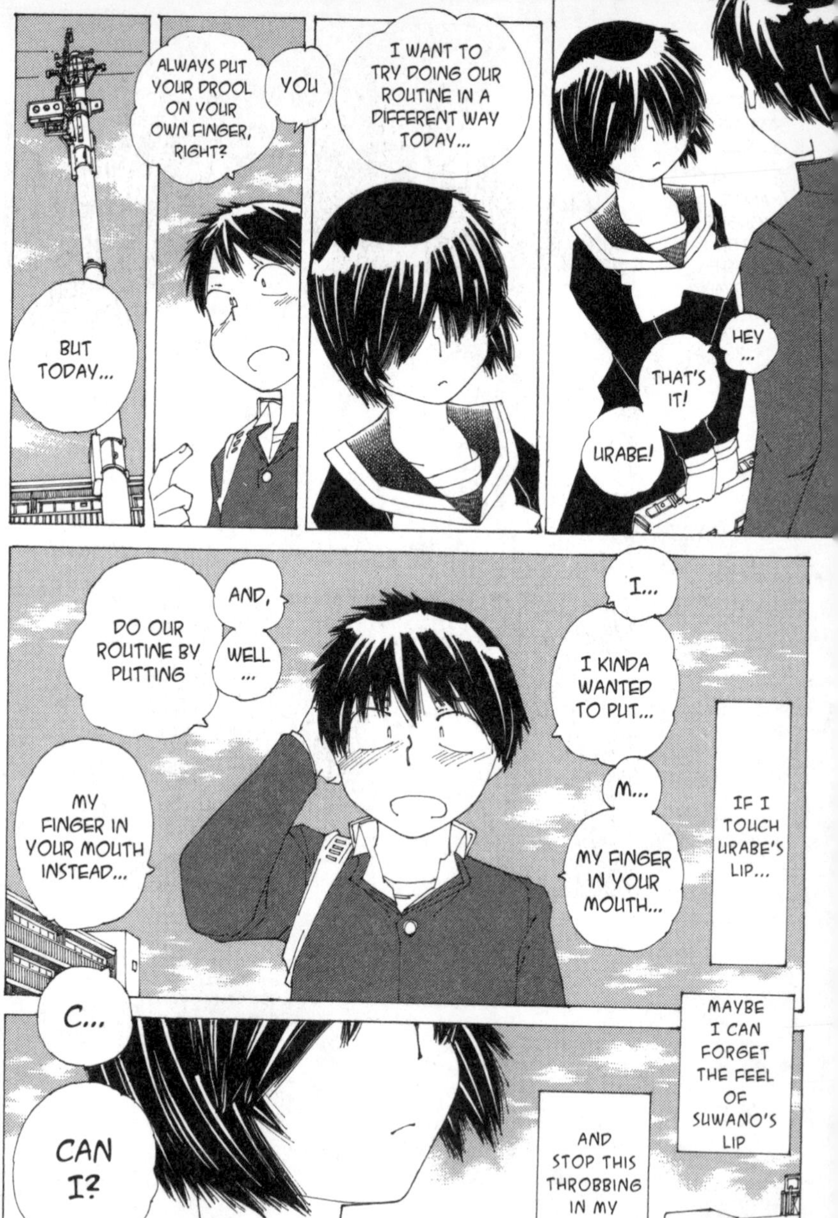

HEY...
THAT'S IT!
URABE!
I WANT TO TRY DOING OUR ROUTINE IN A DIFFERENT WAY TODAY...
YOU
ALWAYS PUT YOUR DROOL ON YOUR OWN FINGER, RIGHT?
BUT TODAY...
IF I TOUCH URABE'S LIP...
I...
I KINDA WANTED TO PUT...
M...
MY FINGER IN YOUR MOUTH...
AND, WELL...
DO OUR ROUTINE BY PUTTING
MY FINGER IN YOUR MOUTH INSTEAD...
MAYBE I CAN FORGET THE FEEL OF SUWANO'S LIP
AND STOP THIS THROBBING IN MY FINGER.
C...
CAN I?

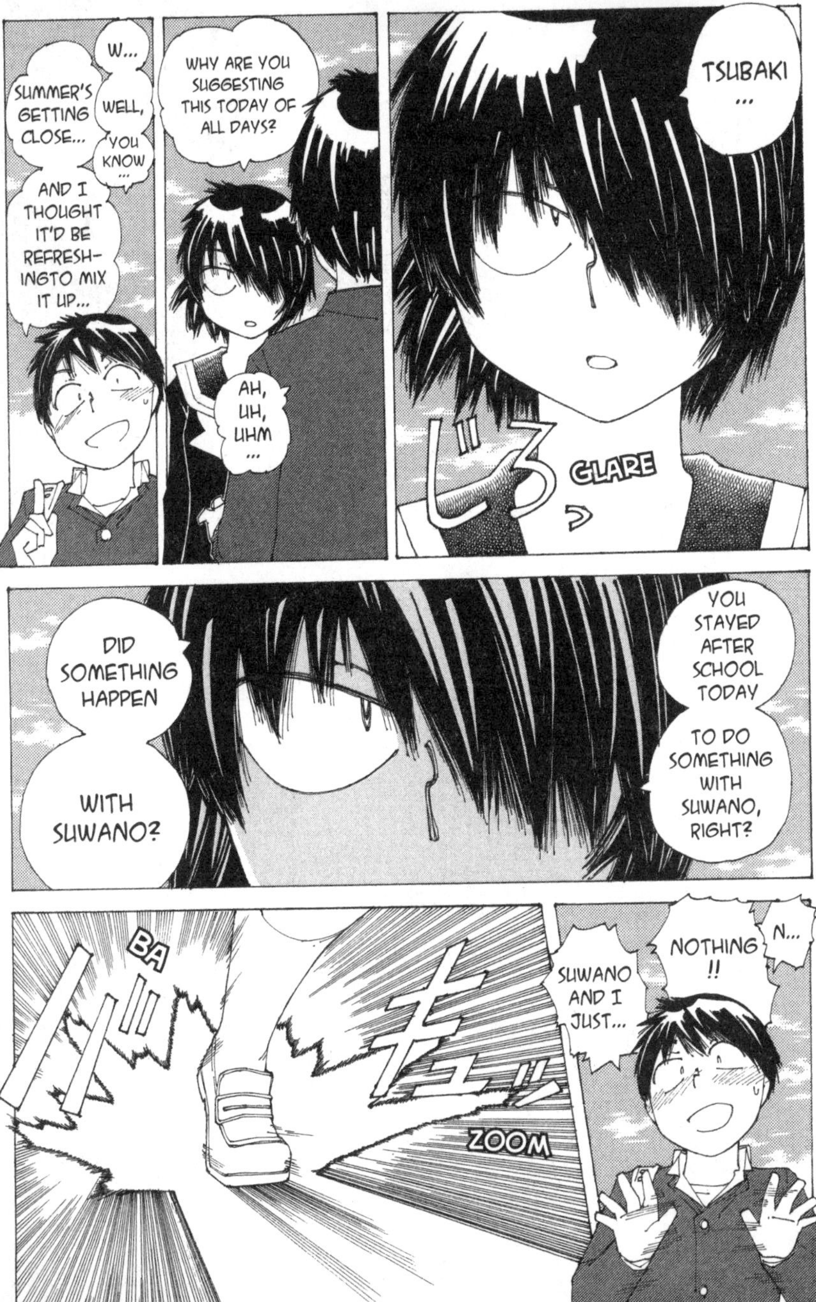
TSUBAKI ...
GLARE
WHY ARE YOU SUGGESTING THIS TODAY OF ALL DAYS?
AH, UH, UHM ...
W...
WELL,
YOU KNOW ...
SUMMER'S GETTING CLOSE...
AND I THOUGHT IT'D BE REFRESH-INGTO MIX IT UP...
YOU STAYED AFTER SCHOOL TODAY
TO DO SOMETHING WITH SUWANO, RIGHT?
DID SOMETHING HAPPEN
WITH SUWANO?
N...
NOTHING !!
SUWANO AND I JUST...
BA
ZOOM

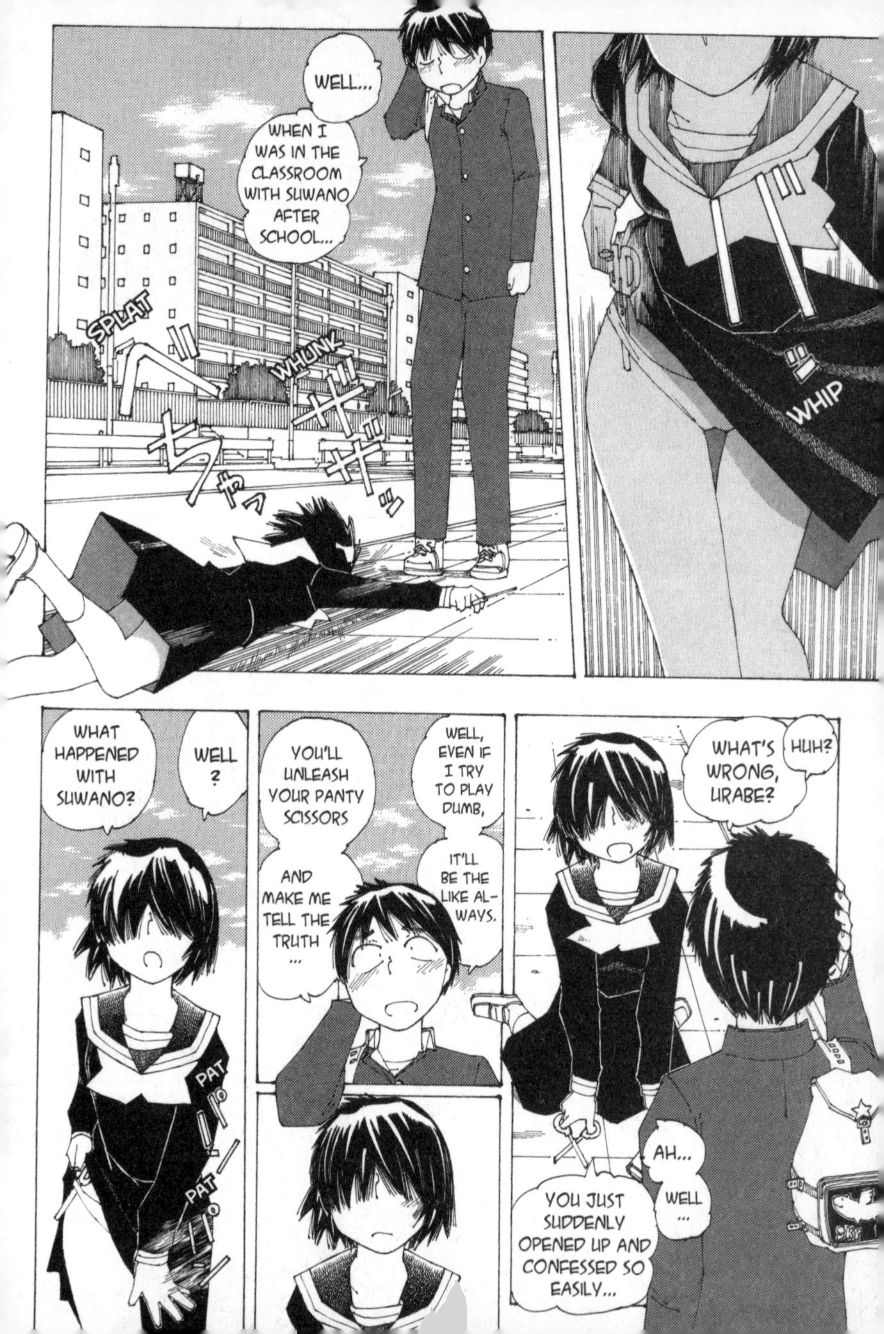
WHIP
WELL...
WHEN I WAS IN THE CLASSROOM WITH SUWANO AFTER SCHOOL...
SPLAT
WHUNK
HUH?
WHAT'S WRONG, URABE?
AH...
WELL ...
YOU JUST SUDDENLY OPENED UP AND CONFESSED SO EASILY...
WELL, EVEN IF I TRY TO PLAY DUMB,
IT'LL BE THE LIKE AL- WAYS.
YOU'LL UNLEASH YOUR PANTY SCISSORS
AND MAKE ME TELL THE TRUTH ...
WELL ?
WHAT HAPPENED WITH SUWANO?
PAT
PAT

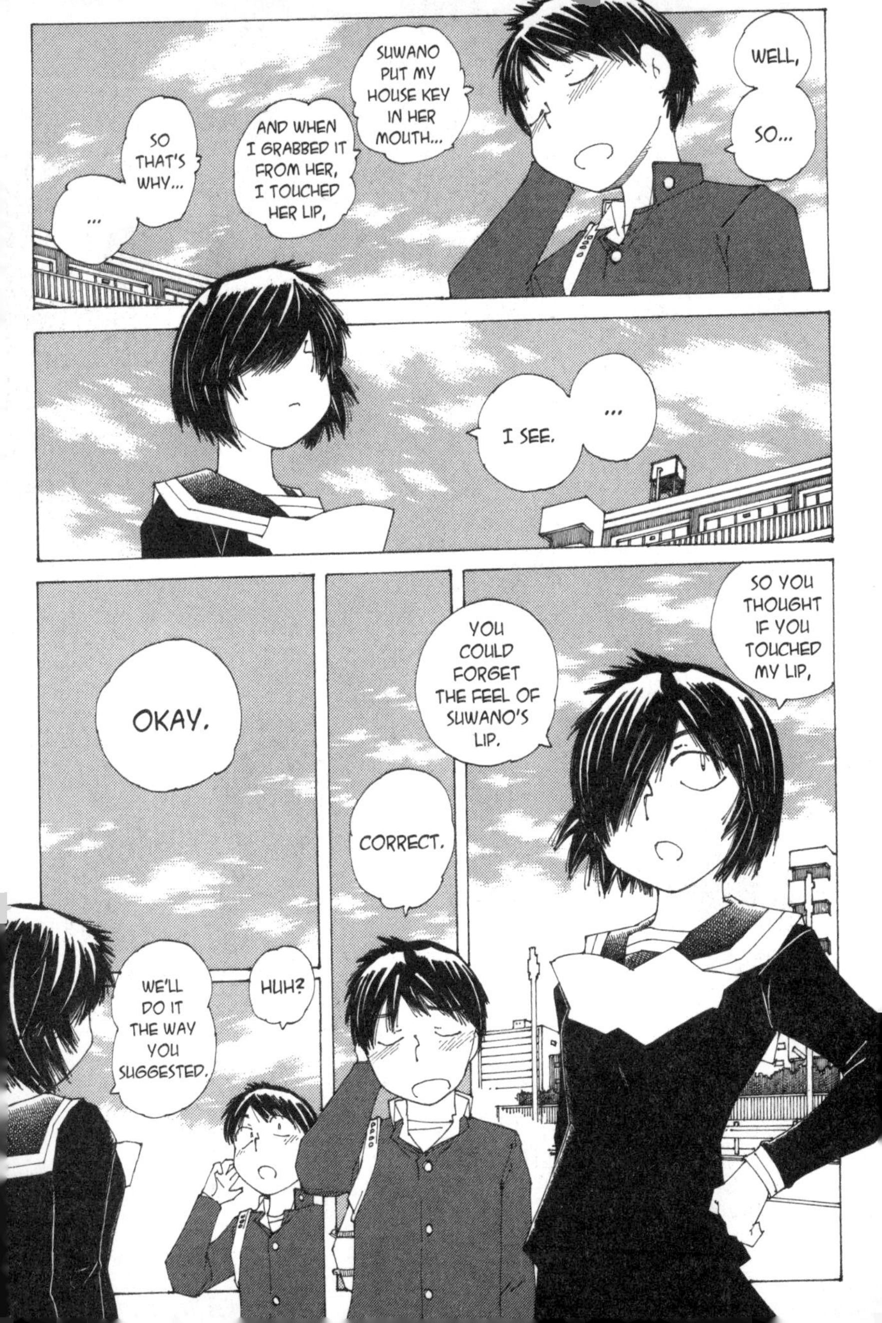
WELL,
SO...
SUWANO PUT MY HOUSE KEY IN HER MOUTH...
AND WHEN I GRABBED IT FROM HER, I TOUCHED HER LIP,
SO THAT'S WHY...
...
...
I SEE.
SO YOU THOUGHT IF YOU TOUCHED MY LIP,
YOU COULD FORGET THE FEEL OF SUWANO'S LIP.
CORRECT.
OKAY.
HUH?
WE'LL DO IT THE WAY YOU SUGGESTED.

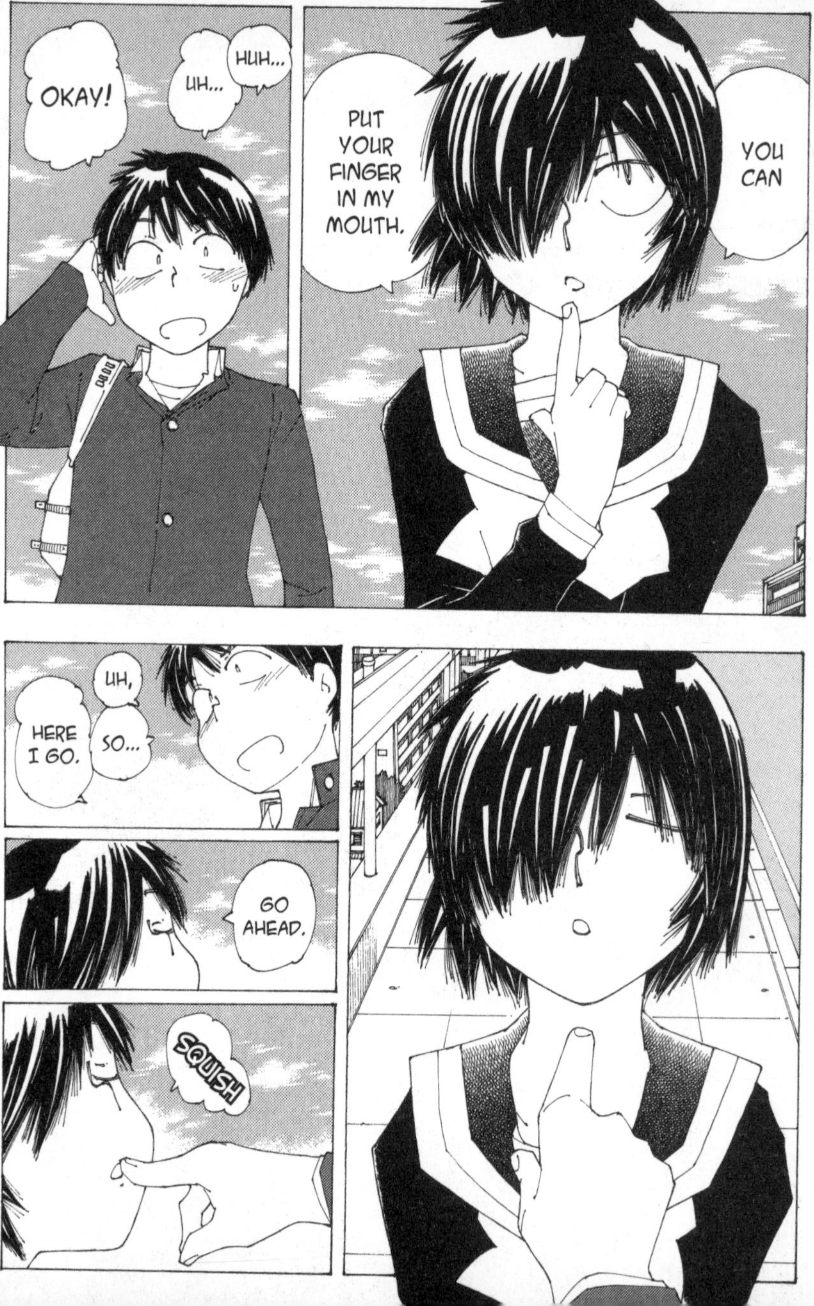
YOU CAN
PUT YOUR FINGER IN MY MOUTH.
HUH...
UH...
OKAY!
UH,
SO...
HERE I GO.
GO AHEAD.
SQUISH

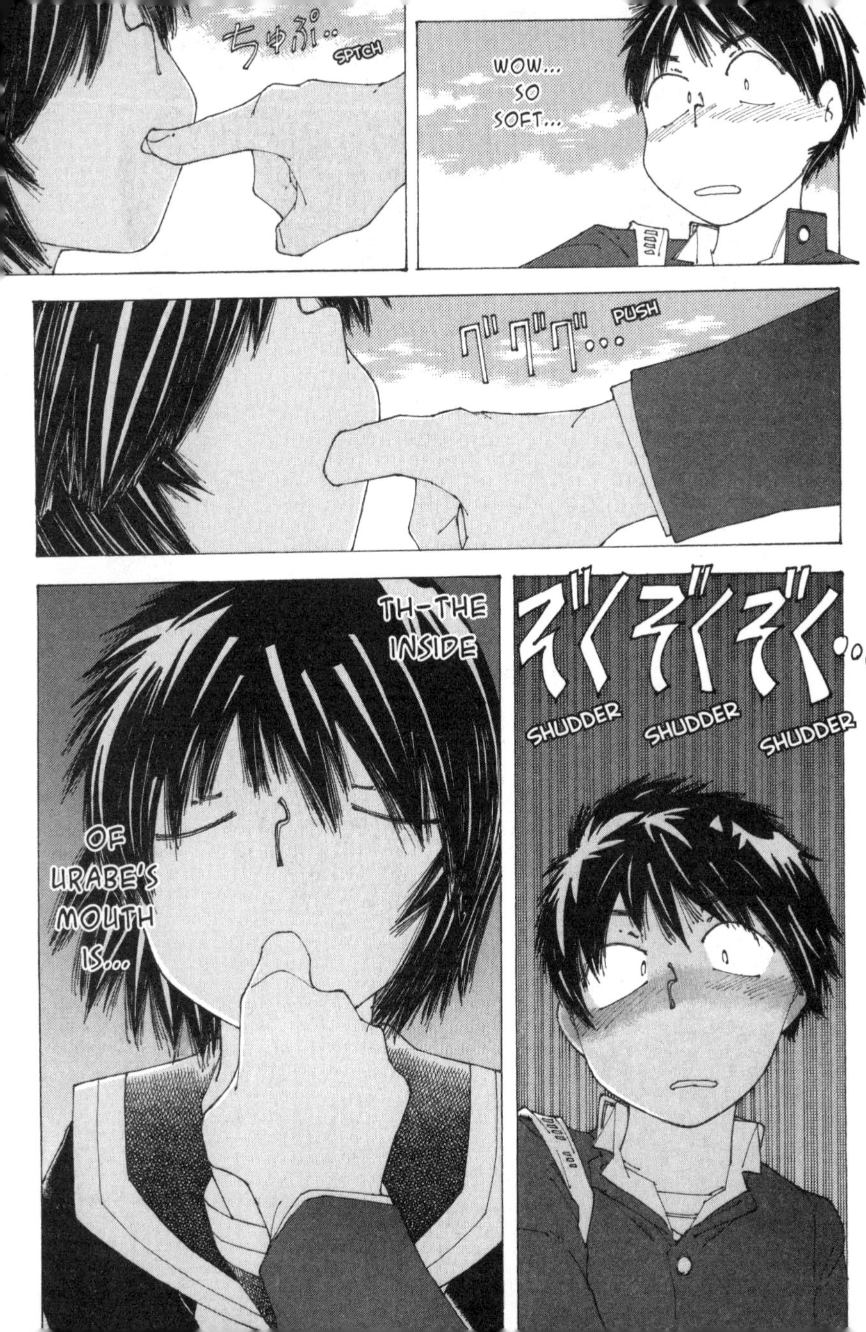
WOW... SO SOFT...
ちゅぷ..
SPTCH
グ゛グ゛グ゛...
PUSH
ぞくぞくぞく...
SHUDDER
SHUDDER
SHUDDER
TH-THE INSIDE
OF URABE'S MOUTH IS...

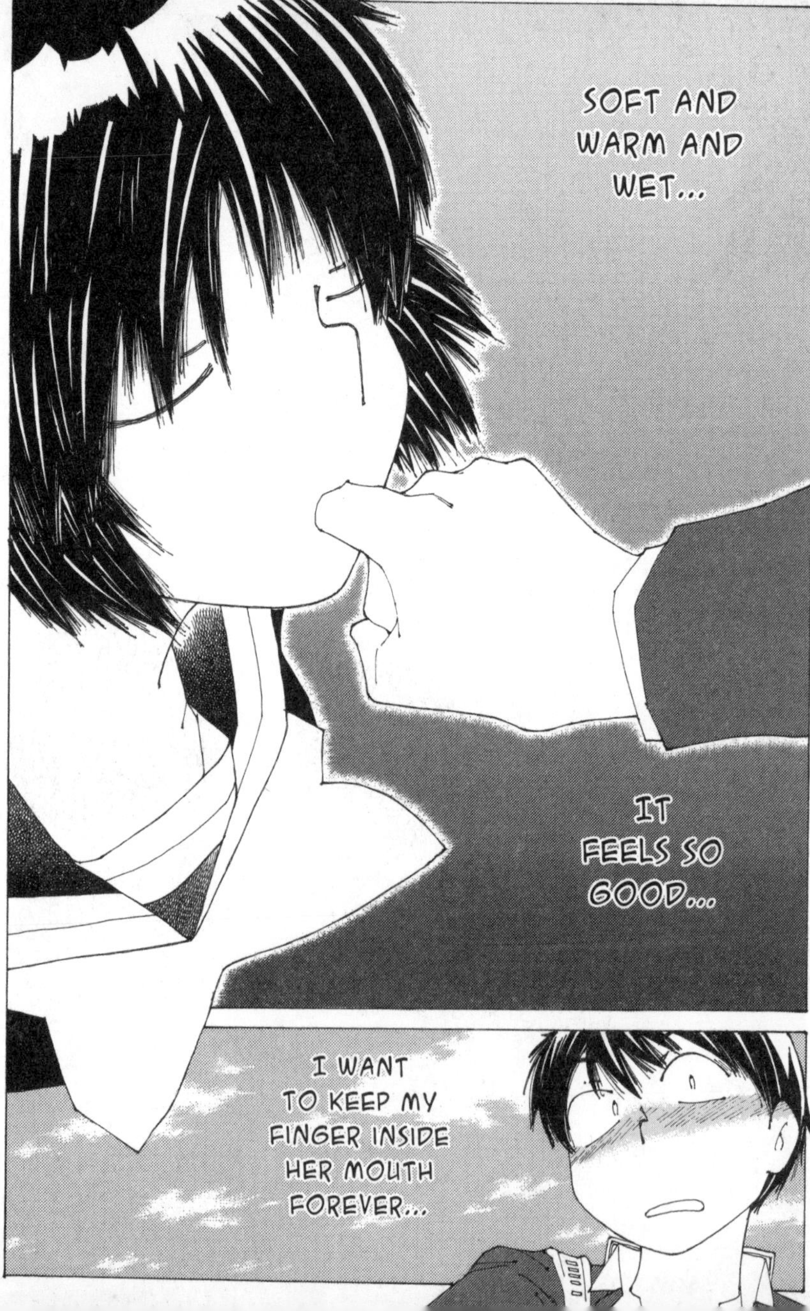
SOFT AND WARM AND WET...
IT FEELS SO GOOD...
I WANT TO KEEP MY FINGER INSIDE HER MOUTH FOREVER...

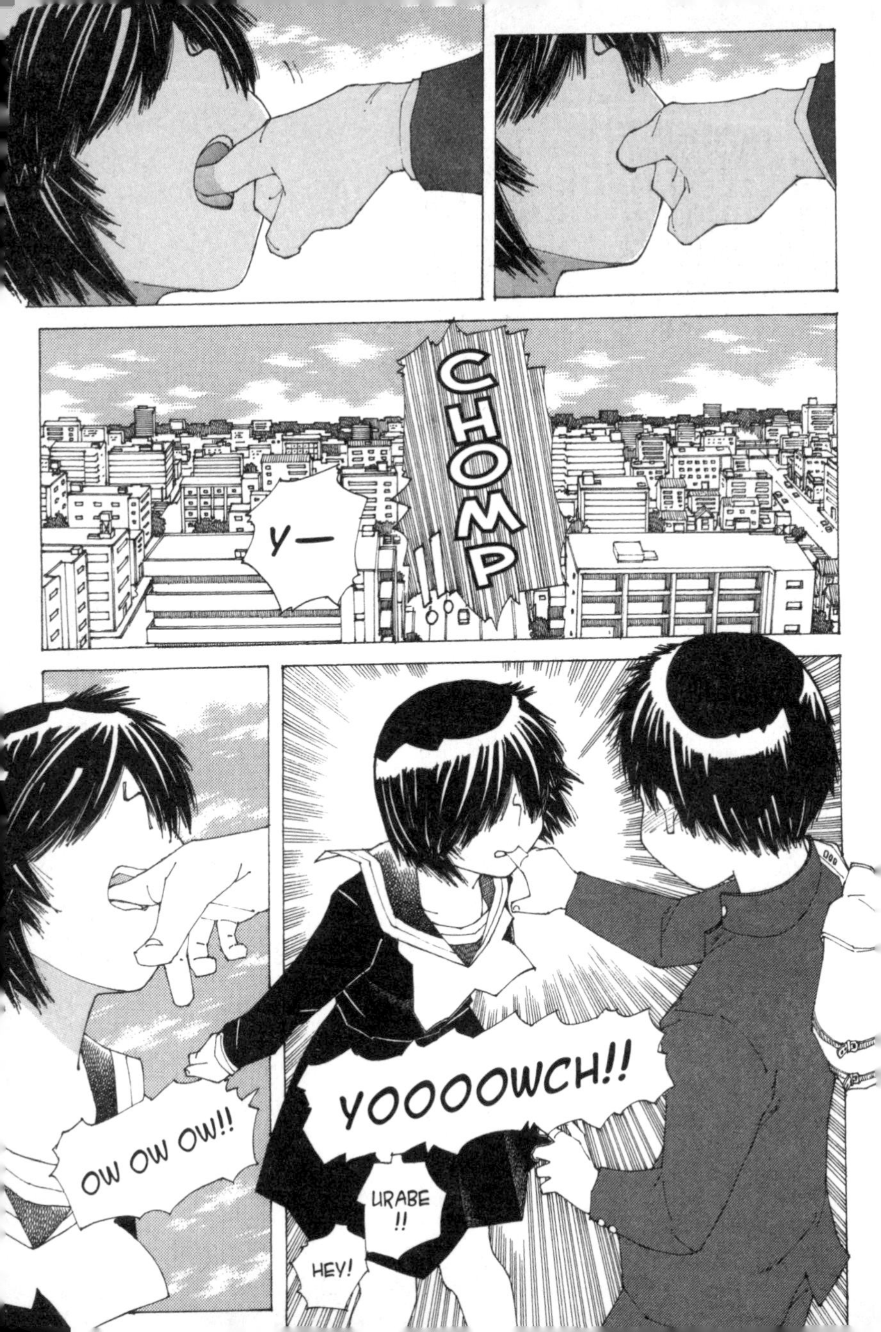
CHOMP
Y—
YOOOOWCH!!
URABE !!
HEY!
OW OW OW!!

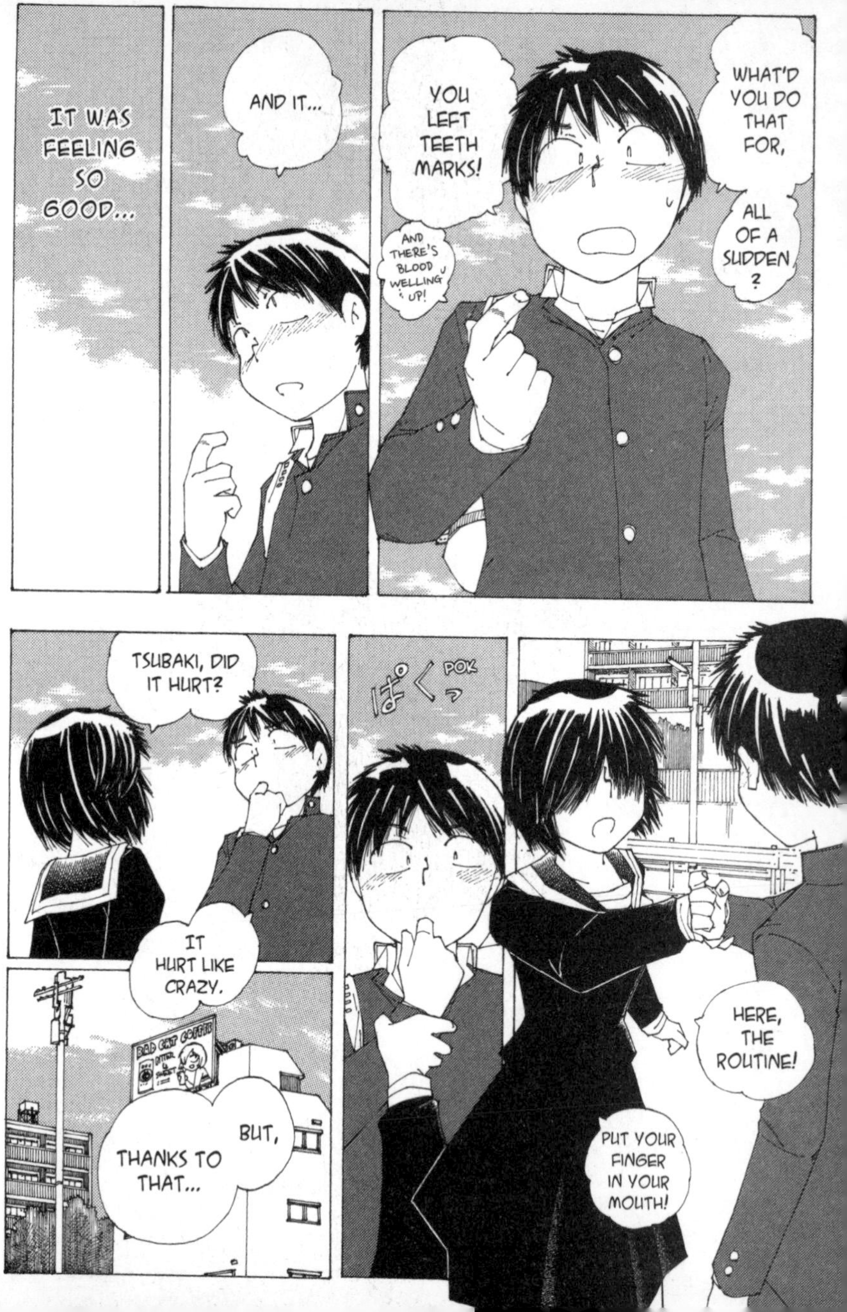
WHAT'D YOU DO THAT FOR,
ALL OF A SUDDEN?
YOU LEFT TEETH MARKS!
AND THERE'S BLOOD WELLING UP!
AND IT...
IT WAS FEELING SO GOOD...
HERE, THE ROUTINE!
PUT YOUR FINGER IN YOUR MOUTH!
ぱくっ POK
TSUBAKI, DID IT HURT?
IT HURT LIKE CRAZY.
BUT,
THANKS TO THAT...

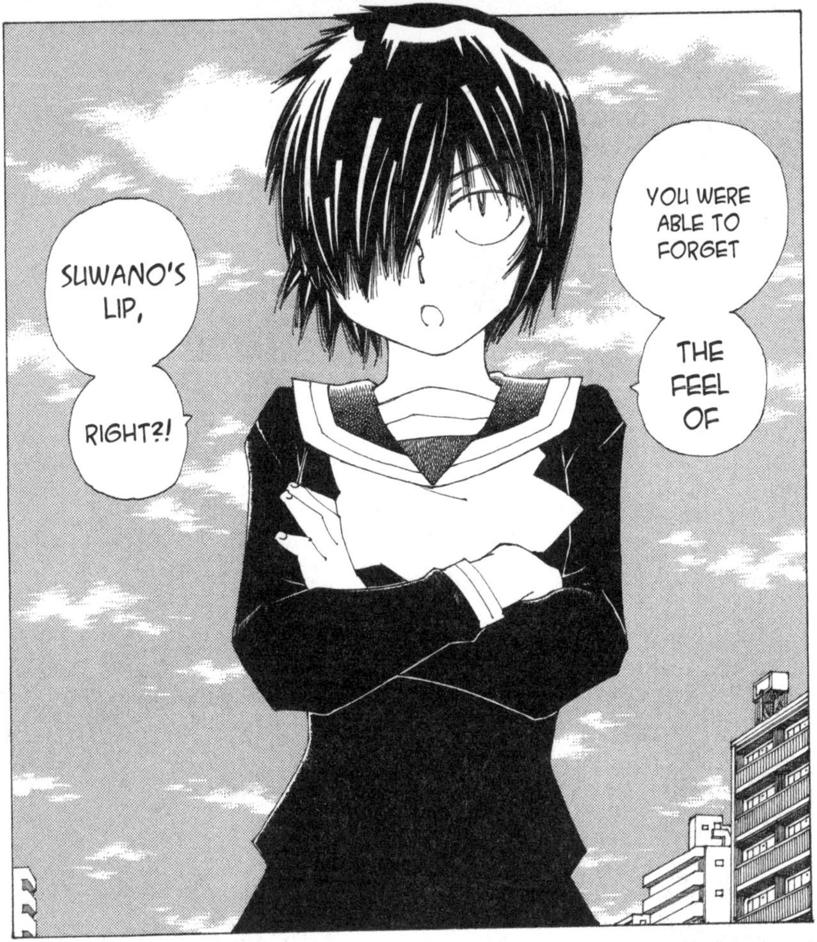
YOU WERE ABLE TO FORGET
THE FEEL OF
SUWANO'S LIP,
RIGHT?!
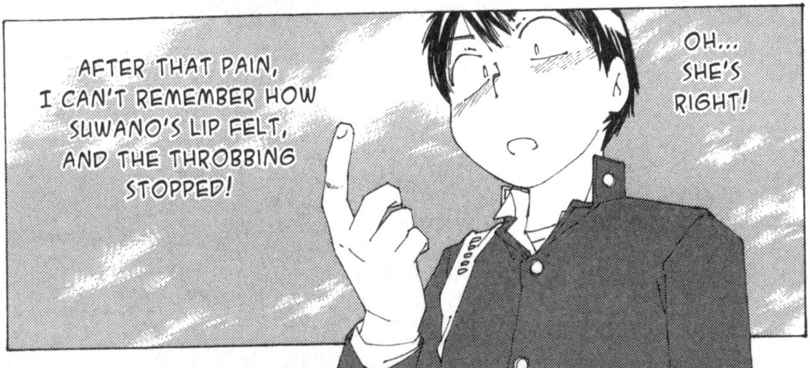
OH... SHE'S RIGHT!
AFTER THAT PAIN, I CAN'T REMEMBER HOW SUWANO'S LIP FELT, AND THE THROBBING STOPPED!

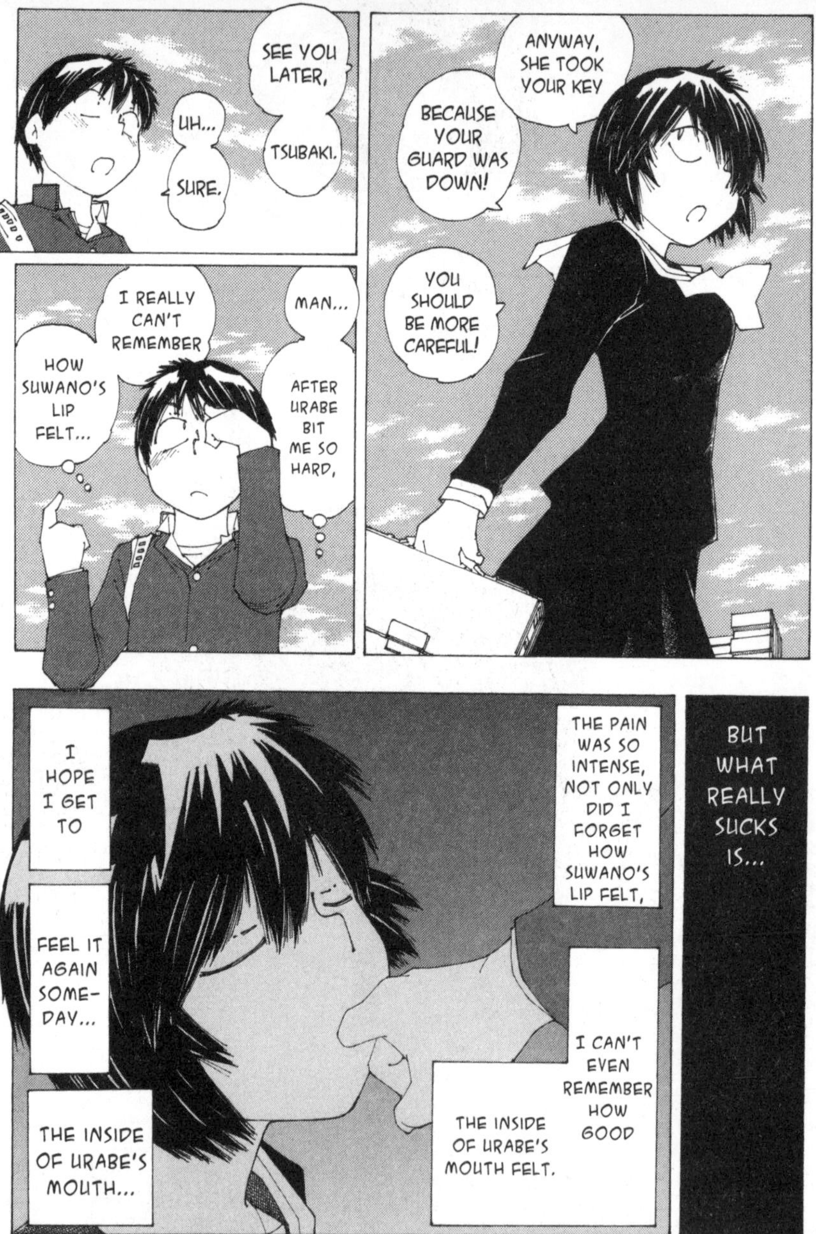
ANYWAY, SHE TOOK YOUR KEY
BECAUSE YOUR GUARD WAS DOWN!
YOU SHOULD BE MORE CAREFUL!
SEE YOU LATER,
TSUBAKI.
UH...
SURE.
MAN...
AFTER URABE BIT ME SO HARD,
I REALLY CAN'T REMEMBER
HOW SUWANO'S LIP FELT...
BUT WHAT REALLY SUCKS IS...
THE PAIN WAS SO INTENSE, NOT ONLY DID I FORGET HOW SUWANO'S LIP FELT,
I CAN'T EVEN REMEMBER HOW GOOD
THE INSIDE OF URABE'S MOUTH FELT.
I HOPE I GET TO
FEEL IT AGAIN SOME-DAY...
THE INSIDE OF URABE'S MOUTH...

END OF CHAPTER 56

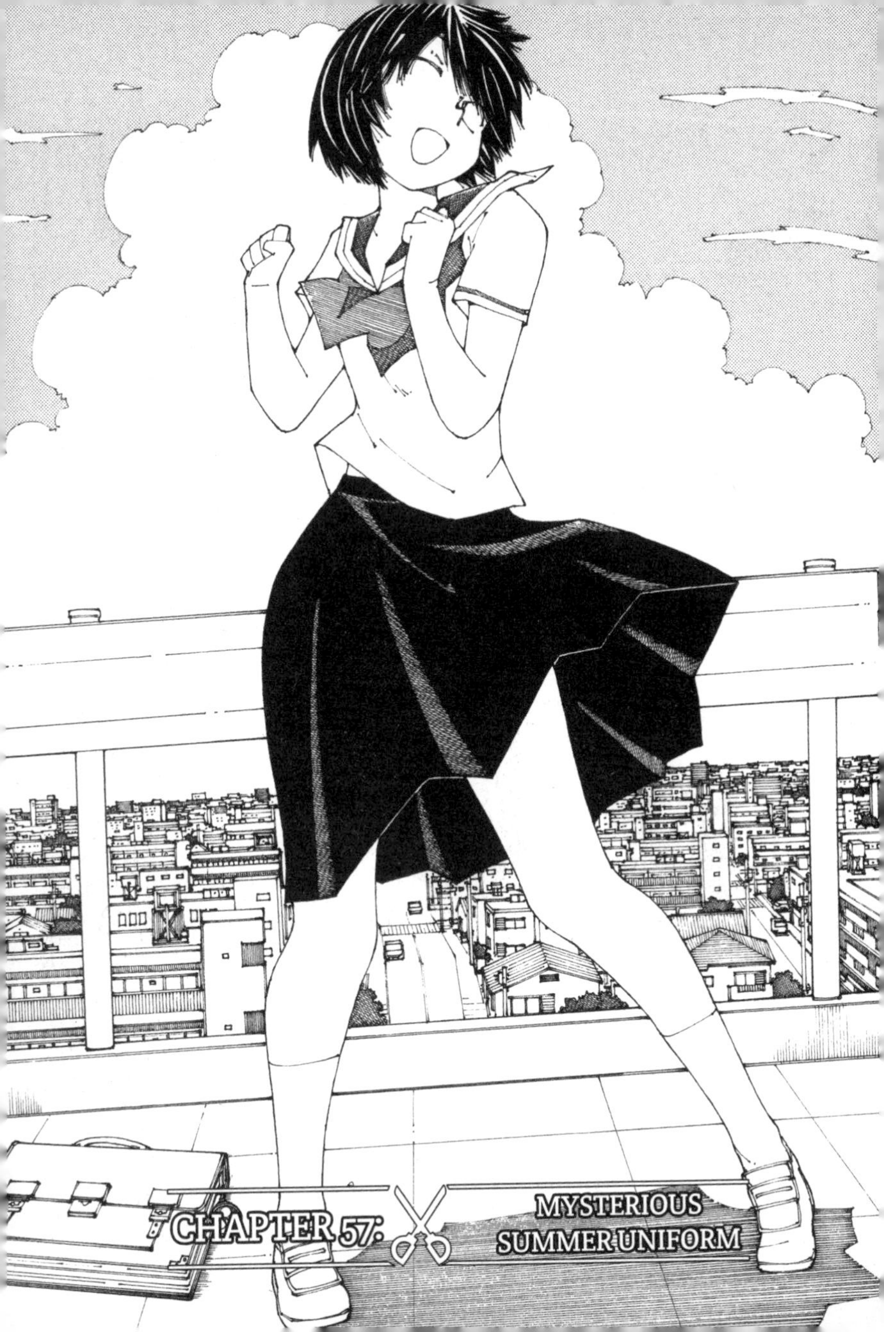
CHAPTER 57:
MYSTERIOUS
SUMMER UNIFORM

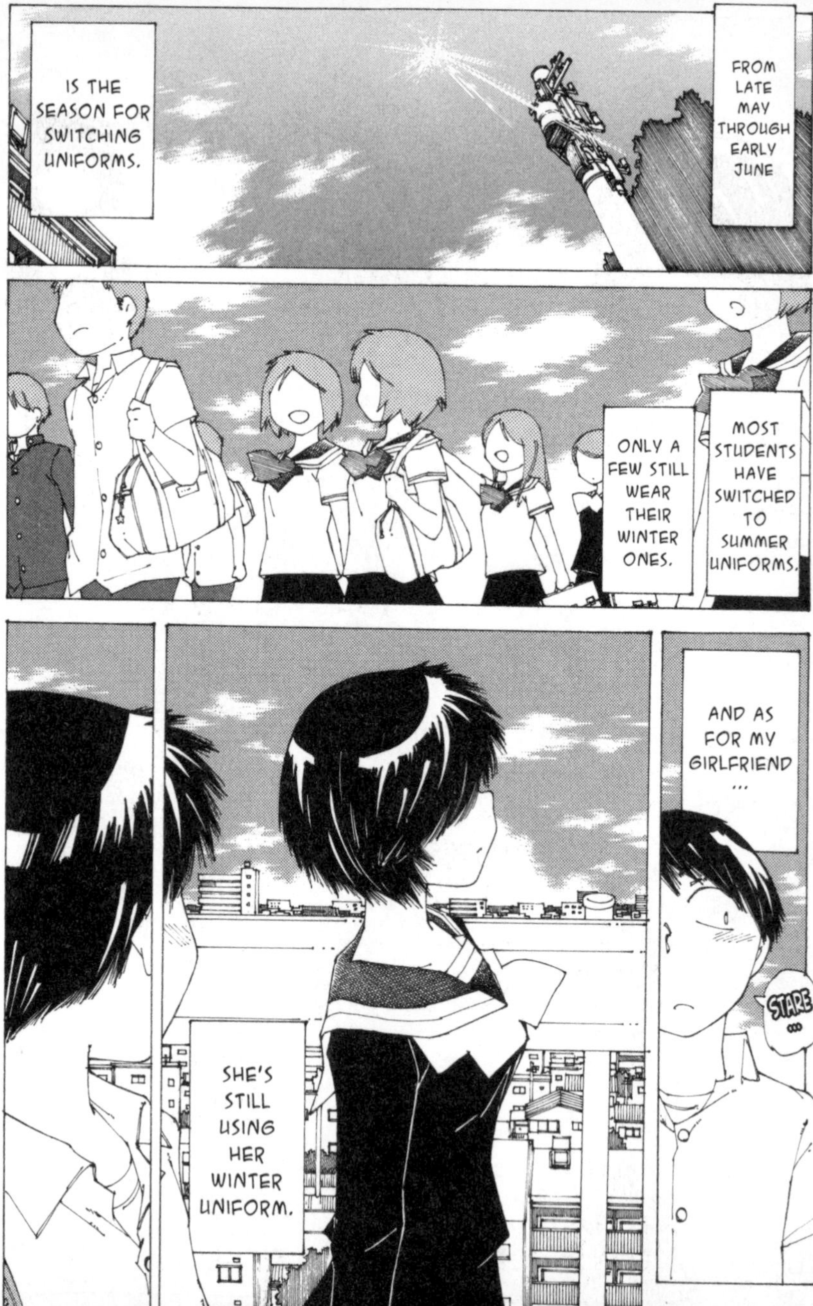
FROM LATE MAY THROUGH EARLY JUNE
IS THE SEASON FOR SWITCHING UNIFORMS.
MOST STUDENTS HAVE SWITCHED TO SUMMER UNIFORMS.
ONLY A FEW STILL WEAR THEIR WINTER ONES.
AND AS FOR MY GIRLFRIEND ...
STARE
SHE'S STILL USING HER WINTER UNIFORM.

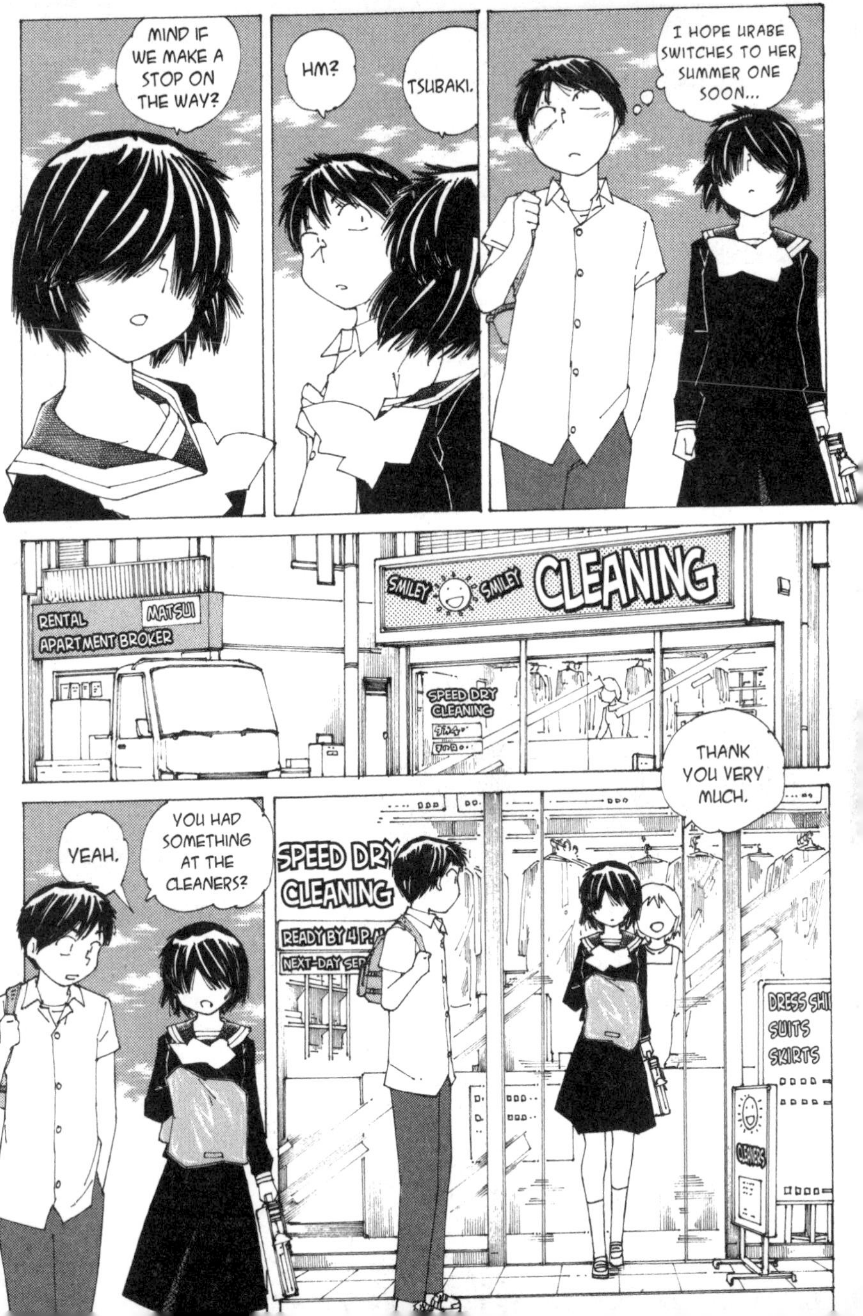
I HOPE URABE SWITCHES TO HER SUMMER ONE SOON...
TSUBAKI.
HM?
MIND IF WE MAKE A STOP ON THE WAY?
SMILEY SMILEY CLEANING
SPEED DRY CLEANING
MATSUI
RENTAL APARTMENT BROKER
THANK YOU VERY MUCH.
SUITS
SKIRTS
CLEANERS
SPEED DRY CLEANING
YOU HAD SOMETHING AT THE CLEANERS?
YEAH.

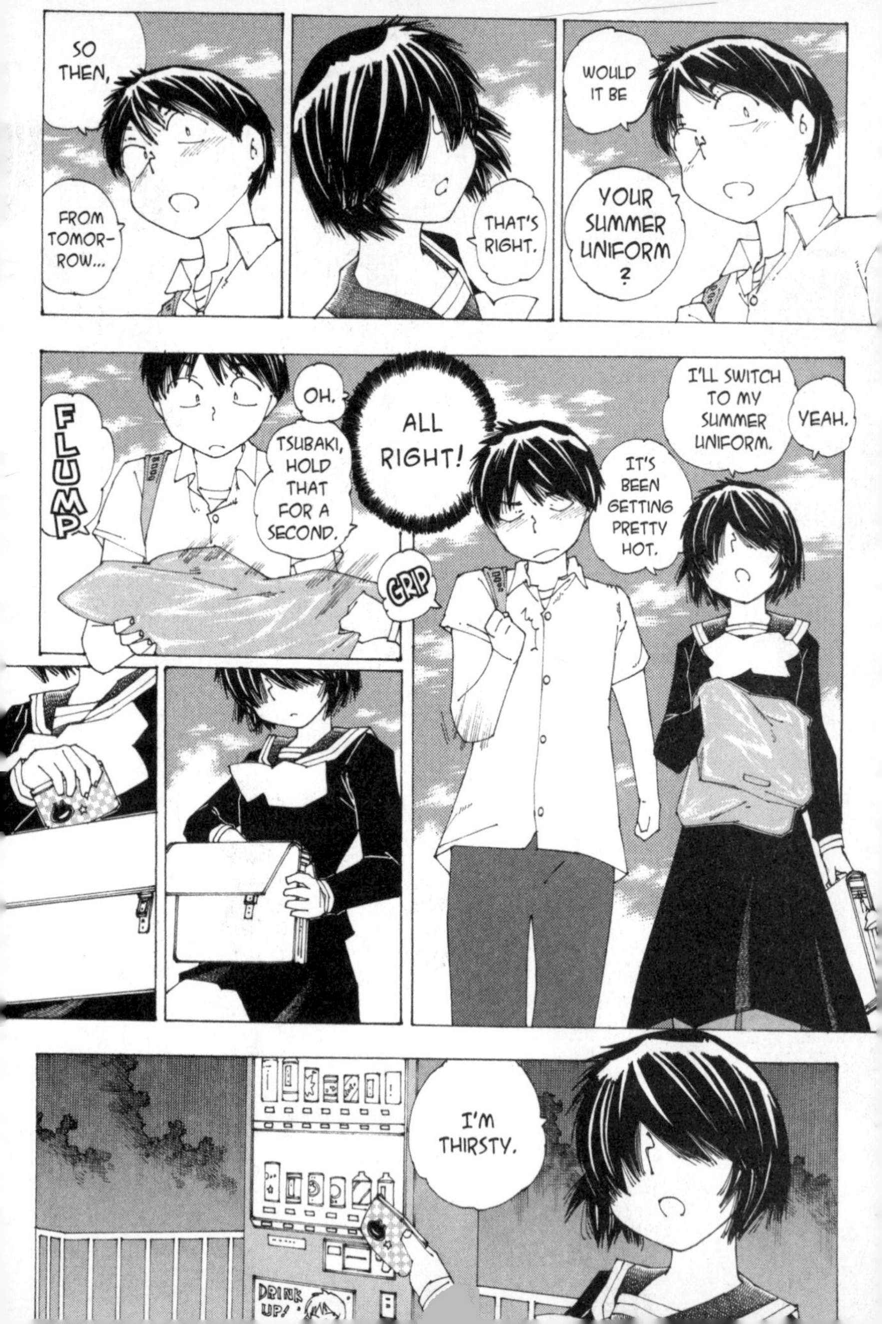
SO THEN,
FROM TOMORROW...
THAT'S RIGHT.
WOULD IT BE
YOUR SUMMER UNIFORM ?
YEAH.
I'LL SWITCH TO MY SUMMER UNIFORM.
IT'S BEEN GETTING PRETTY HOT.
ALL RIGHT!
GRIP
OH.
TSUBAKI, HOLD THAT FOR A SECOND.
FLUMP
I'M THIRSTY.
DRINK UP!

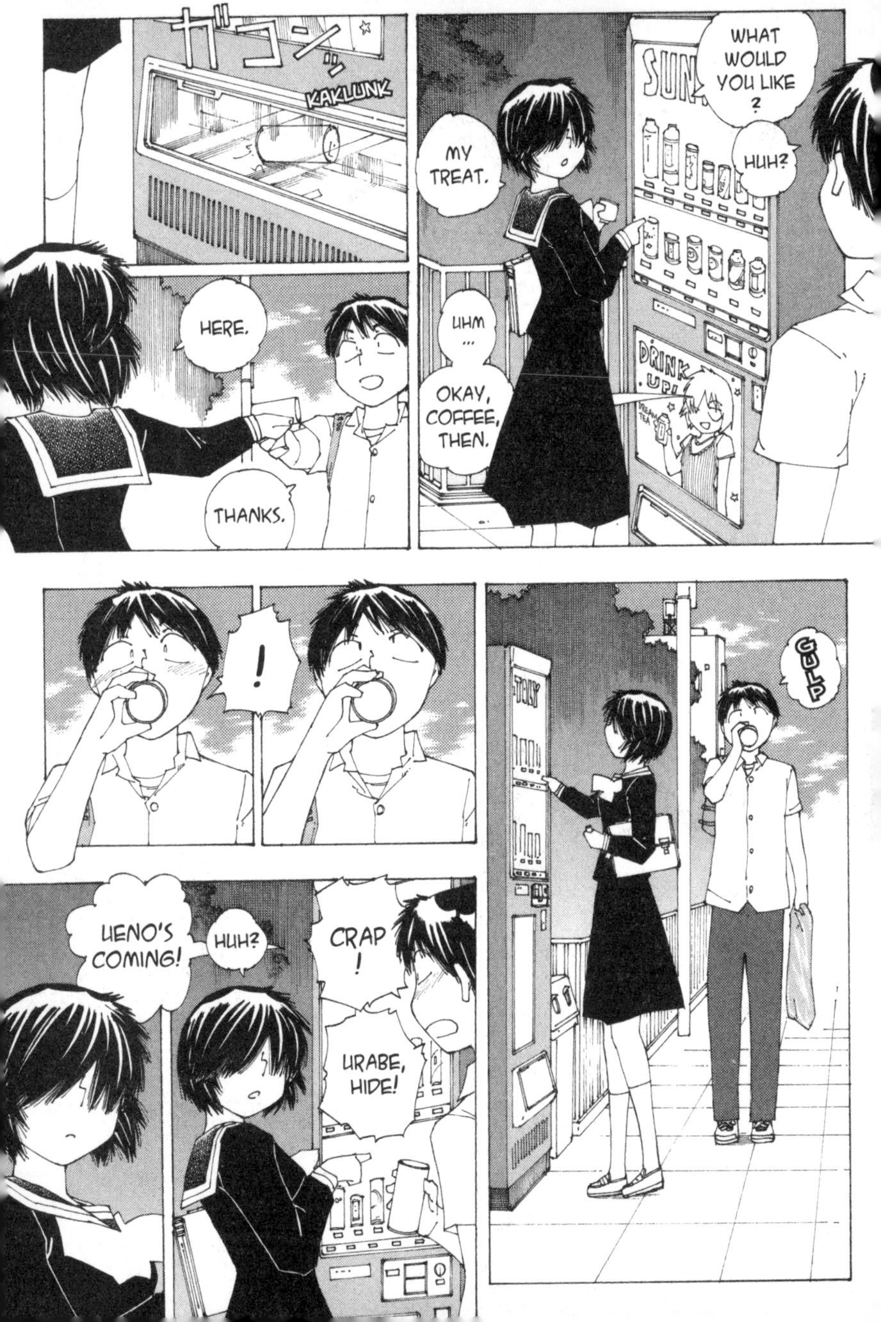
WHAT WOULD YOU LIKE ?
HUH?
MY TREAT.
UHM ...
OKAY, COFFEE, THEN.
KAKLUNK
HERE.
THANKS.
GULP
!
UENO'S COMING!
HUH?
CRAP !
URABE, HIDE!

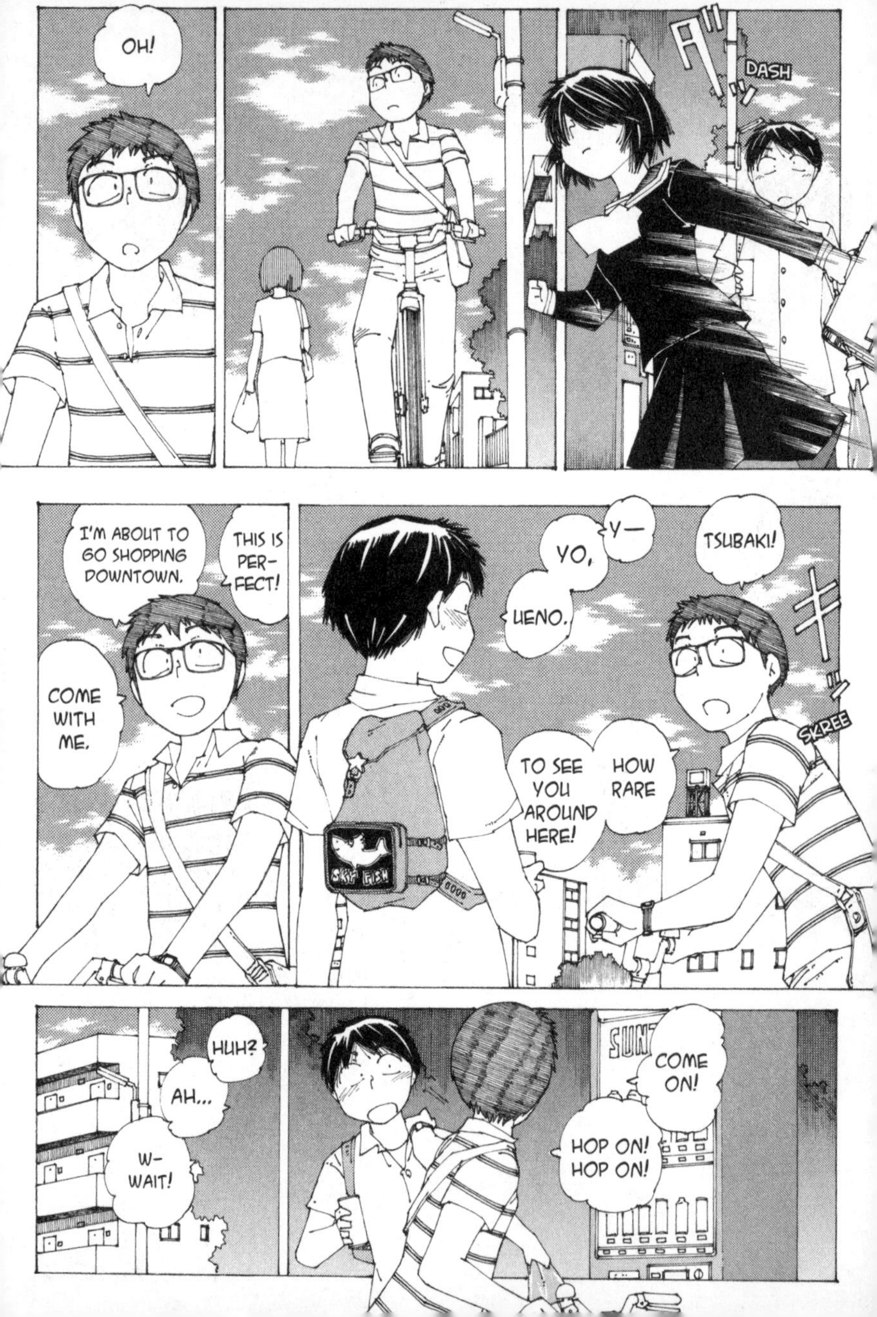
DASH
OH!
TSUBAKI!
SKREE
Y—
YO,
UENO.
HOW RARE
TO SEE YOU AROUND HERE!
THIS IS PER-FECT!
I'M ABOUT TO GO SHOPPING DOWNTOWN.
COME WITH ME.
COME ON!
HOP ON! HOP ON!
HUH?
AH...
W-WAIT!

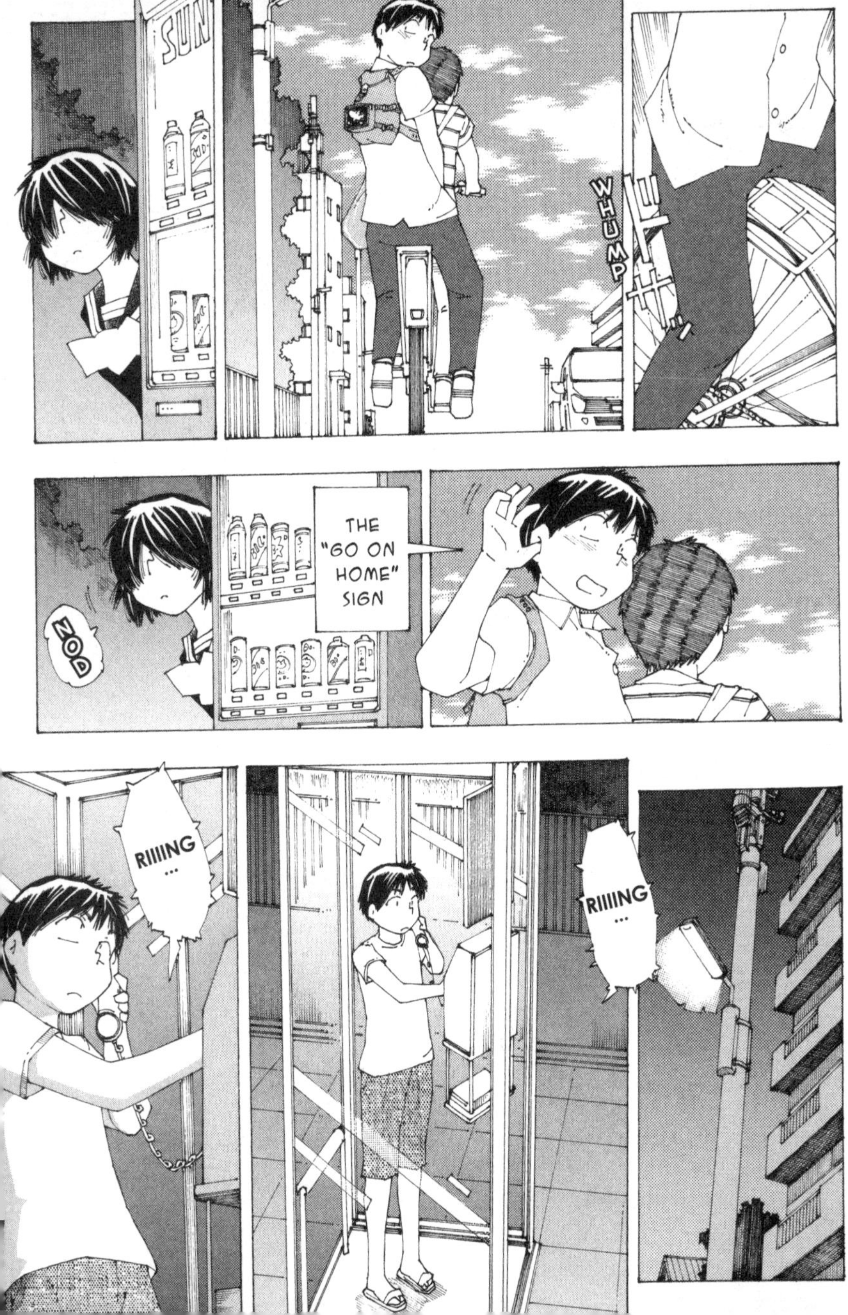
WHUMP
THE "GO ON HOME" SIGN
NOD
RIIIING ...
RIIIING ...

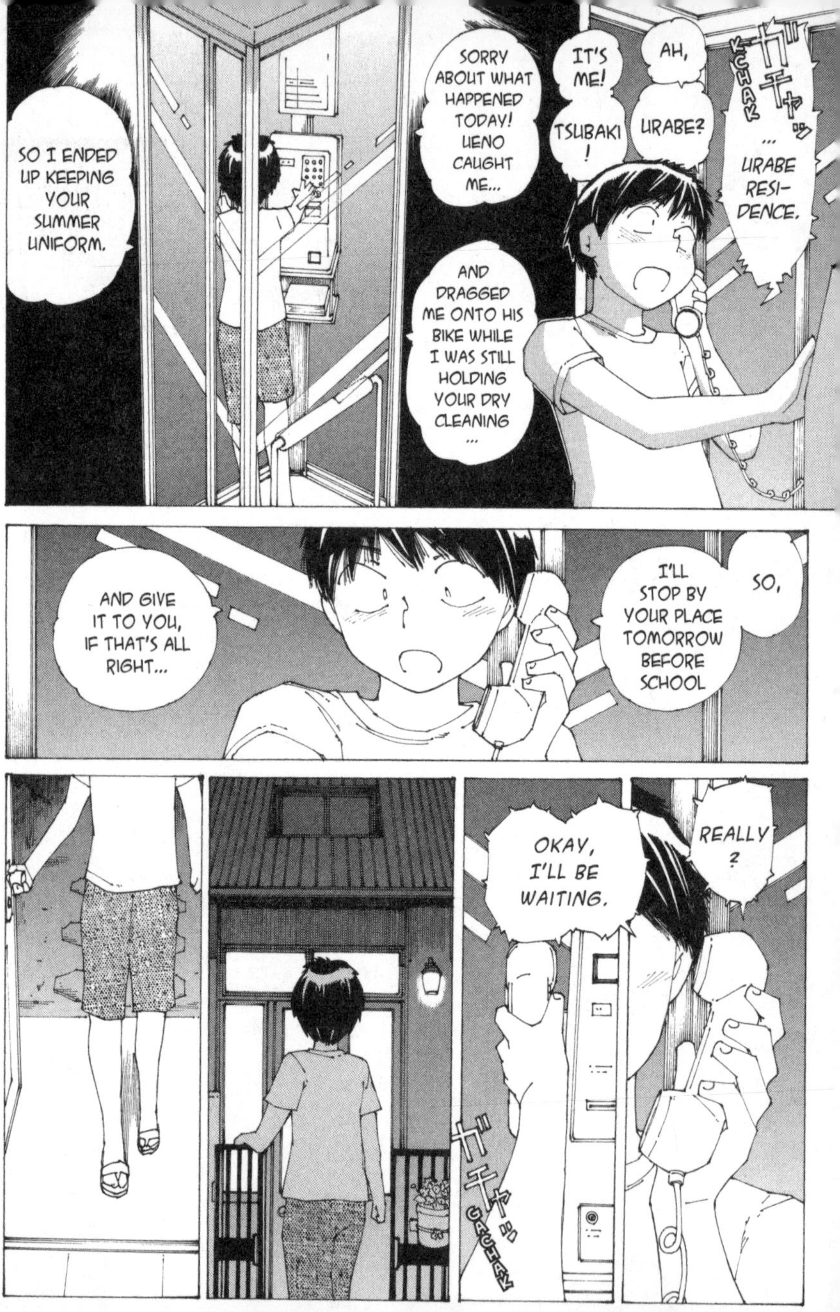
ガチャッ
KCHAK
... URABE RESIDENCE.
AH,
URABE?
IT'S ME!
TSUBAKI!
SORRY ABOUT WHAT HAPPENED TODAY! UENO CAUGHT ME...
AND DRAGGED ME ONTO HIS BIKE WHILE I WAS STILL HOLDING YOUR DRY CLEANING ...
SO I ENDED UP KEEPING YOUR SUMMER UNIFORM.
SO,
I'LL STOP BY YOUR PLACE TOMORROW BEFORE SCHOOL
AND GIVE IT TO YOU, IF THAT'S ALL RIGHT...
REALLY?
OKAY, I'LL BE WAITING.
ガチャッ
GACHAK

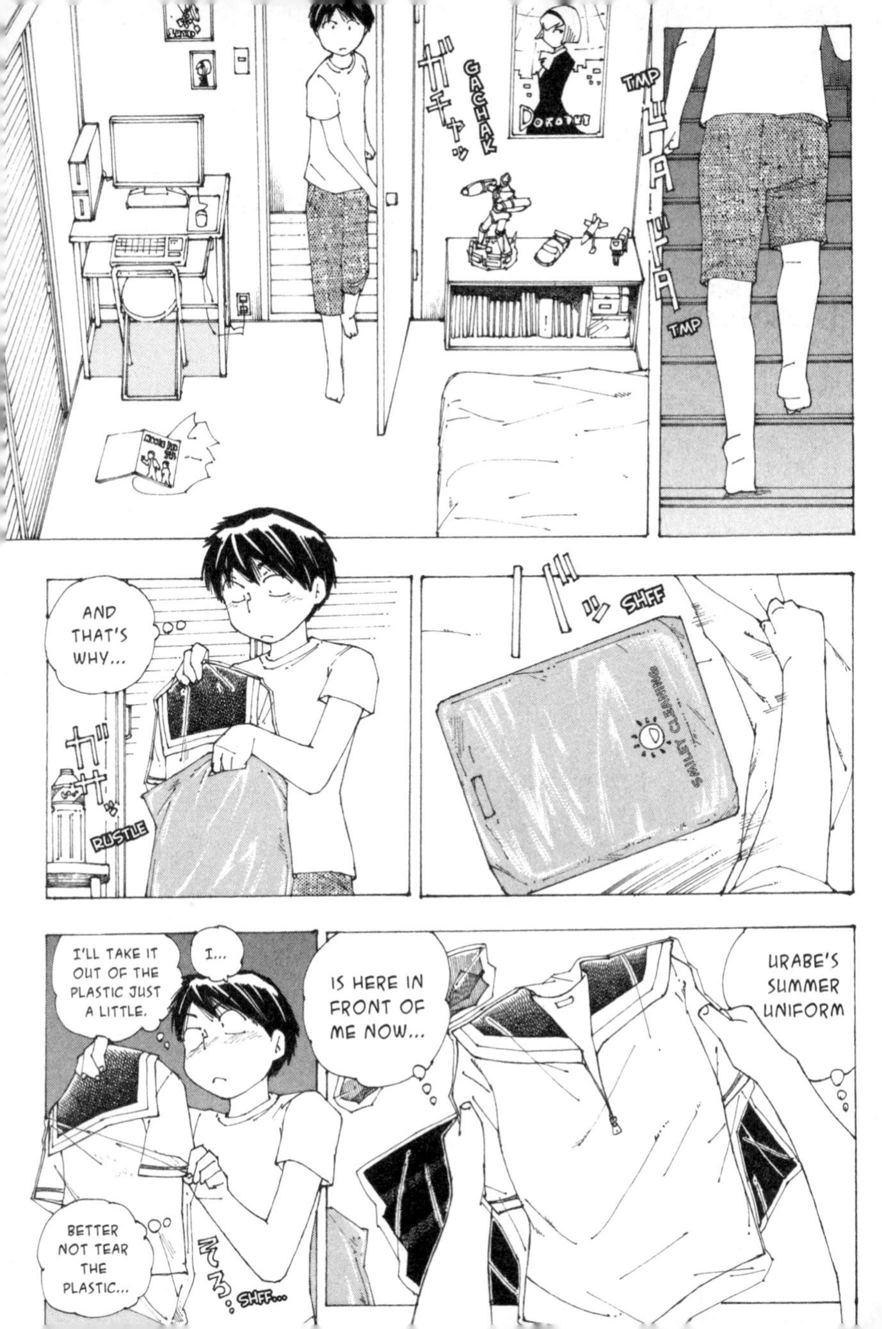
TMP
TMP
ガチャッ
GACHAK
DOROTHY
SHFF
SMILEY CLEANING
AND THAT'S WHY...
RUSTLE
URABE'S SUMMER UNIFORM
IS HERE IN FRONT OF ME NOW...
I...
I'LL TAKE IT OUT OF THE PLASTIC JUST A LITTLE.
BETTER NOT TEAR THE PLASTIC...
SHFF...

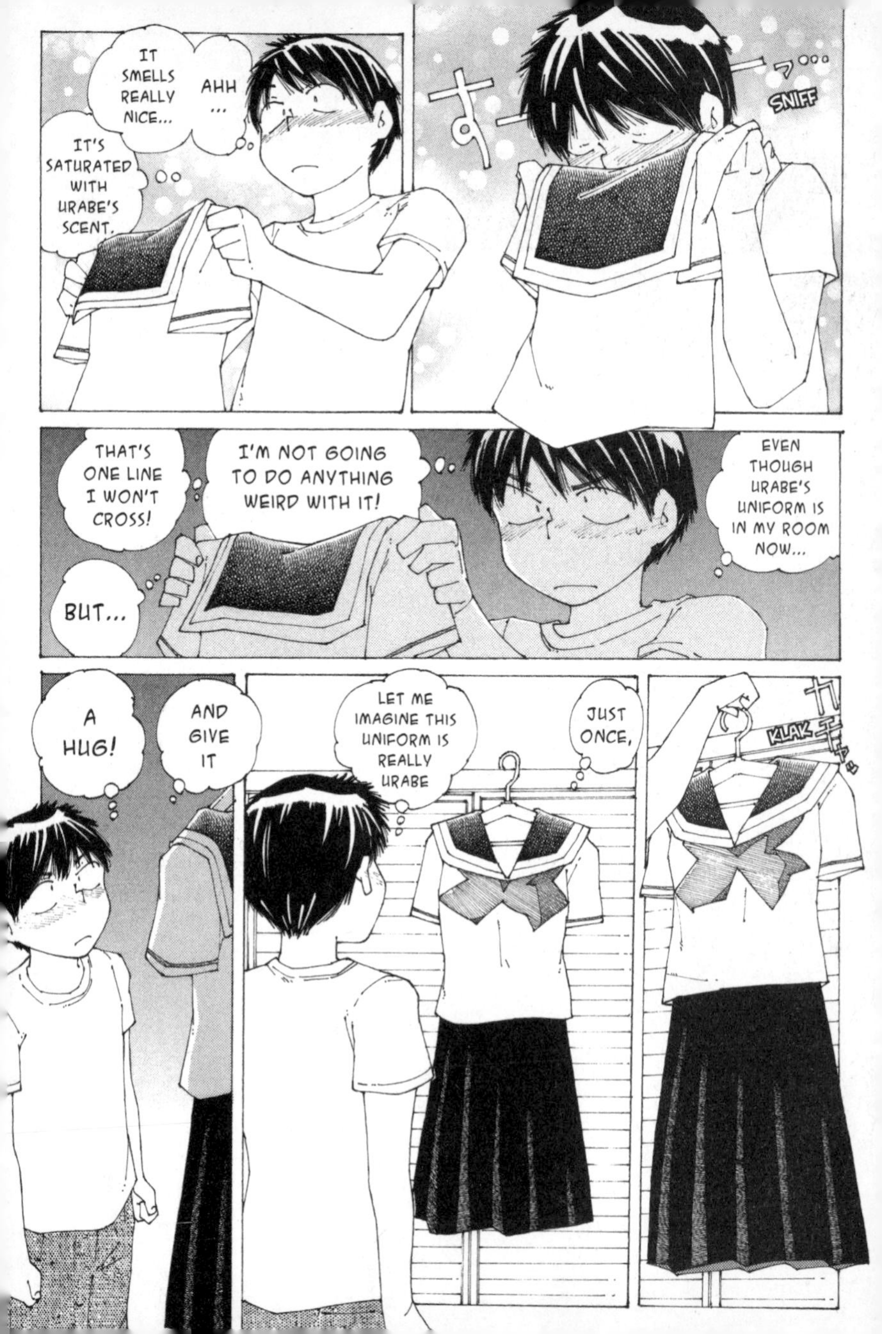
SNIFF
AHH ...
IT SMELLS REALLY NICE...
IT'S SATURATED WITH URABE'S SCENT.
EVEN THOUGH URABE'S UNIFORM IS IN MY ROOM NOW...
I'M NOT GOING TO DO ANYTHING WEIRD WITH IT!
THAT'S ONE LINE I WON'T CROSS!
BUT...
KLAK
JUST ONCE,
LET ME IMAGINE THIS UNIFORM IS REALLY URABE
AND GIVE IT
A HUG!

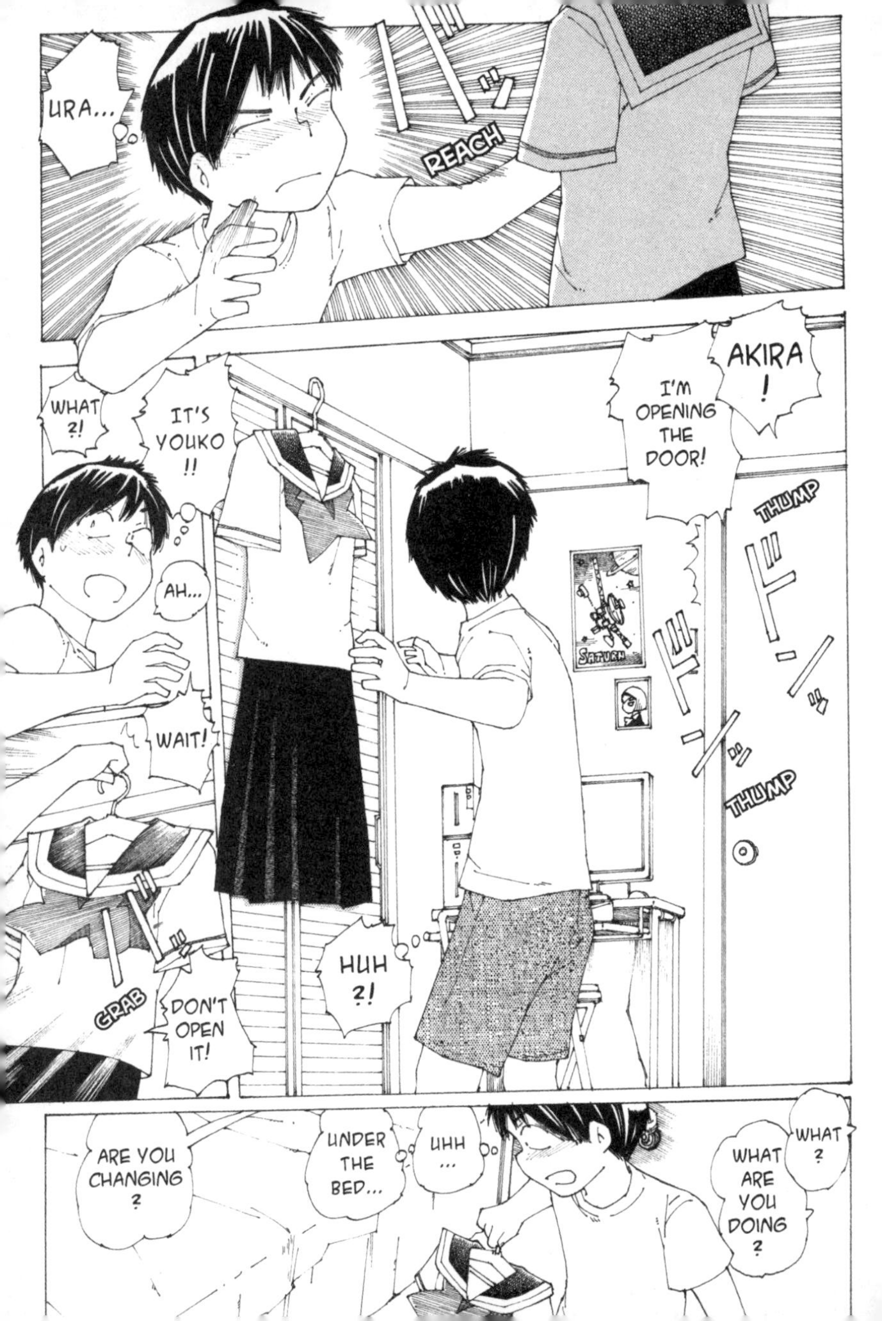
REACH
URA...
AKIRA!
I'M OPENING THE DOOR!
THUMP
THUMP
HUH ?!
IT'S YOUKO !!
WHAT ?!
AH...
WAIT!
DON'T OPEN IT!
GRAB
SATURN
WHAT ?
WHAT ARE YOU DOING ?
UHH ...
UNDER THE BED...
ARE YOU CHANGING ?

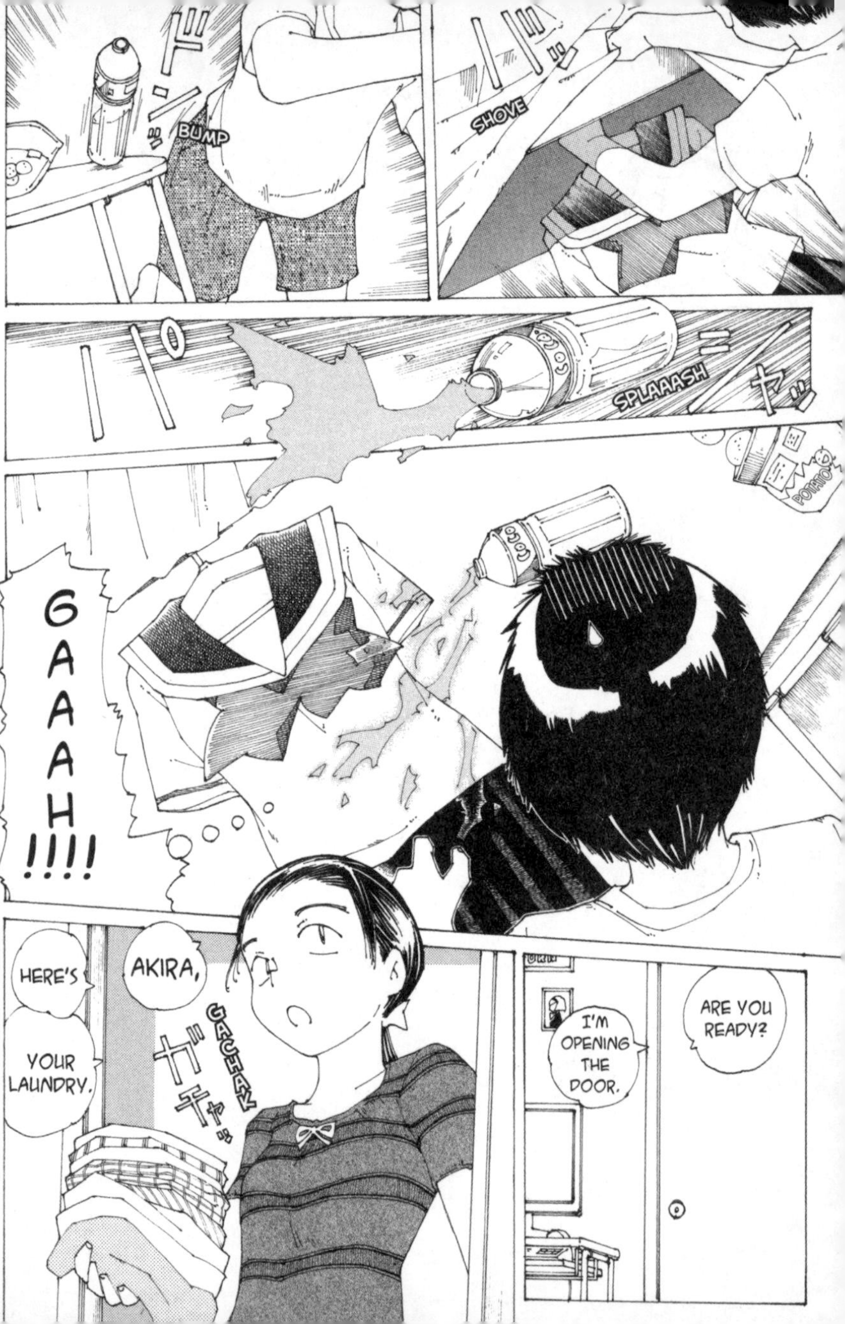
SHOVE
BUMP
COCO
SPLAAASH
POTATO
COCO
GAAAAH!!!!
ARE YOU READY?
I'M OPENING THE DOOR.
GACHAK
AKIRA,
HERE'S YOUR LAUNDRY.

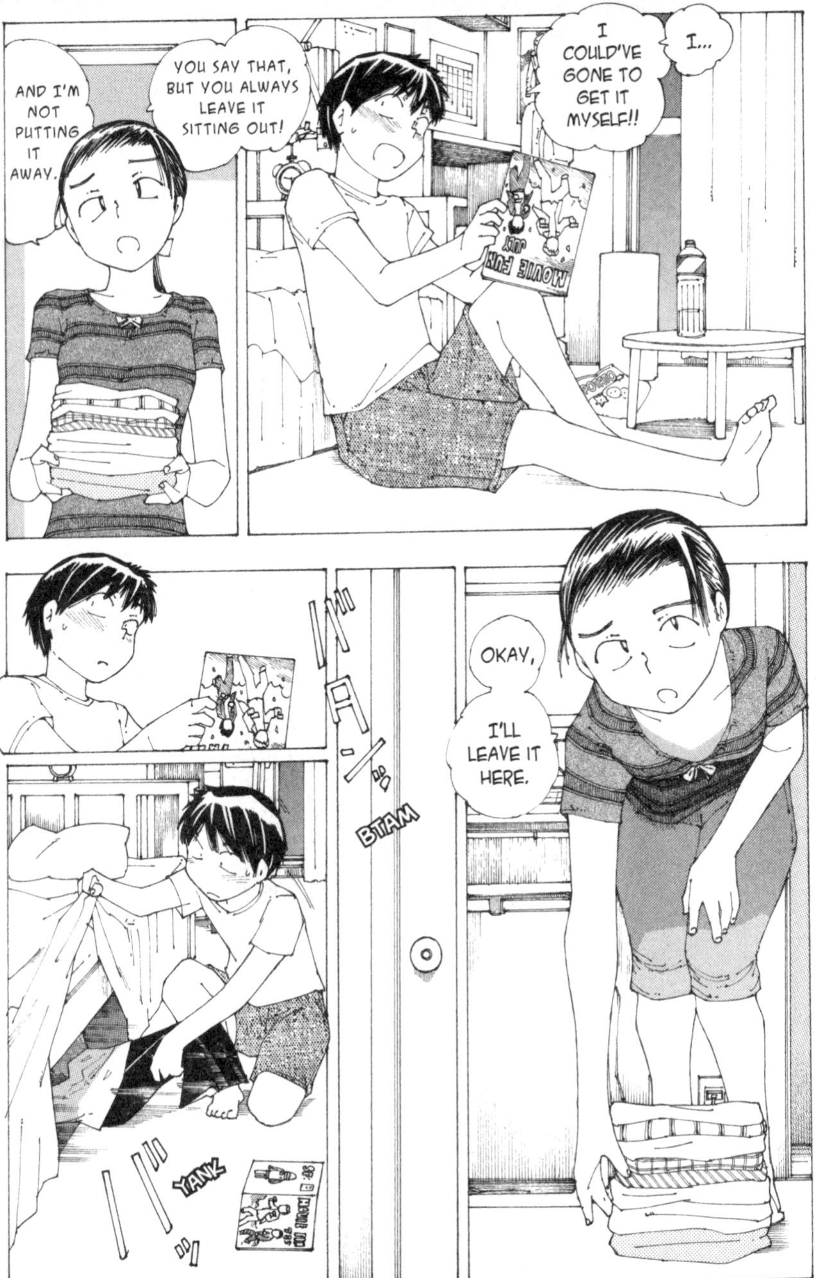
I...
I COULD'VE GONE TO GET IT MYSELF!!
MOVIE FUN
JULY
YOU SAY THAT, BUT YOU ALWAYS LEAVE IT SITTING OUT!
AND I'M NOT PUTTING IT AWAY.
OKAY,
I'LL LEAVE IT HERE.
BTAM
YANK

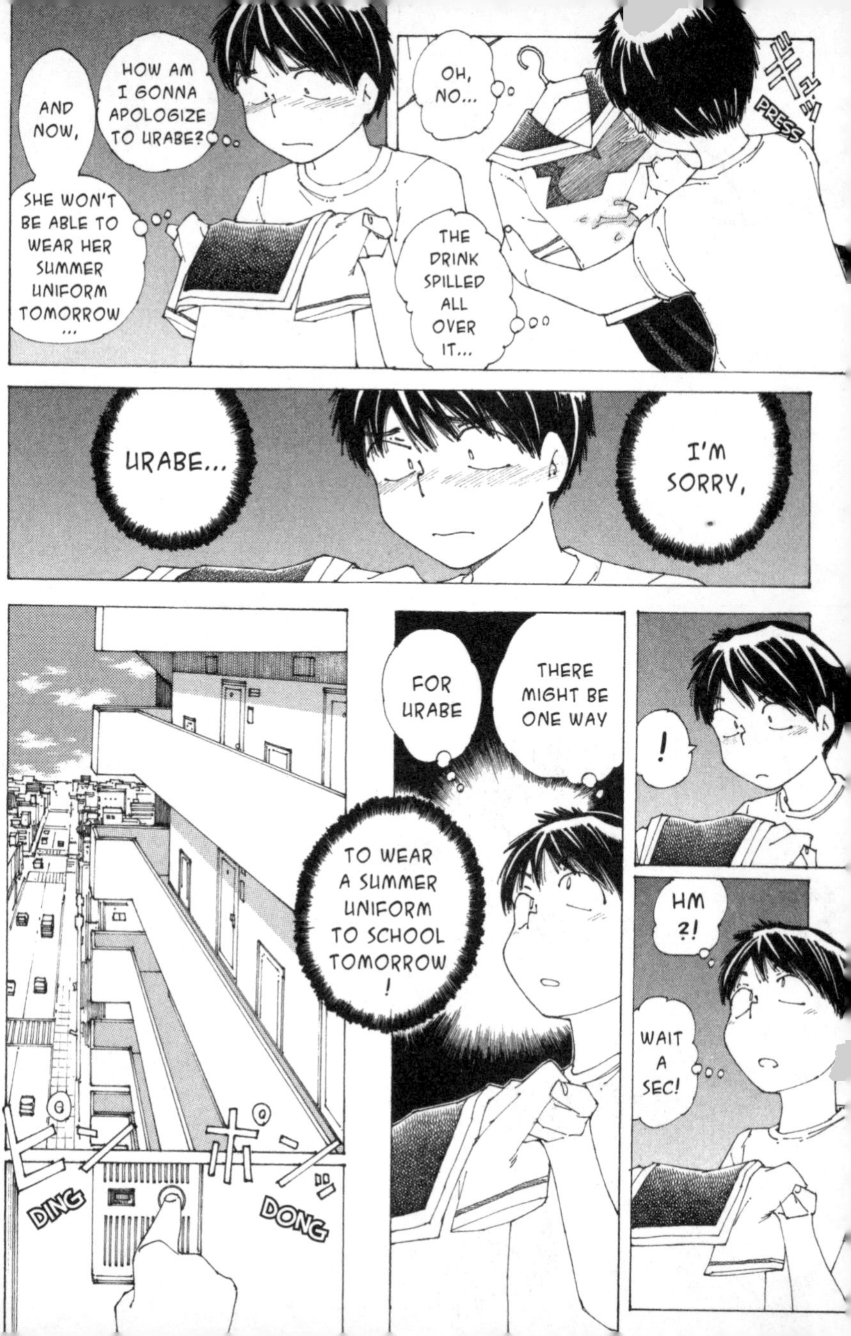
PRESS
OH, NO...
THE DRINK SPILLED ALL OVER IT...
HOW AM I GONNA APOLOGIZE TO URABE?
AND NOW,
SHE WON'T BE ABLE TO WEAR HER SUMMER UNIFORM TOMORROW ...
I'M SORRY,
URABE...
!
HM ?!
WAIT A SEC!
THERE MIGHT BE ONE WAY
FOR URABE
TO WEAR A SUMMER UNIFORM TO SCHOOL TOMORROW !
DING
DONG

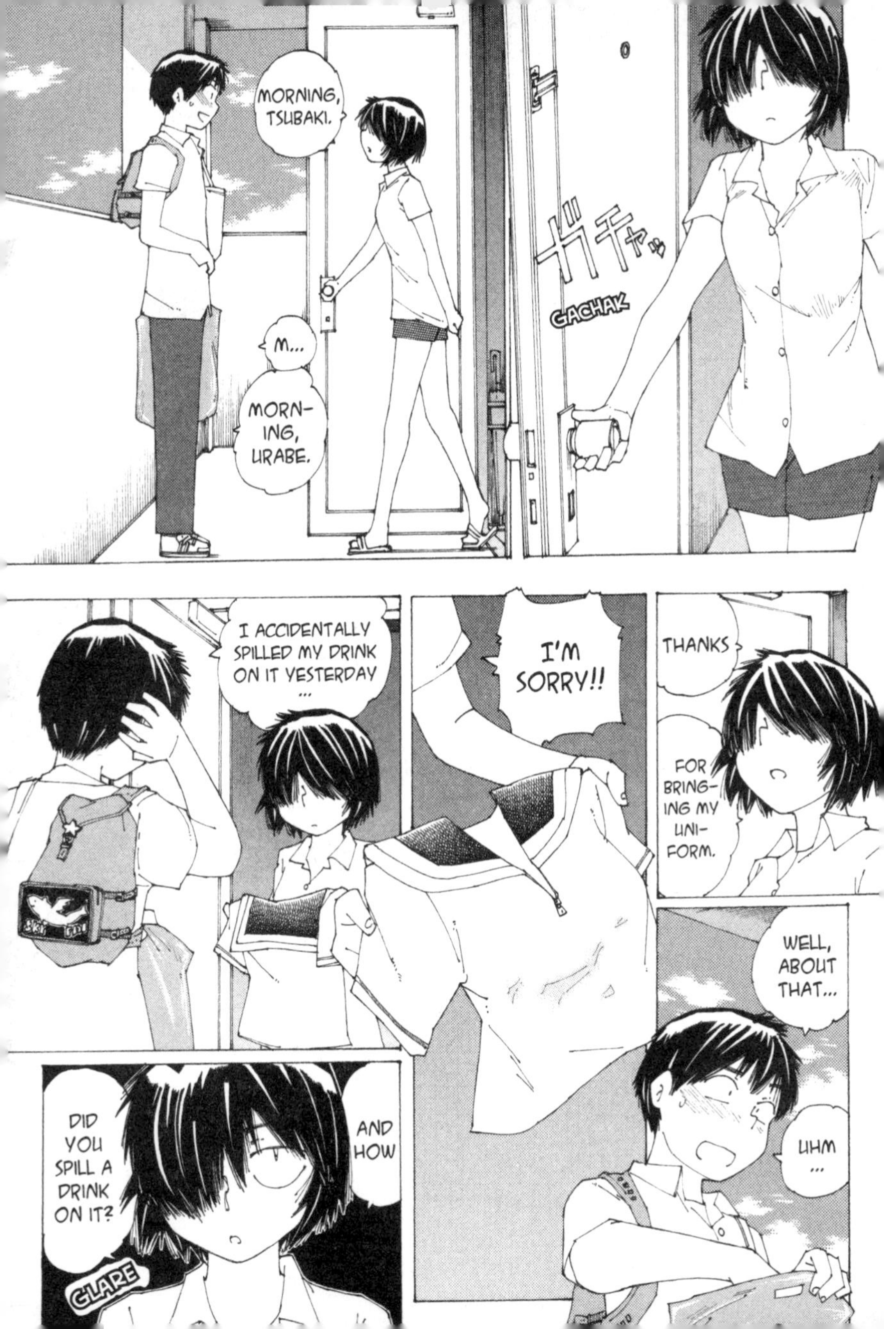

ガチャッ
GACHAK
MORNING, TSUBAKI.
M...
MORNING, URABE.
THANKS
FOR BRINGING MY UNIFORM.
I'M SORRY!!
I ACCIDENTALLY SPILLED MY DRINK ON IT YESTERDAY ...
WELL, ABOUT THAT...
UHM ...
AND HOW
DID YOU SPILL A DRINK ON IT?
GLARE

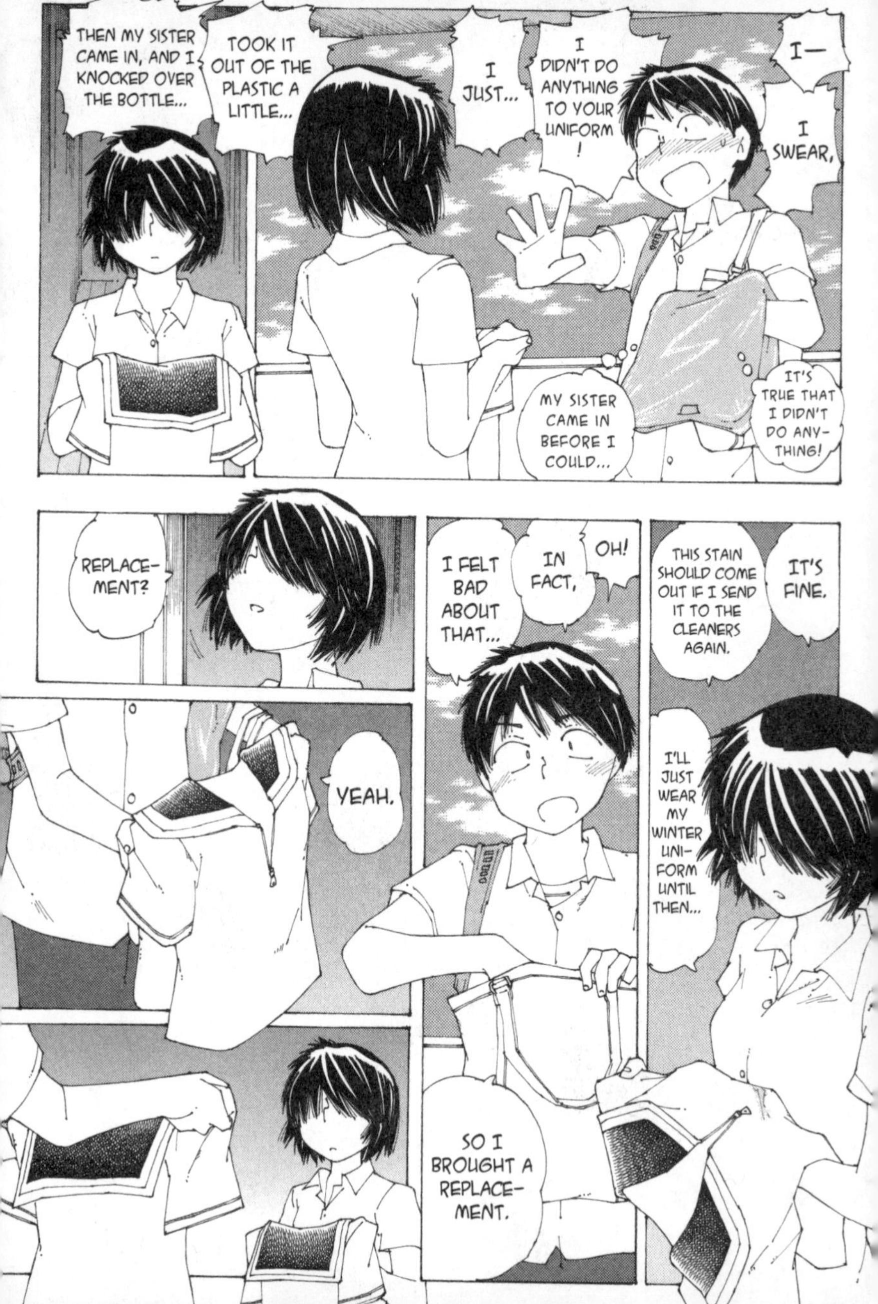
I— I SWEAR,
I DIDN'T DO ANYTHING TO YOUR UNIFORM!
I JUST...
TOOK IT OUT OF THE PLASTIC A LITTLE...
THEN MY SISTER CAME IN, AND I KNOCKED OVER THE BOTTLE...
IT'S TRUE THAT I DIDN'T DO ANY-THING!
MY SISTER CAME IN BEFORE I COULD...
IT'S FINE.
THIS STAIN SHOULD COME OUT IF I SEND IT TO THE CLEANERS AGAIN.
I'LL JUST WEAR MY WINTER UNI-FORM UNTIL THEN...
OH!
IN FACT,
I FELT BAD ABOUT THAT...
SO I BROUGHT A REPLACE-MENT.
REPLACE-MENT?
YEAH.

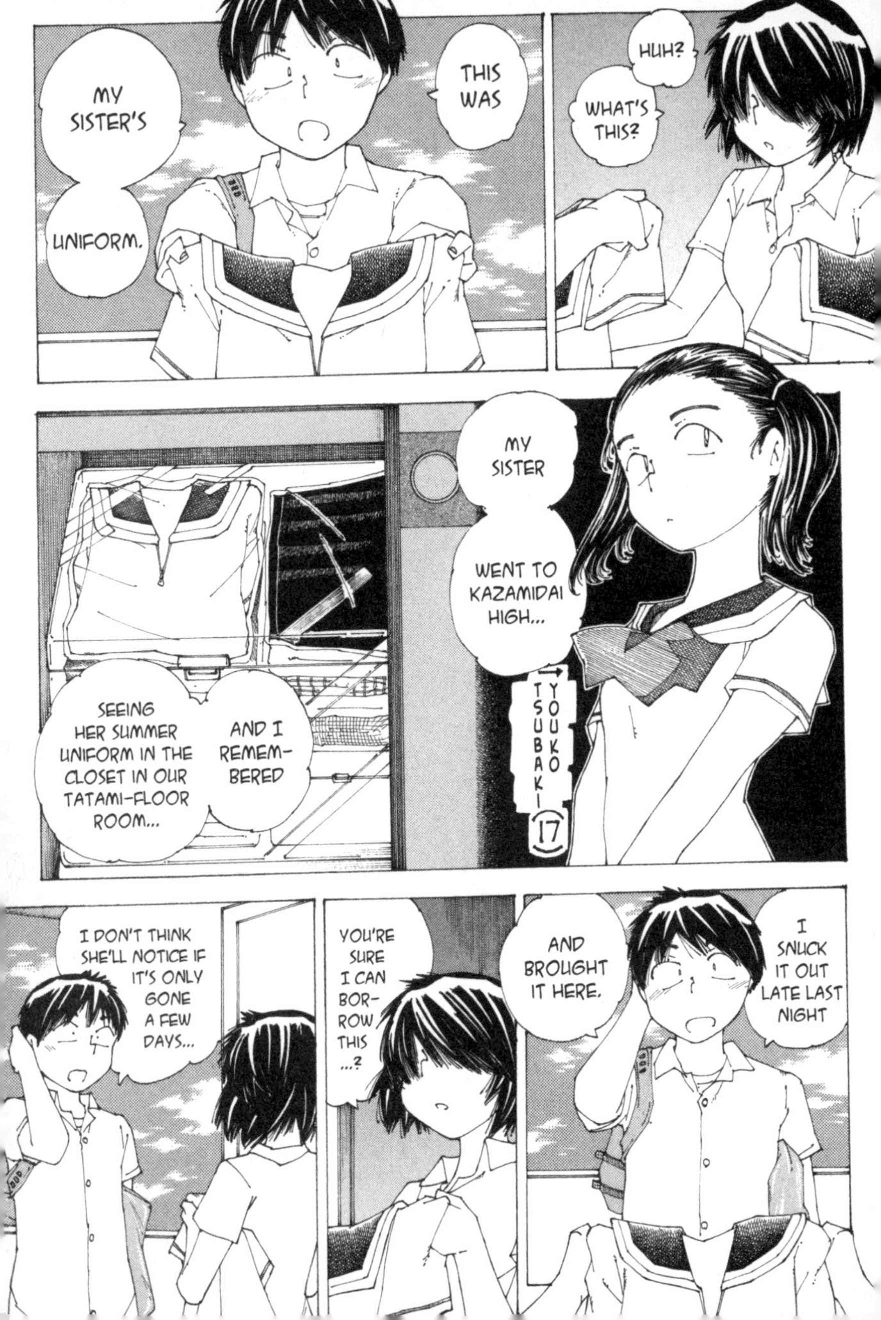
HUH?
WHAT'S THIS?
THIS WAS
MY SISTER'S
UNIFORM.
MY SISTER
WENT TO KAZAMIDAI HIGH...
TSUBAKI YOUKO 17
AND I REMEM-BERED
SEEING HER SUMMER UNIFORM IN THE CLOSET IN OUR TATAMI-FLOOR ROOM...
I SNUCK IT OUT LATE LAST NIGHT
AND BROUGHT IT HERE.
YOU'RE SURE I CAN BOR-ROW THIS ...?
I DON'T THINK SHE'LL NOTICE IF IT'S ONLY GONE A FEW DAYS...

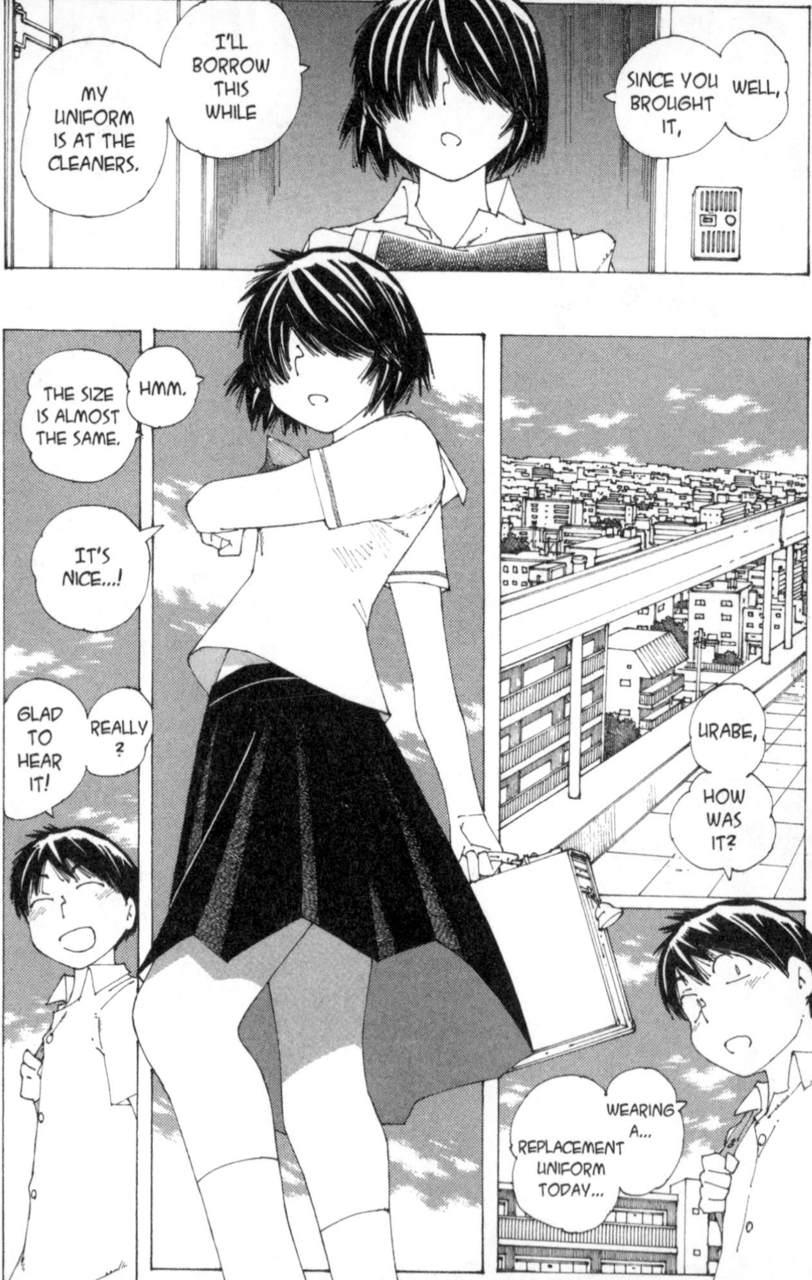
WELL,
SINCE YOU BROUGHT IT,
I'LL BORROW THIS WHILE
MY UNIFORM IS AT THE CLEANERS.
URABE,
HOW WAS IT?
WEARING A...
REPLACEMENT UNIFORM TODAY...
HMM.
THE SIZE IS ALMOST THE SAME.
IT'S NICE...!
REALLY?
GLAD TO HEAR IT!

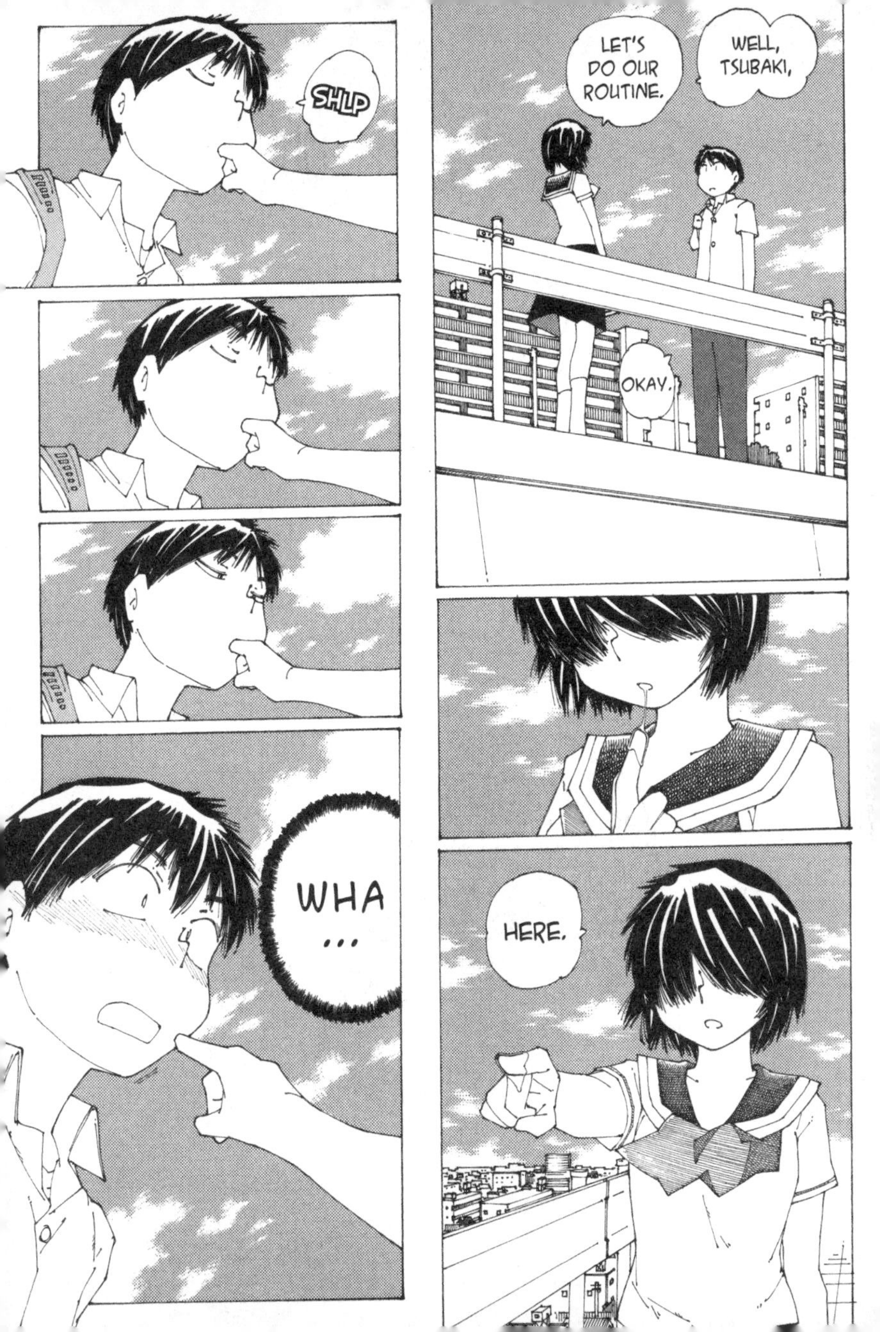
WELL, TSUBAKI,
LET'S DO OUR ROUTINE.
OKAY.
HERE.
SHLP
WHA ...

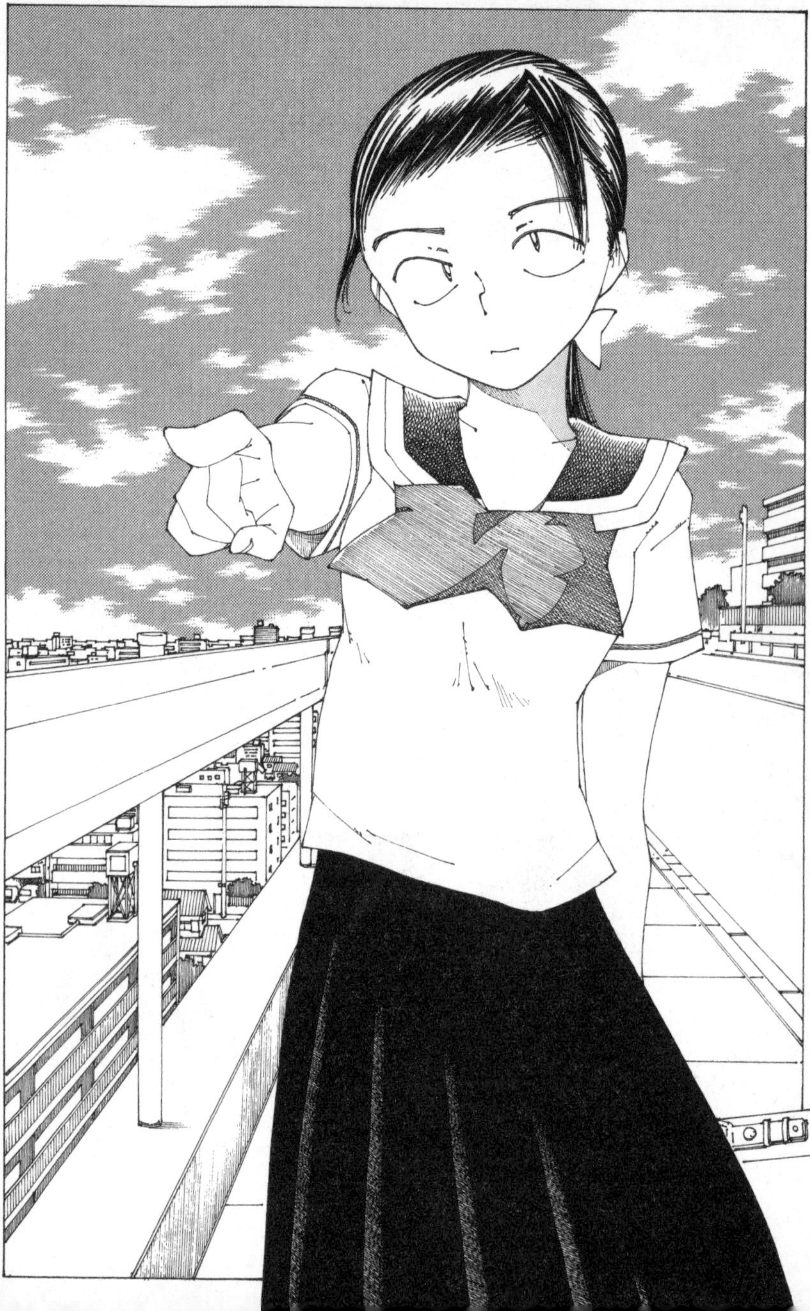

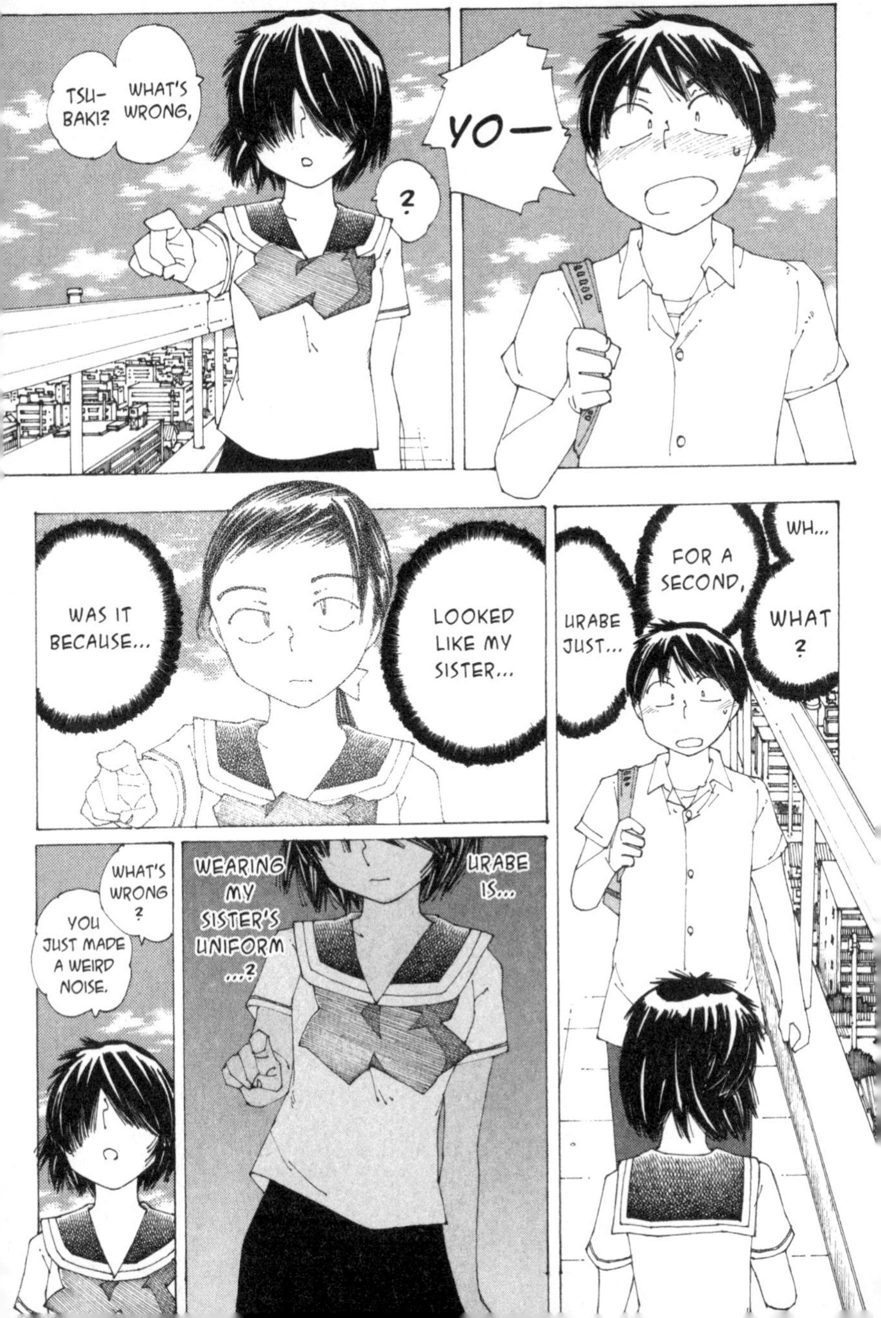

YO—
WHAT'S WRONG, TSU- BAKI?
?
WH... WHAT?
FOR A SECOND,
URABE JUST...
LOOKED LIKE MY SISTER...
WAS IT BECAUSE...
URABE IS...
WEARING MY SISTER'S UNIFORM ...?
WHAT'S WRONG?
YOU JUST MADE A WEIRD NOISE.

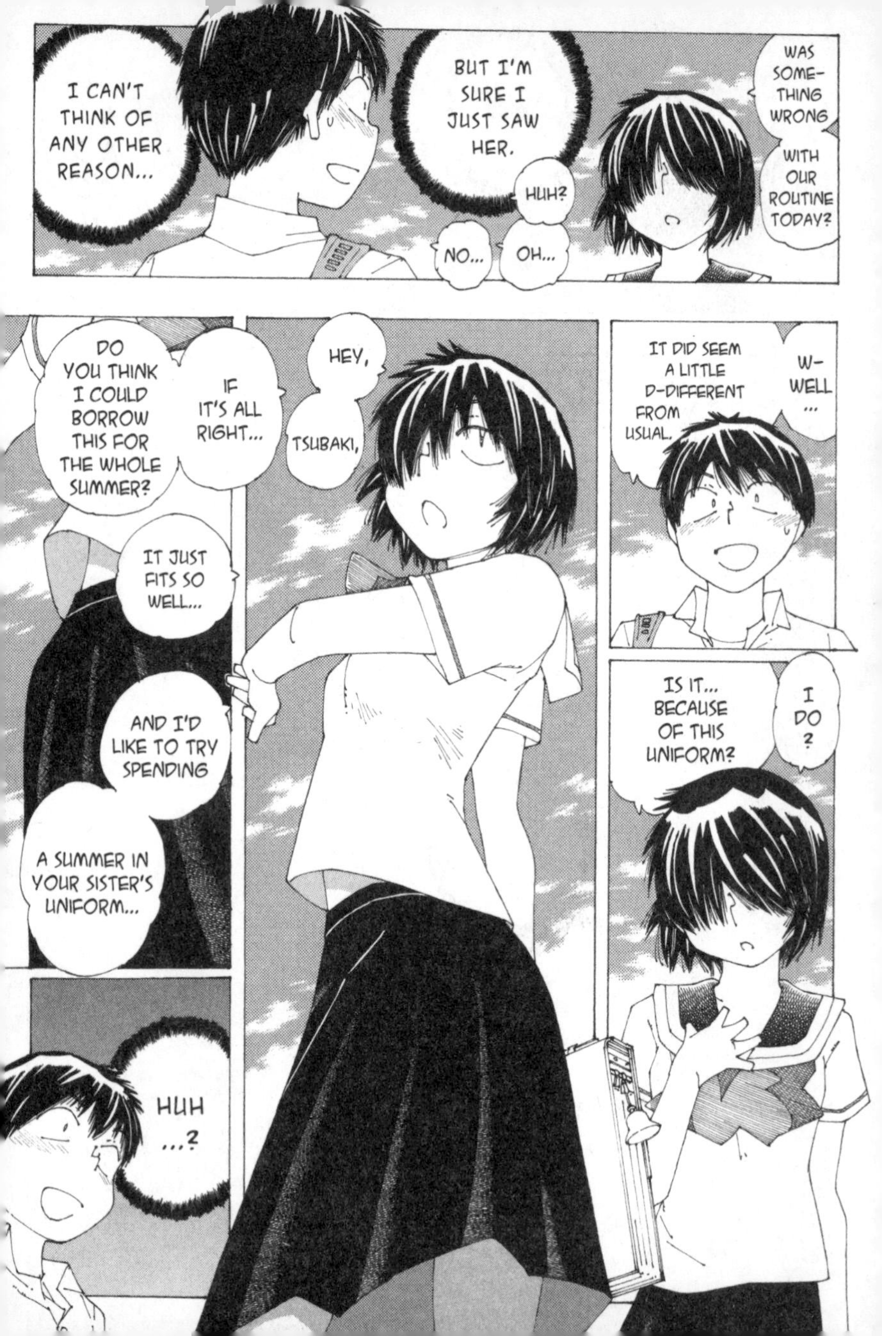
WAS SOME-THING WRONG
WITH OUR ROUTINE TODAY?
HUH?
OH...
NO...
BUT I'M SURE I JUST SAW HER.
I CAN'T THINK OF ANY OTHER REASON...
W-WELL...
IT DID SEEM A LITTLE D-DIFFERENT FROM USUAL.
I DO?
IS IT... BECAUSE OF THIS UNIFORM?
HEY,
TSUBAKI,
IF IT'S ALL RIGHT...
DO YOU THINK I COULD BORROW THIS FOR THE WHOLE SUMMER?
IT JUST FITS SO WELL...
AND I'D LIKE TO TRY SPENDING
A SUMMER IN YOUR SISTER'S UNIFORM...
HUH ...?

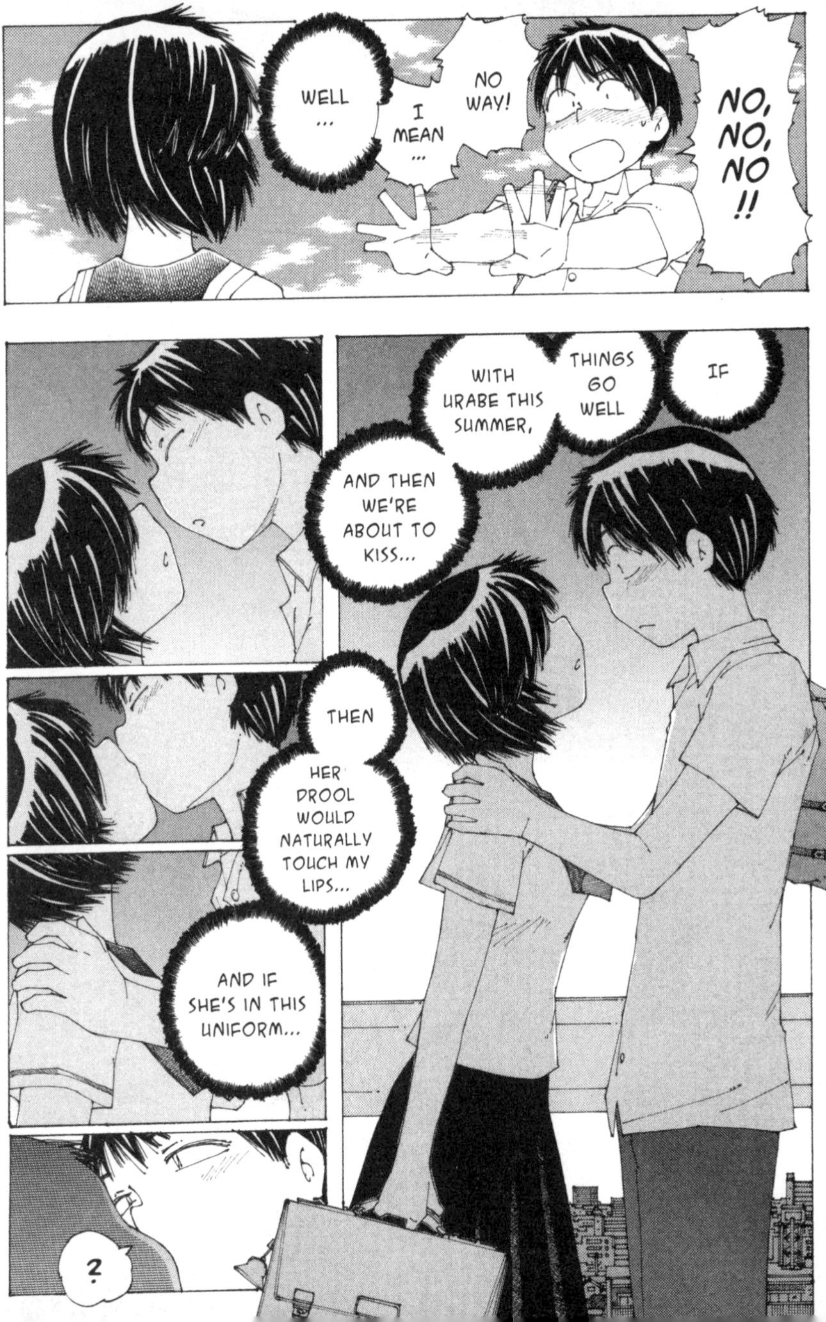
NO, NO, NO!!
NO WAY!
I MEAN...
WELL...
IF
THINGS GO WELL
WITH URABE THIS SUMMER,
AND THEN WE'RE ABOUT TO KISS...
THEN
HER DROOL WOULD NATURALLY TOUCH MY LIPS...
AND IF SHE'S IN THIS UNIFORM...
?

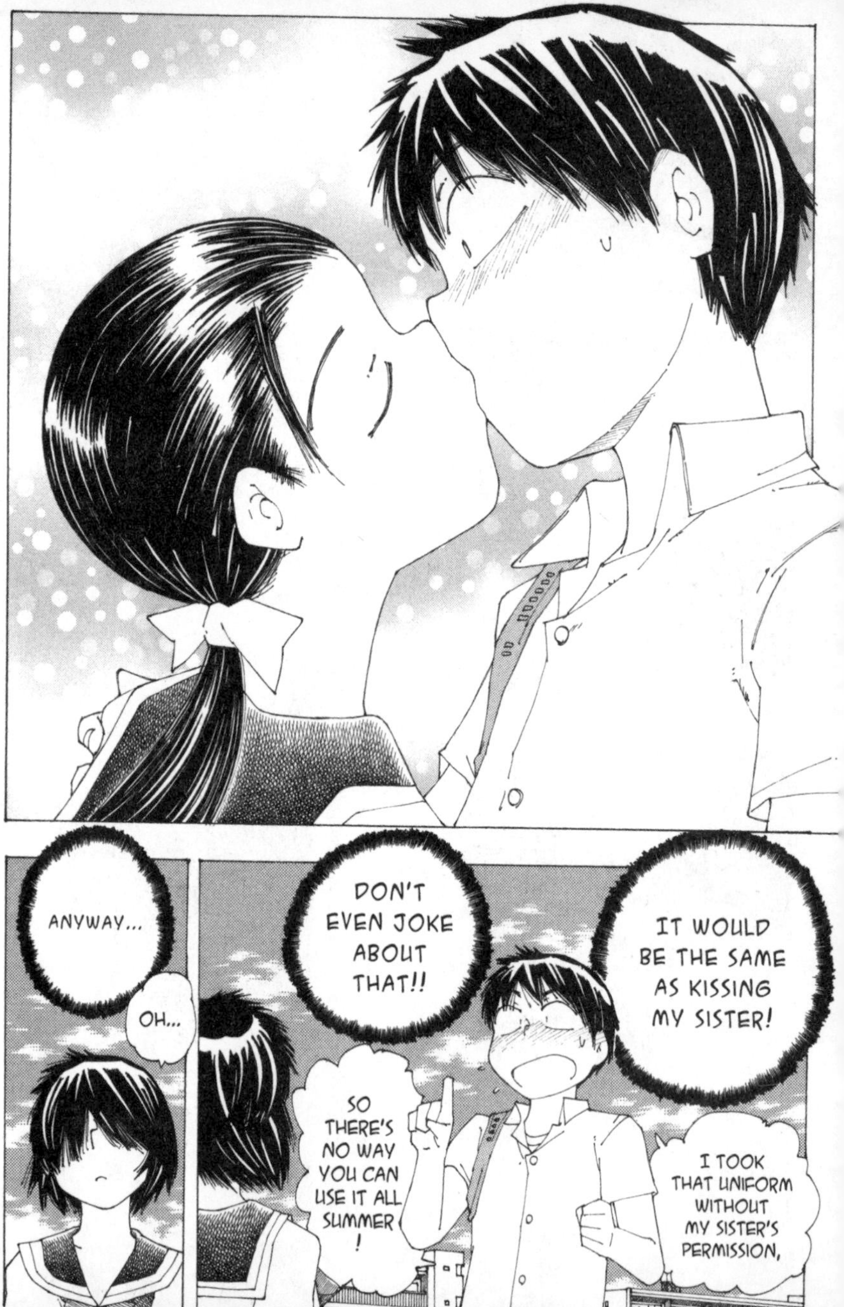
IT WOULD BE THE SAME AS KISSING MY SISTER!
DON'T EVEN JOKE ABOUT THAT!!
I TOOK THAT UNIFORM WITHOUT MY SISTER'S PERMISSION,
SO THERE'S NO WAY YOU CAN USE IT ALL SUMMER!
ANYWAY...
OH...

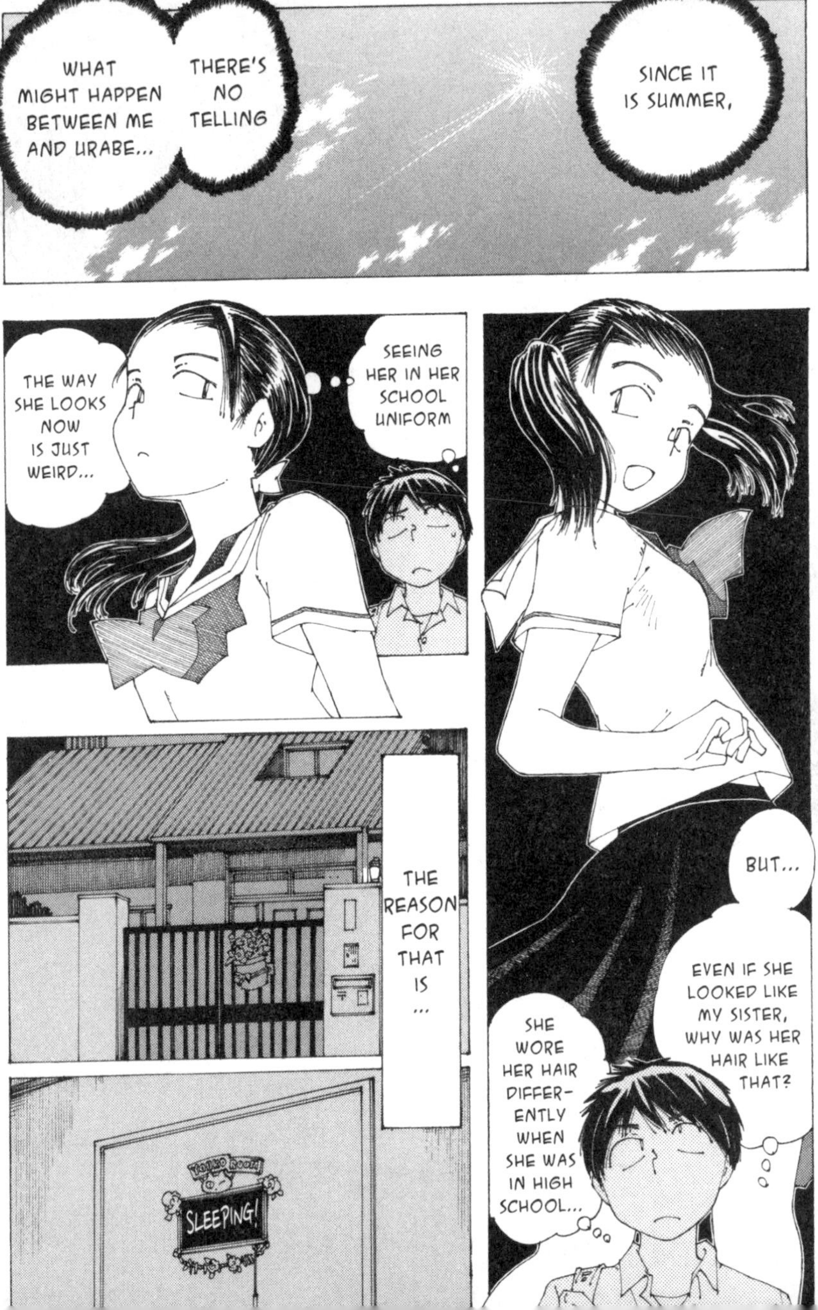
SINCE IT IS SUMMER,
THERE'S NO TELLING
WHAT MIGHT HAPPEN BETWEEN ME AND URABE...
BUT...
EVEN IF SHE LOOKED LIKE MY SISTER, WHY WAS HER HAIR LIKE THAT?
SHE WORE HER HAIR DIFFERENTLY WHEN SHE WAS IN HIGH SCHOOL...
SEEING HER IN HER SCHOOL UNIFORM
THE WAY SHE LOOKS NOW IS JUST WEIRD...
THE REASON FOR THAT IS ...
SLEEPING!

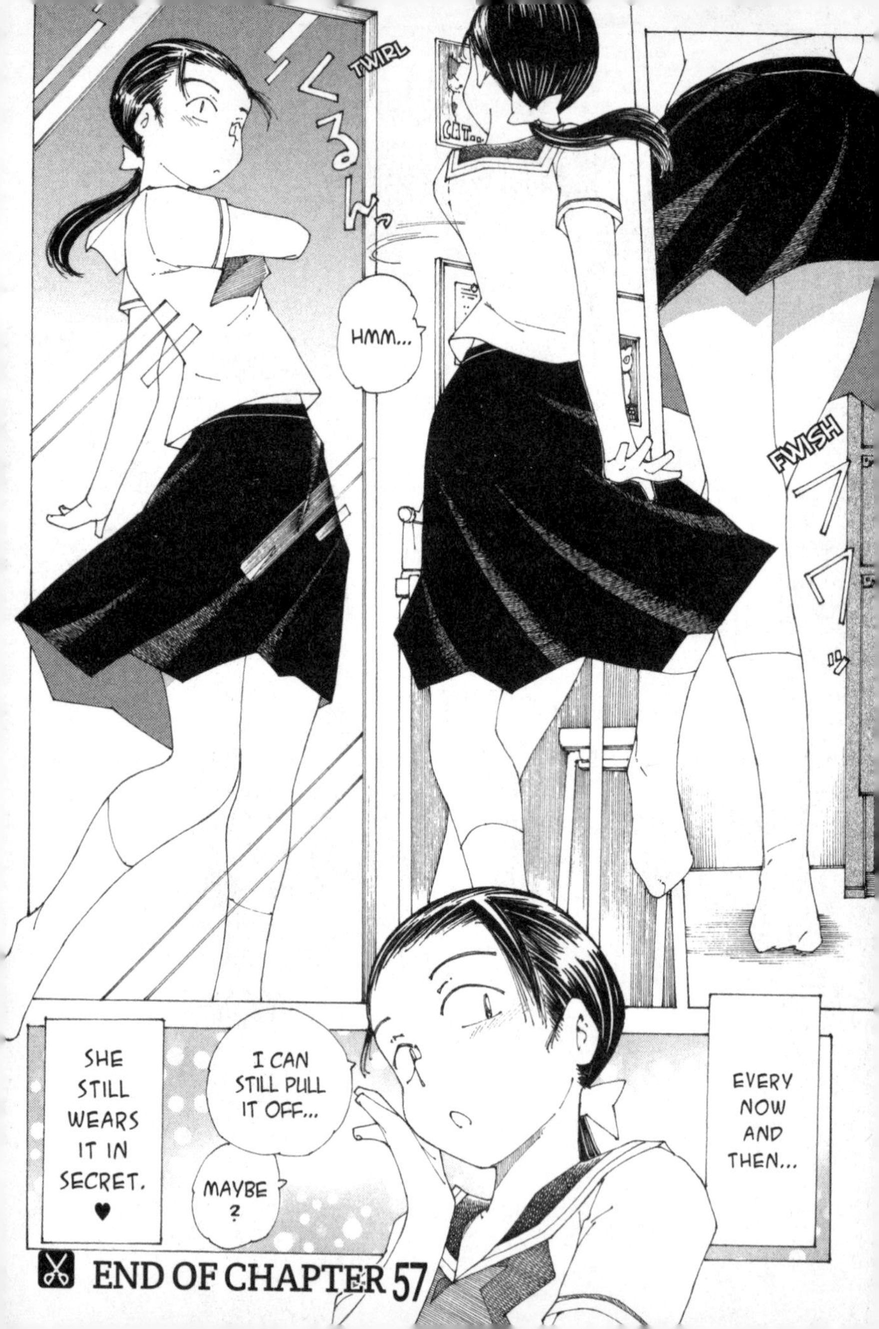
FWISH
CAT...
TWIRL
HMM...
EVERY NOW AND THEN...
I CAN STILL PULL IT OFF...
MAYBE?
SHE STILL WEARS IT IN SECRET. ♥

END OF CHAPTER 57

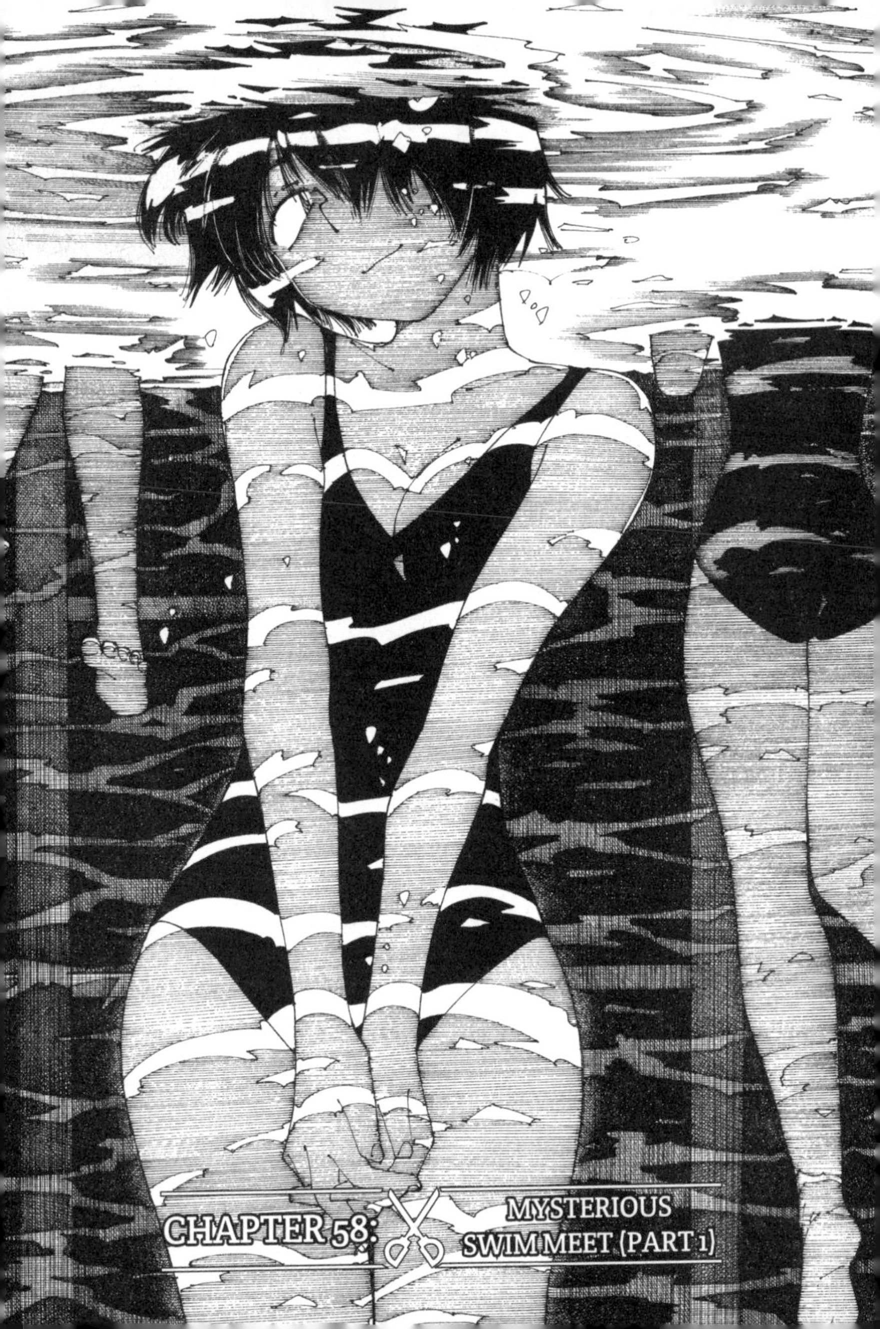
CHAPTER 58:
MYSTERIOUS SWIM MEET (PART 1)

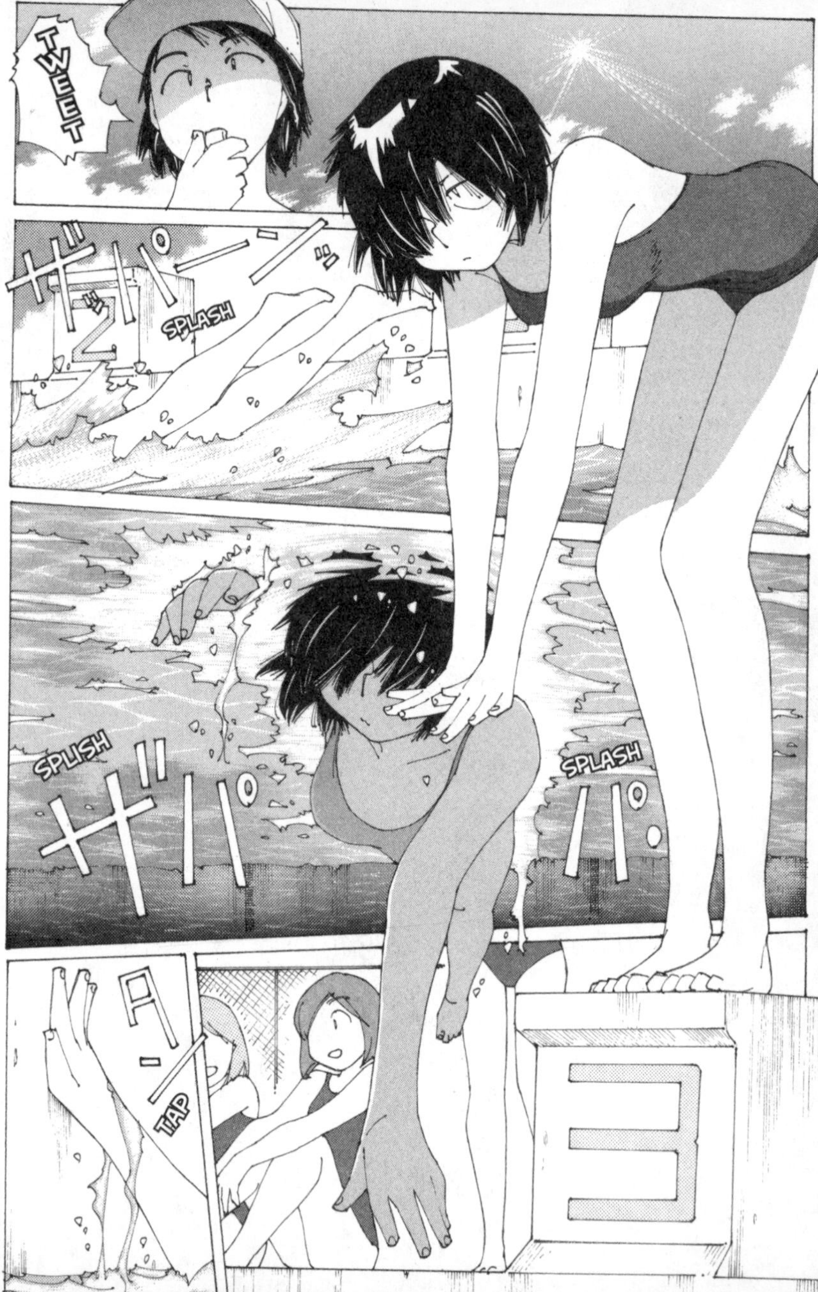
TWEET
SPLASH
SPLASH
SPLISH
TAP

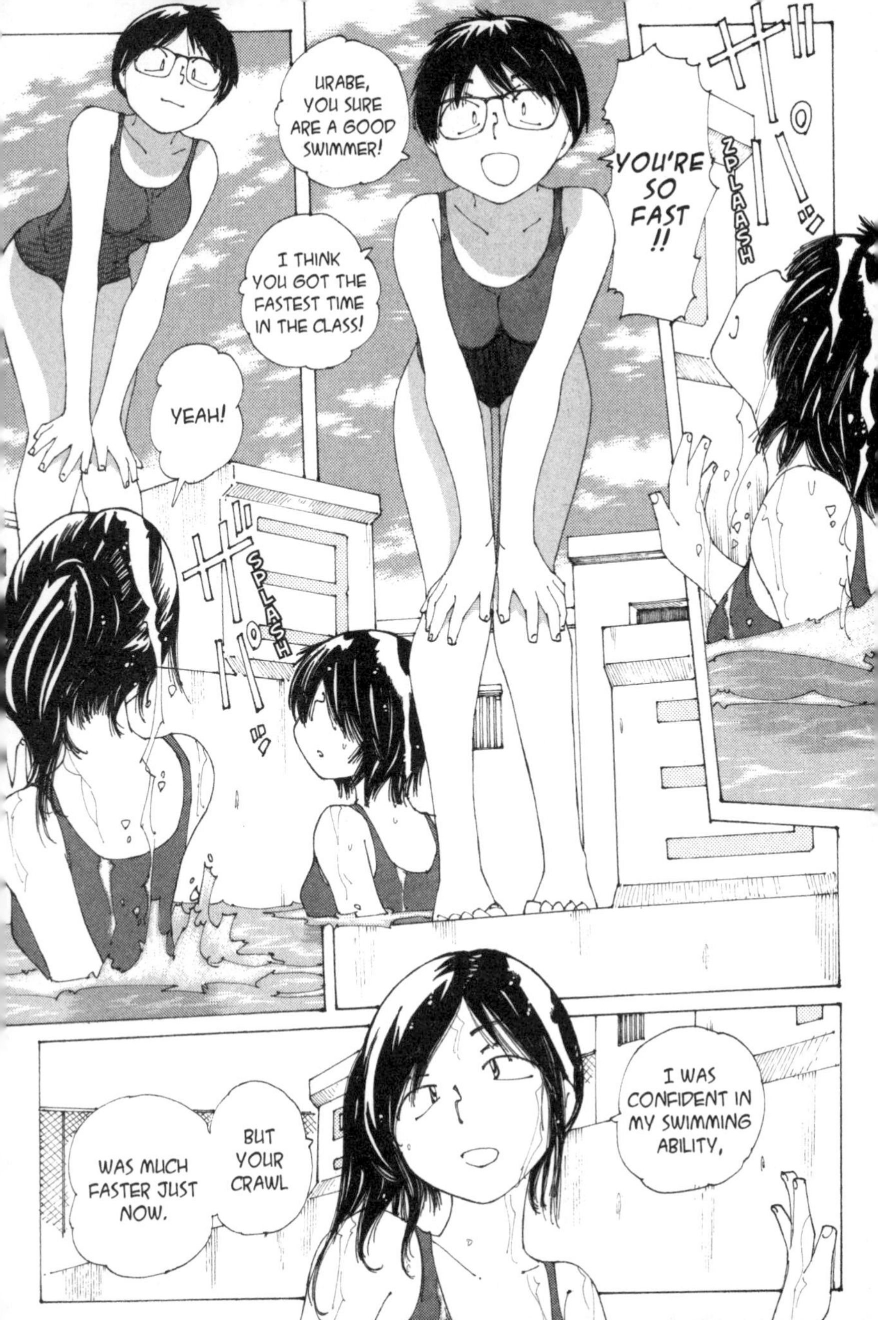
ZPLAASH
YOU'RE SO FAST!!
URABE, YOU SURE ARE A GOOD SWIMMER!
I THINK YOU GOT THE FASTEST TIME IN THE CLASS!
YEAH!
SPLASH
I WAS CONFIDENT IN MY SWIMMING ABILITY,
BUT YOUR CRAWL
WAS MUCH FASTER JUST NOW.

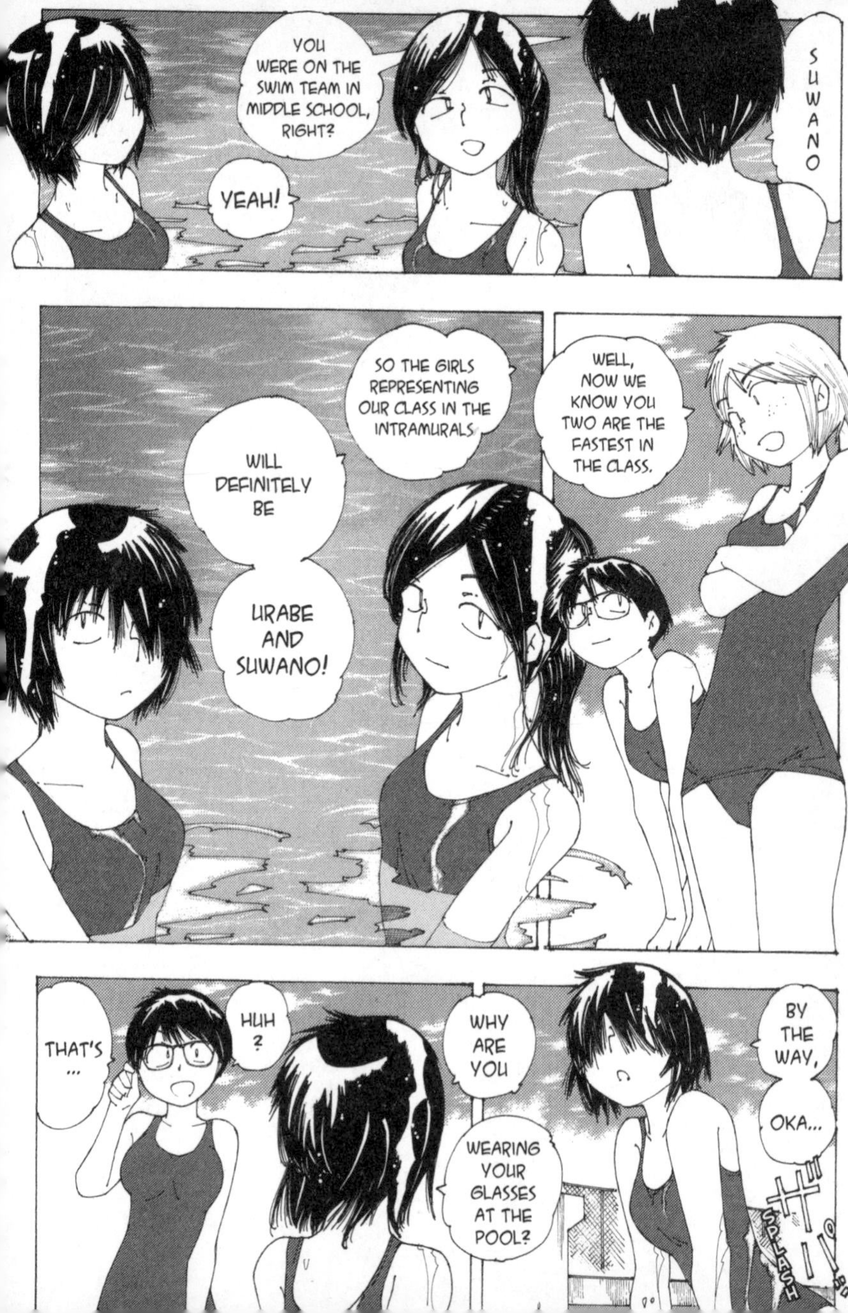
SUWANO
YOU WERE ON THE SWIM TEAM IN MIDDLE SCHOOL, RIGHT?
YEAH!
WELL, NOW WE KNOW YOU TWO ARE THE FASTEST IN THE CLASS.
SO THE GIRLS REPRESENTING OUR CLASS IN THE INTRAMURALS
WILL DEFINITELY BE
URABE AND SUWANO!
BY THE WAY,
OKA...
SPLASH
WHY ARE YOU
WEARING YOUR GLASSES AT THE POOL?
HUH?
THAT'S ...

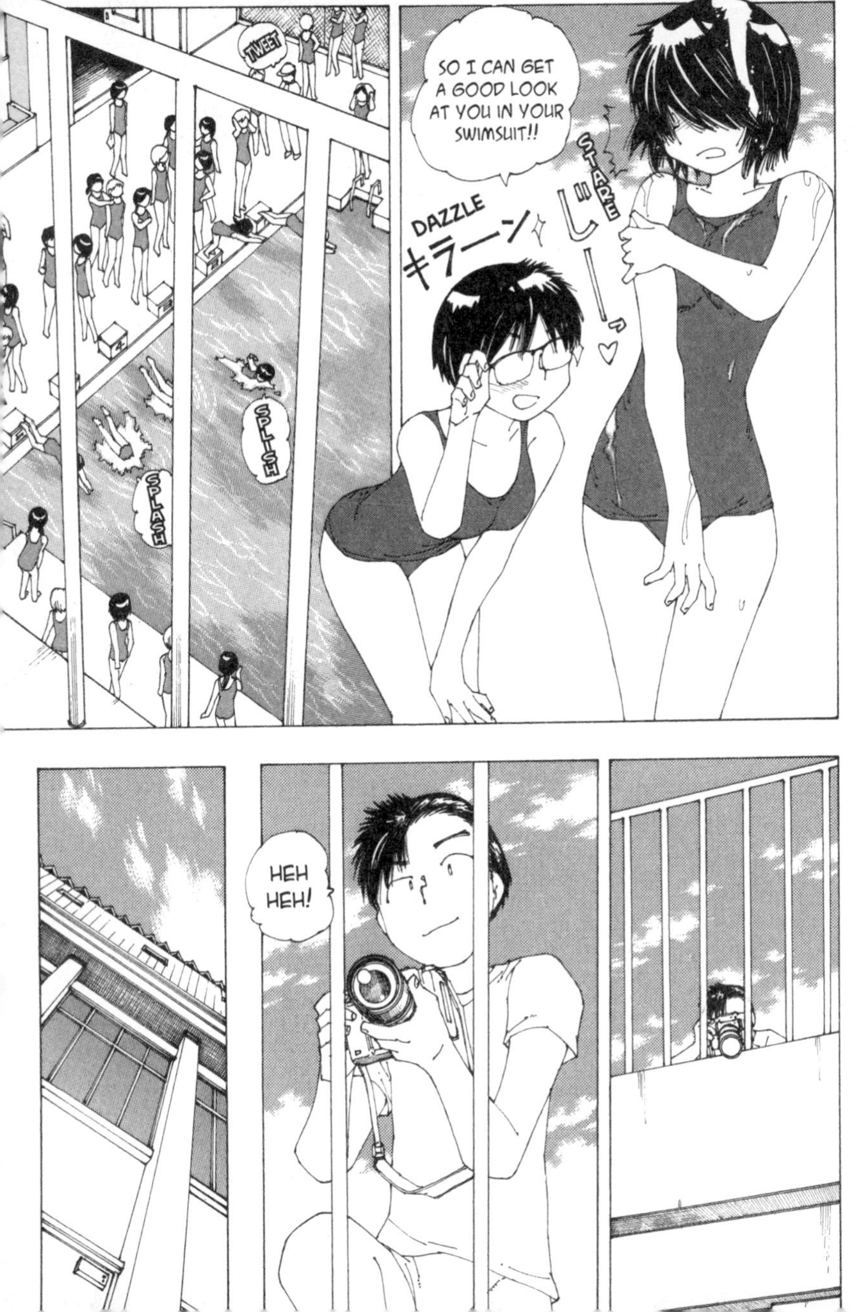
SO I CAN GET A GOOD LOOK AT YOU IN YOUR SWIMSUIT!!
STARE
じー
DAZZLE
キラーン
TWEET
SPLISH
SPLASH
HEH HEH!

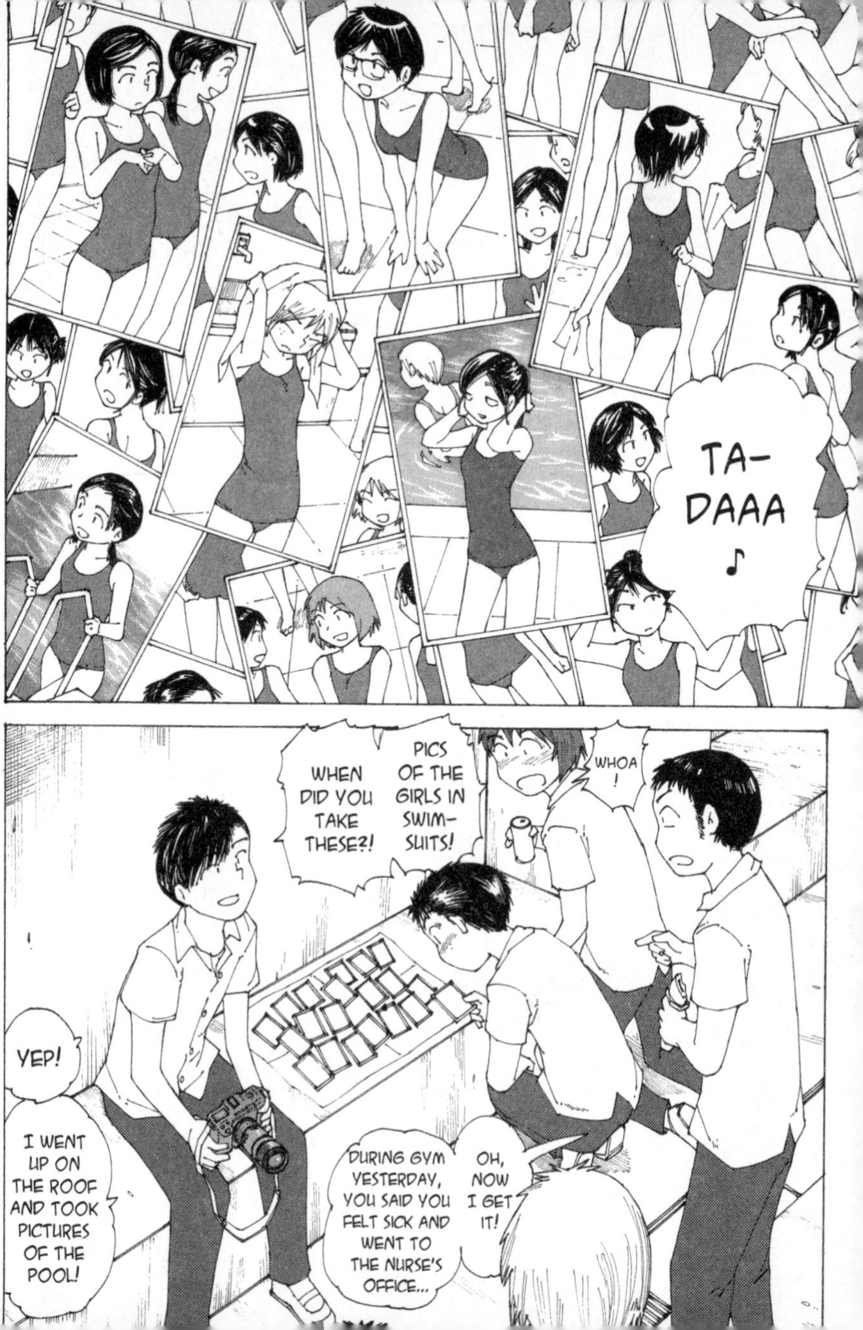
TA-DAAA ♪
WHOA!
PICS OF THE GIRLS IN SWIM-SUITS!
WHEN DID YOU TAKE THESE?!
OH, NOW I GET IT!
DURING GYM YESTERDAY, YOU SAID YOU FELT SICK AND WENT TO THE NURSE'S OFFICE...
YEP!
I WENT UP ON THE ROOF AND TOOK PICTURES OF THE POOL!

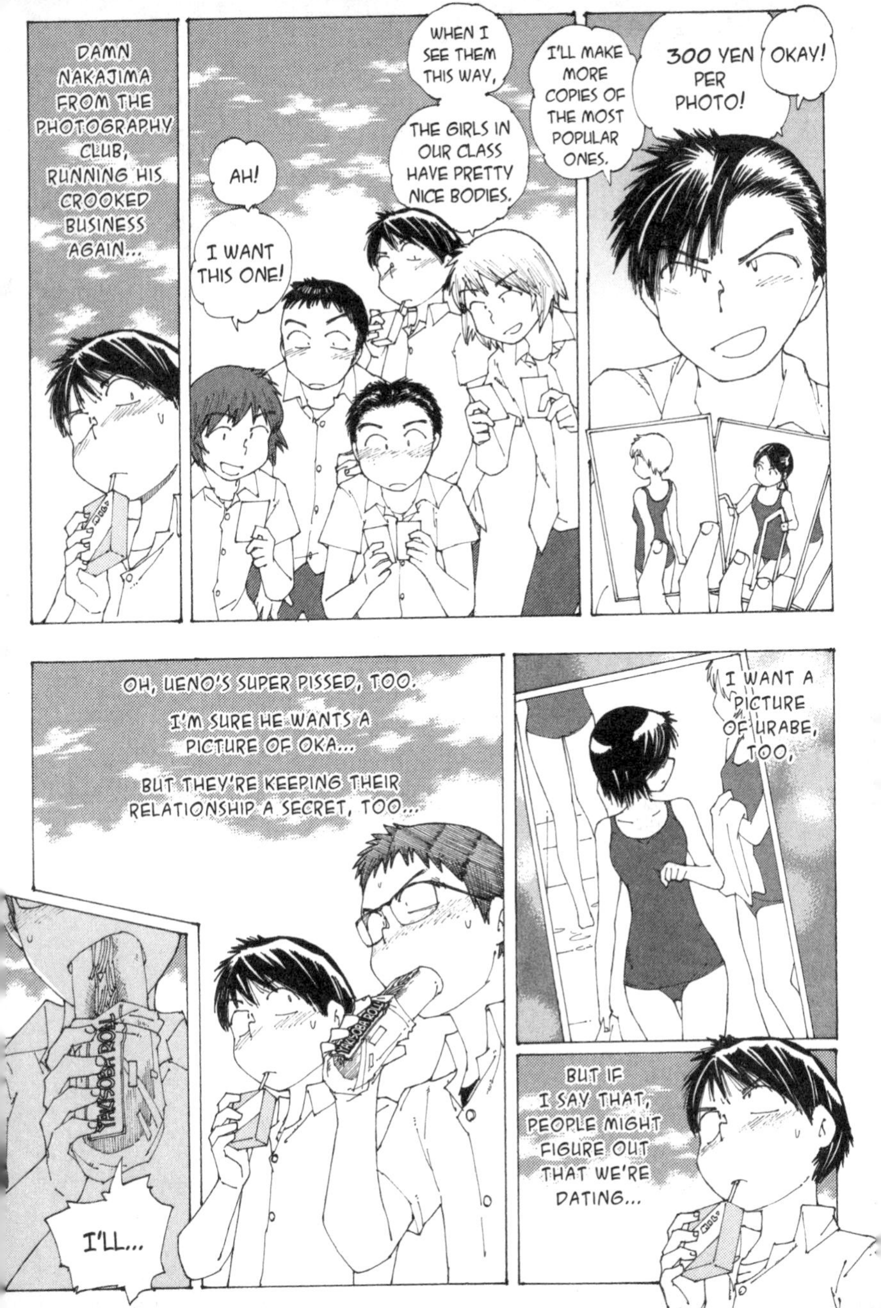
OKAY!
300 YEN PER PHOTO!
I'LL MAKE MORE COPIES OF THE MOST POPULAR ONES.
WHEN I SEE THEM THIS WAY,
THE GIRLS IN OUR CLASS HAVE PRETTY NICE BODIES.
AH!
I WANT THIS ONE!
DAMN NAKAJIMA FROM THE PHOTOGRAPHY CLUB, RUNNING HIS CROOKED BUSINESS AGAIN...
I WANT A PICTURE OF URABE, TOO,
BUT IF I SAY THAT, PEOPLE MIGHT FIGURE OUT THAT WE'RE DATING...
OH, UENO'S SUPER PISSED, TOO.
I'M SURE HE WANTS A PICTURE OF OKA...
BUT THEY'RE KEEPING THEIR RELATIONSHIP A SECRET, TOO...
YAKISOBA ROLL
I'LL...

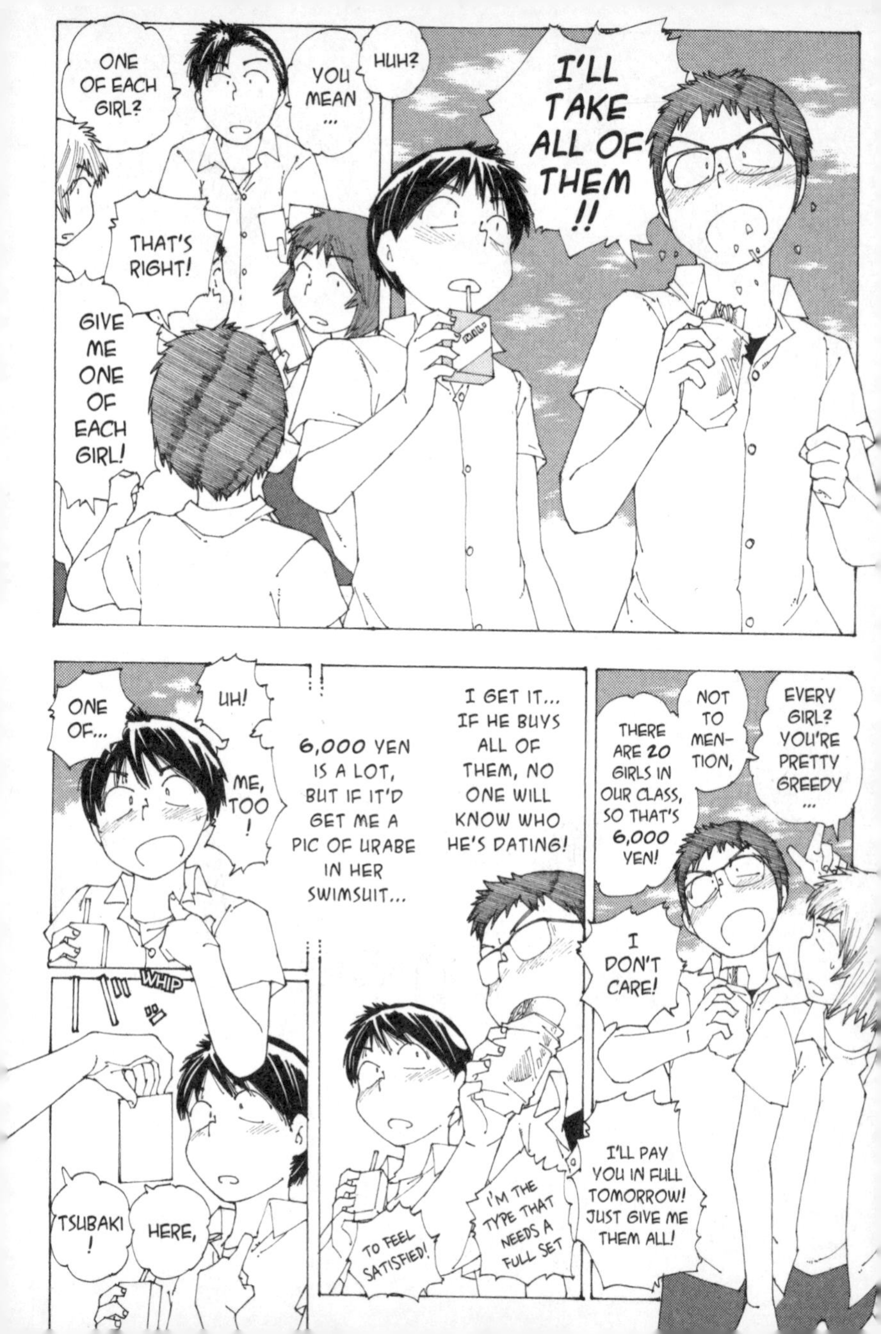
I'LL TAKE ALL OF THEM!!
HUH?
YOU MEAN ...
ONE OF EACH GIRL?
THAT'S RIGHT!
GIVE ME ONE OF EACH GIRL!
EVERY GIRL? YOU'RE PRETTY GREEDY ...
NOT TO MENTION,
THERE ARE 20 GIRLS IN OUR CLASS, SO THAT'S 6,000 YEN!
I DON'T CARE!
I'LL PAY YOU IN FULL TOMORROW! JUST GIVE ME THEM ALL!
I GET IT... IF HE BUYS ALL OF THEM, NO ONE WILL KNOW WHO HE'S DATING!
6,000 YEN IS A LOT, BUT IF IT'D GET ME A PIC OF URABE IN HER SWIMSUIT...
I'M THE TYPE THAT NEEDS A FULL SET
TO FEEL SATISFIED!
UH!
ME, TOO!
ONE OF...
WHIP
HERE,
TSUBAKI!

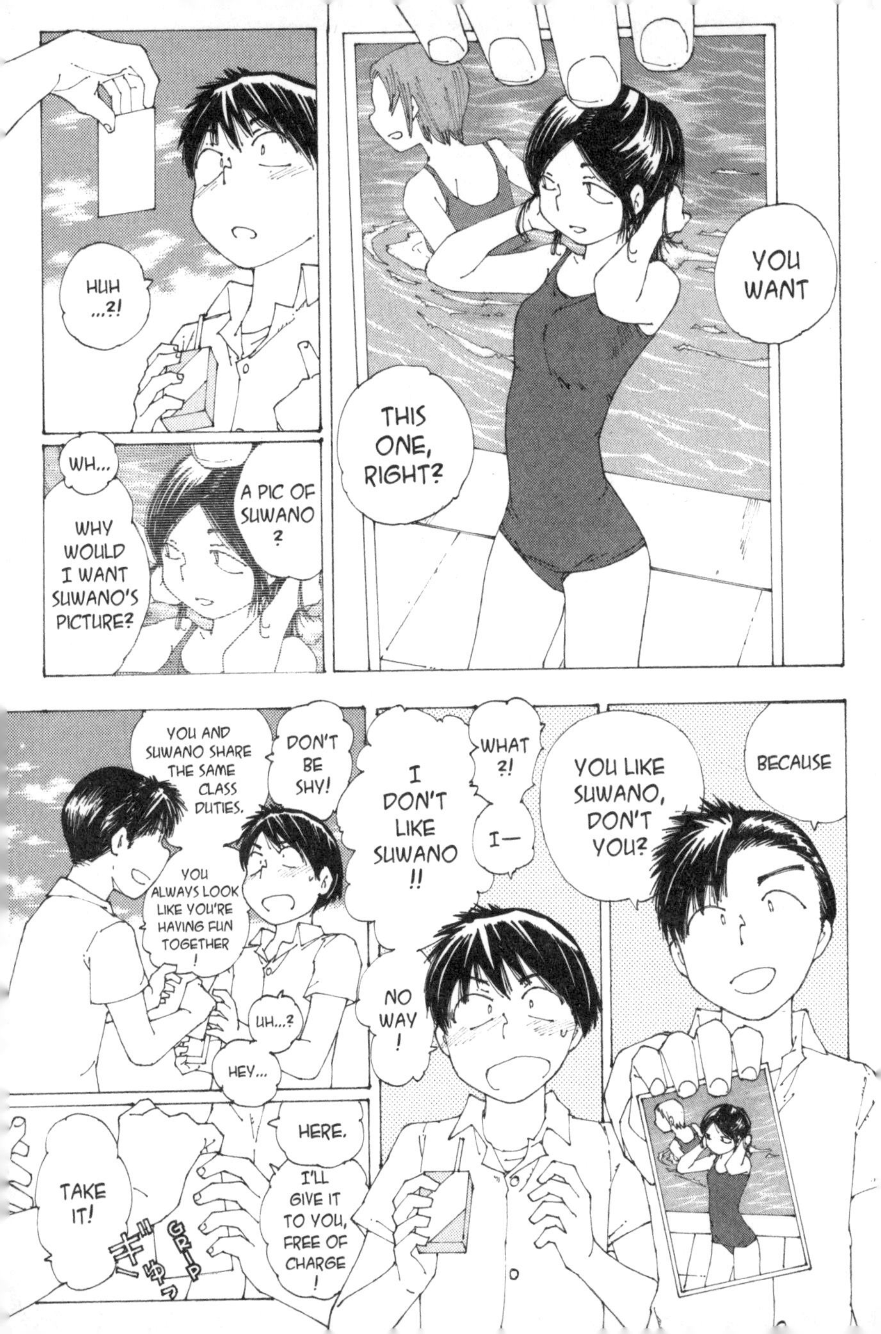
YOU WANT
THIS ONE, RIGHT?
HUH ...?!
A PIC OF SUWANO ?
WH...
WHY WOULD I WANT SUWANO'S PICTURE?
BECAUSE
YOU LIKE SUWANO, DON'T YOU?
WHAT ?!
I—
I DON'T LIKE SUWANO !!
NO WAY !
DON'T BE SHY!
YOU AND SUWANO SHARE THE SAME CLASS DUTIES.
YOU ALWAYS LOOK LIKE YOU'RE HAVING FUN TOGETHER !
UH...?
HEY...
HERE.
I'LL GIVE IT TO YOU, FREE OF CHARGE !
TAKE IT!
GRIP

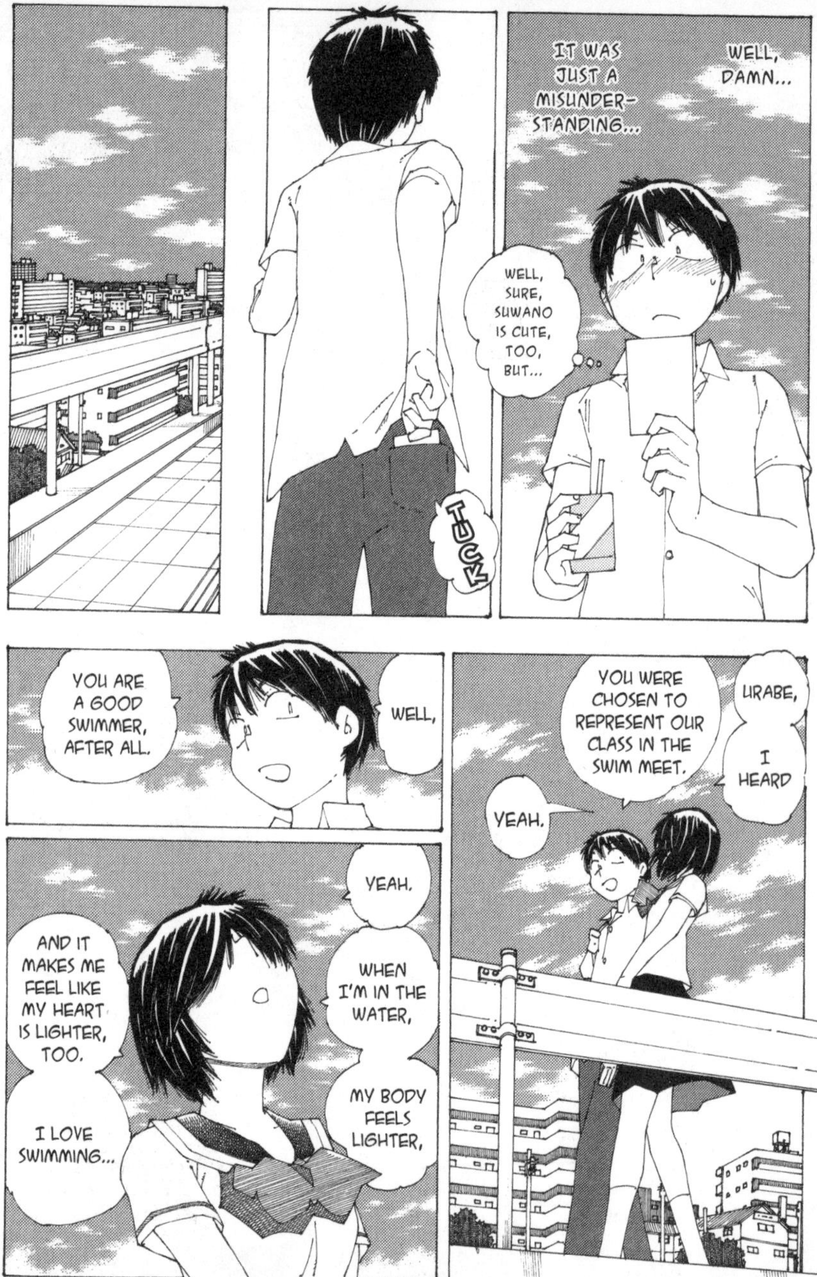
WELL, DAMN...
IT WAS JUST A MISUNDER-STANDING...
WELL, SURE, SUWANO IS CUTE, TOO, BUT...
TUCK
URABE,
I HEARD
YOU WERE CHOSEN TO REPRESENT OUR CLASS IN THE SWIM MEET.
YEAH.
WELL,
YOU ARE A GOOD SWIMMER, AFTER ALL.
YEAH.
WHEN I'M IN THE WATER,
MY BODY FEELS LIGHTER,
AND IT MAKES ME FEEL LIKE MY HEART IS LIGHTER, TOO.
I LOVE SWIMMING...

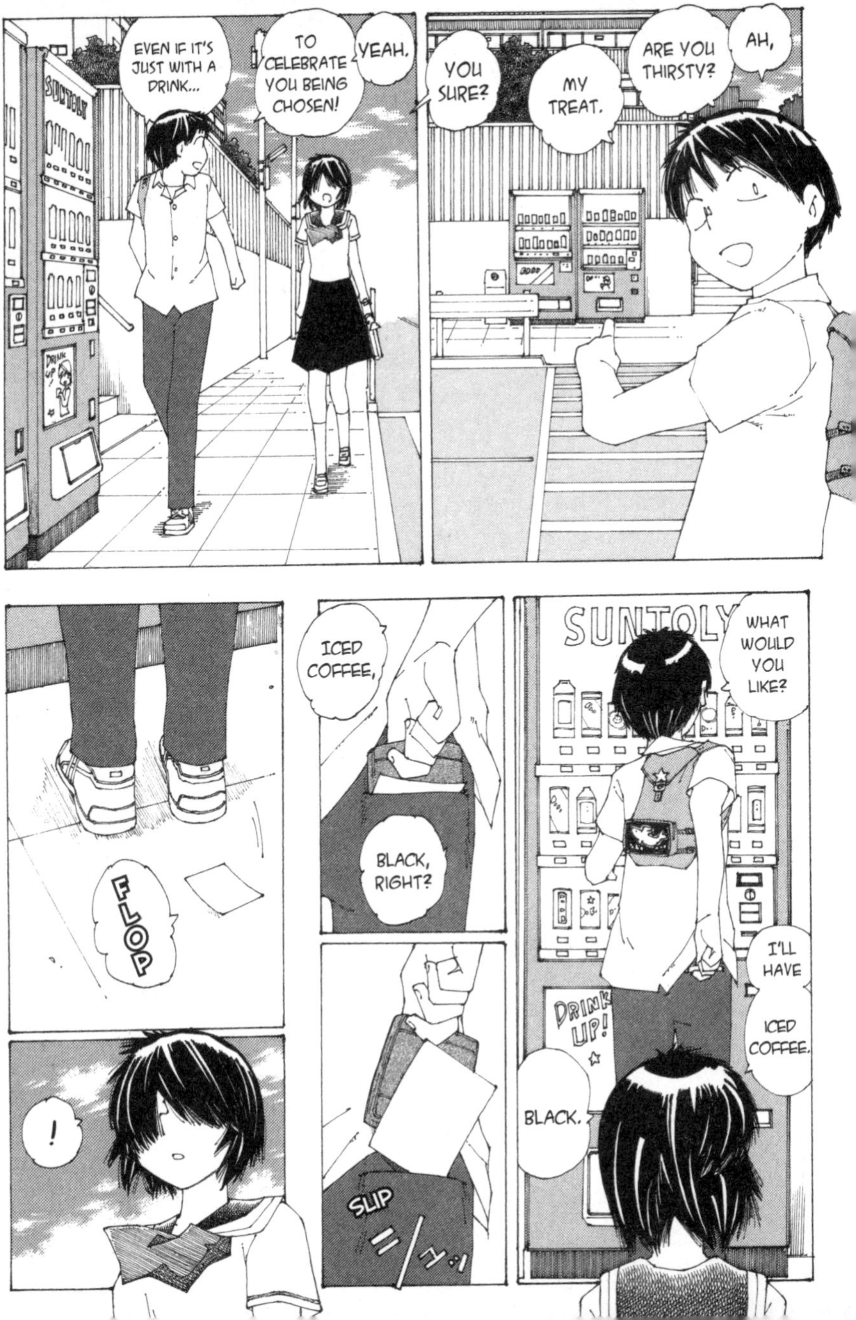
AH,
ARE YOU THIRSTY?
MY TREAT.
YOU SURE?
YEAH.
TO CELEBRATE YOU BEING CHOSEN!
EVEN IF IT'S JUST WITH A DRINK...
SUNTOLY
WHAT WOULD YOU LIKE?
I'LL HAVE
ICED COFFEE.
BLACK.
DRINK UP!
ICED COFFEE,
BLACK, RIGHT?
SLIP
FLOP
!

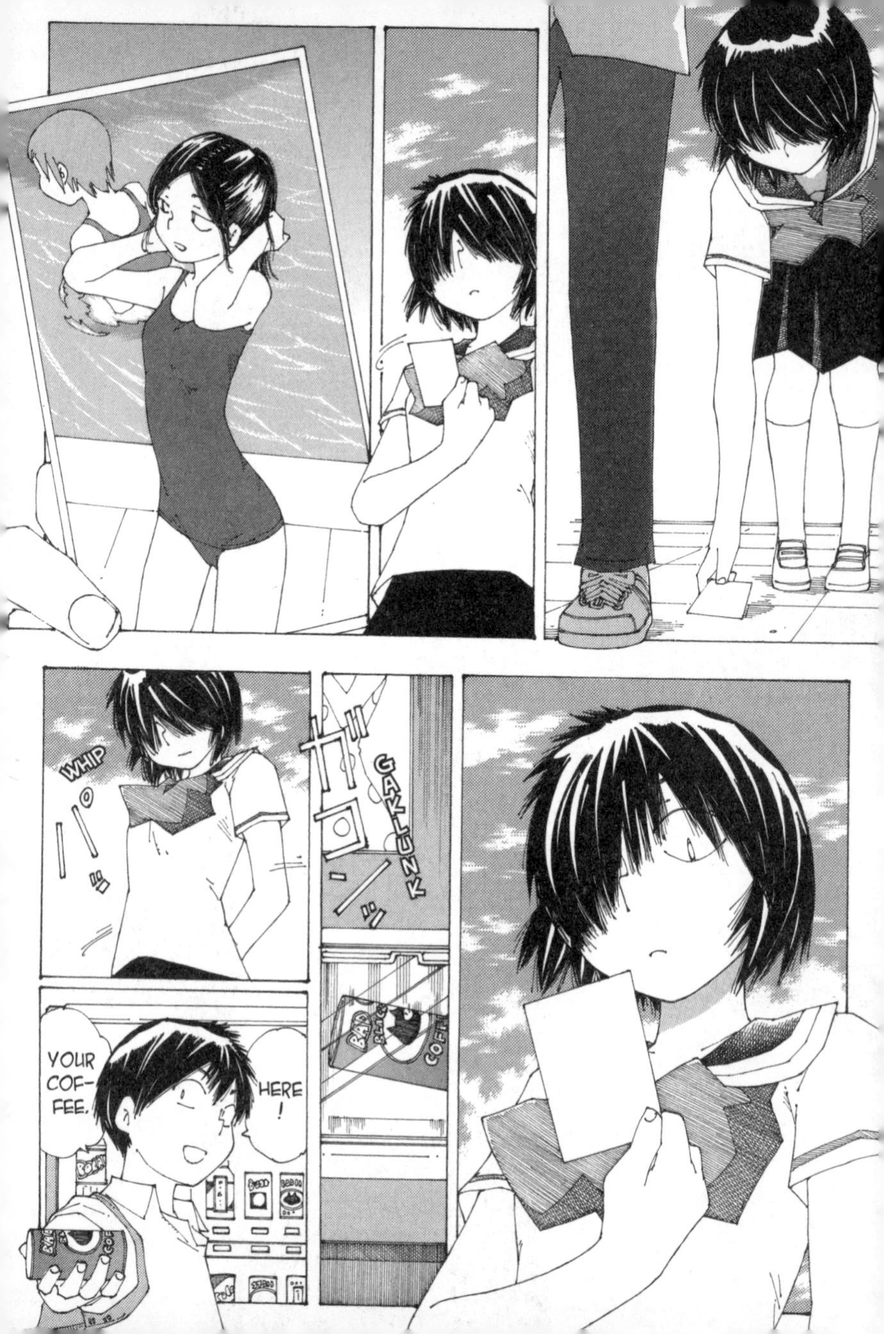
GAKLUNK
WHIP
HERE !
YOUR COF-FEE.

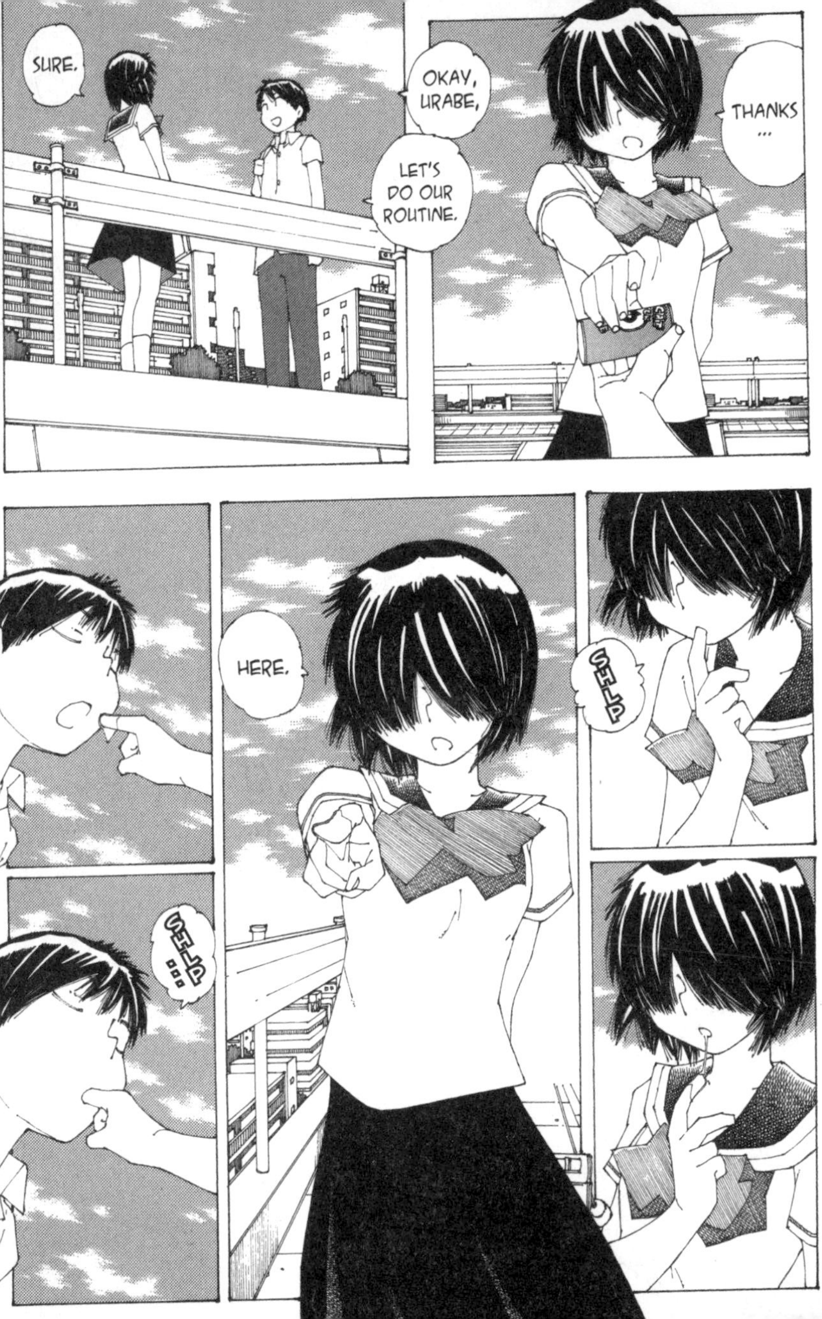
THANKS ...
OKAY, URABE,
LET'S DO OUR ROUTINE.
SURE.
SHLP
HERE.
SHLP ...

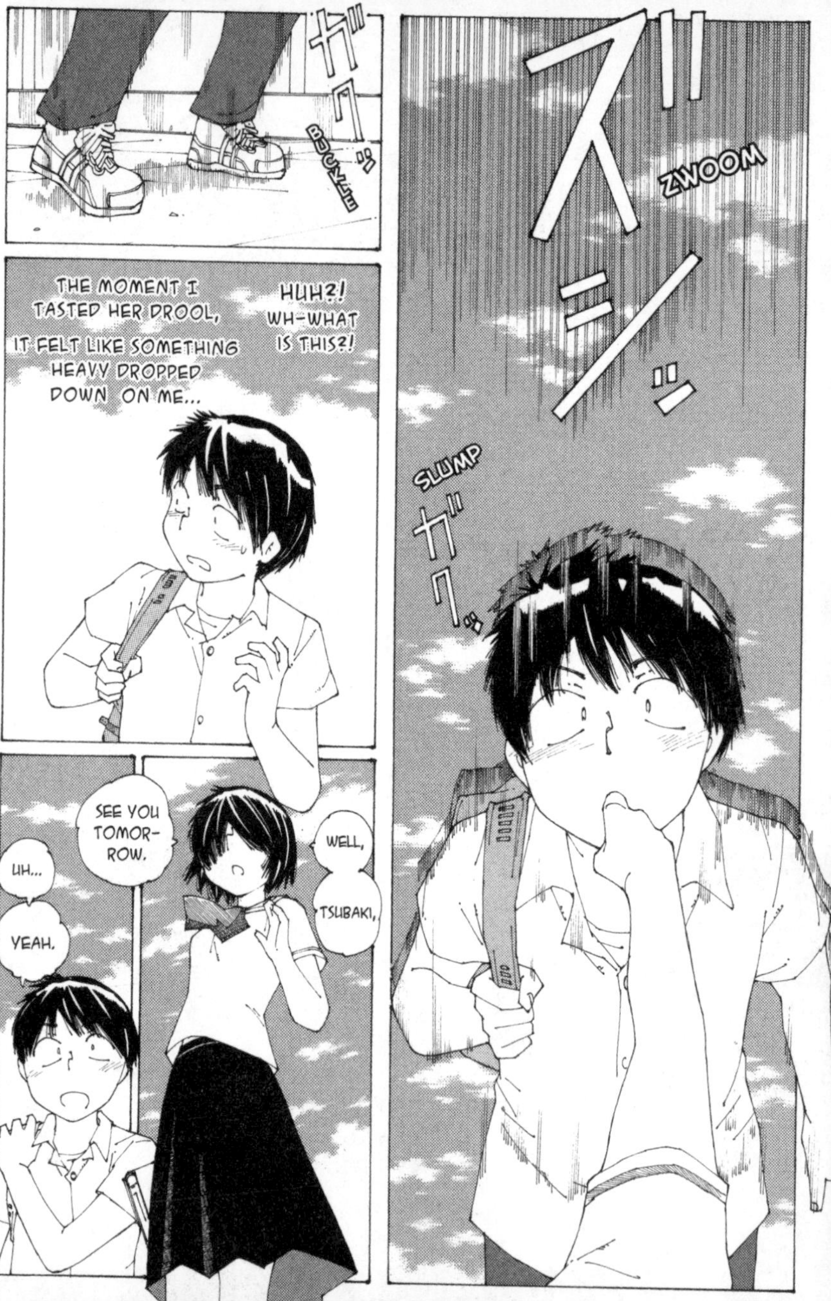
ZWOOM
SLUMP
BUCKLE
THE MOMENT I TASTED HER DROOL, IT FELT LIKE SOMETHING HEAVY DROPPED DOWN ON ME...
HUH?! WH-WHAT IS THIS?!
WELL,
TSUBAKI,
SEE YOU TOMORROW.
UH...
YEAH.

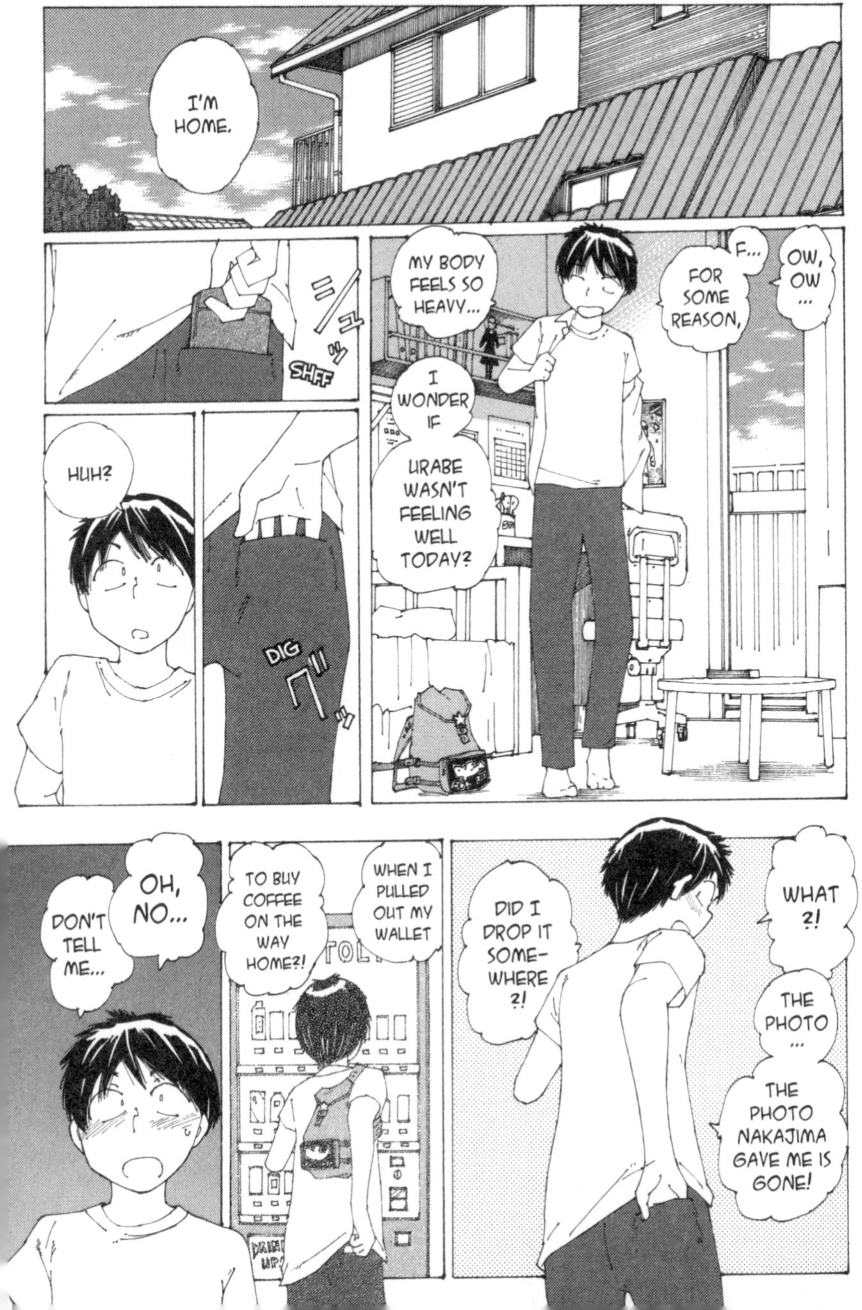
I'M HOME.
OW, OW ...
F... FOR SOME REASON,
MY BODY FEELS SO HEAVY...
I WONDER IF URABE WASN'T FEELING WELL TODAY?
SHFF
DIG
HUH?
WHAT?!
THE PHOTO ...
THE PHOTO NAKAJIMA GAVE ME IS GONE!
DID I DROP IT SOME-WHERE?!
WHEN I PULLED OUT MY WALLET
TO BUY COFFEE ON THE WAY HOME?!
OH, NO...
DON'T TELL ME...

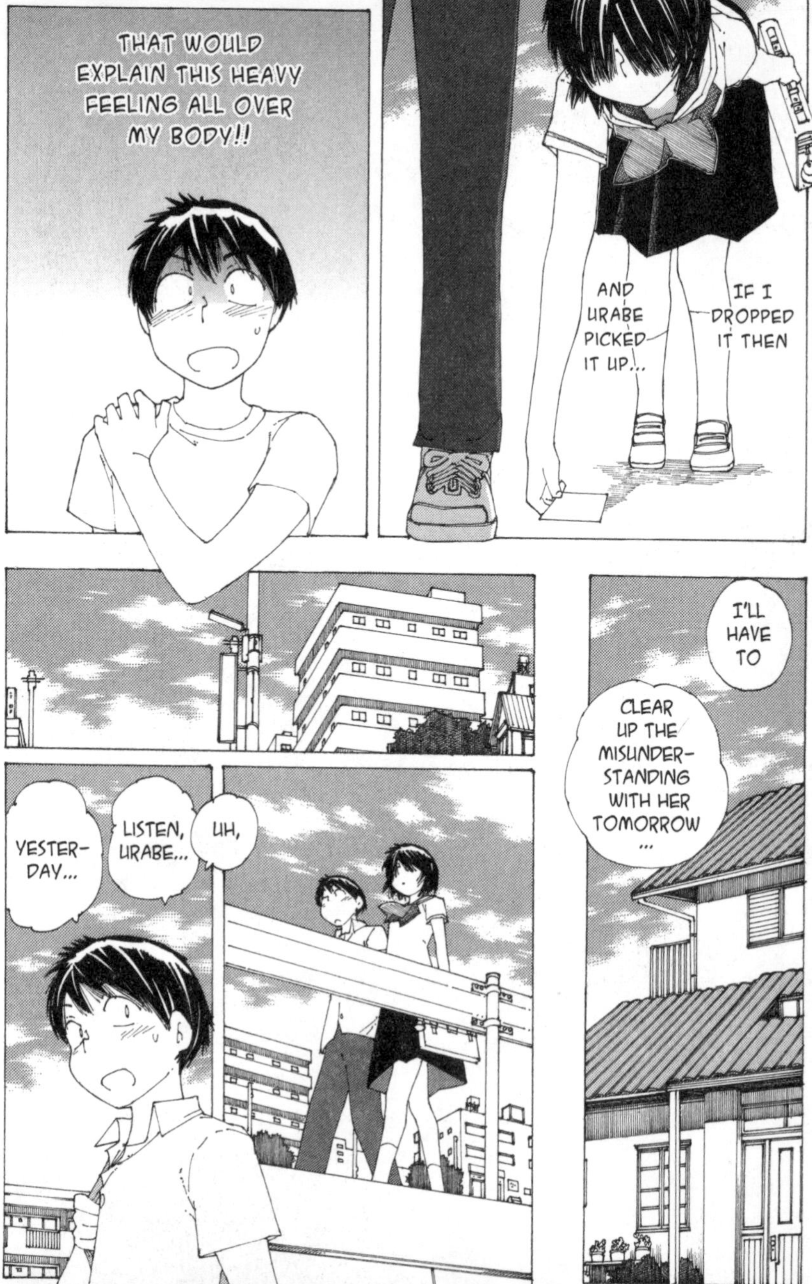
IF I DROPPED IT THEN
AND URABE PICKED IT UP...
THAT WOULD EXPLAIN THIS HEAVY FEELING ALL OVER MY BODY!!
I'LL HAVE TO
CLEAR UP THE MISUNDER-STANDING WITH HER TOMORROW ...
UH,
LISTEN, URABE...
YESTER-DAY...

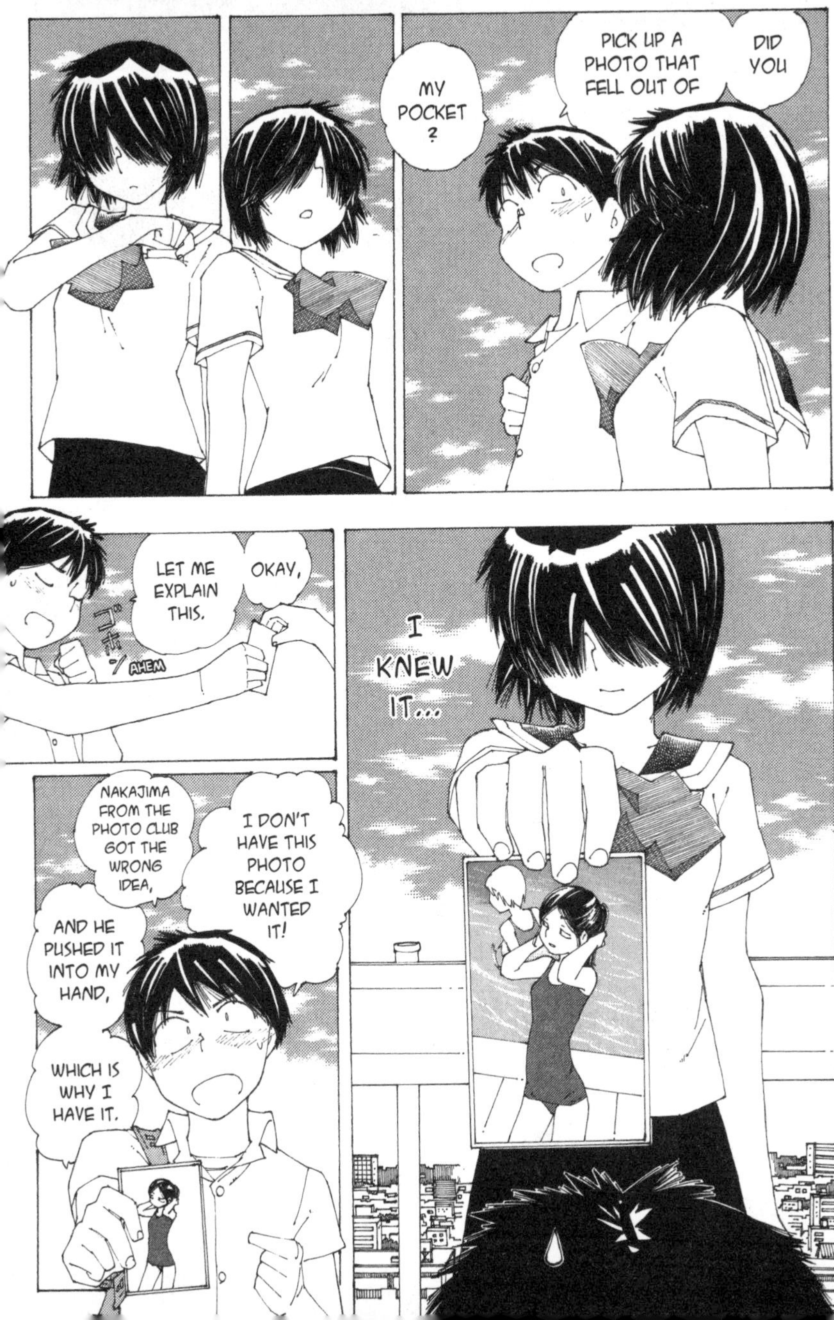
DID YOU
PICK UP A PHOTO THAT FELL OUT OF
MY POCKET ?
I KNEW IT...
OKAY,
LET ME EXPLAIN THIS.
ゴホン
AHEM
I DON'T HAVE THIS PHOTO BECAUSE I WANTED IT!
NAKAJIMA FROM THE PHOTO CLUB GOT THE WRONG IDEA,
AND HE PUSHED IT INTO MY HAND,
WHICH IS WHY I HAVE IT.

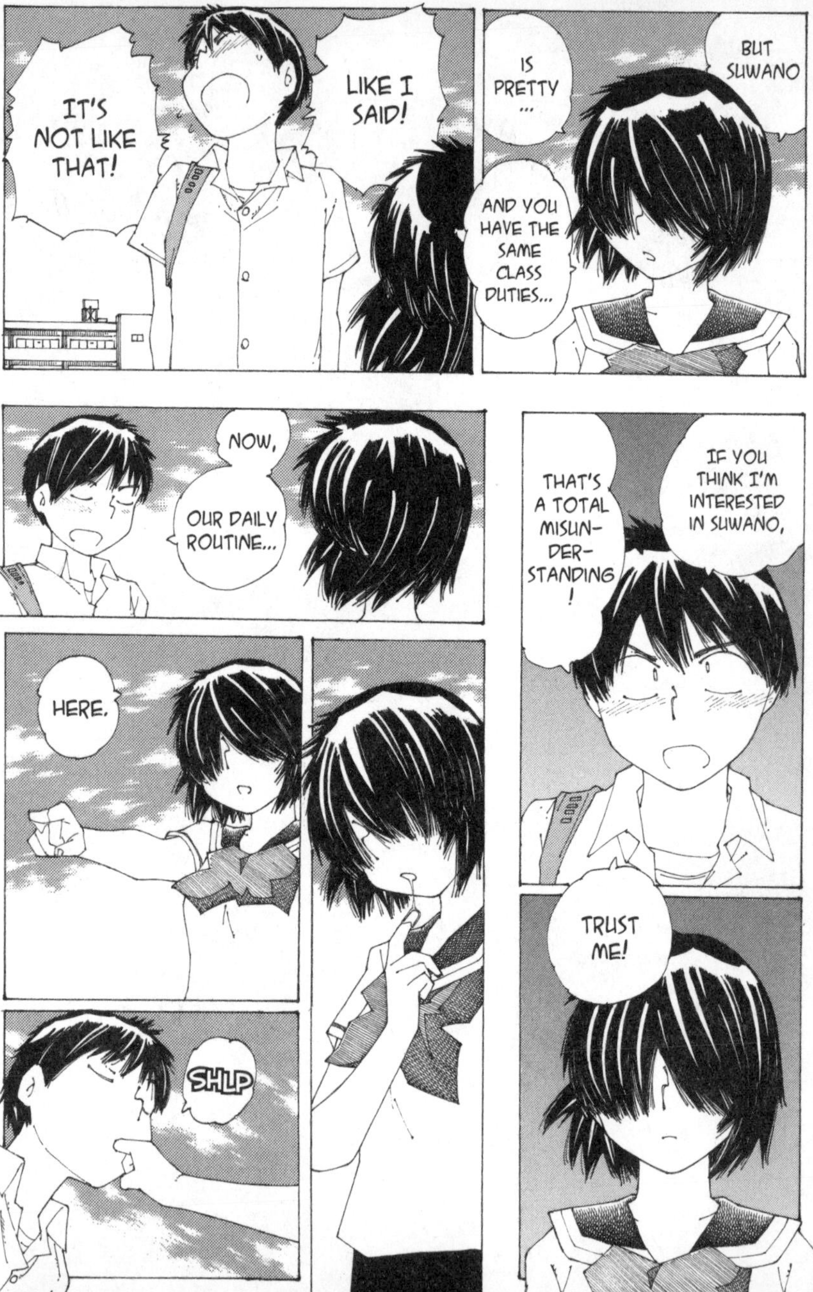
BUT SUWANO
IS PRETTY ...
AND YOU HAVE THE SAME CLASS DUTIES...
LIKE I SAID!
IT'S NOT LIKE THAT!
IF YOU THINK I'M INTERESTED IN SUWANO,
THAT'S A TOTAL MISUNDER-STANDING!
TRUST ME!
NOW,
OUR DAILY ROUTINE...
HERE.
SHLP

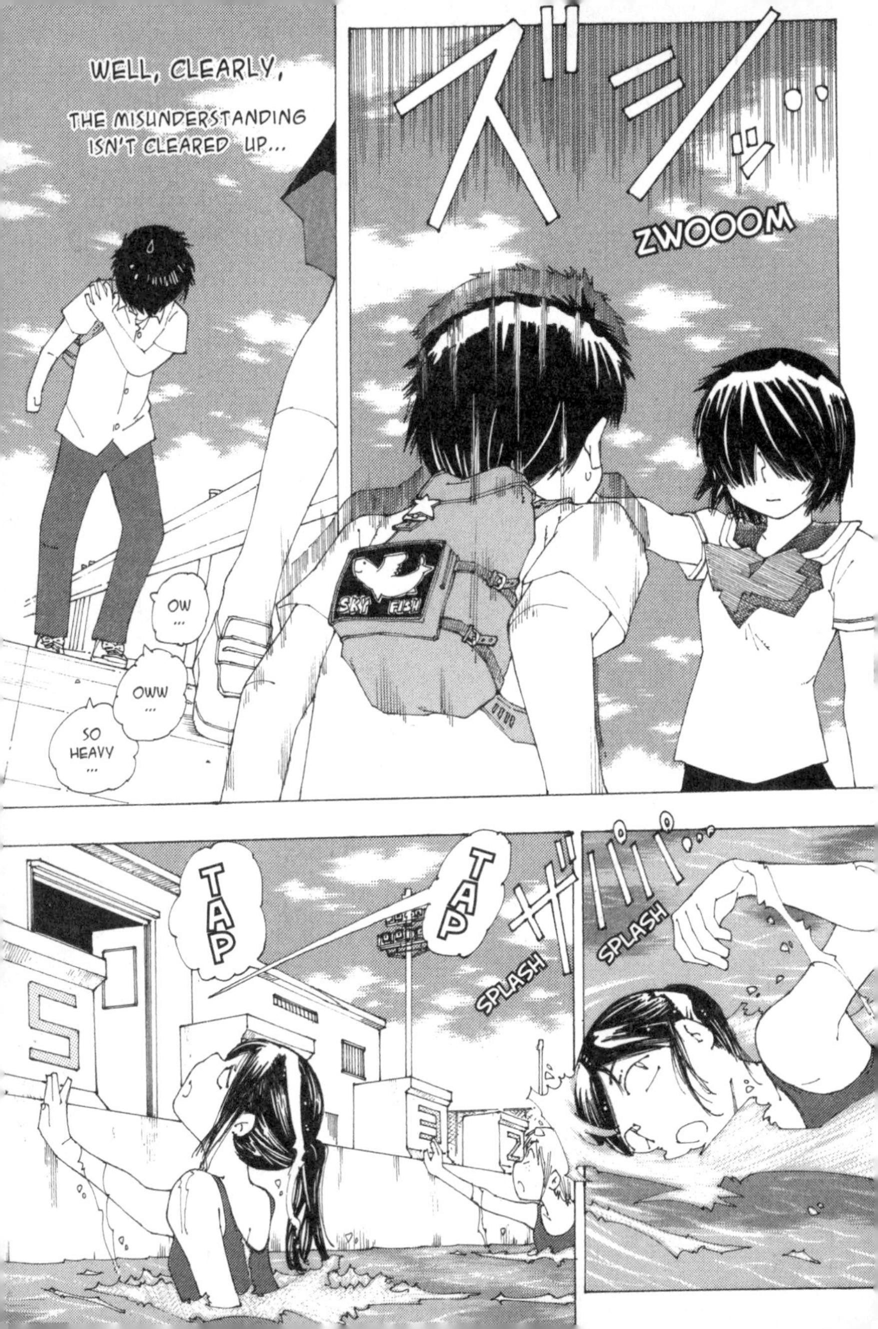
ZWOOOM
SKY FISH
WELL, CLEARLY,
THE MISUNDERSTANDING ISN'T CLEARED UP...
OW ...
OWW ...
SO HEAVY ...
SPLASH
TAP
TAP
SPLASH

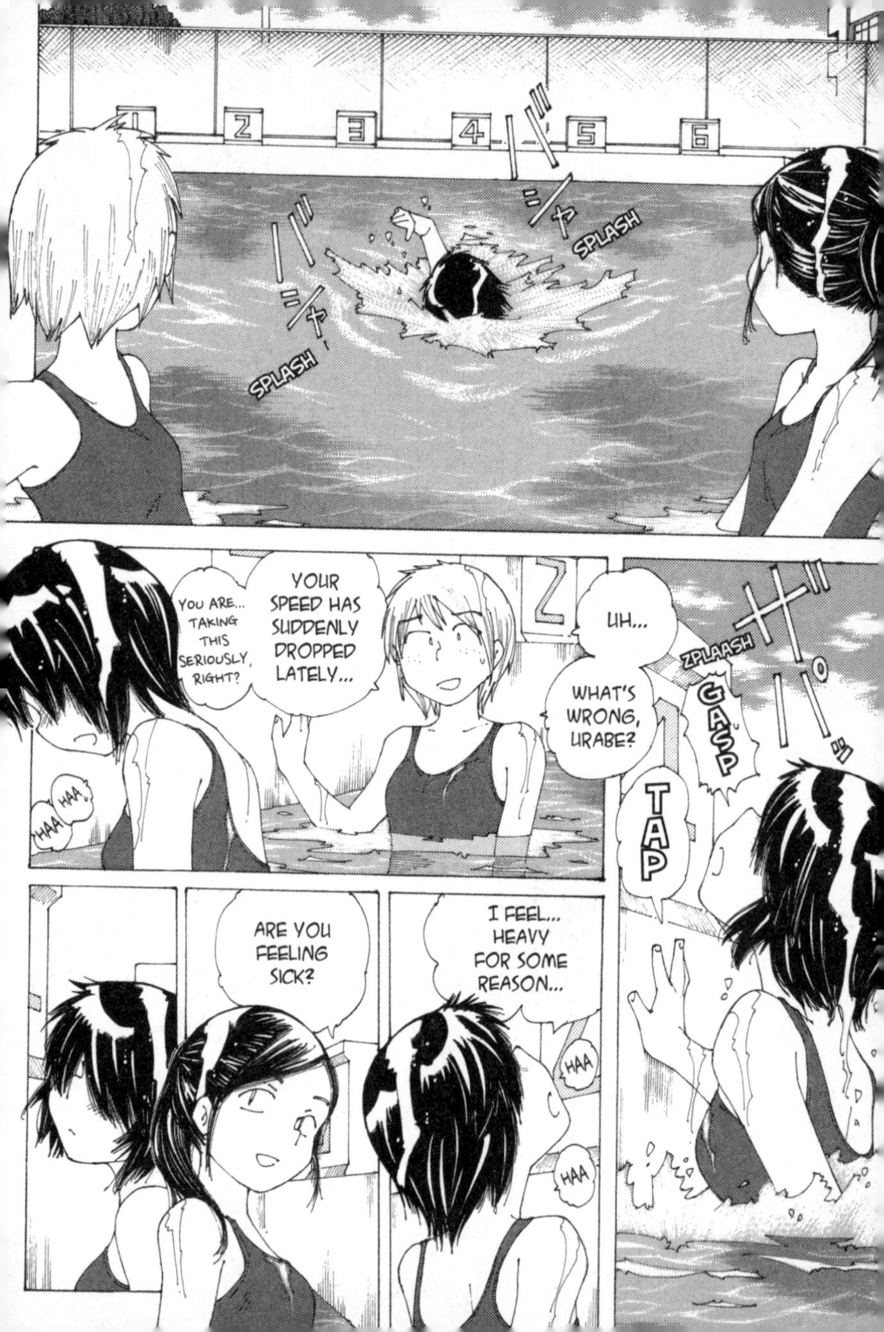
SPLASH
SPLASH
ZPLAASH
GASP
TAP
UH...
WHAT'S WRONG, URABE?
YOUR SPEED HAS SUDDENLY DROPPED LATELY...
YOU ARE... TAKING THIS SERIOUSLY, RIGHT?
HAA HAA
HAA
I FEEL... HEAVY FOR SOME REASON...
HAA
HAA
ARE YOU FEELING SICK?

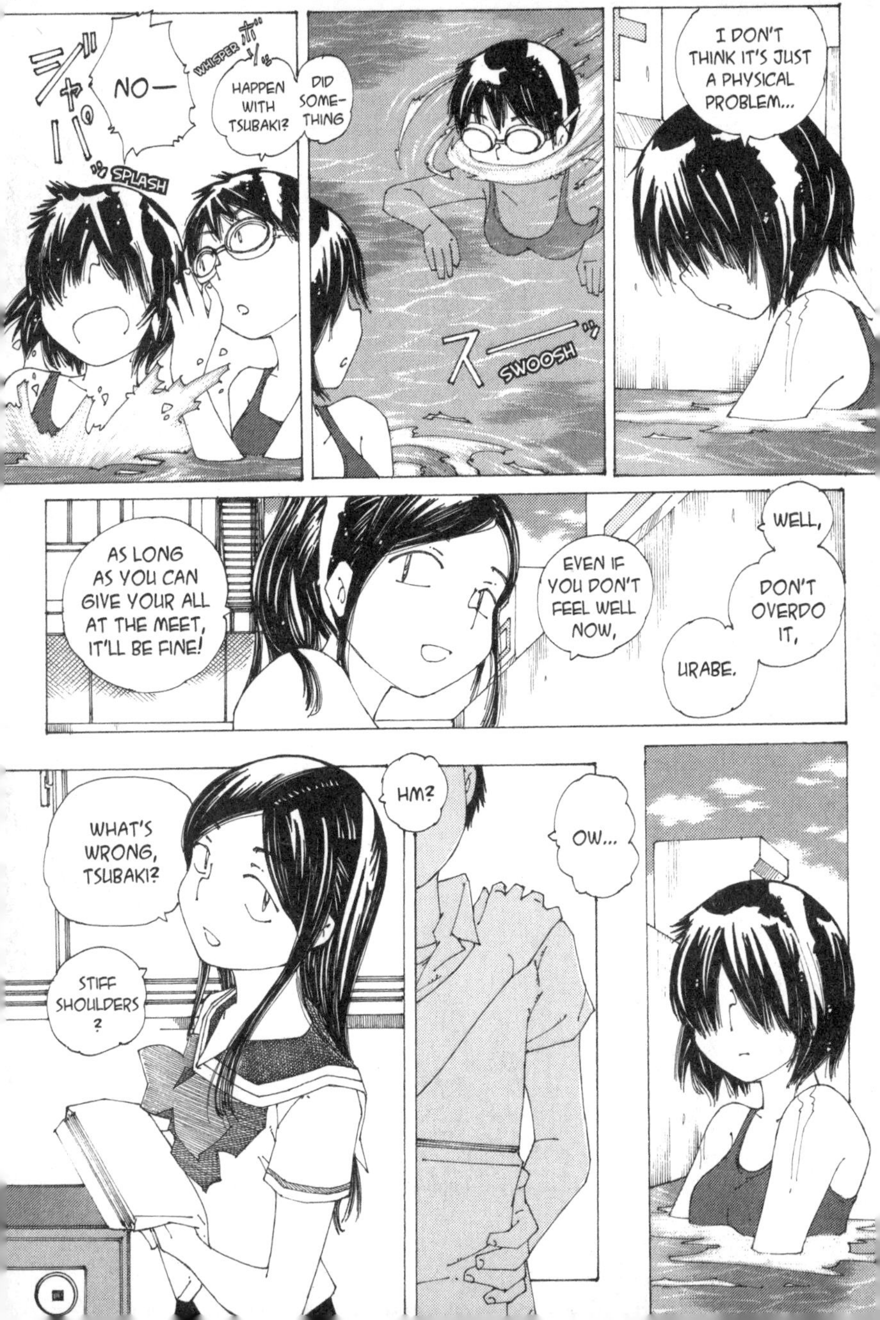
I DON'T THINK IT'S JUST A PHYSICAL PROBLEM...
SWOOSH
DID SOME-THING
HAPPEN WITH TSUBAKI?
WHISPER
NO—
SPLASH
WELL,
DON'T OVERDO IT,
URABE.
EVEN IF YOU DON'T FEEL WELL NOW,
AS LONG AS YOU CAN GIVE YOUR ALL AT THE MEET, IT'LL BE FINE!
OW...
HM?
WHAT'S WRONG, TSUBAKI?
STIFF SHOULDERS?

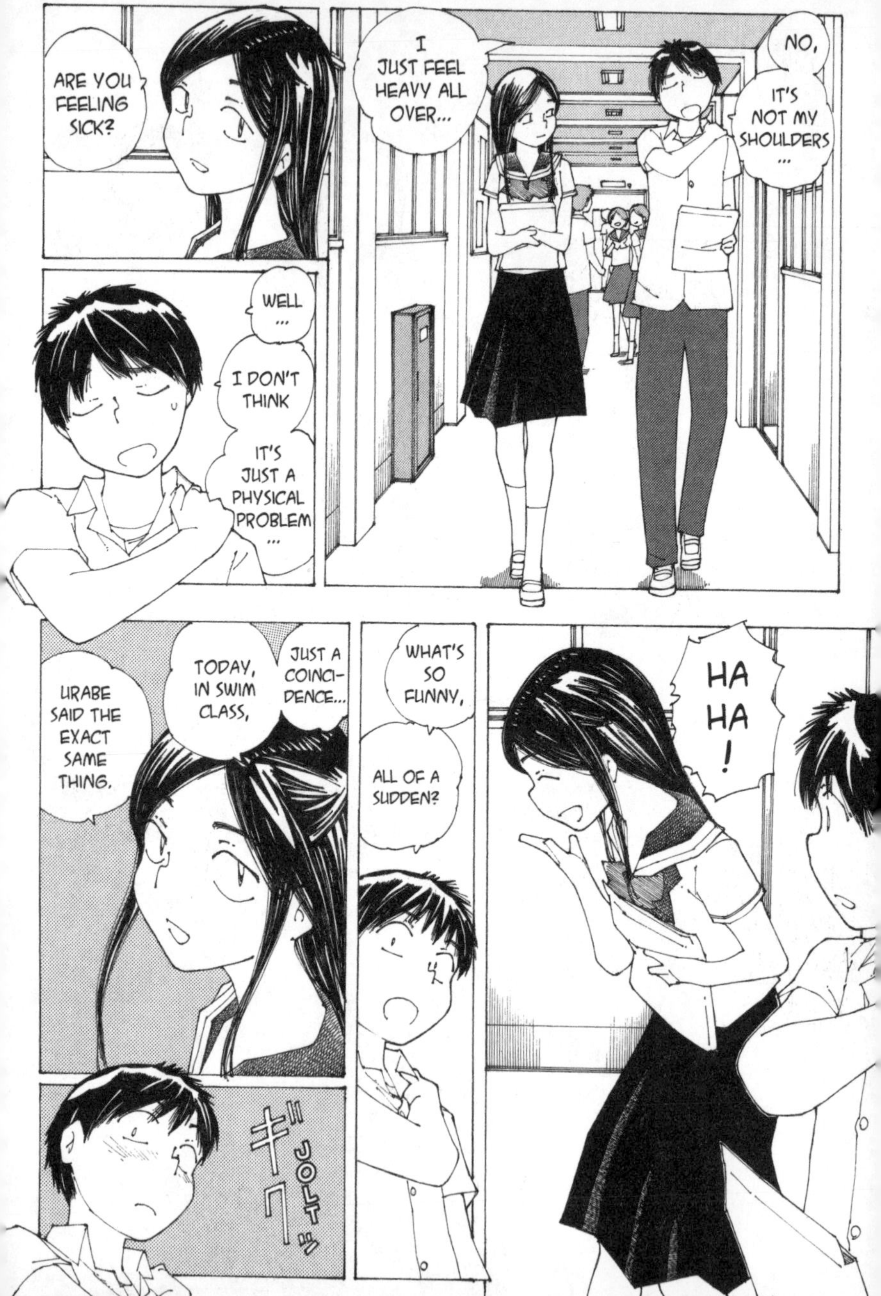
NO,
IT'S NOT MY SHOULDERS...
I JUST FEEL HEAVY ALL OVER...
ARE YOU FEELING SICK?
WELL...
I DON'T THINK
IT'S JUST A PHYSICAL PROBLEM...
HA HA!
WHAT'S SO FUNNY,
ALL OF A SUDDEN?
JUST A COINCIDENCE...
TODAY, IN SWIM CLASS,
URABE SAID THE EXACT SAME THING.
JOLT

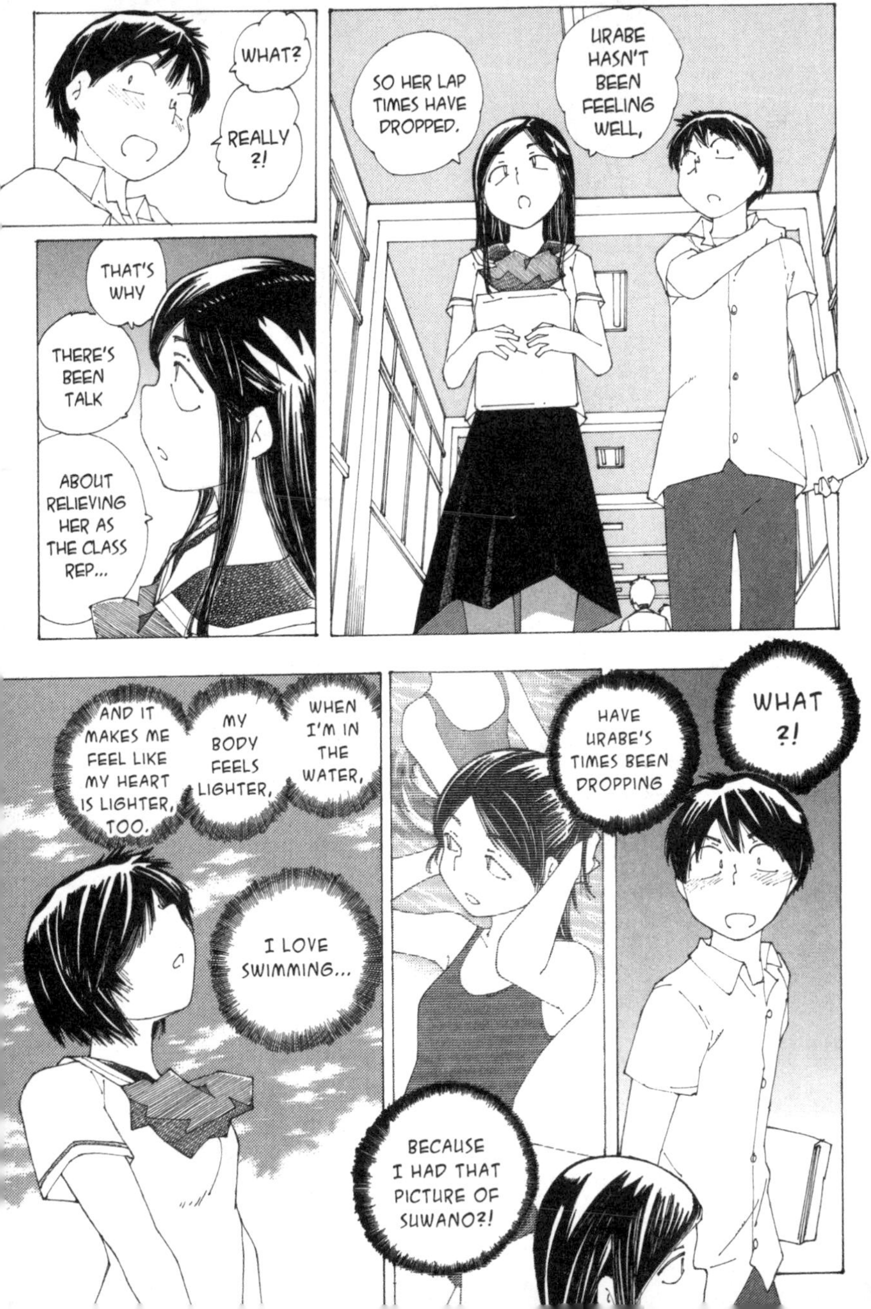
URABE HASN'T BEEN FEELING WELL,
SO HER LAP TIMES HAVE DROPPED.
WHAT?
REALLY?!
THAT'S WHY
THERE'S BEEN TALK
ABOUT RELIEVING HER AS THE CLASS REP...
WHAT?!
HAVE URABE'S TIMES BEEN DROPPING
BECAUSE I HAD THAT PICTURE OF SUWANO?!
WHEN I'M IN THE WATER,
MY BODY FEELS LIGHTER,
AND IT MAKES ME FEEL LIKE MY HEART IS LIGHTER, TOO.
I LOVE SWIMMING...

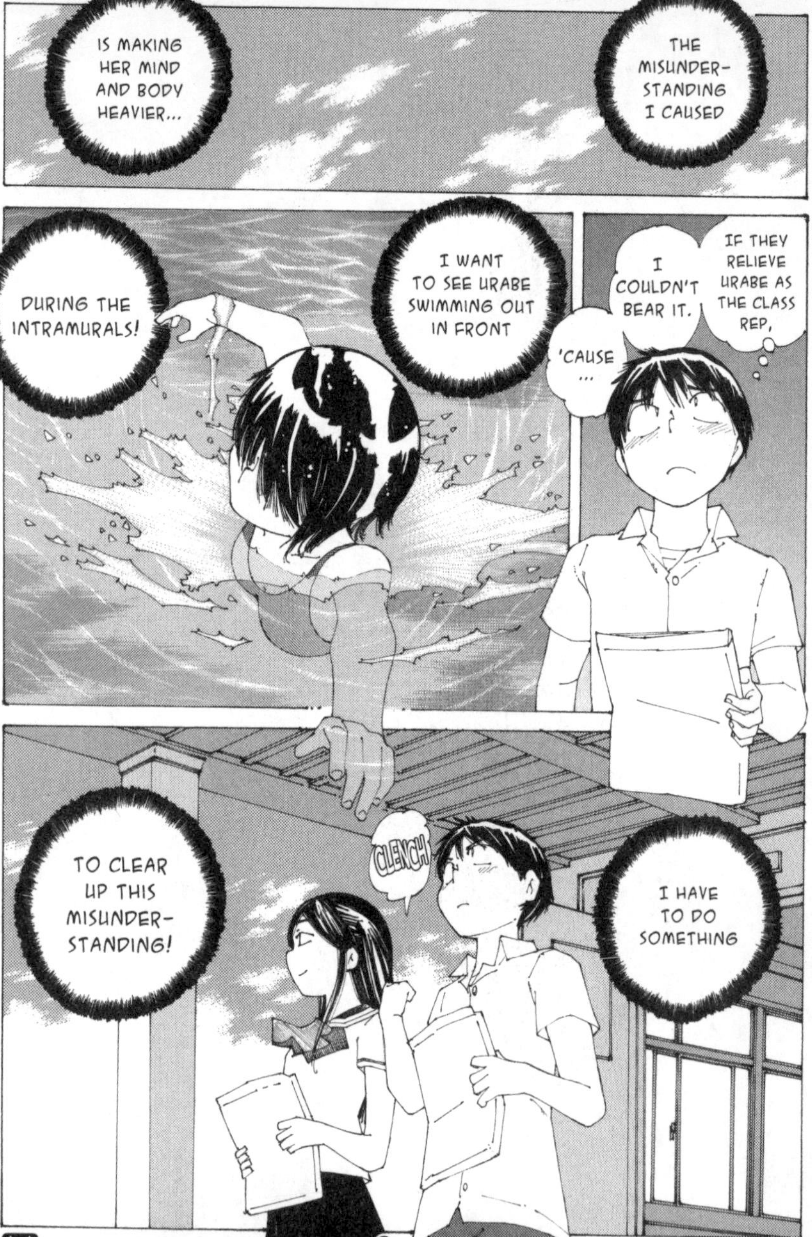
THE MISUNDER-STANDING I CAUSED
IS MAKING HER MIND AND BODY HEAVIER...
IF THEY RELIEVE URABE AS THE CLASS REP,
I COULDN'T BEAR IT.
'CAUSE ...
I WANT TO SEE URABE SWIMMING OUT IN FRONT
DURING THE INTRAMURALS!
I HAVE TO DO SOMETHING
CLENCH
TO CLEAR UP THIS MISUNDER-STANDING!

END OF CHAPTER 58

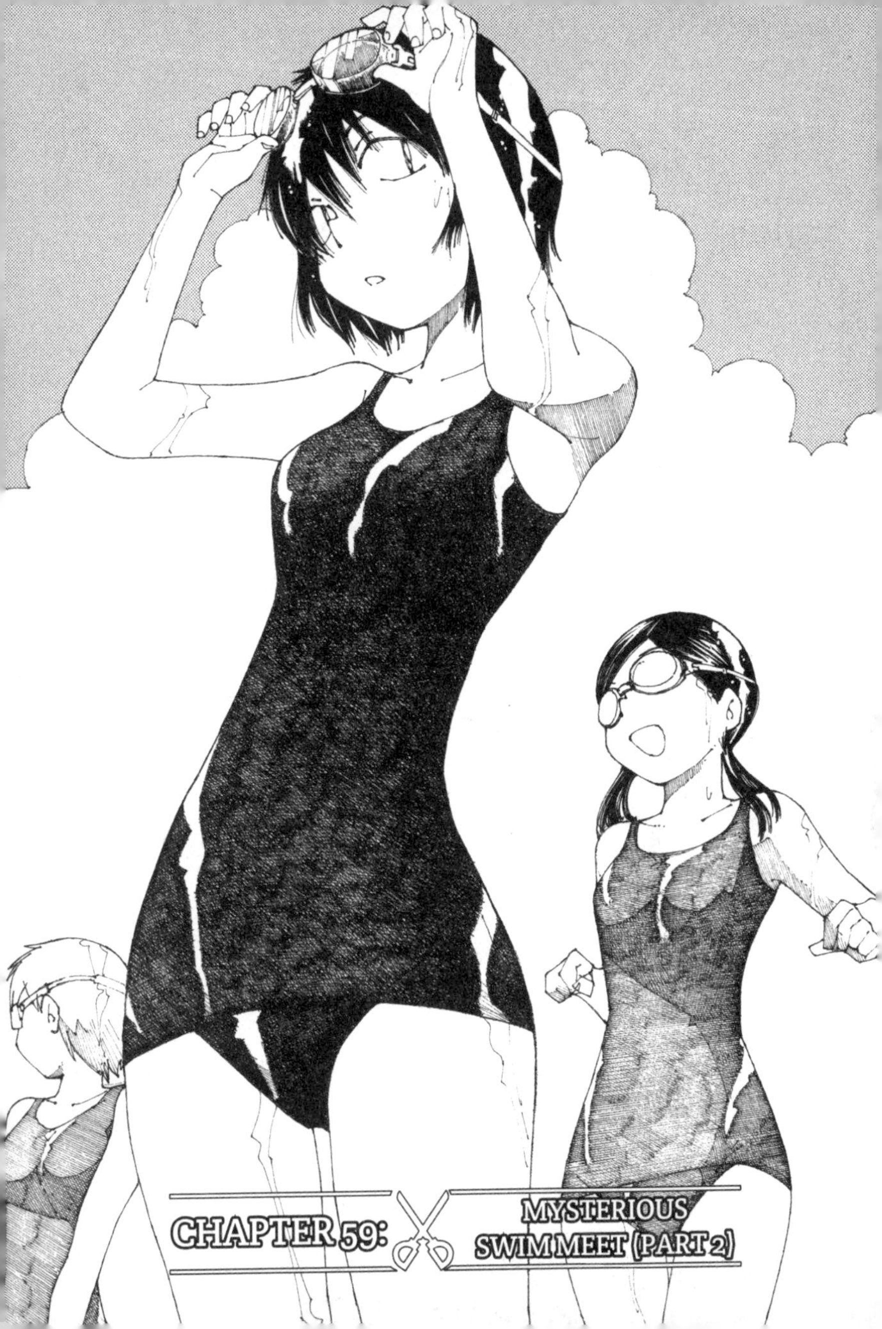
CHAPTER 59:
MYSTERIOUS SWIM MEET (PART 2)

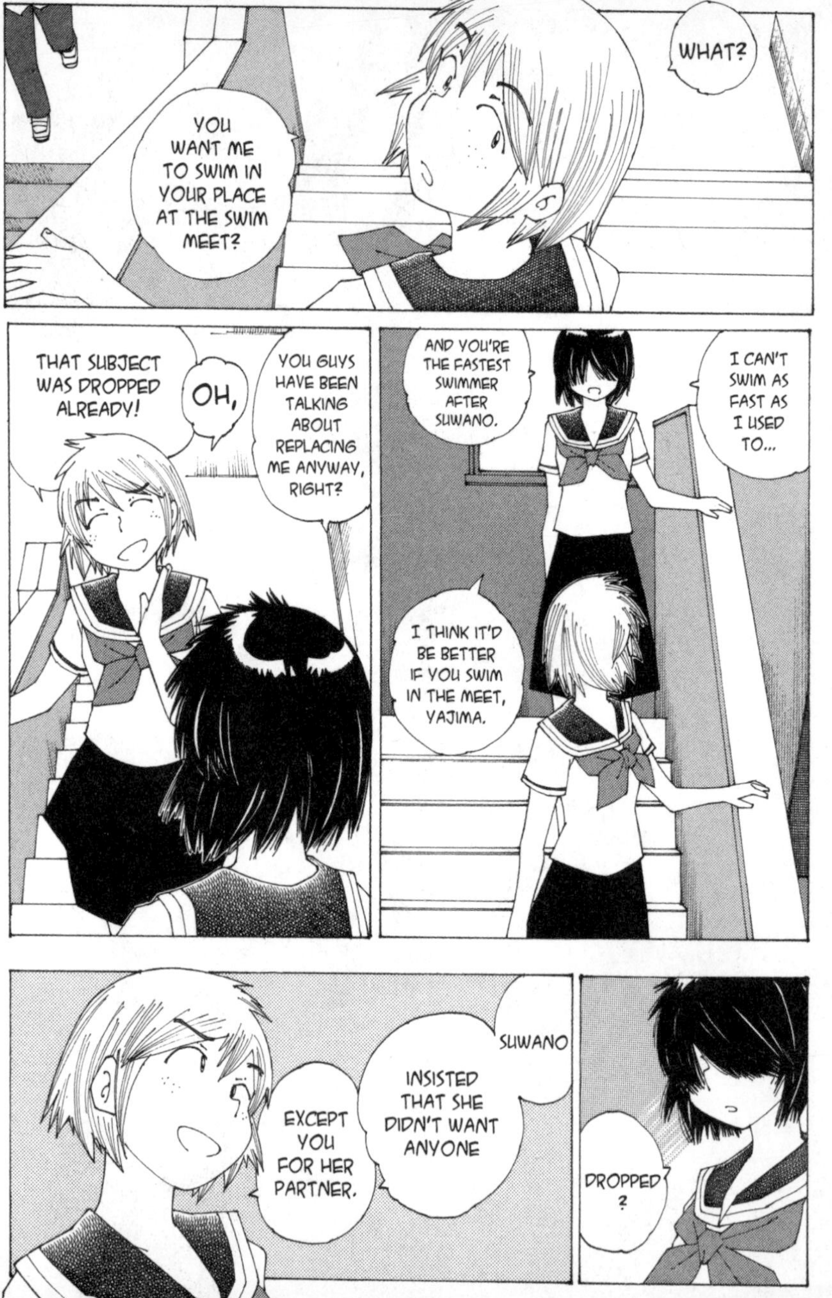
WHAT?
YOU WANT ME TO SWIM IN YOUR PLACE AT THE SWIM MEET?
I CAN'T SWIM AS FAST AS I USED TO...
AND YOU'RE THE FASTEST SWIMMER AFTER SUWANO.
I THINK IT'D BE BETTER IF YOU SWIM IN THE MEET, YAJIMA.
YOU GUYS HAVE BEEN TALKING ABOUT REPLACING ME ANYWAY, RIGHT?
OH,
THAT SUBJECT WAS DROPPED ALREADY!
DROPPED?
SUWANO
INSISTED THAT SHE DIDN'T WANT ANYONE
EXCEPT YOU FOR HER PARTNER.

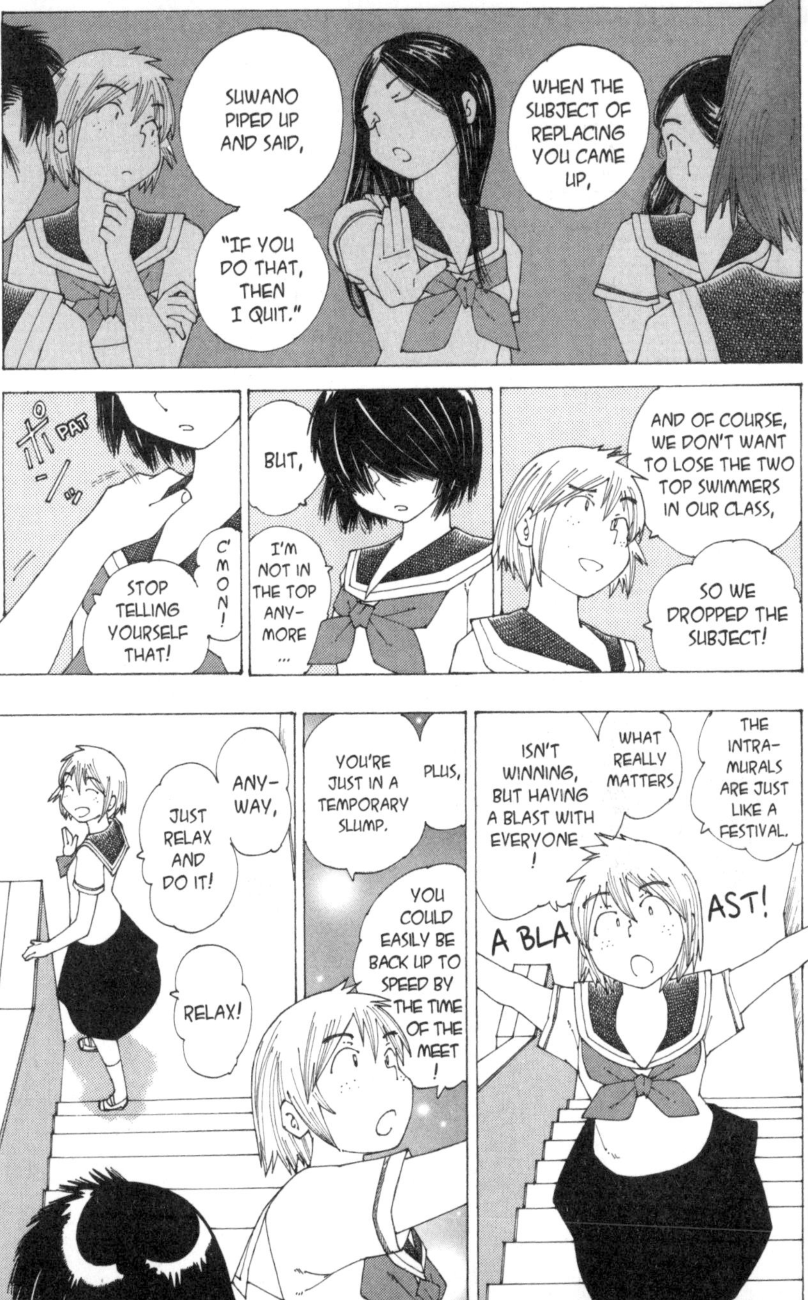
WHEN THE SUBJECT OF REPLACING YOU CAME UP,
SUWANO PIPED UP AND SAID,
"IF YOU DO THAT, THEN I QUIT."
AND OF COURSE, WE DON'T WANT TO LOSE THE TWO TOP SWIMMERS IN OUR CLASS,
SO WE DROPPED THE SUBJECT!
BUT,
I'M NOT IN THE TOP ANYMORE ...
PAT
C'MON!
STOP TELLING YOURSELF THAT!
THE INTRAMURALS ARE JUST LIKE A FESTIVAL.
WHAT REALLY MATTERS
ISN'T WINNING, BUT HAVING A BLAST WITH EVERYONE!
A BLAST!
PLUS,
YOU'RE JUST IN A TEMPORARY SLUMP.
YOU COULD EASILY BE BACK UP TO SPEED BY THE TIME OF THE MEET!
ANYWAY,
JUST RELAX AND DO IT!
RELAX!

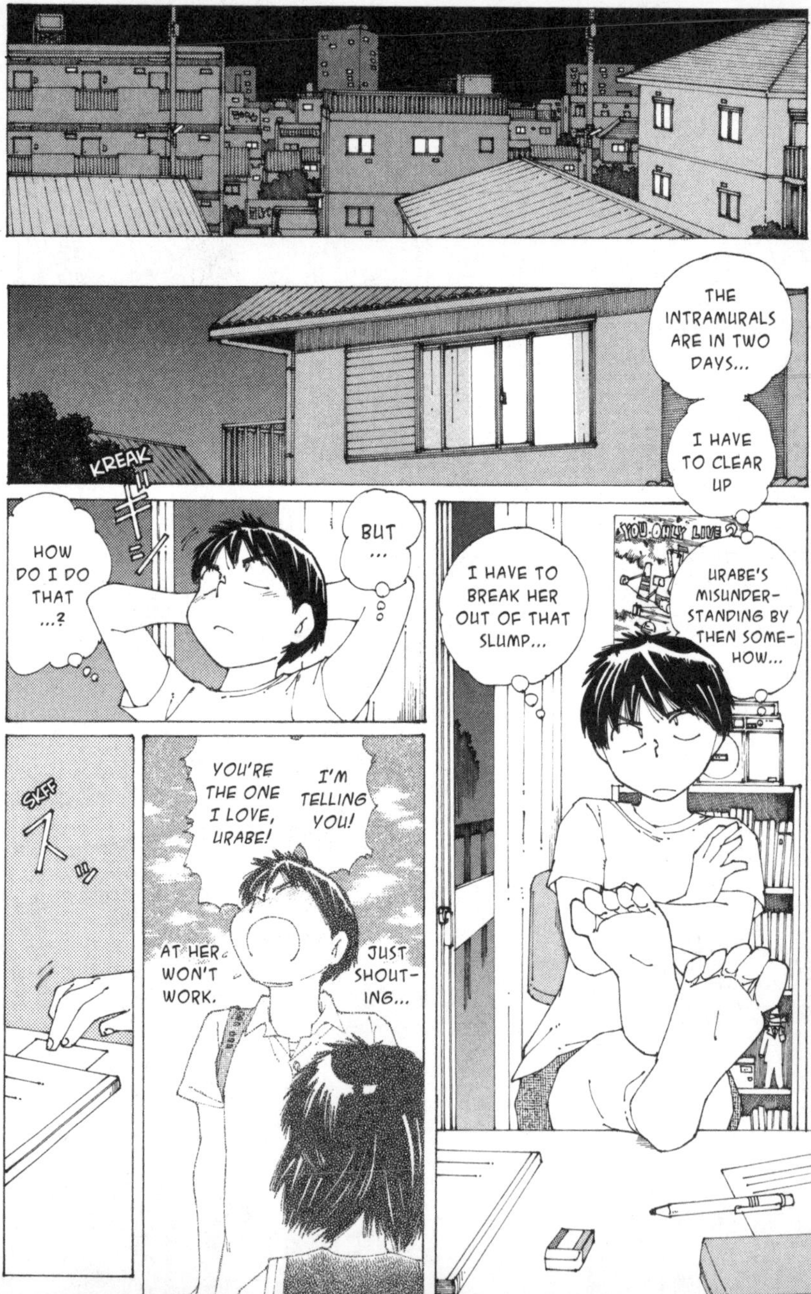
THE INTRAMURALS ARE IN TWO DAYS...
I HAVE TO CLEAR UP
URABE'S MISUNDERSTANDING BY THEN SOMEHOW...
I HAVE TO BREAK HER OUT OF THAT SLUMP...
KREAK
BUT ...
HOW DO I DO THAT ...?
YOU'RE THE ONE I LOVE, URABE! I'M TELLING YOU!
JUST SHOUTING...
AT HER WON'T WORK.
SKFF

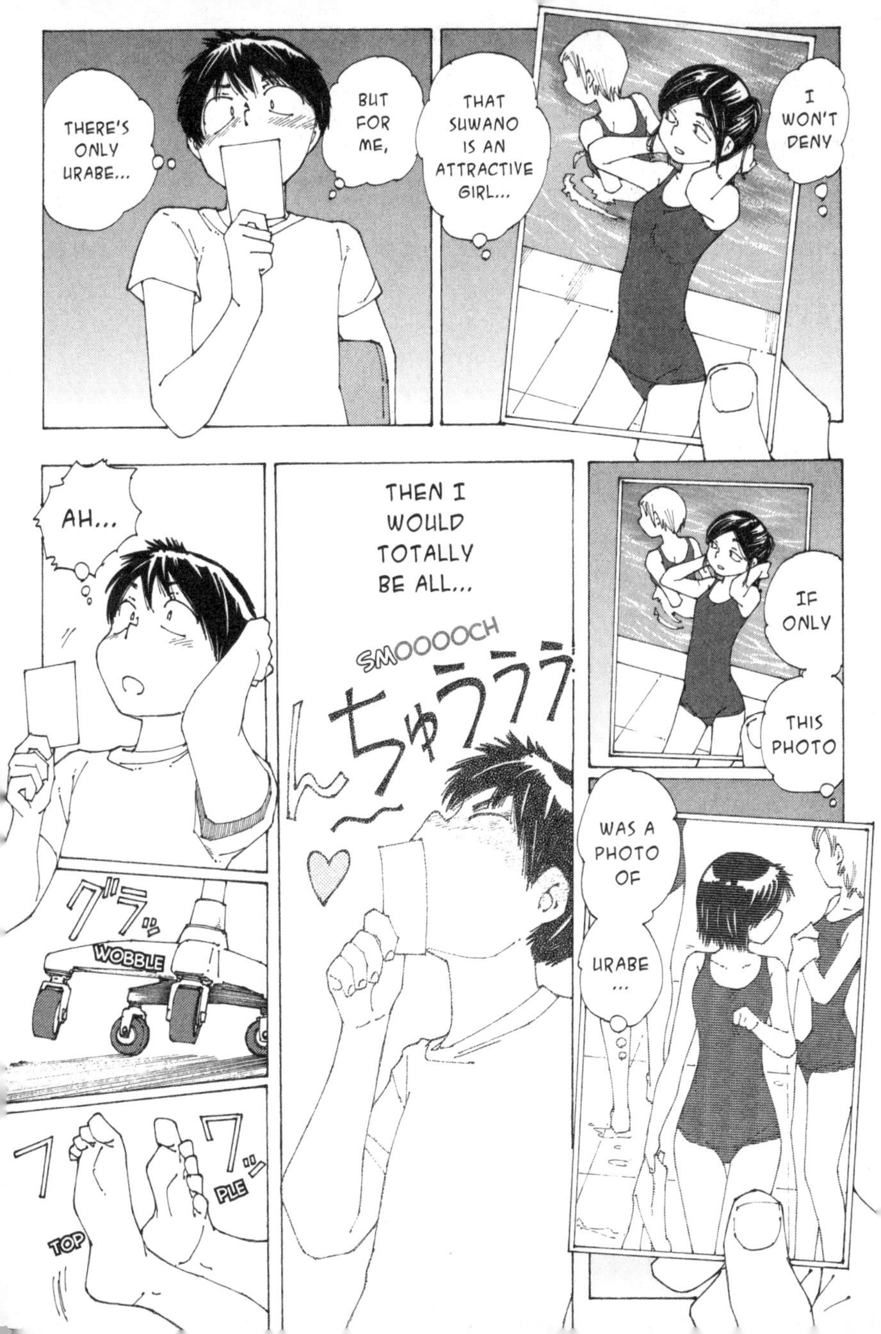
I WON'T DENY
THAT SUWANO IS AN ATTRACTIVE GIRL...
BUT FOR ME,
THERE'S ONLY URABE...
IF ONLY
THIS PHOTO
WAS A PHOTO OF
URABE ...
THEN I WOULD TOTALLY BE ALL...
SMOOOOCH
んちゅううう
AH...
グラッ
WOBBLE
TOP
PLE

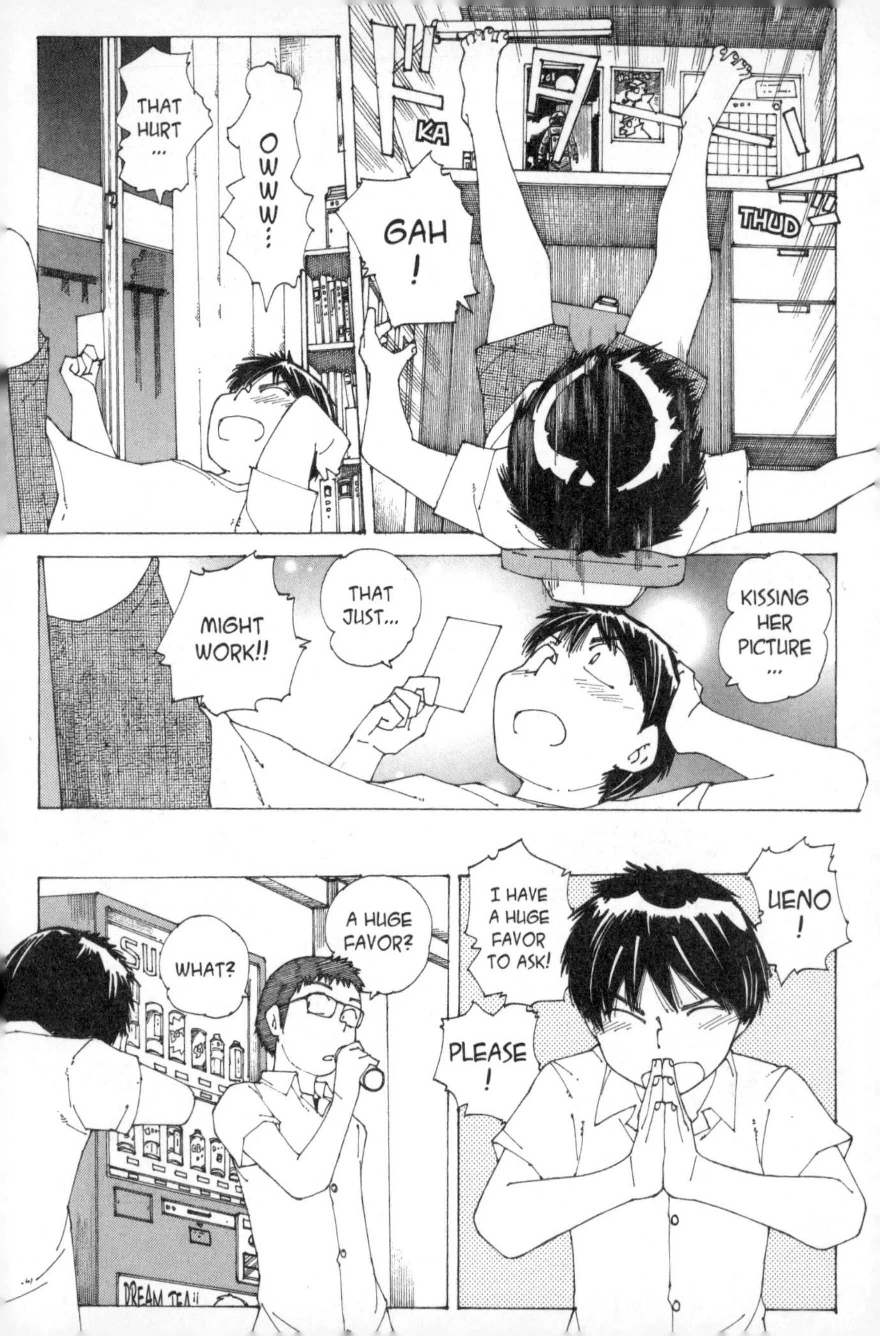
KA
THUD
GAH!
OWWW...
THAT HURT...
KISSING HER PICTURE...
THAT JUST...
MIGHT WORK!!
UENO!
I HAVE A HUGE FAVOR TO ASK!
PLEASE!
A HUGE FAVOR?
WHAT?
DREAM TEA!!

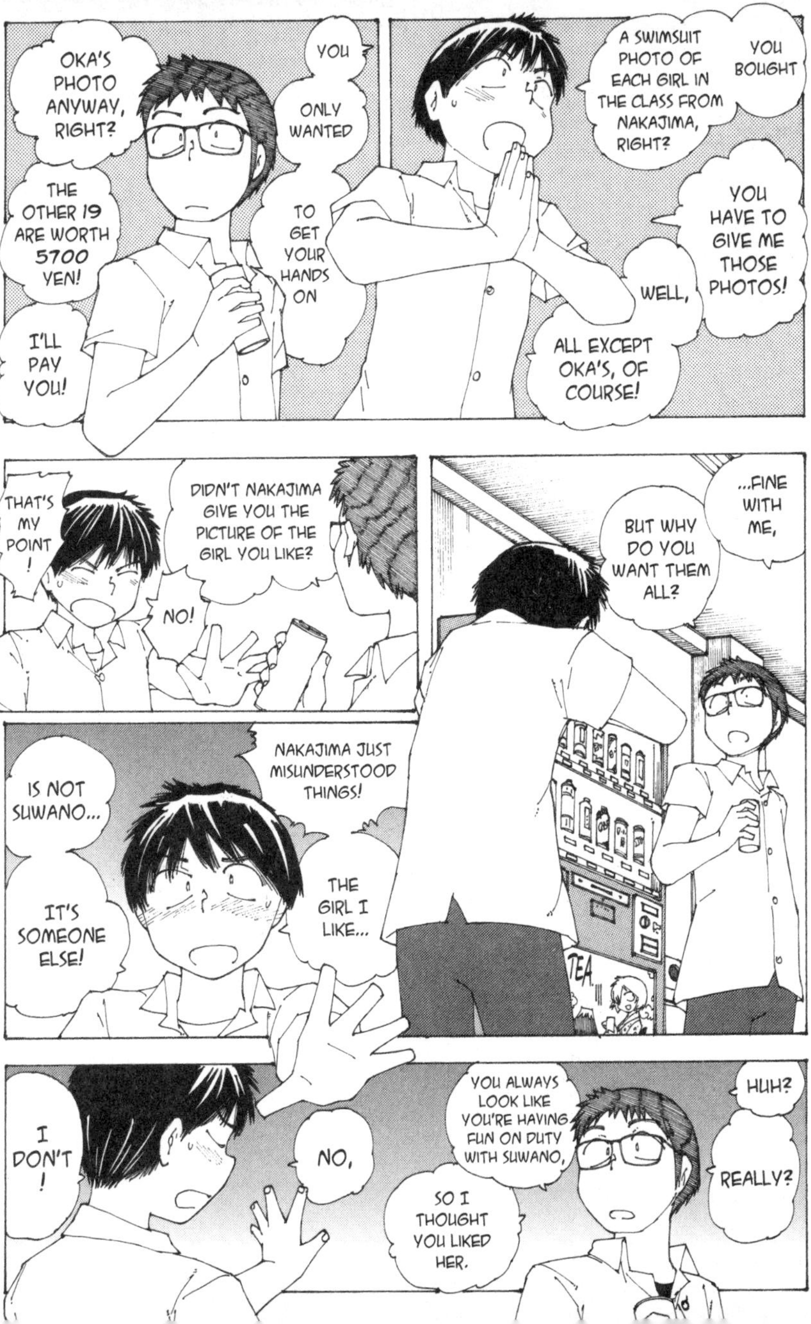

YOU BOUGHT
A SWIMSUIT PHOTO OF EACH GIRL IN THE CLASS FROM NAKAJIMA, RIGHT?
YOU HAVE TO GIVE ME THOSE PHOTOS!
WELL,
ALL EXCEPT OKA'S, OF COURSE!
YOU
ONLY WANTED
TO GET YOUR HANDS ON
OKA'S PHOTO ANYWAY, RIGHT?
THE OTHER 19 ARE WORTH 5700 YEN!
I'LL PAY YOU!
...FINE WITH ME,
BUT WHY DO YOU WANT THEM ALL?
DIDN'T NAKAJIMA GIVE YOU THE PICTURE OF THE GIRL YOU LIKE?
THAT'S MY POINT!
NO!
NAKAJIMA JUST MISUNDERSTOOD THINGS!
THE GIRL I LIKE...
IS NOT SUWANO...
IT'S SOMEONE ELSE!
TEA
HUH?
REALLY?
YOU ALWAYS LOOK LIKE YOU'RE HAVING FUN ON DUTY WITH SUWANO,
SO I THOUGHT YOU LIKED HER.
NO,
I DON'T!

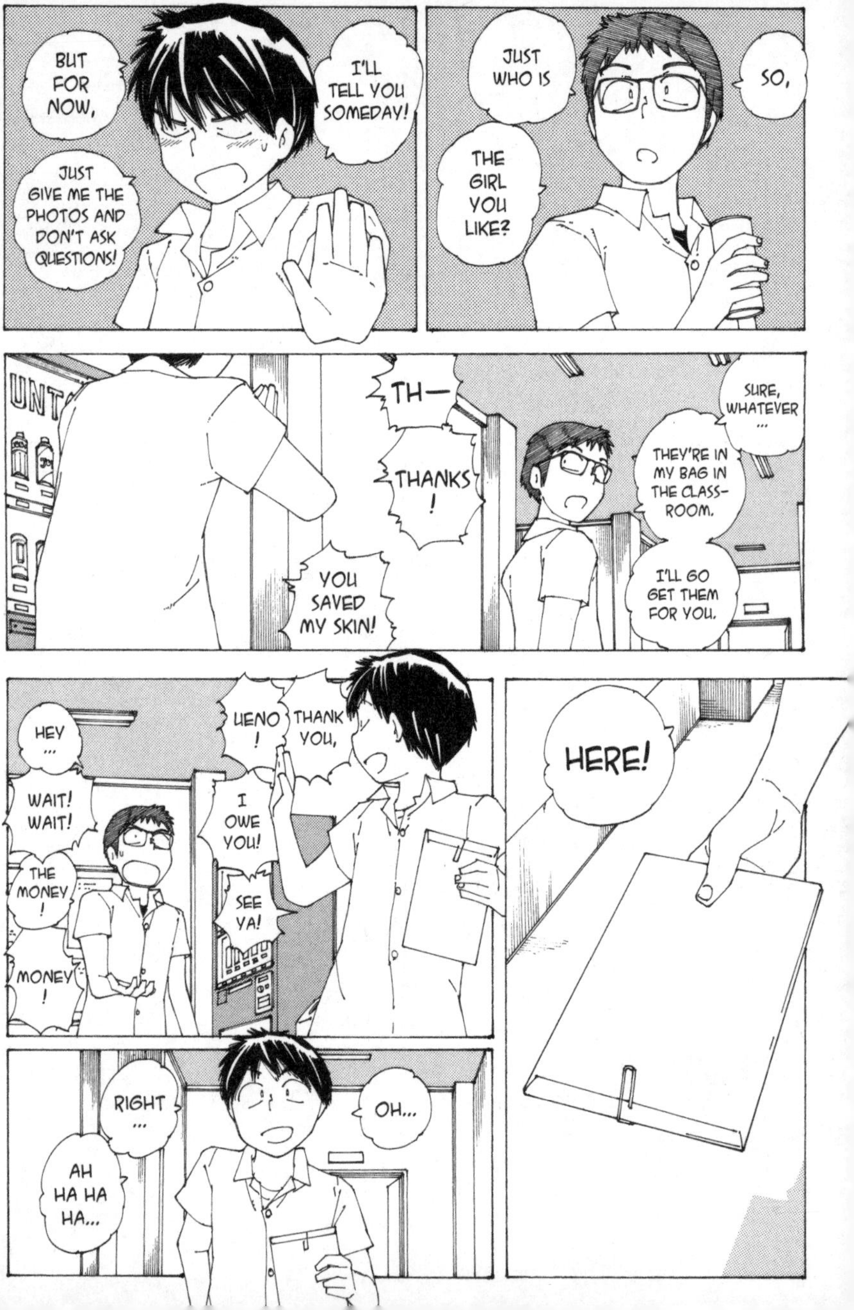
SO,
JUST WHO IS
THE GIRL YOU LIKE?
I'LL TELL YOU SOMEDAY!
BUT FOR NOW,
JUST GIVE ME THE PHOTOS AND DON'T ASK QUESTIONS!
SURE, WHATEVER ...
THEY'RE IN MY BAG IN THE CLASS-ROOM.
I'LL GO GET THEM FOR YOU.
TH—
THANKS!
YOU SAVED MY SKIN!
HERE!
THANK YOU,
UENO!
I OWE YOU!
SEE YA!
HEY ...
WAIT! WAIT!
THE MONEY!
MONEY!
OH...
RIGHT ...
AH HA HA HA...

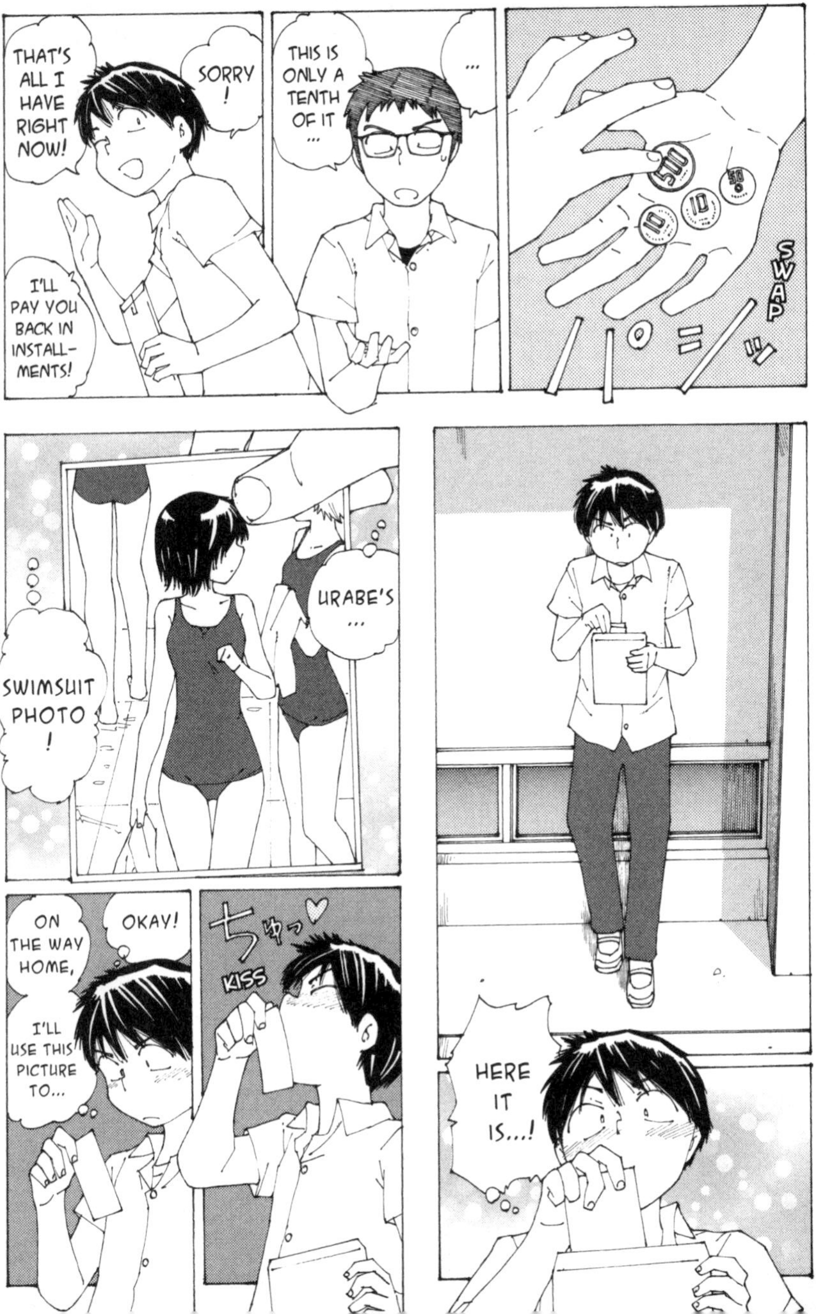
SWAP
...
THIS IS ONLY A TENTH OF IT ...
SORRY!
THAT'S ALL I HAVE RIGHT NOW!
I'LL PAY YOU BACK IN INSTALL-MENTS!
URABE'S ...
SWIMSUIT PHOTO!
HERE IT IS...!
ちゅっ♥
KISS
OKAY!
ON THE WAY HOME,
I'LL USE THIS PICTURE TO...

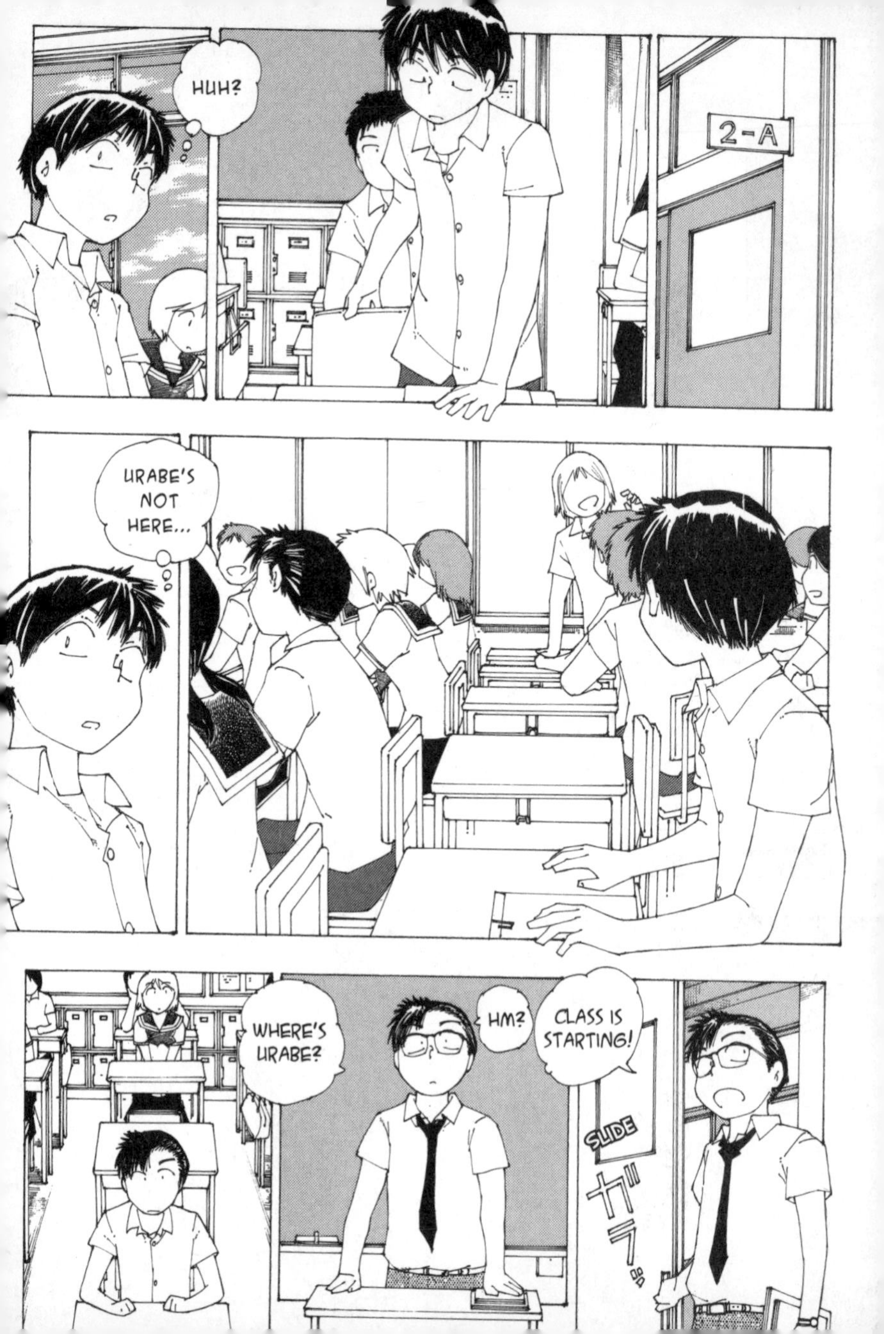
2-A
HUH?
URABE'S NOT HERE...
CLASS IS STARTING!
SLIDE
ガラ
HM?
WHERE'S URABE?

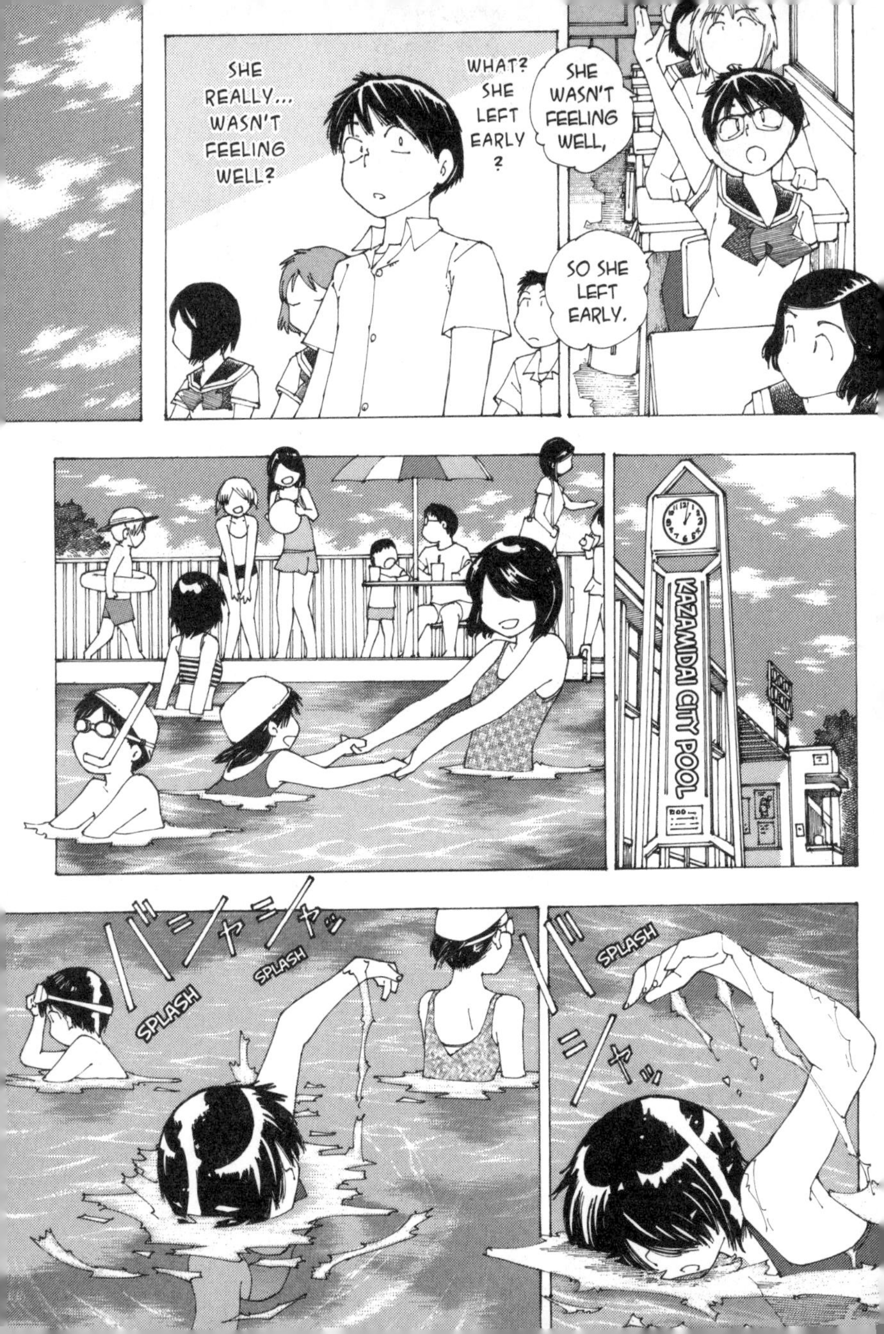
SHE WASN'T FEELING WELL,
SO SHE LEFT EARLY.
WHAT? SHE LEFT EARLY?
SHE REALLY... WASN'T FEELING WELL?
KAZAMIDAI CITY POOL
SPLASH
SPLASH
SPLASH

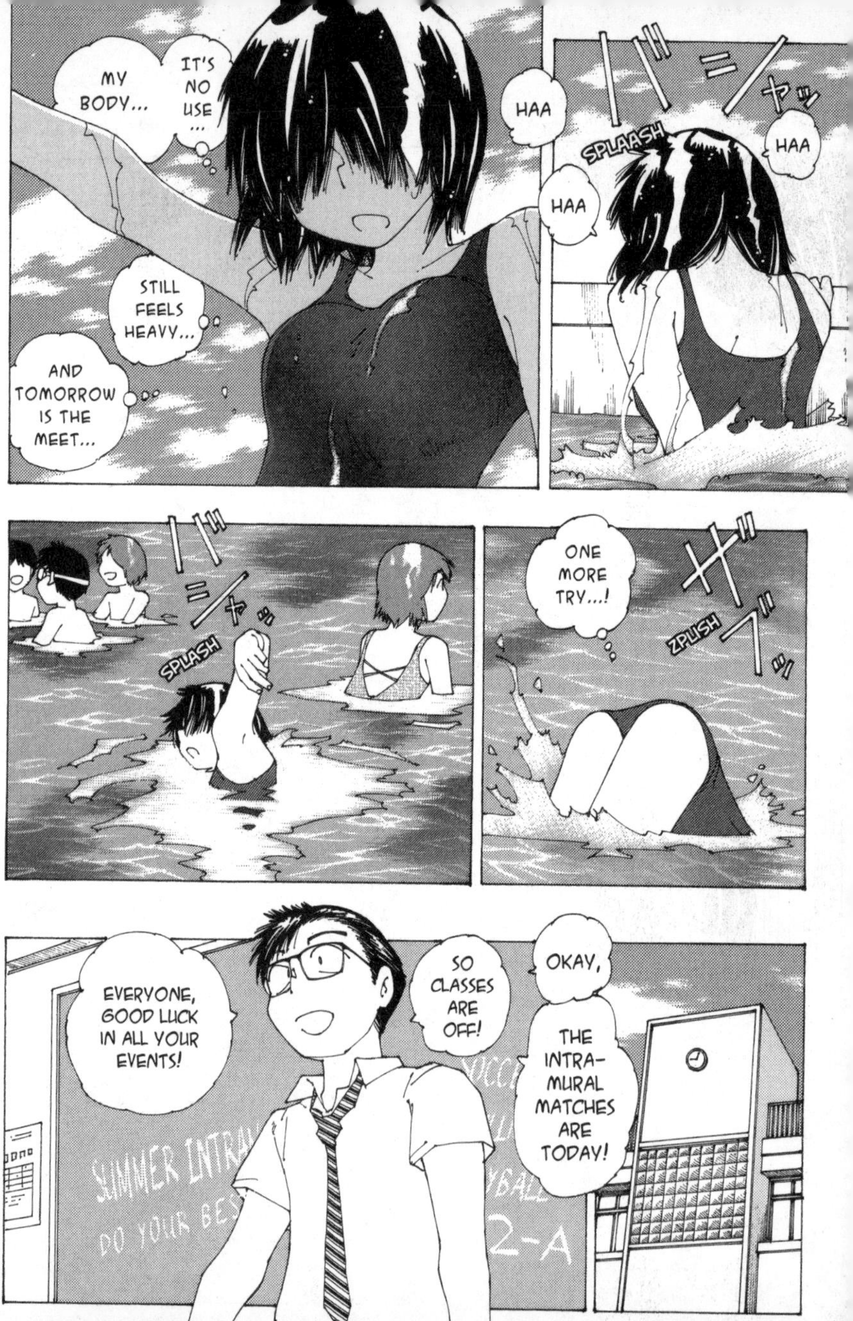
HAA
SPLAASH
HAA
HAA
IT'S NO USE...
MY BODY...
STILL FEELS HEAVY...
AND TOMORROW IS THE MEET...
ONE MORE TRY...!
ZPLUSH
SPLASH
OKAY,
THE INTRA-MURAL MATCHES ARE TODAY!
SO CLASSES ARE OFF!
EVERYONE, GOOD LUCK IN ALL YOUR EVENTS!
2-A

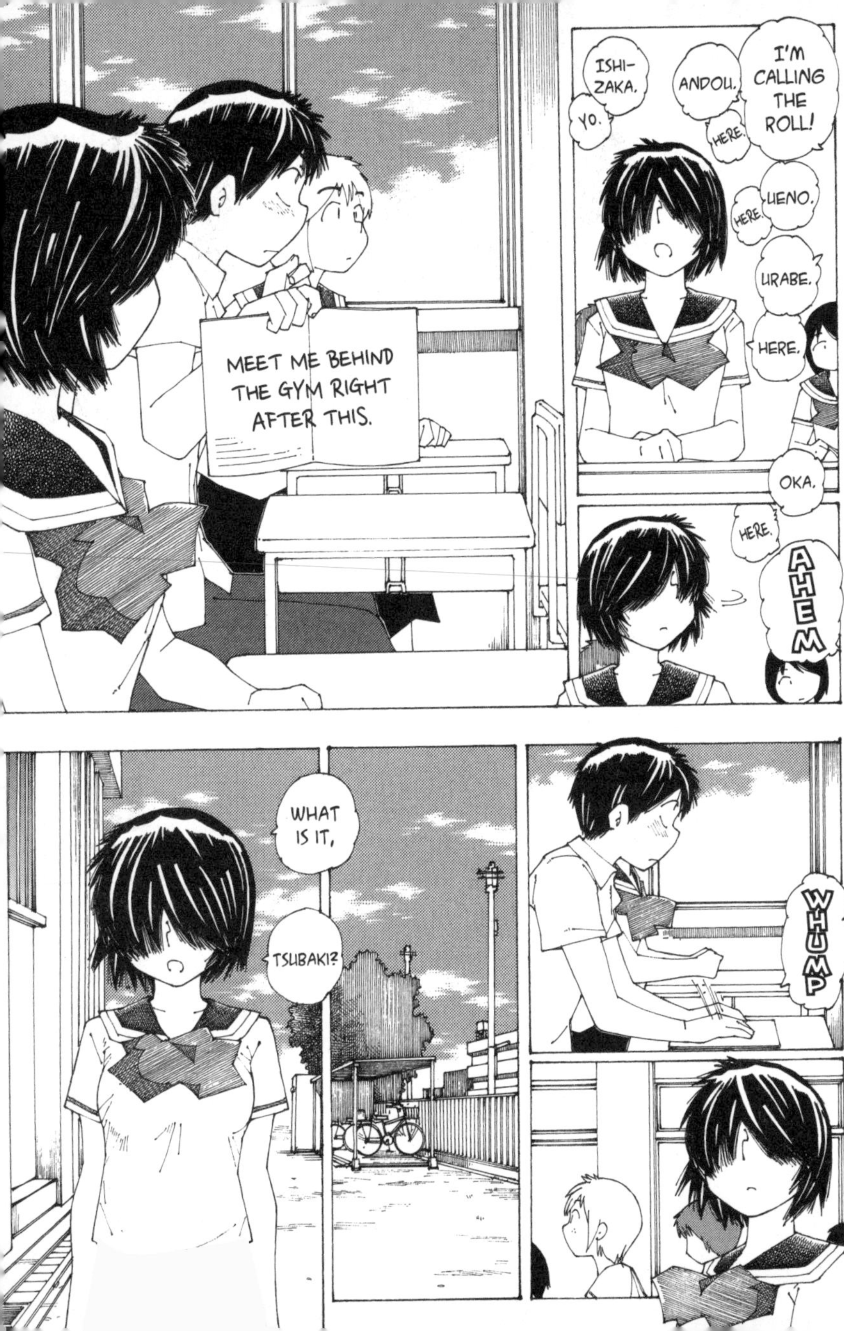
I'M CALLING THE ROLL!
ANDOU.
HERE.
ISHI-ZAKA.
YO.
UENO.
HERE.
URABE.
HERE.
OKA.
HERE.
AHEM
MEET ME BEHIND THE GYM RIGHT AFTER THIS.
WHUMP
WHAT IS IT,
TSUBAKI?

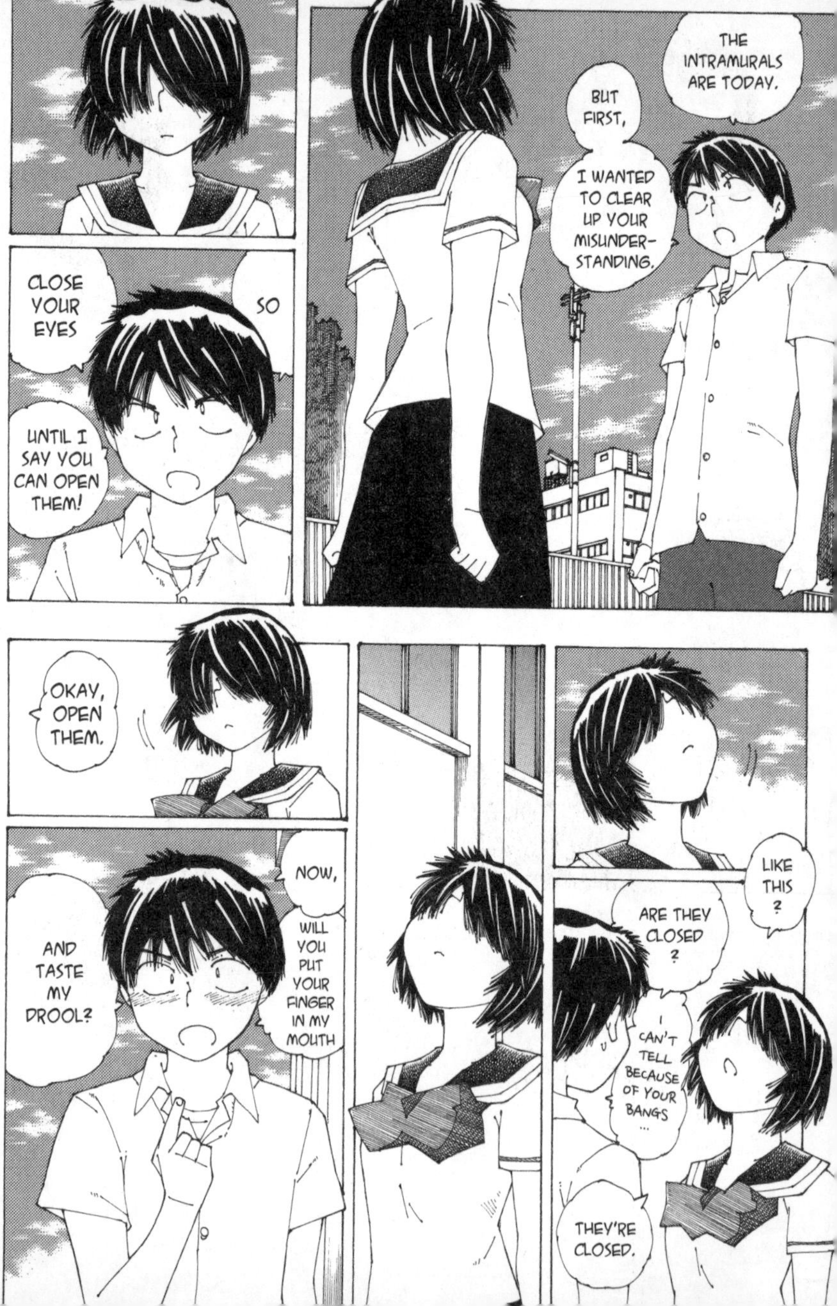
THE INTRAMURALS ARE TODAY.
BUT FIRST,
I WANTED TO CLEAR UP YOUR MISUNDER-STANDING.
SO
CLOSE YOUR EYES
UNTIL I SAY YOU CAN OPEN THEM!
LIKE THIS?
ARE THEY CLOSED?
I CAN'T TELL BECAUSE OF YOUR BANGS...
THEY'RE CLOSED.
OKAY, OPEN THEM.
NOW,
WILL YOU PUT YOUR FINGER IN MY MOUTH
AND TASTE MY DROOL?

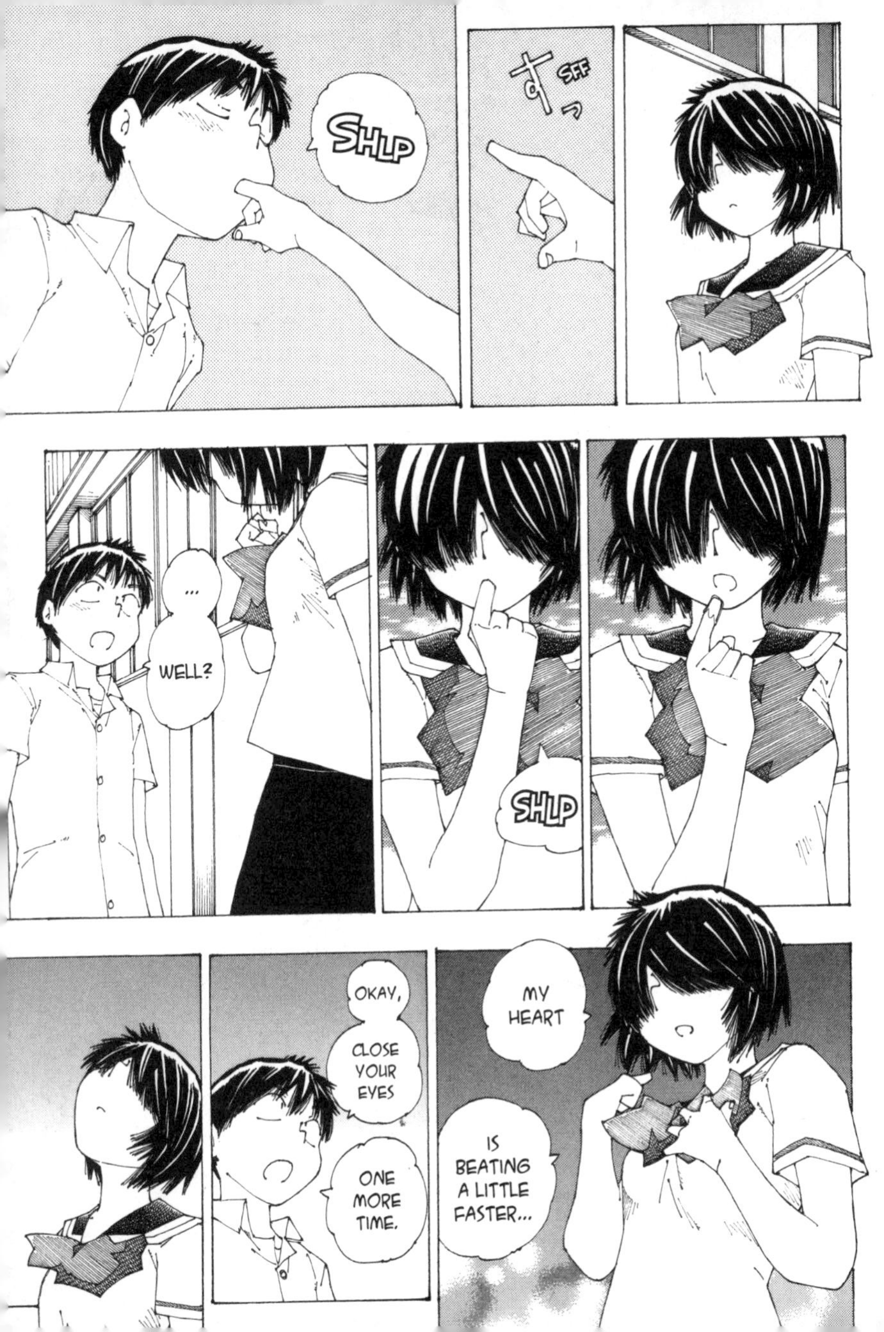
すっ
SFF
SHLP
SHLP
...
WELL?
MY HEART
IS BEATING A LITTLE FASTER...
OKAY,
CLOSE YOUR EYES
ONE MORE TIME.

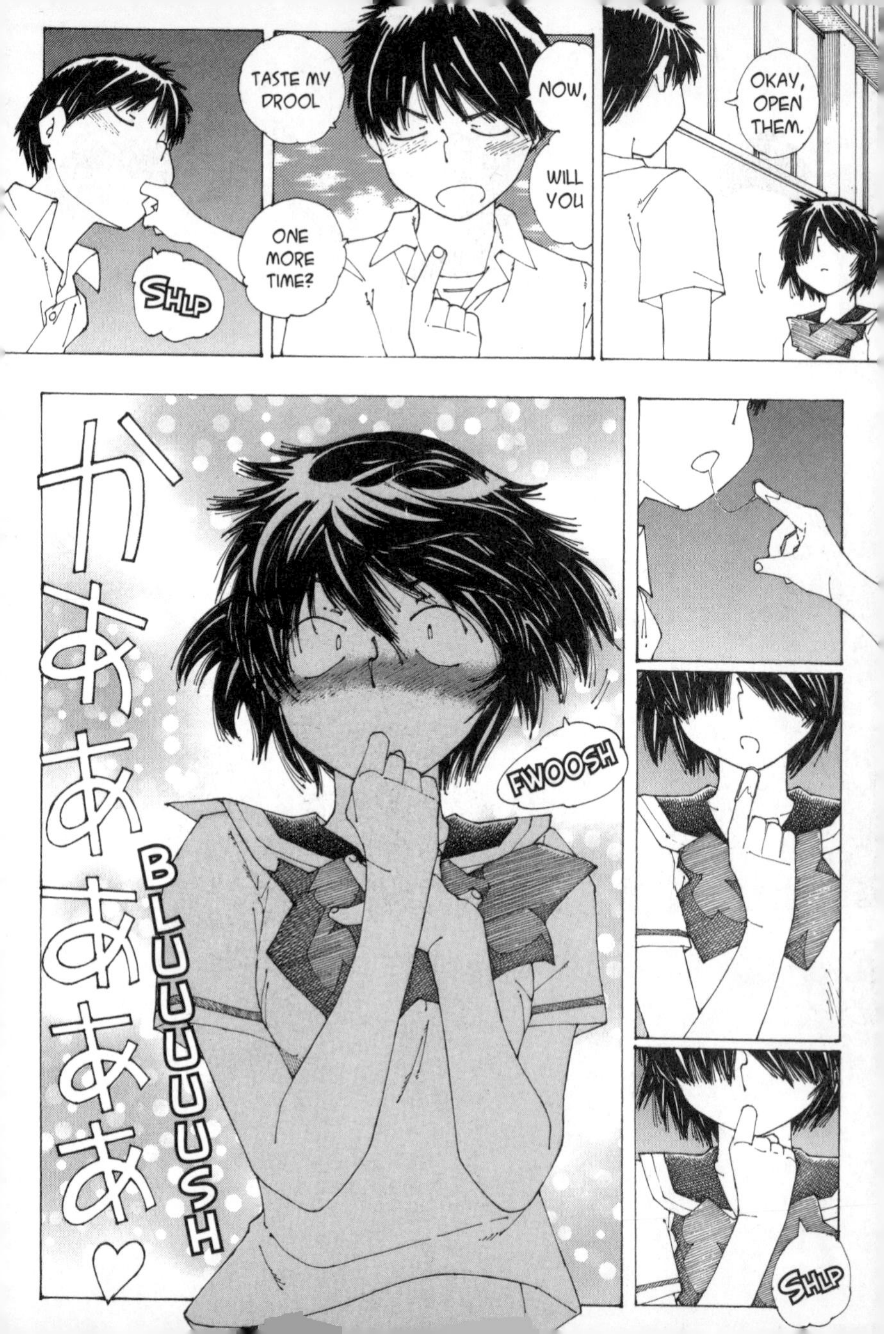
OKAY, OPEN THEM.
NOW,
WILL YOU
ONE MORE TIME?
TASTE MY DROOL
SHLP
SHLP
FWOOSH
かああああ♥
BLUUUUSH

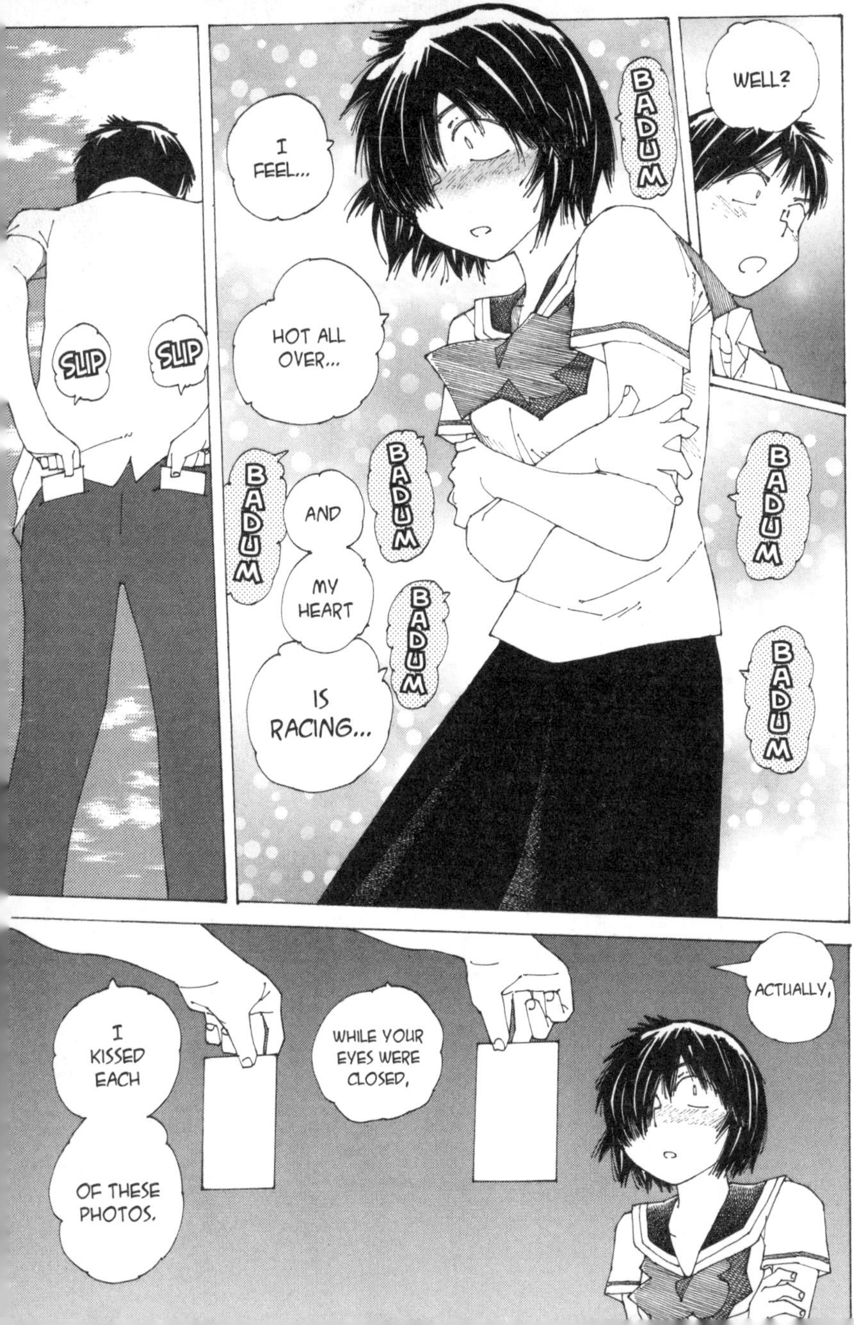
WELL?
BADUM
BADUM
BADUM
BADUM
I FEEL...
HOT ALL OVER...
BADUM
AND
BADUM
MY HEART
IS RACING...
BADUM
SLIP
SLIP
ACTUALLY,
WHILE YOUR EYES WERE CLOSED,
I KISSED EACH
OF THESE PHOTOS.

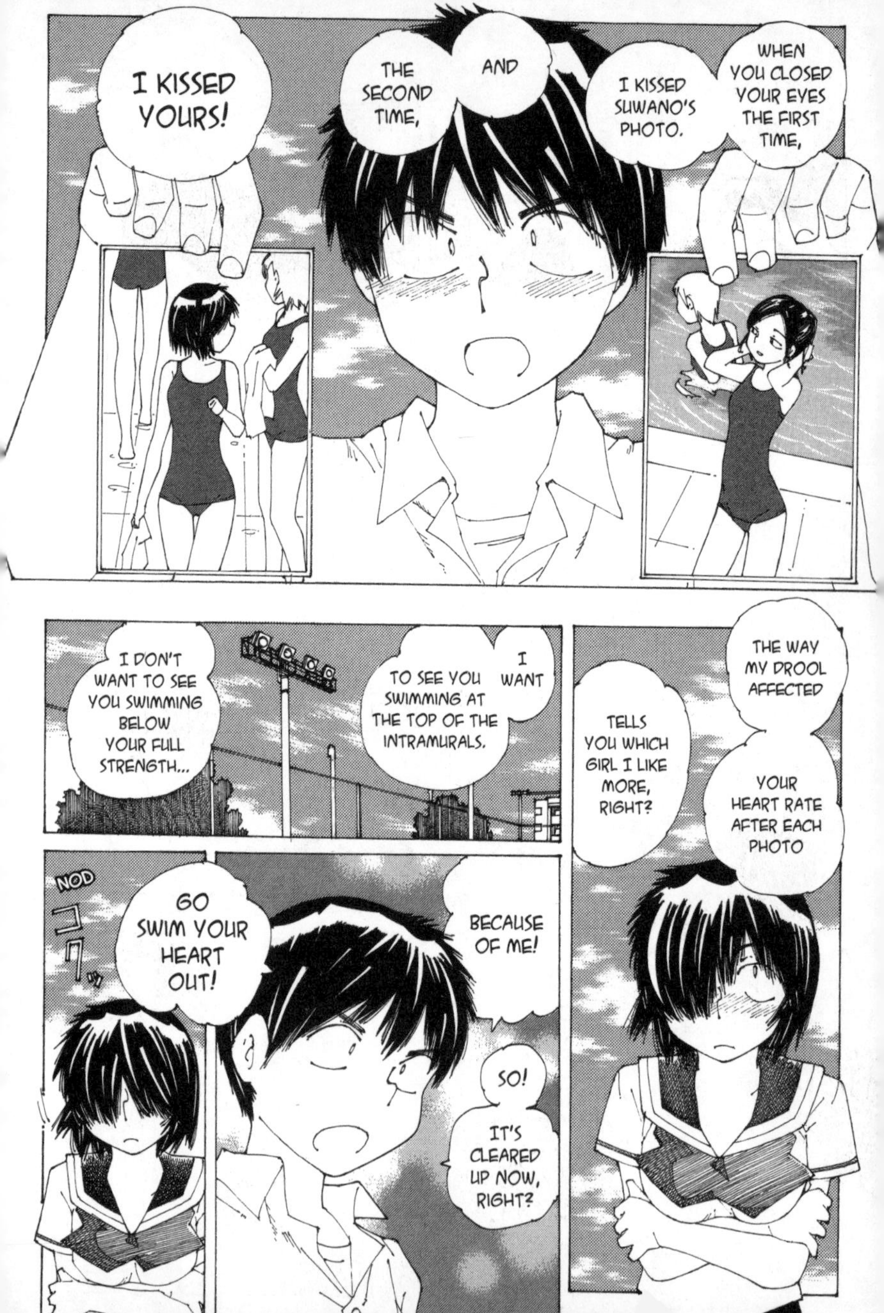
WHEN YOU CLOSED YOUR EYES THE FIRST TIME,
I KISSED SUWANO'S PHOTO.
AND
THE SECOND TIME,
I KISSED YOURS!
THE WAY MY DROOL AFFECTED
YOUR HEART RATE AFTER EACH PHOTO
TELLS YOU WHICH GIRL I LIKE MORE, RIGHT?
I WANT
TO SEE YOU SWIMMING AT THE TOP OF THE INTRAMURALS.
I DON'T WANT TO SEE YOU SWIMMING BELOW YOUR FULL STRENGTH...
BECAUSE OF ME!
SO!
IT'S CLEARED UP NOW, RIGHT?
GO SWIM YOUR HEART OUT!
NOD

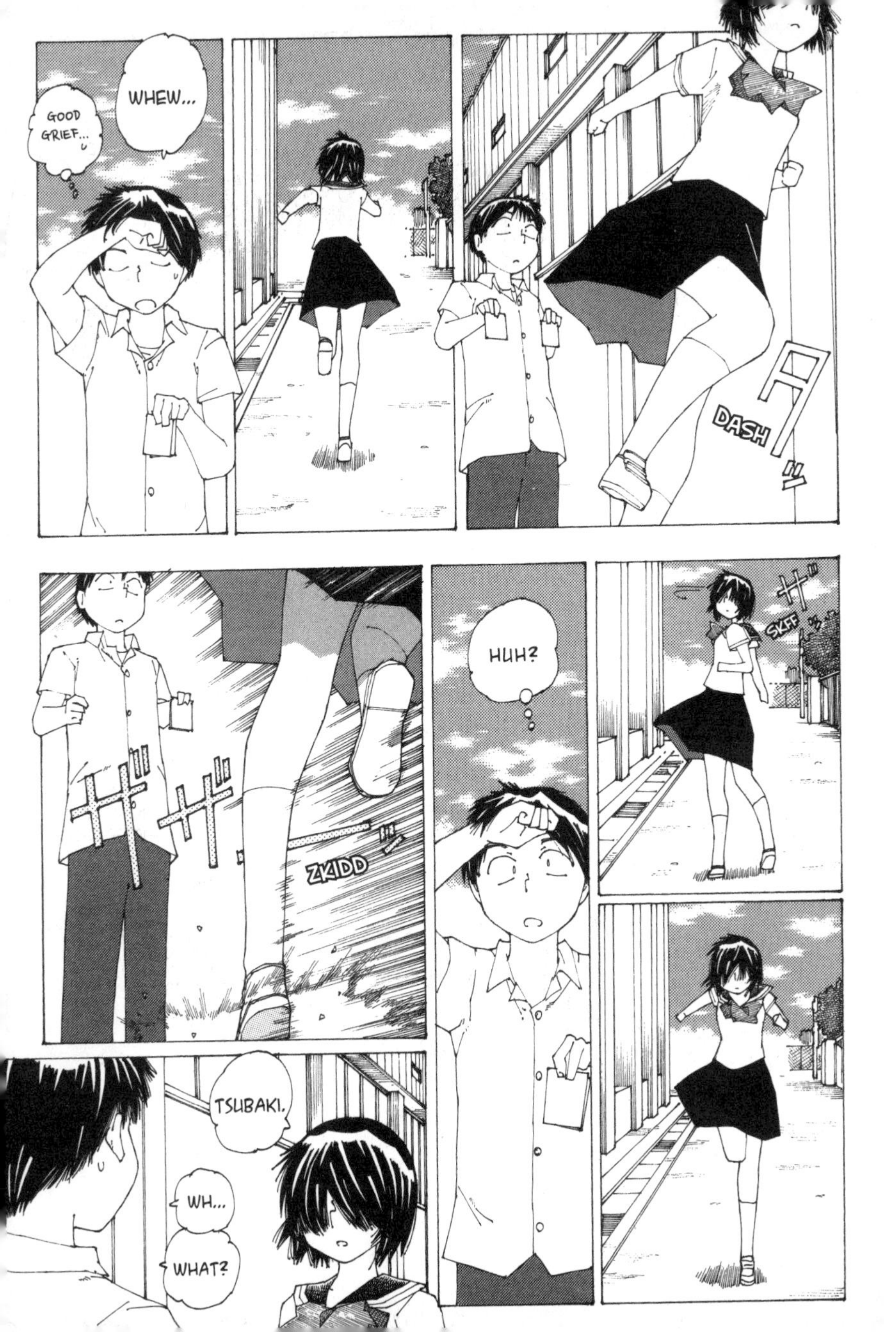
DASH
WHEW...
GOOD GRIEF...
SKFF
HUH?
ZKIDD
TSUBAKI.
WH...
WHAT?

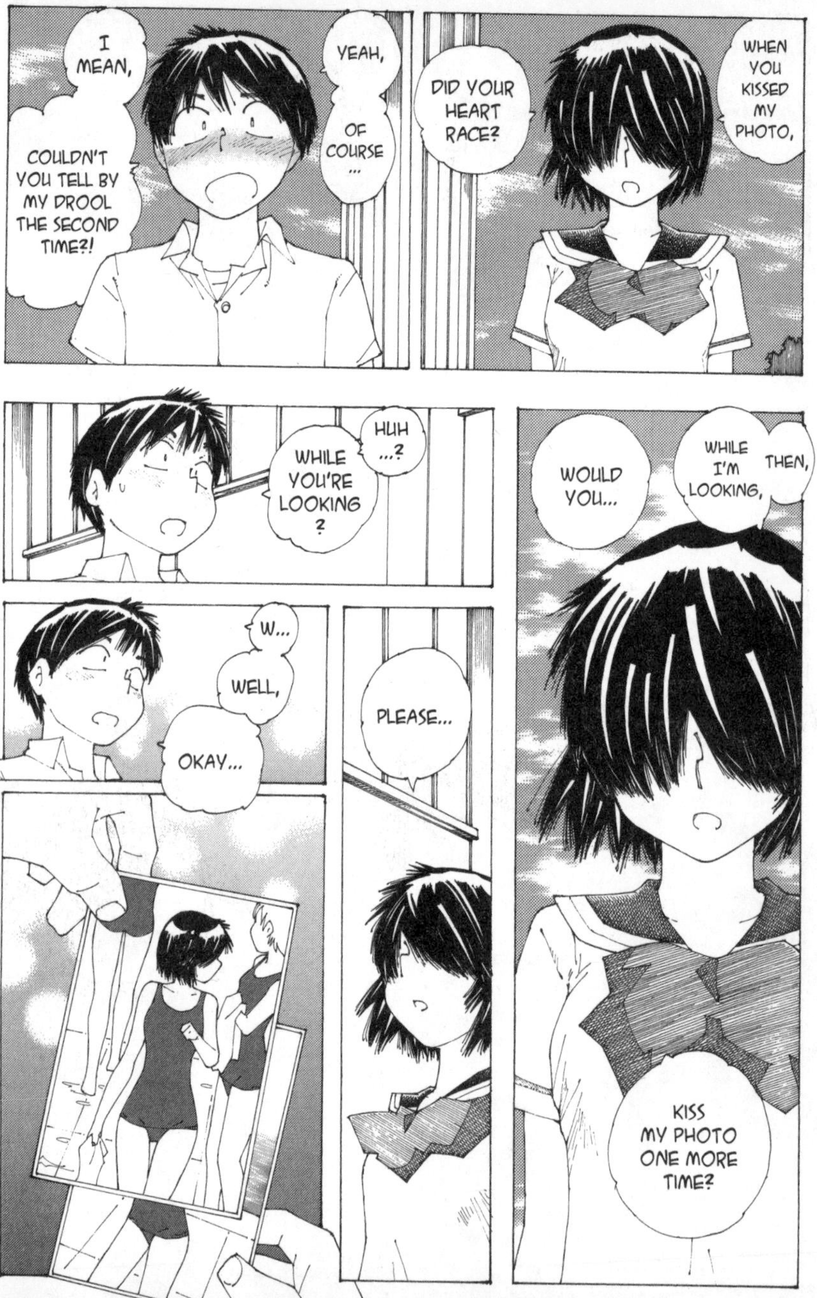
WHEN YOU KISSED MY PHOTO,
DID YOUR HEART RACE?
YEAH,
OF COURSE ...
I MEAN,
COULDN'T YOU TELL BY MY DROOL THE SECOND TIME?!
THEN,
WHILE I'M LOOKING,
WOULD YOU...
KISS MY PHOTO ONE MORE TIME?
HUH ...?
WHILE YOU'RE LOOKING ?
PLEASE...
W...
WELL,
OKAY...

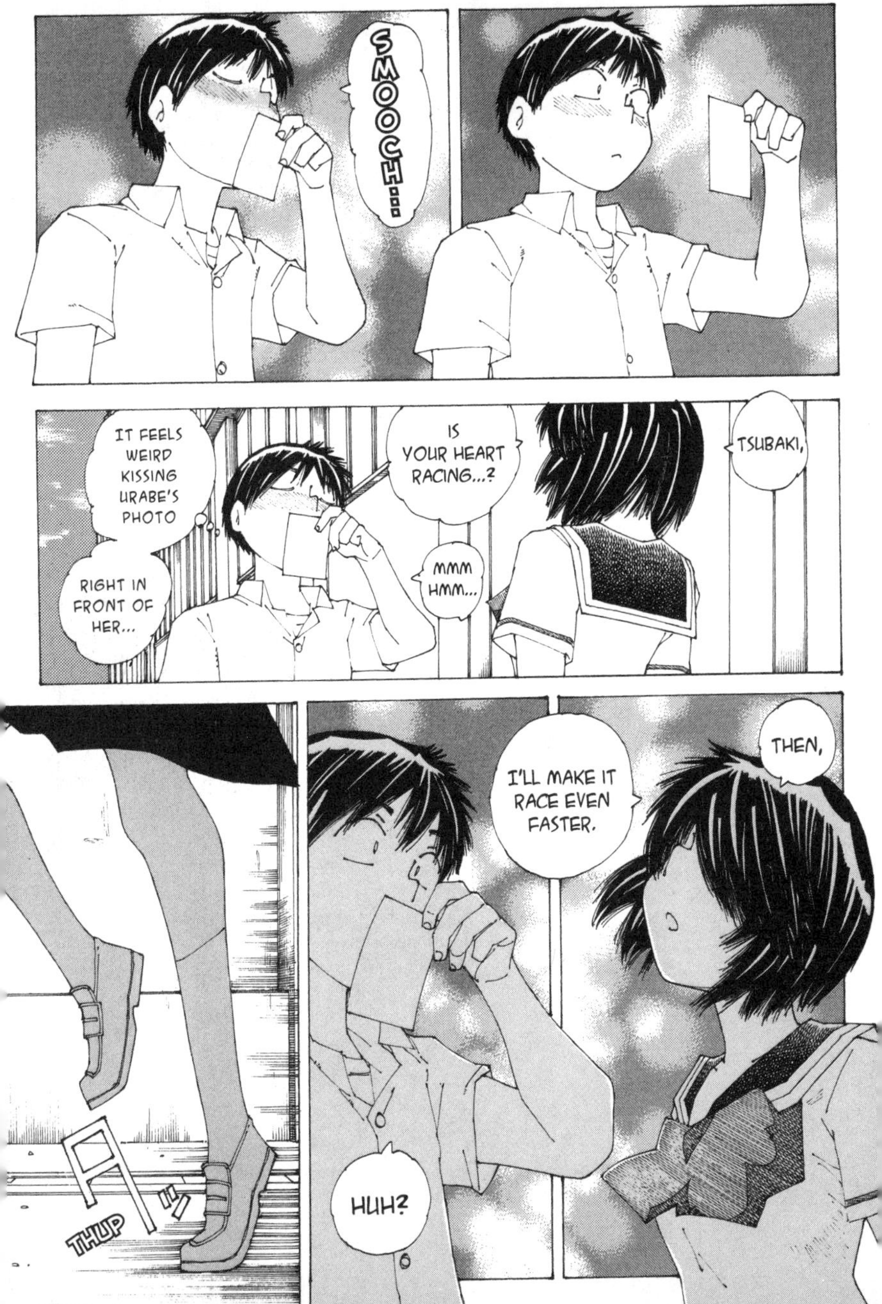
SMOOCH...
TSUBAKI,
IS YOUR HEART RACING...?
MMM HMM...
IT FEELS WEIRD KISSING URABE'S PHOTO
RIGHT IN FRONT OF HER...
THEN,
I'LL MAKE IT RACE EVEN FASTER.
HUH?
THUP

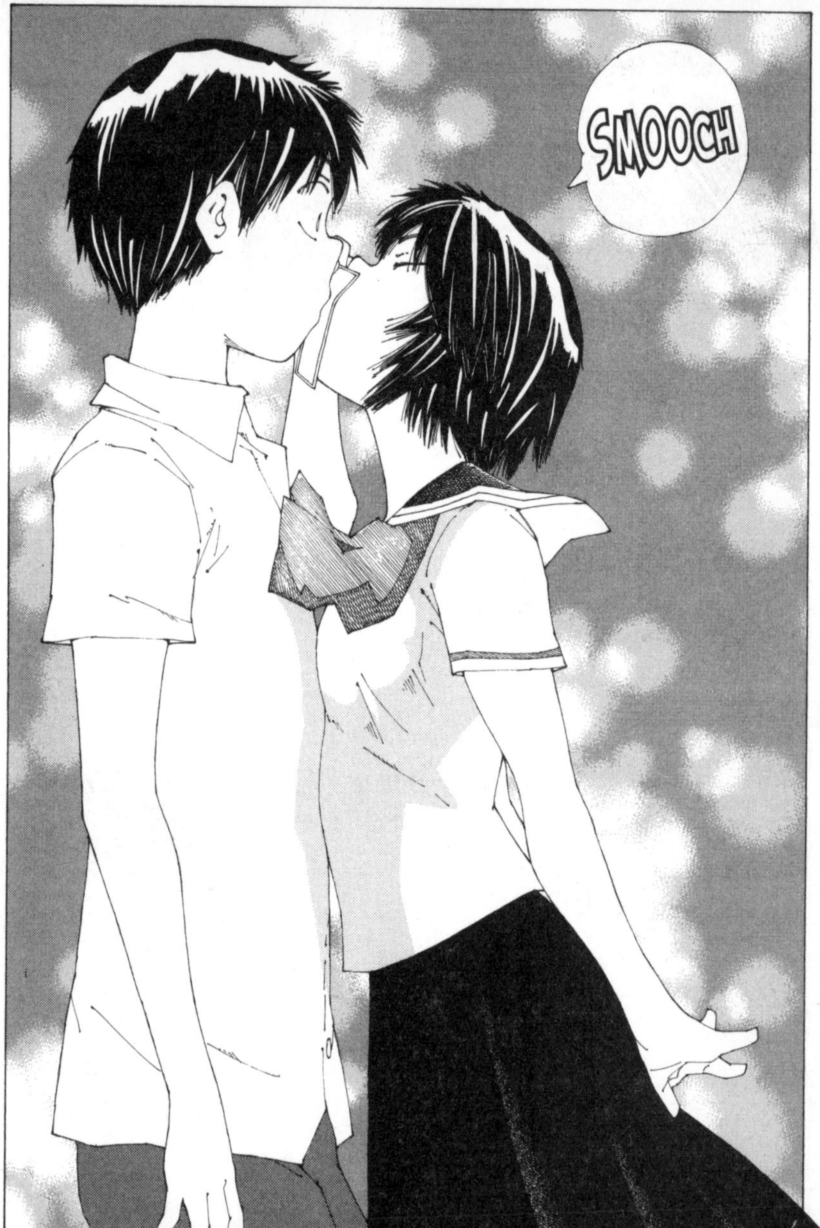
SMOOCH

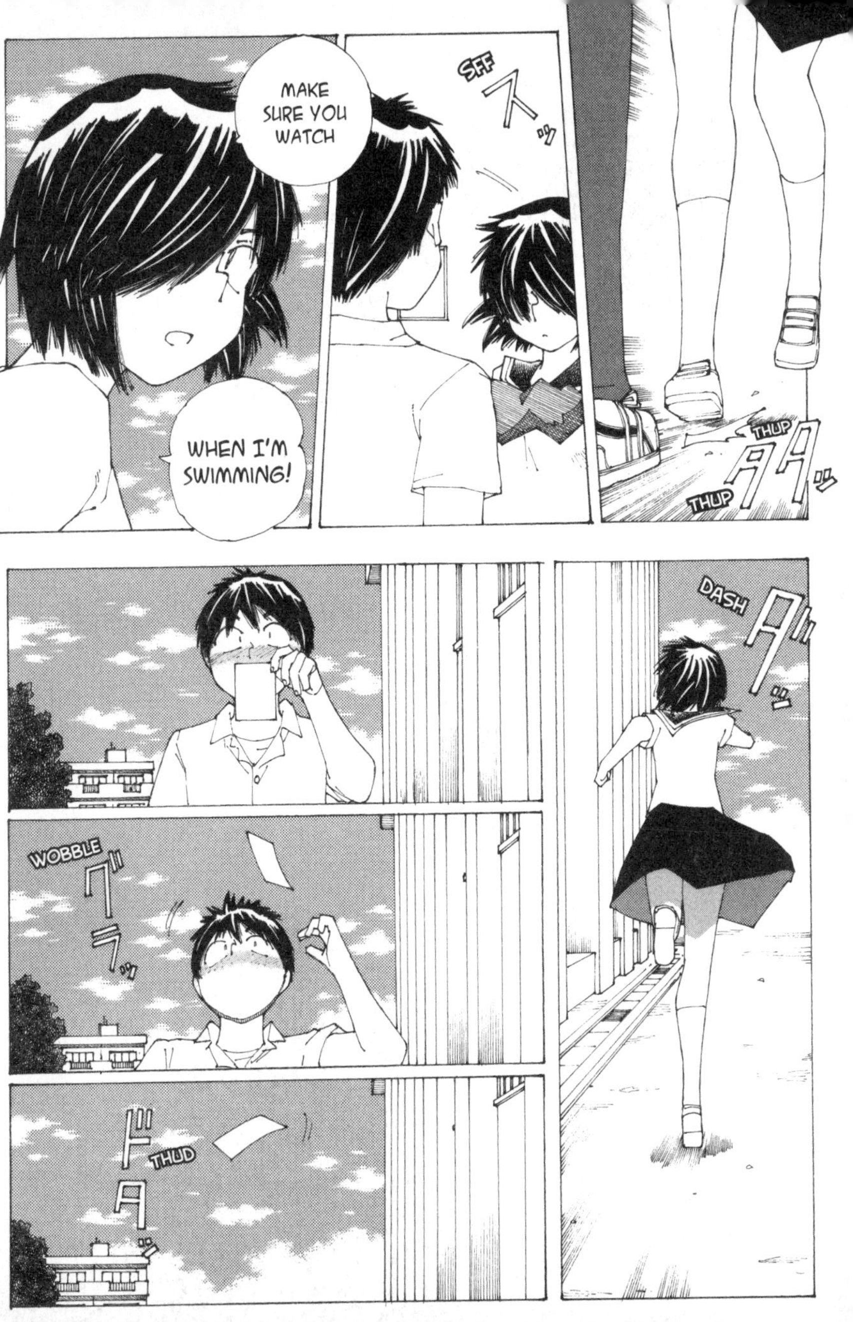
THUP
THUP
SFF
MAKE SURE YOU WATCH
WHEN I'M SWIMMING!
DASH
WOBBLE
THUD

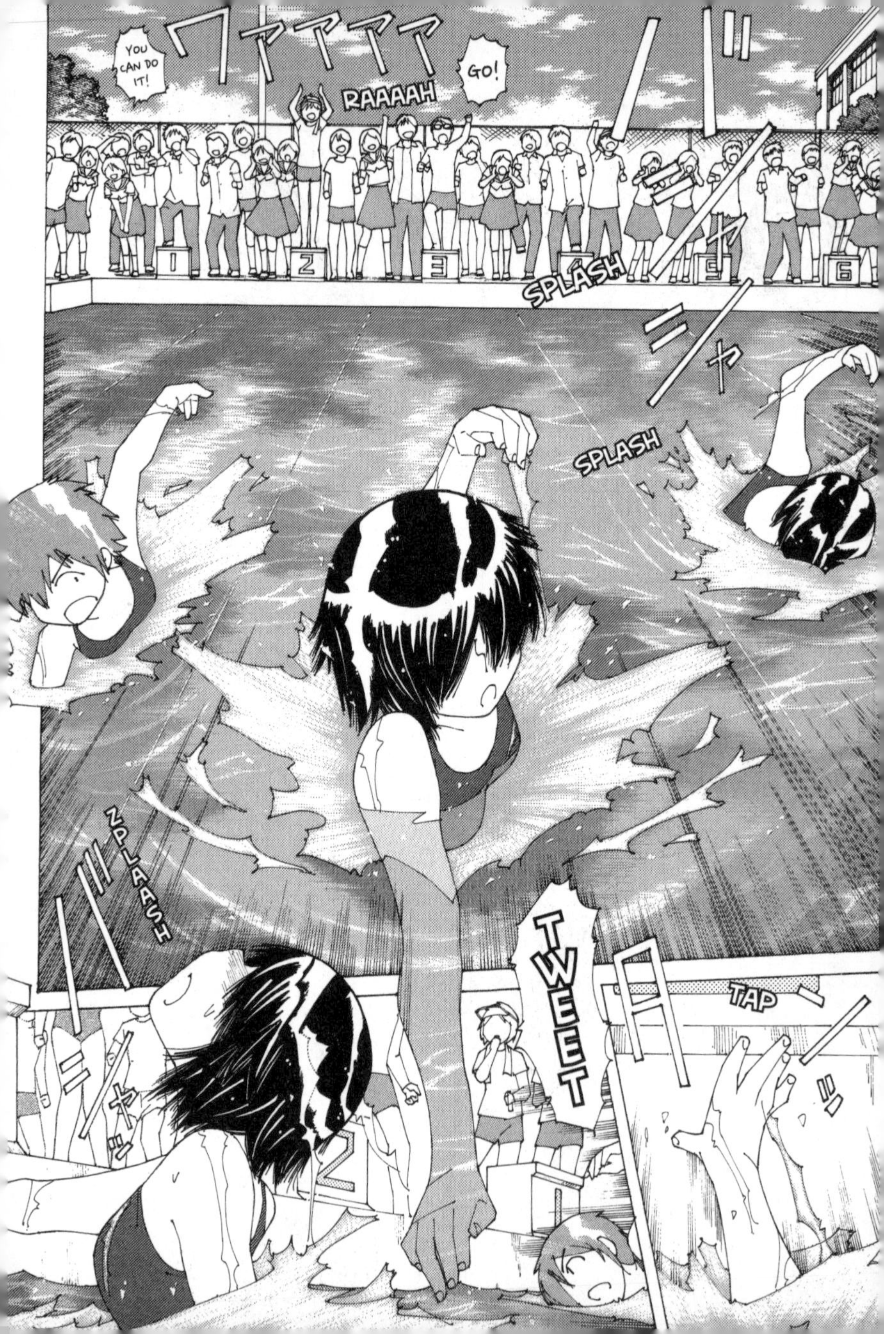
GO!
RAAAAH
ワアアアア
YOU CAN DO IT!
SPLASH
SPLASH
TAP
TWEET
ZPLAAASH

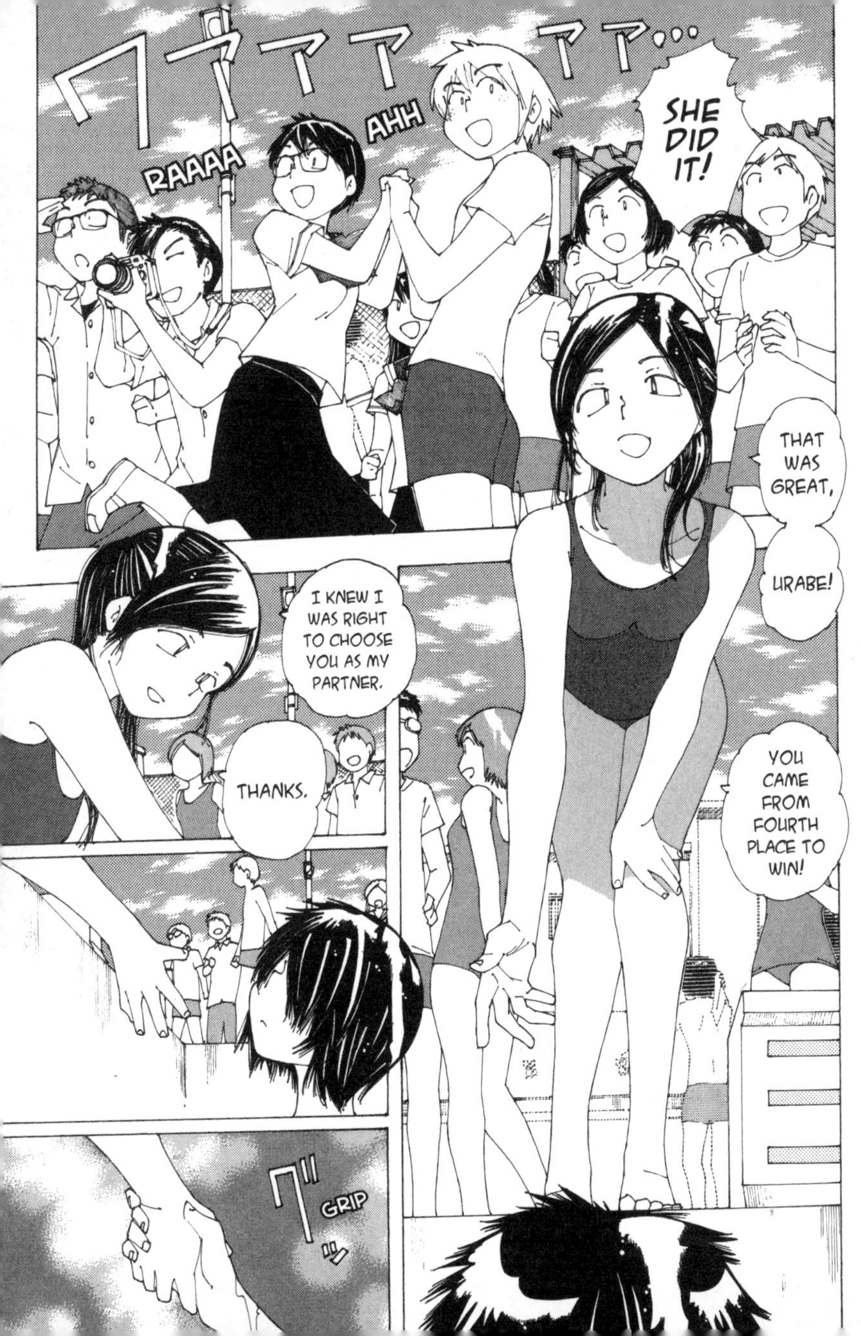
ワァアア アア…
SHE DID IT!
AHH
RAAAA
THAT WAS GREAT,
URABE!
YOU CAME FROM FOURTH PLACE TO WIN!
I KNEW I WAS RIGHT TO CHOOSE YOU AS MY PARTNER.
THANKS.
グッ
GRIP

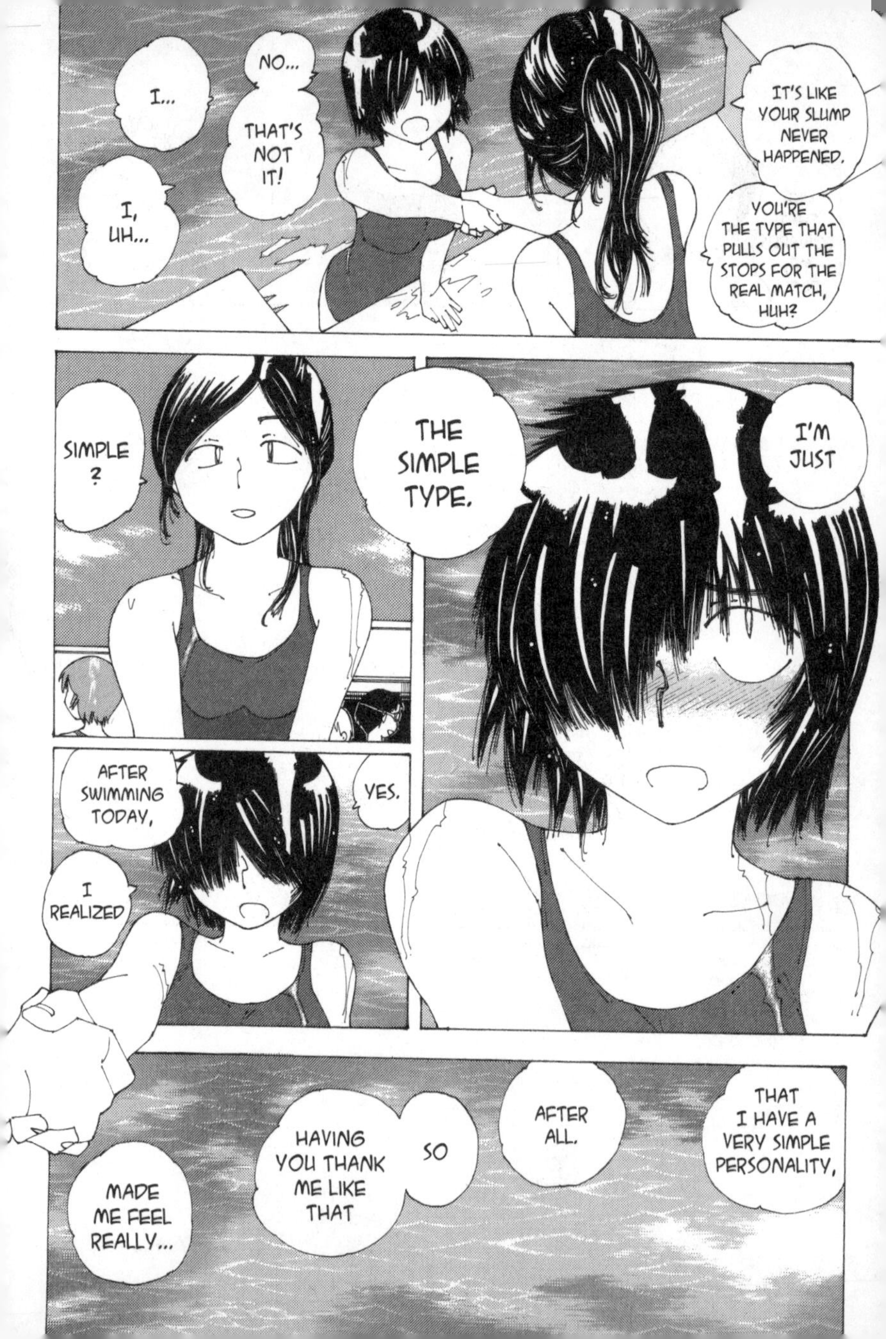
IT'S LIKE YOUR SLUMP NEVER HAPPENED.
YOU'RE THE TYPE THAT PULLS OUT THE STOPS FOR THE REAL MATCH, HUH?
NO...
THAT'S NOT IT!
I...
I, UH...
I'M JUST
THE SIMPLE TYPE.
SIMPLE?
YES.
AFTER SWIMMING TODAY,
I REALIZED
THAT I HAVE A VERY SIMPLE PERSONALITY,
AFTER ALL.
SO
HAVING YOU THANK ME LIKE THAT
MADE ME FEEL REALLY...

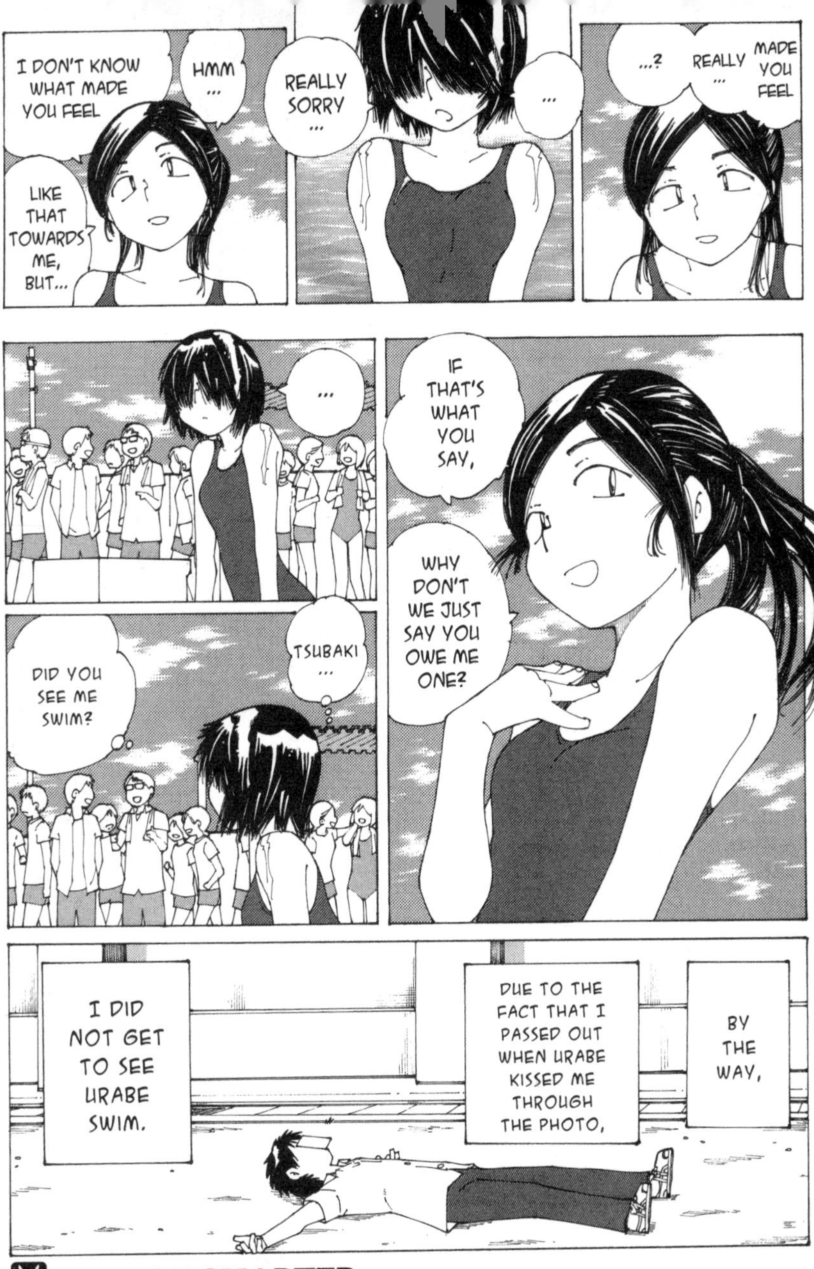
MADE YOU FEEL
REALLY ...
...?
...
REALLY SORRY ...
HMM ...
I DON'T KNOW WHAT MADE YOU FEEL
LIKE THAT TOWARDS ME, BUT...
IF THAT'S WHAT YOU SAY,
WHY DON'T WE JUST SAY YOU OWE ME ONE?
...
TSUBAKI ...
DID YOU SEE ME SWIM?
BY THE WAY,
DUE TO THE FACT THAT I PASSED OUT WHEN URABE KISSED ME THROUGH THE PHOTO,
I DID NOT GET TO SEE URABE SWIM.

END OF CHAPTER 59

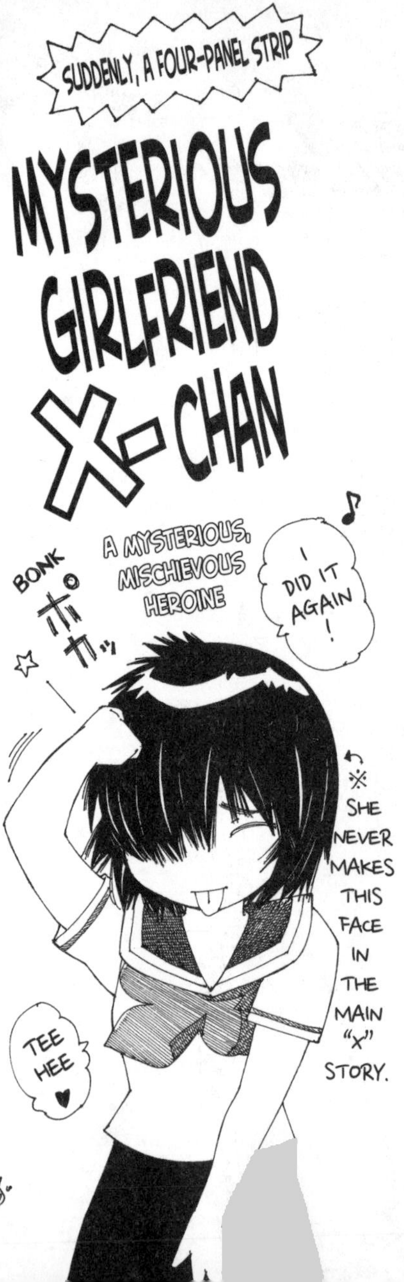
SUDDENLY, A FOUR-PANEL STRIP
MYSTERIOUS GIRLFRIEND X-CHAN
I DID IT AGAIN!
A MYSTERIOUS, MISCHIEVOUS HEROINE
BONK
ポカッ
※ SHE NEVER MAKES THIS FACE IN THE MAIN "X" STORY.
TEE HEE ♥

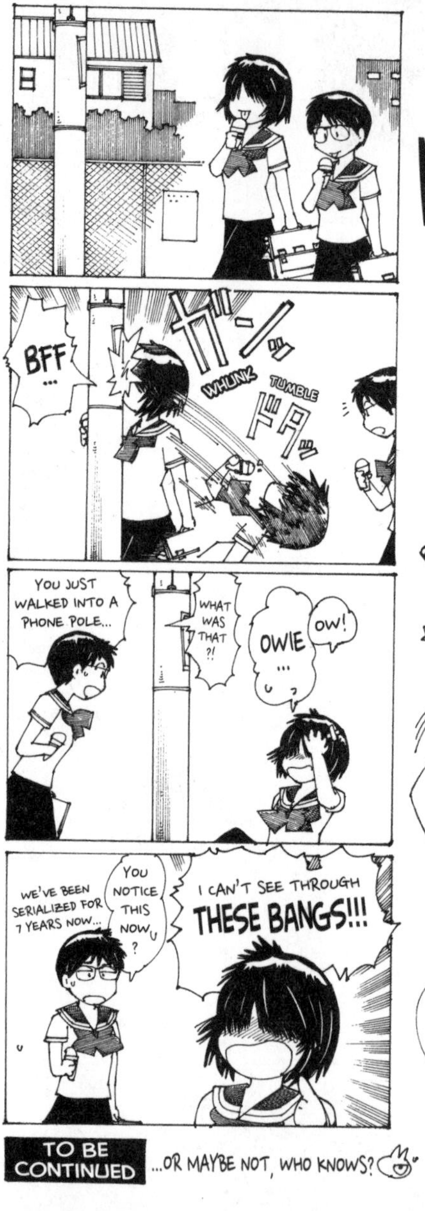
TUMBLE
ドタッ
WHUNK
ガーンッ
BFF...
OW!
OWIE...
WHAT WAS THAT?!
YOU JUST WALKED INTO A PHONE POLE...
I CAN'T SEE THROUGH THESE BANGS!!!
YOU NOTICE THIS NOW?
WE'VE BEEN SERIALIZED FOR 7 YEARS NOW...
TO BE CONTINUED
...OR MAYBE NOT, WHO KNOWS?

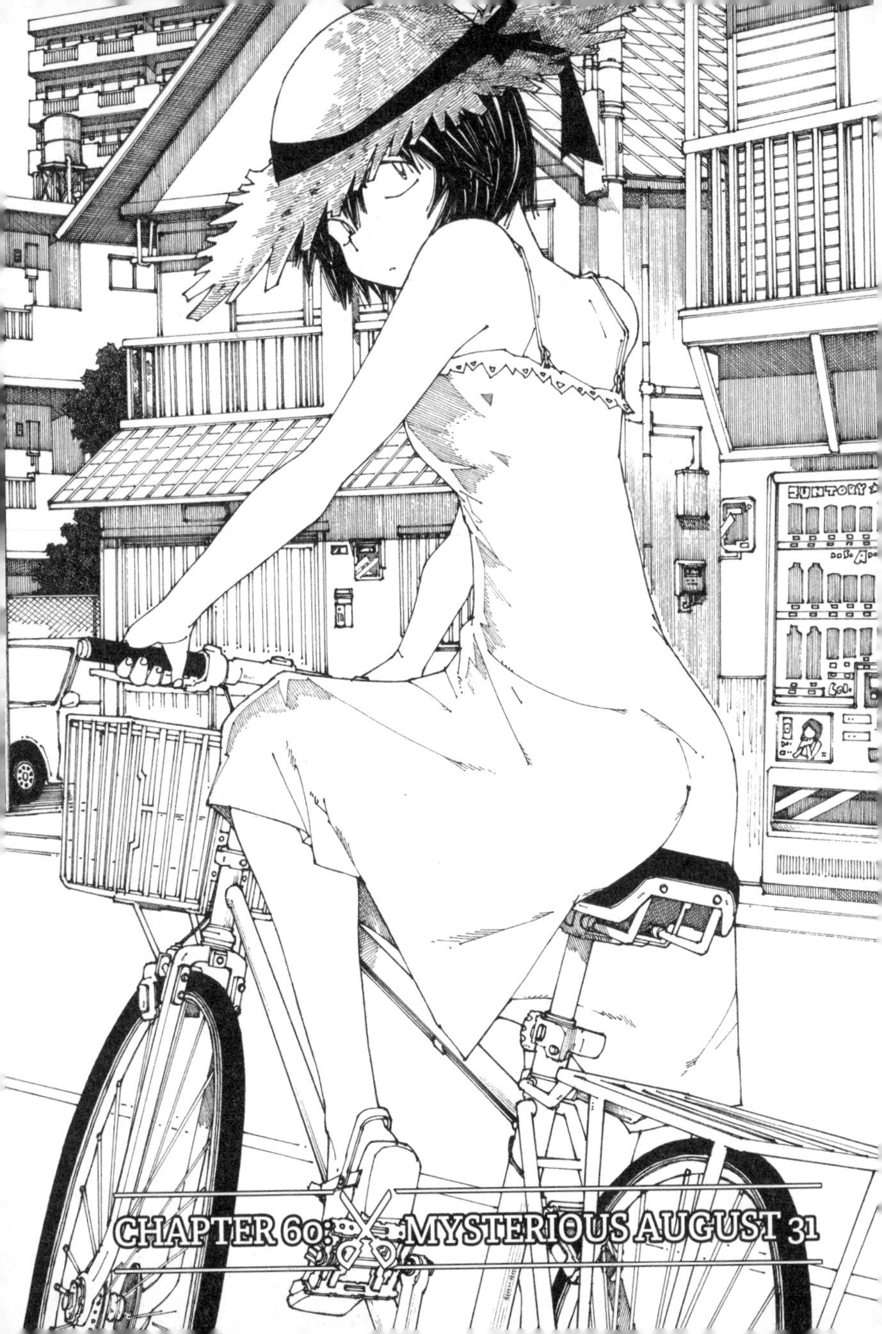
CHAPTER 60: MYSTERIOUS AUGUST 31

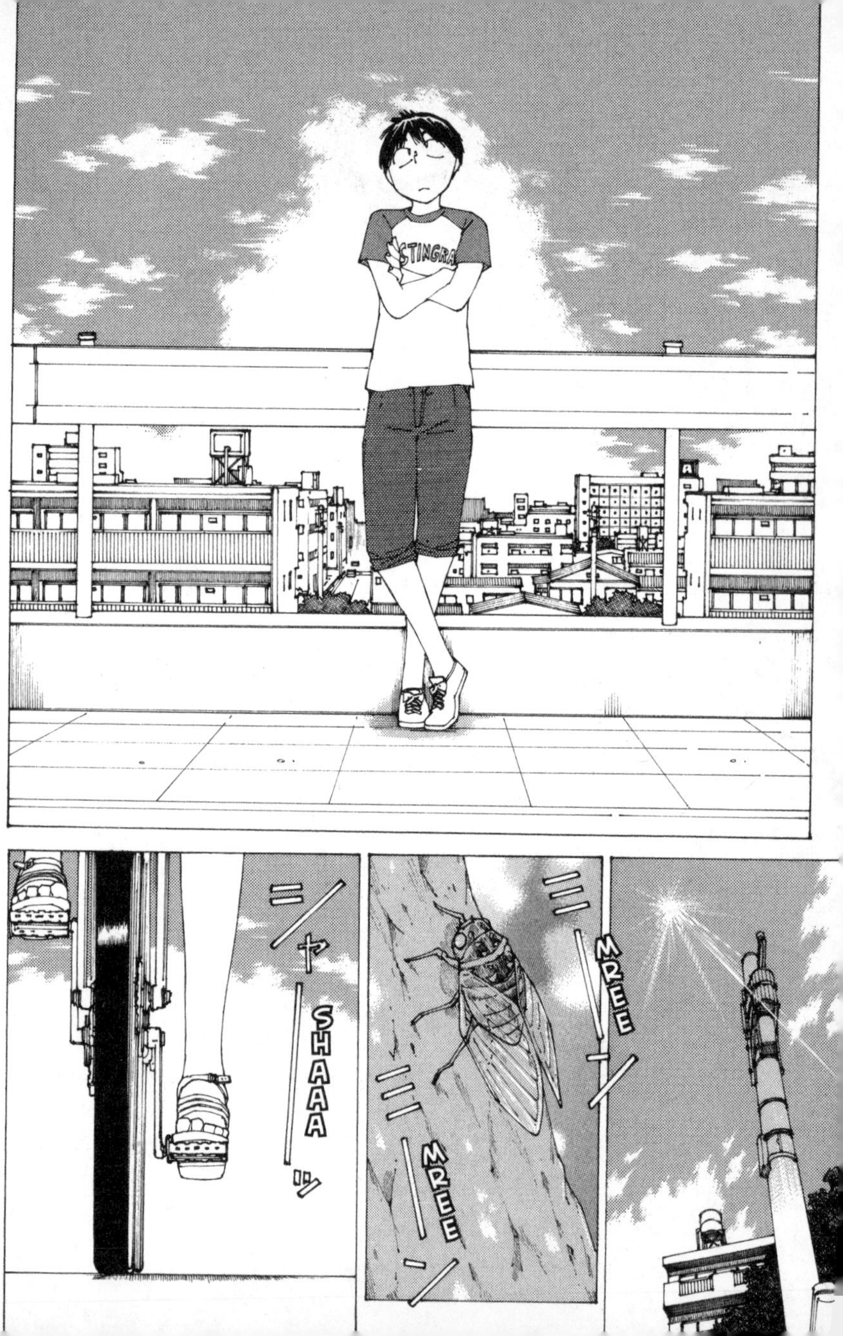
STINGRA
ミー
MREE
ミー
MREE
シャー
SHAAA
ッ

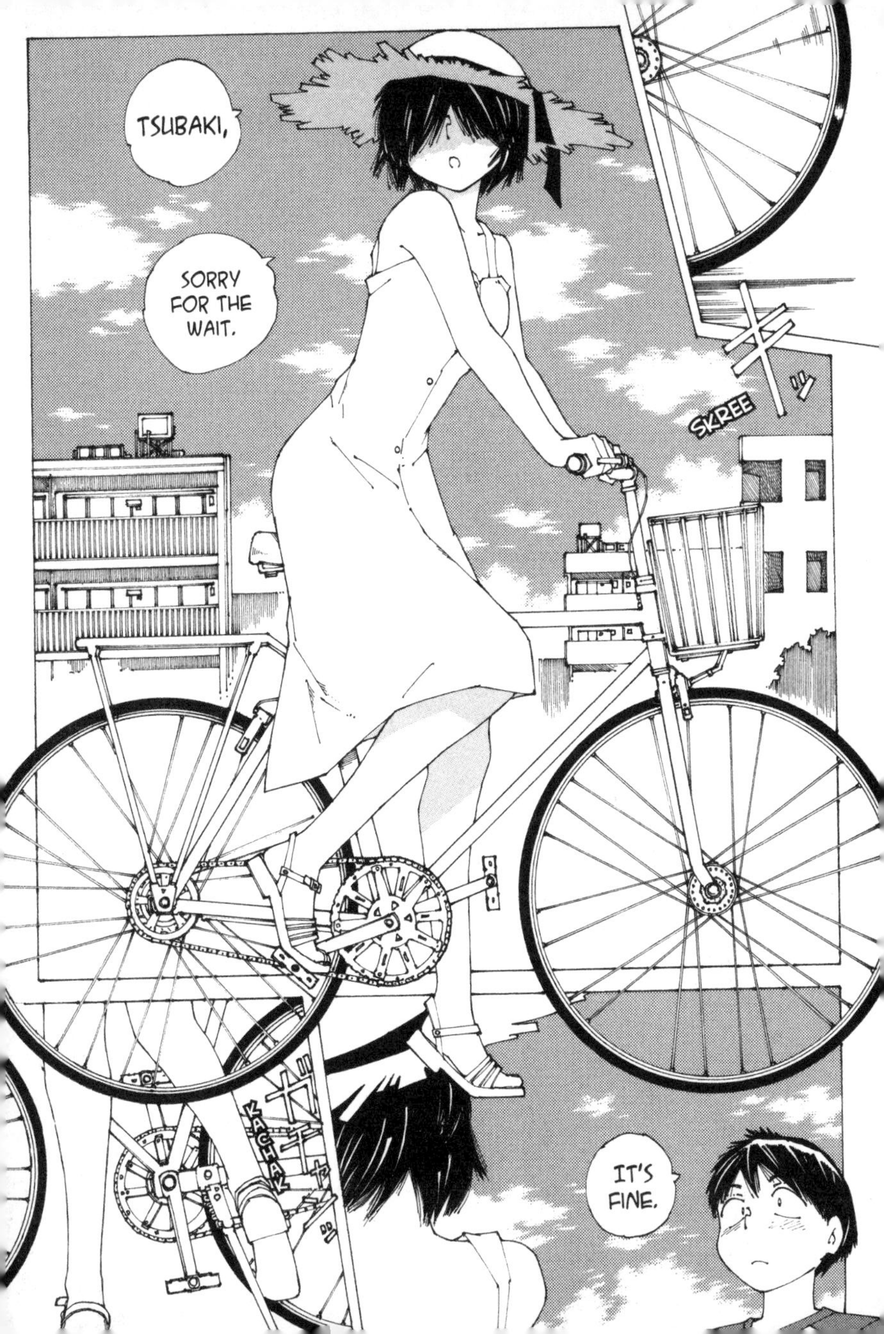
SKREE
TSUBAKI,
SORRY FOR THE WAIT.
KACHAK
IT'S FINE.

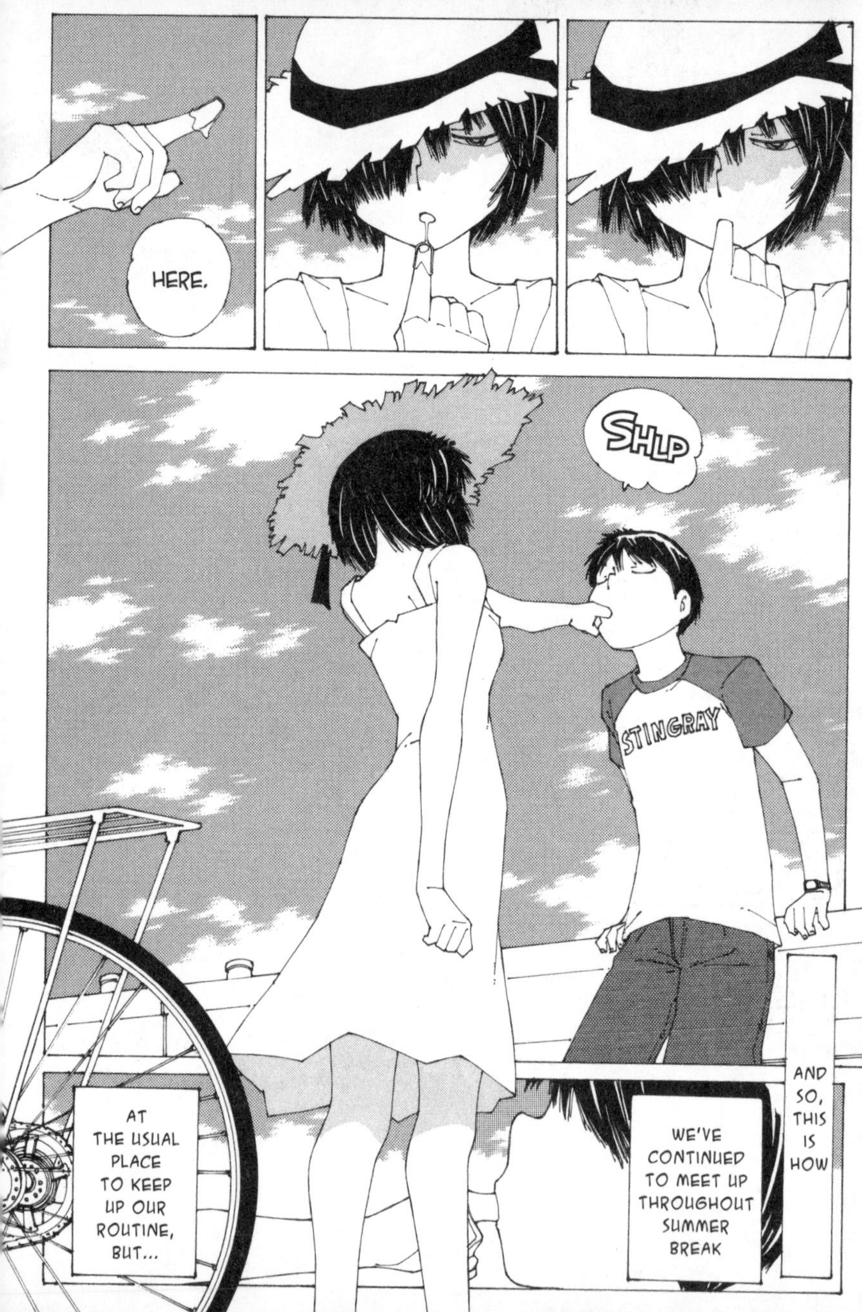
HERE.
SHLP
STINGRAY
AND SO, THIS IS HOW
WE'VE CONTINUED TO MEET UP THROUGHOUT SUMMER BREAK
AT THE USUAL PLACE TO KEEP UP OUR ROUTINE, BUT...

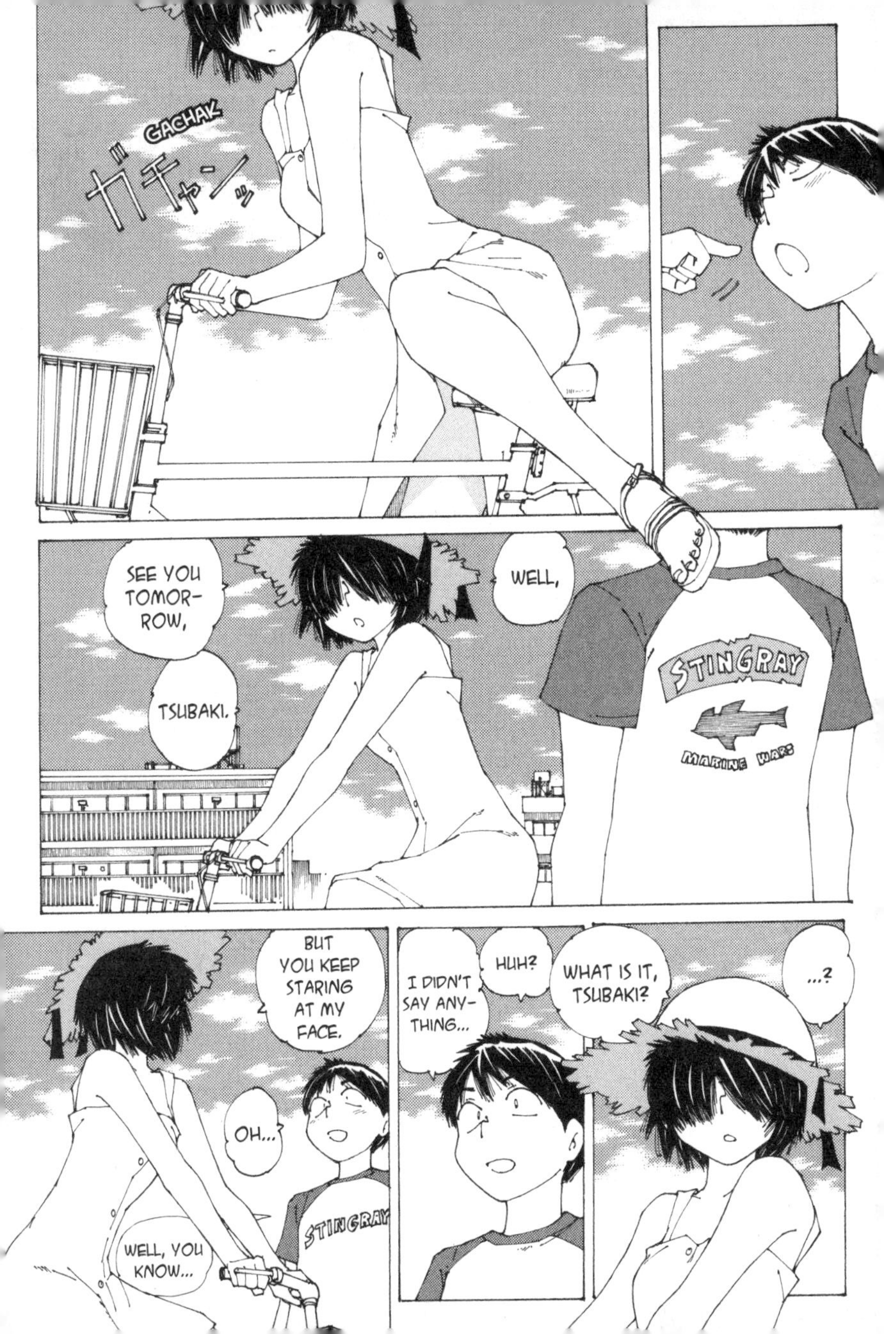
GACHAK
ガチャーンッ
WELL,
SEE YOU TOMORROW,
TSUBAKI.
STINGRAY
...?
WHAT IS IT, TSUBAKI?
HUH?
I DIDN'T SAY ANYTHING...
BUT YOU KEEP STARING AT MY FACE.
OH...
STINGRAY
WELL, YOU KNOW...

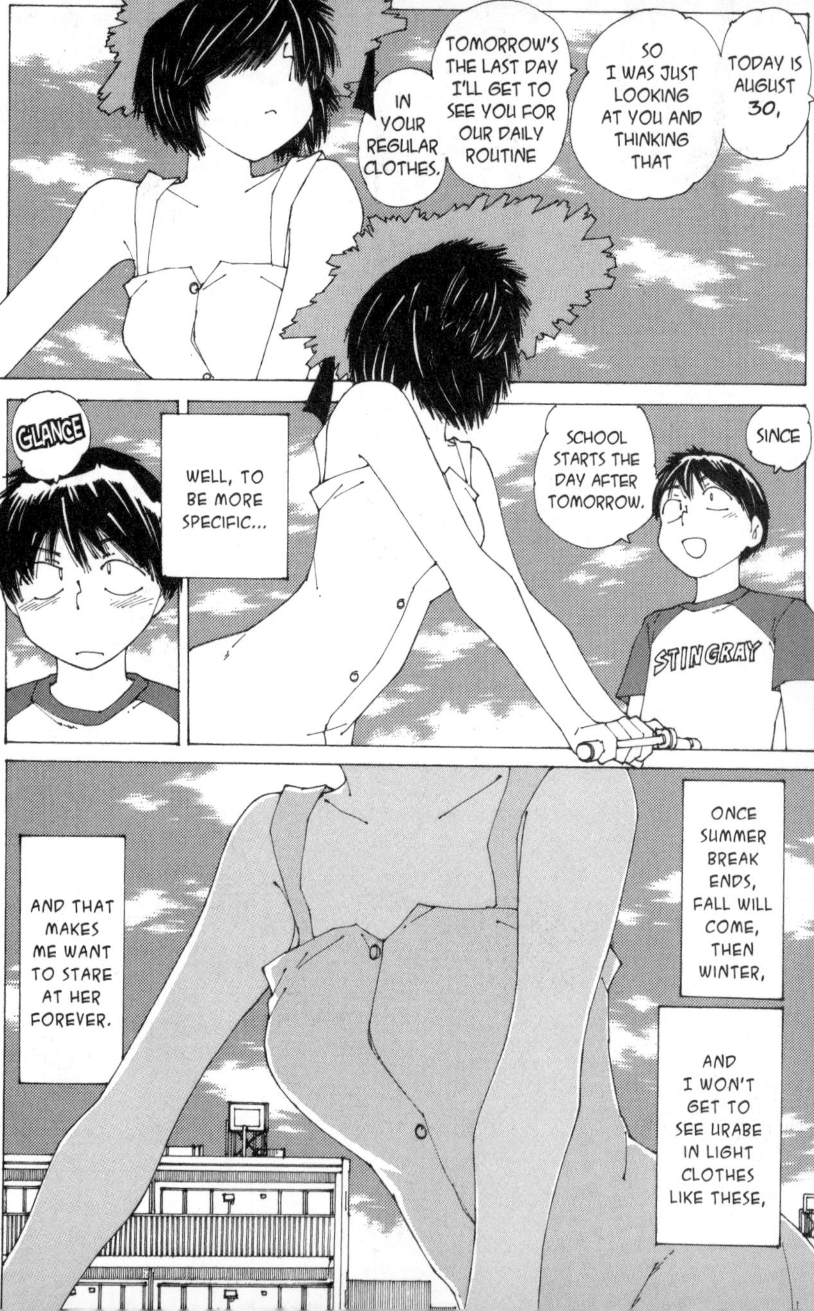
TODAY IS AUGUST 30,
SO I WAS JUST LOOKING AT YOU AND THINKING THAT
TOMORROW'S THE LAST DAY I'LL GET TO SEE YOU FOR OUR DAILY ROUTINE
IN YOUR REGULAR CLOTHES.
SINCE
SCHOOL STARTS THE DAY AFTER TOMORROW.
STINGRAY
WELL, TO BE MORE SPECIFIC...
GLANCE
ONCE SUMMER BREAK ENDS, FALL WILL COME, THEN WINTER,
AND I WON'T GET TO SEE URABE IN LIGHT CLOTHES LIKE THESE,
AND THAT MAKES ME WANT TO STARE AT HER FOREVER.

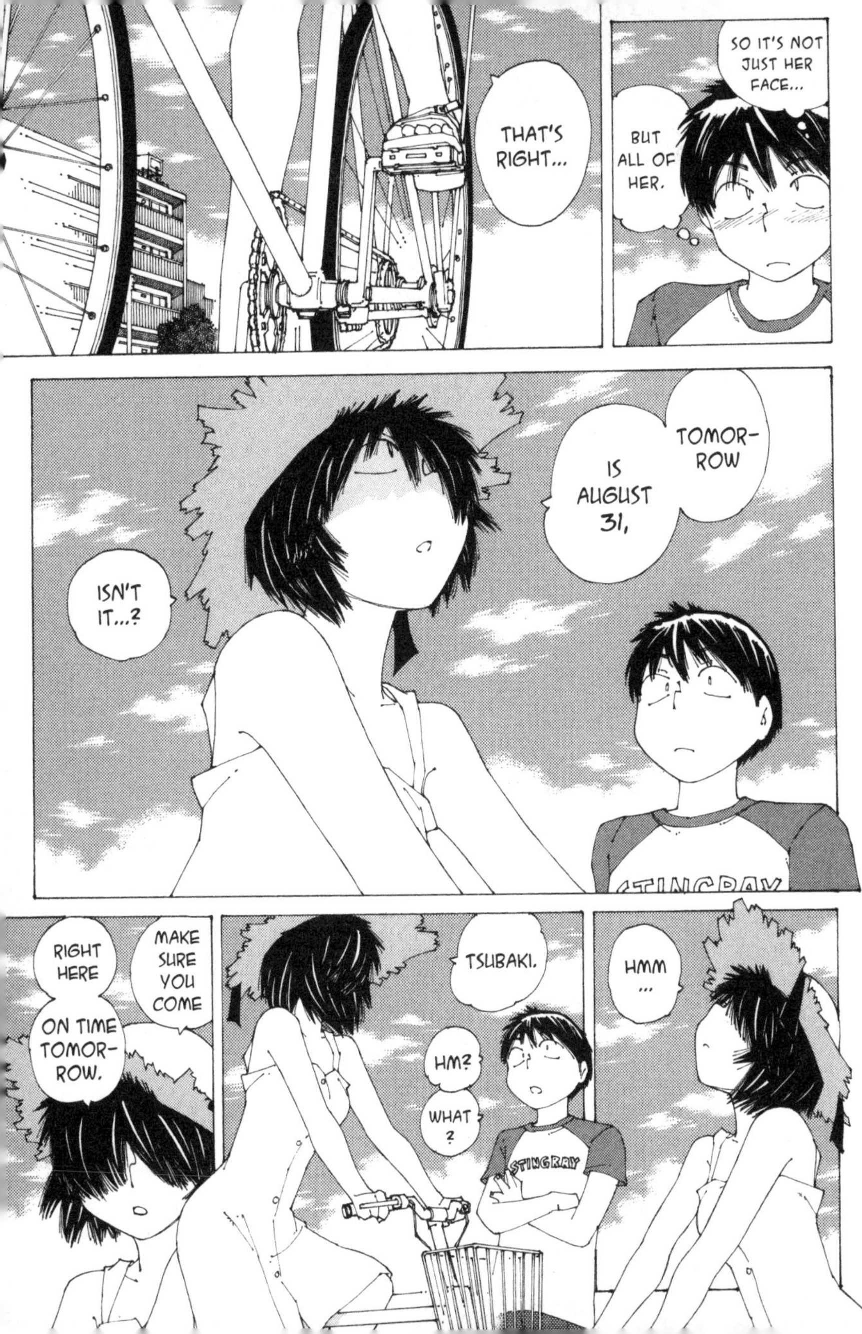
SO IT'S NOT JUST HER FACE...
BUT ALL OF HER.
THAT'S RIGHT...
TOMORROW
IS AUGUST 31,
ISN'T IT...?
HMM ...
TSUBAKI.
HM?
WHAT?
STINGRAY
MAKE SURE YOU COME
RIGHT HERE
ON TIME TOMORROW.

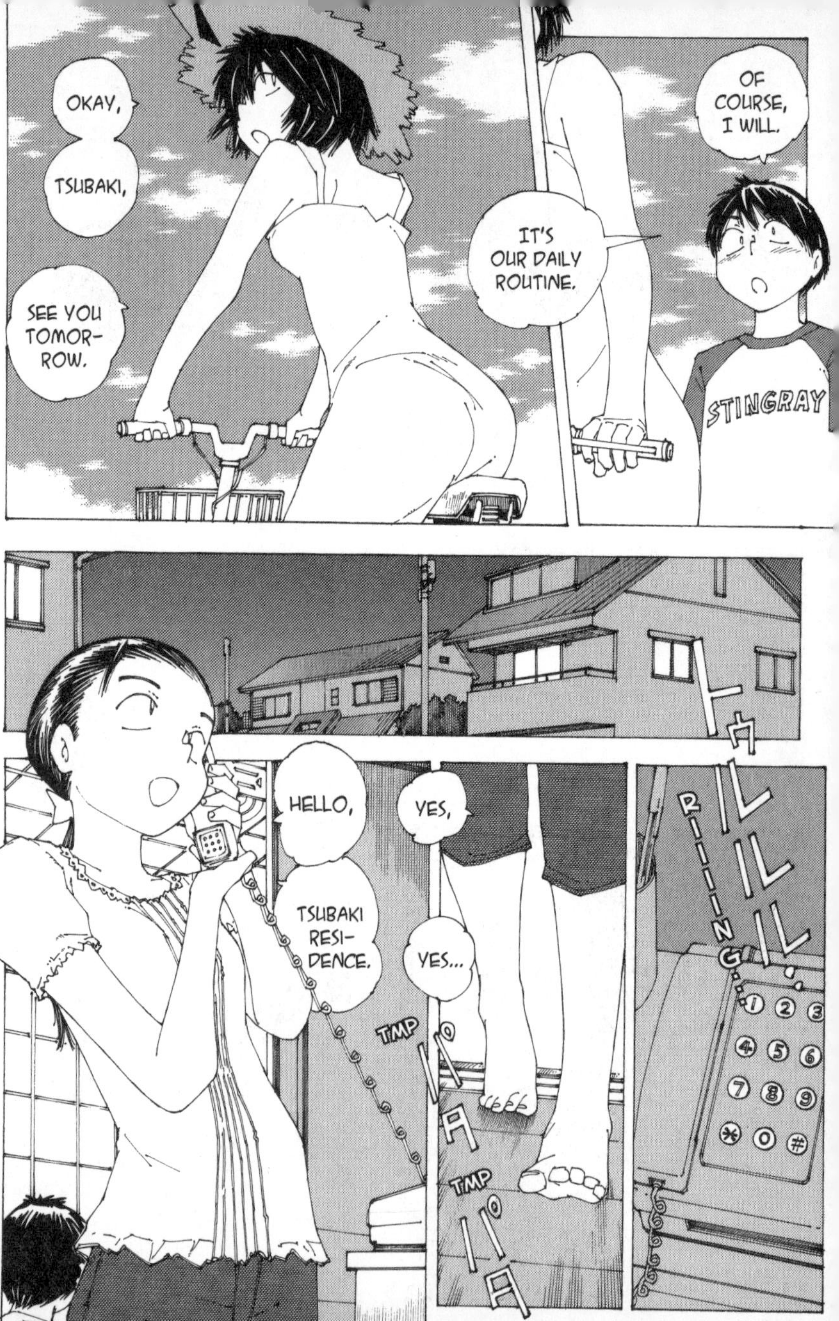
OF COURSE, I WILL.
IT'S OUR DAILY ROUTINE.
OKAY,
TSUBAKI,
SEE YOU TOMORROW.
RIIIING...
TMP
TMP
HELLO,
TSUBAKI RESIDENCE.
YES,
YES...

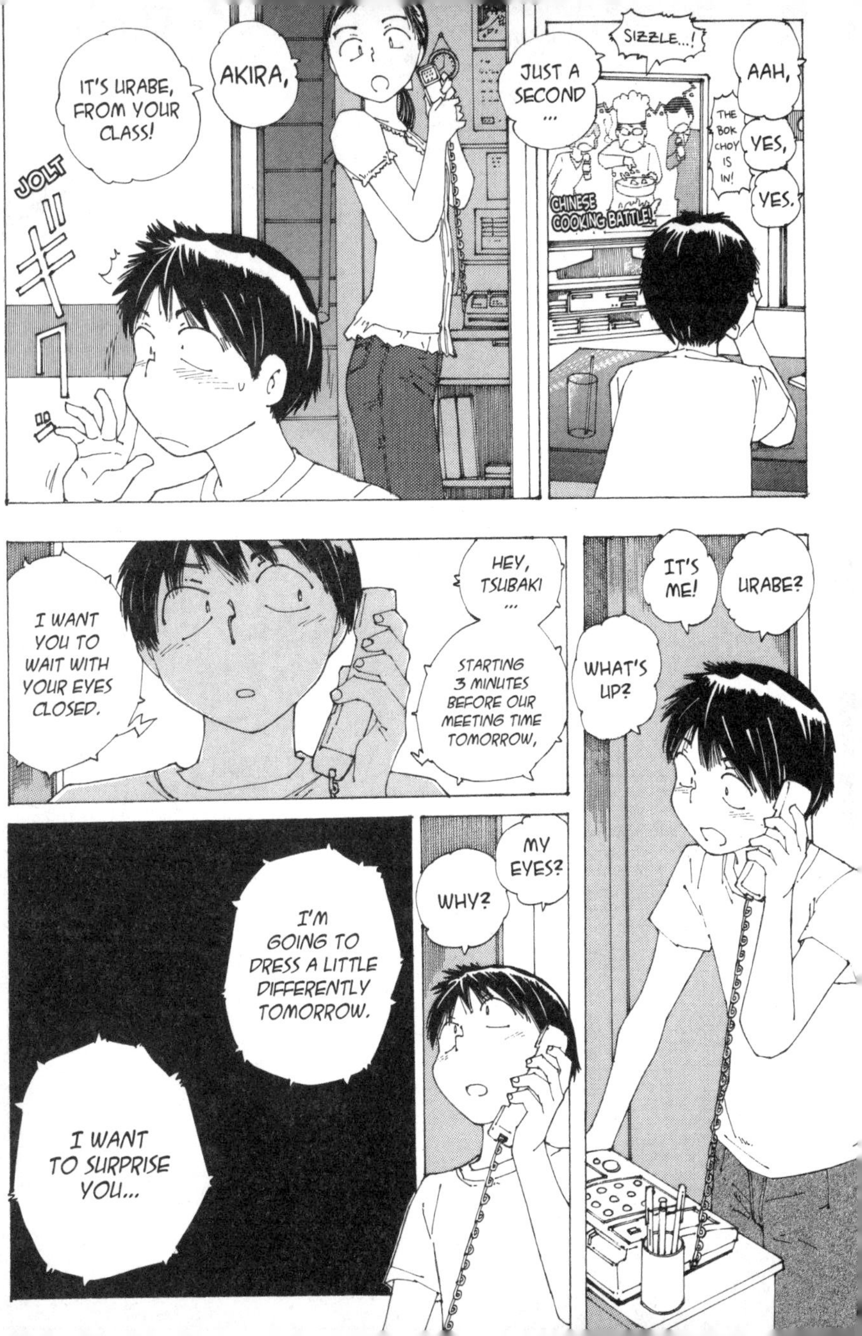
SIZZLE...!
AAH,
YES,
YES.
THE BOK CHOY IS IN!
JUST A SECOND ...
CHINESE COOKING BATTLE!
AKIRA,
IT'S URABE, FROM YOUR CLASS!
JOLT
URABE?
IT'S ME!
WHAT'S UP?
HEY, TSUBAKI ...
STARTING 3 MINUTES BEFORE OUR MEETING TIME TOMORROW,
I WANT YOU TO WAIT WITH YOUR EYES CLOSED.
MY EYES?
WHY?
I'M GOING TO DRESS A LITTLE DIFFERENTLY TOMORROW.
I WANT TO SURPRISE YOU...

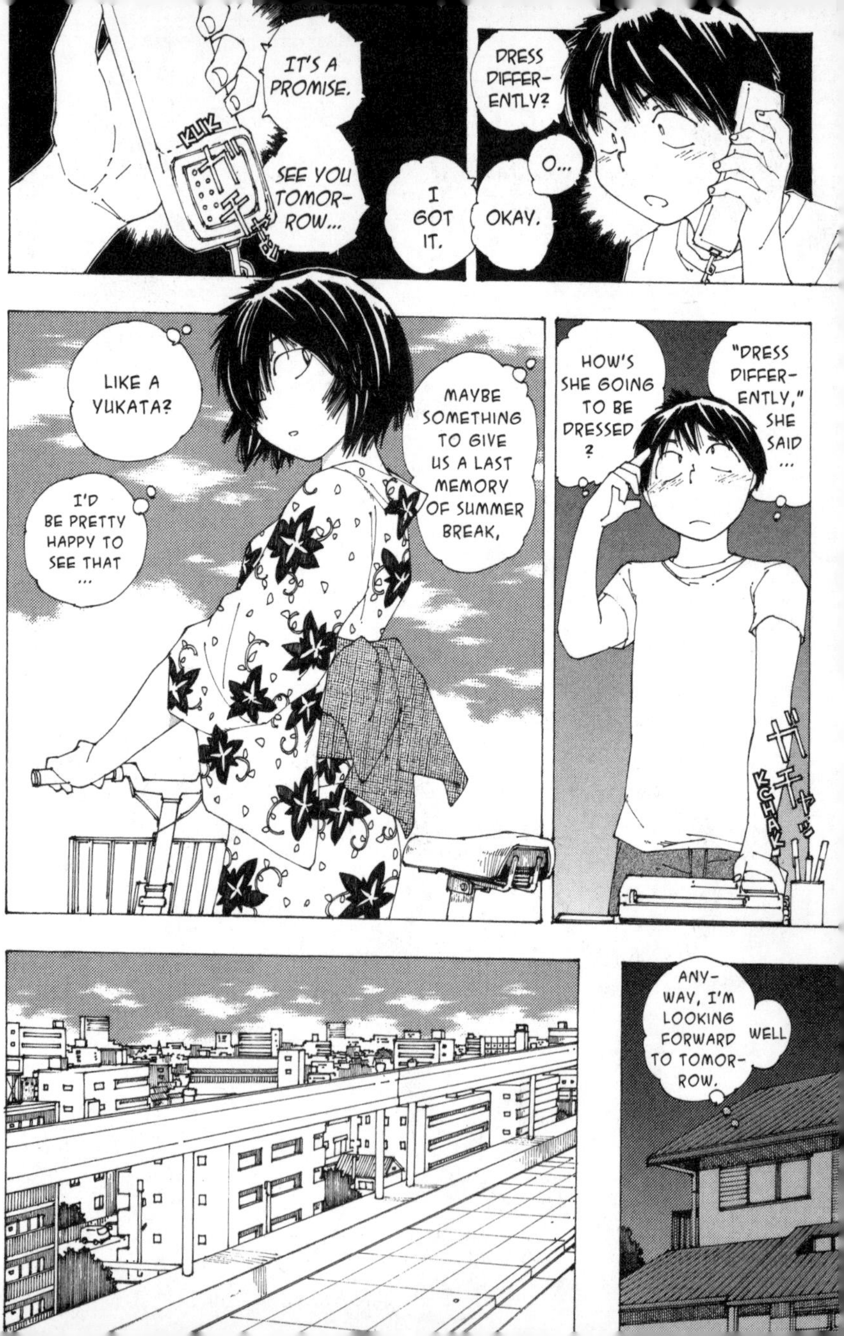
DRESS DIFFER-ENTLY?
O...
OKAY.
I GOT IT.
IT'S A PROMISE.
KLIK
SEE YOU TOMOR-ROW...
"DRESS DIFFER-ENTLY," SHE SAID ...
HOW'S SHE GOING TO BE DRESSED ?
KCHAK
MAYBE SOMETHING TO GIVE US A LAST MEMORY OF SUMMER BREAK,
LIKE A YUKATA?
I'D BE PRETTY HAPPY TO SEE THAT ...
WELL
ANY-WAY, I'M LOOKING FORWARD TO TOMOR-ROW.

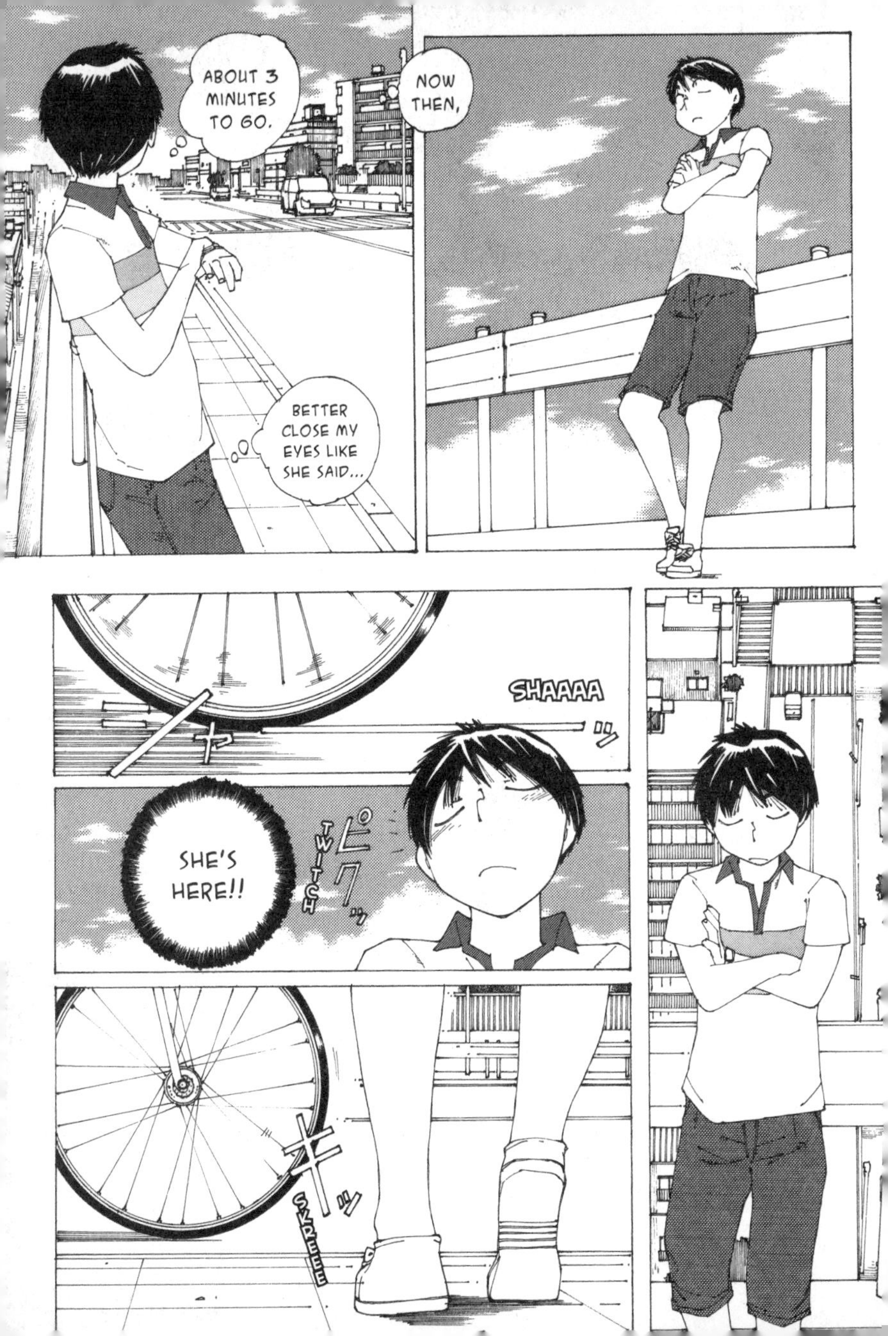
NOW THEN,
ABOUT 3 MINUTES TO GO.
BETTER CLOSE MY EYES LIKE SHE SAID...
SHAAAA
SHE'S HERE!!
ピクッ
TWITCH
キッ
SKREEE

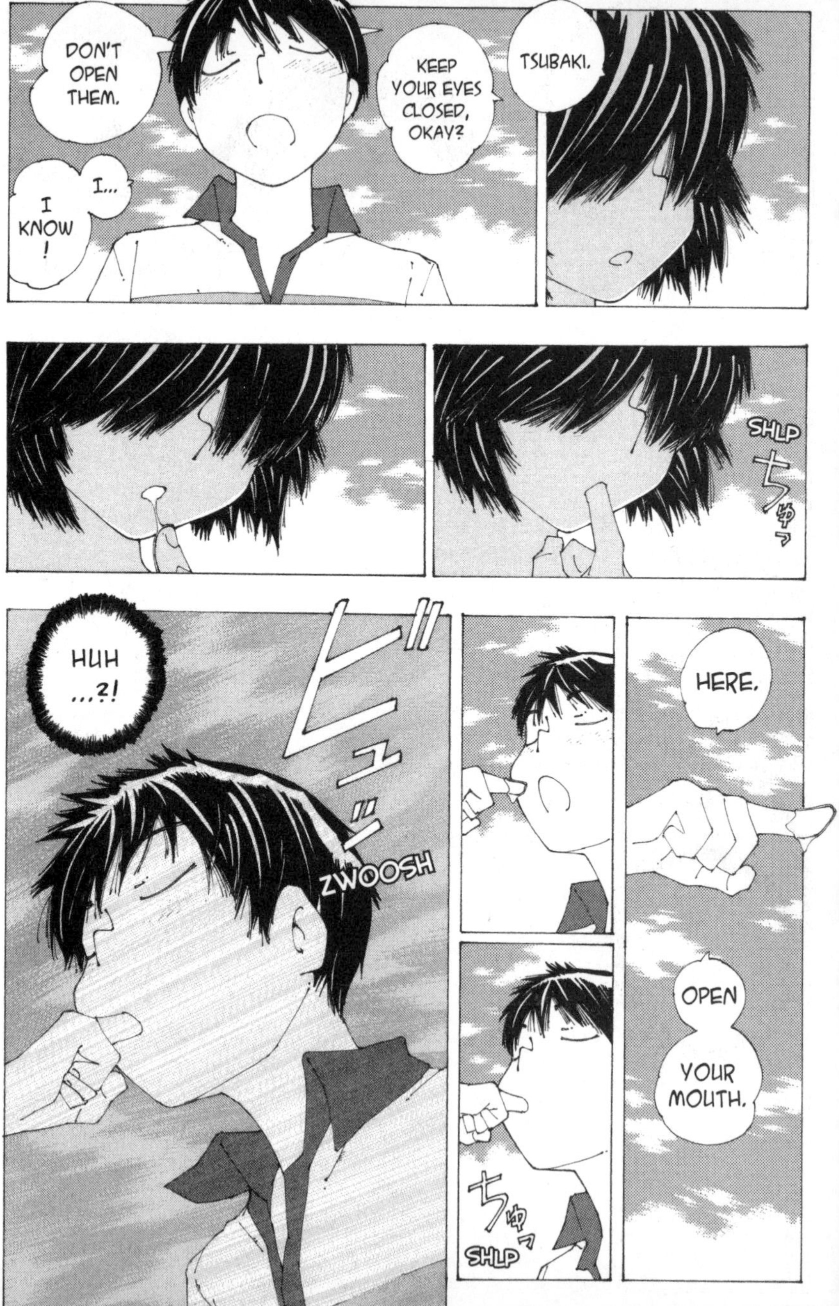
TSUBAKI.
KEEP YOUR EYES CLOSED, OKAY?
DON'T OPEN THEM.
I...
I KNOW!
SHLP
ちゅっ
HERE.
OPEN YOUR MOUTH.
ちゅっ
SHLP
HUH ...?!
ZWOOSH

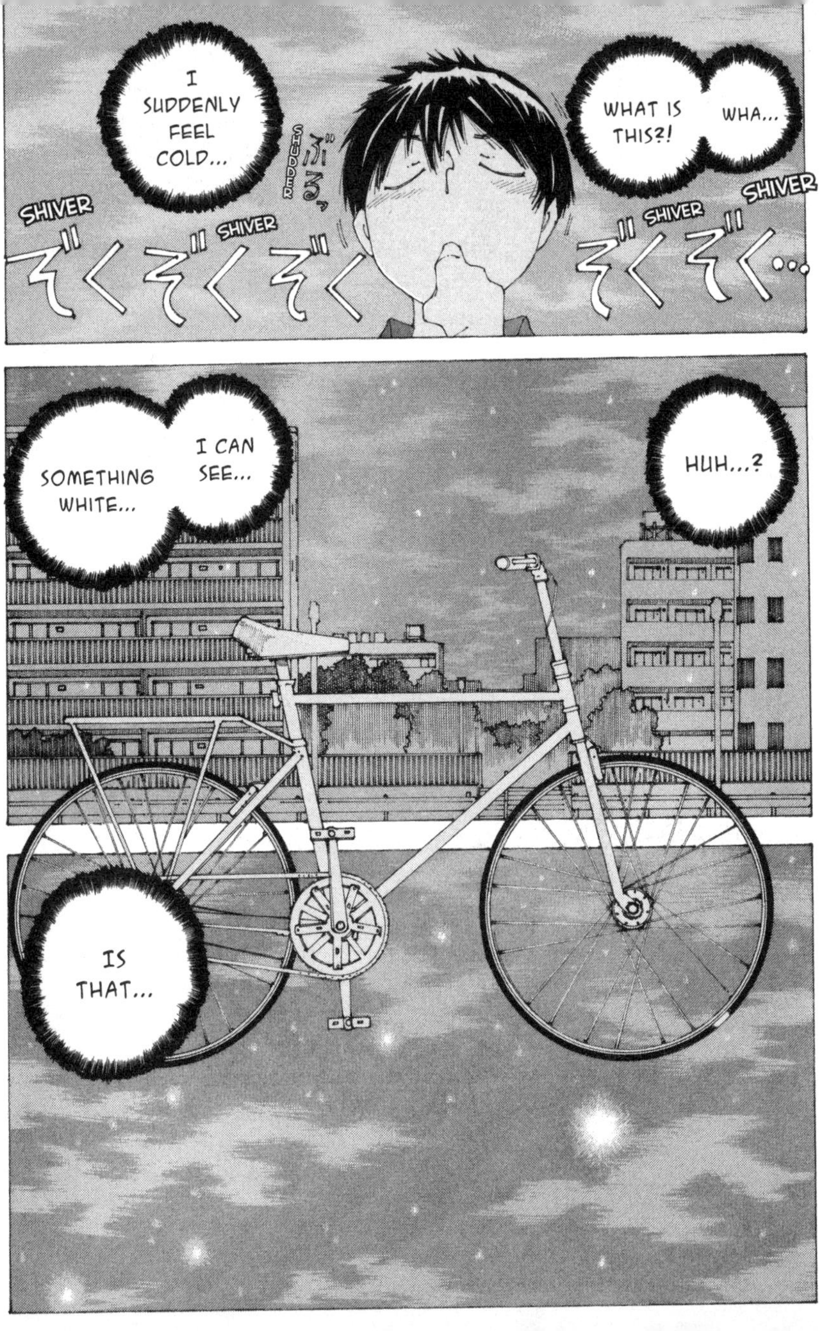
WHA...
WHAT IS THIS?!
SHIVER
SHIVER
ぞくぞく…
ぶるっ
SHUDDER
I SUDDENLY FEEL COLD...
SHIVER
SHIVER
ぞくぞくぞく
HUH...?
I CAN SEE...
SOMETHING WHITE...
IS THAT...

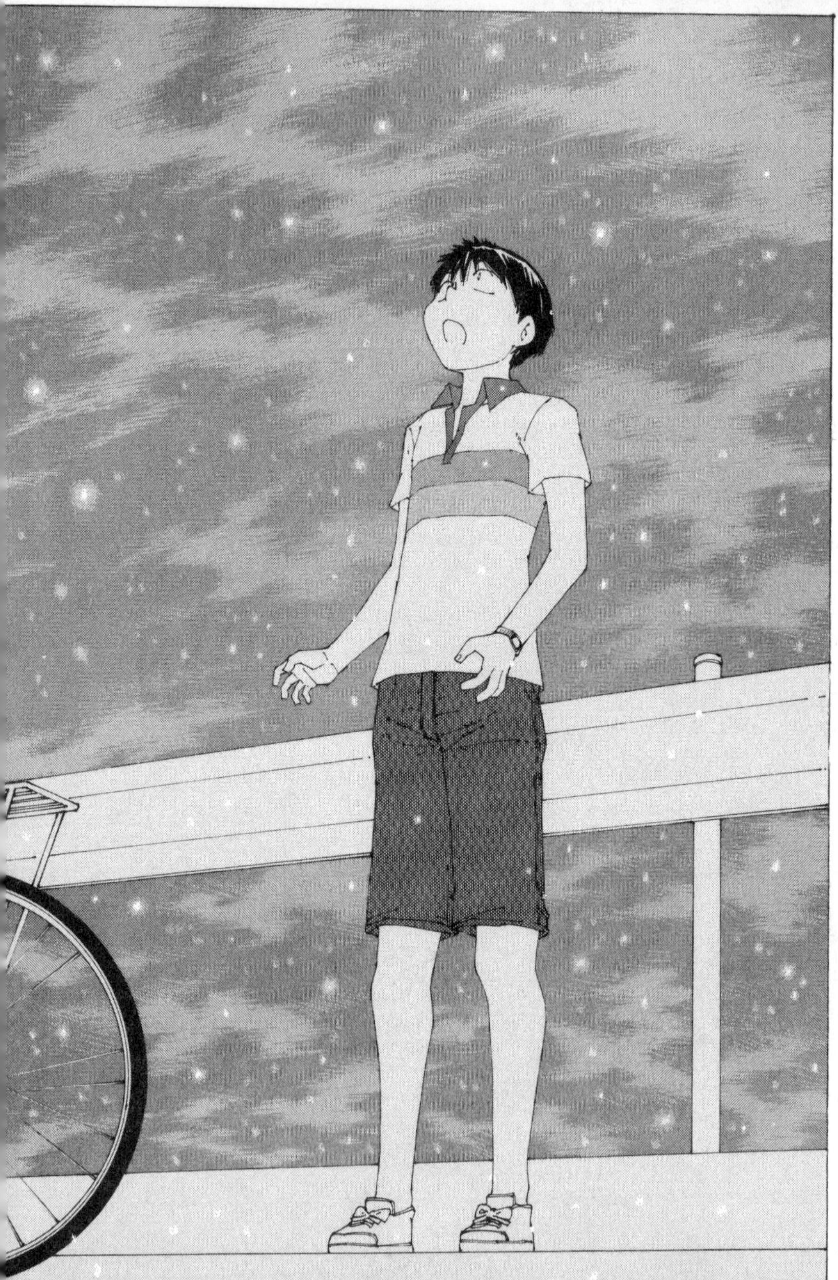

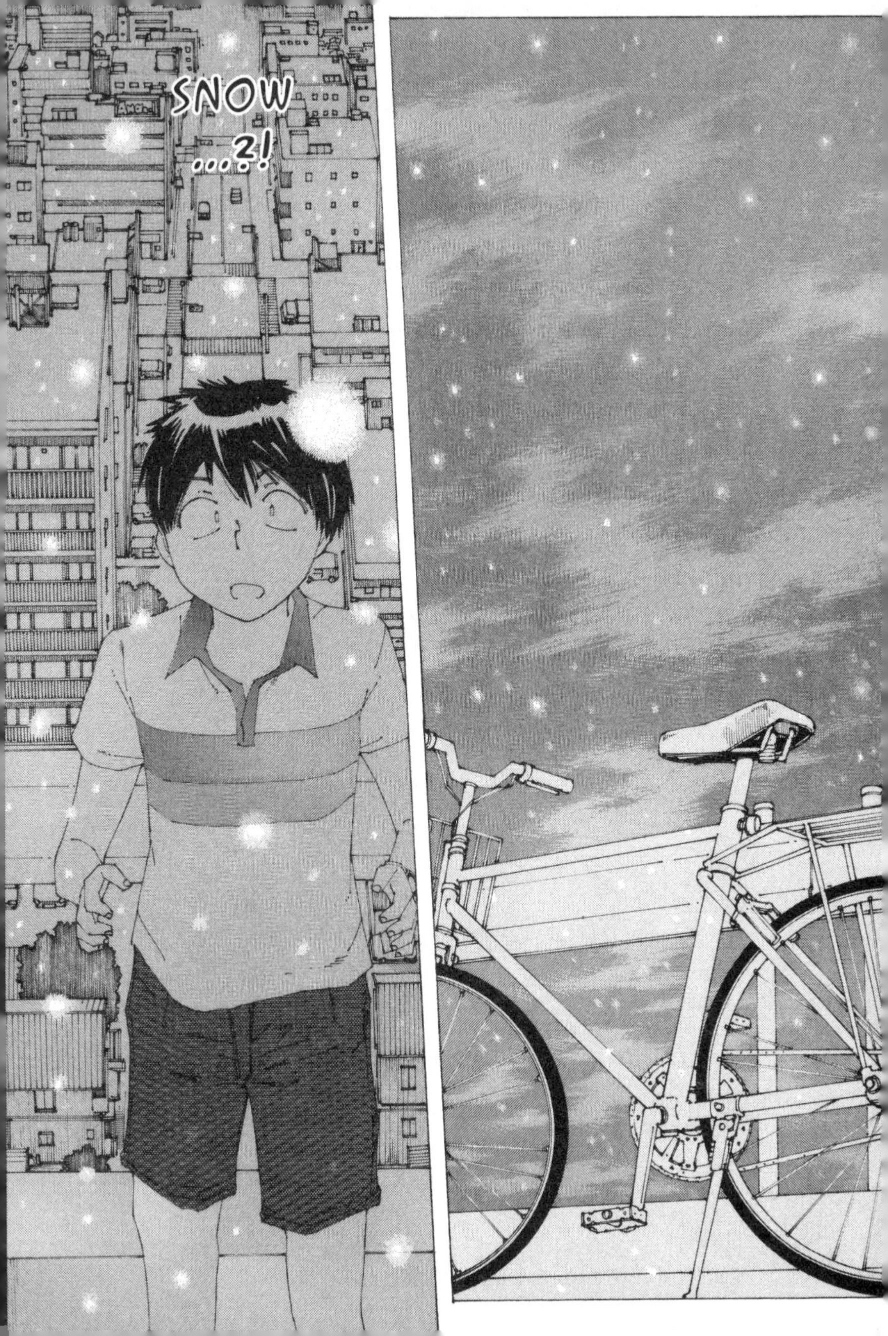
SNOW ...?!

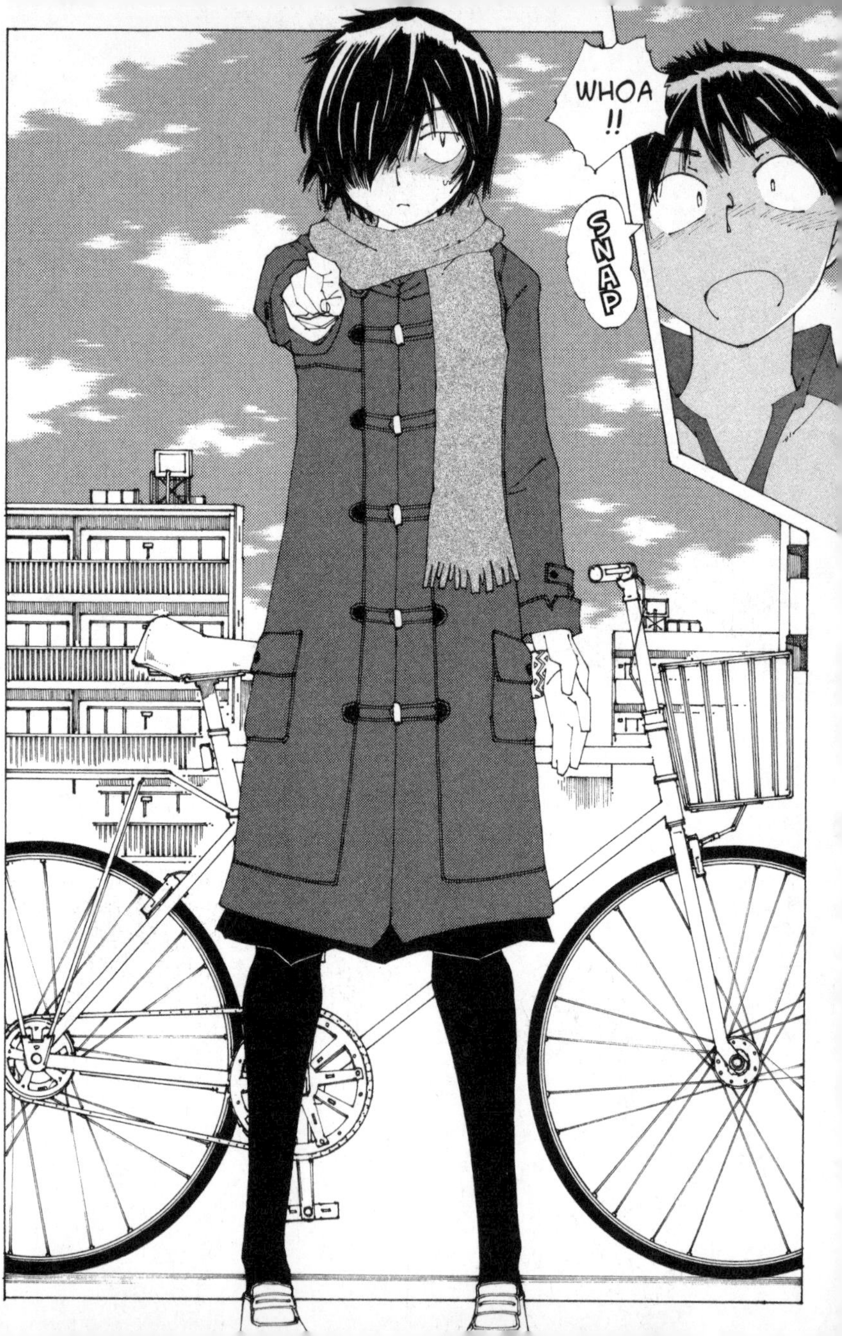
WHOA !!
SNAP

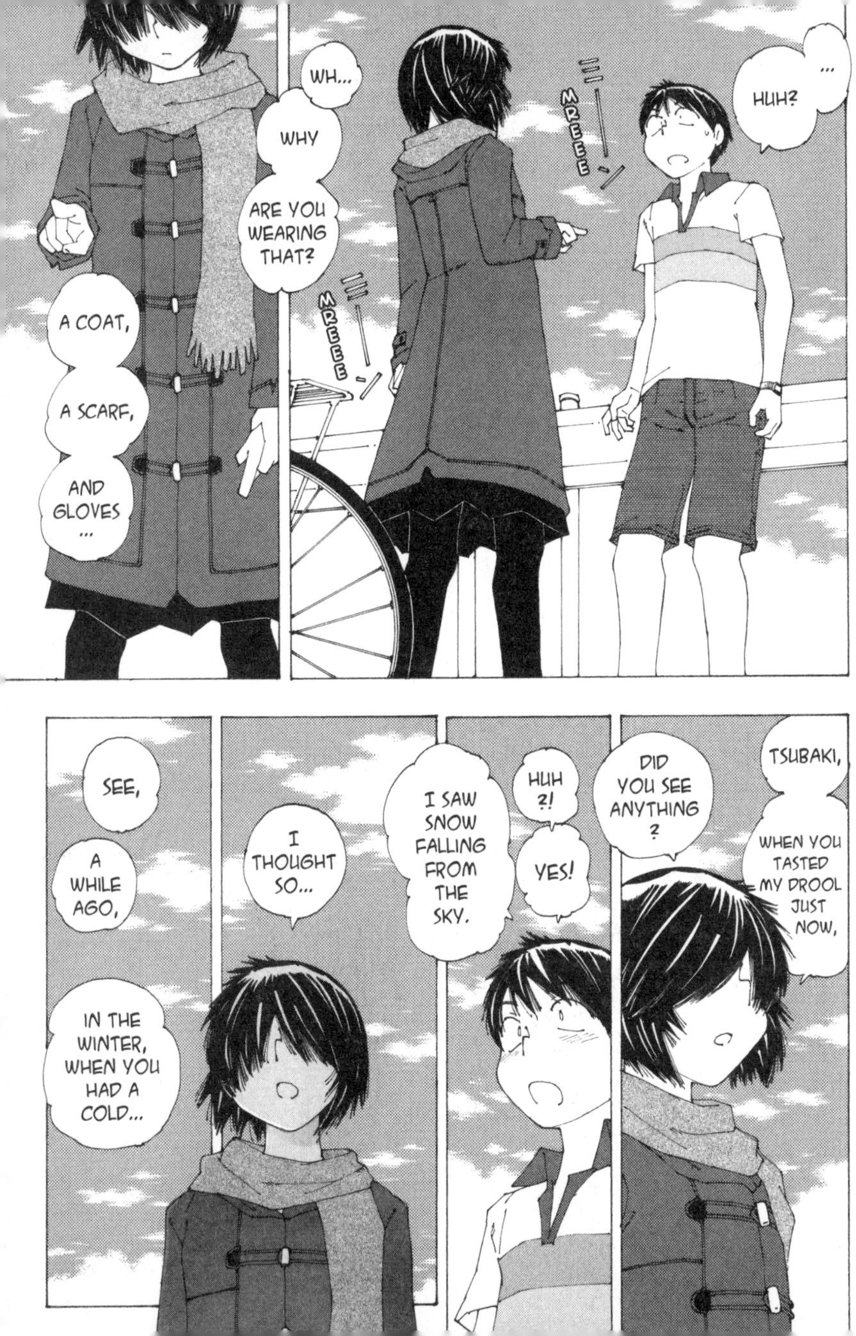
...
HUH?
MREEE
WH...
WHY
ARE YOU WEARING THAT?
MREEE
A COAT,
A SCARF,
AND GLOVES ...
TSUBAKI,
WHEN YOU TASTED MY DROOL JUST NOW,
DID YOU SEE ANYTHING ?
HUH ?!
YES!
I SAW SNOW FALLING FROM THE SKY.
I THOUGHT SO...
SEE,
A WHILE AGO,
IN THE WINTER, WHEN YOU HAD A COLD...

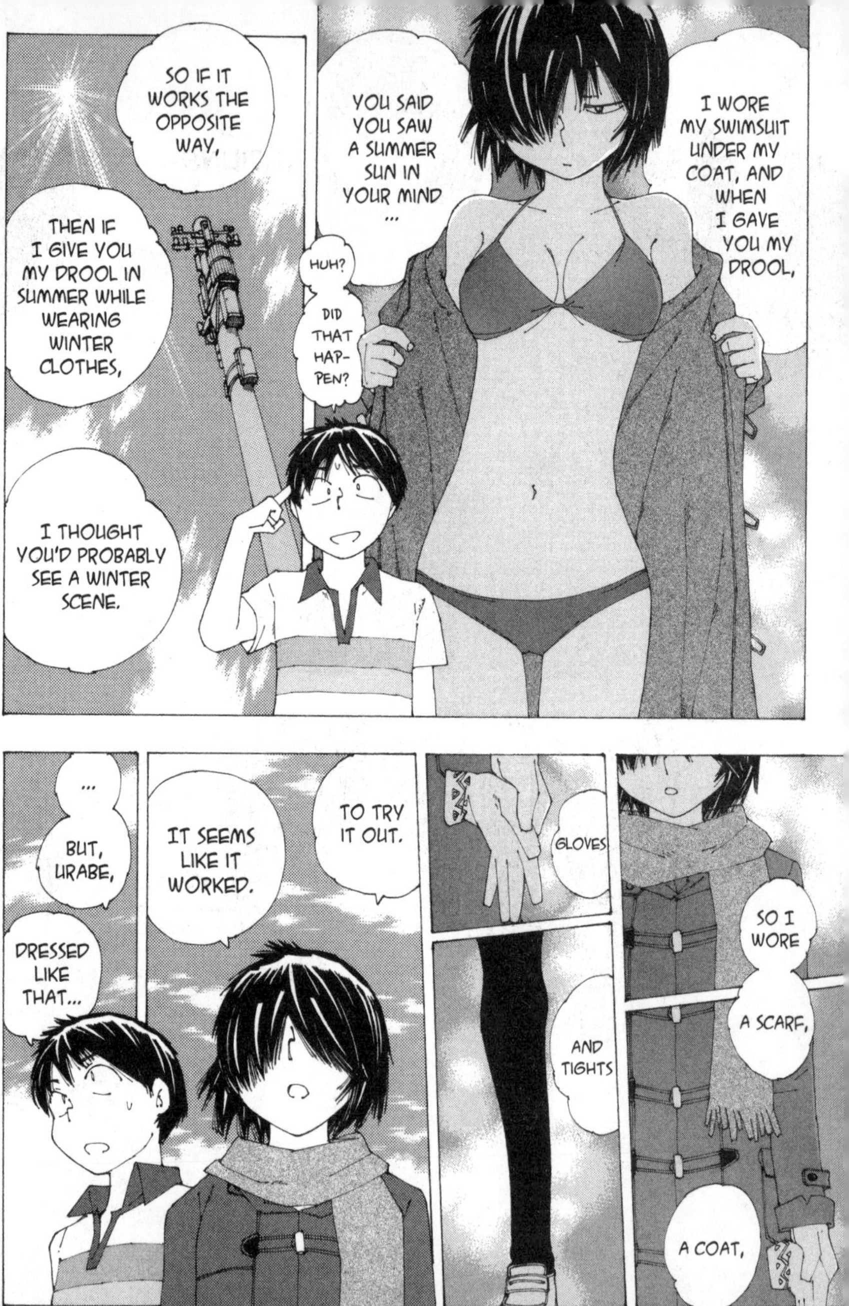
I WORE MY SWIMSUIT UNDER MY COAT, AND WHEN I GAVE YOU MY DROOL,
YOU SAID YOU SAW A SUMMER SUN IN YOUR MIND ...
HUH?
DID THAT HAP- PEN?
SO IF IT WORKS THE OPPOSITE WAY,
THEN IF I GIVE YOU MY DROOL IN SUMMER WHILE WEARING WINTER CLOTHES,
I THOUGHT YOU'D PROBABLY SEE A WINTER SCENE.
SO I WORE
A SCARF,
A COAT,
GLOVES
AND TIGHTS
TO TRY IT OUT.
IT SEEMS LIKE IT WORKED.
...
BUT, URABE,
DRESSED LIKE THAT...

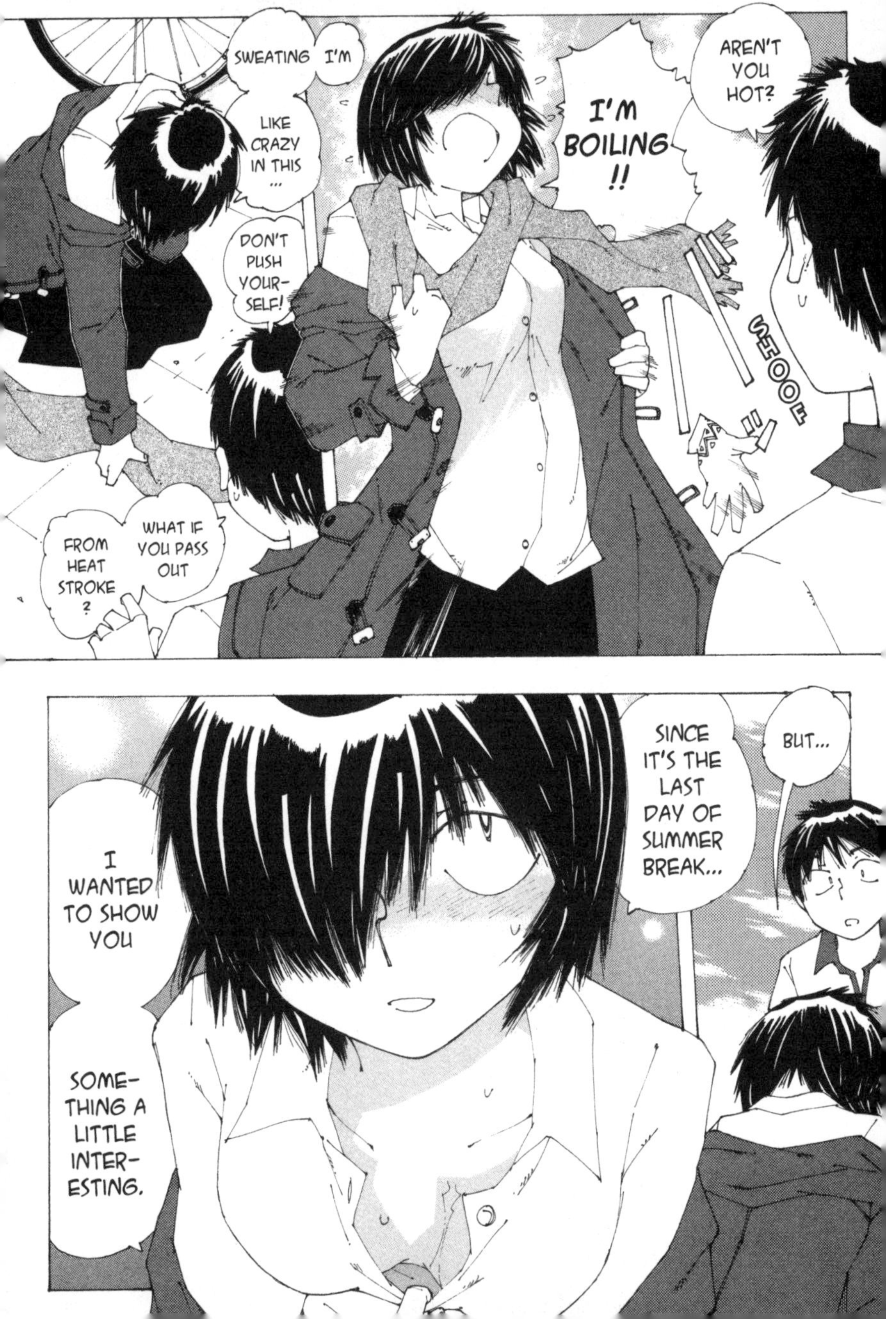
AREN'T YOU HOT?
I'M BOILING!!
SHOOF
I'M SWEATING LIKE CRAZY IN THIS ...
DON'T PUSH YOUR-SELF!
WHAT IF YOU PASS OUT FROM HEAT STROKE?
BUT...
SINCE IT'S THE LAST DAY OF SUMMER BREAK...
I WANTED TO SHOW YOU
SOME-THING A LITTLE INTER-ESTING.

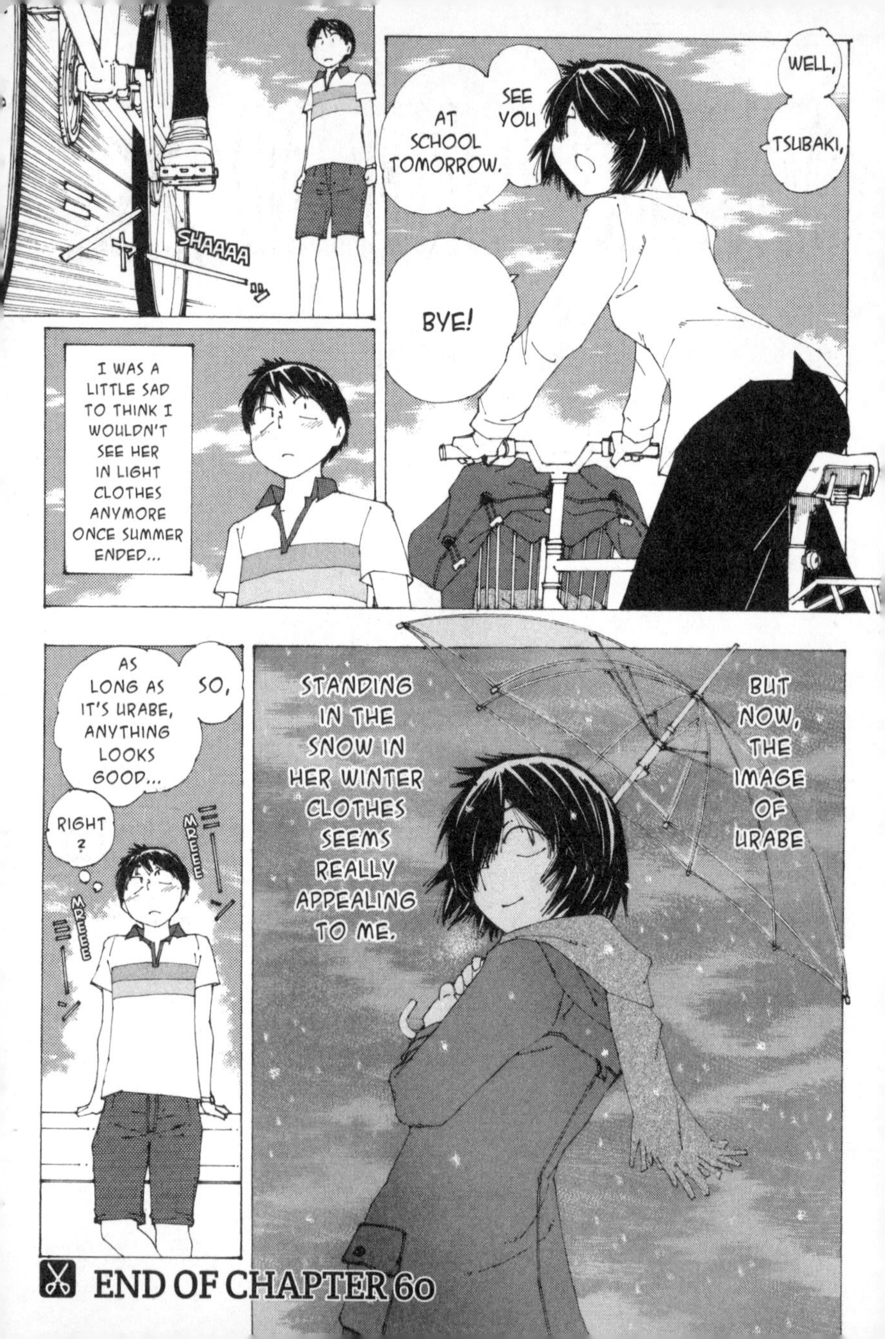
WELL,
TSUBAKI,
SEE YOU AT SCHOOL TOMORROW.
BYE!
SHAAAA
I WAS A LITTLE SAD TO THINK I WOULDN'T SEE HER IN LIGHT CLOTHES ANYMORE ONCE SUMMER ENDED...
BUT NOW, THE IMAGE OF URABE
STANDING IN THE SNOW IN HER WINTER CLOTHES SEEMS REALLY APPEALING TO ME.
SO,
AS LONG AS IT'S URABE, ANYTHING LOOKS GOOD...
RIGHT?
MREEE
MREEE

END OF CHAPTER 60

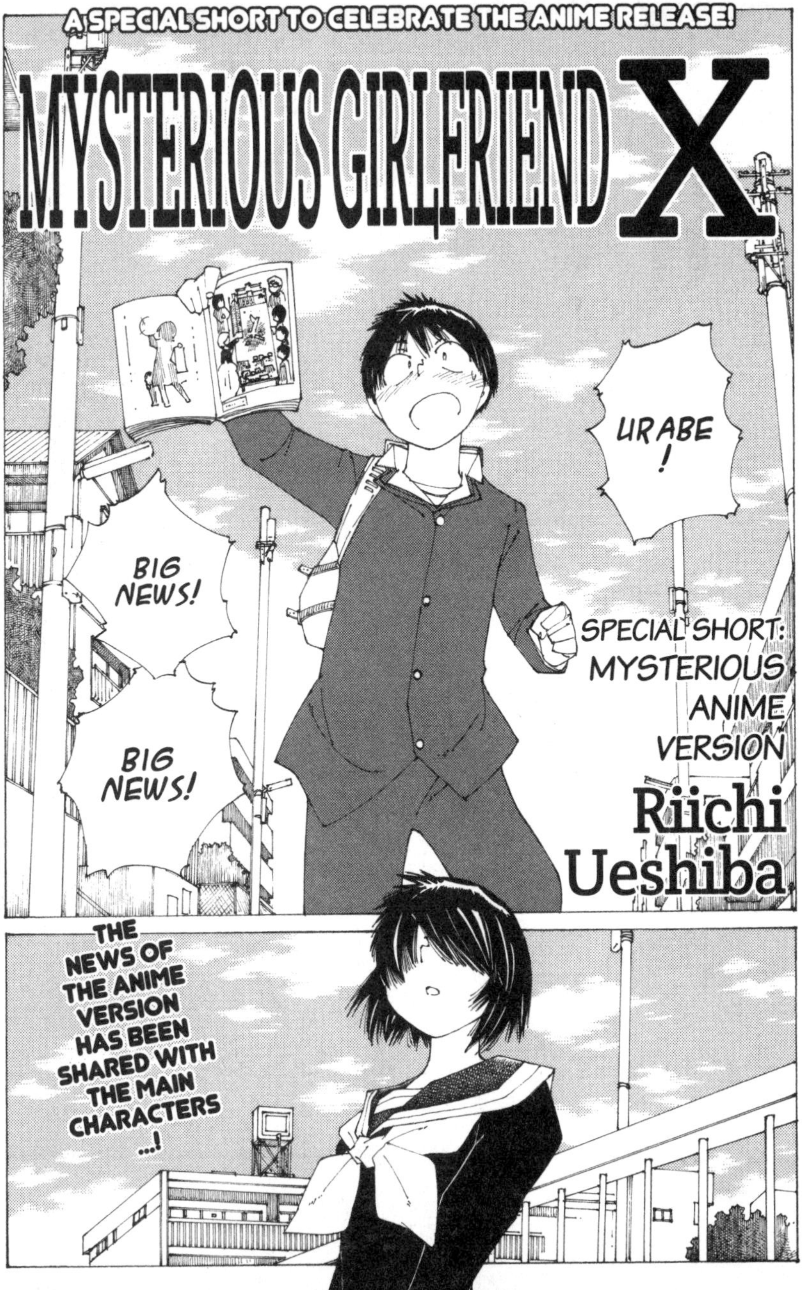
A SPECIAL SHORT TO CELEBRATE THE ANIME RELEASE!
MYSTERIOUS GIRLFRIEND X
URABE!
BIG NEWS!
BIG NEWS!
SPECIAL SHORT: MYSTERIOUS ANIME VERSION
Riichi Ueshiba
THE NEWS OF THE ANIME VERSION HAS BEEN SHARED WITH THE MAIN CHARACTERS ...!

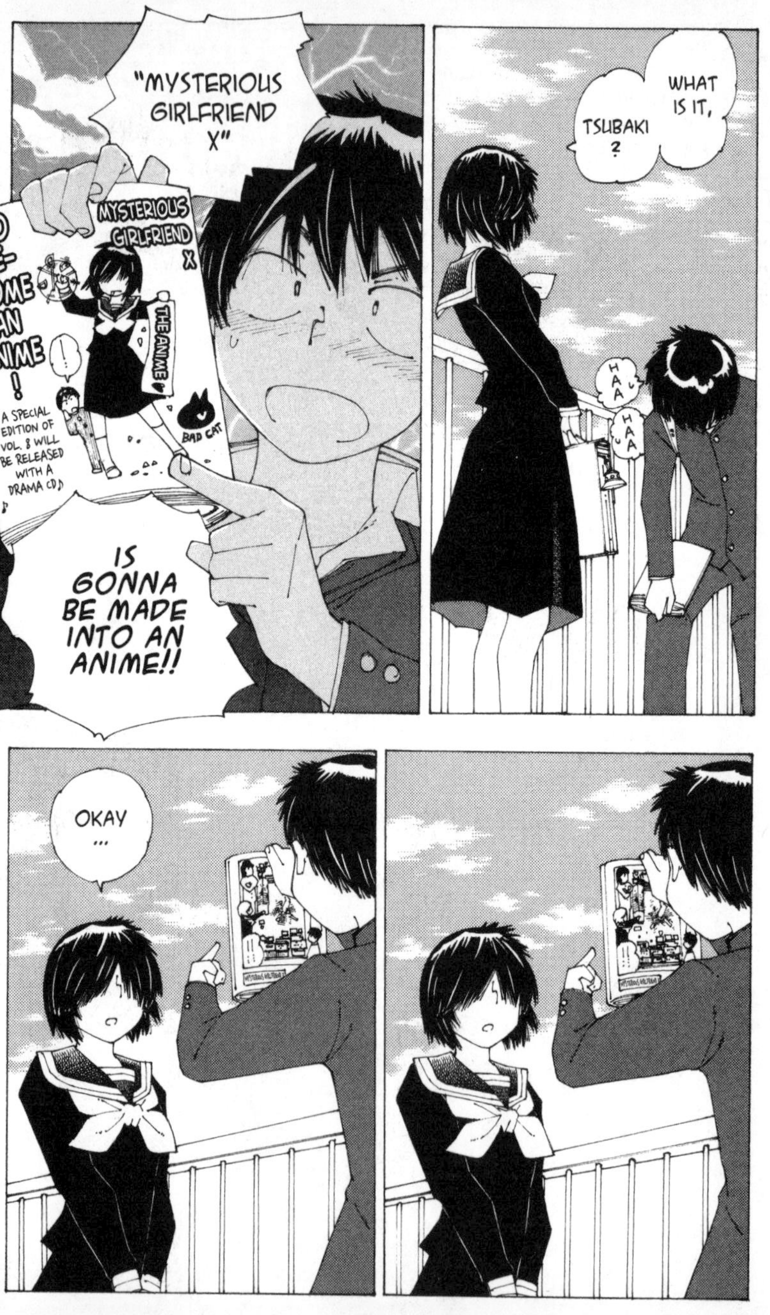
WHAT IS IT, TSUBAKI?
HAA HAA
HAA HAA
"MYSTERIOUS GIRLFRIEND X"
MYSTERIOUS GIRLFRIEND X
TO BE-COME AN ANIME!
THE ANIME
BAD CAT
A SPECIAL EDITION OF VOL. 8 WILL BE RELEASED WITH A DRAMA CD♪
IS GONNA BE MADE INTO AN ANIME!!
OKAY ...

*THIS STORY IS A WORK OF FICTION. RESEMBLANCE TO ANY REAL PERSONS, ORGANIZATIONS, OR TITLES IS PURELY COINCIDENTAL.

The Latest from the Author

Riichi Ueshiba

IN THE '70S AND '80S, IN MY HOMETOWN IN FUKUOKA, THE TV SHOWED RERUNS OF "TOM AND JERRY" ON REPEAT. RECENTLY, I'VE BORROWED RECORDINGS OF THE SHOW FROM A FELLOW FUKUOKA EX-PAT, THE EDITOR MR. N. THE COMPOSITION OF THE PROGRAM IS SO PERFECT THAT IT'S FAR MORE FUN TO WATCH IT THIS WAY THAN ON DVDS RELEASED IN THE MODERN AGE. I'VE BEEN WATCHING THEM ON HEAVY ROTATION.

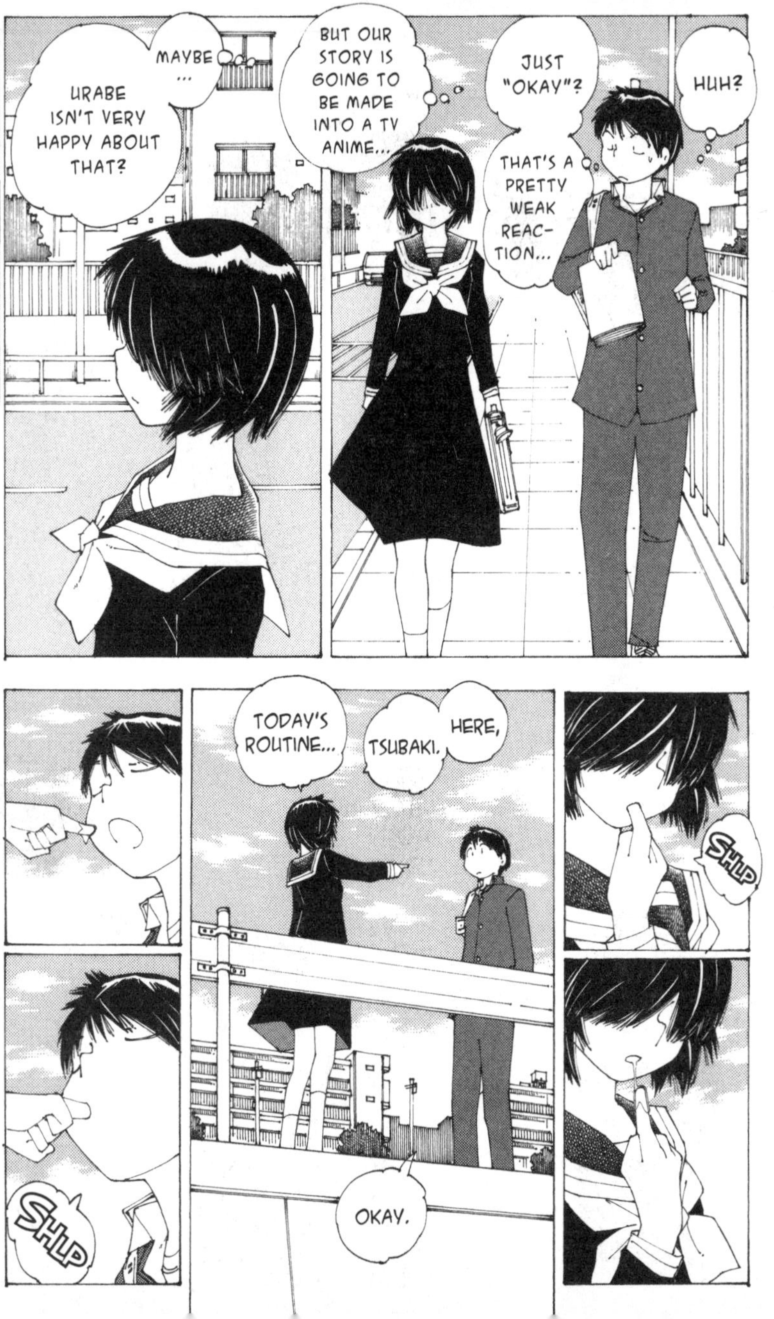
HUH?
JUST "OKAY"?
THAT'S A PRETTY WEAK REACTION...
BUT OUR STORY IS GOING TO BE MADE INTO A TV ANIME...
MAYBE ...
URABE ISN'T VERY HAPPY ABOUT THAT?
SHLP
HERE, TSUBAKI.
TODAY'S ROUTINE...
OKAY.
SHLP

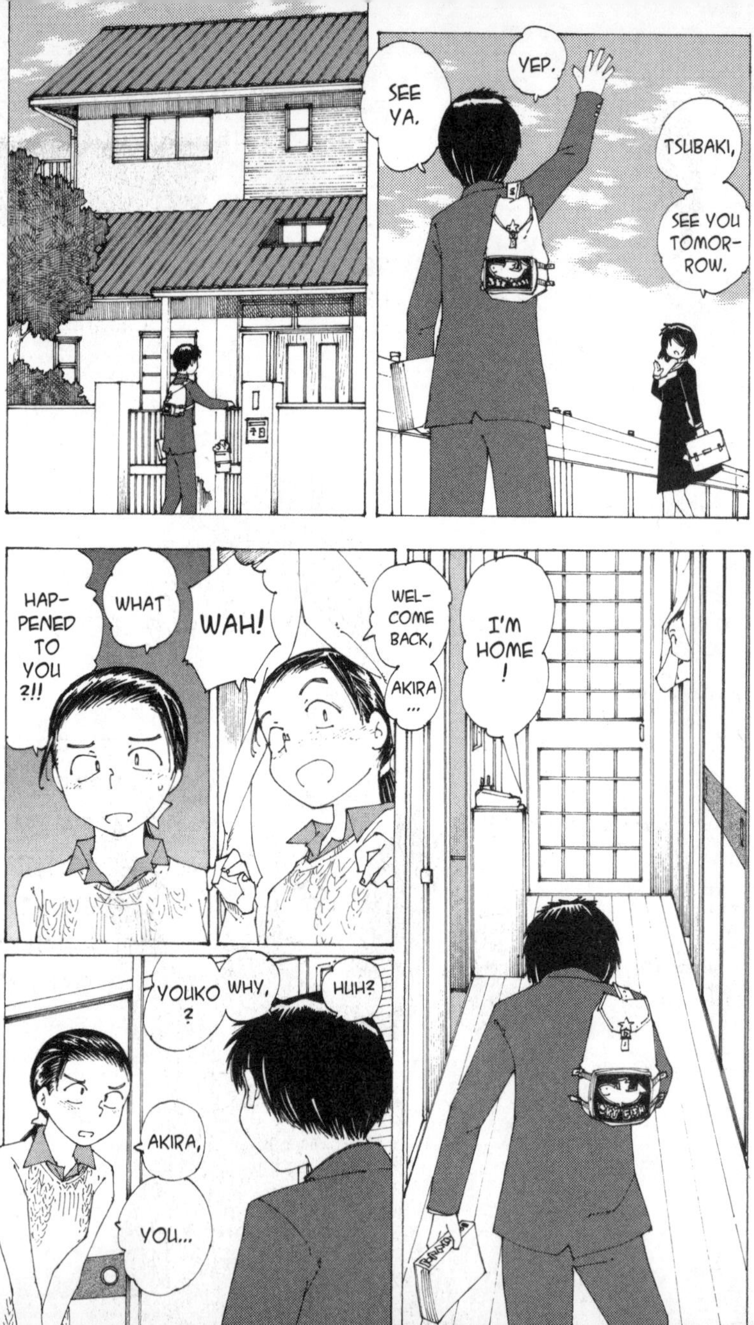
TSUBAKI,
SEE YOU TOMORROW.
YEP.
SEE YA.
I'M HOME!
WELCOME BACK, AKIRA...
WAH!
WHAT HAPPENED TO YOU?!!
HUH?
WHY,
YOUKO?
AKIRA,
YOU...

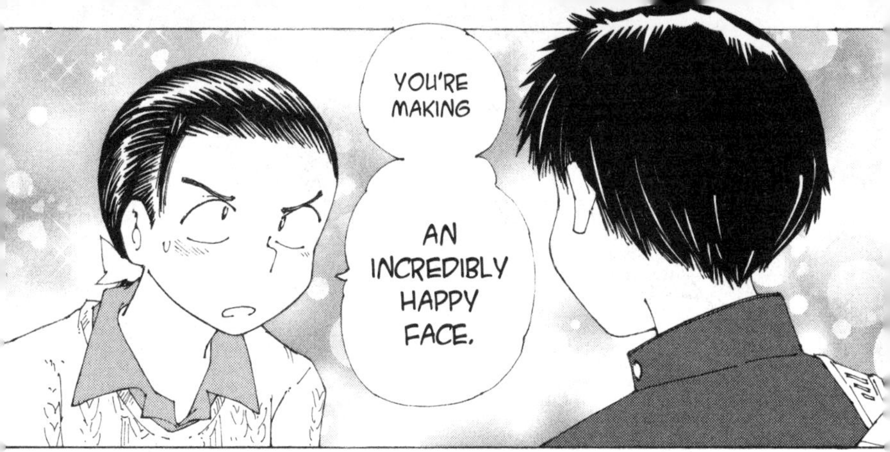
YOU'RE MAKING
AN INCREDIBLY HAPPY FACE.

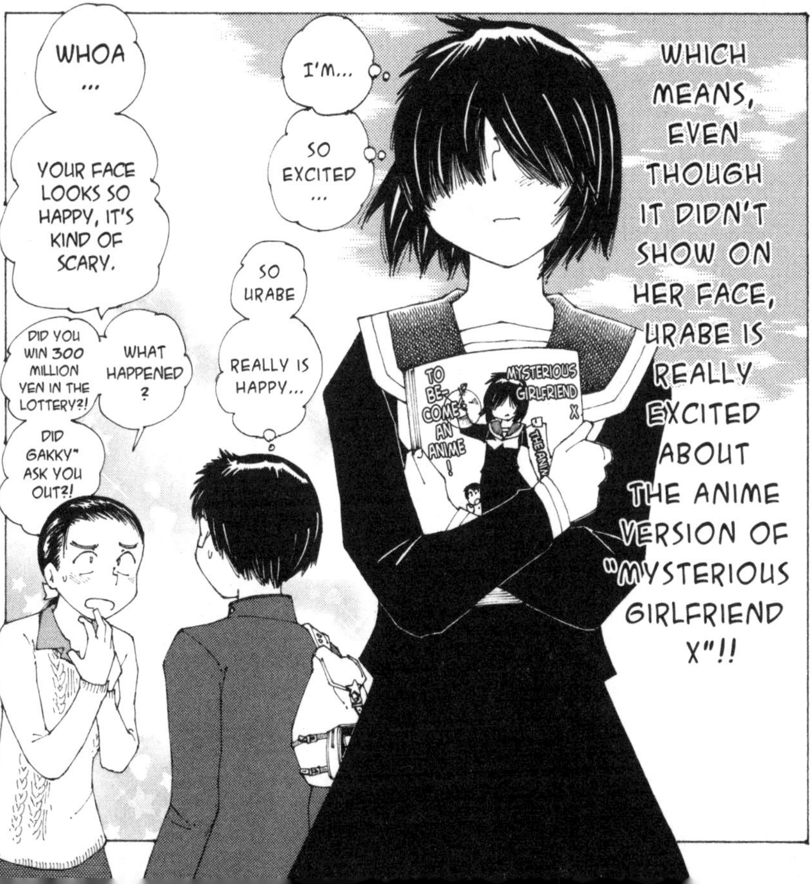
WHICH MEANS, EVEN THOUGH IT DIDN'T SHOW ON HER FACE, URABE IS REALLY EXCITED ABOUT THE ANIME VERSION OF "MYSTERIOUS GIRLFRIEND X"!!
MYSTERIOUS GIRLFRIEND X
TO BE-COME AN ANIME!
I'M...
SO EXCITED...
SO URABE
REALLY IS HAPPY...
WHOA...
YOUR FACE LOOKS SO HAPPY, IT'S KIND OF SCARY.
WHAT HAPPENED?
DID YOU WIN 300 MILLION YEN IN THE LOTTERY?!
DID GAKKY* ASK YOU OUT?!

*Gakky is the nickname of Yui Aragaki, a young actress, model, and singer.

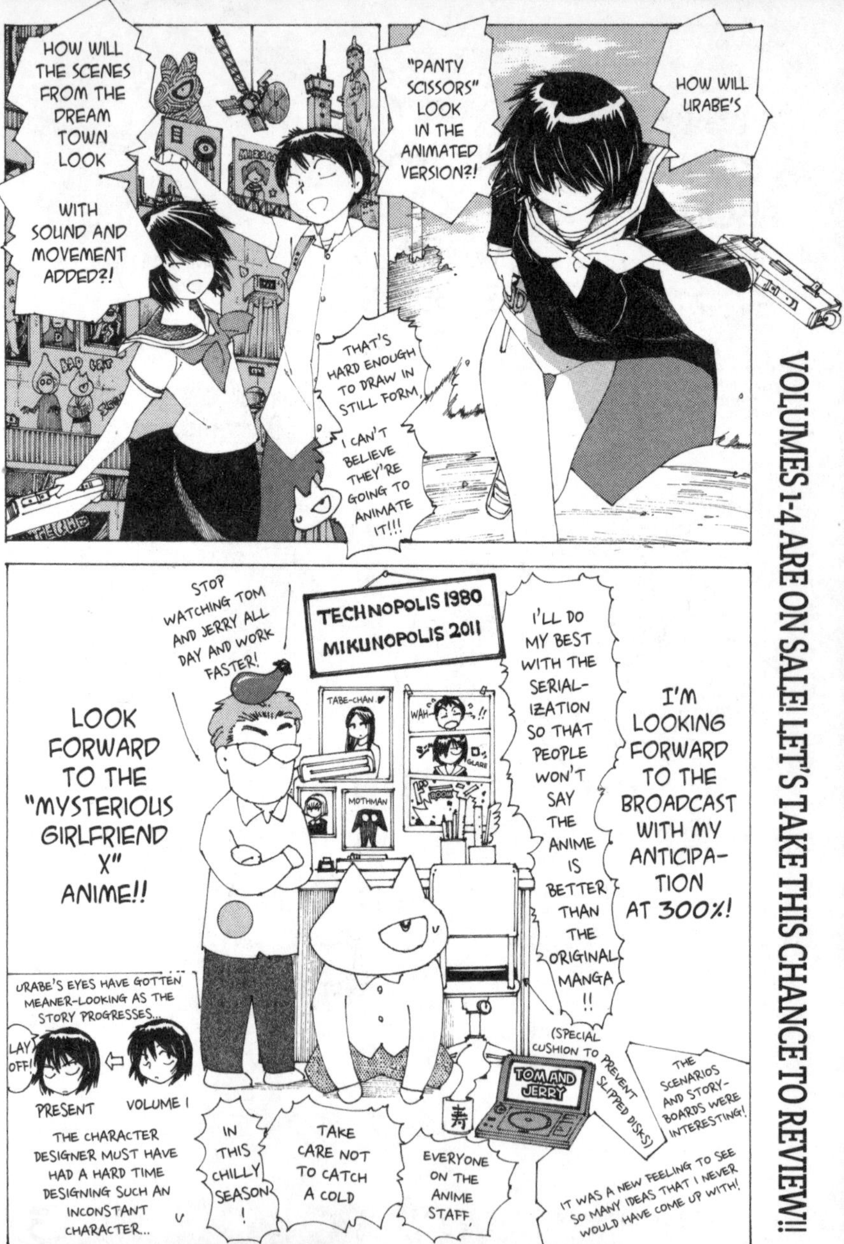
HOW WILL URABE'S
"PANTY SCISSORS" LOOK IN THE ANIMATED VERSION?!
HOW WILL THE SCENES FROM THE DREAM TOWN LOOK
WITH SOUND AND MOVEMENT ADDED?!
THAT'S HARD ENOUGH TO DRAW IN STILL FORM,
I CAN'T BELIEVE THEY'RE GOING TO ANIMATE IT!!!
VOLUMES 1-4 ARE ON SALE! LET'S TAKE THIS CHANCE TO REVIEW!!
I'M LOOKING FORWARD TO THE BROADCAST WITH MY ANTICIPATION AT 300%!
I'LL DO MY BEST WITH THE SERIALIZATION SO THAT PEOPLE WON'T SAY THE ANIME IS BETTER THAN THE ORIGINAL MANGA!!
TECHNOPOLIS 1980
MIKUNOPOLIS 2011
STOP WATCHING TOM AND JERRY ALL DAY AND WORK FASTER!
LOOK FORWARD TO THE "MYSTERIOUS GIRLFRIEND X" ANIME!!
TABE-CHAN
WAH
GLARE
BOOM
MOTHMAN
THE SCENARIOS AND STORYBOARDS WERE INTERESTING!
IT WAS A NEW FEELING TO SEE SO MANY IDEAS THAT I NEVER WOULD HAVE COME UP WITH!
(SPECIAL CUSHION TO PREVENT SLIPPED DISKS)
TOM AND JERRY
EVERYONE ON THE ANIME STAFF,
TAKE CARE NOT TO CATCH A COLD
IN THIS CHILLY SEASON!
URABE'S EYES HAVE GOTTEN MEANER-LOOKING AS THE STORY PROGRESSES...
LAY OFF!
PRESENT
VOLUME 1
THE CHARACTER DESIGNER MUST HAVE HAD A HARD TIME DESIGNING SUCH AN INCONSTANT CHARACTER...

MYSTERIOUS GIRLFRIEND X

END OF SPECIAL SHORT

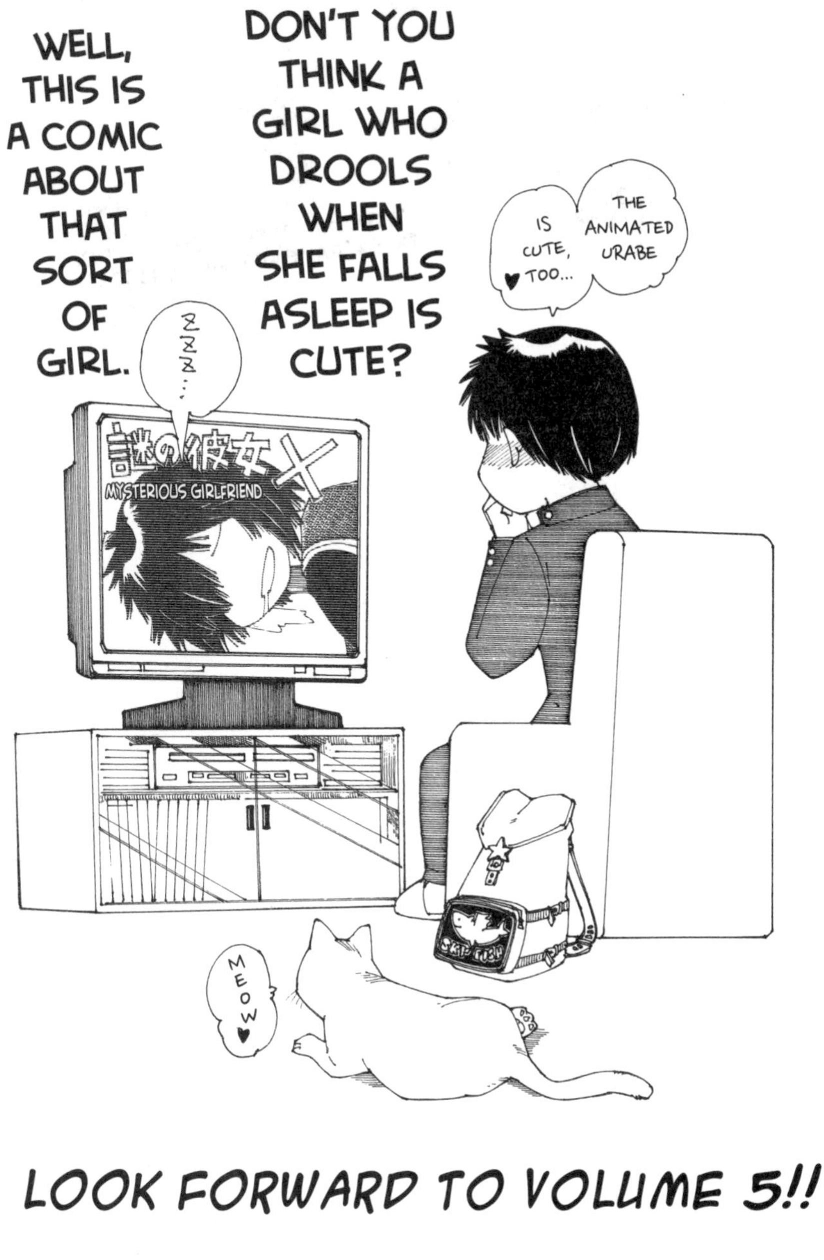
THE ANIMATED URABE
IS CUTE, TOO...
DON'T YOU THINK A GIRL WHO DROOLS WHEN SHE FALLS ASLEEP IS CUTE?
ZZZ...
WELL, THIS IS A COMIC ABOUT THAT SORT OF GIRL.
謎の彼女X
MYSTERIOUS GIRLFRIEND
MEOW
LOOK FORWARD TO VOLUME 5!!

MYSTERIOUS GIRLFRIEND X, VOLUME 4

A Vertical Comics Edition

Translation: Rebecca Cottrill
Production: Risa Cho
        Anthony Quintessenza

© 2016 Riichi Ueshiba. All rights reserved.
First published in Japan in 2011-12 by Kodansha, Ltd., Tokyo
Publication rights for this English edition arranged through Kodansha, Ltd., Tokyo
English language version produced by Vertical, Inc., New York

Published by Vertical Comics, an imprint of Vertical, Inc., New York

Originally published in Japanese as *Nazo no Kanojo X 7* & *8* by Kodansha, Ltd., 2011-12
Nazo no Kanojo X first serialized in *Afternoon*, Kodansha, Ltd., 2004, 2006-2014

This is a work of fiction.

ISBN: 978-1-942993-71-1

Manufactured in Canada

First Edition

Vertical, Inc.
451 Park Avenue South
7th Floor
New York, NY 10016
www.vertical-comics.com

Vertical books are distributed through Penguin-Random House Publisher Services.